RELIGIOUS ACTORS
AND INTERNATIONAL LAW

Religious Actors and International Law

IOANA CISMAS

OXFORD
UNIVERSITY PRESS

OXFORD
UNIVERSITY PRESS

Great Clarendon Street, Oxford, OX2 6DP,
United Kingdom

Oxford University Press is a department of the University of Oxford.
It furthers the University's objective of excellence in research, scholarship,
and education by publishing worldwide. Oxford is a registered trade mark of
Oxford University Press in the UK and in certain other countries

© Ioana Cismas 2014

The moral rights of the author have been asserted

First Edition published in 2014

Impression: 1

Published in the United States of America by Oxford University Press
198 Madison Avenue, New York, NY 10016, United States of America

British Library Cataloguing in Publication Data
Data available

Library of Congress Control Number: 2014934945
ISBN 978–0–19–871282–4

Printed and bound by
CPI Group (UK) Ltd, Croydon, CR0 4YY

Acknowledgements

This book started as a doctoral project at the Graduate Institute of International and Development Studies in Geneva. I owe a debt of gratitude to Professor Andrew Clapham for having accompanied me throughout the writing process, for his trust, patient and kind guidance, and precious advice. But, most of all, I am grateful to Professor Clapham for having introduced me to the complex beauty of international law. I should also like to thank Professor Vera Gowlland-Debbas. I recall with fondness that her classes not only gave me the opportunity to develop and test my first ideas on religious actors and international law, they also provided me with the chance to experience what makes a great woman lawyer. Professor Andrea Bianchi's comments in the early stages of my research were instrumental in that they shaped my thinking on the aim and limits of the research endeavour, and later kept me focused on improving the manuscript. I am thankful to Professor Christina Cerna for her careful reading of the manuscript, her valuable feedback and support.

Thanks go to my former colleagues at the Geneva Academy of International Humanitarian Law and Human Rights, Dr. Annyssa Bellal, Dr. Stuart Casey-Maslen, Dr. Tahmina Karimova, Kamelia Kemileva, Daniela Renggli, Siata Traore, and especially to Dr. Christophe Golay, Alice Priddy, and Ivona Truscan who read parts of the manuscript and provided useful comments. I am grateful to Professor Jean Ziegler for his constant encouragement over the years, and to Professor Paola Gaeta for the opportunities which she offered me in the follow-up of the project.

In the course of drafting this book, at conferences or on other occasions I have met numerous legal scholars, colleagues from other disciplines, and practitioners who showed an interest in the project; my work benefited from their insights, or from materials which they provided me with. In particular, I would like to thank Robert Archer, UN Special Rapporteur Pablo de Greiff, Dr. Turan Kayaoğlu, Prof. Martti Koskenniemi, Dr. Marie Juul Petersen, Dr. Julia Raue, and Prof. Eibe Riedel.

In the final stages of my writing I am enjoying the hospitality of the Center for Human Rights and Global Justice at NYU School of Law. Thanks are due to Professor Philip Alston and Veerle Opgenhaffen, as well as to the Swiss National Science Foundation for the grant which made this scholarly residence possible.

I am immensely grateful to Oxford University Press for expressing an interest in my project and for seeing it come to fruition. Especially, I would like to thank Merel Alstein and Anthony Hinton for their essential advice and support, as well as Dhanuj S. Nair, Yvonne Dixon and Marie Gill. Thanks are also due to the anonymous reviewers who read my book and provided comments which strengthened its argument.

My parents have supported me unfailingly and Céline Glutz has been a wonderful friend: Thank you infinitely. Finally, I wish to thank my husband Daniel Hügli, for his critical thinking and constructive feedback, his immense patience and kindness, and unwavering support.

This book started as an academic project. In parallel it has been my *Bildungsroman*. I dedicate it to Babu, my late grandpa who inspired my interest in religion and its actors.

New York, April 2014
I.C.H.

Contents

II. OPERATIONALIZING THE ANALYTICAL CATEGORY OF RELIGIOUS ACTORS

Table of Cases

EUROPEAN COURT OF HUMAN RIGHTS

INTER-AMERICAN COURT OF HUMAN RIGHTS

INTERNATIONAL COURT OF JUSTICE

INTERNATIONAL CRIMINAL TRIBUNAL
FOR THE FORMER YUGOSLAVIA

INTERNATIONAL CRIMINAL TRIBUNAL FOR RWANDA

UNITED NATIONS COMMITTEE ON THE ELIMINATION
OF RACIAL DISCRIMINATION

UNITED NATIONS HUMAN RIGHTS COMMITTEE

NATIONAL COURTS

Italy

The Philippines

Romania

Table of Treaties, Legislation, and Other Relevant Instruments

List of Abbreviations

AAA	American Anthropological Association
ACHPR	African Charter on Human and Peoples' Rights
ACHR	American Convention on Human Rights
AComHPR	African Commission on Human and Peoples' Rights
ArCHR	Arab Charter on Human Rights
CAT	Convention against Torture and Other Cruel, Inhuman or Degrading Treatment or Punishment
CDHRI	Cairo Declaration on Human Rights in Islam
CEDAW	Convention on the Elimination of All Forms of Discrimination against Women
CERD	International Convention on the Elimination of All Forms of Racial Discrimination
CESCR	Committee on Economic, Social and Cultural Rights
CRC	Convention on the Rights of the Child
CRCI	Covenant on the Rights of the Child in Islam
CRPD	Convention on the Rights of Persons with Disabilities
ECHR	European Convention on Human Rights
EComHR	European Commission on Human Rights
ECtHR	European Court of Human Rights
FSIA	Foreign Sovereign Immunity Act
GA	General Assembly of the United Nations
HRC	United Nations Human Rights Committee
IACtHR	Inter-American Court of Human Rights
IAComHR	Inter-American Commission on Human Rights
ICC	International Criminal Court
ICCPR	International Covenant on Civil and Political Rights
ICESCR	International Covenant on Economic, Social and Cultural Rights
ICJ	International Court of Justice
ICRC	International Committee of the Red Cross
ICTR	International Criminal Tribunal for Rwanda
ILA	International Law Association
ILC	International Law Commission
ILO	International Labour Organization
ILR	International Law Reports
IOR	Institute for the Works of Religion
LGBT	Lesbian, Gay, Bisexual, Transgender Persons
MPEPIL	Max Planck Encyclopedia of Public International Law
OIC	Organization of Islamic Cooperation
OIC IPHRC	OIC Independent Permanent Human Rights Commission

OPSC	Optional Protocol to the Convention on the Rights of the Child on the Sale of Children, Child Prostitution and Child Pornography
UDHR	Universal Declaration of Human Rights
UN	United Nations
UNTS	United Nations Treaty Collection
UNTS	United Nations Treaty Series
UPU	Universal Postal Union
VCDR	Vienna Convention on Diplomatic Relations
VCLT	Vienna Convention on the Law of Treaties
WHO	World Health Organization

Journals:

AJIL	American Journal of International Law
Am. U. Int'l L. Rev.	American University International Law Review
BYBIL	British Year Book of International Law
BYU L. Rev.	Brigham Young University Law Review
Cal. W. Int'l L.J.	California Western International Law Journal
Case W. Res. J. Int'l L.	Case Western Reserve Journal of International Law
Cath. U. L. Rev.	Catholic University Law Review
Col. LR	Columbia Law Review
EJIL	European Journal of International Law
Emory Int'l L. Rev.	Emory International Law Review
Ga. J. Int'l & Comp. L.	Georgia Journal of International and Comparative Law
Geo. Wash. Int'l L. Rev.	George Washington International Law Review
Harv. Hum. Rts. J.	Harvard Human Rights Journal
HRQ	Human Rights Quarterly
ICLQ	International and Comparative Law Quarterly
ILM	International Legal Materials
JCL	Journal of Civil Liberties
J.L. & Relig.	Journal of Law and Religion
Leiden J. Intl. L.	Leiden Journal of International Law
Mich. J. Int'l L.	Michigan Journal of International Law
NYU J.L. & Pol.	New York University Journal of International Law and Politics
Oxford J.L. & Relig.	Oxford Journal of Law and Religion
St. Louis U. L.J.	Saint Louis University Law Journal
U. Pa. J. Int'l L.	University of Pennsylvania Journal of International Law

Introduction

The Shift in Focus

'Action without a name, a "who" attached to it, is meaningless...'

—Hannah Arendt[1]

I. From Religion to Religious Actors

In 2009, Ms Lubna Hussein, a Sudanese journalist and employee of the United Nations (UN) in Khartoum, was charged alongside 12 other women for committing an indecent act: wearing trousers in public.[2] The charges were brought under article 152 of the Sudanese criminal code, which provides that indecent acts and obscene outfits 'shall be punished with flogging which may not exceed forty lashes or with fine or with both', whereby 'the standard of the person's religion' is taken to indicate whether an act is indecent or an outfit obscene.[3] Law enforcement officers and Sudanese courts presume to decide which acts and what clothing deviate from religious standards.[4] Ms Hussein asserted that, as an employee of the UN she enjoyed immunity from prosecution, but she chose to resign 'so that I could face the Sudanese authorities and make them show to the world what they consider justice to be'.[5] Many lessons can be drawn from this

---

[1] H. Arendt, *The Human Condition*, (Chicago: University of Chicago Press, 1958), at 180–181.

[2] J. Copnall, 'Lubna Hussein: "I'm not afraid of being flogged. It doesn't hurt. But it is insulting"', *The Guardian*, 2 August 2009, accessed January 2012, http://www.guardian.co.uk/world/2009/aug/02/sudan-women-dress-code; L. Hussein, 'When I think of my trial, I pray my fight won't be in vain', *The Guardian*, 4 September 2009, accessed January 2012, http://www.guardian.co.uk/commentisfree/2009/sep/04/sudan-woman-trousers-trial; 'Sudan releases woman convicted of wearing tight pants', *CNN*, accessed January 2012, http://www.cnn.com/2009/WORLD/africa/09/08/sudan.journalist.tight.pants/index.html#cnnSTCText. For the position taken by the embassy of Sudan in London, see K. al-Mubarak, 'Lubna Hussein's trial had nothing to do with trousers', *The Guardian*, accessed January 2012, http://www.guardian.co.uk/commentisfree/2009/sep/11/lubna-hussein-sudan-embassy-response.

[3] The full text of article 152 of the Memorandum to the Sudanese Penal Code 1991 can be found in Amnesty International, *Sudan: Amnesty International calls on government to repeal law penalizing women for wearing trousers*, Press Release, 4 September 2009, accessed January 2012, http://www.amnesty.org/en/for-media/press-releases/sudan-amnesty-international-calls-government-repeal-law-penalizing-women.

[4] See note 3.

[5] L. Hussein, 'When I think of my trial, I pray my fight won't be in vain', *The Guardian*, 4 September 2009.

case, but what should be emphasized in this introductory note is the way Ms Hussein framed the situation:

Islam does not say whether a woman can wear trousers or not. The clothes I was wearing when the police caught me—I pray in them. I pray to my God in them. And neither does Islam flog women because of what they wear. If any Muslim in the world says Islamic law or sharia law flogs women for their clothes, let them show me what the Qur'an or Prophet Muhammad said on that issue. There is nothing. It is not about religion, it is about men treating women badly.[6]

She asserts that the Sudanese authorities, not Islam, are responsible for *interpreting* Islam to require the flogging of individuals as a penalty for what *they consider* to be 'indecent acts' and 'obscene outfits'.

This study takes an approach that mirrors the way Ms Hussein framed the situation. It shifts the focus of legal analysis—concentrating on religious actors rather than their religion, and on the rights and obligations of religious actors under international law rather than the compatibility or incompatibility of religion with international law. It is an endeavour that underscores the agency of religious actors in interpreting religion(s) and seeks to establish their legal accountability for these interpretations.

The decision to concentrate on the actions of religious actors was prompted by a certain sense of hopelessness which emerges from studies and articles that portray conflicts between religion(s) and human rights. Religions, and religion in general terms even less, cannot be treated as static, unitary blocs. While religious texts may remain unaltered over centuries, the practice of any religion is dynamic over time and diverse across space. For instance, Exodus 21:12 reads '[h]e that smiteth a man, so that he die, shall be surely put to death'[7] and Leviticus 24:17 confirms that '[h]e that killeth any man shall surely be put to death'.[8] A literal reading of these passages from the Old Testament would imply that, among other religions, Catholicism should support the death penalty. The Catechism of the Catholic Church promulgated by Pope John Paul II admits that 'the traditional teaching of the Church does not exclude recourse to the death penalty...';[9] nonetheless, it goes on to reach the *interpretation* that, because the modern state no longer needs to employ lethal means to protect society, non-lethal means of punishment are 'more in keeping with the concrete conditions of the common good and more in conformity with the dignity of the human person'.[10] Consequently, the US Catholic Bishops' Conference puts itself at the forefront of the campaign to abolish

---

[6] J. Copnall, 'Lubna Hussein: "I'm not afraid of being flogged. It doesn't hurt. But it is insulting"', *The Guardian*, 2 August 2009.

[7] *The Holy Bible. King James Version*, 7th ed., (Peabody, MA: Hendrickson Publishers, 2008), 21:12.

[8] See note 7, 24:17.

[9] *Catechism of the Catholic Church*, 2nd edition, revised in accordance with the official Latin text promulgated by Pope John Paul II, (Libreria Editrice Vaticana, United States Catholic Conference, 2000), para. 2267.

[10] See note 9. See also T. Bjarnason and M. R. Welch, 'Father Knows Best: Parishes, Priests, and American Catholic Parishioners' Attitudes Toward Capital Punishment', 43 *Journal for the Scientific Study of Religion* 1 (2004) 103–118, at 104–105.

the death penalty in the United States.[11] The current interpretation of these biblical texts is not self-evident, nor have Catholic authorities adopted this reading consistently. In the past, the same text was used to justify the Crusades and Inquisition.[12]

With these examples in mind, we understand that religions are constructs that often integrate a range of reflections on a single issue, which contradict and complement one another, and evolve variously over time and across space. It is here where the role of religious actors as interpreters of religion(s) becomes central, because through interpretation they generate the dynamism and diversity of religions. Given these premises, and when the goal is to ensure human rights protection, reiterating that certain aspects of religion(s) are incompatible with legal norms cannot be sufficient or satisfactory. It is therefore necessary to escape the discourse of inevitable conflict between religion and law and replace it with a search for means of securing legal accountability in this area. This is why the present study addresses religious actors. It consciously chooses not to concentrate on religion as a category within which oppressive structures or patterns may exist, but to focus on religious actors who, by their interpretations of religion, uphold and promote or, on the contrary, transform those structures and patterns.

II. Societal Pertinence and Legal Relevance

The relevance of this book's approach and analysis can be affirmed by placing the study in its societal context and reflecting upon existing legal literature.

Evidence from several quarters suggests a renewed prominent role for religion in many areas of contemporary society. Many authors invoke the emergence of religion in public debate following the terrorist attacks of September 2001;[13] however, the resurgence of religion had been heralded before then.[14] In his introduction to a multidisciplinary volume on the *Desecularization of the World* (1999), Peter L. Berger observes: '[T]he assumption that we live in a secularized world is false. The world

---

[11] See Holy Week Campaign to End Death Penalty, accessed March 2011, http://www.americancatholic.org/News/DeathPenalty/BishopsDeath.asp; United States Conference of Catholic Bishops—Catholic Campaign to End the Use of Death Penalty, accessed March 2011, http://www.usccb.org/issues-and-action/human-life-and-dignity/death-penalty-capital-punishment/upload/5-723DEATHBI.pdf.

[12] See Apostolic Letter *Tertio Millennio Adveniente* of His Holiness Pope John Paul II to the Bishops, Clergy and Lay Faithful on Preparation for the Jubilee of the Year 2000, 10 November 1994; 'Pope apologises for church sins', *BBC News*, 12 March 2000, accessed March 2014, http://news.bbc.co.uk/1/hi/world/europe/674246.stm.

[13] Carolyn Evans, for example, argues that the 9/11 attacks have been 'a powerful motivating factor' behind the reconsideration of religion as a public issue. C. Evans, 'Introduction', in P. Cane, C. Evans and Z. Robinson (eds.), *Law and Religion in Theoretical and Historical Context*, (Cambridge: Cambridge University Press, 2008), 1–15, at 1.

[14] R. T. Antoun and M. E. Hegland (eds.), *Religious Resurgence: Contemporary Cases in Islam, Christianity, and Judaism*, (New York: Syracuse University Press, 1987); S. Thomas, 'The Global Resurgence of Religion, International Law and International Society', in M. W. Janis and C. Evans (eds.), *Religion and International Law*, (The Hague: Martinus Nijhoff Publishers, 1999), 321–338; D. Westerlund (ed.), *Questioning the Secular State: The Worldwide Resurgence of Religion in Politics*, (London: Hurst, 1996).

today, with some exceptions…, is as furiously religious as ever, and in some places more so than ever.'[15] Berger ends his remarks with a warning: 'Those who neglect religion in their analyses of contemporary affairs do so at great peril'.[16]

Samuel P. Huntington was also preoccupied by religion when, after the end of the Cold War, he drafted his (in)famous theory on the 'clash of civilizations' to explain the 'remaking of world order'.[17] The late social scientist contended that: '[T]he fundamental source of conflict in this new world will not be primarily ideological or primarily economic. The great divisions among humankind and the dominating source of conflict will be cultural.'[18] It was Huntington's understanding that religion is a defining element of culture and therefore plays an important role in the conflict between civilizations. It is not necessary to report here the methodological, historical, and sociological criticisms of this theory.[19] It may however be useful to illustrate with appeal to the 'Arab Spring' that a complex reality tends to refute any monolithic conception of, in this case, (political) Islam. These recent events have shown that the influence of economic concerns is at least as important as religious allegiance throughout the countries of North Africa.[20] Huntington assumed that cultures (including religious aspects) had fixed identities, rather than being in constant interaction with each other and with economic, social, political, and legal factors. This means that cultures constantly shape and are being shaped by the actions of various actors. The approach taken in this study is partly prompted by academic frustration with the fatalism that simple assumptions and simple categories can generate.

A different argument in support of the claim that religion—or rather its actors—exert social influence in modern society refers to the many links between church and state in Western Europe,[21] a region otherwise portrayed as an exemplar of

---

[15] Berger reports that Western Europe and a 'globalized *elite*' are exceptions to the process of desecularization he describes. However, he is careful to point out that secularization may not describe accurately the reality in France, the United Kingdom, and Scandinavian countries. It would be more precise to speak of 'a shift in the institutional location of religion'. While support for organized religion has fallen away, 'strong survivals of religion' remain. P. L. Berger, 'Introduction', in P. L. Berger (ed.), *The Desecularization of the World: Resurgent Religion and World Politics*, (Washington D.C.: Wm. B. Eerdmans Publishing, 1999), 1–18, at 2 and 9–10.

[16] See note 15, at 18.

[17] S. P. Huntington, *The Clash of Civilizations and the Remaking of World Order*, (New York: Simon & Schuster, 2003); S. P. Huntington, 'The Clash of Civilizations?', *Foreign Affairs*, Summer 1993 22–49.

[18] S. P. Huntington, 'The Clash of Civilizations?', at 22.

[19] See for example A. Mungiu-Pippidi and D. Mindruta, 'Was Huntington Right? Testing Cultural Legacies and the Civilization Border', 39 *International Politics* 2 (2002), 193–213; A. Sen, 'Violence, Identity and Poverty', 45 *Journal of Peace Research* 1 (2008), 5–15.

[20] Considering Egypt, commentators noted the electoral gains of political Islam. However, they also pointed out the divisions between Islamic parties, the absence of a united secular alternative, and the incentive for electors to support the Muslim Brotherhood's political arm because this organization was the only one that offered social and economic support nets during the Mubarak regime. L. Anderson, 'Demystifying the Arab Spring: Parsing the Differences Between Tunisia, Egypt, and Libya', 90 *Foreign Affairs* 3, May/June 2011, 2–7; J. Voll, et al., 'Political Islam in the Arab Awakening: Who Are the Major Players?', 19 *Middle East Policy* 2 (2012), 10–35.

[21] For example, John Madeley shows that European states are committed either *de jure* or *de facto* to support religious organizations or their aims. J. Madeley, 'European Liberal Democracy and the Principle of State Religious Neutrality', 26 *West European Politics* 1 (2003), 1–22. See generally J. Temperman, *State-Religion Relationships and Human Rights Law: Towards a Right to Religiously Neutral Governance*, (Leiden: Martinus Nijhoff Publishers, 2010).

secularism. As Chapter 3 will show, the relationships between church and state account for many of the cases related to religion which are brought before the European Court of Human Rights (ECtHR). Perhaps the most interesting aspect is that secularism itself, while challenging the presence and role of religion and its symbols in public life, may become akin to a religion. In Joseph Weiler's view, for instance, secularism cannot be equated with neutrality, because '*Laïcité* is not an empty category which signifies absence of faith. It is often...a rich world view, a position of conscience. It is not an indifference to religion...[B]ut a "faith" in its own right.'[22] So, while religion is less present in what we regard as secularized societies, it becomes, paradoxically, more visible. The *Lautsi* case illustrates the paradox.[23] Ms Lautsi challenged the display of crucifixes in classrooms of an Italian public school on the grounds that it was 'contrary to the principle of secularism' according to which she wished to raise her children.[24] Even if nothing else is retained in relation to this case at this stage, the flurry of attention which the presence of the crucifix received—from various sectors of society across Europe and beyond, including from politicians, religious figures of various creeds, and indeed legal scholars—should be noted.

The purpose of this book is not to evaluate whether we find ourselves in a post-secular society[25] and measure how prominent religion is in such society; whether resurgence or continuation can be witnessed, or whether the renaissance of religion is merely a perception that may or may not be confirmed by statistical data. Instead the author ventures to suggest that a heightened *perception* of the prominence of religion is sufficient to support this book's focus on religious actors. This is so because when religion is perceived as important, religious actors that interpret it—through constructing meaning and attributing significance to religious texts and practices—are equally significant, or more so. In this sense then, it is in the interest of both the legal scholar and society at large to understand not (only) whether 'God believes in human rights',[26] but whether religious actors do.

This brings us to the second field to which the topic and the book's approach are relevant: legal scholarship. Responding to (perceived) developments in society

---

[22] J. H. H. Weiler, '*Lautsi*: Crucifix in the Classroom Redux', 21 *EJIL* 1 (2010), 1–6, at 4.

[23] A recent book carries the name of this case, which may, as well, be taken as an indication of its notoriety. See J. Temperman (ed.), *The Lautsi Papers: Multidisciplinary Reflections on Religious Symbols in the Public School Classroom* (Leiden: Martinus Nijhoff Publishers, 2012).

[24] *Lautsi and Others v. Italy*, Application no. 30814/06, Grand Chamber, Judgment of 18 March 2011; *Lautsi v. Italy*, Application no. 30814/06, Judgment of 3 November 2009, para. 7. For a discussion of the case see Chapter 1, III.2, in this volume.

[25] See for instance J. Habermas, 'Secularism's Crisis of Faith: Notes on Post-Secular Society', 25 *New Perspectives Quarterly* (2008), 17–29.

[26] This inspired phrase is taken from N. Ghanea, A. Stephens and R. Walden (eds.), *Does God Believe in Human Rights? Essays on Religion and Human Rights*, (Leiden: Martinus Nijhoff Publishers, 2007). Dennis de Jong also identifies *not* God as the one that should believe in human rights, but 'the adherents of religions and beliefs' who 'are bound to human rights law, whether they "believe" in them or not'. It should be noted that the terms 'adherents' and 'religious actors' employed in this study do not necessarily coincide. D. de Jong, 'Freedom of Religion and Belief in the Light of Recent Challenges: Needs, Clashes and Solutions', in N. Ghanea, A. Stephens and R. Walden (eds.), *Does God Believe in Human Rights? Essays on Religion and Human Rights*, (Leiden: Martinus Nijhoff Publishers, 2007) 181–206, at 181.

legal authors have displayed a growing interest in religion and a rather rich literature has recently emerged. A survey of the literature shows that three clusters of topics have attracted the attention of legal scholars.[27]

First, some scholars have studied church-state relations, the principle of state neutrality and secularism, including in relation to the display of religious symbols and the wearing of religious dress in public.[28] A recent volume by Jeroen Temperman makes an important contribution in this area. The author undertook a comprehensive legal analysis of church-state relationships in their different forms, and state practices with regard to them, with the aim of understanding their impact on the implementation of international human rights norms.[29] While recognizing that international legal instruments do not endorse a specific position on established religions, Temperman concludes that some forms of establishment of religion and state atheism 'amount to *ipso facto* violations of international human rights law'.[30] He argues that the 'ramifications' of the obligations of states under human rights law may give rise to a system of state neutrality, understood as the 'self-imposed prohibition of direct discrimination on grounds of religion or belief, supplemented with a lasting commitment to prevent indirect discrimination as well as a durable commitment to redress any instances of inadvertent indirect discrimination'.[31]

---

[27] It is important to note that, although the cluster classification proposed here is useful for analytical purposes, these grand topics which appear in literature should not be perceived as clearly delimited one from the other. On the contrary, they are interrelated. Often an edited book covers in its different parts all three clusters: see for example J. Witte Jr and J. D. Van der Vyver (eds.), *Religious Human Rights in Global Perspective: Legal Perspectives*, (The Hague: Martinus Nijhoff Publishers, 1996) or the remarkable oeuvre N. Ghanea (ed.), *Religion and Human Rights*, vol. I, vol. II, vol. III, vol. IV (New York: Routledge, 2010).

[28] As indicative scholarship, the following can be listed: A. A. An-Na'im, 'The Synergy and Interdependence of Human Rights, Religion and Secularism', in J. Runzo, M. N. Martin and A. Sharma (eds.), *Human Rights and Responsibilities in the World Religions*, (Oxford: Oneworld Publications, 2003), 27–50; W. Brugger and M. Karayanni (eds.), *Religion in the Public Sphere: A Comparative Analysis of German, Israeli, American and International Law*, (Berlin: Springer Verlag, 2007); M. Davies, 'Pluralism in Law and Religion', in P. Cane, C. Evans and Z. Robinson (eds.), *Law and Religion in Theoretical and Historical Context* (Cambridge: Cambridge University Press, 2008), 72–99; D. L. Dreisbach, 'A New Perspective on Jefferson's Views on Church-State Relations: The Virginia Statute for Establishing Religious Freedom in Its Legislative Context', 35 *The American Journal of Legal History* 2 (1991), 172–204; C. Evans and C. Thomas, 'Church-State Relations in the European Court of Human Rights', *BYU L. Rev.* (2006), 699–725; M. Fadel, 'Islamic Politics and Secular Politics: Can They Co-Exist?', 25 *Journal of Law and Religion* 1 (2009), 101–118; D. McGoldrick, *Human Rights and Religion: the Islamic Headscarf Debate in Europe*, (Portland, OR: Hart, 2006); D. Meyerson, 'Why Religion Belongs in the Private Sphere, not the Public Square', in P. Cane, C. Evans and Z. Robinson (eds.), *Law and Religion in Theoretical and Historical Context* (Cambridge: Cambridge University Press, 2008), 44–71; A. Nieuwenhuis, 'European Court of Human Rights: State and Religion, Schools and Scarves. An Analysis of the Margin of Appreciation as Used in the Case of Leyla Sahin v. Turkey, Decision of 29 June 2004, Application Number 44774/98', 1 *European Constitutional Law Review* 3 (2005), 495–510; A. Reuter, 'Säkularität und Religionsfreiheit: ein doppeltes Dilemma', 35 *Leviathan* 2 (2007), 178–192; T. Stahnke and R. C. Blitt, 'The Religion-State Relationship and the Right to Freedom of Religion or Belief: A Comparative Textual Analysis of the Constitutions of Predominantly Muslim Countries', 36 *Georgetown Journal of International Law* (2005), 947–1078.

[29] J. Temperman, *State-Religion Relationships and Human Rights Law: Towards a Right to Religiously Neutral Governance*, at 4.

[30] See note 29, at 340.

[31] See note 29, at 348–349.

A second group of literature examines the relationship between law and religion(s) through a historical, theoretical, doctrinal, or empirical lens. Important work in this category evaluates the contribution of religion to the development of international law, including that on human rights and humanitarian norms in particular,[32] and the compatibility of religion(s) and religious norms with human rights law, as well as the influence of law on religion.[33] Scholars have paid particular attention in recent years to Islam and to gender issues in the context of Islam.[34] Nisrine Abiad's comparative analysis of the role sharia plays in the process of ratification of international human rights treaties is grounded in a thorough understanding of context and manages to capture the complex interactions of human rights and sharia law.[35] The author shows that sharia is sometimes used as an 'excuse' to limit the implementation of human rights law at domestic level; however in other cases legislative amendments have given effect to human rights law within the framework of sharia law, refuting the assumption that the two are necessarily incompatible.[36]

Third, numerous publications analyse the protection that international instruments and national legislation provide to freedom of religion, the prohibition of religious discrimination, and parental rights concerning the religious education of their children. Many scholars examine the jurisprudence of international courts in

---

[32] See for instance chapters 1–8 in M. W. Janis and C. Evans (eds.), *Religion and International Law*, (The Hague: Martinus Nijhoff Publishers, 1999).

[33] Among the works in this field are: P. W. Edge, *Religion and Law: An Introduction*, (Aldershot: Ashgate Publishing, 2006); C. Evans, 'The Double-Edged Sword: Religious Influences on International Humanitarian Law', 6 *Melbourne Journal of International Law* 1 (2005), 1–31; N. Ghanea, A. Stephens and R. Walden (eds.), *Does God Believe in Human Rights? Essays on Religion and Human Rights*, at 19–146; C. W. Howland (ed.), *Religious Fundamentalisms and the Human Rights of Women*, (New York: Palgrave Macmillan, 2001); M. W. Janis and C. Evans (eds.), *Religion and International Law*, (The Hague: Martinus Nijhoff Publishers, 1999); V. Popovski, G. M. Reichberg and N. Turner (eds.), *World Religions and Norms of War*, (New York: United Nations University Press, 2009); J. Runzo, M. N. Martin and A. Sharma (eds.), *Human Rights and Responsibilities in the World Religions*, (Oxford: Oneworld Publications, 2003), at 209–301; A. Whiting and C. Evans (eds.), *Mixed Blessings: Laws, Religions and Women's Rights in the Asia-Pacific Region*, (Leiden: Martinus Nijhoff Publishers, 2006); J. Witte Jr, 'A Dickensian Era of Religious Rights: An Update on Religious Human Rights in Global Perspective', 42 *William & Mary Law Review* (2000), 707–770; J. Witte Jr and J. D. Van der Vyver (eds.), *Religious Human Rights in Global Perspective: Religious Perspectives*, (The Hague: Martinus Nijhoff Publishers, 1996).

[34] See for instance N. Abiad and F. Mansoor, *Criminal Law and the Rights of the Child in Muslim States: A Comparative and Analytical Perspective*, (London: British Institute of International and Comparative Law, 2010); R. Ahdar and N. Aroney (eds.), *Shari'a in the West*, (Oxford: Oxford University Press, 2010); S. A. Aldeeb Abu-Sahlieh, 'Conflits entre droit religieux et droit étatique chez les musulmans dans les pays musulmans et en Europe', 49 *Revue internationale de droit comparé* 4 (1997), 813–834; S. S. Ali, *Gender and Human Rights in Islam and International Law: Equal Before Allah, Unequal Before Man?*, (The Hague: Kluwer Law International, 2000); E. Krivenko Yahyaoui, *Women, Islam and International Law: within the context of the Convention on the Elimination of All Forms of Discrimination against Women*, (Leiden: Martinus Nijhoff Publishers, 2009); F. Raday, 'Culture, Religion, and Gender', 1 *International Journal of Constitutional Law* 4 (2003), 663–715; J. Rehman and S. Breau (eds.), *Religion, Human Rights and International Law*, Martinus Nijhoff Publishers, 2007.

[35] N. Abiad, *Sharia, Muslim States and International Human Rights Treaty Obligations: A Comparative Study*, (London: British Institute of International and Comparative Law, 2008).

[36] See note 35, at xv.

these areas. Topics that have received particular attention are conscientious objection, proselytism, and blasphemy.[37]

In addition to academic publications, UN treaty bodies have produced relevant documents, including the Human Rights Committee's General Comment 22 on the right to freedom of religion enshrined in the International Covenant on Civil and Political Rights (ICCPR), supplemented by the work of Special Procedures and other studies by UN bodies.[38]

This book regards the three clusters of legal literature as its point of departure and draws on many of these studies. At the same time, it takes the analysis in a new direction, through the focus on the agency of religious actors in interpreting religion. It reaches beyond freedom of religion to address a wider array of

[37] See S. Angeletti, *Libertà religiosa e patto internazionale sui diritti civili e politici. La prassi del comitato per i diritti umani delle Nazioni Unite*, (Torino: G.Giappichelli Editore, 2008); B. Dickson, 'The United Nations and Freedom of Religion', 44 *ICLQ* 2 (1995), 327–357; M. D. Evans, 'The United Nations and Freedom of Religion: The Work of the Human Rights Committee', in R. J. Ahdar (ed.), *Law and Religion*, (Aldershot: Ashgate, 2000), 35–62; N. Lerner, 'Proselytism, Change of Religion, and International Human Rights', 12 *Emory Int'l L. Rev* (1998), 477–561; N. Lerner, *Religion, Beliefs, and International Human Rights*, (Maryknoll, New York: Orbis Books, 2000); T. Massis and C. Pettiti (eds.), *La Liberté Religieuse et la Convention Européenne des Droits de l'Homme*, (Bruxelles: Bruylant, 2004); D. J. Sullivan, 'Advancing the Freedom of Religion or Belief through the UN Declaration on the Elimination of Religious Intolerance and Discrimination', 82 *AJIL* 3 (1988), 487–520; B. Tahzib, *Freedom of Religion or Belief: Ensuring Effective International Legal Protection*, (Dordrecht: Martinus Nijhoff Publishers, 1996); P. M. Taylor, *Freedom of Religion: UN and European Human Rights Law and Practice*, (Cambridge: Cambridge University Press, 2005); J. Temperman, 'Blasphemy, Defamation of Religions and Human Rights Law', 26 *Netherlands Quarterly of Human Rights* 4 (2008), 517–545; R. Uitz, *Freedom of Religion in European Constitutional and International Case Law*, (Strasbourg: Council of Europe Publishing, 2007).

[38] Among the general comments of the treaty bodies addressing aspects related to religion, see: CEDAW Committee, *General Recommendation No. 21: equality in marriage and family relations*, 13th session, 1994; CEDAW Committee, *General Recommendation No. 23: women in political and public life*, 16th session, 1997; CESCR, *General Comment No. 13: The right to education (Art.13)*, UN Doc. E/C.12/1999/10, 8 December 1999; CESCR, *General Comment No. 20: Non-Discrimination in Economic, Social and Cultural Rights (art. 2, para. 2)*, UN Doc. E/C.12/GC/20, 10 June 2009; CESCR, *General Comment No. 21: Right of everyone to take part in cultural life (art 15, para. 1(a))*, 20 November 2009, UN Doc. E/C.12/GC/21; HRC, *General Comment No. 11: Prohibition of propaganda for war and inciting national, racial or religious hatred (Art. 20)*, 29 July 1983; HRC, *General Comment No. 18: Non-discrimination*, 10 November 1989; HRC, *General Comment No. 22: The right to freedom of thought, conscience and religion (Art. 18)*, UN Doc. CCPR/C/21/Rev.1/Add.4, 30 July 1993; HRC, *General Comment No. 23: The rights of minorities (Art. 27)*, 8 April 1994; HRC, *General Comment No. 24: Issues relating to reservations made upon ratification or accession to the Covenant or the Optional Protocols thereto, or in relation to declarations under article 41 of the Covenant*, 4 November 1994, UN Doc. CCPR/C/21/Rev.1/Add.6; HRC, *General Comment No. 28: Equality of rights between men and women (article 3)*, UN Doc. CCPR/C/21/Rev.1/Add.10, 29 March 2008. For reports of Special Rapporteurs on the right to freedom of religion or belief, see http://www.ohchr.org/EN/Issues/FreedomReligion/Pages/Annual.aspx, and in particular on gender aspects the Rapport soumis par M. Abdelfattah Amor, Rapporteur spécial, conformément à la résolution 2001/42 de la Commission des droits de l'homme, Additif: *Etude sur la liberté de religion ou de conviction et la condition de la femme au regard de la religion et des traditions*, 5 April 2002, UN. Doc. E/CN.4/2002/73/Add.2. See also: OHCHR, *Study of the United Nations High Commissioner for Human Rights compiling existing legislations and jurisprudence concerning defamation of and contempt for religions*, 5 September 2008, UN Doc. A/HRC/9/25; Report of the Secretary-General, *Combating defamation of religions*, 12 September 2006, UN Doc. A/61/325; and the seminal report of A. Krishnaswami, 'Study of Discrimination in the Matter of Religious Rights and Practices, UN Document (1960)(reprinted)', 11 *NYU J.L. & Pol.* (1978), 227–298.

rights of religious actors, and beyond the incompatibility of religion with law to address the obligations of religious actors under international law. The book will systematically carve out the accountability framework of religious actors—be they non-state entities, international organizations, or states. The ultimate aim is to transcend the deadlock on whether religion is or is not compatible with international law in general, and human rights law in particular, by providing a new narrative that seeks to ensure the compliance of religious actors with international law.

III. From (In)compatibility Towards Accountability

In shifting the focus of the legal analysis away from debates over (in)compatibility of religion and law, the book introduces religious actors as an analytical category.[39] This analytical category presents religious actors as state and non-state entities, which assume the role of interpreters of religion, and draw on a 'special' legitimacy in demanding obedience from their adherents, members, or citizens.

At this stage it is important to express a caveat. The present study does not claim that the interpretation of religion is the exclusive right or attribute of religious actors; elsewhere, I have examined the role of non-religious courts in interpreting religion whilst adjudicating cases involving religious aspects.[40] The difference between non-religious courts and religious actors lies in the type of legitimacy they enjoy. The interpretations of religious actors are not regarded as legitimate by followers primarily because they result from processes of rationalization and have been enacted in a legal way, as is the case with judicial decisions; their legitimacy stems foremost from affect generated by tradition and charisma.[41] If truth be told, this observation is somehow axiomatic, since it is precisely their religious character which places religious actors in a 'special' legitimacy regime compared to other actors.[42] In practice, this 'special' legitimacy translates into influence, which may strengthen human rights and benefit the human rights movement; it may, however, also function as a societal taboo or a symbolic shield against outside interference or critique of manifestations of religious actors.

In the end, it is this, their legitimacy which makes the legal study of the rights and obligations of religious actors under international law so interesting and necessary, and prompts the fundamental question of this book: does the 'special' legitimacy of religious actors translate into a special legality regime?

---

[39] See Chapter 2, I and II.

[40] I. Cismas, 'Whose Belief: the Plaintiff's or the Judge's? Strategies to Preserve the Impartiality of Judicial Decisions in Cases Relating to Religion', European Society of International Law, 5th Research Forum, Amsterdam, 23–25 May 2013.

[41] See Chapter 2, II.2.

[42] For instance, Timothy Macklem attempts to answer why secular societies extend special protection 'to forms of belief that can be called religious' and argues that 'faith, understood as a mode of belief distinct from reason' has a special value since it is capable of contributing to human well-being. See T. Macklem, 'Faith as a Secular Value', 45 *McGill Law Journal* (2000), 1–63, at 1 and 35.

Let us illustrate the relevance of the above question with three cases which span across the state/non-state divide. The first example is ignited by a cautionary statement by the European Court of Human Rights (ECtHR) to the effect that states should refrain from interfering with the autonomy of religious organizations. The Court ruled that 'but for very exceptional cases...the Convention excludes any discretion on the part of the State to determine whether religious beliefs or the means used to express such beliefs are legitimate'.[43] Should this statement be considered to affirm a near-absolute guarantee of church autonomy that discounts the possible duties of religious organizations towards respecting the rights of third parties such as employees or adherents?

Second, the Holy See claims a dual personality in international law, as the government of the Vatican on one hand and, separately, as the government of the Catholic Church on the other. This interpretation opens the door to what this project describes as a shifting of the two international personae. For instance, the Holy See has claimed and benefited from state immunity in relation to civil suits over its handling of clerics involved in cases of child sexual abuse in the US, whereby no differentiation has been made by courts as to the capacity in which the Holy See acted, qua church or qua state.[44] In turn, the review process of the Holy See by the Committee on the Rights of the Child shows that the actor does not assume its obligations under the Convention on the Rights of the Child as a state, but portrays them as moral obligations, drawing on its personality as the government of the Catholic Church.[45] The questions that need to be answered are whether this dual personality is consistent with international law and the practice of states and whether the Holy See enjoys the privileges of a state, but not the corresponding obligations?

Third, the Organization of Islamic Cooperation (OIC) assumed the role of interpreter of human rights in the context of Islam by adopting the Cairo Declaration on Human Rights in Islam to 'serve as a guide for Member States in all aspects of life'.[46] Several of the provisions of the Cairo Declaration diverge from universal human rights standards.[47] Can states escape their international human rights obligations by joining an organization which apparently proposes an alternative understanding of human rights derived from a particular religious interpretation, a sort of 'religionalism'? As important, was this the goal of states in joining the OIC?

Against the backdrop of these three challenging illustrations, the aim of this study is to demonstrate that religious actors do not form an autonomous legal category in international law and, thus, share the accountability framework with their

---

[43] *Hasan and Chaush v. Bulgaria*, Application no. 30985/96, Judgment of 26 October 2000, para. 78.

[44] See Chapter 4, VI.2.3.

[45] See Chapter 4, VI.4.1 and 4.2.

[46] OIC, Resolution No. 49/19-P, Nineteenth Islamic Conference of Foreign Ministers, Cairo, 5 August 1990, para. 1. In the cited resolution OIC member states adopted the Cairo Declaration on Human Rights in Islam, U.N. GAOR, World Conf. on Hum. Rts., 4th Sess., Agenda Item 5, UN Doc. A/CONF.157/PC/62/Add.18 (1993) (hereafter CDHRI or Cairo Declaration).

[47] See Chapter 5, IV.1.

non-religious peers. To make this case, the book will develop in relation to the three types of religious actors—non-state entities, states, and international organizations—the following two central arguments:

- Religious actors do not enjoy special or exclusive rights compared to their non-religious peers.
- Religious actors have the same legal obligations as their respective non-religious peers.

Whilst it ensures a certain balance among the religious actors that it analyses in what concerns the religions which they propagate, this book does not aim to exhaust the entire array of religions—this is perhaps also in an effort to underline that it is not religion that is the focus of study here but the actors. As such, the two central arguments are verified in relation to the three case studies we have just touched upon: a diverse array of religious legal entities under the European Convention regime, the Holy See-Vatican, and the Organization of Islamic Cooperation. As these cases span across the state/non-state spectrum it is possible to envisage extrapolation of the results to actors similar in *genre* which nonetheless expound different religions.

At least two other classes of actors might qualify as religious non-state actors for the purpose of this study, but they are beyond its scope: individual clerics and non-state armed groups with a religious doctrine. Some rights and obligations of clerics are addressed throughout this book, however a chapter specifically dedicated to clerics was considered unnecessary in the light of the research objective. Based on a preliminary assessment and several interviews undertaken in the course of the research it was concluded that the claim to religious legitimacy of a non-state armed groups might have a bearing on the adherence and obedience of the group's members.[48] Appeals to religion by humanitarian workers or negotiators may also facilitate, legitimate, or contribute to the success of humanitarian dialogue with non-state armed groups which have religious inclinations; however nothing specifically indicated that the claim to religious legitimacy had an impact on their position in international law by comparison with non-religious armed groups. These are certainly interesting topics to explore in a future study; they are, however, beyond the ambit of the present project.

Structurally, the study is in two parts. The two chapters in Part I, titled *Religion, Its Actors, and International Law*, lay the foundation on which the legal analysis in Part II builds.

Chapter 1 explores narratives on religion and international law and describes the separation of international law from religion as it asserted itself as a distinct discipline; it also examines the more recent pull towards religion in an attempt to draw upon its legitimating features. The chapter proposes a different narrative by demonstrating that the options at hand are not ignoring or acknowledging

---

[48] In literature see for instance, P. Otis, 'Armed with the Power of Religion: Not Just a War of Ideas', in J.H. Norwitz (ed.), *Armed Groups: Studies in National Security, Counterterrorism, and Counterinsurgency*, (Newport, RI: Naval War College Press, 2008), 215–224.

religion, but rather taking stock of *religious actors* that are present and, to a certain extent, influential in international law. This 'taking stock' narrative seeks to ensure the accountability of religious actors in their engagement with the law. To support this alternative, the chapter also surveys human rights, humanitarian, and criminal law instruments to show their human-centred approach, whereby an individual or individuals acting as a collective enjoys protection of their beliefs, not religion as such.

Chapter 2 introduces the analytical category of religious actors that functions as a heuristic device in this study's endeavour to verify the two central arguments. The chapter provides the definitional contours of religious actors—they transcend the state/non-state divide, assume the role of interpreters of religion, and claim 'special' legitimacy. It clarifies these contours further by analyzing the interaction of religious actors in international fora on issues of sexuality and defamation of religions thereby also showing their potential impact on international law. Last, the chapter discusses the framework of acquisition of rights and obligations in international law of relevance also to religious actors.

Part II has three chapters, each dedicated to one case study aimed at *Operationalizing the Analytical Category of Religious Actors*. The methods and perspectives that the chapters employ are varied. These have been tailored to tackle the particular challenges which the 'speciality' of each religious actor poses: absolute church autonomy in the case of religious organizations, shifting international legal personalities in the case of the Holy See-Vatican, the carving out of exceptions to international human rights standards in the case of the OIC. At the same time, the chosen methods also enhance the potential to make comparisons between each religious actor and its corresponding non-religious peer: religious organizations versus non-religious legal entities, Holy See-Vatican versus non-religious states, OIC versus non-religious intergovernmental organizations.

Chapter 3 utilizes the capacity approach to 'extract' from the jurisprudence of the Strasbourg mechanisms the various rights which religious organizations have claimed under the European Convention on Human Rights and to demonstrate that the process of acquisition of rights functions in a similar fashion to that of non-religious legal entities. A detailed assessment of article 9 jurisprudence discloses why churches and other religious organizations were initially refused the protection granted by the right to freedom of religion under the Convention, and why today they are the exclusive holders of this right among legal entities. It discards this exclusivity—which would otherwise falsify one of the central arguments of the study—by showing that religious organizations enjoy a derivative right based on the freedom of individuals to collectively manifest their religious beliefs. The analysis goes on to look at the positive state obligations in the context of church autonomy, which it argues reveal the existence of human rights responsibilities of religious organizations, including towards employees and adherents, and the scope of such duties.

Chapter 4 examines the Holy See and the Vatican by first exposing the legal challenges posed by the dual personality scenario. One such problem is the shifting nature of the two personalities, which creates a situation in which the actor may legitimately avail itself of the privileges deriving from statehood but may choose when it complies with a state's obligations. In contrast to this dual personality portrayal—dominant in the current literature—the chapter advances a new argument, that of a construct formed by the Holy See and the Vatican which enjoys a single personality grounded in two sources: international custom recognizes the religious legitimacy of the Holy See, while a resemblance of statehood is conferred by the Lateran Treaty. It draws on a variety of methods—legal positivism, jurisprudential analysis, examination of diplomatic practice, insights from social constructivism—in order to first establish the personality of the entities under international law and then discuss the rights and obligations which flow from this personality. By exploring the responsibilities of the Holy See-Vatican under human rights law in the context of child sexual abuse by Catholic clerics in Ireland it illustrates that the actor's obligations do not appear to be different in nature from those of other states, whereas their extraterritorial applicability may be of greater significance.

Chapter 5 seeks to understand what drives the OIC's codification of human rights and reflect upon it within the framework of regionalism under two guises: as an approach aimed at carving out exceptions to universal human rights norms and as a context-sensitive approach to interpreting and applying international human rights standards. The Cairo Declaration on Human Rights in Islam is examined against the background of OIC member states' obligations under international human rights treaties and their commitment to these obligations. In this light, it is submitted that the Cairo Declaration, which subjects the rights entailed therein to sharia law, does not reflect the majority of its member states' understanding of human rights, nor does it succeed in guiding their conduct in this area; by all accounts, this would be a failure for an organization that portrays itself as 'a guide for Member States in all aspects of life'. At the same time, the analysis sheds light on the non-accommodation by international law (its other actors and its mechanisms) of claims to religious exceptionalism made by some OIC states and also on the accountability of the OIC as such. More recent instruments, such as the Covenant on the Rights in Islam and the Statute of the OIC Independent Permanent Human Rights Commission, have a certain potential to promote human rights in the context of the 'Muslim world'[49] in a manner that is context-sensitive, yet more in accordance with the practice of other regional human rights systems.

The findings of the research are appraised in the Conclusions which offer an answer to the central question of the study: does the analytical category of religious actors form an autonomous legal category in international law? The Conclusions also articulate the need for a process of two-sided legitimation: religious actors have come to need the legitimacy of international law to strengthen the legitimacy of their authority to interpret religion, and international law itself may benefit

---

[49] This expression is used here to echo the OIC's own description.

from religious actors fostering its legitimacy in different cultural contexts. In an effort to place Ms. Lubna Hussein's archetypal case in a wider context, an interactional[50] approach to legitimating international law is explored. Such an approach draws on the interpretative role of a variety of actors, including religious ones, and on the recognition that international law itself is dynamic (as is religion) while its 'force' relies on legality and shared understandings of such legality.

---

[50] See J. Brunnée and S. J. Toope, *Legitimacy and Legality in International Law: an Interactional Account*, (Cambridge: Cambridge University Press, 2010).

PART I

RELIGION, ITS ACTORS, AND INTERNATIONAL LAW

1

Religion and International Law
Revisited

'Because we're separated, everything separates us, even our efforts to join each
other.'

—Simone de Beauvoir[1]

I. Introduction

Whilst it embraces a shift in focus, this project is not rooted in a sort of legal evolu-
tionism which discards the existing literature on religion and international law and
the concern with religious freedom. Quite the opposite, the relationship of religion
and international law and the provisions of treaty and customary law related to
religion represent the starting point on which the subsequent analysis builds. For
that reason, this chapter explores narratives on religion and international law, discussing the incentives for legal scholars of discovering the roots of the discipline in
various religions and the reasons for keeping religion and law separate. The chapter
then proposes to recast this debate, by demonstrating that the options at hand do
not concern ignoring or acknowledging *religion*; what is needed instead is a new
narrative which takes stock of the *religious actors* that are present and to a certain
extent influential in international law (II).

Further, the chapter examines relevant provisions of human rights treaties, and
international humanitarian law and criminal law instruments in order to provide
support for this study's focus on religious actors. The review of treaty and customary law categorically demonstrates that the beneficiaries of legal protection are certain actors rather than religion per se. The examination of positive law also initiates
the book's démarche of clarifying the rights and obligations of religious actors (III).

II. Narratives on Religion and International Law

Accounts of religion in the legal history of international law often portray it as
having played a role in the development of the discipline. Two narratives develop

---

[1] S. de Beauvoir, *The Mandarins*, 2 ed., (New York: W.W. Norton & Company, 1999), at 370.

from here. First, there are those scholars who argue that the religious origins of international law should be acknowledged and recuperated to forge legitimacy for that law. Second, and to the contrary, there is the argument that emphasizes the necessity for international law to remain secular, as its crystallization into a separate discipline resulted from its emancipation from religion.

1. Acknowledging and recuperating religion

Yoram Dinstein observes that the present make-up of international law is 'devoid of any religious contents [b]ut religion had a great impact on the genesis of the international legal system'.[2] One author summarizes an apparent agreement of scholarship on the fact that 'much modern international law grew out of Christian civilization' and is quick to add that 'contemporary religious underpinnings are more ecumenical'.[3] Judge Cançado Trindade recalled, on several occasions, the influence of the Spanish theologians of the sixteenth century, Francisco de Vitoria and Francisco Suárez, and also of Hugo Grotius, whom he collectively acclaims as 'the founding fathers of international law', their work having 'propounded an essentially universalist outlook'.[4] In *Brierly's Law of Nations*, Andrew Clapham regards de Vitoria's work as remarkable since it puts forward 'a courageous defence of the rights of the indigenous people conquered' by Spaniards.[5] The contention is that:

Vitoria's teaching marks an important step in the expansion of international law into a world system; for it meant that a law which had its rise among the few princes of European Christendom was not to be limited to them, or to their relations with one another, but was universally valid, founded as it was on a natural law applying equally to all men everywhere.[6]

It is interesting to note that both Cançado Trindade and Clapham implicitly recognize the agency of these actors—indeed religious actors—and do not attribute the beginnings of international law diffusely to Christianity.

Recent scholarship increasingly addresses the role of the religious traditions of Islam, Hinduism, Confucianism,[7] Jainism, Buddhism, and others, in the

---

[2] This link with religion is, in Dinstein's analysis, a feature of primitive legal systems. Y. Dinstein, 'International Law as a Primitive Legal System', 19 *NYU J.L. & Pol.* 1 (1986) 1–32, at 17.

[3] J. A. R. Nafziger, 'The Functions of Religion in the International Legal System', in M. W. Janis and C. Evans (eds.), *Religion and International Law*, (The Hague: Martinus Nijhoff Publishers, 1999), 155–176, at 162. See also Dinstein, 'International Law as a Primitive Legal System', at 17–18.

[4] Separate Opinion of Judge A.A. Cançado Trindade, *Case of the Moiwana Community v. Suriname*, Judgment of 15 June 2005, para. 62. See also Concurring Opinion of Judge A.A. Cançado Trindade, *Juridical Condition and Rights of Undocumented Migrants*, Advisory Opinion OC-18/03, 17 September 2003, paras. 4–12.

[5] A. Clapham, *Brierly's Law of Nations*, 7th ed., (Oxford: Oxford University Press, 2012), at 24. See also D. M. Johnston, *The Historical Foundations of World Order: The Tower and the Arena*, (Leiden: Martinus Nijhoff Publishers, 2008), at 379 ff.

[6] Clapham, *Brierly's Law of Nations*, 7th ed., at 24.

[7] Frederick Tse-shyang Chen notes however that 'Confucianism is not a religion', although it is sometimes mistaken for one. F. Tse-shyang Chen, 'The Confucian View of World Order', in M. W. Janis and C. Evans (eds.), *Religion and International Law*, (The Hague: Martinus Nijhoff Publishers, 1999), 27–50, at 27.

current process of development of international law.[8] In the words of Mashood A. Baderin:

[W]hile Christianity is perceived to have played an almost unilateral role, at least from the European perspective, in the historical development of modern international law, other religions are now asserting their values as relevant factors to be considered in its continued evolution.[9]

In particular, the origins of human rights have received considerable attention. Consequently, '[a]ll major religions lay claim to having fostered the idea of human rights'.[10] The roots of human rights are said to be traceable to early political and philosophical natural law writings of Western thought, as well as Confucian, Hindu, and Buddhist traditions, just as the Bible and the Quran can be read to proclaim not only duties but also rights.[11] Ilias Bantekas observes that the French and American constitutions, and even the Universal Declaration of Human Rights (UDHR), resound with echoes of natural law philosophy. The assertion is that, in as much as natural law coincides with and is a continuation of religion,[12] the claim made by religions to have played an important role in the development of human rights law is supported. In a post-colonial world, struggling with forces of globalization and localism at the same time, the narrative that human rights is a distillation of religious and cultural traditions may appear appealing.

In the context of the development of humanitarian law, several authors have explored not whether, but how far, different religions have served as inspiration.[13] Whereas James Cockayne suggests that the interplay between Islamic and Western civilizations has had an important role in shaping humanitarian law,[14]

---

[8] See for example G. M. Badr, 'A Survey of Islamic International Law', in M. W. Janis and C. Evans (eds.), *Religion and International Law*, (The Hague: Martinus Nijhoff Publishers, 1999), 95–102; S. C. Jain, 'Jainism, War and International Law', 43 *Indian Journal of International Law* 4 (2003), 748–757; V. P. Nanda, 'International Law in Ancient Hindu India', in M. W. Janis and C. Evans (eds.), *Religion and International Law*, (The Hague: Martinus Nijhoff Publishers, 1999), 51–62; R. Shabtai, 'The Influence of Judaism on the Development of International Law—An Assessment', in M. W. Janis and C. Evans (eds.), *Religion and International Law*, (The Hague: Martinus Nijhoff Publishers, 1999), 63–92; Tse-shyang Chen, 'The Confucian View of World Order'; C. Weeramantry, *Universalising International Law*, (Leiden: Martinus Nijhoff Publishers, 2004), at 1–31.

[9] M. A. Baderin, 'Religion and International Law: Friends or Foes?', 5 *European Human Rights Law Review* (2009), 637–658, at 643.

[10] I. Bantekas, 'Religion as a Source of International Law', in J. Rehman and S. Breau (eds.), *Religion, Human Rights and International Law*, (Leiden: Martinus Nijhoff Publishers, 2007), 115–136, at 130. There are several scholarly contributions dealing with the ways in which religions have contributed to the development of human rights. A less cited example can be found in J. B. Leith, 'A More Constructive Encounter: A Bahá'í View of Religion and Human Rights', in N. Ghanea, A. Stephens and R. Walden (eds.), *Does God Believe in Human Rights? Essays on Religion and Human Rights*, (Leiden: Martinus Nijhoff Publishers, 2007), 121–146.

[11] A. Clapham, *Human Rights: A Very Short Introduction*, (Oxford: Oxford University Press, 2007), at 5.

[12] Bantekas, 'Religion as a Source of International Law', at 130.

[13] For an example see M. K. Sinha, 'Hinduism and International Humanitarian Law', 87 *International Review of the Red Cross* 858 (2005), 285–294. See also contributions in the edited volume V. Popovski, G. Reichberg and N. Turner (eds.), *World Religions and Norms of War*, (New York: United Nations University Press, 2009).

[14] J. Cockayne, 'Islam and International Humanitarian Law: From a Clash to a Conversation Between Civilizations', 84 *International Review of the Red Cross* 847 (2002), 597–626.

Judge Weeramantry seeks to 'strengthen' humanitarian law by acknowledging that:

[it] is not a recent invention, nor the product of any one culture. The concept is of ancient origin, with a lineage stretching back at least three millennia... [I]t is deep-rooted in many cultures—Hindu, Buddhist, Chinese, Christian, Islamic and traditional African. These cultures have all given expression to a variety of limitations on the extent to which any means can be used for the purposes of fighting one's enemy.[15]

To substantiate the claims asserting the influence of religion on the development of humanitarian law, Henry Dunant's Christian internationalism,[16] which was at the base of the founding of the International Committee of the Red Cross (ICRC), should be recalled. Undeniably, the history of the ICRC as an organization coincides in many respects with the history, and strengths and weaknesses, of international humanitarian law itself. Anecdotal evidence suggests that ICRC delegates appeal to religious principles in their day-to-day operations on the ground when they promote compliance with the laws of armed conflict. Daniel Thürer sees a great utility in appealing to religions in support of international law, in particular in times of conflict, because 'it can easily be shown that law as such is powerless if it is not backed by forces beyond the legal system, such as customs, public opinion or—religion.'[17] His endeavour is a strategic one, in so far as the goal is to uncover and promote those positive elements which have supported law in times of war, and not those which have endangered it.[18]

As a relatively new discipline, which is intrinsically linked to international law, transitional justice aims to offer redress to victims of human rights and humanitarian law violations by promoting truth-seeking initiatives, criminal prosecutions, reparation programs, and institutional reform in the aftermath of authoritarianism and conflict.[19] Transitional justice mechanisms, and in particular truth commissions, have attracted the participation of clerics as commissioners which can be argued to be important[20]—most-cited is the example of Archbishop Desmond Tutu the appointment of whom is said to have shaped the work of the Truth and Reconciliation Commission of South Africa.[21] One scholar suggests that religious

---

[15] Dissenting Opinion of Judge Weeramantry, *Legality of the Threat or Use of Nuclear Weapons, Advisory Opinion*, ICJ Reports 1996, at 256.

[16] Cockayne, 'Islam and International Humanitarian Law: From a Clash to a Conversation Between Civilizations', at 600.

[17] D. Thürer, *International Humanitarian Law: Theory, Practice, Context*, Collected Courses of the Hague Academy of International Law, vol. 338, (Online ed.: Martinus Nijhoff, 2008), at 167.

[18] See note 17.

[19] See for instance, Report of the Special Rapporteur on the promotion of truth, justice, reparation and guarantees of non-recurrence, Pablo de Greiff, UN Doc. A/HRC/21/46, 9 August 2012, paras. 15–46.

[20] To merely give some examples: in East Timor two of seven commissioners were clerics, and the technical institution set up as a follow up is also headed by a cleric, see http://www.cavr-timorleste. org/en/cavr.htm; the Commission Vérité, Justice et Reconciliation of Togo was chaired by a cleric, see http://www.cvjr-togo.org/fr/cvjr.html#4; and in Guatemala, the Catholic Church set up an independent truth-seeking project, Recuperación de la Memoria Histórica, which is considered to have had a tremendous impact on subsequent transitional justice processes in the country, see L. Bickford, 'Unofficial Truth Projects', 29 *HRQ* 4 (2007), 994–1035, at 1010–1012.

[21] One scholar notes that 'given the presence of Archbishop Desmond Tutu as the Chair [of the truth commission], some of its public hearings had a decidedly religious character. Commentators pointed

actors have been influential in eight out of 15 countries that exercised 'strong' or 'moderately strong' truth seeking initiatives and in two of four countries which pursued moderately strong punitive measures (defined in this case as criminal prosecutions and vetting).[22] Other authors identify four roles that religious actors have played in different transitional justice processes—as makers, adaptors, facilitators, and reflectors of norms.[23] While the limited scholarship on the topic does not allow for generalization, it is not far-fetched to note that religious actors exercised a certain influence on the conceptual and institutional development of transitional justice, including through the direct participation of clerics in transitional justice mechanisms.

It has been indicated, in this review portraying religious interpretations as a factor in the development of international law (and in particular human rights and humanitarian law), that the authors who highlight this factor sometimes have an interest that goes beyond historical precision or political correctness: by unearthing the religious roots of law they hope to strengthen the legitimacy of international law within different religious and cultural contexts.

2. Insisting on the separation of law and religion

To be clear, there are scholars who oppose a démarche aimed at recuperating the religious roots of international law; and it is here that the second narrative takes shape, separating law from religion. During the nineteenth and twentieth century great efforts have been made by legal positivists to keep international law apart from religion and morals.[24] Hilary Charlesworth explains the background:

International law is constantly under challenge as a *legal* system. . . . Perhaps because there is so much anxiety about whether international law can claim to be a branch of law, the topic of the making and sources of international law dominates most introductory works. It is as if pinning down the well-springs of international law will provide certainty and authority for the discipline.[25]

---

out that the hearings frequently resembled a church service more than a judicial proceeding, with a definite "liturgical character."' A. R. Chapman and P. Ball, 'The Truth of Truth Commissions: Comparative Lessons from Haiti, South Africa, and Guatemala', 23 *HRQ* 1 (2001), 1–43, at 18. The influence of Desmond Tutu in the conception and functioning of the South African Truth and Reconciliation Commission has been made the object of both acclaim and critical analysis, see for instance T.A. Borer, 'Reconciling South Africa or South Africans? Cautionary Notes from the TRC', 8 *African Studies Quarterly* 1 (2004), 20–38, at 31–32.

[22] D. Philpott, 'When Faith Meets History: the Influence of Religion on Transitional Justice', in T. Brudholm and T. Cushman (eds.),*The Religious in Response to Mass Atrocity: Interdisciplinary Perspectives*, (Cambridge: Cambridge University Press, 2009), 174–212.

[23] See A. P. Boesenecker and L. Vinjamuri, 'Lost in Translation? Civil Society, Faith-based Organizations and the Negotiation of International Norms', 5 *International Journal of Transitional Justice* 3 (2011), 345–365.

[24] M. W. Janis, 'Introduction', in M. W. Janis and C. Evans (eds.), *Religion and International Law*, (The Hague: Martinus Nijhoff Publishers, 1999) xi–xiii, at xi.

[25] H. Charlesworth, 'Law-making and Sources', in J. Crawford and M. Koskenniemi (eds.), *The Cambridge Companion to International Law*, (Cambridge: Cambridge University Press, 2012) 187–202, at 187.

In other words, it is argued that the divorce from religion has been prompted by an attempt to establish international law as science, or as 'law proper'. On this view, international law is universal law, not because of its origins in natural law, but because states consented to it by means of treaty, or custom (where state practice stemmed from a conviction that a rule is binding), and because it can be rationally discerned from general principles of law 'recognized by civilized nations' and from the jurisprudence and work of 'the most highly qualified publicists of the various nations'.[26] The impetus to see international law as science, distinct from religious considerations, lingers to this day.

A second motive for the insistence on separating law from religion is grounded in historic awareness of the European experience of religious wars in the sixteenth and seventeenth centuries. The feeling is that in a multi-religious and multi-cultural world, to assure equality and non-discrimination, international law, and especially international human rights and humanitarian law, must rest on secular founda-tions.[27] Critical accounts of law and religion observe that despite the promotion of separateness through legal positivism, the narratives of the 'Legal' and the 'Religious' about the self, the other, and each other are strikingly similar, reflecting a continuous interaction.[28] David Kennedy comments that the secular narrative on international law is erroneous, and traces the commencement of international law not to the Peace of Westphalia of 1648 but as follows:

Were we to focus on the evolution of a culturally independent, self-confident legal cul-ture—professionally, doctrinally, institutionally—we would surely need to begin with reli-gion, seeing the roots of law's arrogance, universality, indeed univocality, in the project of canon law and the development of catholicity. Catholicity not as we now regard it, as a virtual synonym for 'general, universal'... but as it developed from the Greek to mean the opinion of the greater, wiser, older, healthier part, in short, the orthodoxy established by council as arbiters of the public good. And we would see in the catholic not merely a pre-cursor but an origin, a companion for international law's generalizing pretense—even unto its roots in the institutional structure of plenary and consent.[29]

There is a third justification of separationist efforts. Forging legitimacy for human rights via their alleged religious roots is opposed by pointing to the deliberately secular nature of human rights law whereby the foundation of human rights in human dignity and human agency is the principal, even exclusive, reason for their success.[30] This is a fundamental philosophical objection that can be difficult to overcome. This staunch defence of the secularism of human rights may however

---

[26] See Statute of the International Court of Justice (1945), art. 38.1.

[27] See Baderin, 'Religion and International Law: Friends or Foes?', at 644–646; Janis, 'Introduction', in M. W. Janis and C. Evans (eds.), *Religion and International Law*, at xi.

[28] D. Kennedy, 'Images of Religion in International Legal History', in M. W. Janis and C. Evans (eds.), *Religion and International Law*, (The Hague: Martinus Nijhoff Publishers, 1999), 145–153, at 153.

[29] See note 28, at 151.

[30] For a discussion of Louis Henkin and Michael Ignatieff's arguments against religious immix-tures in human rights, see S. R. Marks and A. Clapham, *International Human Rights Lexicon*, (Oxford: Oxford University Press, 2005), at 310–312.

also be understood not as a philosophical objection but as a reaction to empirical facts; for instance, the pick-and-choose approach of some states and other actors, who embrace some human rights but relativize or reject others, is sometimes legitimized by appeals to religious considerations.

Current reality also suggests that humanitarian law may be influenced by religious interpretations, with implications for military conduct. Israel, where rabbinic literature on required military conduct is currently flourishing, offers an example. References in the Bible to 'collateral damage' and the prohibition of use of certain types of weapons are missing altogether so some rabbis have transferred principles that were not originally intended for the military context to the latter.[31] In one such instance, it is asserted that, some have sought 'to apply to the Palestinian population the category of *rodef*, the rabbinic term that defines the status of a person who endangers [lit. pursues] the life of another, and who therefore himself constitutes a legitimate target of pre-emptive attack'.[32] Stuart A. Cohen contends that such interpretations may have operational implications for the conduct of the Israel Defense Forces (IDF). According to Cohen, current IDF operations, characterized by small and isolated military units, require at times that single officers make rapid decisions as to permissible targets and as such:

[t]he heavy representation in that cadre of a group that is particularly sensitive to the emergence of the new field of *hilkhot tzavah u-milchamah* [Jewish laws relating to Military and Law], in all its nuances, could well exert a profound influence on the tenor of IDF operations as a whole.[33]

The more recent development of transitional justice which, as pointed out earlier, has witnessed a certain influence by religious actors also raises a number of questions. Anecdotal evidence from Guinea suggests that the imam and archbishop which had been appointed to head a reflection commission on reconciliation have 'transformed the entire country in a mosque and a church' in an attempt to foster forgivingness for the episodes of violence experienced over decades.[34] While this example should be taken as what it is, an anecdote, one of the main concerns of observers is that a religious ethos of forgiveness evidenced in processes where religious actors were involved may legitimize amnesty for perpetrators of human rights violations.[35] For instance, Aaron P. Boesenecker and Leslie Vinjamuri argue that the actions of the Inter-Religious Council of Sierra Leone, which included representation from Muslim, Catholic, Pentecostal, and Protestant denominations, led to the inclusion of amnesty provisions in

---

[31] S. A. Cohen, 'The Re-Discovery of Orthodox Jewish Laws Relating to the Military and War (Hilkhot Tzavah U-Milchamah) in Contemporary Israel: Trends and Implications', 12 *Israel Studies* 2 (2007), 1–28, at 19.

[32] See note 31.   [33] See note 31, at 22.

[34] Interview with UN expert based in Guinea, November 2013, on file with the author.

[35] For an interesting discussion of reconciliation understood as forgiveness in South Africa and the role of Desmond Tutu see Borer, 'Reconciling South Africa or South Africans? Cautionary Notes from the TRC', at 31–32.

the Lomé Peace Accord between the Government of Sierra Leone and the Revolutionary United Front.[36] In a review of the impact of faith-based and local organizations on transitional justice, the authors contend that '[t]hese actors have often been crucial in adapting, displacing or even rejecting international standards of accountability' and that the normative adaptation 'reflects alternative understandings or, sometimes, contestation over the assumptions that underpin liberal-legal accountability strategies.'[37]

The perception that religion is gendered also encourages many to reject any attempt to unearth the religious roots of international law more broadly, and specifically human rights law, or to accept that religious principles may play a role in today's legal setting. Frances Raday's example provides the context for such opposition:

Judaism, Christianity, and Islam, whose religious courts have jurisdiction over marriage and divorce in Israel, all impose patriarchal institutions and norms—both religious and secular—on the women of the three communities. I became convinced that, without a transformation of religious patriarchy by decree of the constitutional system, women could not gain full equality. Furthermore, with time, I came to understand that, without the dismantling of patriarchy within the religions, traditionalist women would have no right to equal religious personhood.[38]

It may be contended that if one were to accept the religious foundations of international law or to allow religion to play any part in the evolution of human rights law or humanitarian norms, this would ultimately mean the importation of patriarchal patterns;[39] however, scholars have shown that even in its most secular form, international law is masculine. Both the organizational and normative structures of the international legal system are dominated by men and by masculine concerns; this has made it possible for issues of particular interest to women to remain ignored, diluted, or undermined.[40] To be clear, various religious texts include patriarchal elements as well as powerful equality clauses. Religious actors choose to emphasize one or the other. The ultimate aim should be, as Raday underlined, to change the patriarchal structures within religions.

A counter-claim to the separationist theory asserts that because the core of the neutrality argument is Eurocentric it lacks universality; that is, it represents the reverse of what it proclaims to achieve. Drawing on the historical experience of Europe, it fails to take into account the experience of other 'civilizations in relation to the accommodation of religious norms within the public sphere of

---

[36] Boesenecker and Vinjamuri, 'Lost in Translation? Civil Society, Faith-based Organizations and the Negotiation of International Norms', at 357–358.

[37] See note 36, at 347.

[38] F. Raday, 'Culture, Religion, and CEDAW's Article 5 (a)', in H. Schöpp-Schilling and C. Flinterman (eds.), *Circle of Empowerment: Twenty-Five Years of the UN Committee on the Elimination of Discrimination against Women*, (New York: Feminist Press, 2007), 68–85.

[39] See F. Raday, 'Culture, Religion, and Gender', 1 *International Journal of Constitutional Law* 4 (2003), 663–715.

[40] For an excellent analysis, see H. Charlesworth and C. Chinkin, *The Boundaries of International Law: A Feminist Analysis*, (Manchester: Manchester University Press 2000); H. Charlesworth, C. Chinkin and S. Wright, 'Feminist Approaches to International Law', 85 *AJIL* 4 (1991), 613–645.

law and governance'.[41] Moreover, as Amy Gutmann rhetorically observes: 'Do plural foundations make a human rights regime philosophically or morally incoherent?'[42] The separationist theory would be the sole coherent theory to adopt 'only if we assume that human rights must rest on a single value—*ur* value, principle, common denominator—that is acceptable to all or most people.'[43] In the absence of such an assumption, and indeed this premise tends not to conform to lived reality, human rights may have a plurality of foundations, be they secular or religious. These foundations nonetheless should not be seen as the ultimate goal, nor should they be 'worshipful, or in other way reverential, let alone idolatrous'.[44]

3. Recasting the debate: religious actors and their accountability framework

Beyond advocacy for the recuperation of religion, the insistence on separation, and subsequent claims to the contrary, what transpires from the reviewed narratives is that religion does play a certain role in international law and this is so, foremost, through the interpretations put forward by religious actors. Francisco de Vitoria, rabbis in Israel, Desmond Tutu in South Africa, or the Inter-Religious Council of Sierra Leone are examples of such actors that influenced the development or the application of the law through their interpretations. As shall be illustrated in Chapter 2, the complex interactions of religious actors in international fora, on topics such as sexuality and reproduction or in relation to the 'defamation of religions' resolutions passed at the UN Human Rights Council and General Assembly over the past decade provide examples of the potential impact of these actors on international law.

It would seem that the question under discussion is not whether religion should or should not play a role in international law; if, as evidence from various quarters suggests, *religious actors* are active in international law, then this *fait accompli* should lead us to a different narrative. Taking stock of such empirical evidence, this book asks a different question: on what terms are religious actors engaging in international fora and do they form a special legal category under international law? In other words, by clarifying the legal framework applicable to religious actors, this study recasts the two previously discussed narratives and argues that the rights and obligations of religious actors ultimately represent the boundaries of their engagement with international law, the limits of what they can do in the system. It is therefore vital to understand whether their rights and obligations are special or by no means different from those of non-religious actors.

---

[41] Baderin, 'Religion and International Law: Friends or Foes?', at 646–647.

[42] A. Gutmann, 'Introduction', in M. Ignatieff (A. Gutmann ed.), *Human Rights as Politics and Idolatry*, (Princeton: Princeton University Press, 2001), at xxii.

[43] Marks and Clapham, *International Human Rights Lexicon*, at 311.

[44] A. Gutmann, 'Introduction', in M. Ignatieff (A. Gutmann ed.), *Human Rights as Politics and Idolatry*, at xxv.

III. Relevant Provisions of International Law

Having reviewed two existing narratives on religion and international law, and argued for an alternative account, it is useful to inquire into the provisions of international and regional human rights treaties, international humanitarian law and criminal law instruments, and customary law in order to establish whether they bear any relevance for religion or religious actors. The aim of this examination is to verify whether postive law assumes an actor-centred approach or makes religion, as such, the beneficiary of legal protection. The former outcome would sanction this study's shift of focus from religion to its actors, while at the same time providing the initial elements of the legal framework applicable to religious actors.

1. International instruments

A generous account of history could pinpoint the seeds of the international human rights system in international agreements from the seventeenth and eighteenth centuries that contained an early political formulation of minority rights as religious freedoms granted to certain Christian communities by the sovereign.[45] In an effort to trace the origins of the legal prohibition of genocide, William Schabas also recalls the early protection from persecution offered by international law to national, racial, ethnic, and religious groups.[46] This prohibition of persecution, he argues, 'runs like a golden thread through the defining moments of the history of human rights'.[47] It is interesting to note that this early codification recognized religious rights—notably for groups, as opposed to religion per se—even if those rights were not the universal human rights we have come to know today.

The modern proclamation of human rights and references related to religion can be found in the Charter of the United Nations. On the 26 June 1945, the UN Charter gave the imprimatur to the non-discrimination clause that has since permeated human rights law instruments at international and regional level.[48] The prohibition of discrimination based on religion, in addition to race, sex, and language appears in article 1.3 in the section setting forth the purposes of the UN. It is among the basic objectives of the trusteeship system in article 76.c, and importantly is reiterated in article 55.c. The latter reads:

---

[45] For an interesting analysis of the early agreements of Westphalia, Vienna, and Berlin which included minority rights centred on religion, and later minority treaties under the League of Nations, see J. Jackson Preece, 'Minority Rights in Europe: From Westphalia to Helsinki', 23 *Review of International Studies* 1 (2001), 75–92.

[46] W. Schabas, *Genocide in International Law: The Crime of Crimes*, (Cambridge: Cambridge University Press, 2000), at 15.

[47] See note 46.

[48] The notable exceptions, which do not include the classic non-discrimination clause are the Convention on the Elimination of All Forms of Discrimination against Women, 1249 UNTS 18 (adopted 18 December 1979, entered into force 3 September 1981, hereafter CEDAW) and the Convention against Torture and Other Cruel, Inhuman or Degrading Treatment or Punishment, 1465 UNTS 85, (adopted 10 December 1984, entered into force 26 June 1987, hereafter CAT).

With a view to the creation of conditions of stability and well-being which are necessary for peaceful and friendly relations among nations based on respect for the principle of equal rights and self-determination of peoples, the United Nations shall promote... universal respect for, and observance of, human rights and fundamental freedoms for all without distinction as to race, sex, language, or religion.[49]

As Eibe Riedel observes in his commentary on article 55.c, those who drafted the UN Charter in Dumbarton Oaks oscillated between making vague references that offered weak support to the 'promotion of the observance of human rights' and inserting an effective human rights protection system.[50] It is perhaps ironic to note that the Soviet Union, a self-proclaimed atheistic state[51] which had opposed the insertion of a human rights clause, became in San Francisco the proponent of the clause that prohibited discrimination based on race, sex, language and, notably, religion.[52] Riedel further asserts that today the non-discrimination clause in article 55.c constitutes a clear legal obligation: 'frequently, it is even regarded as being part of *ius cogens*'.[53]

A chronological approach to the international human rights instruments that proclaim freedom of religion and other rights related to religion must start with the Universal Declaration of Human Rights of 1948 (UDHR). Whilst legally binding only in relation to those provisions that have become customary norms, the UDHR is an important normative standard. Article 18 of the UDHR provides:

Everyone has the right to freedom of thought, conscience and religion; this right includes freedom to change his religion or belief, and freedom, either alone or in community with others and in public or private, to manifest his religion or belief in teaching, practice, worship and observance.[54]

In guaranteeing the right to freedom of religion to 'everyone', it is clear that the UDHR takes an actor-centred approach in so far as individuals and groups of individuals are concerned. The text however does not disclose whether legal entities with religious purposes, such as churches or religious organizations, should also enjoy religious freedom—the analysis of jurisprudence in Chapter 3 will extensively clarify which legal entities enjoy such a right under the European Convention regime.

Noteworthy is the absence of any specific limitation or restriction on religious freedom in article 18. Although the suggested characterization of the right to freedom of religion as 'absolute and sacred' was not included in the article, there was

---

[49] Charter of the United Nations, 1 UNTS XVI (signed on 26 June 1945, entered into force 24 October 1945), arts. 1(3), 76(c) and 55(c). (Hereafter UN Charter).

[50] E. Riedel, 'Article 55(c)', in B. Simma (ed.), *The Charter of the United Nations: A Commentary*, 2nd ed., vol. 2, (Oxford: Oxford University Press, 2002), at 920.

[51] See P. Walters, 'A Survey of Soviet Religious Policy', in S. P. Ramet (ed.), *Religious Policy in the Soviet Union*, (Cambridge: Cambridge University Press, 1993), 3–30.

[52] Riedel, 'Article 55(c)', at 920.

[53] See note 52, at 923.

[54] Universal Declaration of Human Rights, G.A. res. 217A (III), U.N. Doc A/810, (adopted 10 December 1948), art 18. (Hereafter UDHR). On the customary status of religious freedom see section III.4 in this chapter.

a general consensus among the drafters that freedom of religion carried with it a 'metaphysical significance'.[55]

The 1951 Convention relating to the Status of Refugees retains the right to manifest one's religion and specifies the freedom of refugees in regard to the religious education of their children.[56] Of great importance and unquestionably in response to the tragic contemporary events,[57] the Convention lists religion as one of the grounds of non-refoulement.[58] The Convention relating to the Status of Stateless Persons adopted in 1954 mirrors the provisions of the Refugees Convention, and provides for religious rights of stateless persons.[59] The 1965 International Convention on the Elimination of All Forms of Racial Discrimination (CERD), under the general undertaking of state parties to eliminate racial discrimination, guarantees the right of everyone to freedom of thought, conscience, and religion.[60]

Unsurprisingly, among the international human rights instruments, it is the International Covenant on Civil and Political Rights (ICCPR) that has the most elaborate provisions on freedom of religion. Article 18 reads:

1. Everyone shall have the right to freedom of thought, conscience and religion. This right shall include freedom to have or to adopt a religion or belief of his choice, and freedom, either individually or in community with others and in public or private, to manifest his religion or belief in worship, observance, practice and teaching.

2. No one shall be subject to coercion which would impair his freedom to have or to adopt a religion or belief of his choice.

3. Freedom to manifest one's religion or beliefs may be subject only to such limitations as are prescribed by law and are necessary to protect public safety, order, health, or morals or the fundamental rights and freedoms of others.

4. The States Parties to the present Covenant undertake to have respect for the liberty of parents and, when applicable, legal guardians to ensure the religious and moral education of their children in conformity with their own convictions.[61]

The first paragraph closely resembles the UDHR provisions and addresses individuals and groups. The paragraph excludes however the explicit mention of the right to change one's religion as this was a contentious issue during the drafting of the ICCPR. As the *travaux préparatoires* show, the inclusion of the right to change one's religion was contested on several grounds: it was redundant, being

---

[55] See M. Scheinin, 'Article 18', in G. Alfredsson and A. Eide (eds.), *The Universal Declaration of Human Rights: A Common Standard of Achievement*, (The Hague: Martinus Nijhoff Publishers, 1999), 359–378, at 380–382. There remain, of course, the restrictions that are stipulated by the general limitations clause in article 29 of the UDHR.

[56] Convention relating to the Status of Refugees, 18 UNTS 50, (adopted 28 July 1951, entered into force 22 April 1954), art. 4.

[57] The historical context is expressly mentioned in the Convention relating to the Status of Refugees, art. 1.2.

[58] Convention relating to the Status of Refugees, art. 33.1.

[59] Convention relating to the Status of Stateless Persons, 360 UNTS 117, (adopted 28 September 1954, entered into force 6 June 1960), art. 4.

[60] International Convention on the Elimination of All Forms of Racial Discrimination, 660 UNTS 195 (adopted 21 December 1965, entered into force 4 Janaury 1969), art. 5.vii. (Hereafter CERD).

[61] International Covenant on Civil and Political Rights 999 UNTS 171 (adopted 16 December 1966, entered into force 23 March 1976), art. 18. (Hereafter ICCPR).

already implicit in the concept of freedom of religion; it lent support to proselytism, missionaries, and atheistic activities, and was strongly opposed for this reason by Muslim states in particular; it posed difficulties for states that had religious constitutions; and it unbalanced the Covenant because the provision on freedom of thought and conscience was less elaborate.[62] The drafters sought a compromise by proclaiming the right 'to have or to adopt a religion or belief of his choice', whereby the term 'adopt' introduced the possibility of discontinuing one's belief.

Special Rapporteur Arcot Krishnaswami's reading of the missing 'change' was that '[f]reedom to maintain or to change religion or belief falls primarily within the domain of the inner faith and conscience of an individual. Viewed from this angle, one would assume that any intervention from outside is not only illegitimate but impossible.'[63] However, as the Rapporteur acknowledged, 'problems do arise'.[64] This is because the inner and outer circles of religious freedom are inherently interlinked and cannot be surgically kept apart. While the thoughts and beliefs of a person are intimate, implying that changes in religious choice cannot be controlled, the exterior manifestation of those changes can. For example, a woman may be prevented from leaving the organized life of a religion by compelling her to wear certain religious dress or imposing a church tax upon her.

The interpretation of the Human Rights Committee (HRC), upheld in the process of monitoring state obligations,[65] has been that religious change is certainly a component of the *forum internum* of religious freedom. According to the Committee: '[F]reedom to "have or to adopt" a religion or belief necessarily entails the freedom to choose a religion or belief, including the right to replace one's current religion or belief with another or to adopt atheistic views, as well as the right to retain one's religion or belief.'[66] We shall return to this point in Chapter 5 in the context of the analysis of instruments developed by the Organization of Islamic Cooperation (OIC).

---

[62] Annotations on the text of the draft International Covenants on Human Rights, 1 July 1995, UN Doc. A/2929, para. 108, at 48; M. Nowak, *UN Covenant on Civil and Political Rights. CCPR Commentary*, 2nd ed., (Kehl: N.P. Engel, 2005), at 410. See also the drafting reports of the Commission: UN Docs. E/CN.4/SR. 116, 117, 161 of 1949–1950; for the Official Records of the General Assembly Third Committee, see UN Docs. A/C.3/5/SR. 288–290, 302, 306, 367 and 371 of 1950–1951, A/C.3/9/SR. 563–566 of 1954.

[63] Krishnaswami, 'Study of Discrimination in the Matter of Religious Rights and Practices, UN Document (1960)(reprinted)', at 231.

[64] See note 63.

[65] In its Concluding observations on the report of Nepal, the HRC noted 'with concern...the restrictions which apply to the manifestation of religion and to change of religion'. HRC, Concluding observations of the Human Rights Committee: Nepal, UN Doc. CCPR/C/79/Add.42, 11 October 1994, para. 11. With regard to Morocco, it expressed its concern 'about the de facto limitations on the freedom of religion or belief, including the fact that it is impossible, in practice, for a Muslim to change religion. It recalls that article 18 of the Covenant protects all religions and all beliefs, ancient and less ancient, major and minor, and includes the right to adopt the religion or belief of one's choice. The State party should take steps to ensure respect for freedom of religion or belief and to ensure that its legislation and practices are fully in conformity with article 18 of the Covenant.' HRC, Consideration of Reports Submitted by States Parties under Article 40 of the Covenant, Concluding observations: Morocco, UN Doc. CCPR/CO/82/MAR, 1 December 2004, para 21.

[66] HRC, *General Comment No. 22*, para. 5.

Coercion that results in impairing the right to have or adopt a religion or belief is specifically prohibited under the ICCPR in the second paragraph of article 18—which would in turn speak again for the possibility of continuing and discontinuing belief. The approach of the HRC in General Comment 22 was to stress *state* coercion and nothing in this authoritative interpretation of article 18.2 'seems to equate proselytism with coercion'.[67] As such, threat and use of force, penal sanctions, and policies or practices intended to compel believers or non-believers 'to adhere to their religious beliefs and congregations'; or to renounce their belief; or to convert, are considered to be among the coercive acts prohibited by article 18.2 of the ICCPR.[68]

The third paragraph of article 18 has led doctrine and practice to develop the distinction between a *forum internum* and a *forum externum*, where manifestations of religion belong to the second category. In General Comment 22, the HRC enumerates a range of acts which the *forum externum* may include:

The concept of worship extends to ritual and ceremonial acts giving direct expression to belief, as well as various practices integral to such acts, including the building of places of worship, the use of ritual formulae and objects, the display of symbols, and the observance of holidays and days of rest. The observance and practice of religion or belief may include not only ceremonial acts but also such customs as the observance of dietary regulations, the wearing of distinctive clothing or headcoverings, participation in rituals associated with certain stages of life, and the use of a particular language customarily spoken by a group. In addition, the practice and teaching of religion or belief includes acts integral to the conduct by religious groups of their basic affairs, such as the freedom to choose their religious leaders, priests and teachers, the freedom to establish seminaries or religious schools and the freedom to prepare and distribute religious texts or publications.[69]

The paragraph also reveals that the right to manifest one's religion, the *forum externum*, is not absolute. While states cannot derogate from the outer and inner freedoms even in times of public emergency[70] manifestations of religion may be limited under certain conditions. The rationale behind the permissibility of restrictions is explained by appeal to the direct impact on 'society at large' that religious manifestations may have. It follows that states may have 'a legitimate goal of overall social policy' to limit this impact.[71] As Carolyn Evans observes, 'at one extreme, it is clear that a State is not required in the name of religious freedom to tolerate

---

[67] P. M. Taylor, *Freedom of Religion: UN and European Human Rights Law and Practice* (Cambridge: Cambridge University Press, 2005), at 25.

[68] HRC, *General Comment No. 22*, para. 5.

[69] HRC, *General Comment No. 22*, para. 4. In these terms, what for some individuals might seem to be trivial aspects, for others may be vital manifestations of their religious freedom. Consistent with its own interpretation in the cited paragraph, in *Boodoo v. Trinidad and Tobago* the HRC found that 'wearing a beard' was a religious manifestation which deserved protection under article 18 of the Covenant. See Communication No. 721/1996, UN Doc. CCPR/C/74/D/721/1996 (2002), para. 6.6.

[70] HRC, *General Comment No. 22*, para. 1.

[71] R. S. Clark, 'The United Nations and Religious Freedom', 11 *Journal of International Law and Politics* (1978), 197–226, at 216; See also Tahzib-Lie, 'Women's Equal Right to Freedom of Religion or Belief: An Important but Neglected Subject', at 121.

ritual human sacrifice, even if it genuinely is an essential component of a religious practice'.[72] On the contrary, it could be argued that the state would have an obligation to intervene and curb such a manifestation of religious freedom. In reality, most cases do not conform to this extreme situation, and legal provisions and jurisprudential practice are therefore intended to curb 'expansive interpretation at the hands of the cynical state'.[73] Therefore, the principle of legality, the pursuit of legitimate aims, and the necessity to pursue these in a democratic society, are conditions that must be cumulatively fulfilled if restrictions on the right to manifest one's religion are to be lawful.

The first element of the test requires that restrictions on manifestations of religion be prescribed by law. The formula employed by the HRC (and the European Court of Human Rights (ECtHR)) requires that legislation be accessible and sufficiently precise.[74] In addition to factual aspects, the legislation enacting the restriction must also fulfil certain qualitative characteristics in order to be 'compatible with the rule of law'.[75] The HRC observes that '[l]imitations imposed must be established by law and must not be applied in a manner that would vitiate the rights guaranteed in article 18'.[76]

The ICCPR and, as will be shown, the European Convention on Human Rights (ECHR) and the American Convention on Human Rights (ACHR) list identical aims that can be used to limit manifestations of religion. The list of legitimate aims is exhaustive. Additional grounds of restricting manifestations of religion, such as national security, even if allowed as limitations to other rights recognized by these instruments, are not permissible *in casu*.[77] Therefore, a restriction of the right to manifest one's religion is lawful only if it is necessary to protect public safety, order, health or morals, or the (fundamental) rights and freedoms of others. For the current study, it is very relevant that the rights and freedoms of others is a legitimate ground for restricting the external aspects of the right to religious freedom. As will be illustrated, in the context of Chapter 3, states have a positive obligation to protect the rights of others, for example by restricting church autonomy when it impinges on the very substance of the human rights of church employees.[78]

In order to verify whether it is necessary to pursue a legitimate aim, and to assess the validity of that aim a proportionality test has been employed, a variant of which is the margin of appreciation developed by the ECtHR and which arguably is also employed by the HRC.[79]

---

[72] C. Evans, *Freedom of Religion under the European Convention on Human Rights*, (Oxford: Oxford University Press, 2001), at 133.

[73] Clark, 'The United Nations and Religious Freedom', at 217.

[74] *Sunday Times v. The United Kingdom*, Application no. 6538/7, Judgment of 26 April 1979, para. 49.

[75] *James and others v. The United Kingdom*, Application no. 8793/79, Judgment of 21 February 1986, para. 67.

[76] HRC, *General Comment No. 22*, para. 8.

[77] HRC, *General Comment No. 22*, para. 8. For the ECHR, contrast the grounds of limitation in article 9.2 with article 8.2.

[78] See Chapter 3, III.

[79] Dominic McGoldrick contends that 'non-resort to the margin of appreciation by the HRC may, in any event, be no more than a matter of semantics'. D. McGoldrick, *Human Rights and Religion: The Islamic Headscarf Debate in Europe*, (Portland, OR: Hart, 2006), at 169.

In the last paragraph of article 18 of the ICCPR, the liberty of parents to ensure their children's education in conformity with their religion or belief is retained, following in the normative footsteps of the drafters of the UDHR.

Additionally, article 20.2 of the ICCPR prohibits advocacy of national, racial, or religious hatred, which constitutes incitement to discrimination, hostility, or violence.[80] In its General Comment 22, the HRC considers that this prohibition represents an important safeguard 'against infringement of the rights of religious minorities and of other religious groups to exercise the rights guaranteed by articles 18 and 27, and against acts of violence or persecution directed towards those groups'.[81]

Article 27 protects the right of persons belonging to minorities 'in community with the other members of their group, to enjoy their own culture, to profess and practise their own religion, or to use their own language'.[82] Together with the right to manifest religion, these provisions address the collective dimension of religious freedom and are thus of great relevance in particular for religious organizations, such as churches and humanist associations.

Under the 'right to education' heading, the International Covenant on Economic, Social and Cultural Rights (ICESCR) expands on the rights of parents to ensure their children's education in accordance with their religion and convictions.[83] While parents seeking to educate their children in conformity with their beliefs are free to opt for other schools than those established by the authorities, these institutions must conform to 'minimum educational standards' as provided for by the state.[84] This provision should be read in the context of the respect-protect-fulfil framework adopted by the Committee on Economic, Social and Cultural Rights, under which states continue to have a duty to ensure that education services are available, accessible, acceptable, and adapted to need, even when they are devolved or privatized.[85]

Interestingly, the 1979 Convention on the Elimination of All Forms of Discrimination against Women (CEDAW) does not explicitly provide for women's equal right to freedom of religion.[86] In fact, the term religion does not appear at all in the CEDAW. Religious freedom is however certainly included among the rights to which the general prohibition of discrimination against women in article 1 applies.[87] Moreover, as the general recommendations of the CEDAW Committee

---

[80] ICCPR, art. 20.2.   [81] HRC, General Comment No. 22, para. 9.

[82] ICCPR, art. 27.

[83] International Covenant on Economic, Social and Cultural Rights, 993 UNTS 3 (adopted 16 December 1966, entered into force 3 January 1976), art. 13.3. (Hereafter ICESCR).

[84] ICESCR, art. 13.3.

[85] CESCR, General Comment No. 13, paras. 4, 41, 50, 59 and footnote 15. For a summary of the 4As framework developed by Katarina Tomasevski, the first Special Rapporteur on the right to education, see C. Golay, C. Mahon and I. Cismas, 'The Impact of the UN Special Procedures on the Development and Implementation of Economic, Social and Cultural Rights', 15 *The International Journal of Human Rights* 2 (2011), 299–318, at 301.

[86] The same omission is noticeable in the Convention on the Rights of Persons with Disabilities, 2515 UNTS 3, (adopted 13 December 2006, entered into force 3 May 2008). (Hereafter CRPD).

[87] On the lack of an explicit provision relating to religious freedom in the CEDAW, and on how this absence was balanced in practice, see B. G. Tahzib-Lie, 'Women's Equal Right to Freedom of Religion

show, article 2—which provides that states should take appropriate measures, including legislation, to modify or abolish existing laws, regulations, customs, and practices which constitute discrimination against women—is seen as applicable to discriminatory legislation, customs, and practices of a religious nature.[88]

The Convention on the Right of the Child (CRC) stipulates the right of the child to freedom of thought, conscience, and religion. Noteworthy is article 14.2 which requires states to 'respect the rights and duties of the parents... to provide direction to the child in the exercise of his or her right in a manner consistent with the evolving capacities of the child'.[89] This formulation represents 'a sliding scale'—as the child matures her interests in respect to religious education should be taken into account—and was a compromise intended to solve the tension between the right of the child to freedom of religion and 'the sanctioned practice of a child to be reared in the religion of his parents'.[90] Be that as it may, the position of the CRC is progressive compared to other instruments that fail to address the child's interest with regard to religious education.[91]

Another important element related to religion appears in article 20 of the CRC, which lists the 'kafalah of Islamic law' among the childcare alternatives for children who are temporarily or permanently deprived of their family environment.[92] It should be emphasized that the text of the Convention is phrased in such a way so as to ensure the needs of the *child of Muslim faith* who has been deprived temporarily or permanently of her family and not the needs of Islam as a religion. Certainly there is a link between the two; nonetheless, this phrasing demonstrates that positive human rights law distinguishes itself by virtue of recognizing the rights of individuals and groups as opposed to those of religions as categories of thought and practice.

The International Convention on the Protection of the Rights of All Migrant Workers and Members of Their Families follows closely the pattern established by the ICCPR on religious freedom and parental rights concerning religious education.[93]

---

or Belief: An Important but Neglected Subject', in C. W. Howland (ed.), *Religious Fundamentalisms and the Human Rights of Women*, (New York: Palgrave Macmillan, 2001), 117–128, at 117–119.

[88] See for example CEDAW Committee, *General Recommendation No. 21*, specifically paras. 13, 16, 17.

[89] Convention on the Rights of the Child 1577 UNTS 3 (adopted 20 November 1989, entered into force 2 September 1990), art. 14.2. (Hereafter CRC).

[90] C. D. de Jong, *The Freedom of Thought, Conscience and Religion or Belief in the United Nations (1946–1992)*, (Antwerpen: Intersentia, 2000), at 51–55. See also S. Detrick, J. Doek and N. Cantwell, *The United Nations Convention on the Rights of the Child: A Guide to the 'Travaux Préparatoires'*, (Dordrecht: Martinus Nijhoff Publishers, 1992), at 238–248.

[91] See, for example, ICCPR, art. 18(4); Protocol 1, art. 2 of the ECHR; and the Declaration on the Elimination of All Forms of Intolerance and of Discrimination Based on Religion or Belief, GA Res. 36/55, 25 November 1981, arts. 5.1 and 5.2. See also, G. van Bueren, *The International Law on the Rights of the Child*, (The Hague: Martinus Nijhoff Publishers, 1998), at 160 ff.

[92] See more on kafalah and current developments in van Bueren, *The International Law on the Rights of the Child*, at 95.

[93] International Convention on the Protection of the Rights of All Migrant Workers and Members of Their Families, 2220 UNTS 3 (adopted 18 December 1990, entered into force 1 July 2003), art. 12.

The newest addition to the international human rights instruments, the International Convention for the Protection of All Persons from Enforced Disappearance, excludes extradition 'when a state party has substantial ground for believing that the request has been made for the purpose of prosecuting or punishing a person' on grounds of that person's religion.[94]

Efforts to draft and adopt a sectoral human rights convention for the elimination of religious intolerance following the model of instruments on race and on gender have been unsuccessful.[95] These efforts have materialized instead in the non-binding UN Declaration on the Elimination of All Forms of Intolerance and of Discrimination Based on Religion or Belief,[96] which seeks to uphold the right to freedom of religion and to prohibit discrimination based on religion. In relation to the *forum externum*, article 6 of the Declaration on the Elimination of All Forms of Intolerance and of Discrimination Based on Religion or Belief usefully provides a non-exhaustive list of freedoms, where the collective dimension of manifestation of religion is evident:

(a) To worship or assemble in connection with a religion or belief, and to establish and maintain places for these purposes;

(b) To establish and maintain appropriate charitable or humanitarian institutions;

(c) To make, acquire and use to an adequate extent the necessary articles and materials related to the rites or customs of a religion or belief;

(d) To write, issue and disseminate relevant publications in these areas;

(e) To teach a religion or belief in places suitable for these purposes;

(f) To solicit and receive voluntary financial and other contributions from individuals and institutions;

(g) To train, appoint, elect or designate by succession appropriate leaders called for by the requirements and standards of any religion or belief;

(h) To observe days of rest and to celebrate holidays and ceremonies in accordance with the precepts of one's religion or belief;

(i) To establish and maintain communications with individuals and communities in matters of religion and belief at the national and international levels.[97]

It should be noted that the Declaration departs from the UDHR and ICCPR language in that it expressly stipulates only the right to have a religion, while the aspect concerning change of religion is absent. On the other hand, according to article 8 '[n]othing in the present Declaration shall be construed as restricting or derogating from any right defined in the Universal Declaration of Human Rights and the International Covenants on Human Rights'.[98] This compromise sought to

---

[94] International Convention for the Protection of All Persons from Enforced Disappearance, A/61/488, (adopted 20 December 2006, entered into force 23 December 2010), art. 13.7.

[95] Manfred Nowak believes that the 'controversial character' of religious freedom is responsible for the lack of success of adopting a sectoral treaty. Nowak, *UN Covenant on Civil and Political Rights. CCPR Commentary*, 2nd ed., at 409.

[96] Other soft-law instruments relevant in this context are the 1992 Declaration on the Rights of Persons Belonging to National or Ethnic, Religious and Linguistic Minorities and the 2007 Declaration on the Rights of Indigenous Peoples.

[97] Declaration on the Elimination of All Forms of Intolerance and of Discrimination Based on Religion or Belief, art. 6.

[98] Declaration on the Elimination of All Forms of Intolerance and of Discrimination Based on Religion or Belief, art. 8.

accommodate Muslim opposition to the formal guarantee of the right to change one's religion, while upholding actual protection of the right at stake.[99] Therefore, while the Declaration differs from the UDHR with respect to the phrasing of the right to religious change, this is arguably not the case substantively.[100]

2. Regional human rights instruments

At the regional level, the European Convention on Human Rights (ECHR) protects freedom of religion in article 9.[101]

1. Everyone has the right to freedom of thought, conscience and religion; this right includes freedom to change his religion or belief and freedom, either alone or in community with others and in public or private, to manifest his religion or belief, in worship, teaching, practice and observance.
2. Freedom to manifest one's religion or beliefs shall be subject only to such limitations as are prescribed by law and are necessary in a democratic society in the interests of public safety, for the protection of public order, health or morals, or for the protection of the rights and freedoms of others.

The stipulations of the first paragraph, which refer to the internal and external fora of the right are identical to those of article 18 in the UDHR.[102] The limitations clause in the second paragraph is very similar to that of the ICCPR (or, if due respect is paid to the chronology of the drafting process, the ICCPR mirrors the provisions of the European Convention).[103] Protocol 1 to the ECHR, includes the rights to property, education, and free elections, (rights that were difficult to agree upon during the drafting of the Convention itself[104]) and stipulates in its article 2:

In the exercise of any functions which it assumes in relation to education and to teaching, the State shall respect the right of parents to ensure such education and teaching in conformity with their own religions and philosophical convictions.[105]

---

[99] See C. Walter, 'Religion or Belief, Freedom of, International Protection', in R. Wolfrum (ed.), *MPEPIL*, (Online edition: Oxford University Press, 2008), para. 7.

[100] See Implementation of the Declaration on the Elimination of All Forms of Intolerance and of Discrimination Based on Religion or Belief, Report by Abdelfattah Amor, Special Rapporteur, E/CN.4/1997/91, 30 December 1996, paras. 70–80.

[101] Convention for the Protection of Human Rights and Fundamental Freedoms (European Convention on Human Rights), Council of Europe Treaty Series No. 5, art. 9 (adopted 4 November 1950, entered into force on 3 September 1953, text as amended by Protocols No. 11 and No. 14). (Hereafter ECHR).

[102] The only difference is in respect to the position of the word 'worship'. In the ECHR, 'worship' appears before teaching and practice, while in the UDHR it comes after.

[103] While the legitimate grounds for limiting the right to manifest one's religion are identical, the mention of necessary 'in a democratic society' which appears in the ECHR cannot be found in the ICCPR.

[104] On the problematic aspects that were raised during the drafting of the ECHR, and which led to the non-inclusion of the rights mentioned above in the Convention, see S. C. Greer, *The European Convention on Human Rights: Achievements, Problems and Prospects*, (Cambridge: Cambridge University Press, 2006), at 18–20.

[105] ECHR, Protocol 1, art. 2.

We should pause at this stage to briefly discuss the margin of appreciation as it has been developed by the European Court, and replicated by other mechanisms in pro-portionality assessments. In Chapter 5, we shall build on this discussion in crafting a set of recommendations in relation to a possible proportionality test which could be employed by the OIC Independent Permanent Human Rights Commission.

In *Handyside v. the United Kingdom*, a case principally concerned with freedom of expression,[106] the ECtHR outlined the test that it continued to apply in later cases in relation to other rights of the Convention, including religious freedom. First, the Court recognizes the principle of subsidiarity in respect to the protection of the rights and freedoms of the Convention, submitting that 'State authorities are in principle in a better position than the international judge to give an opin-ion on the exact content of these requirements as well as on the "necessity" of a "restriction" or "penalty" intended to meet them'.[107] Thus, the Court gives a certain discretion to the state to make 'the *initial* assessment' concerning 'the reality of the pressing social need implied by the notion of "necessity"'.[108] Second, the ECtHR retains its role as ultimate supervisor since it gives states some, but not unconfined, discretion;[109] whereby the proportionality of the interference plays an important role in determining a violation of the Convention rights.

It becomes evident that the application of this doctrine is inherently contextual, hence the difficulty of assessing the width of the margin of appreciation, either in general or as a matter of principle. The much-debated *Lautsi v. Italy* case presents some of the factors that shape the margin of appreciation doctrine and the pitfalls it may create in particularly in freedom of religion cases.[110] In reversing the unani-mous decision of the Court, the Grand Chamber held that Italy was not in viola-tion of the Convention by allowing a crucifix to be displayed in the classroom of a public Italian school. In his persuasive dissenting opinion Judge Malinverni noted that the Grand Chamber could have not reached the decision it did, if it had not granted a large margin of appreciation to the respondent state. He commented:

Whilst the doctrine of the margin of appreciation may be useful, or indeed convenient, it is a tool that needs to be handled with care because the scope of that margin will depend on a great many factors: the right in issue, the seriousness of the infringement, the existence of a European consensus, etc. The Court has thus affirmed that "the scope of this margin of appreciation is not identical in each case but will vary according to the context.... Relevant factors include the nature of the Convention right in issue, its importance for the individual and the nature of the activities concerned". The proper application of this theory will thus depend on the importance to be attached to each of these various factors. Where the Court decrees that the margin of appreciation is a narrow one, it will generally find a violation of

---

[106] *Handyside v. The United Kingdom*, Application no. 5493/72, Judgment of 7 December 1976.

[107] *Handyside v. The United Kingdom*, para 48.

[108] *Handyside v. The United Kingdom*, para 48 (emphasis added).

[109] See *National Union of Belgian Police v. Belgium*, Application no. 4464/70, Judgment of 27 October 1975, para. 49; *Case 'relating to certain aspects of the laws on the use of languages in education in Belgium'*, Application no 1474/62; 1677/62; 1691/62; 1769/63; 1994/63; 2126/64, Judgment of 23 July 1968, para. 9.

[110] See Dissenting Opinion of Judge Malinverni Joined by Judge Kalaydjieva, *Lautsi and Others v. Italy*, Application no. 30814/06, Grand Chamber, Judgment of 18 March 2011.

the Convention; where it considers that the margin of appreciation is wide, the respondent State will usually be "acquitted".[111]

The dissenting judge argues that in the case at hand the Court's deferral to Italy has been accorded on a false premise, because it relied mainly on the absence (as opposed to the presence) of a European consensus as to whether the display of crucifixes should be permitted in public schools.[112] Moreover, it was pointed out that the Court had failed to take into consideration the fact that article 9 and article 2 of Protocol 1 give rise to a positive obligation 'to create a climate of tolerance and mutual respect among their population', which are more pressing when the rights of a minority are at stake—given these positive obligations the margin of appreciation should have been reduced.[113]

As underlined earlier, a number of factors contribute to widening or reducing the margin of appreciation. Among them are the extent to which the matter interferes with the core of an applicant's private life, the importance of the right in a democratic, pluralistic society, and the level of consensus among European states on the issues at hand.[114] However, an over-reliance on the concept of European consensus, to the detriment of the other factors, produces skewed results. Instead, the international adjudicative mechanism may be inclined to defer to states where it feels that a solid democratic process underpins a decision, in order to avoid alienating the respondent state. It may, at times, also lend an ear to the pulse of society. Yet, this contextual analysis which the ECtHR embraces, as does the HRC in all but name, requires the supervisory organ not only to understand the position of the state that imposes the restriction and the interest of society or religious majority, but also the importance attached by the individual, religious minority, or church to the right which has been interfered with. As Peter Edge points out:

If the State is often in the best place to evaluate the vital forces at work within the religious make-up of its territory, is the individual believer not better placed than an international tribunal to determine whether a particular action causes conflict with his or her religious principles?[115]

Moreover, the application of the margin of appreciation requires judges, at domestic, regional and international levels, to distance themselves from their own religious understandings in an effort not to project these onto a complainant's religious

---

[111] Dissenting Opinion of Judge Malinverni Joined by Judge Kalaydjieva, *Lautsi and Others v. Italy*, Application no. 30814/06, Grand Chamber, Judgment of 18 March 2011, para. 1.

[112] In reality, it is suggested that only two states and certain German *Länder* have specific provisions requiring the presence of religious symbols. In addition, the democratic legitimacy underpinning the display of the crucifix in Italian schools was lacking because no law had been enacted by Parliament. The regulation stemmed from an 1860 royal decree, a fascist circular of 1922, and two other royal decrees from the late 1920s. Dissenting Opinion of Judge Malinverni Joined by Judge Kalaydjieva, *Lautsi and Others v. Italy*, Application no. 30814/06, Grand Chamber, Judgment of 18 March 2011, para. 1.

[113] Dissenting Opinion of Judge Malinverni Joined by Judge Kalaydjieva, *Lautsi and Others v. Italy*, Application no. 30814/06, Grand Chamber, Judgment of 18 March 2011, para. 1.

[114] Evans, *Freedom of Religion under the European Convention on Human Rights*, at 143.

[115] P. W. Edge, 'The European Court of Human Rights and Religious Rights', 47 *ICLQ* 3 (2008), 680–687, at 686.

beliefs. Given the complexity of such exercise it seems unsurprising that the ECtHR has cautioned state authorities against assessing the legitimacy of religious belief.[116] Ironically, the ECtHR's own case law, in particular *Dahlab v. Switzerland*, provides evidence that when a court ventures into religious interpretation it runs the risk of misinterpreting concepts and even patronizing communities of gender and faith.[117]

In Chapter 5, when exploring critically the margin of appreciation doctrine as a tool to be used by the OIC Independent Permanent Human Rights Commission, we suggest that it can be reversed to show bias in favour of the individual, and the rule can be guided by the maxim *in dubio pro libertate*.[118]

It should be remembered that the ECHR does not contain an equivalent clause to article 20.2 of the ICCPR, which prohibits advocacy of religious hatred that constitutes incitement to discrimination, hostility, or violence.

The American Convention on Human Rights (ACHR), while leaving out 'thought' from the usual formula 'freedom of thought, conscience and religion', protects religious choice and manifestation of one's religion 'either individually or together with others, in public or in private' in article 12.[119] The second paragraph of article 12 does not speak of coercion—as is the case in the ICCPR—but of the prohibition on 'restrictions that might impair his freedom to maintain or to change his religion or beliefs'.[120] The last two paragraphs are similar to those of the ICCPR and address the admissible limitations of manifestation of religion and religious education of one's children.[121]

The 1981 African [Banjul] Charter on Human and Peoples' Rights (ACHPR) has less detailed provisions on freedom of religion compared to its regional counterparts. Article 8 reads:

Freedom of conscience, the profession and free practice of religion shall be guaranteed. No one may, subject to law and order, be submitted to measures restricting the exercise of these freedoms.[122]

---

[116] *Hasan and Chaush v. Bulgaria*, Application no. 30985/96, Judgment of 26 October 2000, para. 78.

[117] In *Dahlab v. Switzerland*, a primary school teacher wishing to wear a headscarf while teaching was prohibited from doing so by the school authorities, and the prohibition was subsequently upheld by Swiss courts, and the ECtHR. In an infamous passage the ECtHR held that: '[I]t cannot be denied outright that the wearing of a headscarf might have some kind of proselytising effect, seeing that it appears to be imposed on women by a precept which is laid down in the Koran and which, as the Federal Court noted, is hard to square with the principle of gender equality. It therefore appears difficult to reconcile the wearing of an Islamic headscarf with the message of tolerance, respect for others and, above all, equality and non-discrimination that all teachers in a democratic society must convey to their pupils.' *Dahlab v. Switzerland*, Application no. 42393/98, Decision of 15 February 2001. Given the Court's crude characterization of what the Quran supposedly requires from women, we can only subscribe to Taylor's observation that 'the message which the children are more likely to note is one of the State's intolerance not only towards Muslim dress but Islam more general'. Taylor, *Freedom of Religion: UN and European Human Rights Law and Practice*, at 172.

[118] See Chapter 5, IV.3.1.

[119] American Convention on Human Rights, OAS Treaty Series No. 36, 1144 UNTS 123, (adopted 22 November 1969, entered into force 18 July 1978), art. 12.1. (Hereafter ACHR).

[120] ACHR, art. 12.2.   [121] ACHR, arts. 12.3 and 12.4.

[122] African [Banjul] Charter on Human and Peoples' Rights OAU Doc. CAB/LEG/67/3 rev. 5, 21 *ILM* 58 (1982) (adopted 27 June 1981, entered into force 21 October 1986), art. 8. (Hereafter ACHPR).

The ACHPR is silent on the aspect of changing one's religion. Recourse was not made to the ICCPR's compromise formulation 'to have or to adopt' a religion or belief of one's choice. Furthermore, it is not clear from the text whether restrictions may be applied only to the manifestation aspect or equally to the *forum internum*. Unlike other instruments, the ACHPR does not provide an exhaustive list of legitimate grounds for limiting religious freedom. The clause 'subject to law and order' nonetheless may be read to require that restrictions must be prescribed by law. Be that as it may, it should be observed that the work of the African Commission on Human and Peoples' Rights (AComHPR) has often supplemented, through jurisprudential interpretation, the at times vague text of the Charter.[123] For instance, the Commission considered in *Amnesty International, Comité Loosli Bachelard and others v. Sudan*, that limitations may not be imposed on the inner circle of religious freedom in spite of the elusiveness of the African Charter on the issues at hand.[124]

The (Revised) Arab Charter on Human Rights presents one particularity in the architecture of human rights instruments in so far as it makes specific mention in its preamble of the 'divinely-revealed' religions, and in particular Islam. It is noteworthy that the religious rights stipulated by the Charter are characterized by a number of claw-back clauses. Freedom of religion is provided for in article 30.1 as follows: '[e]veryone has the right to freedom of thought, conscience and religion and no restrictions may be imposed on the exercise of such freedoms except as provided for by law'.[125] The second paragraph specifies the usual grounds for limiting manifestations of religious freedom.[126] It states that restrictions must be prescribed by law and be 'necessary in a tolerant society that respects human rights and freedoms'.[127] Thus, if the first paragraph is read in the light of the second, only the *forum externum* would be subject to restrictions, however, a disjunctive reading of the two stipulations seems to have been the intention.[128] This implies restrictions to both fora, amounting to an unprecedented development in the realm of provisions on religious freedom. The third paragraph of article 30 guarantees the freedom of parents or guardians to provide for the religious and moral education of their children.[129] Article 25, which stipulates that minorities are 'not [to] be denied

---

[123] See in particular K. Olaniyan, 'Civil and Political Rights in the African Charter: Articles 8-14', in M. D. Evans and R. Murray (eds.), *The African Charter on Human and Peoples' Rights: The System in Practice, 1986–2006*, (Cambridge: Cambridge University Press, 2008), 213–243, at 215–219. More generally on claw-back clauses in the ACHPR and the work of the Commission, see G. J. Naldi, 'Limitation of Rights under the African Charter on Human and Peoples' Rights: The Contribution of the African Commission on Human and Peoples' Rights', 17 *South African Journal on Human Rights* (2001), 109–118.

[124] *Amnesty International, Comité Loosli Bachelard, Lawyers Committee for Human Rights, Association of Members of the Episcopal Conference of East Sudan v. Sudan*, Communication nos. 48/90-50/91-52/91-89/93 (1999) paras. 71–76.

[125] Arab Charter on Human Rights, 12 Int'l Hum. Rts. Rep. 893 (2005) (adopted 22 May 2004, entered into force 15 March 2008), art. 30.1. Notably, the right to change one's religion is absent from the provision. (Hereafter ArCHR).

[126] These are: public safety, public order, public health or morals, or the fundamental rights and freedoms of others. ArCHR, art. 30.2.

[127] ArCHR, art. 30.2.

[128] M. Rishmawi, 'The Arab Charter on Human Rights and the League of Arab States: An Update', 10 *Human Rights Law Review* 1 (2010), 169–178, at 171–172.

[129] ArCHR, art. 30.3.

the right to enjoy their own culture, to use their own language and to practice their own religion' is subject to a wide claw-back clause.[130] Lastly, the provision on equality of men and women 'within the framework of the positive discrimination established in favour of women by the Islamic Shariah [and] other divine laws' should be noted.[131]

This overview of treaty provisions regarding religious aspects in international law could not conclude without mentioning the two human rights instruments developed within the framework of the OIC. While Chapter 5 will give greater attention to the non-binding Cairo Declaration on Human Rights in Islam and the Covenant of the Rights of the Child in Islam, it should be observed at this stage that neither document affirms the right to freedom of religion.

3. International humanitarian law and criminal law instruments

International humanitarian law deals with manifestations of religion in a rich and detailed manner. The codified law appears to respond to the continued importance that individuals and communities attach to religion in times of war.[132] Reference to religious-related aspects is made in the Hague Conventions of 1899 and 1907, all four Geneva Conventions of 1949, and the three Additional Protocols. It may be useful at this point to cluster and discuss the provisions related to religion in international humanitarian law.

To start with, the prohibition of religious discrimination in the application of humanitarian norms appears in the four Geneva Conventions.[133] Paragraph 1 of common article 3, which has crystallized into a customary norm[134] and is applicable in times of non-international armed conflict, reads as follows:

Persons taking no active part in the hostilities, including members of armed forces who have laid down their arms and those placed *hors de combat* by sickness, wounds, detention, or any other cause, shall in all circumstances be treated humanely, without any adverse distinction founded on race, colour, religion or faith, sex, birth or wealth, or any other similar criteria.[135]

---

[130] The clause reads: 'The exercise of these rights shall be governed by law'. ArCHR, art. 25.

[131] It is also noteworthy that in addition to reaffirming the principles contained by the UN Charter and the Bill of Rights, the preamble of the ArCHR 'has regard' to the Cairo Declaration on Human Rights in Islam (CDHRI). For a good analysis, see M. Rishmawi, 'The Revised Arab Charter on Human Rights: A Step Forward?', 5 *Human Rights Law Review* 2 (2005), 361–376.

[132] See S. Lunze, 'Serving God and Caesar: Religious Personnel and their Protection in Armed Conflict', 86 *International Review of the Red Cross* 853 (2004), 69–91, at 69.

[133] Geneva Convention I for the Amelioration of the Condition of the Wounded and Sick in Armed Forces in the Field, 75 UNTS. 31 (1949), art. 12; Geneva Convention II for the Amelioration of the Condition of Wounded, Sick and Shipwrecked Members of Armed Forces at Sea, 75 UNTS 8 (1949), art. 12; Geneva Convention III relative to the Treatment of Prisoners of War, 75 UNTS 135 (1949), art. 16; Geneva Convention IV relative to the Protection of Civilian Persons in Time of War, 75 UNTS 287 (1949), art. 13.

[134] J. M. Henckaerts and L. Doswald-Beck, *Customary International Humanitarian Law: Rules*, vol. I, (Cambridge: Cambridge University Press, 2009), rule 88, at 308.

[135] Geneva Conventions I, II, III and IV, art. 3.

The prohibition of 'adverse distinction' is the expression used to denote non-discrimination. It underlines that, while discrimination on other grounds except medical urgency is prohibited, priority may be given to those most in need of medical care.[136] The human-centred approach of the provision, as opposed to a religion-centred one, is unmistakable.

Second, both international humanitarian treaty law and custom proclaim that 'the convictions and religious practices of civilians and persons *hors de combat* must be respected' and that 'the personal convictions and religious practices of persons deprived of their liberty must be respected'.[137] These rules are recognized as customary in both international and non-international armed conflict.[138] The ICRC Study on Customary International Humanitarian Law lists over 20 countries which have provisions protecting religious freedom in their military manuals, and asserts that 'countless' domestic laws provide for the right to freedom of religion and of conscience. Among these states are Bangladesh, Bosnia and Herzegovina, Colombia, Croatia, Kuwait, the United Kingdom, and the United States of America.[139] National jurisprudence and the practice of international organizations also support the customary character of this right.[140] A series of remarkably detailed provisions of the Geneva Conventions are intended to ensure the necessary conditions for the manifestation of religious freedom for prisoners of war and civilians.[141]

Third, the norms refer to religious personnel as one of the groups specifically protected under humanitarian law in both international and non-international armed conflict.[142] Rule 27 of ICRC Study on Customary International Humanitarian Law reads:

Religious personnel exclusively assigned to religious duties must be respected and protected in all circumstances. They lose their protection if they commit, outside their humanitarian function, acts harmful to the enemy.[143]

---

[136] Henckaerts and Doswald-Beck, *Customary International Humanitarian Law: Rules*, at 309.

[137] See note 136, rule 104 at 375, and rule 127 at 449.

[138] See note 136.

[139] J. M. Henckaerts and L. Doswald-Beck, *Customary International Humanitarian Law: Practice*, vol. II, part 2, (Cambridge: Cambridge University Press, 2009), at 2512–2525.

[140] See note 139.

[141] See Geneva Convention III relative to the Treatment of Prisoners of War, arts. 34, 72, 120, 125; Geneva Convention IV relative to the Protection of Civilian Persons in Time of War, arts. 23, 50, 58, 86, 93, 130, 142.

[142] Relevant provisions regarding religious personnel are to be found in Geneva Convention I for the Amelioration of the Condition of the Wounded and Sick in Armed Forces in the Field, arts. 24, 25, 26, 27, 28, 30; Geneva Convention II for the Amelioration of the Condition of Wounded, Sick and Shipwrecked Members of Armed Forces at Sea, arts. 36, 37; Geneva Convention III relative to the Treatment of Prisoners of War, arts. 33, 36, 125; Geneva Convention IV relative to the Protection of Civilian Persons in Time of War, arts. 17, 93, 142; Protocol Additional (I) to the Geneva Conventions of 12 August 1949, and relating to the Protection of Victims of International Armed Conflicts (1977), arts. 8.d, 15, 18, 23; Protocol Additional (II) to the Geneva Conventions of 12 August 1949, and relating to the Protection of Victims of Non-International Armed Conflicts (1977), arts. 9, 12; Protocol Additional (III) to the Geneva Conventions of 12 August 1949, and relating to the Adoption of an Additional Distinctive Emblem (2005), arts. 2, 5.

[143] Henckaerts and Doswald-Beck, *Customary International Humanitarian Law: Rules*, rule 27, at 88.

The term 'religious personnel' covers both military and civilian personnel who are exclusively engaged in ministry and attached to the armed force of a party to the conflict.[144] The Dutch authorities consider 'humanist counsellors' to be covered equally by the definition of religious personnel.[145] It should be noted that religious personnel generally enjoy the same privileges as medical personnel and, like the latter, they lose protection if they engage in acts hostile to the enemy.[146] This provision provides support for the direction of our hypothesis: religious legitimacy that attaches to ministers and priests does not translate into a different legality regime for this category of personnel by loosening the rules of war, on the contrary, while their special role is acknowledged, the same rules apply.

Lastly, the laws of war require respect and protection to be accorded to cultural property, which includes religious buildings, 'unless they are military objectives'.[147] Intentionally directing attacks against buildings which are dedicated to religion, art, science, education, or charitable purposes, if they are not military objectives, represents a serious violation of the laws and customs applicable in armed conflict of both international and non-international character, and thus amounts to a war crime.[148] So far this study's review has shown that stipulations related to religion in international law are generally human-centred. The provisions just mentioned, which offer protection to religious sites per se, are rather exceptional in the architecture of international law. Even this protection of religious property however is justified by its 'great importance to the cultural heritage of every *people*'.[149]

Norms of international criminal law reinforce the human rights and humanitarian law stipulations concerning religious freedom and the prohibition of discrimination based on religion.[150] Criminal law addresses the 'victims [who] are defaced even to their own eyes as they cannot exert their rights or refer to some symbolic order capable of representing them and humanizing their relationship with others'.[151] In this context it could be argued that international criminal law takes religious freedom to another level, since it deals with crimes of another level.

Notably, the Convention on the Prevention and Punishment of the Crime of Genocide defines genocide as killing, causing serious bodily or mental harm, and

---

[144] Henckaerts and Doswald-Beck, *Customary International Humanitarian Law: Rules*, at 90.

[145] See note 144.

[146] See note 144, at 91. The ICRC *Study on Customary International Humanitarian Law* considers that there is sufficient state practice to support the application to religious personnel, *mutatis mutandis*, of provisions on the equipment of medical personnel with light individual weapons. Religious personnel may be able to use such weapons in self-defence or to defend wounded, sick, and shipwrecked persons in their care. See a more nuanced view in Lunze, 'Serving God and Caesar: Religious Personnel and their Protection in Armed Conflict', at 76.

[147] Henckaerts and Doswald-Beck, *Customary International Humanitarian Law: Rules*, rule 38, 39 at 127–132; Laws and Customs of War on Land (Hague II) (1899), art. 27.

[148] Rome Statute of the International Criminal Court, 2187 UNTS 90 (adopted 17 July 1998, entered into force 1 July 2002), arts. 8.2.(b)(ix), 8.2.(e)(iv). (Hereafter Rome Statute).

[149] Henckaerts and Doswald-Beck, *Customary International Humanitarian Law: Rules*, at 127. (Emphasis added.)

[150] See discussion in Marks and Clapham, *International Human Rights Lexicon*, at 317–318.

[151] See A. Ceretti, 'Collective Violence and International Crime', in A. Cassese (ed.), *The Oxford Companion to International Criminal Justice*, (Oxford: Oxford University Press, 2009), 5–15, at 11.

other serious acts 'committed with intent to destroy, in whole or in part, a national, ethnical, racial or *religious group*'.[152] A religious group is one 'whose members share the same religion, denomination or mode of worship'.[153] This definition reflects a theist conception of belief, yet it may cover non-religious and atheist groups, based on the latter's 'internal "beliefs" (i.e., that there is no God) or their functional "mode of worship" (i.e., choosing not to worship at all)'.[154]

Fifty years after the adoption of the Genocide Convention, the Rome Statute brings under the jurisdiction of the International Criminal Court (ICC) not only the crime of genocide but also crimes against humanity. One of the latter crimes refers to persecution of a religious group or collectivity 'committed as part of a widespread or systematic attack directed against any civilian population, with knowledge of the attack' in connection with other crimes against humanity, genocide, or war crimes.[155]

In the introduction to this volume clerics have been identified as religious actors, whilst it was clarified that a special chapter will not be dedicated to the treatment of their rights and obligations under international law; nonetheless, in the context of the current review of international criminal law, some observations on the recognition of clerical privilege would be useful. The rules of procedure of the ICC and two hybrid courts, the East Timor Special Panel for Serious Crimes and the Court of Bosnia and Herzegovina, include specific provisions related to clerical privilege.[156] The ICC's Rules of Procedure and Evidence recognize that the relationship between a person and a cleric, like the relationships between legal counsel and client and between medical doctor and patient, belongs to 'a class of professional or other confidential relationships'.[157] The communications between a person and a member of the clergy are to be recognized as privileged in as far as they occur in the course of a 'confidential relationship producing a reasonable expectation of privacy and non-disclosure', where 'confidentiality is essential to the nature and type of relationship between the person and the confidant', and as long as this would 'further the objectives of the Statute and the Rules'.[158] Based on

---

[152] Convention on the Prevention and Punishment of the Crime of Genocide, 78 UNTS 277, (adopted 9 December 1948, entered into force 12 January 1951), art. 2. (Emphasis added.)

[153] *Prosecutor v. Akayesu*, Case No. ICTR-96-4-T, ICTR Trial Chamber, Judgment of 2 September 1998, para. 515.

[154] D. L. Nersessian, 'The Razor's Edge: Defining and Protecting Human Groups under the Genocide Convention', 36 *Cornell International Law Journal* (2003), 293–327, at 300–301. But see F. Martin, 'The Notion of 'Protected Group' in the Genocide Convention and its Application', in P. Gaeta (ed.), *The UN Genocide Convention: A Commentary*, (Oxford: Oxford University Press, 2009), 112–127, at 119.

[155] Rome Statute, art. 7.1(h). Persecution is defined as the intentional and severe deprivation of fundamental rights contrary to international law by reason of the identity of the group or collectivity, in Rome Statute, art. 7.2(g).

[156] See P. Murphy and L. Baddour, 'International Criminal Law and Common Law: Rules of Evidence', in K. Khan, C. Buisman and C. Gosnell (eds.), *Principles of Evidence in International Criminal Justice*, (New York: Oxford University Press, 2010), 96–156, at 145.

[157] International Criminal Court Rules of Procedure and Evidence, Adopted by the Assembly of States Parties, First session, New York, 3–10 September 2002, Official Records ICC-ASP/1/3 rule 73.

[158] International Criminal Court Rules of Procedure and Evidence, rule 73.2.

these principles, one may conclude that not all communications between a person and a cleric fall automatically within the category of privileged communications. For example, a communication may not be privileged if there is an unreasonable expectation of non-disclosure, as we shall illustrate later. Rule 73.3 of the ICC introduces a further differentiation, whereby the Court is to give particularly privileged protection to communications made in a sacred confession where it is an integral part of the practice of that religion.[159] Under the Transitional Rules of Criminal Procedure of the East Timor Special Panel for Serious Crimes it was possible to waive clerical privilege but only if the accused consented.[160]

It is interesting to note in this context that in the *Media Case*[161] before the International Criminal Tribunal for Rwanda (ICTR), clerical privilege—which is not stipulated by the Rules of Procedure and Evidence of that court—was nonetheless seen as having a limitable application.[162] Claude Buchard, deputy commander of the UN Detention Facility, was called to testify about what an imam had told him concerning an alleged threatening letter which he had received from the accused, Hassan Ngeze, and delivered to another inmate, Omar Serushago. The defence attorney argued that the imam refused to be a witness, invoking clergy-penitent privilege, and posited that allowing Mr Bouchard to testify would amount to a violation of the privilege.[163] While the imam was not called to give evidence, the Chamber allowed the prosecution to call Mr Buchard as witness because the chain of communication of the letter in question was in dispute.[164] At a domestic level, in the context of child sexual abuse by Catholic clerics (an issue that will be discussed in Chapter 4),[165] the clergy-penitent privilege has come under pressure in some of the countries where it is protected by law.[166]

Last, like any other individual who commits international crimes, clerics may be held criminally responsible at international level.[167] It goes beyond the capacity and ambition of this study to dwell on issues of international criminal responsibility, however, this section could not end without mentioning that in recent years the

---

[159] International Criminal Court Rules of Procedure and Evidence, rule 73.3.

[160] Regulation no. 2000/30 on Transitional Rules of Criminal Procedure, UNTAET/REG/2000/30, 25 September 2000, art. 35.3(a).

[161] For the judgment, see *Prosecutor v. Ferdinand Nahimana, Jean-Bosco Barayagwiza and Hassan Ngeze*, Case No. ICTR-99-52-T, Trial Chamber, Judgment and Sentence of 3 December 2003.

[162] For a position in favour of the recognition by international criminal courts of clerical privilege, see R. J. Araujo, 'International Tribunals and Rules of Evidence: The Case for Respecting and Preserving the Priest-Penitent Privilege under International Law', 15 *Am. U. Int'l L. Rev.* (1999), 639–666.

[163] Minutes of Proceedings, *Prosecutor v. Ferdinand Nahimana*, Jean-Bosco Barayagwiza and Hassan Ngeze, Case No. ICTR-99-52-T, 30 November 2001.

[164] Minutes of Proceedings, *Prosecutor v. Ferdinand Nahimana*. See also Radio Netherlands Worldwide, 'Who Really Runs the UN Detention Facility?', 3 December 2001, accessed May 2012, http://www.rnw.nl/international-justice/article/who-really-runs-un-detention-facility?id=2066.

[165] See Chapter 4, VI.2.3. and 4.4.

[166] See R. Durrant, 'Where There's Smoke, There's Fire (and Brimstone): Is It Time to Abandon the Clergy-Penitent Privilege', 39 *Loyola of Los Angeles Law Review* (2006), 1339–1368; P. Counihan, 'Irish priests say they will disobey new confession box law on child abuse', *IrishCentral*, accessed May 2012, http://www.irishcentral.com/news/Irish-priests-say-they-will-disobey-new-confession-box-law-on-child-abuse-149029005.html#ixzz1vVWh8tJ0.

[167] See Rome Statute, art. 25.

ICTR has convicted a number of clerics for their involvement in the Rwandan genocide. Elizaphan Ntakirutimana, a pastor of the Seventh Day Adventist Church, was
the first cleric to have been convicted by the ICTR. The Trial Chamber found that
Ntakirutimana had transported militias to the Mugonero complex where they killed
hundreds of Tutsi refugees.[168] On appeal, the cleric was sentenced to 10 years impris-
onment for aiding and abetting genocide, and for extermination as a crime against
humanity.[169] In April 1994, Athanase Seromba actively participated in the destruction
of the Nyange church where he was a Catholic priest and where Tutsis had sought ref-
uge; at least 1,500 Tutsis died in the demolition of the church by means of a bulldozer.
The Appeals Chamber of the ICTR found Seromba guilty of committing genocide—
as well as extermination as a crime against humanity—and sentenced him to life in
prison.[170] This leads us to the acknowledgment that no one is above the law, not even,
in the case at hand, men of God.

4. Freedom of religion—a customary norm?

As noted in the previous section, the prohibition of discrimination, including based
on religious grounds, is regarded today as forming an integral part of international
custom; some authors even regard it as a peremptory norm.[171] The religious right—
which raises most questions as to its customary character, yet is fundamental for religious non-state actors—is freedom of religion. In the quest to establish the customary
character of a norm it is common to look for the two elements of international custom: 'extensive and virtually uniform' state practice and *opinio juris*.[172]

The first argument for the customary character of the right to freedom of
religion relies on wide domestic codification of this right. According to a comparative study, the right to freedom of religion is absent from the domestic legislation of only nine states.[173] Admittedly, the recognition of religious freedom in
some countries is imperfect. On Jeroen Temperman's 'state-religion identification spectrum' an incomplete protection of religious freedom appears to be more
prevalent among those states that have a positive identification with religion.[174]
Partial protection may refer to the recognition of only the *forum externum*, to
the incomplete codification of only the freedom to worship, or to the *de facto*

---

[168] *Prosecutor v. Elizaphan Ntakirutimana and Gérard Ntakirutimana*, Cases No. ICTR-96-
10 & ICTR-96-17-T, Trial Chamber I, Judgment and Sentence of 21 February 2003; *Prosecutor
v. Elizaphan Ntakirutimana and Gérard Ntakirutimana*, Cases No. ICTR-96-10-A & ICTR-96-17-A,
Appeals Chamber, Judgment of 13 December 2004.

[169] *Prosecutor v. Elizaphan Ntakirutimana and Gérard Ntakirutimana*, Cases No. ICTR-96-10-A &
ICTR-96-17-A, Appeals Chamber, Judgment of 13 December 2004.

[170] *Prosecutor v. Athanase Seromba*, Case No. ICTR-2001-66-A, Appeals Chamber, Judgment
of 12 March 2008; *Prosecutor v. Athanase Seromba*, Case No. ICTR-2001-66-I, Trial Chamber III,
Judgment of 13 December 2006.

[171] Riedel, 'Article 55(c)', at 920.

[172] *North Sea Continental Shelf*, Judgment, ICJ Reports 1969, p. 3, para. 74. See also A. Cassese,
International Law, 2nd ed., (Oxford: Oxford University Press, 2005), at 157–160.

[173] J. Temperman, *State-Religion Relationships and Human Rights Law: Towards a Right to Religiously
Neutral Governance*, (Leiden: Martinus Nijhoff Publishers, 2010), at 206.

[174] See note 173.

exclusion of certain religious minorities from the protection offered by the right to religious freedom.[175] At the other end of the spectrum, secular states generally recognize both the inner and outer circles of the right, but some allow limitations on grounds that are not on the exhaustive list enshrined in international human rights instruments.[176]

This brings us to the extensive codification of religious freedom at regional and international level. To reiterate what has been previously illustrated, the right to freedom of religion is stipulated in the ICCPR, most of the sectoral human rights treaties and all regional human rights conventions, with the exception of the Covenant on the Rights of the Child in Islam (not yet in force). As such, each of the 193 UN member states, (bar the newest member, South Sudan[177]) are party to at least one of these instruments and therefore are bound to respect the right to freedom of religion. Notably, in its General Comment 24, the HRC lists the right to freedom of thought, conscience, and religion as one of the provisions of the ICCPR that has achieved the status of international custom.[178] One can also note here Switzerland's objection from 28 June 2011 to the reservation entered by Pakistan to article 18 of the ICCPR, which reads:

The Swiss Federal Council has examined the reservations made by the Islamic Republic of Pakistan upon its accession to the International Covenant on Civil and Political Rights of 16 December 1966, with regard to articles 3, 6, 7, 18 and 19 of the Covenant. The reservations to the articles, which refer to the provisions of domestic law and Islamic Sharia law, do not specify their scope and raise doubts about the ability of the Islamic Republic of Pakistan to honour its obligations as a party to the Covenant. Furthermore, the Swiss Federal Council emphasizes that the third sentence of article 6, paragraph 1; article 7; and *article 18, paragraph 2,* constitute *jus cogens* and therefore enjoy absolute protection.[179]

In Switzerland's view, therefore, the prohibition of coercion that would impair the freedom of an individual to have, or to adopt, a religion or belief of his choice, represents a peremptory norm.

The Restatement of the Foreign Relations Law of the United States lists 'denial of freedom of conscience and religion' as offending against one of the rights of a customary nature, when it amounts to 'a consistent pattern of gross violations'.[180] The commentary explains that it includes as customary law 'only

---

[175] Temperman, *State-Religion Relationships and Human Rights Law: Towards a Right to Religiously Neutral Governance*, at 207–210.

[176] See note 175, at 222–223.

[177] As of December 2013, see however United Nations Mission in South Sudan, 'Parliament passes bill to ratify child rights convention', 20 November 2013, http://unmiss.unmissions.org/Default.aspx?tabid=3465&ctl=Details&mid=6047&ItemID=2338858&language=en-US.

[178] HRC, *General Comment No. 24*, para. 8.

[179] Objection of Switzerland to Pakistan's reservation to the ICCPR, accessed June 2012, UNTC, Online Database, Chapter IV: Human Rights, International Covenant on Civil and Political Rights. (Emphasis added).

[180] *Restatement (Third) of the Foreign Relations Law of the United States*, vol. 2 (1987), para. 702, at 161, 166–167.

those human rights whose status as customary law is generally accepted (as of 1987) and whose scope and content are generally agreed'.[181] Read in the light of the interpretation provided by the HRC in General Comment 22—which clarifies the scope and content of the right to freedom of religion—and in the light of the Committee's finding in General Comment 24 as to the customary character of the right, the Restatement appears overtly restrictive when it contends that religious freedom is customary only when its denial reflects a consistent pattern of gross violations.

Non-binding instruments may provide an indication as to the customary character of religious freedom. A number of rights enshrined in the UDHR have emerged as norms of customary law, and the UDHR is used by the International Court of Justice (ICJ) and other international courts either as an interpretative tool or as outright evidence of the customary nature of some rights.[182] Martin Scheinin's contribution on article 18 in Alfredsson and Eide's leading commentary to the UDHR does not mention the customary character of the right to freedom of religion or of any of its components.[183] It is true that Alfredsson and Eide explicitly caution that they have not set out to establish in their seminal commentary which rights have become customary and which have not,[184] therefore, a negation of the customary character of religious freedom cannot be inferred based on the absence of reference to it in their work. Fania Domb, citing Yoram Dinstein in support, appears certain that:

Freedom of religion—in article 18 of the Declaration—was already declared as part of Law of Nations in the past century... and today it is customary in all its four meanings, namely: 'freedom of religious choice, freedom of religious observance, freedom of religious teaching, and freedom of propagating in faith'.[185]

The Declaration on the Elimination of All Forms of Intolerance and of Discrimination Based on Religion or Belief was adopted by the UN General Assembly in 1981 by consensus. It may therefore be regarded as reflecting a broad common understanding among states concerning the right to freedom of religion

---

[181] *Restatement (Third) of the Foreign Relations Law of the United States*, vol. 2 (1987), para. 702, at 161–162. Note Bruno Simma and Philip Alston's observation that '[t]he interpretation which the Restatement applies to this category is a particularly striking instance of assuming that American values are synonymous with those reflected in international law'. B. Simma and P. Alston, 'The Sources of Human Rights Law: Custom, *Jus Cogens*, and General Principles', 12 *Australian Yearbook of International Law* (1988), 82–108, at 94.

[182] See A. Eide and G. Alfredsson, 'Introduction', in G. Alfredsson and A. Eide (eds.), *The Universal Declaration of Human Rights: A Common Standard of Achievement*, (The Hague: Martinus Nijhoff Publishers, 1999), xxv–xxxv, at xxxi–xxxii.

[183] See M. Scheinin, 'Article 18', in G. Alfredsson and A. Eide (eds.), *The Universal Declaration of Human Rights: A Common Standard of Achievement*, (The Hague: Martinus Nijhoff Publishers, 1999), 379–392.

[184] Eide and Alfredsson, 'Introduction' in G. Alfredsson and A. Eide (eds.), *The Universal Declaration of Human Rights: A Common Standard of Achievement*, at xxxii.

[185] F. Domb, 'The Gaza and Jericho Autonomy and Human Rights', 25 *Israel Yearbook on Human Rights* (1995), 21–49, at 41. See also P. W. Mason, 'Pilgrimage to Religious Shrines: An Essential Element in the Human Right to Freedom of Thought, Conscience, and Religion', 25 *Case W. Res. J. Int'l L.* (1993), 619–652, at 624.

and the protection it accords to individuals and groups. In 'the most fundamental aspects', at least, it constitutes customary international law.[186] Article 1, which is certainly fundamental, reads:

1. Everyone shall have the right to freedom of thought, conscience and religion. This right shall include freedom to have a religion or whatever belief of his choice, and freedom, either individually or in community with others, and in public or private, to manifest his religion or belief in worship, observance, practice and teaching.
2. No one shall be subject to coercion which would impair his freedom to have a religion or belief of his choice.
3. Freedom to manifest one's religion or belief may be subject only to such limitations as are prescribed by law and are necessary to protect public safety, order, health or morals, or the fundamental rights and freedoms of others.[187]

As has already been noted, during the drafting process of the Declaration some Muslim states opposed the inclusion of a formal guarantee of the right to change one's religion. This would suggest that the *opinio juris* element is not fully present. However, a compromise was sought by including a clause in article 8 which requires compatibility with the UDHR provisions, and therefore protects change of religion. In the understanding of this author, the prohibition of coercion against having a religion of one's choice includes a dynamic element. Based on the text of the Declaration it is difficult to draw a definitive conclusion as to the customary status of the right to change one's religion. It is equally difficult to deny this status. It is clear nonetheless that the *forum internum* is protected by means of custom at least in respect to the right to have a religion or belief, which certainly includes non-theistic and atheistic beliefs. Similarly, the right to manifest religion subject to a restricted number of legitimate limitations, and freedom from coercion, are customary norms.

Finally, the strongest argument for the customary character of religious freedom is one of logic. It is instructive that customary international humanitarian law protects freedom of religion in its two dimensions, with regard to convictions and with regard to religious manifestations by civilians, persons *hors de combat* and persons deprived of their liberty.[188] How could a human right be customary in times of international and non-international armed conflict and yet lose this character in times of peace?

IV. Conclusion

We began by exploring two existing narratives on religion and international law, which led us to an understanding of the reasons why some scholars acknowledge certain religious roots of the international legal system while others are reluctant

---

[186] C. Walter, 'Religion or Belief, Freedom of, International Protection', *MPEPIL* (2008), para. 8.

[187] Declaration on the Elimination of All Forms of Intolerance and of Discrimination Based on Religion or Belief, art. 1.

[188] Henckaerts and Doswald-Beck, *Customary International Humanitarian Law: Rules*, rule 104 at 375, and rule 127 at 449. See also section III.3 in this chapter.

to draw upon these. With respect to human rights and international humanitarian law attitudes vary. Appeals to religious origins and principles are made provided they strengthen the legitimacy of human rights and humanitarian norms in various cultural contexts. At the same time, there is a certain unwillingness to elaborate links with religion because the human rights movement considers that its success is due precisely to its areligiosity. Beyond these claims and counter-claims, the analysis suggested that for the most part religious actors—not religion as a diffuse term—are active in international fora and they have a certain influence on international law. The first point which therefore deserves emphasis refers to the search for a new narrative which takes stock of this empirical evidence. The suggestion put forward in this study was that the new narrative would need to inquire into the rights and obligations of religious actors, as such a legal framework constitutes the boundary of their engagement with, and influence on, international law.

The inquiry into provisions of positive law reveals a second element. International and regional human rights treaties, and international humanitarian and criminal law stipulate non-discrimination clauses, affirm the right to freedom of religion and the right of parents to educate their children in accordance with their religions and convictions, prohibit incitement to religious hatred, and require non-refoulement when life is threatened based on religious grounds. In other words, international law provisions generally take a human-centred approach, whereby religion is protected as the apanage of the individual (acting singly or collectively) and not vice-versa; religion is not protected as such. This represents further evidence that the actor-centred approach of this book, as opposed to a religion-centred one, is justified.

In our attempt to establish which are the rights and obligations of religious actors we are a small step further as it appears clear that individuals and groups benefit from a number of religious rights. At the same time, it is obvious that a mere review of treaty and customary law, such as the one performed previously, reveals relatively little about the entire panoply of rights and the possible corresponding obligations of religious actors if these are understood to include, in addition to individuals and groups, legal non-state entities, international organizations, and states. Therefore, important questions remain unanswered. Does a religious legal entity as opposed to a group of individuals enjoy religious rights? Which religious rights? Does a non-religious legal entity have such rights? What about religious actors that are states or international organizations? Beyond religious rights, what other rights do religious actors enjoy and indeed, of great importance, which obligations do they incur? It becomes evident that in our démarche of clarifying the legal framework of religious actors, it is first necessary to define the analytical category of religious actors and subsequently to operationalize it by drawing on a number of different methods and perspectives, including jurisprudential analysis.

2

Religious Actors as an Analytical Category

'So fear not I shall falter. I shall not grow conservative with age.'

—Elizabeth Cady Stanton[1]

I. Introduction

The term 'actor' is not autochthonous to international law.[2] International lawyers borrowed the notion from social sciences and used it, typically preceded by the qualification 'non-state', in a pragmatic attempt to respond to the increased activity, and perceived importance in international law, of entities that are not states. Today the term has become part of the mainstream vocabulary of international legal scholars; the expression 'religious actors', on the other hand, is rarely used in international law.[3] In its attempt to shift the focus from religion and the (in)compatibility of religion with law to avenues where the agents that interpret religion are held accountable under the law, this study introduces and relies on an analytical category of religious actors. Given the anonymity of the term religious actors in international law, and its particular use in this book as an analytical device, some conceptual foundations must be laid out at this stage in order to facilitate the further research démarche.

The utility of an analytical category is recognized, for instance, by feminist scholars in relation to gender, and stems from its function as a heuristic device that

---

[1] T. Stanton and H. Stanton Blatch (eds.), *Elizabeth Cady Stanton as Revealed in Her Letters, Diary and Reminiscences*, vol. 2, (New York: Harper & Brothers, 1922), at 83, accessed June 2012, http://archive.org/stream/elizabethcadyst00blatgoog#page/n11/mode/2up.

[2] After searching for studies on the actors of international law, Andrea Bianchi concludes that 'there is no such thing in the general theory of international law'. A. Bianchi, 'Introduction: Relativizing the Subjects or Subjectivizing the Actors: Is That the Question?', in A. Bianchi (ed.), *Non-state Actors and International Law*, (Dartmouth: Ashgate Publishing, 2009), xi–xxx at xii.

[3] Some works of political science and international relations employ the term religious actors to refer to clergy, social movements and other non-state actors, whether national or transnational. See for instance J. Heynes, *Religious Transnational Actors and Soft Power* (Aldershot: Ashgate, 2012); J. Heynes and A. Hennig (eds.), *Religious Actors in the Public Sphere: Means, Objectives, and Effects* (London: Routledge, 2011); G. Shani, 'Transnational Religious Actors and International Relations', in J. Heynes (ed.), *Routledge Handbook of Religion and Politics* (New York, NY: Routledge, 2011), 308–322.

'identifies puzzles or problems in need of exploration or clarification and provides concepts, definitions and hypotheses to guide research'.[4] Relying on the same heuristic function of the analytical category, this chapter will provide the definitional contours of religious actors (II), clarify these contours further by identifying some current contexts in which religious actors' action may have potential impact on international law (III) and discuss the framework of acquisition of rights and obligations in international law (IV). All this, in order to prepare for the three case studies of the following chapters which will verify the hypothesis according to which religious actors are *not* an autonomous or special legal category in international law. Or, differently put, the analytical device is constructed here and employed in this study in order to demonstrate that the regime of rights and obligations which attaches to religious actors is similar, when compared to actors which, simply put, are not religious.

II. Definitional Contours of Religious Actors

In delineating the analytical category of religious actors, this part will draw on an empirical approach, constitutional and statutory analyses, as well as insights from sociology.

1. Transcending the state/non-state divide and assuming the role of interpreters of religion

As a point of departure an empirical approach may be useful in illustrating some characteristics of religious actors. Let us therefore start with the following enumeration: the Islamic Republic of Iran, the Holy See-Vatican, the Organization of Islamic Cooperation (OIC), the Russian Orthodox Church, Jehovah's Witnesses, and Rabbi Shlomo Goren.

No extraordinary observation skills are needed to notice one difference between the entries and one important shared feature. First, some entities are states, one is an international organization, others are non-state actors and one is an individual—transcending therefore the state/non-state divide. Second, all entries have a strong link to religion, presenting several of the following characteristics: a religious organizational structure, religious doctrine, religious motivation or religious overarching goal, or a predominately religious discourse. At the most general level, it would seem that regardless of whether they are states or non-state entities, actors which grant religion a central place in their functioning can be considered religious actors.

---

[4] See Mary Hawkesworth who describes gender as an analytical category in M. Hawkesworth 'Confounding Gender' 22 *Signs* 3 (1997), 649–685, at 655, drawing on the work of Imre Lakatos. I. Lakatos, 'Falsification and the methodology of scientific research programmes' in I. Lakatos and A. Musgrave (eds.), *Criticism and the Growth of Knowledge* (Cambridge, Cambridge University Press: 1970), 91–195.

Before anything else, a clarification is in order. It is evident that an empirical method which offers indicia as to whether an actor can be considered a religious one relies on observation and social perception. The process involves prior experience, motivations, expectations, and the filtering of information through such lenses.[5] In the case at hand, this may mean that the definition of a religious actor will be affected by evaluations of what a specific religion is understood to be, or should be, in terms of good or bad, true or false religion. Such an outcome certainly goes against the intention of this study and the use of religious actors as an analytical category. As an analytical device, the category of religious actors does not assert any commonalities in values, nor does it negate the many differences that there may be among these entities, including in relation to the different religions they propagate. The examples enumerated in the opening paragraph of this section have been chosen intentionally so as to expound different religions. The intention was precisely to clarify that this book is not interested in passing value judgments in relation to religion(s) but instead wishes to operationalize an analytical category of actors with certain common functional or operational characteristics of which shared values are not one. In order to correct any bias which the empirical method may import into the category of religious actors this method must be supplemented by an analysis of constitutional texts and statues of the actors themselves and by insights from sociology which trace the type of legitimacy upon which they rely.

An analysis of constitutional texts and statutes can be useful in clarifying what the actors' strong link to religion is taken to mean for the purpose of this study. In the case of states, some of their constitutions reveal that they accord a central role to religion.[6] The constitutional text of Iran is such a paradigmatic case. Said Amir Arjomand asserts that the clerical drafters of the Constitution of Iran claimed judicial prerogatives and supervisory power over legislation, and introduced 'a clericalist claim: the right to rule on behalf of God'.[7] The Principles of Governance of the Just Holy Person that are set forth in the constitutional text substantiate Arjomand's assessment:

In keeping with the principles of governance and the perpetual necessity of leadership, the Constitution provides for the establishment of leadership by a holy person possessing the necessary qualifications and recognized as leader by the people (this is in accordance with the saying *The direction of affairs is in the hands of those who are learned concerning God and are trustworthy in matters pertaining to what He permits and forbids*). Such leadership will prevent any deviation by the various organs of State from their essential Islamic duties.[8]

---

[5] See a review of social psychologists' works on the idea that social perception can be affected by biases and errors: L. Jussim, *Social Perception and Social Reality: Why Accuracy Dominates Bias and Self-Fulfilling Prophecy* (Oxford: Oxford University Press, 2012), at 19–22.

[6] See generally Temperman, *State-Religion Relationships and Human Rights Law: Towards a Right to Religiously Neutral Governance*, at 12–31.

[7] S. A. Arjomand, 'Constitution-Making in Islamic Iran: The Impact of Theocracy on the Legal Order of a Nation-State', in J. Starr and J. Collier Fishburne (eds.), *History and Power in the Study of Law: New Directions in Legal Anthropology*, (New York: Cornell University Press, 1989), 113–126, at 125.

[8] Constitution of the Islamic Republic of Iran (adopted on 24 October 1979, entered into force 3 December 1979, as amended on 28 July 1989), accessed June 2012, http://www.verfassungsvergleich. de, preamble and arts. 5, 107–112.

In other words, in Iran, the Just Holy Person is empowered constitutionally to act as *the* interpreter of Islam, whereby his voice is to guide the affairs of the state.

While Chapter 4 will extensively delve into the question of statehood in relation to the Holy See, the Vatican, and the construct formed by the two entities, it is sufficient to note here that the Lateran Treaty of 1929, the Fundamental Law of the State of the Vatican City, as well as canon law 'approximate...most faithfully the ideal-typical conception of a theocratic Roman Catholic state'.[9] The Pope, who is head of state and of the Catholic Church,[10] and the bishops in communion with him, are said to have been entrusted with the task 'of *interpreting* the Word of God authentically'.[11]

These two examples clarify that what is of interest for this study is not the mere enunciation of religion in a constitution, but the authority conferred upon legislative, executive, and judicial organs to interpret religion. For the purposes of this book, state religious actors are considered to be actors that assume the authority to interpret religion—who use religion as an important or primary source of law, whose executive and judiciary enforce religious laws, or who grant religious authorities a principal role in the executive. According to a comprehensive comparative constitutional analysis the following states can be considered religious: the Islamic Republic of Afghanistan, the Kingdom of Bahrain, the Nation of Brunei, the Abode of Peace (Brunei Darussalam), the Islamic Republic of Iran, the Islamic Republic of Mauritania, the Sultanate of Oman, the Islamic Republic of Pakistan, the Kingdom of Saudi Arabia, the Republic of Yemen, and the Vatican City State.[12] In this sense, any of these states could have been listed in the opening enumeration of religious actors.

States which provide a form of establishment, those which have less explicit forms of religion-state entanglement, and indeed secular states, are of interest to this study; in those cases, the focus will be on established churches, other churches and religious organizations, and the state's obligations towards these and third parties will be addressed.

Among intergovernmental organizations, the OIC is unique in so far as its religious contours are concerned. Chapter 5 will present arguments for including this international organization in the analytical category of religious actors; it is sufficent to note at this point that the Organization's constitutive charter of 1972 and

---

[9] Temperman, *State-Religion Relationships and Human Rights Law: Towards a Right to Religiously Neutral Governance*, at 17. The Lateran Treaty, the Fundamental Law of the Vatican City State and other relevant legislative acts will be examined at length in Chapter 4 to unearth the complex relationship of the Vatican with the Holy See. See Chapter 4, IV.

[10] Fundamental Law of the Vatican City State, 26 November 2000, accessed January 2013, http://www.vaticanstate.va/content/dam/vaticanstate/documenti/leggi-e-decreti/Normative-Penali-e-Amministrative/FundamentalLaw1.pdf, art. 1.1.

[11] *Catechism of the Catholic Church*, 2nd ed., revised in accordance with the official Latin text promulgated by Pope John Paul II, (Libreria Editrice Vaticana, United States Catholic Conference, 2000), para. 100. (Emphasis added).

[12] Temperman, *State-Religion Relationships and Human Rights Law: Towards a Right to Religiously Neutral Governance*, at 17–25.

the revised Charter of 2008 accord an important place to religion, and that the OIC has assumed the role of interpreter of human rights in the context of Islam.[13]

In the case of non-state actors, it is often their statutes that reveal their religious character, religious structure, and the authority they assume to lay down principles, rules, doctrine, and policy for their adherents and clergy. For example, the Statute of the Russian Orthodox Church stipulates that the Church exercises its activities on the basis of the Holy Scriptures and Holy Tradition, as well as the canons and rules issued by the Local Council, the Bishops' Council, and the Holy Synod headed by the Patriarch of Moscow and All Russia, while doing so 'with respect of and adherence to the acting laws' of every state where it has canonical jurisdiction.[14] The Statute clarifies that the Church has jurisdiction over persons of Orthodox confession living in 12 countries and over individuals of other countries who wish to voluntarily join this juridiction.[15] The Statute provides for ecclesiastical courts and prohibits the access of clergymen and laymen 'to the bodies of state authority and to civil court on the matters pertaining to internal church life, including those of canonical governance, church order, liturgical and pastoral activities'.[16] This latter provision is interesting given that it lays out the understanding of the Russian Orthodox Church as to the extent of its autonomy. As church autonomy is a key right of religious organizations that raises questions concerning a possible special status of these actors under international law in comparison to their non-religious peers, it will be extensively discussed in Chapter 3.

In the absence of statutory and constitutive documents, clues for the religious character of some organizations must be sought in their history and publications. This would be the case for the Jehovah's Witnesses, a movement which emerged from a Bible study group in Pennsylvania in 1872, which distinguishes itself through an 'apocalyptic hope'.[17] Today, flagship publications such as *The Watchtower* or *Awake!* provide information to followers on the doctrine and teachings and serve as support material in the proselytizing activities of the Witnesses.[18]

Some individuals—as is suggested in the opening enumeration—may also be included in the category of religious actors. For example, Rabbi Shlomo Goren, the first Chief Rabbi of the Israel Defense Force (IDF), is said to be the architect of the corpus of Jewish law concerning war and the military by both shaping the role of the IDF Rabbinate and issuing a number of *halakhic* (religious) rulings on military conduct.[19]

---

[13] See Chapter 5, II.

[14] Department for External Church Relations of the Russian Orthodox Church, Statute of the Russian Orthodox Church, 2 February 2013, accessed October 2013, https://mospat.ru/en/documents/ustav/i/, art. 4.

[15] Statute of the Russian Orthodox Church, 2 February 2013, art. 3.

[16] Statute of the Russian Orthodox Church, 2 February 2013, arts. 8–9.

[17] D. A. Weddle, 'Jehovah's Witnesses', in Eugene V. Gallagher and W. Michael Ashcraft (eds.), *Introduction to New and Alternative Religions in America*, vol. 2 (Westport, Connecticut: Greenwood, 2006), 62–66, at 62.

[18] See R. S Ellwood and G.D. Alles, *Encyclopedia of World Religions*, revised edition, (New York, NY: Infobase Publishing, 2009), at 235. For the description of the two publications see http://www.jw.org/en/publications/magazines/, accessed October 2013.

[19] See A. Edrei, 'Divine Spirit and Physical Power: Rabbi Shlomo Goren and the Military Ethic of the Israel Defense Forces', 7 *Theoretical Inquiries in Law* 1 (2006), 255–297.

As a result of his interpretation of religion, and that of subsequent military rabbis, it is contended that:

[R]eligion does not exist as a segmented subculture within the overall Israeli military fabric. Rather, it constitutes one of the IDF's integral components. Within the force, traditional Jewish rites and symbols intrude on life in numerous spheres and at various levels.... [T]hey generate a symbiosis between religion and military service that, even if not altogether unique, is certainly more pervasive than that experienced in other modem armed forces.[20]

Based on an empirical approach and analysis of constitutional and statutory texts, this study has so far argued that state and non-state entities which act as interpreters of religion can be considered religious actors. A question which arises is how far interpretations of religion by religious actors differ from similar such interpretations by non-religious actors.

2. Claiming 'special' legitimacy

Sociological insights may shed light on what it is about religious actors' claims to have the legitimate authority to interpret religion that sets them apart from similar claims by non-religions actors. The underlining question is why do adherents, members, citizens, and other individuals obey the doctrine and rules, follow the guidelines, and act upon legal norms that are put forward by religious actors.

To start with, the relationship between religious actors and adherents, members, and citizens is one of command-obedience between an authority (a power-holder) and power-subjects. Authorities, whether they take the form of religious or non-religious actors, seek to convince power-subjects that their commands are legitimate or 'rightful' so that the latter will obey them; in doing so authorities appeal to various sources of legitimation.[21] Before addressing those sources, however, it should be recalled that legitimate authority is not the only form of command. It is, however:

a less 'costly' form of authority than either coercive or reward-based authority. In the case of coercive authority, only constant surveillance and supervision can ensure that subordinates completely comply with commands, for subordinates will comply only when they face the prospect of punishment for non-compliance. In the case of reward-based authority, obedience has to be 'purchased' through the offer of rewards for compliance. Legitimate

---

[20] S. A. Cohen, 'From Integration to Segregation The Role of Religion in the IDF', 25 *Armed Forces & Society* 3 (1999), 387–405, at 389. The permeation of religion in the military—as well as the fact that religious courts (rabbinic, sharia, christian, druze) are run by their respective religious communities and are vested by the government with powers to decide personal status matters—discloses a complex entanglement between religion and state in Israel. Unsurprisingly perhaps, among legal doctrine and Jews themselves, it is controversial whether Israel is a Jewish state in a religious or ethnic sense. See S. Goldstein, 'Israel: A Secular or a Religious State?', 36 *St. Louis U. L.J.* 1 (1991), 143–161; Y. Merin, 'The Right to Family Life and Civil Marriage Under International Law and Its Implementation in the State of Israel', *bepress Legal Series* 275 (2004), 1–51.

[21] C. Matheson, 'Weber and the Classification of Forms of Legitimacy', 38 *The British Journal of Sociology* 2 (1987), 199–215, at 200.

authority obviates the need for surveillance and rewards, since subordinates feel obliged to obey no matter whether there is a 'reward' for compliance or not.[22]

Mattei Dogan observes that reality can rarely be described in terms of legitimacy or illegitimacy and concludes that 'legitimacy must come in degrees';[23] this is an observation shared by legal scholars in relation to norms of international law.[24] Nonetheless, there seems to be a convention that a rule is illegitimate if a majority believes it to be so.[25] What needs to be remembered is that *any* authority, including religious actors when they issue religious interpretations, strives to justify or to *legitimate* its commands, as such, legitimacy designates a sense of duty or an 'oughtness' towards rules or legal norms issued by an authority.[26] The power-subjects feel obliged to obey these rules or legal norms because of the legitimate character of the command-obedience relation, and their 'belief' that the authority's conduct is rightful.[27] Of interest for this study are the sources of legitimacy on which religious actors draw to legitimate their authoritative interpretations of religion.

Max Weber famously developed three *Idealtypen* of legitimate authority.[28] Legitimacy may be ascribed on traditional grounds, 'resting on an established belief in the sanctity of immemorial traditions and the legitimacy of those exercising authority under them'; this corresponds to traditional authority.[29] In a second category, legitimacy is ascribed on charismatic grounds, whereby an authority draws upon emotions and faith that validate a model to follow, or devotion to the 'exceptional sanctity' and 'the normative patterns or order revealed or ordained by him'; this corresponds to charismatic authority.[30] Third, legal-rational legitimacy results from the 'belief in the legality of enacted rules and the right of those elevated to authority under such rules to issue commands'; this corresponds to legal authority.[31]

---

[22] See note 21.

[23] M. Dogan, 'Conceptions of Legitimacy', in M. Hawkesworth and M. Kogan (eds.), *Encyclopedia of Government and Politics*, 2 ed., vol. I, (London: Routledge 2004), 110–120, at 114.

[24] See T. M. Franck, *The Power of Legitimacy Among Nations*, (New York: Oxford University Press, 1990), chapter 3.

[25] Dogan, 'Conceptions of Legitimacy', at 117.

[26] M. E. Spencer, 'Weber on Legitimate Norms and Authority', 21 *The British Journal of Sociology* 2 (1970), 123–134, at 126.

[27] Dogan, 'Conceptions of Legitimacy', at 116–117; Matheson, 'Weber and the Classification of Forms of Legitimacy', at 200.

[28] Weber's typology is lacking one type of authority that would correspond to value-rational legitimacy (Wertrational). Scholars have since considered that value-rational legitimacy may correspond to an ideological authority. See D. E. Willer, 'Max Weber's Missing Authority Type', in J. Scott (ed.), *Power: Critical Concepts*, (London, New York: Routledge, 1994), 131–139. For instance, Roberta Lynn Satow considers the authority of professional organizations, in law and medicine, is ideological, ascribed through value-rational legitimacy. R. L. Satow, 'Value-Rational Authority and Professional Organizations: Weber's Missing Type', 20 *Administrative Science Quarterly* 4 (1975), 526–531.

[29] M. Weber, *Economy and Society* (G. Roth *and* C. Wittich *eds.*), (Berkeley: University of California Press, 1978), at 215. See also H. H. Gerth and C. Wright Mills (eds.), *From Max Weber: Essays in Sociology*, (New York: Oxford University Press, 1975), at 296.

[30] Weber, *Economy and Society*, at 33 and 215. See also Spencer, 'Weber on Legitimate Norms and Authority', at 123.

[31] Weber, *Economy and Society*, at 215. See also Matheson, 'Weber and the Classification of Forms of Legitimacy', at 209–210.

It should be emphasized that these are *Idealtypen* and that in practice authorities draw on several of these sources to legitimate their commands.[32] One could paraphrase Dogan and speak of degrees of legitimating sources. As mentioned already, authorities also draw on coercion and material rewards, which further depicts a complex reality marked by degrees of legitimacy. To emphasize this complex reality this study sometimes refers to a religious actor's 'claim to legitimacy' or 'claim to legitimate authority' to interpret religion; these expressions suggest that the claim of religious actors may or may not be validated by power-subjects. When adherents, members, or citizens respectively validate such claims to legitimacy, they obey the religious interpretations. In the absence of validation by power-subjects, the commands may still be followed, but on illegitimate grounds, because of fear of punishment or interest in rewards.

Reviewing the different sources of legitimacy, it is important to observe that religious actors draw *primarily* on traditional and charismatic sources. Rational-legal features, while certainly present, are not primarily emphasized for the purpose of convincing power-subjects to follow religious interpretations. The example of Iran could be recalled since it offers a fitting illustration. The Grand Ayatollah Khomeini, who led the 1979 Iranian Revolution, and was responsible for its constitutional design, is considered in sociological literature to be *the* paradigmatic example of a charismatic authority.[33] While the Constitution itself was subject to a referendum and provided rational-legal features to legitimate authority in Iran, it is beyond doubt that religion is the main anchor of legitimacy for the Iranian political system and its clerical jurists. Saudi Arabia and Morocco are among states cited as examples of traditional authority, whereas monarchies such as the United Kingdom, Spain, Belgium, Sweden, Norway, the Netherlands, and Japan are legitimized contemporaneously on rational-legal grounds and only in a very subsidiary manner by appeal to tradition.[34] The legitimate authority of the Holy See is also seen as mainly grounded in Christianity and its tradition. Jean-Philippe Lecomte explains:

Ainsi l'obéissance des chrétiennes au Pape ne découle que très secondairement de la personne du souverain pontife et prioritairement de l'adhésion au dogme, aux valeurs du christianisme ainsi qu'à l'institution ecclésiale et aux règles de dévolution du pouvoir au sein de l'organisation.[35]

Religious organizations draw on a combination of the three sources. Charismatic authority typically plays an important role in the case of new religions.[36] Rational-legal features should not be discarded, since many religious organizations

---

[32] J.-P. Lecomte, *Sociologie Politique*, (Paris: Gualino éditeur, 2005), at 84–85.

[33] Dogan, 'Conceptions of Legitimacy', at 118.

[34] See note 33.

[35] Lecomte, *Sociologie Politique*, at 80. (This author's translation: Thus, the obedience of Christians towards the Pope derives only secondarily from the person of the Sovereign Pontiff, but primarily from their adherence to dogma, the values of Christianity as well as from the ecclesial institution and the rules of devolution of power within the organisation.)

[36] P. E. Hammond, L. Salinas and D. Sloane, 'Types of Clergy Authority: Their Measurement, Location, and Effects', 17 *Journal for the Scientific Study of Religion* 3 (1978), 241–253, at 243–245; J. R. Lewis, *Legitimating New Religions*, (New Jersey: Rutgers University Press, 2003), at 13–14.

assume a bureaucratic form. Nonetheless, the inclination of adherents of the Jehovah's Witnesses, by way of example, to obey the prohibition on extra-marital sex cannot be explained as being the outcome of a process of rationalization. Similarly, it is of little relevance whether the prohibition can be seen to have been enacted in a legal way, much rather, as Andrew Holden puts it:

Watch Tower teachings on sexual conduct provide an excellent example of the usage of purity to combat the risk of contamination posed by modernity. The belief that sex is strictly a heterosexual affair which should be practised only within marriage suggest that the Witnesses are heirs of the...*absolutist* model of sexual morality rooted in the Judeo-Christian tradition.... This approach regards sex as potentially dangerous and anti-social and contrasts sharply with the *libertarian* position in which sexual desire is seen as benign and life-enhancing.[37]

It follows that the Governing Body of the Witnesses draws upon religious tradition to guide the adherents' conduct in accepting a prohibition on extra-marital sex.

The OIC taps into traditional legitimacy when it assumes the role of constructing international law in accordance with what it considers to be the Muslim tradition. At the same time state consent is paramount for the development of norms within the OIC, which is a strong rational-legal feature.

To summarize this definitional exercise, the analytical category of religious actors covers states and non-state entities which share certain operational characteristics: they assume the role of interpreters of religion and in doing so they claim a 'special' or religious legitimacy which relies primarily on tradition or charisma.

In the end, one major question arises: outside the command-obedience relationship between religious actors as authority and adherents, members, and citizens as power subjects, what is the impact of the 'special' or religious legitimacy of religious actors? How do states, treaty monitoring mechanisms, and international courts respond to this legitimacy? Do they grant extra rights to religious actors and loosen their legal obligations to accommodate religious interpretations that may depart from international law norms? As is becoming evident this is *the* research question of the present book. The legal analysis in Chapters 3, 4 and 5 aims precisely to enhance our understanding of the impact of the legitimacy of religious actors on their rights and obligations under international law.

III. Religious Actors' Cooperation and Divergence in International Fora

Whilst this study is not primarily concerned with charting the array of interactions of religious actors in international fora, by examining some instances of these interactions a number of aspects related to the analytical category, as employed here, can be further clarified. First, this part will demonstrate that the inclusion

---

[37] A Holden, *Jehovah's Witnesses: Portrait of a Contemporary Religious Movement* (London: Routledge, 2002), at 53.

of entities in the analytical category (because they share certain operational characteristics) does not automatically presume cooperation in the international arena or elsewhere. Second, and related, it will clarify that entities which share the same religion and values can cooperate, but can also diverge on various issues; conversely, actors of different religious affiliations may well cooperate. This demonstrates that it is the interpretative role of religious actors and the claim to a special legitimacy, which warrants their unification in the analytical category and not whether they share a religion or values. A third aspect shows that religious actors can have an impact on the current development of international law standards—hindering or advancing such development. Such evidence ties into the findings of Chapter 1 in relation to the presence of religious actors in international fora and the need to search for a new narrative that takes stock of this *fait accompli*.

1. Sexuality and reproduction

In international conferences and UN fora initiatives to clarify and advance sexual and reproductive rights have become the most visible areas where religious actors cooperate to oppose normative development—the same initiatives, however, present strong examples of divergence among religious actors of shared religious affiliation. This can be a baffling occurrence if one does not understand the role of these actors as interpreters of religion.

In the mid-1990s observers noted the convergence of action of the Holy See, some Catholic states, and some Muslim states (in particular Pakistan and Iran), on the occasions of the International Conference on Population and Development in Cairo and the Fourth World Conference on Women in Beijing.[38] The Holy See's aim was to remove language on contraception, abortion, and gender identity from the respective outcome documents to the extent that during preparatory meetings it square-bracketed any reference to 'gender', 'gender equality', 'sexual orientation', 'lifestyle', 'contraception', 'unwanted pregnancy', or reproductive healthcare which included unsafe abortion.[39] Muslim states were rather concerned with sexual rights which were not only recognized for the 'couple', but also for the individual, thereby extending to sexual relations outside the confines of marriage between a men and a woman.[40]

While consensus had been reached in 1994 on the Cairo Programme of Action and in 1995 on the Beijing Platform for Action, the two documents were joined

---

[38] M. Pentikäinen, 'The Right to Speak for the Women's Cause: May Also Women Participate? The Case of the Holy See in the UN' in J. Petman, and J. Klabbers (eds.) *Nordic Cosmopolitanism: Essays in International Law for Martti Koskenniemi* (Leiden: Martinus Nijhoff Publishers, 2003), 141–154, at 144–145.

[39] For an extensive account of the Holy See's position and action before, during, and after the two conferences see Y. Abdullah, 'The Holy See at United Nations Conferences: State or Church?', 96 *Col. LR* 7 (1996) 1835–1875, at 1844–1854.

[40] Programme of Action of the International Conference on Population and Development, Cairo 5–13 September 2013, A/CONF.171/13/Rev.1, Part II, Statements and Reservations on the Programme of Action. See also Abdullah, 'The Holy See at United Nations Conferences: State or Church?', at 1847, footnote 99.

by a myriad of interpretative statements and reservations. El Salvador's reservation is relevant in as much as it specifically uses the religious argument in interpreting the text by claiming that 'We Latin American countries...are mainly Christian, we consider that life is given by the Creator and cannot be taken unless there is a reason which justifies it being extinguished'.[41] Other states have entered reservations to the text in part or in its entirety requesting compliance with the 'nature' and 'particular mission' of the Holy See, Sharia law, Islam, 'ethical values', and other such qualifications.[42]

Beyond the two world conferences, a number of studies identify two opposing alliances in relation to reproductive rights as well as the rights of lesbian, gays, bisexual, and transgender persons (LGBT). Of utmost interest is the fact that the rift does not trace religious lines, but rather sets up a 'conservative' side and a 'progressive' side, both of which cut across religious affiliations.[43]

As such, on one side, a loose coalition was formed by Catholic, Evangelical, and Mormon non-governmental organizations, mostly based in the US; the Russian Orthodox Church; conservative Muslim states, sometimes acting on behalf of the OIC; and at its centre, the Holy See—opposing normative developments on reproductive and LGBT rights.[44] A study by the Norwegian Agency for Development Cooperation analyses their interaction at the UN and argues that the action of these actors is driven by a 'critical and defensive stand against modern socio-political developments' including secularization, the feminist movement, and the sexual revolution.[45] Such developments are regarded by the actors as a threat to religion and society more broadly, as they believe society 'depends for its stability on traditional moral values and a patriarchal social order, framed as "family values" and conceived as absolute moral standards laid down in pre-modern sacred texts or authoritative religious teachings'.[46] In this context, one could draw on Doris Buss and Didi Herman's exercise, where they contrast verses from the New Testament that portray 'the Jesus movement' as a clear alternative community to the biological family (which in a sense was repudiated) with statements from the Catechism that describe the family as a man and a women united in marriage with their children.[47] In Buss and Herman's account, today's conservative Christian organizations

---

[41] See Programme of Action of the International Conference on Population and Development, Cairo 5–13 September 1994, A/CONF.171/13/Rev.1, Part II, Statements and Reservations on the Programme of Action; Report of the Fourth World Conference on Women, Beijing, 4–15 September 1995, A/CONF.177/20/Rev.1, at 154ff.

[42] See note 41.

[43] See for instance D. Buss and D. Herman, *Globalizing Family Values. The Christian Rights in International Politics* (Minneapolis, MN: University of Minnesota Press, 2003); M. Juul Petersen, 'International Religious NGOs at The United Nations: A Study of a Group of Religious Organizations', *The Journal of Humanitarian Assistance* (2010); J. Heynes, *Faith-based Organisations at the United Nations*, European University Institute Working Papers, RSCAS 2013/70, 2013.

[44] Heynes, *Faith-based Organisations at the United Nations*, at 12.

[45] Norwegian Agency for Development Cooperation, *Lobbying for Faith and Family: A Study of Religious NGOs at the United Nations*, NORAD Report 7/2013, at 4.

[46] See note 45.

[47] Buss and Herman, *Globalizing Family Values. The Christian Rights in International Politics*, at 2–4.

choose to emphasize the latter portrayal of the family, basing their interpretation not so much on biblical authority but on the tradition of the last century.[48] If nothing else, this example speaks for the role which conservative religious actors assume as interpreters of religion and their agency in interpreting texts and tradition in a certain way as opposed to another.

On the other side, a different group of religious organizations were joined by secular non-governmental organizations, and supported by some Western and Latin American governments. Among the most vocal organizations were Catholics for a Free Choice—which, as we shall see in Chapter 4, questions the role of the Holy See as a state given that, according to them, statehood grants, to what essentially is a church, undue influence in international fora. Ecumenical Women, another 'progressive' organization integrating Anglican, Presbyterian, Lutheran, and Methodist groups, asserted its vision statement as follows:

Within our Biblical interpretation, Jesus' ministry of healing and community with women and other marginalized peoples, indicates a deep respect for and equality with women.... It is our understanding that the church at its best can be a center which models policies which reinforce gender equality... and which develops networks of women and men who resist systems of patriarchy, domination and abuse. We believe that the church is a powerful transformative vehicle for the teaching, protection and enforcement of women's rights and gender equality when its constituents and leadership are informed and empowered.[49]

It is important to note that groups which share the same faith diverge on fundamental issues of their religion, such as the meaning of the family. This divergence provides evidence that religious actors assume an interpretative role of their religion and values, as indeed is expressly recognized by Ecumenical Women in their vision statement. It is this which allows them to bridge institutional differences and indeed religious divides, by emphasizing those interpretations of their various religious texts which reflect a 'conservative' or on the contrary a 'progressive' standpoint.

The acknowledgment that it is actors' interpretation of religion, and not religion as such, which clash may assuage fears related to the (in)famous clash of civilizations theory. Beyond academic interest, however, where does the importance of this acknowledgment lie? As interpretations are not fixed, but vary according to time and context, two areas are of practical importance. First, the interpretation of a religious actor of a certain issue may change in time and hence their opposition to the advancement of standards on issues such as gender equality and sexual orientation may lessen. Perhaps the strongest indication of the potential for interpretative change comes from Pope Francis who declared in a 2013 interview:

I said that if a homosexual person is of good will and is in search of God, I am no one to judge. By saying this, I said what the catechism says. Religion has the right to express its opinion in the service of the people, but God in creation has set us free: it is not possible

[48] Buss and Herman, *Globalizing Family Values. The Christian Rights in International Politics*, at 4.
[49] Ecumenical Women website accessed October 2013, http://ecumenicalwomen.org/about/ (emphasis added).

to interfere spiritually in the life of a person.... We cannot insist only on issues related to abortion, gay marriage and the use of contraceptive methods. This is not possible. I have not spoken much about these things, and I was reprimanded for that. But when we speak about these issues, we have to talk about them in a context. The teaching of the church, for that matter, is clear and I am a son of the church, but it is not necessary to talk about these issues all the time.... The dogmatic and moral teachings of the church are not all equivalent. The church's pastoral ministry cannot be obsessed with the transmission of a disjointed multitude of doctrines to be imposed insistently.[50]

An example of change, which predates Pope Francis' indication, or promise, of a new direction, comes from Ecuador. In 1994, Ecuador, reflecting the position of the strong Catholic Church in the country, 'entered a reservation [to the Cairo Programme of Action] concerning certain unnatural concepts relating to the family, inter alia, which might undermine the principles contained in its Constitution'.[51] In 2011, Ecuador has voted in favour of the Human Rights Council resolution on Human rights, sexual orientation and gender identity which recognizes that acts of violence and discrimination are committed in all regions of the world against individuals because of their sexual orientation and gender identity.[52] Certainly, normative change is a complex process involving multiple factors beyond the interpretative position of a religious actor, hence it will not occur overnight, but rather incrementally, and its directionality is not always guaranteed.

Second, the interpretation of a religious actor may vary with context and the issue at hand. As will be shown in the following section, allies in opposing normative developments at the UN on sexual identity may not find themselves sharing the same opinions in relation to the 'defamation of religions'.

2. 'Defamation of religions'

Let us start with three observations in relation to religious actors that are allies in their opposition to normative developments on issues of sexuality and reproduction yet choose different paths in relation to the defamation of religions topic. First, the English language website of the Department for External Church Relations of the Russian Orthodox Church, presents in its 'Documents' section the document entitled 'The Russian Orthodox Church's Approach to Willful Public Blasphemy and Slander against the Church'. This may suggest, and the text of the document confirms, that the Russian Orthodox Church nurtures a certain attachment to initiatives aimed at combating 'defamation of religions'.[53] Second, from the website of the *Guardian* newspaper we learn, in the words of a US diplomat, that at the 64th

---

[50] A. Spadaro, S.J, 'The Exclusive Interview with Pope Francis: A Big Heart Open to God', *America, the National Catholic Weekly*, 30 September 2013, at 24 and 26.

[51] See Programme of Action of the International Conference on Population and Development, Cairo 5-13 September 1994, A/CONF.171/13/Rev.1, Part II, Statements and Reservations on the Programme of Action.

[52] See Human Rights Council resolution 17/19, Human rights, sexual orientation and gender identity, UN Doc. A/HRC/RES/17/19, 17 June 2011.

[53] See https://mospat.ru/en/documents/, accessed October 2013.

session of the UN General Assembly, '[t]he Vatican observer mission lobbied actively and influentially in the corridors and in informal consultations...especially on the Defamation of Religions resolution, where they are allies [of the US]. Their long-term view of this issue coincides with ours...'[54]; and an observer of the works of UN fora could add that the view of the Holy See/Vatican on 'defamation of religions' diverges from that of Russia, and the Russian Orthodox Church. The last piece of this puzzle on shifting allegiances is offered by the OIC website, which lists three items under the heading 'Basic International Documents on Human Rights': the International Covenant on Civil and Political Rights (ICCPR), and two UN resolutions on 'combating intolerance, negative stereotyping, stigmatization, discrimination, incitement to violence and violence against persons, based on religion or belief'.[55] It is striking that the OIC as initiator of the 'defamation of religions' resolutions, did not choose to highlight these, but opted instead to emphasize those consensual resolutions which formally put an end to the defamation debates at the UN.[56]

The suggestion of this study is that the key to solving this puzzle on shifting allegiances lies in acknowledging the interpretative role of religious actors in this context and how it shaped, and has been shaped by, other actors along the years in the international arena. This section will therefore focus on unearthing the construction of the religious actors' arguments, while Chapter 3 will address in detail questions related to blasphemy and religious actors' rights to freedom of expression and religion, and their duties in this context.

In 1999, Pakistan, on behalf of the OIC, proposed an initial resolution intended to curb the 'defamation of Islam' at the UN Commission for Human Rights. At that time, Mr Akram noted that:

manifestations of intolerance and misunderstanding, not to say hatred, of Islam and Muslims in various parts of the world...might become as widespread and endemic as anti-semitism had been in the past. There was a tendency in some countries and in the international media to portray Islam as a religion hostile to human rights, threatening to the Western world and associated with terrorism and violence.... No other religion received such constant negative media coverage. That defamation campaign was reflected in growing intolerance towards Muslims.[57]

The OIC identified the cause of intolerance, discrimination, and hatred towards Muslims in the very fact of 'defaming' Islam. Following this line of argument it requested that protection be granted to Islam as such. It should be recalled that

---

[54] 'US embassy cables: Vatican's 'active and influential' role at UN general assembly', *The Guardian*, 10 December 2012, http://www.theguardian.com/world/us-embassy-cables-documents/240914, accessed October 2013.

[55] See http://www.oic-oci.org/oicv2/page/?p_id=260&p_ref=89&lan=en, accessed October 2013.

[56] Note, however the observation entailed by the Washington Draft Report of the Committee on Islamic Law and International Law of the International Law Association: 'the OIC has expressly stated that it intends to use this alternative resolution as a means of keeping the "defamation of religion" issue alive until such time as it can reappear on the international agenda'. International Law Association, Committee on Islamic Law and International Law, Draft Conference Report Washington, April 2014, at 25–6 http://www.ila-hq.org/en/committees/index.cfm/cid/1006, accessed April 2014.

[57] See Commission on Human Rights, Summary Record of the 61st Meeting, 55th session, Geneva, 29 April 1999, UN Doc. E/CN.4/1999/SR.61, 19 October 1999, para. 1.

the review of legal provisions in Chapter 1 demonstrated that in international law the beneficiariaries of protection are individuals and groups of individuals and not religion(s); in this context, the OIC's initiative would seem atypical, if not revolutionary. In 1999, the response of many of the European countries, but not exclusively,[58] had been to point to the imbalanced nature of the resolution, not primarily on grounds that it protected religion as a category—as opposed to the rights of individuals to religious freedom and to non-discrimination on religious grounds—but that it protected a specific religion, Islam—in contrast to religions more broadly. As a consequence, Germany, on behalf of the European Union, introduced certain amendments to the text proposed by Pakistan. The UN Commission's resolution was thus adopted without a vote and inter alia expressed deep concern: 'at the negative stereotyping of religions'; 'that Islam is frequently and wrongly associated with human rights violations and with terrorism'; and, at the use of media 'to incite acts of violence, xenophobia or related intolerance and discrimination *towards Islam and any other religion*'.[59] A similar resolution was adopted by consensus the following year, despite the palpable unease that persisted among various delegations.[60] In hindsight, one has to note that while the OIC had been the initiator of a resolution which was atypical in human rights law—in as far as it protected religion per se as opposed to the holders of religious rights—it was the consensual nature of the 1999 and 2000 resolutions which may have posed the most serious implications for the human-centred paradigm on which the human rights system rests.[61]

In 2001, the Belgian representative, on behalf of the European Union, raised the awaited objection: 'dans le texte à l'examen, l'accent est mis sur la protection des religions plutôt que sur celle des droits de l'homme des individus adeptes de ces religions.'[62] The same year the resolution on 'combating defamation of religions' was passed by the Commission by vote;[63] the majority decreased consistently in

---

[58] For instance, the Guatemalan delegate noted that '[h]e entirely shared the OIC countries' concern at the negative stereotyping of Islam and agreed on the need to promote religious tolerance and dialogue among civilizations and cultures with a view to promoting international understanding and avoiding a "clash of civilizations". But he also shared the concerns of those who felt that negative stereotypes, which were rooted in religious extremism, affected all religions.' It is interesting to observe that Huntington's terminology has gained access in UN fora. Commission on Human Rights, Summary Record of the 62nd Meeting, 55th session, Geneva, 30 April 1999, UN doc. E/CN.4/1999/SR.62, 17 November 1999, para. 5.

[59] Commission on Human Rights resolution 1999/82, Defamation of religions, 62nd meeting, 55th session, U.N. Doc. E/CN.4/Res/1999/82, art. 1–4 (emphasis added).

[60] Commission on Human Rights, Summary Record of the 67th Meeting, 56th session, Geneva, 26 April 2000, UN Doc. E/CN.4/2000/SR.67, 1 December 2000, para. 72; Commission on Human Rights resolution 2000/84, 67th Meeting, 56th session, UN Doc. E/CN.4/Res/2000/84, 26 April 2000.

[61] On the complexity of consensus-based decision-making and the implications for normative development see A.N. Pronto, 'Some Thoughts on the Making of International Law', 19 *EJIL* 3 (2008), 601–616.

[62] Commission on Human Rights, Summary Record of the 6st Meeting, 57th session, Geneva, 18 April 2001, UN Doc. E/CN.4/2001/SR.61, 4 December 2001, para. 5. (This author's translation: in the text under consideration, the focus is on the protection of religions rather than on the rights of individuals followers of these religions).

[63] Commission on Human Rights resolution 2001/4, 67th Meeting, 56th session, UN Doc. E/CN.4/RES/2001/4, 18 April 2001.

2002, 2003, 2004, 2005,[64] and the same trend was evident at the Human Rights Council—the Commission's successor—in 2007, 2008, 2009, and 2010.[65] Having been tabled at the General Assembly in 2006, the resolution on 'defamation of religions' has been adopted by vote, with decreasing support every year until 2010 inclusive.[66]

It is noteworthy that in terms of construction of arguments over the years, the OIC drafters sought to fuse religious arguments (the defamation of Islam as such) with human rights arguments (the rights of Muslims to freedom of religion, not to be discriminated against or not to be made the target of incitement to violence). In terms of substance, nonetheless, this fusion has resulted in confusion as to whether the 'defamation of religions' could lead to discrimination against individuals or represented discrimination as such, could lead to racism or was racism as such, or could lead to incitement to violence or represented incitement to violence as such.[67] In a forthcoming article, Turan Kayaoğlu argues that the OIC adopted 'liberal-secular categories' to translate its Islamic demands in 'acceptable language'.[68] This in turn exposed the religious actor to mostly Western states' critique of terminology such as the precise definitions of 'defamation' and 'race', challenges concerning 'the necessity and feasibility of anti-defamation norms' in international human rights law, and indeed vulnerability in relation to member states practices' such as blasphemy laws that are used to silence or discriminate against non-Muslims and Muslim communities.[69] According to the author, 'the initial Islamic argument: combating Islamophobia can be a means of protecting Muslims' rights in the West', was lost in translation.[70]

Whereas this critique may capture certain realities, it is also important to recall that the relationship of Western states with religion is a rather complex one. As Chapter 3 will show, European states are far from being totally abandoned in the arms of secularism, and as such they struggle themselves with terminology and balancing religion and law. In this vein, it should be noted that the United Kingdom abolished its blasphemy law as late as in 2008.[71]

Another aspect deserves attention. Western states, human rights organizations and legal scholars have expressed concern at the 'defamation of religions' resolutions as setting undue limitations on freedom of speech and conflating race and

---

[64] See Commission on Human Rights, Reports on the 57th, 58th, 59th, 60th, 61st sessions, UN Doc. E/CN.4/2001/167, E/CN.4/2002/200, E/CN.4/2003/135, E/CN.4/2004/127, E/CN.4/2005/135.

[65] For the resolutions and voting records see Report of the Human Rights Council 4th, 7th, 10th, 13th session, UN Doc. A/HRC/4/123, A/HRC/7/78, A/HRC/10/29, A/HRC/13/56. The margin in 2010 was 20 to 17 with 8 abstentions.

[66] General Assembly resolutions 60/150 of 20 January 2006; 61/164 of 21 February 2007; 62/154 of 6 March 2008; 63/171 of 24 March 2009; 64/156 of 8 March 2010; 65/224 of 11 April 2011.

[67] For the peak of the fusion of arguments and substantive confusion see General Assembly resolution 60/150 of 20 January 2006.

[68] T. Kayaoğlu, 'Giving an Inch only to Lose a Mile: Muslim States, Liberalism, and Human Rights in the UN', 36 *HRQ* 1 (2014, forthcoming).

[69] See note 68.   [70] See note 68.

[71] See Criminal Justice and Immigration Act 2008, sec. 79.

religion as discriminatory grounds[72]—all of these actors could be argued to master the liberal and secular discourse. In addition to them however, religious organizations of all affiliations have also challenged the 'defamation' resolutions.[73] Among the religious actors were the voices of various allies of the 'conservative' coalition— this was the case with some Evangelical organizations which may have feared that their proselytizing activities would come under the scrutiny of blasphemy laws legitimized by the 'defamation of religions' resolutions and it was the case with the Holy See. The Representative of the Holy See at the General Assembly declared the following:

> My delegation remains concerned that, in its implementation, the concept of 'defamation' has given rise to States enacting laws which undermine this fundamental right to freedom of religion and conscience, particularly for religious minority groups. We call, therefore, on all States to ensure full respect for the human dignity and fundamental rights of all.[74]

In this case, religious actors of 'conservative' orientation have exercised their discretion in interpreting blasphemy laws—which, after all, are conservative devices aimed at protecting religious tenets and conserving the prevailing social order[75]— as contrary to their religious interest.

All the while, Russia remained the staunch ally of the OIC, as evidenced by its consistent vote in favour of the 'defamation' resolutions in both UN fora.[76] It may be unexpected that a resolution which set out to highlight the uniqueness of the intolerance

---

[72] A selection of articles which analyse—some in more lucid terms, others in rather alarmist terms— the various challenges posed by the 'defamation' resolutions includes J. Temperman, 'The Emerging Counter-defamation of Religion Discourse: a Critical Analysis', 4 *Droit et Religions: Annuaire* (2009), 553–559; R. J. Dobras, 'Is the United Nations Endorsing Human Rights Violations: An Analysis of the United Nations' Combating Defamation of Religions Resolutions and Pakistan's Blasphemy Laws', 37 *Ga. J. Int'l & Comp. L.* (2009), 339–380; A. G. Belnap, 'Defamation of Religions: A Vague and Overbroad Theory that Threatens Basic Human Rights', *BYU L. Rev.* (2010), 635–685; J. Rehman and S. E. Berry, 'Is "Defamation of Religions" Passé? The United Nations, Organisation of Islamic Cooperation, and Islamic State Practices: Lessons from Pakistan', 44 *Geo. Wash. Int'l L. Rev.* (2012), 431–539; L. Langer, 'The Rise (and Fall?) of Defamation of Religions', 35 *Yale J. Int'l L.* (2010), 257–533. L. Bennett Graham contextualizes and offers the most complete picture of the various challenges posed by the resolutions: the problematic transposition of the legal concept of defamation utilized to protect individuals' livelihood and reputation to religion, essentially a category of practice, thoughts and texts such as religion, and the corresponding burden placed on the shoulders of judges to define religion and the truth about it; the high threshold of article 20(2) ICCPR which provides for the prohibition of advocacy of national, racial or religious hatred that constitutes incitement to discrimination, hostility, or violence; the conflation of race, an immutable category, with religion, which according to human rights law can be changed although some Muslim countries have at times objected to this provision; the less than favourable record of domestic implementation of blasphemy laws and their legitimization through the 'defamation of religions' resolutions. See L. B. Graham, 'Defamation of Religions: The End of Pluralism', 23 *Emory Int'l L. Rev* (2009), 69–84.

[73] See Heynes, *Faith-based Organisations at the United Nations*, at 22.

[74] Statement of the Holy See in Explanation of Position, Resolution on Defamation of Religions A/C.3/65/L.46/Rev.1, Third Committee of the 65th session of the UN General Assembly, New York, 23 November 2010.

[75] For a history of the blasphemy law in the United Kingdom see I. Bryan, 'Suffering Offence: The Place, Function and Future of the Blasphemy Laws Revisited' 4 *JCL* (1999), 332–363, at 336–340.

[76] See earlier notes 65–66 for the records of vote. It should be noted that the Russian Federation is an observer state of the OIC since 2005, see 'Observers', accessed October 2013, http://www.oic-oci. org/oicv2/page/?p_id=179&p_ref=60&lan=en.

faced by Muslims attracted support from a country with a strong Orthodox following. Some observers seek to provide the context in which the Russian support to the OIC could be understood. According to Robert C. Blitt, in recent years the influence of the Russian Orthodox Church has increasingly shaped not only domestic but also foreign policy issues.[77] Blitt contends that among the Church's priority areas—transposed by Russian diplomats in the international arena—are the prohibition on defamation of religion and a 'retrograde effort to contextualize other existing rights protections in light of so-called "traditional" and "religious" values.'[78] Another observer explains that support for the 'defamation of religion' resolutions is part of the Russian Orthodox Church's 'struggle against present-day Western secularism'; 'key tactics' in this struggle include the cooperation with 'the conservative non-Orthodox Christian bodies and…Muslim bodies in defense of traditional religiosity and adjacent social and legal norms'.[79] Against these observations, it should be noted that the document explicating the Church's approach on the topic of blasphemy is not dissimilar to the 'defamation of religions' resolutions in as far as it amalgamates religious grounds with human rights terms.[80] It also emphasizes that 'blasphemy and slander are used more often as a means of struggle against religion justified by references to freedom of conscience, expression or creative work.'[81] The 2013 Russian law criminalizing blasphemy can be read to sanction the Church's position.[82]

In 2011, a change of course was registered at the Human Rights Council, and subsequently the General Assembly, with the adoption by consensus of the OIC-sponsored resolutions on 'Combating intolerance, negative stereotyping and stigmatization of, and discrimination, incitement to violence and violence against, persons based on religion or belief'.[83] In Geneva, on the corridors of the Palais

---

[77] According to the author: 'The Patriarch today enjoys the ear of Russia's Foreign Ministry and plays a key role in both formulating and advancing Russian interests abroad.' R. C. Blitt, 'Russia's Orthodox Foreign Policy: The Growing Influence of the Russian Orthodox Church in Shaping Russia's Policies Abroad', 33 *U. Pa. J. Int'l L.* 2 (2011), 363–460, at 365.

[78] Blitt, 'Russia's Orthodox Foreign Policy: The Growing Influence of the Russian Orthodox Church in Shaping Russia's Policies Abroad', at 405.

[79] A. Zolotov, 'Russia, Defamation of Religion & Free Speech: Implications for Media', accessed November 2013, http://themediaproject.org.

[80] See *The Russian Orthodox Church's Approach to Willful Public Blasphemy and Slander against the Church*, adopted on 4 February 2011, by the Bishops' Council of the Russian Orthodox Church, accessed November 2013, https://mospat.ru/en/documents/otnoshenie-russkojj-pravoslavnojj-cerkvi-k-namerennomu-publichnomu-bogokhulstvu-i-klevete-v-adres-cerkvi/.

[81] See note 80.

[82] For criticism of the law see Article 19, 'Russia: Religious insult laws a threat to free expression', Press Release, 10 June 2013, accessed September 2013, http://www.article19.org/resources.php/resource/37100/en/russia:-religious-insult-laws-a-threat-to-free-expression#sthash.iTxNOz2g.dpuf.

[83] Human Rights Council resolution 16/18, Combating intolerance, negative stereotyping and stigmatization of, and discrimination, incitement to violence and violence against, persons based on religion or belief, 24 March 2011, UN Doc. A/HRC/RES/16/18; General Assembly resolution 66/167, Combating intolerance, negative stereotyping, stigmatization, discrimination, incitement to violence and violence against persons, based on religion or belief, 19 December 2011, UN Doc. A/RES/66/167. See also the subsequent Human Rights Council resolutions 19/25, 23 March 2012, A/HRC/19/L.7 and 22/31, 22 March 2013, A/HRC/22/L.40, as well as General Assembly resolution 67/178, 20 December 2012, A/RES/67/178.

des Nations, speculation as to the change of heart of the OIC pointed to the success of the anti-anti-defamation of religions campaign; to the increased tensions within the OIC itself, where certain member states objected to what seemed to be the undertaking of a few hardliners; or to the proper engagement of Western governments, including the United States, in finding solutions to what was a real problem, that of increasing discrimination against Muslims within the boundaries of their states.

The 'combating of incitement to violence' resolutions depart from the defamation discourse as they take a decidedly human-centred approach instead of identifying religion as the beneficiary of legal protection under human rights law. They are premised on the fact that 'enhance[d] implementation of existing legal regimes that protect individuals against discrimination and hate crimes, increase[d] interfaith and intercultural efforts and…[the expansion of] human rights education are important first steps in combating incidents of intolerance, discrimination and violence against individuals on the basis of religion or belief'.[84] The OIC ownership of this resolution is signalled by the central reference to the speech of the OIC Secretary-General in which he proposed a series of measures aimed at fostering 'a domestic environment of religious tolerance, peace and respect'.[85]

One should observe that the search for alternatives to the 'defamation of religions' resolutions and the adoption of the 'combating of incitement to violence' resolutions set in motion a process of high-level meetings: the Istanbul Process for Combating Intolerance, Discrimination and Incitement to Hatred and/or Violence on the Basis of Religion or Belief.[86] OIC initiatives to establish an international monitoring mechanism on the topic have been more controversial.[87] In this context, the Rabat Plan of Action on the prohibition of advocacy of national, racial or religious hatred that constitutes incitement to discrimination, hostility or violence—which resulted from expert workshops organized by the Office of the High Commissioner for Human Rights (OHCHR)—opens the debate on an area of human rights law which has long remained dormant and the implementation of which is lacking in many respects.[88] The document resets the terms of discussion away from 'defamation of religions', not incidentally recommending the repeal of blasphemy laws. It proposes comprehensive anti-discrimination legislation, while

[84] See A/HRC/RES/16/18, preambular paragraph, and the similar phrasing in A/RES/66/167.

[85] See note 84, para 5 in both resolutions.

[86] See for instance, Joint Statement by the Co-Chairs of the Ministerial on Implementation of UN Human Rights Council Resolution 16/18 on Combating Intolerance, Discrimination, and Violence Based on Religion or Belief, 15 July 2011, accessed November 2013, http://www.state.gov/r/pa/prs/ps/2011/07/168653.htm.

[87] See for instance Article 19 and Cairo Institute for Human Rights Studies, 'UN Human Rights Council must consolidate consensus on 16–18', 20 March 2013, http://www.article19.org/resources.php/resource/3672/en/un-human-rights-council-must-consolidate-consensus-on-16-18#sthash.ZWeHe2Ep.dpuf, accessed August 2013.

[88] Report of the United Nations High Commissioner for Human Rights on the expert workshops on the prohibition of incitement to national, racial or religious hatred, Annex, Rabat Plan of Action on the prohibition of advocacy of national, racial or religious hatred that constitutes incitement to discrimination, hostility or violence, UN Doc. A/HRC/22/17/Add.4, 11 January 2013.

recommending a high-threshold in the reading of article 20.2 of the ICCPR on the prohibition of advocacy of national, racial or religious hatred that constitutes incitement to violence by linking it to article 19 and its three part test of limitations (legality, proportionality, and necessity).

As noted in the opening puzzle, on its website, the OIC claims ownership of the 'combating of incitement to violence' resolutions as opposed to the myriad 'defamation of religions' resolutions. In this sense, it would seem that the religious actor interprets its efforts to put Islamophobia on the agenda of UN fora as a 'gain in translation', despite the rejection of its initial religion-centred approach.

This brief and, hence necessarily, arbitrary review of instances of interaction of religious actors has revealed that one certainly cannot speak of an *express adherence* to the same category of religious actors of the Holy See, Iran, Pakistan, the OIC, and the various churches and religious organizations; however, all these actors, when they put forward interpretations that pose challenges to international law—whether to current standards or the development of new ones—tend to emphasize the central role which religion plays in their functioning together with the claim of legitimate authority to interpret religion as central arguments setting them aside from the law. It is this *common claim to be special or exceptional due to their religious characteristics*, which warrants their unification under the analytical category of religious actors and not an express adherence, or shared set of values.[89] Against this backdrop then, it is necessary to return to the research question of this study and endeavour to examine whether the claim for speciality of religious actors is accommodated by the international legal system through the acknowledgement of special rights and lesser obligations.

IV. The Acquisition of Rights and Obligations in International Law

To verify whether religious actors benefit from a special or exceptional framework of rights and obligations, the first question that requires an answer is how do actors, in general, acquire rights and obligations in international law. 'As in any

---

[39] It is difficult to find another category—particularly one which cuts across the state/non-state spectrum—comprising actors which claim 'speciality' in international law. One possible example comes from Latin America and refers to members of the military. In the transition from military dictatorships to democratic regimes, Latin American states granted amnesty to military leaders so that civil courts lacked jurisdiction for human rights violations perpetrated by these. In the 1990s, many victims of human rights violations of the military regimes sought out justice with international human rights bodies and in particular the Inter-American human rights system. The result, as Laplante explains, was that 'international human rights law jurisprudence ... strengthened recognition of individual rights while slowly chipping away at absolute state sovereignty' in what appeared like a human rights coup targeting amnesty laws. See L.J. Laplante, 'Outlawing Amnesty: The Return of Criminal Justice in Transitional Justice Schemes', 50 *Virginia Journal of International Law* 1 (2009), 915–984, at 917. Consequently, the exclusivity or specialty of members of the military, which saw themselves outside the confines of human rights law, has been dismantled. This example is different from that of religious actors, in as far as the category of members of the military in Latin America did not extend beyond the individual to comprise international organizations or states. It is similar in as far as a given characteristic—military, religious respectively—has been invoked to interpret the law applicable to non-military and non-religious peers.

other legal system', Hersch Lauterpacht contended, 'so also in the international sphere the subjects of law are the persons, national and juridical, upon whom the law confers rights and imposes duties'.[90] Hence, by making an analogy with the domestic system, the subjects of international law have rights and duties by virtue of their international legal personality. Ian Brownlie—while stressing the circularity of the definition of the subject of international law, 'since the *indicia* referred to depend on the existence of a legal person'—added another definitional element: the capacity of the subject to maintain its rights by bringing international claims.[91]

Consequently, in examining the rights and obligations of religious actors one would prima facie need to establish whether a specific religious actor is a subject of international law. It can be assumed that states would present relatively few hurdles. Religious state actors are incontestably subjects of international law by virtue of the fact that they are states. Less obvious is the case of the Holy See, which claims a dual personality as the government of the Catholic Church and the government of the Vatican, and for this reason Chapter 4 will engage extensively with the personality question and the rights and obligations which flow therefrom. Beyond states, what rights and duties for international organizations, or indeed for non-state actors?

A theory concerning the acquisition of rights and obligations under international law must respond to several important challenges. Two are identified here. First, there is a need for flexibility because, even if it is accepted that categories other than states may be subjects of international law, not all of these subjects have the same rights and obligations, and not all of these rights and obligations can be enforced in a similar fashion to those of states.[92] For example, international organizations are recognized as subjects of international law yet lack the *capacity* to enjoy some of the rights of states, such as the right to territorial integrity. It is also notoriously difficult to enforce the human rights obligations that international organizations are said to have in the absence of international courts that have general jurisdiction over international organizations. Approaches have therefore been proposed that assert that 'international organizations should "account" for their performance in a much broader way than only on the basis of clear violations of their obligations established under international law'.[93] Chapter 5 will address these issues in the context of an analysis of the OIC. Second, a theory on the acquisition of rights and obligations in the international legal system needs to be responsive to context. The

---

[90] H. Lauterpacht, 'General Rules of the Law of Peace', in E. Lauterpacht (ed.), *International Law Being the Collected Papers of Hersch Lauterpacht*, vol. I, The General Works, (Cambridge: Cambridge University Press, 1970), at 136.

[91] I. Brownlie, *Principles of Public International Law*, 7th ed., (Oxford: Oxford University Press, 2008), at 52.

[92] See also J. Klabbers, '(I Can't Get No) Recognition: Subjects Doctrine and the Emergence of Non-State Actors', in J. Petman and J. Klabbers (eds.), *Nordic Cosmopolitanism. Essays in International Law for Martti Koskenniemi*, (Leiden: Martinus Nijhoff Publishers, 2003), 351–369, at 363.

[93] I. F. Dekker, 'Accountability of International Organisations: An Evolving Concept?', in J. Wouters, et al. (eds.), *Accountability for Human Rights Violations by International Organisations*, (Antwerp: Intersentia, 2010), 21–36, at 22–23.

driving force behind attempts to include non-state actors within the framework of the international legal system stems from the need to account for their growing importance in norm creation and implementation.[94] In the concluding remarks to a 2011 volume that brought together multiple perspectives on non-state actors in international law, Jean d'Aspremont asserts that 'there is not a single area of international law where law-making and law-enforcement—including compliance monitoring—has not been affected by these [non-state] actors'.[95] Specifically, the need for *accountability* of these entities, in contexts where they exercise power and affect the human rights of individuals, represents a significant argument for their inclusion in the system.[96]

Several attempts have been made to address the rights and obligations of non-state actors, the most challenging category to accommodate within international law. The 'subjects doctrine' has been adjusted to accommodate non-state entities, either by 'relativizing the subjects or subjectivizing the actors'.[97] Alternatively, the 'capacity approach', a pragmatic, inductive approach has been advocated, insisting that certain non-state actors possess the 'requisite legal capacity directly to acquire rights and obligations under international law'.[98] The process of accommodating non-state actors within international law has been described as a 'constant swing of the pendulum between . . . two opposite poles, the normative construct of the subjects and the descriptive approach of the actors'.[99] Certainly, what these observations bring to the fore is that conferring, bestowing, or acquiring rights and obligations in international law is a complex and hence much debated matter. Yet, to paraphrase Martti Koskenniemi, complexities are part of the beauty of international law.[100]

This part will provide an overview of the subjects doctrine, discuss the capacity approach, and engage with Janne Elisabeth Nijman's efforts to retrace the original meaning of international legal personality and unearth its relevance for current

[94] See Bianchi, 'The Fight for Inclusion: Non-state Actors and International Law', at 41–42; A. C. Cutler, 'Critical Reflections on the Westphalian Assumptions of International Law and Organization: a Crisis of Legitimacy', 27 *Review of International Studies* 2 (2001), 133–150, at 137 ff.

[95] J. d'Aspremont, 'Inclusive Law-Making and Law-Enforcement for an Exclusive International Legal System', in J. d'Aspremont (ed.), *Participants in the International Legal System: Multiple Perspectives on Non-State Actors in International Law*, (London: Routledge, 2011), 425–439, at 425.

[96] See for example L. Cameron, 'Private Military Companies: their Status under International Humanitarian Law and its Impact on their Regulation', 88 *International Review of the Red Cross* 863 (2006), 573–598; A. Clapham, 'Human Rights Obligations of Non-state Actors in Conflict Situation', 88 *International Review of the Red Cross* 863 (2006), 491–523; A. Clapham, 'Extending International Criminal Law Beyond the Individual to Corporations and Armed Opposition Groups', 6 *Journal of International Criminal Justice* 5 (2008), 899–926; C. Jochnick, 'Confronting the Impunity of Non-state Actors: New Fields for the Promotion of Human Rights', 21 *HRQ* (1999), 56–79. For an overview on sectoral studies on non-state actors, see Bianchi, 'The Fight for Inclusion: Non-state Actors and International Law', at 47–48.

[97] As critically discussed in Bianchi, 'Introduction: Relativizing the Subjects or Subjectivizing the Actors: Is That the Question?', xi–xxx.

[98] A. Clapham, *Human Rights Obligations of Non-State Actors*, (Oxford: Oxford University Press, 2006), at 71.

[99] Bianchi, 'The Fight for Inclusion: Non-state Actors and International Law', at 38.

[100] M. Koskenniemi, 'Address at the New York University School of Law', 4 April 2006, quoted in C. Leathley, 'An Institutional Hierarchy to Combat the Fragmentation of International Law: Has the ILC Missed an Opportunity?', 40 *NYU J.L. & Pol.* 1 (2007), 259–306, at 270.

times. The aim is to offer insights into how this book will approach the acquisition of rights and obligations under international law by religious actors, including religious non-state entities.

1. The (still) dominant narrative: the subjects doctrine

Mainstream international legal scholarship moved away from the paradigm that portrayed states as *the sole subjects* of international law. States are regarded now as *the sole full subjects* of international law, whereas the rest of actors are just that, the rest, although with nuances of tolerated and tolerable subjectivity.[101] The international law manual of the late Antonio Cassese regards 'States' as the 'fundamental or primary' subjects in international law.[102] 'Quite understandably', it is asserted, 'the latter seek to keep under control the legal processes that take place in an international community in which they are still deemed to be the main actors'.[103]

The convention of capitalizing the term 'state' can perhaps be seen as the orthographic attestation of the centrality attributed to the state in the international legal system. Conversely, defining actors in terms of what they are not—i.e. non-state—beyond being 'euphemistic', or so Philip Alston convincingly argues, introduces a relational element, a gravitation of all other actors around the state.[104] The central role of states is explained by appeal to two aspects: states control territories in a stable and permanent way, and states exercise the fundamental lawmaking and executive functions.[105]

States, therefore, are the backbone of the community. They possess full *legal capacity*, that is, the capacity to be vested with rights, powers, and obligations. Were they to disappear, the present international community would either fall apart or change radically.[106]

If the criteria for statehood are the same as those for subjectivity, as suggested above, then there appears to be little space for any other subjects of international law. However, as Michel Virally noted, 'il y a toujours été difficile de refuser absolument la qualité de sujet de droit à ceux qui vivent habituellement à l'intérieur du groupe'.[107] Such refusal to admit non-state actors is less and less justifiable today, since recent decades have witnessed an increasing role being played by such actors in international law, in particular 'in the shaping of

---

[101] See P. Alston, 'The "Not-a-Cat" Syndrome: Can the International Human Rights Regime Accommodate Non-State Actors?', in P. Alston (ed.), *Non-state Actors and Human Rights*, (New York: Oxford University Press, 2005), 3–36, at 19.

[102] A. Cassese, *International Law*, 2nd ed., (Oxford: Oxford University Press, 2005), at 71.

[103] A. Bianchi, 'Globalization of Human Rights: The Role of Non-state Actors', in G. Teubner (ed.), *Global Law without a State*, (Aldershot: Dartmouth, 1997), 179–212, at 180.

[104] Alston, 'The "Not-a-Cat" Syndrome: Can the International Human Rights Regime Accommodate Non-State Actors?', at 3–4.

[105] Cassese, *International Law*, 2nd ed., at 71.

[106] See note 105.

[107] M. Virally, *La Pensée Juridique*, (Paris: LGDJ, 1960), at 122. (This author's translation: it has always been difficult to refuse in an absolute manner the subjectivity of those who habitually live within the group). See also M. Cosnard, 'Avant-propos', *Le Sujet en Droit International: Colloque du Mans*, (Paris: Editions A. Pedone, 2005), at 3.

international human rights doctrine, deeply infringing on the once indisputable prerogatives of the nation-states';[108] but can the subjects doctrine accommodate these developments?

When discussing subjectivity, it is difficult to avoid citing the 1949 *Reparation for Injuries* Advisory Opinion. The International Court of Justice (ICJ) was asked to advise whether the United Nations, as an international organization, had the capacity to bring an international claim against a state when a UN agent suffered injuries in the performance of his duties in circumstances involving a state's international responsibility. The Court held that the United Nations had 'objective international personality... together with the capacity to bring international claims'.[109] In a famous passage, the Court explained its reasoning:

The subjects of law in any legal system are not necessarily identical in their nature or the extent of their rights, and their nature depends upon the needs of the community. Throughout history, the development of international law has been influenced by the requirements of international life and the progressive increase in the collective activities of States has already given rise to instances of action upon the international plane by certain entities which are not States.[110]

The *Reparation for Injuries* Advisory Opinion is considered to assert what Prosper Weil terms 'l'étrange théorie de la personnalité relative'.[111] This theory has been re-confirmed and at the same time confined in more recent times. In 1993, the World Health Organization (WHO) asked the Court for an opinion on whether— in view of its health and environmental effects—the use of nuclear weapons by a state in times of armed conflict would constitute a breach of that state's obligations under international law, including under the WHO Constitution. The ICJ declared that the WHO lacked standing, stating:

That the WHO, as a subject of international law, should be led to apply the rules of international law or concern itself with their development is in no way surprising; but it does not follow that it has received a mandate, beyond the terms of its Constitution, itself to address the legality or illegality of the use of weaponry in hostilities.[112]

It follows that although international organizations are subjects of international law, they are so in the light of a derivation principle: 'that is to say, they are invested

---

[108] Bianchi, 'Globalization of Human Rights: The Role of Non-state Actors', at 180. See also Cutler, 'Critical Reflections on the Westphalian Assumptions of International Law and Organization: a Crisis of Legitimacy', 133–150.

[109] *Reparation for injuries suffered in the service of the United Nations*, Advisory Opinion, ICJ Reports 1949, p. 174, at 185.

[110] *Reparation for injuries suffered in the service of the United Nations*, at 178.

[111] P. Weil, 'Le Droit International en Quête de son Identité: Cours Général de Droit International Public', 237 *Recueil des Cours de l'Académie de Droit International de la Haye* (1992-VI), 9–370, at 100–101. (This author's translation: the strange theory of relative personality). See also H. Ruiz Fabri, 'Les Catégories de Sujets du Droit International', *Le sujet en droit international: Colloque du Mans*, (Paris: Editions A. Pedone, 2005), 55–71, at 71.

[112] *Legality of the Use by a State of Nuclear Weapons in Armed Conflict*, Advisory Opinion, ICJ Reports 1996, p. 66, at 82, para. 27.

by the States which create them with powers, the limits of which are a function of the common interests whose promotion those States entrust to them'.[113]

It becomes clear from the preceding paragraphs that an interplay between a 'necessity' argument and a 'recognition' aspect in respect to the subjectivity of different actors is taking place. As Jan Klabbers observes, there are considerations of necessity which determine states, as 'the gate-keepers' of the international system, to accommodate non-state entities.[114] The necessity argument is perhaps most evident in relation to international organizations that states set up to overcome problems of cooperation by, for example, reducing communication costs, fostering community values, or addressing issues that single states cannot deal with effectively.[115] The shared understanding among states that it is a necessity to establish effective international organizations has made it easier to recognize these non-state entities as international subjects, albeit, with limited legal capacity in respect of rights and obligations and their actual ability to operate or put into effect their rights.

Setting the question of 'capacity' aside, since it will be addressed in the next section, one has to note that the problem with subjectivity of most other non-state actors—notably national liberation movements, armed groups, companies, and NGOs—rarely concerns the necessity argument and more often concerns the recognition aspect.[116] In other words, while there are diverse and at times imperative reasons to treat non-state actors as subjects, and therefore incorporate them in the international legal framework, the acceptance or recognition of their subjectivity is withheld by states and by doctrine—not necessarily in that order. Commenting on the reasons why legal scholarship failed to accept non-state actors at the 'top table' of international law, Philip Alston enumerates:

[A]n intrinsic lack of imagination; a natural affinity with the status quo; a deeply rooted professional affinity with internationalism, albeit one premised on the continuity of the system of sovereign equality; a reluctance to bite the hand that feeds; or simply the conviction that respect for that system has taken a great deal of time and human suffering to achieve and that it continues to offer a better prospect than any alternative that has so far been put forward.[117]

Some authors argue that it is the embedded politics within the subjects doctrine which makes it difficult, if not impossible, for the paradigm to accommodate non-state actors.[118] According to Klabbers, the 'subjects doctrine displays highly

---

[113] *Legality of the Use by a State of Nuclear Weapons in Armed Conflict*, at 78, para. 25.

[114] Klabbers, '(I Can't Get No) Recognition: Subjects Doctrine and the Emergence of Non-State Actors', at 50–51.

[115] See K. W. Abbott and D. Snidal, 'Why States Act through Formal International Organizations', 42 *The Journal of Conflict Resolution* 1 (1998), 3–32.

[116] See Klabbers, '(I Can't Get No) Recognition: Subjects Doctrine and the Emergence of Non-State Actors', at 365.

[117] Alston, 'The "Not-a-Cat" Syndrome: Can the International Human Rights Regime Accommodate Non-State Actors?', at 21.

[118] Klabbers, '(I Can't Get No) Recognition: Subjects Doctrine and the Emergence of Non-State Actors', at 369.

political characteristics... [It] forms the clearing house between sources and substance: it is through subjects doctrine that the international allocation of values takes place, and as any political scientist knows, the authoritative allocation of values is one of the main political functions'.[119] To exemplify the point let us focus on one of the main objections raised in relation to a 'privatization' of human rights law that seeks to regulate the conduct of non-state actors—the legitimation argument.[120] There is a lingering fear, implicitly or explicitly apparent both in scholarly articles and the discourses of diplomats and politicians, that elevating a non-state actor to the status of subject would legitimate its goals and actions. This argument is made in particular in relation to non-state armed groups and corporations.[121] In the view of this study, legitimation may indeed take place; however, one needs to understand and emphasize that the resulting legitimation is that of the actor as rights-holder *and* duty-bearer, not of its goals and conduct. The recognition of an actor as a subject of international law by no means triggers an automatic endorsement of its objectives and conduct. Its uncontested status as an international legal subject did not legitimate Nazi Germany's goals and actions. The lack of subjectivity of al-Qaeda did not prevent the organization from enjoying legitimacy in certain circles. In both cases it would be absurd to affirm otherwise and mistaken to point to any direct links between subjectivity and the legitimation of the actions of these entities.

Another disadvantage of the subjects doctrine, perhaps its greatest, is that it fails to indicate which obligations flow directly from the status of the international subject. The 'étrange' label attributed by Weil to the 'relative legal personality' could be read to illustrate the uncertainty concerning which rights and obligations a non-state actor would have, once it was recognized as a subject of international law. Klabbers is also pessimistic when he asserts that 'personality in international law, like "subjectivity", is but a descriptive notion: useful to describe a state of affairs, but normatively empty, as neither rights nor obligations flow automatically' from a grant of personality.[122]

In conclusion, even though subjectivity may remain instructive for understanding the rights and obligations of states and arguably international organizations, the subjects doctrine appears unappealing at present for the legal study of non-state actors, and as such also for our concern with religious non-state actors. Given the previously highlighted challenges to accommodating non-state actors, and the uncertain implications of subjectivity in terms of providing a substantive normative framework for this type of actors, several authors have avoided the subjects doctrine altogether and preferred to approach the topic of rights and obligations of non-state actors from a more pragmatic angle. Whether embracing this inductive method amounts to the emancipation of legal studies from the dominance of

---

[119] See note 118.

[120] See Clapham, *Human Rights Obligations of Non-State Actors*, at 33–55.

[121] See note 120, at 46–55.

[122] J. Klabbers, *An Introduction to International Institutional Law*, 2nd ed., (Cambridge: Cambridge University Press, 2009), at 51.

positivism remains to be seen. It is promising that eminent legal scholars have recognized that the subjects doctrine is a social construct,[123] and that its coordinates might therefore be alterable, or its overall utility might be denounced and another paradigm constructed.

2. The 'capacity approach' and the 'reconceptualization' of international legal personality

The heading of this section might strike observers as conceptually cacophonous, since the 'capacity approach' seemingly tries to do away with subjectivity and international legal personality, while the latter part of the heading attempts to bring legal personality back into the analytical focus. It will be shown, however, that the capacity approach and a 'reconceptualized' international personality complete each other. The suggestion made here is that a 'doctrine of actors' could be possible by acknowledging and drawing on this linkage.

The section starts by examining the meaning of 'capacity', drawing on the two main questions that Andrew Clapham's analysis of human rights obligations of non-state actors addressed.

First, does the entity have the requisite legal capacity directly to acquire rights and obligations under international law? And, second, in what circumstances do these actors have the capacity to be party to a claim (either as a claimant or as a defendant) at international level?[124]

This would seem to bring us back to the definition of subjectivity as a 'double-capacity' line of reasoning: capacity to possess legal rights and duties, and capacity to bring an international claim to maintain the rights in question. Why is it necessary to use the capacity narrative instead of subjectivity, if *de facto* they are taken to mean the same?

In order to understand that this inconsistency is illusory, it is necessary to comprehend the existence of two distinct analytical planes, one operational and one of values. Certain values are attached to capacity as an integral element of the concept of subjectivity. These values portray an *Idealtyp* of subject, the characteristics of which amount to statehood; hence, using capacity via the subjects doctrine is circumscribed by the elements of statehood. If this hurdle can be overcome by relativizing the subject, a different, but related obstacle has to be faced; this obstacle, as shown previously, flows from the legitimacy embedded in the concept of subject. When capacity is understood as an operational concept, an actor no longer needs to conform to the attributes of statehood to obtain rights and obligations under international law. At the same time unwanted issues of legitimation are avoided. In short:

---

[123] Rosalyn Higgins' metaphor 'we have erected an intellectual prison of our own choosing' is a pointed exemplification of the acknowledgement that the subjects doctrine has been socially constructed. R. Higgins, *Problems and Process: International Law and How We Use It*, (Oxford: Oxford University Press, 1995), at 49.

[124] Clapham, *Human Rights Obligations of Non-State Actors*, at 71.

When we leave the arena of treaty-making, diplomatic relations and immunity before the courts we see a panoply of possible legal rights and obligations which can be applied to non-state actors without suggesting that they have state-like qualities or privileges.[125]

When efforts are made to develop a normative framework for non-state actors, authors often compare the situation with the capacity of individuals to acquire rights and obligations under human rights law and international humanitarian law. Human rights treaty and customary law, and international humanitarian norms that address individuals, make the capacity of individuals to bear rights indisputable. In a parenthesis, one cannot help but notice that, even though states are portrayed to be the full subjects of rights, they lack the capacity to enjoy the most celebrated of all rights: human rights. Ironically, human rights law may probably represent the main conceptual challenge to the full subjectivity of states in the international legal system. Moreover, it is now 'clear to the point of triteness' that 'international legal duties of natural persons extend at a very minimum to those derived from the narrow class of human rights norms that comprise international criminal law'.[126] If an individual can have certain obligations at international level, why would an organized group of individuals be unable to bear such obligations?[127] Plain logic suggests that such an organized group could bear certain obligations.

Scholars increasingly identify rights and responsibilities of non-state actors by 'extracting' capacity from an analysis of human rights treaty and customary provisions and the jurisprudence of international courts and monitoring bodies. A starting point for this approach is suggested by Steven Ratner in the context of corporate responsibility. 'The first true example of international human rights law [the Protocol to the 1926 Slavery Convention] was a response to *commercially* orientated violations of rights'.[128] Some authors have pointed out that the Advisory Opinion on the *Accordance with international law of the unilateral declaration of independence in respect of Kosovo* reflects the ICJ's adoption of a pragmatic capacity approach, since the Court had emphasized the obligations of non-state actors without inquiring into their subjectivity.[129] Another recent example comes from the Report of the Independent Commission of Inquiry on Syria set up by the UN Human Rights Council, which 'endeavoured to reflect violations

---

[125] Clapham, *Human Rights Obligations of Non-State Actors*, at 80.

[126] A. J. Wilson, 'Beyond *Unocal*: Conceptual Problems in Using International Norms to Hold Transnational Corporations Liable under the Alien Tort Claims Act', in O. de Schutter (ed.), *Transnational Corporations and Human Rights*, (Portland, Oregon: Hart Publishing, 2006), at 48–49. The Rome Statute of the International Criminal Court may in fact confirm a state of affairs that no longer needs confirmation.

[127] As Andrew Clapham argues: 'As long as we admit that individuals have rights and duties under customary human rights law and international humanitarian law, we have to admit that legal persons may also possess the international legal personality necessary to enjoy some of these rights, and conversely to be prosecuted or held accountable for violations of the relevant international duties'. Clapham, *Human Rights Obligations of Non-State Actors*, at 79.

[128] S. Ratner, 'Corporations and Human Rights: a Theory of Legal Responsibility', 111 *Yale Law Journal* (2001) 443–546, at 465. (Emphasis added).

[129] See d'Aspremont, 'Inclusive Law-Making and Law-Enforcement for an Exclusive International Legal System', at 432.

and abuses on all sides'.[130] In the absence of an armed conflict capable of triggering the application of international humanitarian law over the period covered by the inquiry (March 2011–February 2012), the applicable law was that of human rights. In the words of the report:

> The commission carefully reviewed the information gathered on the operations and activities to date of FSA [Free Syrian Army] groups. In this regard, the commission notes that, at a minimum, human rights obligations constituting peremptory international law (ius cogens) bind States, individuals and non-State collective entities, including armed groups. Acts violating ius cogens—for instance, torture or enforced disappearances—can never be justified.[131]

The Commission asserted that in addition to 'a widespread and systematic pattern of gross violations committed by State forces—in conditions of impunity', it also found 'instances of gross abuses committed by anti-Government armed groups'.[132] The report of the Commission does not refer to the legal status or international personality of the Free Syrian Army or of other opposition armed groups. One has to conclude that the Commission effectively embraced a capacity approach in relation to these armed groups.

One objection that can be raised in relation to the modality of extracting capacity from the case law of courts and monitoring bodies is that, in essence, the capacity of a non-state actor to bring an international claim may merely reflect domestic personality.[133] While not wanting to give away too much in relation to the capacity of religious organizations to bring an international claim (see Chapter 3), at this stage, some comparative illustrations are important to underline the general point that the capacity approach operates on a different plane to domestic personality. Let us start from the following assertion: the European Court of Human Rights (ECtHR) takes up freedom of religion cases invoked by religious legal entities because such cases have been decided at municipal level, and hence capacity is a reflection of the entities' domestic personality. On the one hand, it is clear that the ECtHR is concerned with organizational article 9 cases because they arise at domestic level. This is so not least because the configuration of regional and international human rights adjudication systems demands a prior treatment of cases at the domestic level—the requirement of the exhaustion of domestic remedies is one of the admissibility criteria of all international human rights regimes. On the other hand, there are other admissibility criteria (such as the non-governmental or individual requirement and the victim criterion) which have to be met for a religious organization to be capable to claim a freedom of religion case under an

---

[130] Report of the Independent International Commission of Inquiry on the Syrian Arab Republic, UN Doc. A/HRC/19/69, 22 February 2012, para. 7.

[131] Report of the Independent International Commission of Inquiry on the Syrian Arab Republic, para. 106.

[132] Report of the Independent International Commission of Inquiry on the Syrian Arab Republic, para. 83.

[133] This is an interesting objection which was suggested by one of the reviewers of this manuscript, Review on file with the author.

international instrument. It is submitted that the admissibility criteria, and the way courts and monitoring bodies interpret them, determine the capacity of a non-state legal entity to bring a claim under a specific instrument regardless of the entity's domestic personality. As we shall see in Chapter 3, the Strasbourg mechanisms had *initially* denied the right of a church to bring a freedom of religion claim because it was deemed that as 'a legal, and not a natural person' it was 'incapable of having or exercising the rights mentioned in Article 9, paragraph 1 of the Convention, or Article 2 of the First Protocol'.[134] In other words, despite it having personality under domestic law the entity was not deemed to have the *capacity* to claim the right to freedom of religion under the European Convention. In more recent cases brought against the Russian Federation[135] the matter at stake was precisely a denial or weakening of legal personality at domestic level of religious organizations; nevertheless, the ECtHR found that the entities had the capacity to bring, inter alia, an article 9 claim under the European Convention.

Let us take this exercise a step further and transpose our initial statement from the European regime to the ICCPR regime. It would read as follows: the Human Rights Committee (HRC) takes up organizational freedom of religion cases under article 18 because they have already been decided on a municipal level, thereby reflecting the domestic personality of churches. The HRC's jurisprudence however renders the first part of this transposition invalid. The Committee does not take up church autonomy cases, as the communication procedure under the Optional Protocol to the ICCPR is restricted to 'individuals' who claim to be victims of a violation[136] and it chooses to read the term literally. As such, churches and religious associations are barred from direct access to remedies for violations of their rights under the Covenant.[137] Can we, by turning our initial proposition on its head, infer from the rejection of organizational article 18 cases that the HRC denies the domestic personality of these legal entities—as it certainly does not seem to reflect it in its jurisprudence? We are suggesting that the only thing the Committee is denying is the capacity of religious organizations to bring article 18 cases under the ICCPR. Beyond that little can be said about their capacity under other regimes, or indeed about the domestic personality of these organizations.

Although the capacity approach is flexible and responsive to context—the two elements identified at the start as essential for a theory concerning the acquisition of rights and obligations under international law—it is felt by some authors that proceeding on an operational plane is insufficient. Something else is needed, or felt

---

[134] *Church of X v. the United Kingdom*, Application no. 3798/68, Decision of 7 December 1968, at 6–8.

[135] *Jehovah's Witnesses of Moscow v. Russia*, Application no. 302/02, Judgment of 10 June 2010; *Church of Scientology Moscow v. Russia*, Application no. 18147/02, Judgment of 5 April 2007; *Moscow Branch of the Salvation Army v. Russia*, Application No. 72881/01, Judgment of 5 October 2006.

[136] Optional Protocol to the International Covenant on Civil and Political Rights, 1976 UNTS 14668 (adopted 16 December 1966, entered into force 23 March 1976), arts. 1 and 2.

[137] See M. Nowak, *UN Covenant on Civil and Political Rights. CCPR Commentary*, 2nd ed., (Kehl: N.P. Engel, 2005), at 830–831.

to be needed.[138] It is here that the link with a reconceptualized international legal personality becomes most evident.

By showing how legal thinkers of the past centuries have been using the concept of international legal personality, Janne Elisabeth Nijman demonstrates that the original concept differs from the traditional understanding according to which states are the only international personae on the international legal scene.[139] Nijman reveals that the traditional state-centred concept of international legal personality is not the original one, but rather a construct imposed by a later positivist tradition. This traditional concept has itself been altered (as shown earlier), and today's understanding is that states are the only *full* legal persons, rather than the only legal persons.

At this stage, it is essential to cite the definition of international legal personality as it was imagined by Gottfried Wilhelm Leibniz (1646–1716), the first scholar to use the term.

He possesses a personality in international law who represents the public liberty, such that he is not subject to the tutelage or the power of anyone else, but has in himself the power of war and of alliances; although he may perhaps be limited by the bonds of obligations towards a superior and owe him homage, fidelity and obedience. If his authority, then, is sufficiently extensive, it is agreed to call him a potentate, and he will be called a sovereign or a sovereign power.... Those are counted among sovereign powers, then, and are held to possess sovereignty, who can count on sufficient freedom and power to exercise some influence in international affairs, with armies or by treaties...[140]

What this definition discloses may come as a surprise to some. The concept of international legal personality did not emerge in the context of what is perceived today to be the traditional Westphalian concept of *absolute sovereignty*, but in relation to Leibniz's concept of *relative sovereignty*.[141] In fact, the term international legal personality was coined precisely to accommodate changes set in motion in 1648 that were still continuing when Leibniz was writing.[142] As Nijman concludes,

---

[138] For example, Andrea Bianchi points to the need for a theoretical discourse about non-state actors in international law, which should underpin the current sectoral narratives taking place in different contexts on a small-scale. Bianchi, 'Introduction: Relativizing the Subjects or Subjectivizing the Actors: Is That the Question?', at xiii; Bianchi, 'The Fight for Inclusion: Non-state Actors and International Law', at 39–40. Jan Klabbers, similarly, expressed his dissatisfaction with the current state of affairs and points to the risk that creating 'rights and obligations, left, right and centre' without a 'clear grounding' opens the door to a constant challenge from non-state actors concerning the authority of international law over them. Klabbers, '(I Can't Get No) Recognition: Subjects Doctrine and the Emergence of Non-State Actors', at 368.

[139] J. E. Nijman, *The Concept of International Legal Personality: An Inquiry into the History and Theory of International Law*, (The Hague: TMC Asser Press, 2004), at 25.

[140] P. Riley (ed.), *Leibniz: Political Writings*, 2nd ed., (Cambridge: Cambridge University Press, 1988), at 175. See also J. E. Nijman, *The Concept of International Legal Personality*, at 58–59.

[141] J. E. Nijman, 'Leibniz's Theory of Relative Sovereignty and International Legal Personality: Justice and Stability or the Last Great Defence of the Holy Roman Empire', *IILJ Working Paper No. 2004/2* (2004), at 3.

[142] Janne Elisabeth Nijman challenges the assertion that the paradigm of absolute sovereignty came into being *instantly* after the Peace of Westphalia. She argues that the 1648 Treaties should be regarded as signals of transition, which by definition is neither an instant process nor one characterized by shared understandings. Such periods are marked by sharp oscillation between old and alternative ways of thinking. Nijman, *The Concept of International Legal Personality: An Inquiry into the History and Theory of International Law*, at 11–12.

the concept was 'aimed at facilitating the international system's flexibility'.[143] In a period when German princes with extensive *de facto* powers were waging a struggle to be recognized as sovereigns on the same stage as the German Emperor, when France was powerful and expansionist, and the Holy Roman Empire as the approximation of the *Respublica Christiana* was crumbling, Leibniz sought to put forward a concept of international legal personality infused by political realism *and* firmly grounded in natural law and justice. The coupling of capacity with responsibility was paramount. *Ab initio*, the construction of the concept had at its core the need to ensure that German princes were accountable. The *legitimate participation* of these new actors was made *dependent* upon them conducting their international affairs within the limits of *positive law* and in conformity with the moral requirement to act justly, in accordance with *natural law*.[144]

While keeping due proportion and respecting the historical context, it is striking to what extent today's globalized and localized, universalized and fragmented, secular and religious world resembles the context Leibniz was describing. At the same time, it is likely that a contextual analysis of the writings of most authors would disclose a similar preoccupation with upheaval; in short, crises are ubiquitous in the eyes of those writing about contemporary events.[145] At first sight, this assertion might seem potentially self-defeating, at least from the point of view of those that believe that non-state actors need to be accommodated within the international legal framework because we live in exceptional times. Nonetheless, it is submitted that the perception of necessity—and not whether a 'real' necessity exists which could potentially be demonstrated based on a comparison of the current context with past ones—should be determinant for accepting non-state actors at the 'top table'.[146]

Against the existing background of a commonly perceived imperative to (somehow) deal with non-state actors, it is extremely helpful to draw on Leibniz's concept of legal international personality. On Nijman's interpretation, Leibniz attempted to promote 'a law of nations that is binding upon those entities which are able to employ international power and are therefore obliged to take into account the common interest of a universal human society and pursue universal justice'.[147]

---

[143] Nijman, 'Leibniz's Theory of Relative Sovereignty and International Legal Personality: Justice and Stability or the Last Great Defence of the Holy Roman Empire', at 3.

[144] See Nijman, *The Concept of International Legal Personality: An Inquiry into the History and Theory of International Law*, at 65–80.

[145] Here it would appear that we depart from the methodological lens proposed above by Nijman at 17–18. As Anthony Carty observes, since 'the context of the author's work and goals is outside him or herself', for Nijman, 'it follows that the interpreter must pursue the author into that context in order to understand the author'. A. Carty, 'Review Essay: International Legal Personality and the End of the Subject: Natural Law and Phenomenological Responses to New Approaches to International Law', 6 *Melbourne Journal of International Law* 2 (2005), 534–552, at 536. We submit that there is a dialogue between the context and the writer. The context influences the writer and the writer responds to the context, and both construct 'reality'.

[146] The use of the word 'perception' is not intended to imply lack of actual necessity. Rather, it underlines the importance of shared understandings when individuals interpret a context or situation.

[147] Nijman, *The Concept of International Legal Personality: An Inquiry into the History and Theory of International Law*, at 449.

It is clear from these lines that the value of Leibniz's concept of international legal personality does not lay in its ability to give practical insights into *how* non-state actors should be included in the international legal system—the capacity approach already meets that need. However, a 'reconceptualized'[148] international legal personality that traces Leibniz's early intentions provides a philosophical foundation for contemporary pragmatic approaches to non-state actors and could therefore lend significance to these approaches as part of a wider project on actors in international law. In conclusion, to use Nijman's own words as the author who unearthed the original meaning of international legal personality, the recuperation of this concept could serve to build 'just international institutions and just international law'.[149] It is interesting to observe, as have others, that initiatives to build international law on moral fundaments are gaining momentum.[150]

V. Conclusion

This may be an optimistic ending: there is no place for naivety, however. If some states and elements of doctrine find the capacity approach dangerous because it implies the legitimation of non-state actors, and allegedly their goals and actions, the concept of an international legal personality grounded in a theory of justice may seem an even greater threat. Nonetheless, a refusal of scholars to provide deeper foundations for today's international law by recuperating Leibniz's international legal personality and linking it to the capacity approach, may confirm the view that legal theory (to recall the opening epigraph of this chapter) has grown conservative with age.

Similarly, an insistence on pursuing the two dominant narratives on law and religion, as long as they fail to examine which are the rights and obligations of religious actors under international law, but rather focus on whether religion should or not be accepted as playing a certain role in the development of law, may confirm that legal theory has grown ignorant with age. Let us therefore put the analytical category of religious actors, as defined here, to good use by revealing the accountability framework of these actors—be they non-state entities, states, or international organizations—and therefore the boundaries of their engagement with the law.

---

[148] Nijman's own expression. See J. E. Nijman, 'Paul Ricoeur and International Law: Beyond 'The End of the Subject'. Towards a Reconceptualization of International Legal Personality', 20 *Leiden J Intl L* 1 (2007), 25–64.

[149] Nijman, 'Paul Ricoeur and International Law: Beyond 'The End of the Subject'. Towards a Reconceptualization of International Legal Personality', at 25.

[150] For some examples, see M. Koskenniemi, 'The Fate of Public International Law: Between Technique and Politics', 70 *Modern Law Review* 1 (2007), 1–30; and S. Singh, 'The Potential of International Law: Fragmentation and Ethics', 24 *Leiden J Intl L* 1 (2011), 23–43.

PART II

OPERATIONALIZING THE ANALYTICAL CATEGORY OF RELIGIOUS ACTORS

3

Religious Organizations Under the European Convention Regime

'To enjoy freedom we have to control ourselves.'

—Virginia Woolf[1]

I. Introduction

In the quest to examine the rights and obligations of religious actors under international law, the operationalization of the analytical category must start with what are intuitively considered to be such actors—religious organizations.

Religious organizations are non-state actors: inevitably, any attempt to examine their rights and obligations is confronted by challenges relating to their subjectivity. However, as discussed in Chapter 2, scholars have developed alternatives to the subjects doctrine,[2] such as the capacity approach which offers a pragmatic and valuable method of 'extracting' rights and obligations of non-state actors from treaty and customary law and jurisprudence. When applying Andrew Clapham's capacity test to religious non-state actors, the first question that needs to be answered in this chapter has two parts: Do religious organizations have the legal capacity to directly acquire rights and obligations under international law? Do they have the capacity to be party to an international claim, in a similar fashion to their non-religious peers?

In Chapter 2 it was asserted that efforts to recuperate the original meaning of Leibniz's international legal personality may provide a theoretical underpinning to the capacity approach, one that portrays 'a law of nations that is binding upon those entities which are able to employ international power and are therefore obliged to take into account the common interest of a universal human society and pursue universal justice'.[3] While this chapter opts for the pragmatic capacity

---

[1] The citation is taken from *Women's History*, accessed March 2012, http://womenshistory.about.com/od/quotes/a/Virginia-Woolf.htm.

[2] See Chapter 2, IV.

[3] Nijman, *The Concept of International Legal Personality: An Inquiry into the History and Theory of International Law*, at 449.

approach—and is hence unconcerned with whether religious organizations are subjects of international law, or enjoy international legal personality—its focus on church autonomy certainly takes inspiration from Leibniz's philosophy. As will be demonstrated, church autonomy or religious autonomy is a right exclusive to religious organizations, which derives, however, from the right of individuals to collectively manifest religion. Religious autonomy refers to the right of a religious organization to self-administer or self-govern itself in the legislative, administrative, and ministerial realms, and in matters of adjudication.[4] In this context, it would appear that religious organizations as interpreters of religion are granted legal guarantees that might shield their religious interpretations from judicial review. As one scholar summarizes: 'Although in large part the right of religious autonomy comprises claims that the state should not interfere in the affairs of religious organizations in such matters, *it can also potentially conflict with the rights of individuals within those organizations.*'[5] This is where the second question emerges: Does such a powerful right insulate religious organizations from obligations that their non-religious peers may have, or is the right to church autonomy matched by human rights responsibilities?

In seeking to respond to these two central questions, this chapter adopts a jurisprudential approach by examining the case law of the European Commission on Human Rights (EComHR) and the European Court of Human Rights (ECtHR). For comparative purposes, domestic and international cases decided by other jurisdictions will be used; nonetheless, the focus is on the practice of the Strasbourg mechanisms, which provides the most detailed picture of the capacities of religious organizations to hold and claim human rights. The EComHR and ECtHR also developed the positive obligations of states in the context of church autonomy, through which, it is submitted, the scope of the obligations of religious organization can be discerned. An effort to demystify the portrayal of the European continent as profoundly, or even exclusively, secular by exposing the rather complex relations between state and church represents another reason why the focus here is on the European system.

The chapter starts with an analysis of the capacity of religious organizations to bring a human rights claim under the European Convention on Human Rights (ECHR), by examining the non-governmental criterion and the victim requirement. Because article 9 is the basis of protection of church autonomy, the chapter carefully examines which non-state actors have been found to have capacity to bring a claim under its provisions. The aim is to understand why and how non-profit organizations with religious or philosophical objects have become the exclusive holders of the right to freedom of religion (II). Subsequently, the analysis concentrates on church autonomy as a crucial right of religious organizations,

---

[4] N. Doe, *Law and Religion in Europe: A Comparative Introduction*, (Oxford: Oxford University Press, 2011), at 114–138; I. Leigh, 'Balancing Religious Autonomy and Other Human Rights under the European Convention', 1 *Oxford Journal of Law and Religion* 1 (2012) 109–125, at 112–113.

[5] Leigh, 'Balancing Religious Autonomy and Other Human Rights under the European Convention', at 110. (Emphasis added).

which receives protection under article 9 read in the light of article 11 of the ECHR. The case law of the EComHR will be contrasted with that of the ECtHR, to illustrate the different approaches taken to limiting religious autonomy. The analytical focus will be on examining positive obligations in the context of church autonomy, and therefore the scope of the responsibilities of religious organizations themselves (III). The concluding remarks (IV) summarize the findings and offer an answer to the key concern of the research: do religious organizations, by way of their special legitimacy, enjoy a special legality regime which is different from that of their non-religious peers?

II. Religious Organizations as Claimants of Rights Under the European Convention

Churches and religious associations have brought many more cases before the European human rights system compared to the African and Inter-American systems and international treaty bodies. It was by no means clear however in the early days of the European system that religious organizations had the capacity to bring a freedom of religion claim under article 9 of the ECHR, which may well be the right most vital to the interests of religious organizations. Indeed, as we shall see, it is the right in which church autonomy is grounded.

The former article 25 of the ECHR stipulated that the EComHR may receive petitions from:

any person, non-governmental organization or group of individuals claiming to be the victim of a violation by one of the High Contracting Parties of the rights set forth in this Convention, provided that the High Contracting Party against which the complaint has been lodged has declared that it recognizes the competence of the Commission to receive such petitions.[6]

Protocol 11 to the ECHR altered the human rights machinery by abolishing the EComHR and allowing direct access to the ECtHR; however, the standing formula has been retained in the current article 34, which superseded article 25.

The Court may receive applications from any person, non-governmental organisation or group of individuals claiming to be the victim of a violation by one of the High Contracting Parties of the rights set forth in the Convention or the protocols thereto.[7]

It is clear from these provisions of the Convention that two issues are at stake. First, for an application by a church or other religious association to be admissible under the ECHR, the actor must be a non-governmental organization. Second, the capacity of religious organizations to bring a claim under this instrument presupposes that the applicant is a victim of a violation of a right stipulated by the ECHR.

---

[6] ECHR, art. 25, before amendment through Protocol 11, E.T.S. 155, entered into force 1 November 1998.
[7] ECHR (text as amended by Protocols No. 11 and No. 14), art. 34.

1. The non-governmental requirement and established churches

Prima facie, churches, religious associations, or humanist organizations would not encounter a hurdle in fulfilling the non-governmental requirement for the purposes of article 34 of the ECHR (or former article 25); yet, the wide spectrum of religion-state relations in Europe presents a potential challenge, that of established churches. The rationale behind established religion, as Jeroen Temperman observes, is one of 'mutual interest: to foster a religio-ethical legitimization of state authority in return for financial, ethical, pragmatic and other forms of support for the religion in question'.[8] The development of established churches is to be understood as interlinked with the history of royal houses,[9] and is context specific to a particular state. A contextual analysis is therefore necessary to understand the entanglement between church and state authorities and, against this background, the functions and powers which an established church fulfils.

For example, the tension within the Church of England over theological and liturgical issues are said to have contributed to the outbreak of the English Civil War, when the established Church was associated with Royalists.[10] After the restoration of the monarchy, the Toleration Act of 1689 formed the basis of the 'constitutional position of the Church of England... with a range of particular legal privileges and responsibilities'.[11] The entanglement of state and church is evident if one considers that the British monarch carries the title of the Supreme Governor of the Church of England and has the prerogative to appoint the Church's bishops; that the so-called Lords Spiritual serve in the House of Lords; and that the state is, to a certain extent, involved in the law-making process of the Church.[12]

Another example comes from Greece, where the Constitution stipulates that 'the prevailing religion in Greece is that of the Eastern Greek Orthodox Church of Christ'.[13] In *Holy Monasteries v. Greece*, the ECtHR was faced with defining what the non-governmental requirement means in a case brought by eight Greek Orthodox monasteries claiming violations of their rights under articles 6, 9, 11, 13, and 14 of the ECHR, and of article 1 of Protocol 1.[14] The Greek government

---

[8] Temperman, *State-Religion Relationships and Human Rights Law: Towards a Right to Religiously Neutral Governance*, at 31.

[9] See note 8, at 44.

[10] See The Church of England, Detailed History, accessed May 2012, http://www.churchofengland.org/about-us/history/detailed-history.aspx.

[11] See note 10.

[12] Doe, *Law and Religion in Europe: A Comparative Introduction*, at 33 and 126; Temperman, *State-Religion Relationships and Human Rights Law: Towards a Right to Religiously Neutral Governance*, at 61.

[13] Constitution of Greece (2001), art. 3. Winfried Brugger describes the state-religion system in Greece as a state church. W. Brugger, 'On the Relationship between Structural Norms and Constitutional Rights in Church-State-Relations', in W. Brugger and M. Karayanni (eds.), *Religion in the Public Sphere: A Comparative Analysis of German, Israeli, American and International Law*, (Berlin: Springer Verlag, 2007), 21–86, at 43.

[14] *Holy Monasteries v. Greece*, Application Nos. 13092/87 and 13984/88, Judgment of 9 December 1994, para. 1.

challenged the jurisdiction *ratione personae* of the Court on several counts, asserting that the Orthodox monasteries were not non-governmental organizations within the meaning of (former) article 25.[15] First, Greece pointed to the entanglement between the Greek Orthodox Church and the state as reflected in the Hellenic Constitution and other legislation, and to the significant influence of the Church on state activities. Second, it was emphasized that:

the Greek Orthodox Church and its institutions played a direct, active part in public administration; they took enforceable administrative decisions whose lawfulness was subject to review by the Supreme Administrative Court like any other public authority's decisions. The monasteries were hierarchically integrated into the organic structure of the Greek Church...[16]

The government also underlined that the Church and its constituent parts, including the monasteries, were public law entities, albeit separate ones.

The ECtHR dismissed the government's jurisdictional objection. It read the term non-governmental in a narrow manner, that is the non-participation in the exercise of governmental powers. In the view of the judges, the fact that the monasteries were public entities reflected merely the 'special links between the monasteries and the State' and not the attribution of governmental powers.[17] The Court went on to focus on the objectives of the monasteries, which were 'essentially ecclesiastical and spiritual ones, but also cultural and social ones in some cases' and 'are not such as to enable them to be classed with governmental organisations established for public administration purposes'.[18] Finally, in relation to exercised powers, the Court chose to focus on the monasteries as entities distinguishable from the Greek Orthodox Church; they therefore disregarded the powers of the Church entity, of which the monasteries are certainly an integral part. It is unclear whether the Court might have reached a different conclusion if it had considered the monasteries to be constituent parts or institutions of the Greek Orthodox Church, since the latter arguably plays a direct role in public administration. In the view of this author, it was correct to consider the objectives and powers of the monasteries as separate from those of the Greek Orthodox Church in a generic sense, because the two entities have separate legal personalities. In essence, the Court undertook a contextual analysis, which, given the context-specificity of establishments in Europe, seems to this author to be the only appropriate one.

In *Hautaniemi v. Sweden*, the EComHR relied on the *Holy Monasteries* case and concluded, without entering into any factual analysis, that the established Church of Sweden 'cannot be considered to have been exercising governmental powers' and was therefore a non-governmental organization for the purpose of the ECHR.[19] This could be considered a generally laconic decision and the lack of contextualization, in particular, is problematic when the matter at stake arguably

---

[15] *Holy Monasteries v. Greece*, para. 48.   [16] *Holy Monasteries v. Greece*, para. 48.
[17] *Holy Monasteries v. Greece*, para. 49.   [18] *Holy Monasteries v. Greece*, para. 49.
[19] *Finska församlingen i Stockholm and Teuvo Hautaniemi v. Sweden*, Application No. 24019/94, Decision of 11 April 1996, EComHR, Decisions and Reports, vol. 62, at 97.

demanded a thorough contextual examination. As a consequence of *Hautaniemi v. Sweden*, it would seem that established churches are automatically considered to fulfil the non-governmental requirement without a contextual analysis; in this sense, the direct state responsibility framework under the ECHR was weakened. The presumption being that a state would incur responsibility only if it fails to prevent or punish human rights abuses by established churches, under the positive obligations doctrine. To Charlotte Smith, the current non-differentiating and non-contextual approach to established churches under the ECHR appears unsatisfactory since it:

creates problems with regard to national, constitutional and legal treatment of Established Churches. It does so by wilfully closing its eyes to existing relationships between state signatories and churches. It tends to ignore institutional relationships between church and state and to assume that the rights which it guarantees are exercised on a level playing field. It provides little guidance on how to proceed when this is not the case.[20]

It is interesting to return to the example of the Church of England and to scrutinize the impact that this Strasbourg jurisprudence is said to have had on a House of Lords judgment.[21] The case—*Parochial Church Council of the Parish of Aston Cantlow and Wilmcote with Billesley, Warwickshire (Appellants) v. Wallbank and another (Respondents)*—concerned the distinction between a religious entity's 'publicness' and its 'governmental powers'. Mr and Ms Wallbank were freehold owners of land that was part of the rectory of the parish. The Parochial Church Council of the Church of England sought to enforce the duty, which the owners incurred under a 1932 law, to pay for chancel repairs. The owners complained before the Court of Appeal that the Parochial Church Council was a public authority for the purposes of section 6 of the Human Rights Act 1998 and that by serving notice the council had acted in violation of their rights under article 1 of Protocol 1 alone and in conjunction with article 14.[22]

It should be noted at this point that the Human Rights Act 1998, which entered into force in 2000, gives 'further effect' in domestic law to the rights enshrined in the ECHR. The rights scheduled under the Human Rights Act 1998 can be directly enforced against public authorities, defined as 'any person certain of whose functions are functions of a public nature'.[23] Under section 6.1, public authorities are under an obligation to act in a way which is compatible with the ECHR.[24] In relation to religious organizations, section 13.1 of the Act provides that:

---

[20] C. Smith, 'A Very English Affair: Establishment and Human Rights in an Organic Constitution', in P. Cane, C. Evans and Z. Robinson (eds.), *Law and Religion in Theoretical and Historical Context* (Cambridge: Cambridge University Press, 2008), 157–185, at 183.

[21] *Parochial Church Council of the Parish of Aston Cantlow and Wilmcote with Billesley, Warwickshire (Appellants) v Wallbank and another (Respondents)* [2003] UKHL 37.

[22] *Parochial Church Council of the Parish of Aston Cantlow and Wilmcote with Billesley, Warwickshire v. Wallbank* [2001] EWCA Civ 713, para. 6.

[23] Human Rights Act 1998, s. 6.3.(b).

[24] Wadham, et al., *Blackstone's Guide to the Human Rights Act 1998*, 4th ed., (Oxford: Oxford University Press, 2007), paras. 4.44 and 4.45.

If a court's determination of any question arising under this Act might affect the exercise by a religious organisation (itself or its members collectively) of the Convention right to freedom of thought, conscience and religion, it must have particular regard to the importance of that right.[25]

Section 13 sought to reassure religious organizations that in general they would not be regarded as public authorities and 'thus [not be] susceptible of claims under the Act with the exception of where they stood in the place of State providing a public service'.[26]

The Court of Appeal in *Aston Cantlow*—like many other higher courts before and subsequently[27]—made no mention of section 13. Instead, in finding that the Parochial Church Council was 'inescapably' a public authority—at least when enforcing the chancel repair obligation—the appeals court relied on the fact that the council was not a voluntary association but a statutory corporation, that its functions included both spiritual and civil matters and were established by a measure which had the force of primary legislation, and that its actions were binding on individuals that were not members of the Church.[28]

The House of Lords reversed the decision of the Court of Appeal in *Aston Cantlow*. Lord Hope's opinion portrays the influence that the ECHR and the Strasbourg jurisprudence had in the internal logic of the judgment.[29] Lord Hope agreed that the Parochial Church Council had statutory powers, which it could exercise against persons who appear to be liable notwithstanding whether they were residents of the parish or members of the Church of England, and concluded that '[i]n that context, perhaps, it may be said in a very loose sense to be a public rather than a private body'.[30] He went on to assert:

[N]one of these characteristics indicate that it is a governmental organisation, as that phrase is understood in the context of article 34 of the Convention. It plainly has nothing whatever to do with the process of either central or local government. It is not accountable to the general public for what it does.[31]

---

[25] Human Rights Act 1998, s.13.1.

[26] Mark Hill et al. recount that section 13 resulted from the lobbying of a number of religious organizations, including Evangelical Christians, the Roman Catholic Church, the Chief Rabbi, the Church of Scotland, and the Plymouth Brethren. Scholars are doubtful about the possibility of giving a greater weight to the right to freedom of religion when balanced against the rights of others: 'since the whole scheme of the Convention is to give particular regard to a prima facie right, permitting derogations from it only if they are necessary, proportionate, and so on, the effect of this section is really to add political comfort to religious interest rather than to add anything in terms of practical effect': M. Hill, R. Sandberg and N. Doe, *Religion and Law in the United Kingdom*, (Alphen an den Rijn: Kluwer Law International, 2011), at 61; Wadham, et al., *Blackstone's Guide to the Human Rights Act 1998*, 4th ed., para. 4.37.

[27] See Hill, Sandberg and Doe, *Religion and Law in the United Kingdom*, at 67.

[28] See D. Feldman, 'Standards of Review and Human Rights in English Law', *Oxford Principles of English Law: English Public Law*, 2nd ed., (Oxford: Oxford University Press, 2009), 317–378, at 360; [2001] EWCA Civ 713, paras. 32-35; Smith, 'A Very English Affair: Establishment and Human Rights in an Organic Constitution', at 178.

[29] See Smith, 'A Very English Affair: Establishment and Human Rights in an Organic Constitution', at 179.

[30] *Parochial Church Council of the Parish of Aston Cantlow and Wilmcote with Billesley, Warwickshire (Appellants) v Wallbank and another (Respondents)* [2003] UKHL 37, para. 58.

[31] [2003] UKHL 37, para. 59. (Emphasis added.)

It can certainly be argued that the Law Lords were encouraged to adopt this approach by the 'extraordinary conclusion' that would have resulted from an opposite finding.[32] Had they found that the Parochial Church Council was a public authority, it would have meant that the council could not have been considered a victim of a human rights violation under the Human Rights Act 1998. The concern was that the Council would have lost the benefit of the right to freedom of religion and the autonomy that this freedom guarantees to churches.[33] The Law Lords' decision means that the Church of England and its institutions may not be regarded as 'core public authorities' for the purpose of the Human Rights Act 1998; however, when institutions or components of the Church are 'hybrid public authorities', and exercise public functions (such as, arguably, the conduct of marriage services), human rights might be enforced against them under the Act.[34]

The distinction developed by the House of Lords between 'core public authorities' and 'hybrid public authorities' could prove useful in the context of the ECHR, to counter the lack of contextuality that currently prevails in relation to established churches. The hybrid category would only bar established churches from bringing a claim under the Convention when they exercise public functions of a governmental nature. This is a compromise solution which, on one hand, reflects reality (established churches or their components do in certain circumstances exercise public functions of a governmental manner) and, on the other, responds to the vital need of these organizations to enjoy rights under the ECHR. This would allow for the conduct of established churches, where they are exercising public functions of a governmental nature, to be attributed to the state for purposes of direct responsibility under the ECHR.[35]

For the purposes of a comparison on admissibility criteria the conservative approach of the First Optional Protocol to the ICCPR should be mentioned. The

---

[32] [2003] UKHL 37, para. 15.

[33] Lord Nicholls of Birkenhead comments: 'The contrary conclusion, that the church authorities in general and parochial church councils in particular are "core" public authorities, would mean these bodies are not capable of being victims within the meaning of the Human Rights Act. Accordingly they are not able to complain of infringements of Convention rights. That would be an extraordinary conclusion. The Human Rights Act goes out of its way, in section 13, to single out for express mention the exercise by religious organisations of the Convention right of freedom of thought, conscience and religion. One would expect that these and other Convention rights would be enjoyed by the Church of England as much as other religious bodies.' [2003] UKHL 37, para. 15.

[34] Hill, Sandberg and Doe, *Religion and Law in the United Kingdom*, at 65; and [2003] UKHL 37, para. 11.

[35] For example in *Young and James v. the United Kingdom*, the EComHR dismissed the UK Government's contention that the British Railways Board, which was responsible for the dismissal of the two applicants, was an autonomous institution and therefore the responsibility of the state could not be engaged. It noted that 'under the provision of the Transport Act 1962 the British Railways Board was constituted as a public authority and had the task of running the railways although certain powers were conferred on the Minister of the Government. Whatever the division of rights and duties between the Board and the respective Minister may be, in the Commission's opinion, there can be no doubt that the Government of the United Kingdom is responsible for their public authorities and thus for the acts of the British Railways Board.' *Young and James v. the United Kingdom*, Application no. 7601/76, Decision of 11 July 1977, at 144.

communication procedure under this mechanism is restricted to 'individuals' who claim to be victims of a violation.[36] The Human Rights Committee (HRC) has embraced a literal reading of 'individuals' and, as a result, legal persons—including churches and religious associations—are barred from direct access to remedies for violations of their rights under the Covenant.[37] In certain cases, such as those concerning the prohibition or censorship of religious orgaizations, individual victims can be identified to file a petition, therefore granting churches and religious associations 'indirect' standing.[38] For instance, in *Malakhovsky et al v. Belarus,* two members of the Minsk Vaishnava community of Krishna Consciousness authored a communication, due to the fact that the restrictive admissibility criteria under the First Protocol prevented the community itself from doing so. In their communication before the HRC, they argued that the refusal of the authorities to register their religious association amounted to a violation of their freedom to manifest religion and their freedom of association under the ICCPR. Interestingly, the Committee considered that 'the *author* has sufficiently substantiated *his* claims under articles 18, paragraphs 1 and 3, and article 22, paragraphs 1 and 2, for purposes of admissibility' and proceeded to find a violation of the right to manifest religion on merit.[39] The use of the singular is almost certainly a spelling mistake, but the symbolism cannot be overlooked: the rights at stake are foremost those of the Krishna community of Belarus.

At the other end of the admissibility spectrum are the African and Inter-American procedures, where indigenous people and 'tribal communities' have found standing to take account of their communal ways of manifesting religious freedom, linked to ownership and use of property.[40]

2. The victim requirement and the rights invoked by religious organizations

The victim requirement is another admissibility criterion that religious organizations have to meet in order to be able to claim rights under the ECHR. We are fundamentally inclined to think that only human beings can be considered victims of human rights violations. In relation to corporations Marius Emberland identifies 'voices of dissent' speaking against their recognition as victims of violations of human rights under the ECHR: it is argued that because human rights are for human beings, companies would gain a disproportional advantage in litigation,

---

[36] Optional Protocol to the ICCPR (1966), arts. 1 and 2. The CAT follows the *locus standi* model of the ICCPR. CAT, art. 22.

[37] See Nowak, *UN Covenant on Civil and Political Rights. CCPR Commentary,* 2nd ed., at 830–831.

[38] See note 37, at 831.

[39] *Malakhovsky et al v. Belarus,* Communication No. 1207/2003, UN Doc. CCPR/C/84/D/1207/2003 (2005).

[40] Case of *Plan de Sánchez Massacre v. Guatemala,* Judgment of 29 April 2004; Case of the *Moiwana Community v. Suriname,* Judgment of 15 June 2005; *Centre for Minority Rights Development (Kenya) and Minority Rights Group International on behalf of Endorois Welfare Council v. Kenya,* Communication No. 276/2003, 27th Activity Report of the AComHPR 2009.

given their financial capacities and their profit-oriented inclination; in addition, companies are themselves often human rights abusers.[41] The latter objection is particularly interesting because it is precisely what Michael Addo reads in reverse:

Another compelling reason for seeking to allow corporations to claim benefits under human rights standards is what may be termed the double-edge value of human rights. In getting corporations to appreciate the value of human rights, especially in seeking to give credibility to corporate duties in the field of human rights, it is also important to recognize the corresponding claims and entitlements of these corporations. Such an approach will give the corporations a stake in the human rights regime upon which one can build a relationship of co-operation in the effective protection of human rights. For, after all, it would be insincere for corporations to claim rights under the human rights regime yet deny their duties and responsibilities in that field.[42]

While this argument may be correct from a strategic point of view, it remains clear that legal entities, including churches and other associations that pursue religious or philosophical objects, cannot be deprived of their 'human' life in the sense of article 2 and cannot be subjected to torture, degrading, or inhuman treatment in the sense a human being may be.[43] In this context, Robin C.A. White and Clare Ovey observe that 'a corporate body has some but not all of the rights of individuals'.[44] It is recognized that due process rights, the right to property, freedom of expression, and aspects of the right to privacy may be held and exercised by legal entities.[45]

In relation to legal entities the EComHR has interpreted the victim requirement as follows:

[A]n applicant cannot claim to be the victim of a breach of one of the rights or freedoms protected by the Convention unless there is a sufficiently direct connection between the applicant as such and the injury he maintains he suffered as a result of the alleged breach.[46]

---

[41] It should be clarified that Emberland argues that companies are, and should be, able to claim rights under the ECHR. M. Emberland, *The Human Rights of Companies: Exploring the Structure of ECHR Protection*, (Oxford: Oxford University Press, 2006), at 26–32.

[42] M. K. Addo, 'The Corporation as a Victim of Human Rights Violations', in M. K. Addo (ed.), *Human Rights Standards and the Responsibility of Transnational Corporations*, (The Hague: Kluwer Law, 1999), 187–196, at 192–193.

[43] A decision of the Romanian National Council on Combating Discrimination is interesting in this context. The Council found that the Ministry of Education had violated the right to dignity 'of the Bahá'í community' in Romania, because it authorized a schoolbook for religion which presented the community in pejorative terms as a 'proselytizing sect'. The formulation of the complaint and the case suggests, however, that the Council referred in fact to the dignity of members of the community, not *a* dignity of the association itself. Consiliul Naţional pentru Combaterea Discriminării, *Hotărârea nr. 279/02.10.2007*. See also Emberland, *The Human Rights of Companies: Exploring the Structure of ECHR Protection*, at 27–28.

[44] R. C. A. White and C. Ovey, *The European Convention on Human Rights*, 5th ed., (Oxford: Oxford University Press, 2010), at 31.

[45] See for example *OAO Neftyanaya Kompaniya Yukos v. Russia*, Application no. 14902/04, Judgment of 20 September 2011, which refers to a company's complaint of violations of articles 6, 7, 13, and article 1 of Protocol 1 in conjuction with article 14; *Özgür Gündem v. Turkey*, Application no. 23144/93, Judgment of 16 March 2000 concerns a complaint by a newpaper of an article 10 violation. See also White and Ovey, *The European Convention on Human Rights*, 5th ed., at 31. It should also be noted that article 1 of Protocol 1 specifically mentions that legal entities hold the right to peaceful enjoyment of possessions. ECHR, Protocol 1, art. 1.

[46] *Asociacion de Aviadores de la Republic, Mata et al v. Spain*, Application no. 10733/84, Decision of 11 March 1985, at 222.

An *actio popularis*, or an abstract complaint, is excluded for purposes of article 34. A less strict interpretation has been given to the notion of victim in some applications, to cover claims of a 'partly abstract' character, in an attempt to give effective protection to the rights of individual applicants.[47] There is no express provision in article 34 (or in former article 25) allowing an individual, a group of individuals, or a non-governmental organization to bring a claim 'on behalf' of a victim;[48] nonetheless, it would seem that an organization may bring a complaint on behalf of its members,[49] though the procedure is onerous. For example, in *Confédération des Syndicats Médicaux Français, Fédérations Nationale des Infirmiers v. France*,[50] two medical trade unions represented medical personnel who were alleged to be victims of an article 8 violation under the Convention, because of an accounting formality that required them to disclose the identities of patients. The Commission held that the unions must identify all the medical personnel in question, to demonstrate that they had been granted 'specific instructions from each of them'.[51]

The extensive review of jurisprudence undertaken for this chapter did not reveal even one case in which the Strasbourg mechanisms admitted an application by a church only after they had requested and received a list of the members whom the church claimed to represent or proof of its authority to act on their behalf. The applications of religious organizations were either dismissed as manifestly ill founded, because they were deemed not to fulfil the victim requirement, or accepted *sui juris*. It is safe to conclude that, as a result of the victim requirement in the European system, a religious organization's capacity to bring a claim is made dependent on the capacity to bear rights under the ECHR. The procedure under the ECHR therefore conflates the two capacities of the capacity test employed in this study. This observation would not hold true in the Inter-American or African systems, which have more permissive admissibility criteria, under which a petitioner may or may not be a victim of the violation of the rights set forth by the

---

[47] See van Dijk and van Hoof, *Theory and Practice of the European Convention on Human Rights*, 3rd ed., at 46–60; White and Ovey, *The European Convention on Human Rights*, 5th ed., at 31–33.

[48] Several of the international treaty body mechanisms may receive communications 'from and on behalf of individuals and groups of individuals' alleging to have suffered a violation of the rights set forth in the respective instruments. International Convention for the Protection of All Persons from Enforced Disappearance (adopted 20 December 2006, entered into force 23 December 2010), art. 31; Optional Protocol to the Convention on the Elimination of All Forms of Discrimination against Women 2131 UNTS 83, (adopted 6 December 1999, entered into force 22 December 2000), art. 2; Optional Protocol to the Convention on the Rights of Persons with Disabilities, A/61/611, (adopted 13 December 2006, entered into force on 3 May 2008), art. 1; Optional Protocol to the Convention on the Rights of the Child on a communications procedure, A/RES/66/138, (adopted 19 December 2011, not entered into force), art. 5; Optional Protocol to the International Covenant on Economic, Social and Cultural Rights, A/63/435, (adopted 10 December 2008, entered into force 5 May 2013), art. 2. The problematic aspect for organizations in the context of these instruments is interpretation of the term 'groups of individuals': can it be understood to include a legal entity? The CERD Committee has responded in the affirmative in *Zentralrat Deutscher Sinti und Roma et al v. Germany*, Communication No. 38/2006, UN Doc. CERD/C/72/D/38/2006, 3 March 2008, para. 7.2.

[49] See White and Ovey, *The European Convention on Human Rights*, 5th ed., at 31.

[50] *Confédération des Syndicats Médicaux Français, Fédérations Nationale des Infirmiers v. France*, Application no. 10983/84, Decision of 12 May 1986.

[51] *Confédération des Syndicats Médicaux Français, Fédérations Nationale des Infirmiers v. France*, at 229.

respective regional instruments.[52] For instance, it cannot be concluded, based solely on the fact that the petition of Les Témoins de Jehovah against the Democratic Republic of Congo was admitted by the African Commission on Human and Peoples' Rights (AComHPR),[53] that the religious organization in question is a rights-holder under the Banjul Charter.

The following section will review the rights that have been claimed successfully[54] by religious organizations. It needs to be stressed that the primary concern of this segment of analysis is not the duties which may arise for religious organizations under the provisions of the ECHR, as distilled in case law—those aspects will be dealt with in part III. The main purpose here is to establish the capacity of religious organizations to bear rights under the ECHR and bring a claim in relation to those rights.

2.1. *Religious organizations as claimants of rights under articles 6, 13, 10, 11 and article 1 of Protocol 1*

Like other legal entities, religious organizations have invoked the right to a fair trial under article 6[55] and the right to an effective remedy under article 13.[56] For example, in a case brought by the Ligue du monde islamique and Organisation islamique mondiale du secours islamique, France was found in breach of article 6.[57] The two organizations, based in Saudi Arabia, which had religious goals, intended to bring defamation claims against a French newspaper; however, French courts declared the cases inadmissible. According to the provisions of a 1901 law, a foreign organization may bring a claim before French courts only after it has made a declaration before the local authorities of the organization's principal place of business in France. The two Saudi organizations had no business in France and, in consequence, no principal place of business. The ECtHR found that the

---

[52] ACHPR, art. 56; ACHR, art. 44. See also Nmehielle, *The African Human Rights System: Its Laws, Practice, and Institutions*, at 203–204; D. R. Pinzon, 'The Victim Requirement, the Fourth Instance Formula and the Notion of Person in the Individual Complaint Procedure of the Inter-American Human Rights System', 7 *ILSA Journal of International & Comparative Law* 1 (2000), 369–386, at 372–376.

[53] In finding a violation of article 8 (freedom of conscience) and article 6 (right to liberty and security of person), the AComHPR referred to the 'believers of this religion' and not to the Jehovah's Witnesses as an organization. *Free Legal Assistance Group, Lawyers' Committee for Human Rights, Union Interafricaine des Droits de l'Homme, Les Témoins de Jehovah v. DRC*, Communication nos. 25/89-47/90-56/91-100/93 (1995), para. 45.

[54] The term 'successfully' does not refer to the merits of a case but to the recognized capacity of a religious entity to claim a right before the EComHR and the ECtHR.

[55] See, for example, a case where the Greek Catholic Church was unable to take legal proceedings as a result of the refusal of civil courts to acknowledge that it had legal personality. *Case of the Canea Catholic Church v. Greece*, Application no. 25528/94, Judgment of 16 December 1997.

[56] By way of example, in *Metropolitan Church of Bessarabia and Others v. Moldova*, Application no. 45701/99, Judgment of 13 December 2001, paras. 135–140, the applicants' church was unable to obtain redress from a national authority in respect of its complaint relating to the right to the freedom of religion, specifically to have the church recognized.

[57] *Ligue du monde islamique et Organisation islamique mondiale du secours islamique v. France*, Requêtes nos 36497/05 et 37172/05, Arrêt du 15 janvier 2009.

requirements of the 1901 law were more than a simple formality necessary for the protection of public order and the rights of others, as argued by the government, and represented serious restrictions affecting the substance of the two organizations' right of access to courts.[58]

In section III.2.2. it will be examined whether, and to what extent, due process guarantees enshrined in the Convention can give rise to obligations for religious organizations in the context of church autonomy.

Freedom of expression under article 10 has been claimed by a number of organizations with religious or philosophical objects. In *Church of Scientology v. Sweden,* the EComHR considered that advertisements of a purely commercial nature, even if disseminated by a religious organization, fall outside the scope of article 9.1 but within the ambit of article 10. Under article 10.2, the right to freedom of expression of a religious organization is balanced against the rights of others, including consumer rights.[59]

As we shall see, church autonomy is grounded in the right of individuals to collectively manifest their religion, read in light of the freedom of association.[60] It is not surprising, therefore, that a variety of claims concerning registration and recognition have been brought by religious organizations under article 11 in conjunction with article 9.[61] In the case of the *Church of Scientology Moscow v. the Russian Federation,*[62] the ECtHR found that the state party had violated the right to freedom of association of the applicant. Pursuant to a 1997 law, all religious associations that had previously been granted legal status in Russia (including the applicant) had to bring their articles of association into conformity with the new act. The Church of Scientology in Moscow submitted its documentation to the authorities, but its re-registration was repeatedly refused on the grounds that criminal charges were pending against the then president of the organization; that the Church had committed unspecified violations of Russian law; and that its documents were incomplete (without indicating what was required to fulfil official criteria). The ECtHR used strong language when finding that a violation had occurred: 'In denying registration to the Church of Scientology of Moscow, the Moscow authorities did not act in good faith and neglected their duty of neutrality and impartiality vis-à-vis the applicant's religious community.'[63]

The right to association and assembly is not an absolute right. Governments are entitled to require religious bodies that wish to register and to be recognized by the state to furnish 'a document setting out the fundamental principles of their religion', so that the authorities can assess whether the body is acting in accordance with legal provisions; that it represents no danger to a democratic society; and that its activity is not directed against the interests of public safety, public order,

---

[58] *Ligue du monde islamique et Organisation islamique mondiale du secours islamique v. France,* para. 58.

[59] *Church of Scientology v. Sweden,* Application No. 7805/77, Decision of 5 May 1979.

[60] See Part III in this chapter.

[61] See Part III in this chapter.

[62] *Church of Scientology Moscow v. Russia,* Application no. 18147/02, Judgment of 5 April 2007.

[63] *Church of Scientology Moscow v. Russia,* para. 97.

health, morals, or the rights and freedoms of others.[64] A religious organization has an obligation to act in accordance with the law, and not to undertake activities that are against the interest of the state or the rights of others, if it wishes to be registered and recognized. In this context, it is interesting to mention the case of the *Mouvement Raelien Suisse v. Switzerland*, where the two dissenting judges of the first instance pointed out an inconsistency in the conduct of Switzerland: by registering the Raelian movement, the state party had recognized that the organization's goals were legal, yet it limited the expression of those goals as illegal.[65]

The limits on the right to freedom of association of religious organizations have also been addressed by the Inter-American Commission on Human Rights (IAComHR), in the context of terrorism, in its Report on Terrorism and Human Rights. The Commission concluded that, in the absence of clear evidence of a threat to public safety or security, governments were prohibited from banning participation in faith-based groups or organizations.[66]

It has been recognized on numerous occasions that the right to peaceful possession of property under article 1 of Protocol 1 may be invoked by churches or religious associations.[67] By way of example, Norman Doe asserts that there are at least 300 Romanian churches with outstanding property claims in Strasbourg.[68] This is anecdotal evidence to suggest that the capacity to bring a claim before the Strasbourg mechanisms has become a justice strategy for religious organizations in the absence of effective remedies at a national level to address the consequences of nationalization during the communist regime (with reference to Romania). The right to property is often invoked by religious organizations in connection with articles 6 and 14. It seems fitting therefore to conclude with a case that deals with the first right listed in this section (fair trial) and the last (right to property), and adds non-discrimination to our survey of rights successfully claimed by religious organizations. *Paroisse Greco Catholique Sâmbata Bihor v. Romania*[69] involved a

---

[64] *Cârmuirea Spirituală a Musulmanilor din Republica Moldova*, Application no. 12282/02, Decision of 14 June 2005.

[65] See Dissenting Opinion of Judges Rozakis and Vajić, *Mouvement Raelien Suisse v. Switzerland*, Application no. 16354/06, Judgment of 13 January 2011, para. 3.a. The case concerned the ban on displaying posters in a public space owing to immoral conduct of the publishing organization and reference to a cloning internet site. The Court found no violation of article 10, and its decision was upheld by the Grand Chamber with 9 votes in favour and 8 against. For a critical account of the Grand Chamber's arguments see the dissenting opinions of Judges Tulkens, Sajo, Lazarova-Trajkovska, Bianku, Power-Forde, Vucinic, Yudkivska, and Albuquerque, *Mouvement Raelien Suisse v. Switzerland*, Application no. 16354/06, Grand Chamber, Judgment of 13 July 2012. See also G. Guillemin, 'Case Law, Strasbourg: Mouvement Raelien Suisse v Switzerland, Of Aliens and Flying Saucers', *Strassbourg Observers*, http://strasbourgobservers.com/2012/07/31/case-law-strasbourg-mouvement-raelien-suisse-v-switzerland-of-aliens-and-flying-saucers/.

[66] IAComHR, *Report on Terrorism and Human Rights*, OEA/Ser.L/V/II.116, 22 October 2002, paras. 358–364. See also L. Doswald-Beck, *Human Rights in Times of Conflict and Terrorism*, (Oxford: Oxford University Press, 2011), at 424–425.

[67] See, for example, a complex situation regarding the property of eight Greek Orthodox monasteries, *Holy Monasteries v. Greece*, Application Nos. 13092/87 and 13984/88, Judgment of 9 December 1994.

[68] Doe, *Law and Religion in Europe: A Comparative Introduction*, at 170.

[69] *Paroisse Greco Catholique Sâmbata Bihor c. Roumanie*, Requête no 48107/99, Arrêt du 12 janvier 2010.

Greek Catholic (Uniate) parish that had been refused access to domestic courts concerning a restitution claim. A church building in which the Sâmbata Uniate priest officiated was nationalized in 1948 under the communist regime, and transferred to the Romanian Orthodox Church. Under 1990 legislation, joint committees of the two churches were to settle the status of properties under dispute. In this case, however, the dispute could not be resolved and the Orthodox Church representatives refused a proposal for the two denominations to hold alternate services in the church in Sâmbata. While a court of first instance sided with the Uniate church and ordered that alternate services should be introduced in an equitable manner, an appeals court reversed the decision on the grounds that disputes concerning church ownership were within the exclusive jurisdiction of the joint committees. The ECtHR found a violation of article 6.1 and 14. Interestingly, it was the unjustified difference in treatment vis-à-vis other Uniate parishes—whereby some were granted access to court while others were not—which represented the central argument in the finding of a violation of article 14.[70]

To sum up, religious organizations have been successful in invoking, and hence are recognized to hold rights under, articles 6, 13, 10, 11 of the ECHR; article 1 of Protocol 1; and under the non-discrimination clause in article 14 in connection with some of the enumerated rights.

2.2. Non-profit legal entities pursuing religious or philosophical objects as exceptional right holders under article 9

While legal entities pursuing religious or philosophical objects were initially denied the right to freedom of religion, today these may enjoy and claim the proection of article 9. This section aims to deconstruct the reasoning behind this judicial development as it is highly relevant for the book's argument which claims that religious actors do not enjoy special or exclusive rights under international law.

In 1968, the Church of X alleged that the United Kingdom had violated its right to freedom of religion under article 9.1, and—taken together with the non-discrimination provision in article 14—the right to fair trial in article 6, and the right to effective remedy in article 13. The EComHR *ex officio* considered an alleged violation of the right to education in article 2 of Protocol 1.[71] In reply to a parliamentary inquiry regarding the activities of scientologists in the UK, the Minister of Health described the Church of X as a 'pseudo-philosophical cult the practice of which was potentially harmful to its adherents' and explained that, although the government had no power under existing legislation to prohibit the practice of scientology, it would take 'all steps within their power to curb its growth'.[72] These steps included de-registering educational establishments dedicated to the study

---

[70] *Paroisse Greco Catholique Sâmbata Bihor c. Roumanie*, paras. 80–81.

[71] *Church of X v. the United Kingdom*, Application no. 3798/68, Decision of 7 December 1968, at 4–5.

[72] *Church of X v. the United Kingdom*, at 3.

of scientology, denying entry into the UK of foreign nationals who wanted to work and study with the church, and denying the renewal of work and study permits.[73] The EComHR declared the case inadmissible. It held that Church X as a corporation was a non-governmental organization, however, it was 'a legal, and not a natural person' and therefore 'incapable of having or exercising the rights mentioned in Article 9, paragraph 1 of the Convention, or Article 2 of the First Protocol'.[74]

Carolyn Evans observes, correctly in this author's opinion, that the EComHR failed to acknowledge in its early jurisprudence that a 'church may be the appropriate and effective body to enforce the provisions relating to freedom of religion, especially in cases where the government has undertaken an explicit campaign to limit the effectiveness of a religious group rather than to restrict the rights of individual members.'[75]

The late 1970s, however, saw the EComHR's jurisprudence change course regarding the standing of churches. In *X and Church of Scientology v. Sweden*, the Commission revised its position and ruled that the distinction between a church and its members under article 9.1 of the Convention was artificial.

When a church body lodges an application under the Convention, it does so in reality, on behalf of its members. It should therefore be accepted that a church body is capable of possessing and exercising the rights contained in Article 9(1) in its own capacity as a representative of its members. . . . Accordingly, the Church of Scientology, as a non-governmental organisation, can properly be considered to be an applicant within the meaning of Article 25(1) of the Convention.[76]

The EComHR's finding with respect to the church's capacity to bear and exercise rights 'in its own capacity as a representative of its members' could seem rather confusing. One would assume that if a church has the right to freedom of religion in its own capacity, this capacity cannot at the same time be dependent on the representation of its members. A way of understanding this less than fortunate wording of the EComHR would be to consider that the 'aggregating of the rights'[77] of individuals lies at the *origin* of the right of the church to manifest religion.[78] That does not mean however that a perfect representation of the interests of the members is needed for this right to continue to exist. One can imagine situations where it would be difficult for a church to exercise *its* right to freedom of religion if the right were conditioned by a perfect representation function. The EComHR has dealt with precisely such cases in both *X v. Denmark*[79] and *Hautaniemi*

---

[73] See also Evans, *Freedom of Religion under the European Convention on Human Rights*, at 12–13.

[74] However, in respect to article 6.1, the argumentation was different. The EComHR found that the official measures, and the refusal to hold an inquiry and disclose evidence, were of an administrative nature and did not involve the determination of a civil right within the meaning of art. 6.1 of the ECHR. The issues in relation to articles 13 and 14 had no basis in the light of the findings on article 9. *Church of X v. the United Kingdom*, Application no. 3798/68, Decision of 7 December 1968, at 6–8.

[75] Evans, *Freedom of Religion under the European Convention on Human Rights*, at 13.

[76] *Church of Scientology v. Sweden*, Application No. 7805/77, Decision of 5 May 1979, at 70.

[77] Evans, *Freedom of Religion under the European Convention on Human Rights*, at 14.

[78] van Dijk and van Hoof, Theory and Practice of the European Convention on Human Rights, 3rd ed., at 552.

[79] *X v. Denmark*, Application No. 7374/76, Decision of 8 March 1976, at 158.

v. Sweden,[80] where a clergyman and members of a parish dissented from the general practice of the church. Despite the dissent and the implied frustration of representation, the EComHR accepted the church's right to manifest religion; thereby the Commission acknowledged that the function of representation may be imperfect and the right of the church to freedom of religion would continue to exist if representation were frustrated.[81]

In conclusion, the right of a church to manifest religion is derived from the right of individuals to collectively manifest their religion. Without this link, the non-human nature of a legal entity that prevents it from exercising the right to life, for example, would similarly prevent a church from manifesting religion or a humanist organization from exercising beliefs. In later cases the ECtHR and EComHR dropped the explicit mention of the representation nexus.[82] To admit today that a church has *its own* right to manifest religion is not to deny that the collective right of individuals lies at the origin of the church's right. At the same time, it certainly does not mean that a perfect representation of the interests of church members must exist, which ultimately admits the possibility of splinter groups or even schisms.

A variety of churches, religious associations, and other legal entities with religious or philosophical objects have been acknowledged to be capable of possessing and exercising the right to freedom of religion. Among them are churches and associations of various Christian denominations, including established churches,[83] the Jehovah's Witnesses,[84] the Salvation Army,[85] and Islamic,[86] Judaic,[87] Hindu,[88] and humanist associations.[89] Others have also been found to have the capacity to bring a claim under article 9 including the Church of Scientology,[90] the Secular Order of Druids,[91] Divine Light Zentrum,[92] the Osho Movement,[93] and the Mouvement Raelien Suisse.[94]

---

[80] *Finska församlingen i Stockholm and Teuvo Hautaniemi v. Sweden*, Application No. 24019/94, Decision of 11 April 1996, EComHR, Deicisions and Reports, vol. 62.

[81] *X v. Denmark*, Application No. 7374/76, Decision of 8 March 1976, at 158.

[82] *Finska församlingen i Stockholm and Teuvo Hautaniemi v. Sweden*, Application No. 24019/94, Decision of 11 April 1996, EComHR, Deicisions and Reports, vol. 62; *Holy Monasteries v. Greece*, Application Nos. 13092/87 and 13984/88, Judgment of 9 December 1994.

[83] *Holy Monasteries v. Greece*, Application Nos. 13092/87 and 13984/88, Judgment of 9 December 1994.

[84] *Association Les Témoins de Jéhovah c. France*, Requête no 8916/05, Arrêt du 30 juin 2011.

[85] *Moscow Branch of the Salvation Army v. Russia*, Application No. 72881/01, Judgment of 5 Ocotber 2006.

[86] *Supreme Holy Council of the Muslim Community v. Bulgaria*, Application no. 39023/97, Judgment of 16 March 2005.

[87] *Cha'are Shalom Ve Tsedek v. France*, Application no. 27417/95, Judgment of 27 June 2000.

[88] *ISKCON et al. v. the United Kingdom*, Application No. 20490/92, Decision of 8 March 1994.

[89] *Kustannus Oy Vapaa Ajattelija AB et al. v. Finland*, Application No. 20471/92, Decision of 15 April 1996, EComHR, Decisions and Reports, vol. 85A.

[90] *Church of Scientology v. Sweden*, Application No. 7805/77, Decision of 5 May 1979.

[91] *A.R.M. Chappel v. the United Kingdom*, Application No. 12587/86, Decision of 14 July 1987.

[92] *Omkarananda and Divine Light Zentrum v. Switzerland*, Application No. 8118/77, Decision of 19 March 1981.

[93] *Leela Förderkreis E.V et al., v. Germany*, Application No. 58911/00, Judgment of 6 November 2008.

[94] *Mouvement Raelien Suisse v. Switzerland*, Application no. 16354/06, Judgment of 13 January 2011.

2.2.1. Freedom of religion and belief denied to profit-making corporations

The Strasbourg mechanisms have drawn the line of admissibility of article 9 applications at corporations. In *Company X v. Switzerland*, the applicant, a limited liability company, complained that the ecclesiastical taxes imposed by the cantonal authorities for the benefit of Catholic and Protestant Churches, represented an infringement of its rights under article 9. The EComHR summarily dismissed the application, as follows:

> Even supposing that the applicant's claim may fall within the ambit of Article 9 of the Convention, the Commission is nevertheless of the opinion that a limited liability company given the fact that it concerns a profit-making corporate body, can neither enjoy nor rely on the rights referred to in Article 9, paragraphe 1 [sic], of the Convention.[95]

The decision of the EComHR begs a question: is it the profit-seeking character of the legal person that denies it the capacity to hold the right enshrined in article 9? Given the succinctness of this particular finding one is left to speculate about the reasoning behind the proposed profit/non-profit distinction applied to legal entities for the purpose of article 9. It is unlikely that the Commission's intention would have been to suggest that profit and religion are incompatible. It is relevant at this point to analyse the Swiss context which gave rise to the *Company X* case and may have contributed to shaping the ECHR mechanisms' approach to the non-admissibility of article 9 cases brought by for-profit entities.

Swiss companies have repeatedly taken up in domestic courts the issue of religious tax benefitting established churches of the various cantons.[96] The first noteworthy aspect is that the Swiss Federal Tribunal reaffirmed its earlier jurisprudence and, additionally, relied on the later finding of the EComHR to deny the application of the right to freedom of religion to legal entities in general.[97] In a 2010 case, the single shareholder and employee of a profit-making company, X, stressed that she was a firm opponent of the church and given that she had to personally ensure the transfer of the church tax this amounted to an indignity and insult.[98] As such, the complainant insisted that it was necessary to consider the rights of the natural person behind the legal person, arguing that 'die Berufung auf die Religionsfreiheit dürfte nicht an der formalen Konstruktion der juristischen Person scheitern'.[99]

---

[95] *Company X v. Switzerland*, Application No. 7865/77, Decision of 27 February 1979, at 87.

[96] In Switzerland, the cantons have the authority to levy religious tax. Most cantons impose religious taxes upon both natural and legal persons for the benefit of the Protestant Church, the Roman Catholic Church, and the Christlichkatholische Kirche der Schweiz respectively, or a combination thereof. However, some cantons impose such taxes only on natural persons (Schaffhausen, Aargau) and others do not impose church taxes on either natural or legal persons (Vaud). One canton makes a profit/non-profit distinction, and exempts only non-profit activities of a religious legal person from the imposition of the ecclesiastical tax. See Steuerkonferenz SSK, Kirchensteuern. Stand der Gesetzgebung: 1. Januar 2009, Abteilung Grundlagen/ESTV Bern, 2009.

[97] *i.S. Model AG gegen Steuerverwaltung und Verwaltungsgericht des Kantons Thurgau*, Urteil des Bundesgerichts vom 13. Juni 2000, BGE 126 I 122; *Urteil des Bundesgerichts, 2C_71/2010* vom 22. September 2010.

[98] *Urteil des Bundesgerichts, 2C_71/2010* vom 22. September 2010, para. 5.

[99] Author's own translation: 'the invocation of the right to religious freedom should not fail because of the formal construct of the legal person'. *Urteil des Bundesgerichts, 2C_71/2010* vom 22. September 2010.

The court explained the general reasoning behind the imposition of church taxation upon legal persons: by judicially separating part of its wealth through the establishment of a legal person, an individual is enjoying a number of benefits, while certain obligations ensue for the legal entity.[100] Taxes are one of the obligations, including, where cantons so decide, church taxes. Because legal persons are independent subjects for the purpose of taxation, with a separate existence from that of the natural persons involved in their activities, the religious freedom of the natural persons behind the activity of a legal person is therefore not relevant in taxation cases.[101]

Second, the Federal Tribunal made an exemption from religious taxation for legal persons that pursue religious or church-related goals. The court held:

[w]enn auch juristische Personen im allgemeinen und Erwerbsgesellschaften im besondern unter dem Gesichtswinkel der Besteuerung sich nicht auf die Glaubens- und Gewissensfreiheit berufen können, so wäre es anderseits—bei aller formalen Logik—absurd, juristischen Personen mit religiöser oder kirchlicher Zwecksetzung...der Besteuerung durch Kirchen Andersgläubiger zu unterwerfen.[102]

In other words, while the right to freedom of religion is expressly denied to legal entities in general, it is specifically accepted in the case of legal entities which themselves pursue religious or church-related goals. The court acknowledged the apparent incoherence and sought to justify it in a case in which a *Freikirche* (a non-established church) challenged the levying of the religious tax.[103] In the *Freikirche* case, the Federal Tribunal concluded that the imposition of church taxes for the benefit of established churches would have a disproportionate effect on members of the *Freikirche*. Interestingly, the freedom of religion of members of the non-established church was seen as *the* relevant issue here, whereas the relevance of the rights of natural persons behind legal entities in general has been consistently denied. This in turn supports, in a domestic context, the observation made in relation to the Strasbourg mechanism: the religious freedom of a church is a right derived from the right of individuals to manifest their religion collectively.

To return to the Swiss *Freikirche* case, the disproportionate effect, which the Tribunal identified, is due to the fact that the tax must be collected from the church's members, and as such potentially threatening the church's survival.

---

[100] *Urteil des Bundesgerichts, 2C_71/2010* vom 22. September 2010, para. 4.1. See also *i.S. Model AG gegen Steuerverwaltung und Verwaltungsgericht des Kantons* Thurgau, Urteil des Bundesgerichts vom 13. Juni 2000, BGE 126 I 122, at 130.

[101] *Urteil des Bundesgerichts, 2C_71/2010* vom 22. September 2010, para. 7.1.

[102] This author's translation: Although legal persons in general and profit-making entities in particular cannot rely on the right to freedom of religion and conscience in the context of taxation, it would be by all means absurd—notwithstanding formal logic—to impose upon a legal person with religious or church objects ecclesiastical taxes intended for churches of different denominations. *i.S. Buchdruckerei Elgg AG gegen evangelisch-reformierte Kirchgemeinde Elgg und Verwaltungsgericht des Kantons Zürich*, Urteil des Bundesgerichts vom 6. Oktober 1976, BGE 102 I 468, at 477.

[103] *i.S. Neuapostolische Kirche in der Schweiz gegen Evangelische Landeskirche, Katholische Landeskirche und Steuerrekurskommission des Kantons Thurgau*, Urteil des Bundesgerichts vom 9. Juli 1969, BGE 95 I 350.

Dadurch würden die Mitglieder und Anhänger der Freikirchen in einer Weise betroffen, die mit der in Art. 49 Abs. 1 BV enthaltenen Garantie der Glaubens- und Gewissensfreiheit und mit der in Abs. 6 zu ihrem Schutz errichteten Schranke der Erhebung von Kultussteuern in einem nicht mehr zu vereinbarenden Widerspruch steht. Es entspricht daher Sinn und Geist des Art. 49 BV, den juristischen Personen, die selber einen religiösen oder kirchlichen Zweck verfolgen, im Gegensatz zu andern juristischen Personen die Berufung auf Art. 49 Abs. 6 BV zu gestatten.[104]

The court's logic seems to be strengthened by the fact that *Freikirchen* have few other ways available to support themselves financially. It is possible that the 1979 decision of the EComHR in *Company X v. Switzerland* had precisely this in mind when it made the profit/non-profit distinction and found that profit-making entities could not rely on article 9 to be exempted from church taxes. A profit-making entity does not depend on the monetary contributions of its members to function; on this ground, exemption would not be justified.

Of course, there remain outlier cases which conform only marginally to the described conditions. In such cases it seems illegitimate to refuse to take the right to freedom of religion of the person behind the legal entity into consideration merely because the entity is profit-making. In a 2010 case brought by the *single* shareholder and employee of company X, who was a firm opponent of the church, one can note the uneasiness of the Swiss Federal Tribunal: whereas it denied the company's right to freedom of religion, it also engaged in what looked like a proportionality test. It held that the sole shareholder of firm X did not clarify the circumstances which would give rise to the personal concern, and that, in any event, the monetary amount of the church tax was rather modest.[105]

Similar unease, this time of the EComHR, can be discerned in the case of *Kustannus Oy Vapaa Ajattelija AB et al. v. Finland*.[106] The first applicant was a Finnish publishing company owned by the second applicant, the registered umbrella association of Finnish freethinkers; the third applicant was the manager of the publishing company and member of the Finnish freethinkers association. The applicants argued that the company was set up with the aim of publishing and selling books reflecting and promoting the aims of the freethinkers' movement and that, while it carried out 'certain modest economic activities, it does not aim at producing profit but at having the Church separated from the State'.[107] They

---

[104] This author's translation: Members and followers of the *Freikirche* would thereby be in a way affected that cannot be reconciled with their right to freedom of religion and conscience enshrined in art. 49 para. 1 of the Federal Constitution and the limit upon the levy of religious tax of para 6 which is intended for their protection. It is therefore in accordance with the object and purpose of art. 49 of the Federal Constitution, to allow legal persons which themselves pursue religious or church-related goals, in contrast to other legal persons, to invoke art. 49, para. 6 of the Constitution. (Note that the citation refers to the Federal Constitution of Switzerland of 1874, which was superseded in 1999 by a new Constitution. The relevant references from the new Federal Constitution are paras. 2 and 4 of art. 14). i.S. *Neuapostolische Kirche in der Schweiz gegen Evangelische Landeskirche, Katholische Landeskirche und Steuerrekurskommission des Kantons Thurgau*, Urteil des Bundesgerichts vom 9. Juli 1969, at 355.

[105] *Urteil des Bundesgerichts, 2C_71/2010* vom 22. September 2010, para. 7.1.

[106] *Kustannus Oy Vapaa Ajattelija AB et al. v. Finland*, Application No. 20471/92, Decision of 15 April 1996, EComHR, Decisions and Reports, vol. 85A.

[107] *Kustannus Oy Vapaa Ajattelija AB et al. v. Finland*, at 39.

further pointed out that, under Finnish law, a limited liability company is not required to be a profit-making body but could be established to serve religious or philosophical purposes. The applicants therefore complained that the religious tax levied on the applicant company violated their right to freedom of religion. The EComHR accepted that:

The company form may have been a deliberate choice on the part of the applicant association and its branches for the pursuance of part of the freethinkers' activities. Nevertheless, for the purposes of domestic law this applicant was registered as a corporate body with limited liability. As such it is in principle required by domestic law to pay tax as any other corporate body, regardless of the underlying purpose of its activities on account of its links with the applicant association and its branches and irrespective of the final receiver of the tax revenues collected from it. Finally, it has not been shown that the applicant association would have been prevented from pursuing the company's commercial activities in its own name. The Commission therefore concludes that in the circumstance of the present case the applicant company cannot rely on the rights referred to in Article 9 para 1.[108]

In other words, while it was accepted that the company may have pursued philosophical objects, the for-profit form it chose disqualified it from invoking article 9. One important aspect must be noted here: the EComHR underlined the fact that the applicants failed to substantiate that it would have been impossible to pursue commercial activities in the association's name. Would the Commission have accepted that the company (despite its profit-making character) could rely on article 9, if the applicants had proved that they had no alternative to setting up a commercial entity if they wished to print and publish books promoting the aims of Finnish freethinkers? One is inclined to reply in the affirmative, for otherwise the observation of the EComHR would be illogical.

To summarize the findings of this section, the right to freedom of religion has been denied to profit-making entities yet recognized for religious organizations. The explanation for the different treatment accorded to religious organizations is that their right to religious freedom is understood to derive or extend from the right of individuals to manifest religion collectively. The fact that only profit-making entities are required to pay ecclesiastical taxes, while religious bodies are exempt, further buttresses this derivative link.

2.2.2. Freedom of conscience denied to non-profit organizations

This section will explore the reasons why, in the view of the ECtHR, non-profit organizations without religious or philosophical objects may not invoke article 9.

The *Verein 'Kontakt-Information-Therapie' (KIT) and Siegfried Hagen v. Austria* case reveals that is not enough for a legal entity to have a non-profit character in order to enjoy article 9 rights. KIT, a non-profit-making organization, sought to rely on the right to freedom of conscience enshrined in article 9.[109] The association ran rehabilitation centres for young drug abusers. Criminal proceedings

---

[108] *Kustannus Oy Vapaa Ajattelija AB et al. v. Finland*, at 43–44.
[109] *Verein 'Kontakt-Information-Therapie' (KIT) and Siegfried Hagen v. Austria*, Application No. 11921/86, Decision of 12 October 1988, EComHR, Decisions and Reports, vol. 57.

were brought against a former patient of a KIT-centre and the Austrian authorities summoned two of the centre's therapists to appear as witnesses. In invoking article 9 of the ECHR, the applicants (KIT and one of the two therapists summoned) contended that the case involved 'a confrontation between demands of the State and the dictates of individual conscience'.[110] While they agreed that in a democratic society the state's recognition of the freedom to act in accordance with one's conscience may be limited, and that combating drug abuse through criminal prosecution was a legitimate aim, the applicants argued that the treatment of young drug addicts in the early stages of their drug dependence also constituted a legitimate aim and served a pressing social need. They concluded that by imposing fines for their refusal to give evidence in court the authorities had interfered disproportionally with the freedom of conscience of the centre and its therapists.[111]

Interestingly, the EComHR did not make any reference to the profit/non-profit distinction, and instead found that article 9 by its nature was not capable of being exercised by a legal person such as a private association. The EComHR however continued by proposing that a distinction must be made between freedom of conscience and freedom of religion, whereby the latter right can also be exercised by a church.[112] Some authors have argued that this distinction is a 'metaphysical impossibility'.[113] Malcolm D. Evans explains the apparent incoherence of the argument: 'A church, as an organization, is neither more nor less capable of having a religion or belief than any other legal person is of having conscience'.[114] Evans resolves the inconsistency by explaining that the distinction between 'thought and conscience' and 'religion and belief' is essential to the architecture of article 9: only *manifestations of religion and belief* are protected under the article.[115] So, while an individual enjoys absolute freedom of thought and conscience, only if they amount to a belief would their manifestation be protected under article 9.2. Otherwise the expression of thought and of conscience would be protected under article 10.2.[116] In conclusion, there is no collective right of individuals to manifest their conscience under article 9 if that conscience does not amount to a belief.[117] Essentially this means that only non-profit organizations that have religious and philosophical objects are able to appeal to article 9 under the European Convention.

[110] *Verein 'Kontakt-Information-Therapie' (KIT) and Siegfried Hagen v. Austria*, at 86.
[111] *Verein 'Kontakt-Information-Therapie' (KIT) and Siegfried Hagen v. Austria*, at 86.
[112] *Verein 'Kontakt-Information-Therapie' (KIT) and Siegfried Hagen v. Austria*, at 88.
[113] White and Ovey, *The European Convention on Human Rights*, 5th ed., at 409.
[114] See note 114, (Cambridge: Cambridge University Press, 1997), at 288.
[115] See note 114, at 288.
[116] See note 114, at 289–290.
[117] In the *Campbell and Cosans* case the ECtHR found that in order for 'ideas', 'opinions', or views to qualify as beliefs they had to reach 'a certain level of cogency, seriousness, cohesion and importance.' Specifically in relation to 'philosophical convictions' which would give rise to manifestations protected under article 9, these should be 'worthy of respect in a "democratic society"' and not 'be incompatible with human dignity'. *Campbell and Cosans v. the United Kingdom*, Application nos. 7511/76; 7743/76, Judgment of 25 February 1982, para. 36.

2.3. A right of religious organizations not to have their religious feelings offended?

Having established that article 9 may be claimed by legal entities that pursue religious and philosophical aims, we turn to the issue of whether these actors may claim the right not to have their religious feeling offended or insulted. The heading is perhaps misleading. It would be more precise to say that the problem that needs to be tackled here is whether *anyone* enjoys a right to be free from offence to his or her religious feelings? We must first establish whether such a right exists per se, before inquiring whether religious organizations may claim it.

As enshrined in article 9, the right to freedom of thought, conscience, and religion protects the absolute right to have, change, or adopt a religion or belief: it is understood that the article covers theistic, non-theistic, and atheistic beliefs[118] and also protects the qualified right to manifest religion. Article 9 does not stipulate that an individual, a group of individuals or a legal entity has the right to be free, or protected, from blasphemy. The controversy arose at the European level as a result of applications filed by individuals and legal entities, complaining that their right to freedom of expression had been breached by interfering governments. The EComHR and the ECtHR understood the situation to be a conflict between the right of the applicants to freedom of expression on the one hand, and 'the right of citizens not be offended in their religious feelings'[119] or 'insulted in their religious feelings'[120] on the other. In many respects the blasphemy controversy is of the Strasbourg mechanisms own making, and it echoes surprisingly with some aspects of the 'defamation of religions' initiatives supported by the Organization of Islamic Cooperation in UN fora, as reviewed in Chapter 2. As dissenting judges acknowledged in *İ.A. v. Turkey*:

The time has perhaps come to "revisit" this case law [*Otto-Preminger-Institut* and *Wingrove*], which in our view seems to place too much emphasis on conformism or uniformity of thought and to reflect an overcautious and timid conception of freedom of the press.[121]

A case concerning the publication *Gay News* was the first one where the EcomHR was confronted with a freedom of expression claim resulting from the application of UK blasphemy laws. A publication and its editor complained that their conviction of the common law offence of blasphemous libel was in violation of their article 10 rights. Their conviction followed the publication of a poem that 'purported to describe in explicit detail acts of sodomy and fellatio with the body of Christ immediately after His death and ascribed to Him during His lifetime promiscuous

---

[118] *Kokkinakis v. Greece*, Application no. 14307/88, Judgment of 25 May 1993, para. 31.

[119] *Otto-Preminger-Institute v. Austria*, Application no. 13470/87, Judgment of 20 September 1994, para. 48.

[120] *Wingrove v. the United Kingdom*, Application no. 17419/90, Judgment of 25 November 1996, para. 47.

[121] Joint Dissenting Opinion of Judges Costa, Cabral Barreto and Jungwiert, *İ.A. v. Turkey*, Application no. 42571/98, Judgment of 13 September 2005, para. 8.

homosexual practices with the Apostles and other men'.[122] The Commission held that:

the offence of blasphemous libel as it is construed under the applicable common law in fact has the main purpose to protect *the right of citizens not to be offended in their religious feelings* by publications.... The Commission therefore concludes that the restriction was indeed covered by a legitimate purpose recognised in the Convention, namely the protection of the rights of others. *If it is accepted* that the religious feelings of the citizen *may deserve* protection against indecent attacks on the matters held sacred by him, then it can also be considered as necessary in a democratic society to stipulate that such attacks, if they attain a certain level of severity, shall constitute a criminal offence triable at the request of the offended person.[123]

The sentiment evoked by this decision is that the EComHR saw the 'right of citizens not to be offended in their religious feelings' as confined to the UK context of this particular case, and that, therefore, it may not be a right of general application under the ECHR. The use of the term 'citizen' rather than 'individual' supports this reading. A more general observation that can be made in relation to the blasphemy case law of the Strasbourg mechanisms is that it is unspecific about the holders of this alleged right. Is the right held by citizens, as *Gay News* implied, or by believers,[124] or more generally by individuals, groups of individuals, or legal entities? Use of the term 'feelings', which can be applied to human beings but not associations, adds to the uncertainly. Can a legal entity claim the right? Similarly, it is unclear whether 'religious' feelings include those of atheists and humanists.

Almost a decade after the decision in *Gay News*, the EComHR was confronted in *Choudhury v. United Kingdom*[125] with the reverse issue concerning the application of the UK blasphemy law. It concerned a complaint by Mr Choudhury whose application to bring a criminal prosecution for blasphemy against Salman Rushdie and the publishing company of his book 'The Satanic Verses' had been dismissed.[126] Mr Choudhury filed the complaint under article 9 of the ECHR, claiming that the lack of protection 'against abuse or scurrilous attack' afforded to Islam under the UK blasphemy law limited the enjoyment of religious freedom.[127] He also alleged that the fact that protection was granted only to the Christian religion represented a violation of article 14. In a succinct decision, that was unsatisfactory to the extent that it failed to analyse the UK blasphemy law,[128] the EComHR dismissed the case. It held that article 9 does not 'extend to guarantee a right to bring any specific

---

[122] *X. Ltd and Y v. the United Kingdom*, Application no. 8710/79, Decision of 7 May 1982, at 78.

[123] *X. Ltd and Y v. the United Kingdom*, at 83, paras. 11–12. (Emphasis added).

[124] *Otto-Preminger-Institute v. Austria*, Application no. 13470/87, Judgment of 20 September 1994, para. 47.

[125] *Choudhury v. United Kingdom*, Application No. 17439/90, Decision of 5 March 1991.

[126] For a detailed analysis of the case before UK courts, see A. Clapham, *Human Rights in the Private Sphere*, (Oxford: Oxford University Press, 1993), at 314–322.

[127] *Choudhury v. United Kingdom*, Application No. 17439/90, Decision of 5 March 1991.

[128] See P. G. Danchin, 'Islam in the Secular *Nomos* of the European Court of Human Rights', 32 *Mich. J. Int'l L.* (2011), 663–747, at 665–666.

form of proceedings against those who, by authorship or publication, offend the sensitivities of an individual or of a group of individuals'.[129] In other words, in the view of the EComHR, the state did not have a positive obligation under the ECHR to protect religious sensitivities.[130] In the light of this finding, subsequent article 10 jurisprudence, which continues in the tradition of *Gay News*, appears incomprehensible. It is difficult to see how article 9 does not give rise to a positive obligation for the state to protect the religious feelings of individuals, but article 10 can be limited to protect the religious feelings of individuals under article 9. We will therefore take a careful look at case law on article 10 that relates to blasphemy in an attempt to understand the reasoning behind the Strasbourg mechanisms' rulings, and their implications.

In *Otto-Preminger-Institut v. Austria* (which concerned the seizure and forfeiture of the movie 'Das Liebeskonzil', considered blasphemous under Austrian law) and *Wingrove v. the United Kingdom* (where an 18-minute video entitled 'Visions of Ecstasy' was not accorded classification by the British Board of Film Classification for contravening the UK blasphemy laws, preventing distribution of the movie), the Commission and Court came to different conclusions in finding, and respectively not finding, a violation of article 10.[131] The treatment by the EComHR of the two cases, and in particular its decision to grant a narrower margin of appreciation to the respondent states, reveals an uneasiness on its part: it had affirmed the right of citizens not to be offended in their religious feelings in *Gay News*, and now had to grapple with the consequences of that ruling.[132] The ECtHR, on the other hand, pointed to the wording of article 10.2, which stipulates the 'duties and responsibilities' that are to be taken into consideration by non-state actors when exercising their right to freedom of expression:

Amongst them—in the context of religious opinions and beliefs—may legitimately be included *an obligation* to avoid as far as possible expressions that are gratuitously offensive to others and thus an infringement of their rights, and which therefore do not contribute to any form of public debate capable of furthering progress in human affairs. This being so, as a matter of principle it may be considered necessary in certain democratic societies to sanction or even prevent improper attacks on objects of religious veneration...[133]

In *Wingrove* the 'obligation' of non-state actors became the 'duty to avoid as far as possible an expression that is, in regard to objects of veneration, gratuitously offensive

---

[129] *Choudhury v. United Kingdom*, Application No. 17439/90, Decision of 5 March 1991.

[130] P. Kearns, 'The End of Blasphemy Law', 76 *Amicus Curiae: Journal for the Society for Advanced Legal Studies* (2008) 25–27, at 26. See also van Dijk and van Hoof, *Theory and Practice of the European Convention on Human Rights*, 3rd ed., at 551.

[131] *Otto-Preminger-Institute v. Austria*, Application no. 13470/87, Judgment of 20 September 1994; *Wingrove v. the United Kingdom*, Application no. 17419/90, Judgment of 25 November 1996.

[132] See Evans, *Religious Liberty and International Law in Europe*, at 335 and 339.

[133] *Otto-Preminger-Institute v. Austria*, Application no. 13470/87, Judgment of 20 September 1994, para. 49. (Emphasis added). See also the analysis in Clapham, *Human Rights Obligations of Non-State Actors*, at 402–405.

to others and profanatory'.[134] This duty—to take the more recent term—could have unusual implications if applied to a religious non-state actor. One can see how some 'citizens' of Christian faith may take great offence and feel deep outrage when exposed to expressions denying the existence of Jesus, a central tenet of their system of belief; however, the opinion that Jesus was 'a most important personality who intervened in world history in a grand way', but was *not* the son of God, the messiah, or a prophet, forms part of the belief of individuals and organizations of Judaic faith.[135] In today's European *espace juridique* and beyond, it is not possible, and it is certainly not desirable, to expect Jewish non-state actors to avoid giving expression to their opinion concerning Jesus in order to avoid offending the most venerated figure of Christianity. This example shows that the duty imposed on non-state actors is legally, but also logically, untenable and is highly questionable at a common sense level.

In *Otto-Preminger-Institut*, and later in *Murphy v. Ireland*,[136] the ECtHR conflated articles 9 and 10. The analysis is perhaps less than clear and consequently its effects more uncertain.[137] How far would such a duty imposed on religious non-state actors extend? We submit that the consequence of an alleged right not to be offended in one's religious feelings is a corresponding duty on religious non-state actors to avoid as far as possible offensive and profanatory expressions. In this context, the potential positive obligation of states to ensure respect for religious feelings may have the most dire consequences for precisely those which it was seemingly intended to protect, religious actors—it would involve state interference with their autonomy. The problem with the alleged right not to be offended in one's religious feelings is that it leads to absurd situations. For example, the right not to be insulted in one's religious feeling could be interpreted as barring proselytism when the proselytized would feel offended by the proselytizer's bearing witness. It is hoped that the Court will not accept such an interpretation and rather rely on its case law on proselytism. In *Kokkinakis v. Greece*,[138] the ECtHR rightly accepted that restrictions may be imposed on the right to proselytize. However, the Court ruled that the use of 'improper means' to proselytize would justify restricting this right and not mere expressions that might offend or insult. It further suggested that improper means could:

take the form of activities offering material or social advantages with a view to gaining new members for a Church or exerting improper pressure on people in distress or in need; it may even entail the use of violence or brainwashing.[139]

A gratuitously offensive or profanatory expression may well be considered as 'shocking, offending or disturbing'[140] to religious individuals but it is difficult

---

[134] *Wingrove v. the United Kingdom*, Application no. 17419/90, Judgment of 25 November 1996, para. 52.

[135] See S. Heschel, *Abraham Geiger and the Jewish Jesus*, (Chicago: Chicago University Press, 1998), at 71.

[136] *Murphy v. Ireland*, Application no. 44179/98, Judgment of 10 July 2003.

[137] See Concurring Opinion of Judge Pettiti, *Wingrove v. the United Kingdom*, Application no. 17419/90, Judgment of 25 November 1996, para. 65; *Murphy v. Ireland*, Application no. 44179/98, Judgment of 10 July 2003. See also Taylor, *Freedom of Religion: UN and European Human Rights Law and Practice*, at 95.

[138] *Kokkinakis v. Greece*, Application no. 14307/88, Judgment of 25 May 1993.

[139] *Kokkinakis v. Greece*, para. 48; *Larissis and others v. Greece*, Application nos. 23372/94; 26377/94; 26378/94, Judgment of 24 February 1998, para. 51. See also Evans, *Religious Liberty and International Law in Europe*, at 336.

[140] *Otto-Preminger-Institute v. Austria*, Application no. 13470/87, Judgment of 20 September 1994, para. 49.

to equate it with 'incitement to violence'. As is suggested by doctrine,[141] and consistent with the article 10 case law of the Convention mechanisms that does not relate to blasphemy,[142] the ECtHR should have focused its analysis not on whether public expressions offended religious feelings but on whether they incite to violence, hostility, and discrimination against (in this case) religious communities.[143] The approach of the HRC in *Ross v. Canada* is illustrative. The Committee was concerned not only with the fact that the Jewish community may find the statements of Malcolm Ross—a teacher and author—gratuitously offensive, but that he had called 'upon true Christians to not merely question the validity of Jewish beliefs and teachings but to hold those of the Jewish faith and ancestry in contempt as undermining freedom, democracy and Christian beliefs and values'.[144] The HRC examined the nature of Mr Ross' opinions and their effect, not as much on the religious feelings of the pupils or Jewish community, but on 'the reaction or potential reaction of persons that read the publications vis-à-vis the group or persons targeted by the publication...and which may indeed be incited to act upon it'.[145]

One may argue that the HRC was at an advantage: it had interpreted the right to freedom of expression enshrined in article 19 of the ICCPR and the 'special duties and responsibilities' which individuals carry while exercising it in the light of the readily available article 20.2 which stipulates that 'any advocacy of national, racial or religious hatred that constitutes incitement to discrimination, hostility or violence shall be prohibited by law'.[146] As noted in Chapter 1, the ECHR does not have a provision equivalent to article 20, however, one would have hoped and expected the European mechanisms to interpet the text of the Convention coherently with other international instruments, and as such in a manner that focuses on the need to protect religious individuals and communities from religious hatred and the intention to incite violence rather than on the protection of religious feelings. The crux of the matter is that the right to have one's religious feelings respected lacks a basis in law and the Convention

---

[141] Evans, *Religious Liberty and International Law in Europe*, at 335–341; van Dijk and van Hoof, *Theory and Practice of the European Convention on Human Rights*, 3rd ed., at 551.

[142] See *Vereinigung demokratischer Soldaten Österreichs and Gubi v. Austria*, Application no. 15153/89, Judgment of 19 December 1994, para. 34 and 38. Judge Nohmus notes in his dissenting opinion in *Wingrove* that the Court acted inconsistently with its article 10 jurisprudence in granting a wide margin of appreciation to the UK. See Dissenting Opinion of Judge Lohmus, *Wingrove v. the United Kingdom*, Application no. 17419/90, Judgment of 25 November 1996, para. 6.

[143] For yet a different approach to blasphemy see *'The Last Temptation of Christ' (Olmedo-Bustos et al.) v. Chile*, Inter-American Court of Human Rights, Judgment of 5 February 2001 and the Opinion of Judge Roux Rengifo in that case.

[144] *Malcolm Ross v. Canada*, Communication No. 736/1997, UN Doc. CCPR/C/70/D/736/1997 (2000), para. 11.5. See also the discussion of *Faurisson v. France* in A. Conte and R. Burchill, *Defining Civil and Political Rights: the Jurisprudence of the United Nations Human Rights Committee*, 2nd ed., (Aldershot: Ashgate, 2009), at 91.

[145] J. Temperman, 'Freedom of Expression and Religious Sensitivities in Pluralist Societies: Facing the Challenge of Extreme Speech', *BYU L. Rev.* (2011), 729–757, at 743–744.

[146] ICCPR, art. 19.3 and 20.2.

mechanisms' reading of such a right in article 9 is, as some scholars have put it, 'mistaken'.[147]

In its 2011 General Comment 34 on the right to freedom of opinion and expression in the ICCPR, the HRC unequivocally asserted:

Prohibitions of displays of lack of respect for a religion or other belief system, including blasphemy laws, are incompatible with the Covenant, except in the specific circumstances envisaged in article 20, paragraph 2, of the Covenant. Such prohibitions must also comply with the strict requirements of article 19, paragraph 3, as well as such articles as 2, 5, 17, 18 and 26. Thus, for instance, it would be impermissible for any such laws to discriminate in favour of or against one or certain religions or belief systems, or their adherents over another, or religious believers over non-believers. Nor would it be permissible for such prohibitions to be used to prevent or punish criticism of religious leaders or commentary on religious doctrine and tenets of faith.[148]

One should equally note that the United Kingdom, the respondent state in the case that coined the right to respect the religious feelings of citizens, has abolished its blasphemy laws[149] and replaced them through the Racial and Religious Hatred Act 2006, whereby 'a person who uses threatening words or behaviour, or displays any written material which is threatening, is guilty of an offence if he intends thereby to stir up religious hatred'.[150] It is worth noting that intention is a required element.

It is evident from the previous paragraphs, and from the review of the evolution of the 'defamation of religions' resolutions in Chapter 2, that international and some domestic fora have moved away from protecting individuals and religious communities or organizations from blasphemy towards protecting them from religious hatred, in which intentional incitement to violence plays an important role. The more recent judgments of the ECtHR concerning the application of blasphemy laws, and (outside the blasphemy context) racial hatred, engender hope that a new approach is gaining footing in the European context as well.

For instance, in *Klein v. Slovakia*, a recent case where the application of blasphemy laws was alleged to have resulted in an article 10 violation, the ECtHR appeared to grant a less generous margin of appreciation to the state in pursuing 'the legitimate aim of protection of the rights of other persons whose religious feelings...had been offended by the applicant's article'.[151] The Court actually found in favour of the applicant. In *Mouvement Raelien Suisse v. Switzerland*, the government invoked, as a legitimate aim of its interference with the right to freedom

---

[147] van Dijk and van Hoof, *Theory and Practice of the European Convention on Human Rights*, 3rd ed., at 551.

[148] HRC, *General Comment 34*, para. 48. See also Report of the Special Rapporteur on the promotion and protection of the right to freedom of opinion and expression, Ambeyi Ligabo, UN Doc. A/HRC/7/14, 28 February 2008, paras. 63–66.

[149] Criminal Justice and Immigration Act 2008, s. 79.

[150] Public Order Act 1986, s. 29B(1) as amended by the Racial and Religious Hatred Act 2006.

[151] *Klein v. Slovakia*, Application no. 72208/01, Judgment of 31 October 2006. In cases from 2003 and 2005, the Court had still granted a wide margin of appreciation. See *Murphy v. Ireland*, Application no. 44179/98, Judgment of 10 July 2003, para. 67; *I.A. v. Turkey*, Application no. 42571/98, Judgment of 13 September 2005, para. 25.

of expression of the applicant, the offence to the religious feelings of certain persons.[152] Yet the Grand Chamber drew only marginally on blasphemy related case law and did not portray the situation as a conflict between the right to freedom of expression and the right not to be offended in one's feelings.[153] Outside the context of blasphemy, the ECtHR had to consider in *Jersild v. Denmark* whether the respondent state was in violation of the applicant's right to freedom of expression. The applicant, who was a journalist, had interviewed a group of people in his programme who made racist comments. The question which the court set out to answer was not whether the Danish population or immigrants (to whom the racist comments were addressed) felt offended in their feelings, but whether the journalist's intention was to advocate racial hatred in a programme. It found that the applicant had no such intention, therefore Denmark was in violation of article 10 of the ECHR.[154]

In conclusion, in the absence of a successful application filed by a religious legal entity[155] that has claimed the right not to be offended in its religious feelings, the existence of such a right cannot be inferred. On the contrary, in the light of the EComHR's early finding in *Choudhury v. United Kingdom* where it held that article 9 does not give rise to a positive obligation of the state to protect religious sensitivities of individuals or group of individuals, one is persuaded to deny the existence of such a right for churches and other religious organizations.

The ECtHR's most recent article 10 judgments on racial hatred and, although more timidly, also on blasphemy, step away from a reading of article 9 that takes account of an individual's right not to be offended in her religious feelings, and step towards affirmation of the right not to be subjected to religious hatred. Such a shift would also imply that individuals and organizations themselves have a duty, by virtue of article 10.2, not to advocate religious hatred. The intent and effect of expressions of religious hatred should play a role in the proportionality test

---

[152] *Mouvement Raelien Suisse v. Switzerland*, Application no. 16354/06, Judgment of 13 January 2011, para. 39. It should be noted that no blasphemy accusations were brought in domestic courts, therefore in a sense this case is different from *Otto-Preminger-Institute* and the like.

[153] See specifically the comments of dissenting Judges Sajó, Lazarova Trajkovska and Vučinić, at para 2.1, *Mouvement Raelien Suisse v. Switzerland*, Application no. 16354/06, Grand Chamber, Judgment of 13 July 2012.

[154] *Jersild v. Denmark*, Application no. 15890/89, Judgment of 23 September 1994, para. 33. See also *Erbakan c. Turquie*, Requête no 59405/00, Arrêt du 6 juillet 2006, para. 68; and Center for Inquiry-International (CFI), The European Court of Human Rights and the interpretation of 'advocacy of religious hatred that constitutes incitement to discrimination, hostility or violence', Written Statement, UN Human Rights Council, 10th Session, March 2009, accessed March 2012, http://www.centerforinquiry.net/uploads/attachments/CFI_statement_on_advocacy_of_religious_hatred.pdf.

[155] The *Choudhury v. United Kingdom* case, which was dismissed as manifestly-ill founded by the EComHR, was brought by an individual. Note, however that the right of an *organization* not to be offended in one's religious 'feelings' could have been tested in 2006. A Moroccan national, together with the Moroccan National Consumer Protection League and the Moroccan Child Protection and Family Support Association complained under articles 9, 14, 10, and 17 that Denmark had permitted the publication of what the applicants considered to be offensive caricatures of the Prophet Muhammad. The application was declared inadmissible because the Court saw no jurisdictional link between the three Moroccan applicants and Denmark: *Ben el Mahi and Others v. Denmark*, Application no. 5853/06, Decision of 11 December 2006.

undertaken by the ECtHR. We would argue that this should certainly be the track taken by the ECtHR in future, one consistent with its article 10 jurisprudence with regard to racism. Finally, even the most ardent advocates for the recognition of the rights of non-state actors may feel a philosophical unease with ascribing feelings to legal entities, even religious ones.

2.4. Parental rights under article 2 of Protocol 1 for religious organizations?

Religious education is understandably an issue of great importance for organizations pursuing religious and philosophical objects. On a number of occasions, the European Convention mechanisms have been asked to decide whether religious organizations may rely in their applications on the second sentence in article 2 of Protocol 1 to the ECHR, which affirms the right of parents to ensure the education of their children in conformity with their own religious and philosophical convictions.[156]

The right was first invoked in *Karnell and Hardt v. Sweden*, where a religious legal entity, the Evangelical Lutheran Church in Sweden, was initially the sole applicant, later joined by Mr and Ms Karnell, and Mr and Ms Hard, to complain of a violation of article 2 of Protocol 1. Interestingly:

The applicants claimed that, in the first place, the application should be recognised as being made by the Church as representative of all its members as well as on its own behalf.[157]

In 1970, the King of Sweden denied the request of the applicant church to be authorized to provide religious education in schools. The applicant church had relied inter alia on parental rights under article 2 of Protocol 1. The Swedish legislation provided for the exemption from religious education for children whose parents 'adhere to a faith and concept of life which essentially belongs to a different civilisation than our own. For such parents, almost exclusively immigrants, the form of religious instruction provided in Swedish schools seems alien and difficult to understand.'[158] The complaint before the Commission turned on the issue of exemption from the religious education class, which Sweden was granting only to some children, as noted in the quotation. The case was never discussed on its merits, because the parties reached an agreement that granted an exemption from religious education in public schools to children belonging to the Evangelical Lutheran Church. It also made the parents of the exempted children responsible for providing them with a religious education that, while accommodating religious differences, was comparable to the one provided for in public schools.[159] Before the parties reached this amicable agreement, the EComHR had the opportunity

---

[156] ECHR, Protocol 1, art. 2.

[157] *Karnell and Hardt v. Sweden*, Application no 4733/71, 14 Yearbook of the ECHR (1971), at 686.

[158] *Karnell and Hardt v. Sweden*, at 670.

[159] See Report of the Commission of 28 May 1973, *Karnell and Hardt v. Sweden*, Application no 4733/71, http://skola.gr8.se/dokument/Juridik/EU%20Court%20cases/KARNELL%20AND%20 HARDT%20v.%20SWEDEN.pdf, at 1–2.

to pronounce itself on admissibility and held that the application was inadmissible 'insofar as it has been brought by the Church itself, the Church being incapable of having or exercising the rights mentioned in Art. 2 of Protocol No.1'[160] No further explanation as to why a church would not be capable of enjoying the right was given.

This position was maintained by the EComHR in *Ingrid Jordebo Foundation of Christian Schools and Ingrid Jordebo v. Sweden*, where Mrs Jordebo was applying as a parent alongside a legal entity that she headed. Although the representation link may arguably be more obvious in this case, the EComHR held that the complaint could only be examined in so far as it was brought by Mrs Jordebo, i.e. an individual and parent.

The Foundation cannot claim to be a 'victim' of a breach of Article 2 of Protocol no. 1 within the meaning of Article 25 of the Convention. Insofar as this complaint is brought by the Foundation it follows that the complaint is incompatible *ratione personae* with the provisions of the Convention and must be rejected...[161]

Even when the applicant is an individual the bar is very high with respect to parental rights in terms of representation before international mechanisms. The HRC's approach in *Erkki Hartikainen v. Finland* is relevant in this context. Mr Hartikainen, a Finnish schoolteacher, submitted a communication 'on his own behalf and also in his capacity as General Secretary of the Union of Free Thinkers in Finland and on behalf of other alleged victims, members of the Union'.[162] He claimed that Finnish education law was in violation of article 18.4 of the ICCPR,[163] given that it stipulated obligatory attendance to classes on the history of religion and on ethics— including by children whose parents were atheists—and the textbooks used for instruction were religious in nature.[164] The HRC refused to accept the communication in so far as it had been submitted by the author 'in his capacity as General Secretary of the Union of Free Thinkers in Finland',[165] instead, he had to provide a list of names and addresses of persons he claimed to represent, together with proof of his authority to act on their behalf.

As the text of article 2 of Protocol 1 clearly stipulates, parental rights are to be exercised by parents; the lack of capacity of an organization with religious or philosophical aims to claim this right before the Strasbourg mechanisms stems from its

---

[160] *Karnell and Hardt v. Sweden*, at 686.

[161] *Ingrid Jordebo Foundation of Christian Schools and Ingrid Jordebo v. Sweden*, Application No. 11533/85, Decision of 6 March 1987, EComHR, Decisions and Reports, vol. 51, para. 128.

[162] *Erkki Hartikainen v. Finland*, Communication No. 40/1978, UN Doc. CCPR/C/OP/1 (1984), para. 1.

[163] Article 18.4 of the ICCPR reads: 'the States Parties to the present Covenant undertake to have respect for the liberty of parents and, when applicable, legal guardians to ensure the religious and moral education of their children in conformity with their own convictions.'

[164] *Erkki Hartikainen v. Finland*, Communication No. 40/1978, UN Doc. CCPR/C/OP/1 (1984), para. 2.1.

[165] *Erkki Hartikainen v. Finland*, paras. 3 and 4.

nature as a legal entity and its incapacity to be a parent. The clearest articulation of this point by the ECtHR was in *Savez crkava 'Riječ života' and Others v. Croatia*.

The Court reiterates that solely the members of a religious community, as individuals, can claim to be victims of a violation of the right to marry or the right to education, rights which by their nature are not susceptible of being exercised by a religious community itself. Therefore, the applicant churches as religious communities cannot themselves allege a violation of either of these rights...[166]

Another important aspect should be mentioned at this point. The right of parents to ensure the education of their children in conformity with their religion and philosophical convictions differs from the right of individuals to manifest their religion. There is no collective aspect of the parental right, as such, the right of a church to speak on children's religious education cannot be derived in the same manner that church autonomy was derived from collective religious freedom. In addition, one would be inclined to deny that article 2 of Protocol 1 could be interpreted in that sense, if a coherent reading with the provisions of the Convention on the Rights of the Child (CRC) is sought. In the architecture of the CRC, the child is a full subject of rights and parental direction of a child's exercise of her right to freedom of religious education shall be 'in a manner consistent with the evolving capacities of the child'.[167] Were the right to be transferred, in some sense, from the parent (proximate) to the church (more distant and with more complex interests), there would be a serious risk that the voice of the child would not be properly heard.

The consistent denial of parental rights to associations with religious and philosophical objects may have prompted a reassessment of the utility of entering such claims. In the context of two sister applications before the ECtHR and the HRC, the Norwegian Humanist Association withdrew its application, initially made alongside 9 parents and children in *Ingebjørg Folgerø and Others against Norway*,[168] and may have been discouraged from joining the petitioner parents and children in *Leirvåg et al. v. Norway*.[169]

But why have religious organizations been interested in the first place in asserting parental rights, given that the text of article 2 of Protocol 1, indicating who holds the right, is very clear? It is submitted that considerations related to strategic litigation may provide part of the explanation. As such, in *Karnell and Hardt v. Sweden*, the religious organization sought a solution not for a particular parent and her child but for a community of faith; arguing that it represented the Evangelical Lutheran community of parents, the church attempted to obtain a general exemption for all pupils of this faith, as well as the right to provide instruction itself.

---

[166] *Savez crkava 'Riječ života' and Others v. Croatia*, Application no. 7798/08, Judgment of 9 December 2010, para. 125.

[167] CRC, para. 14.2. See also van Bueren, *The International Law on the Rights of the Child*, at 159.

[168] *Ingebjørg Folgerø and Others v. Norway*, Application no. 15472/02, Partial Decision of 26 October 2004.

[169] *Leirvåg and Others v. Norway*, Communication No. 1155/2003, CCPR/C/82/D/1155/2003 (2004).

The Evangelical Lutheran Church of Sweden in this case, and other associations in other cases, may have attempted to invoke article 2 of Protocol 1, as opposed to freedom to manifest religion under article 9, given that, arguably, the former belong to the *forum internum*; parental rights to ensure religious and philosophical education in accordance with their convictions are thus 'intended to be free of limitation' and the Convention mechanisms would be barred from providing discretion to states on such matters.[170] Be that as it may, the EComHR and the ECtHR consistently denied that churches could act as a representative of parents in the way they sought, and affirmed that rights under article 1 of Protocol 2 were attributed solely to parents.

While not having the capacity to claim parental rights under the second sentence of article 1, Protocol 2, religious organizations have assumed another role before the Strasbourg Court. In the *Lautsi* case, where a mother and two children complained that the display of a crucifix in the classroom of a public Italian school violated their rights under article 2 of Protocol 1 and article 9 and 14 of the ECHR, five organizations with religious and humanist aims were given leave to intervene in the written procedure.[171] Given the 'physical' impossibility of exercising parental rights, the position of *amicus curiae* may be an appropriate position for a religious organization seeking to advance its interests in legal proceedings.

In conclusion, it should be noted that the second sentence of article 2, Protocol 1 'in addition to [establishing a] primarily negative undertaking, implies some positive obligation on the part of the State.'[172] In *Campbell and Cosans v. the United Kingdom*, the respondent government was found to have violated article 2 of Protocol 1, because it had disrespected the convictions of the two applicants who did not want their children subjected to corporal punishment as a disciplinary measure in their schools in Scotland. The word 'respect' implied positive obligations and the government's policy to move gradually towards the abolition of corporal punishment fell short of meeting those obligations.[173] The question is whether, in the context of parental rights, such positive obligations of the state extend to private/independent school systems and therefore impose an obligation

---

[170] See in particular Taylor, who critically analyses case law of the European mechanisms on article 2, Protocol 1 and contrasts it to decisions of the HRC on article 18.4 and to General Comment 22, para 8. Taylor, *Freedom of Religion: UN and European Human Rights Law and Practice*, at 162–182, and citation at 177. Others assert that the right is 'substantive, yet of a limited nature'. Evans, *Religious Liberty and International Law in Europe*, at 354–355. In contrast to doctrine, in a recent case where a parent invoked article 2, Protocol 1, the Grand Chamber asserted that states enjoy a wide margin of appreciation 'in determining the steps to be taken to ensure compliance with the Convention with due regard to the needs and resources of the community and of individuals'. Therefore strategic considerations (based on a presumed *forum internum*) which may determine applicants to bring a case under article 2, Protocol 1, instead of article 9 may be frustrated. *Lautsi and Others v. Italy*, Application no. 30814/06, Grand Chamber, Judgment of 18 March 2011, para. 61.

[171] *Lautsi and Others v. Italy*, Application no. 30814/06, Grand Chamber, Judgment of 18 March 2011, paras. 51, 52 and 55.

[172] *Campbell and Cosans v. the United Kingdom*, Application nos. 7511/76; 7743/76, Judgment of 25 February 1982, para. 37.

[173] *Campbell and Cosans v. the United Kingdom*, para. 37.a.

on religious schools to eschew corporal punishment? This issue did not arise before the ECtHR under article 2 of Protocol 1.[174]

The issue was brought before the House of Lords in a reverse fashion. Teachers of four Christian schools, and parents, supported use of corporal punishment and objected to the statutory ban that had applied to both public and private (independent) schools since 1998.[175] The Law Lords found that the ban on corporal punishment did not represent a violation of the right of teachers and parents to manifest their religion, nor of the rights of parents under article 2 of Protocol 1. As a result, one could argue that, in the UK, religious schools have an obligation not to use corporal punishment. The House of Lords drew inter alia on the famous case of *Christian Education South Africa v. Minister of Education*. Certainly, a different historical context informed Judge Sachs' analysis, and the constitutional provisions were different to article 9 and article 2 of Protocol 1, yet the case centred around a similar issue.[176] Judge Sachs' thoughtful legal examination masterfully concludes with a statement of the obligation that religious schools and parents have in South Africa's democracy.

I do not wish to be understood as underestimating in any way the very special meaning that corporal correction in school has for the self-definition and ethos of the religious community in question. Yet their schools of necessity function in the public domain so as to prepare their learners for life in the broader society. Just as it is not unduly burdensome to oblige them to accommodate themselves as schools to secular norms regarding health and safety, payment of rates and taxes, planning permissions and fair labour practices, and just as they are obliged to respect national examination standards, so is it not unreasonable to expect them to make suitable adaptations to non-discriminatory laws that impact on their codes of discipline. The parents are not being obliged to make an absolute and strenuous choice between obeying a law of the land or following their conscience. They can do both simultaneously. What they are prevented from doing is to authorise teachers, acting in their name and on school premises, to fulfill what they regard as their conscientious and biblically-ordained responsibilities for the guidance of their children. Similarly, save for this one aspect, the appellant's schools are not prevented from maintaining their specific Christian ethos.[177]

To summarize, Part II of this study has found that, like any other legal entities in the European human rights system, religious organizations enjoy the rights to fair

---

[174] It did arise in the context of articles 3, 8 and 13 in a private school setting in *Costello-Roberts v. the United Kingdom*, Application no. 13134/87, Judgment of 25 March 1993. Contrast with *A. v. the United Kingdom* in the confines of the child's home: *A. v. the United Kingdom*, Application no. 25599/94, Judgment of 23 September 1998.

[175] *Regina v. Secretary of State for Education and Employment and others (Respondents) ex parte Williamson (Appellant) and others* [2005] UKHL 15.

[176] Christian Education of South Africa, representing 196 independent Christian schools, complained that the ban on corporal punishment introduced in 1996 through the South African Schools Act violated the right of parents to freedom of religion, the right to establish independent schools, the right to participate in the cultural life of their choice, and the right to enjoy their culture and to practice their religion. *Christian Education South Africa v. Minister of Education*, CCT4/00 [2000], Decision of 18 August 2000, paras. 67–68.

[177] *Christian Education South Africa v. Minister of Education*, CCT4/00 [2000], Decision of 18 August 2000, para. 51.

trial and to an effective remedy, freedom of expression, freedom of association and assembly, and the right to property. It has also been shown that organizations with religious and philosophical objects may enjoy and claim feedom of religion under article 9, as a derivation from the right of individuals to collectively manifest religion. Considerable doubt was expressed that religious organizations have a right not to be offended in their religious feelings. Finally, religious bodies do not enjoy parental rights under article 2 of Protocol 1.

III. Positive Obligations of States and the Responsibilities of Religious Organizations in the Context of Church Autonomy

We turn in this part to the substantive protection which article 9 affords to religious organizations and the limitations on their conduct. Whereas the European Convention is silent on the right to autonomy of a religious organization, the jurisprudence of the EComHR and ECtHR provides ample evidence of the existence of such a right, inferred from article 9 and read in conjunction with article 11.[178] In this study we argue that the right to church autonomy is derived from the right of individuals to collectively manifest religion; the aim here is to analyse the interplay between the limitations on church autonomy and the positive obligations of states in this context, and examine the scope of the obligations of religious organizations that can be inferred from the latter.

A growing literature on the obligations of non-state actors under the ECHR reveals four important aspects that should be mentioned at this stage. First, non-state actors can infringe the Convention rights of other non-state actors. Influential analyses have been proposed to prove this assertion as a point of departure for establishing the scope of the obligations of non-state actors under the ECHR.[179] At the same time, this acknowledgement is a matter of inverse logic: if states have positive obligations to prevent and punish human rights abuse by non-state actors, non-state actors can and do violate human rights.[180]

Second, in an attempt to ensure the effectiveness of the Convention rights, the ECHR mechanisms have sought to develop the positive obligations of states to protect the human rights of individuals from interference by non-state actors, 'to the point where virtually all the standard-setting provisions of the Convention now have a dual aspect in terms of their requirements, one negative and the other positive'.[181] Pursuant to this, state responsibility arises if a contracting party to

---

[178] In *Hasan and Chaush*, the Court has expressly found that the right to 'organizational autonomy' of a religious community is protected by article 9 of the ECHR. *Hasan and Chaush v. Bulgaria*, Application no. 30985/96, Judgment of 26 October 2000, para. 104.

[179] See in particular Clapham, *Human Rights Obligations of Non-State Actors*, at 349–420; D. Spielmann, 'Obligations positives et effet horizontal des dispositions de la Convention', in F. Sudre (ed.), *L'interprétation de la Convention Européenne des droits de l'homme*, (Bruxelles: Bruylant, 1998), 133–174, at 152.

[180] Spielmann, 'Obligations positives et effet horizontal des dispositions de la Convention', at 134.

[181] Akandji-Kombe, *Positive Obligations under the European Convention on Human Rights*, at 9.

the ECHR does not take the legal or administrative measures to prevent a human rights violation by a non-state actor or fails to provide for effective remedies in the event of a violation.[182]

Third, the theory of positive obligations underpins the move towards extending the scope of the Convention to private relationships between individuals and legal entities (in other words, the horizontal effect theory).[183] Various authors caution however that 'the ability of the national judge to apply the Convention in disputes between private parties may depend on the terms of the incorporating legislation';[184] in turn, this variance in national legal orders gives rise to situations where non-state actors are able to enforce their Convention rights against other non-state actors in some countries, whereas in other domestic jurisdictions this is more difficult.[185]

The fourth aspect underlined by scholars is that the case law of the Strasbourg mechanisms on positive obligations of states reveals the scope of obligations of non-state actors.[186] The rich vein of jurisprudence on church autonomy, and its most recent developments, throws light on the scope of obligations that religious organizations incur under the ECHR. It is this aspect which takes centre-stage in the remainder of the chapter.

As to the structure of this part: first, the right to church autonomy is defined and the rationale behind it examined; second, the early jurisprudence of the EComHR and recent case law of the ECtHR is analysed, to clarify the limits of church autonomy, the positive obligations of states and the duties of religious entities that can be inferred from them.

1. The right to religious autonomy

The concept of church autonomy or religious autonomy refers to the right of a religious organization to govern, administer, or organize its own affairs, generally in the following domains: legislative (the promulgation of religious law, the acquisition of legal personality, the setting up of schools, hospitals or other associations, the owning of property); administrative and ministerial (the formulation and implementation of policy, proclamation of the faith in teaching and practice, designation of religious leadership and employment of staff); and matters of adjudication (the running of an ecclesiastic courts system).[187] The degree of autonomy,

---

[182] Akandji-Kombe, *Positive Obligations under the European Convention on Human Rights*, at 14; White and Ovey, *The European Convention on Human Rights*, 5th ed., at 100.

[183] The horizontal effect is defined as 'the extent to which the Convention itself can create obligations for individuals and private entities (non-state actors) which may be justiciable in the internal legal orders of the states parties to the Convention'. Clapham, *Human Rights Obligations of Non-State Actors*, at 349. See also Akandji-Kombe, *Positive Obligations under the European Convention on Human Rights*, at 14–15; and various authors engaging with the question in D. Oliver and J. Fedtke (eds.), *Human Rights and the Private Sphere: A Comparative Study*, (New York: Routledge, 2007).

[184] Clapham, *Human Rights Obligations of Non-State Actors*, at 350.

[185] Clapham, *Human Rights Obligations of Non-State Actors*, at 350 and 437–440; van Dijk and van Hoof, *Theory and Practice of the European Convention on Human Rights*, 3rd ed., at 24.

[186] See in particular Clapham, *Human Rights Obligations of Non-State Actors*, at 352.

[187] See Doe, *Law and Religion in Europe: A Comparative Introduction*, at 114–138; D. Laycock, '"The Things that are not Caesar's: Religious Organizations as a Check on the Authoritarian

and exactly what each domain of self-administration covers, varies according to the relationship between the state and religion concerned (state religion, state church or established church; cooperation or accommodation; separation).[188] This relationship is influenced by history, politics, and social expectations of the state, among other factors.[189]

Notwithstanding the variety of the state-religion relationships and their contextuality, the concept of church autonomy is enshrined in one form or another in the legislation of many states and also developed through national case law.[190] It is sufficient to provide some examples here. For instance, in Germany the *Grundgesetz* (Basic Law) includes a disestablishment clause which stipulates that '[t]here shall be no state church'.[191] Church autonomy is also enshrined in constitutional law, which provides that 'religious societies shall regulate and administer their affairs independently within the limits of the law that applies to all'.[192] One author asserts that the separation of church and state has not prevented Germany from entering into a 'rather sophisticated partnership with religions'.[193] Other scholars see this partnership as a 'limping separation', which was established during the Weimar Republic against the background of a long period of mutual influence between church and state.[194] This cooperation arrangement is illustrated by the collection of an ecclesiastical tax from adherents by the state on behalf of those religious organizations that have the status of a 'corporation under the public law'.[195] As a result, Germany's constitutional provisions regarding the relationship between the state and religion should not be perceived to surgically separate them. The *Grundgesetz* sought rather to achieve a neutral form of cooperation between the state and various religions.

The Romanian Constitution stipulates that 'religious cults shall be free and organized in accordance to their own statutes under the terms laid down by law', and that they are 'autonomous from the state, while enjoying the support of the state, including through the facilitation of religious service in the army, hospital,

---

Pretensions of the State": Church Autonomy Revisited', 7 *Georgetown Journal of Law and Public Policy* (2009), 253–278, at 254; Leigh, 'Balancing Religious Autonomy and Other Human Rights under the European Convention', at 112–113.

[188] See Doe, *Law and Religion in Europe: A Comparative Introduction*, at 116–117.

[189] C. Evans and A. Hood, 'Religious Autonomy and Labour Law: A Comparison of the Jurisprudence of the United States and the European Court of Human Rights', *Oxford Journal of Law and Religion* (2012), 1–27, at 14; Temperman, *State-Religion Relationships and Human Rights Law: Towards a Right to Religiously Neutral Governance*, at 131–132.

[190] Doe, *Law and Religion in Europe: A Comparative Introduction*, at 116.

[191] Deutscher Bundestag, Basic Law for the Federal Republic of Germany, as at October 2010, accessed March 2012, https://www.btg-bestellservice.de/pdf/80201000.pdf, art. 137.1.

[192] Basic Law for the Federal Republic of Germany, art. 137.3.

[193] Temperman, *State-Religion Relationships and Human Rights Law: Towards a Right to Religiously Neutral Governance*, at 132.

[194] The term used is 'hinkende Trennung'. J. Ziegler, '"Die Gleichheit aller » versus « die Individualität eines jeden". Das Prinzip der Trennung von Kirche und Staat in Deutschland und Frankreich im Spiegel der Kopftuchdebatte', in F. Heidenreich, J. C. Merle and W. Vogel (eds.), *Staat und Religion in Frankreich und Deutschland/L'Etat et la religion en France et en Allemagne*, (Berlin: LIT Verlag, 2008), 158–175, at 159–160.

[195] See note 194. See also Temperman, *State-Religion Relationships and Human Rights Law: Towards a Right to Religiously Neutral Governance*, at 132.

prison facilities, retirement homes and orphanages'.[196] Recognized cults enjoy fiscal facilities and, importantly, support towards the costs of the salaries of clerics, auxiliary personnel, and teachers of religious education in schools.[197] While church and state have been separate in Romania since 1989, the relationship is one of cooperation, and complex political underpinnings in particular concern the Romanian Orthodox Church, the denomination of the majority population. Lavinia Stan and Lucian Turcescu place the contemporary relationship between religion and state in the context of Romania's communist past.

Under the communist regime [the Romanian Orthodox] Church and [the] state established a *modus vivendi* which allowed the Church to be enlisted as an unconditional supporter of communist policies in return for the government's toleration of a certain level of ecclesiastical activity.... Compared with other religious denominations the Romanian Orthodox Church had indeed a privileged position, but continued to be only a privileged servant of the state.[198]

In the United Kingdom church autonomy is not stipulated by law: While 'there is no systematic provision made for the autonomy of churches...in the main, a self-denying ordinance of neutrality predominates'.[199] UK courts have established that '[a] Court of Law will not interfere with the rules of a voluntary religious association unless to protect some civil right or interest which is said to be infringed by their operation'.[200] It is said that the reluctance of the courts to interfere with self-administration of the various religious organizations has been given expression in section 13 of the Human Rights Act 1998, albeit its effect in giving emphasis to religious freedom remains contested.[201] The Human Rights Act has certain consequences for religious organizations, in particular the established Church of England that could find itself in a vulnerable position.[202] For instance, the Measures (which the Church of England uses to legislate) are considered under the Act as primary legislation and consequently they are to be interpreted in a manner which is compatible with ECHR rights.[203] As discussed in section II.1 of this chapter, the Church of England 'remains an essentially religious organisation'

---

[196] Constituția României, modificată și completată prin Legea de revizuire a Constituției României nr. 429/2003, publicată în Monitorul Oficial al României, Partea I, nr. 758 din 29 octombrie 2003 (2003), arts. 27.3 and 27.5 (own translation).

[197] Asociatia pentru Apărarea Drepturilor Omului în România—Comitetul Helsinki, *Stat și religii în România: o relație transparentă?*, București, 2008.

[198] L. Stan and L. Turcescu, 'The Romanian Orthodox Church and Post-Communist Democratisation', 52 *Europe-Asia Studies* 8 (2000) 1467–1488, at 1468 and 1470.

[199] M. Hill, 'Church Autonomy in the United Kingdom', in G. Robbers (ed.), *Church Autonomy: A Comparative Survey*, (Frankfurt am Main: Peter Land, 2001), 267–283, at 267.

[200] Doe, *Law and Religion in Europe: A Comparative Introduction*, at 125.

[201] M. Hill, *Interpreting the European Convention on Human Rights in the United Kingdom Courts: The Impact for Religious Organisations*, European Consortium for Church and State Research, Cyprus, November 2007, at 4. See also II.1 in this chapter.

[202] M. Hill, 'The Permissible Scope of the Legal Limitations on the Freedom of Religion or Belief in the United Kingdom', 19 *Emory Int'l L. Rev* (2005) 1129–1185, at 1144.

[203] M. Hill, *Interpreting the European Convention on Human Rights in the United Kingdom Courts: The Impact for Religious Organisations*, at 2–3.

rather than a governmental one,[204] although when components of the Church (or other religious organizations in the UK) are 'hybrid public authorities' that exercise governmental functions, human rights might be enforced against them under the Act.[205] Finally, 'to the extent that a court is itself a public authority, prohibited from acting in a way incompatible with Convention rights, such rights will fall to be considered in resolving private disputes between individual litigants', including when religious organizations are concerned.[206]

1.1. The scope of religious autonomy

Given that church autonomy is sanctioned by legislation or jurisprudence in many European states, there is a question about how it has developed in the ECHR system, especially in the absence of an express provision in the Convention. According to Norman Doe, church autonomy is mainly justified by the collective right of individuals to manifest their religion.[207] Indeed, in *Hasan and Chaush v. Bulgaria*, the ECtHR anchors church autonomy in article 9, read in the light of article 11. The court held:

Where the organisation of the religious community is at issue, Article 9 of the Convention must be interpreted in the light of Article 11, which safeguards associative life against unjustified State interference. Seen in this perspective, the believers' right to freedom of religion encompasses the expectation that the community will be allowed to function peacefully, free from arbitrary State intervention. Indeed, the autonomous existence of religious communities is indispensable for pluralism in a democratic society and is thus an issue at the very heart of the protection which Article 9 affords. It directly concerns not only the organisation of the community as such but also the effective enjoyment of the right to freedom of religion by all its active members. Were the organisational life of the community not protected by Article 9 of the Convention, all other aspects of the individual's freedom of religion would become vulnerable.[208]

It is clear that in the eyes of the ECtHR religious autonomy represents a guarantee of pluralism, the latter being a principal value of democratic society,[209] therefore, not only traditional religions should enjoy this autonomy but all denominations, old or new. The ECtHR has prompted an inclusive transformation of the concept of church autonomy: the privilege of self-administration, traditionally granted to

---

[204] *Parochial Church Council of the Parish of Aston Cantlow and Wilmcote with Billesley, Warwickshire (Appellants) v Wallbank and another (Respondents)* [2003] UKHL 37, para. 13.

[205] M. Hill, *Interpreting the European Convention on Human Rights in the United Kingdom Courts: The Impact for Religious Organisations*, at 5.

[206] M. Hill, *Interpreting the European Convention on Human Rights in the United Kingdom Courts: The Impact for Religious Organisations*, at 3.

[207] Doe, *Law and Religion in Europe: A Comparative Introduction*, at 117–120.

[208] *Hasan and Chaush v. Bulgaria*, Application no. 30985/96, Judgment of 26 October 2000, para. 62.

[209] Christopher McCrudden observes that 'guaranteeing freedom of religion was seen as a means of maintaining civil peace' and that the origin of the idea 'dates at least from the need to resolve the religious wars in Europe that scarred much of the seventeenth and eighteenth centuries'. C. McCrudden, 'Multiculturalism, Freedom of Religion, Equality, and the British Constitution: The JFS Case Considered', 9 *International Journal of Constitutional Law* 1 (2011), 200–229, at 222.

a specific church by virtue of historic affinities with the state, has become the right of all religious organizations.

The Court has found arbitrary state interference in the religious autonomy of organizations in a number of cases, which in turn has thrown light on the scope of the right to church autonomy. In the *Hasan v. Chaush* case, where Bulgarian authorities had replaced the leadership of the Bulgarian Muslim community, the ECtHR found 'that the leadership of the faction led by Mr. Hasan were unable to mount an effective challenge to the unlawful State interference in the internal affairs of the religious community and to assert their right to organisational autonomy, as protected by Article 9 of the Convention'.[210] The Court has also held different governments to be in violation of religious autonomy when they intervened in the internal leadership dispute in the Bulgarian Orthodox Church;[211] denied re-registration as a legal entity to the Moscow Branch of the Salvation Army[212] and the Church of Scientology of Moscow;[213] dissolved the religious community of Jehovah's Witnesses of Moscow and refused re-registration;[214] and denied recognition to the Metropolitan Church of Bessarabia.[215] In many of these cases, the violations concerned religious associations that were not the church of the majority population:[216] in other words, the right to religious autonomy has functioned to protect newer or non-dominant religious communities.

It is evident from the ECtHR's judgments that it grounds church autonomy in the collective right of individuals to manifest religion. In the European system, religious autonomy is therefore the exclusive right of entities akin to a church, whether unincorporated or incorporated. In respect of incorporated organizations, this conclusion is supported by the fact that article 9 can be exercised and relied upon only by legal entities with religious or philosophical objects.

The question that arises is whether religious autonomy is a qualified right under the ECHR. From a legal standpoint, the existence of a *forum internum* of religious autonomy defined as an 'untouchable... sphere which is completely (theoretically)

---

[210] *Hasan and Chaush v. Bulgaria*, Application no. 30985/96, Judgment of 26 October 2000, para. 104.

[211] *Holy Synod of the Bulgarian Orthodox Church (Metropolitan Inokentiy) et al. v. Bulgaria*, Applications nos. 412/03 and 35677/04, Judgment of 22 January 2009.

[212] *Moscow Branch of the Salvation Army v. Russia*, Application No. 72881/01, Judgment of 5 October 2006.

[213] *Church of Scientology Moscow v. Russia*, Application no. 18147/02, Judgment of 5 April 2007.

[214] *Jehovah's Witnesses of Moscow v. Russia*, Application no. 302/02, Judgment of 10 June 2010.

[215] *Metropolitan Church of Bessarabia and Others v. Moldova*, Application no. 45701/99, Judgment of 13 December 2001.

[216] In this context, it deserves mention that most of the respondent countries were part of the former communist bloc, where the Orthodox religion (as the religion of the majority population) resurfaced strongly after the fall of atheist communism and where the entanglement of religion with the state is complex. Giovanni Barberini notes that 'as a general rule these former Communist countries adopt a line of defence, at times hostile, that particularly manifests itself in the procedures for legal recognition.... New religions are considered to be unknown subjects and interlocutors and therefore also potential factors of destabilization, strangers to the culture and to the tradition of the nation, within a democratic system still fragile and not experienced in pluralism.' G. Barberini, 'Religious Freedom in the Process of Democratization of Central and Eastern European States', in S. Ferrari, C. W. Durham and E. A. Sewell (eds.), *Law and Religion in Post-Communist Europe*, (Leuven: Peeters, 2003), 7–22, at 19.

shielded off from State interference'[217] is not supported. As already underlined, the right originates in the individuals' right to collectively manifest religion, which is qualified under article 9.2; moreover, reading article 9 in the light of freedom of association, which again is a qualified right, also speaks for the absence of an unrestricted *forum internum*. These are unmistakable indicia that church autonomy covers solely a *forum externum* that in turn is not absolute.

Various works of scholars support the assertion just made.[218] Merlin Kiviorg, for instance, examined which areas receive absolute protection in practice and are therefore able to exclude any interference on the part of states. First, she attempted to delineate a set of issues that may be deemed exclusively internal to the religious organization; second, she tried to identify fully-protected core areas, by comparing practices in several European countries; and, finally, she started from the premise that, in a particular context, what falls within the competence of religious communities is already known.[219] Kiviorg's conclusion doubts the existence of a *forum internum* of religious autonomy. She observed that in practice it is possible to identify areas where religious communities have 'broad, but not absolute autonomy'; conversely:

One could argue that at the collective level everything constitutes a manifestation of religion or belief—whether by individuals collectively, or by an institution finding its legitimacy (in human rights terms) in the collective will/choice of individuals. If everything at the collective level constitutes a manifestation of religion or belief, then it should be subject to limitations under Article 9 (2).[220]

Although it lacks a *forum internum* and is not absolute, church autonomy has received a high degree of protection in the European system. The ECtHR has championed a two-pronged approach to the protection of church autonomy. First, religious organizations are granted wide discretion to interpret their religion, and thereby to identify what is central to its manifestation:

[b]ut for very exceptional cases, the right to freedom of religion as guaranteed under the Convention excludes any discretion on the part of the State to determine whether religious beliefs or the means used to express such beliefs are legitimate.[221]

In effect, as put in *Svyato-Mykhaylivska Parafiya v. Ukraine* case: '[t]he State's duty of neutrality and impartiality, as defined in the Court's case law, is incompatible with any power on the State's part to assess the legitimacy of religious beliefs'.[222]

---

[217] M. Kiviorg, 'Collective Religious Autonomy under the European Convention on Human Rights: the UK Jewish Free School Case in International Perspective', 40 *EUI Working Paper* (2010), 1–14, at 4.

[218] See Doe, *Law and Religion in Europe: A Comparative Introduction,* at 114–137.

[219] M. Kiviorg, 'Religious Autonomy in the ECHR', IV *Derecho y Religión* (2009), 131–144, at 135–137; Kiviorg, 'Collective Religious Autonomy under the European Convention on Human Rights: the UK Jewish Free School Case in International Perspective', at 4–7.

[220] Kiviorg, 'Collective Religious Autonomy under the European Convention on Human Rights: the UK Jewish Free School Case in International Perspective', at 4 and 7.

[221] *Hasan and Chaush v. Bulgaria*, Application no. 30985/96, Judgment of 26 October 2000, para. 78.

[222] *Svyato-Mykhaylivska Parafiya v. Ukraine*, Application no. 77703/01, Judgment of 14 June 2007, para. 13.

Second, limitations to church autonomy must be construed strictly.[223] It is sensible to expect that church autonomy is subjected to the same restrictions that are placed on individuals' right to manifest religion collectively, since religious autonomy receives protection under article 9 of the ECHR. Those limitations should be prescribed by law; pursue one of the legitimate aims of protecting public safety, public order, health, or morals, or protecting the rights and freedoms of others; and be necessary in a democratic society, which invariably includes a measure of proportionality. Thus, this second element of the ECtHR's two-pronged approach requires that the state may limit the right only when it pursues legitimate aims and its interference is proportional.

This approach of the ECtHR functions satisfactorily in those cases where a state is required to abstain from interfering with church autonomy. For instance, in *Manoussakis and Others v. Greece*, the Court granted a narrow margin of appreciation to the state. The applicants, Jehovah's Witnesses, were prosecuted and convicted for having operated a place of worship under a private agreement, lacking the specific authorization required by law. While acknowledging the discretion that it accords to states as a matter of principle, the ECtHR asserted that, in defining the width of the margin of appreciation in the present case, 'it must have regard to what is at stake, namely the need to secure true religious pluralism, an inherent feature of the notion of a democratic society'.[224] Declaring that the right to freedom of religion 'excludes any discretion on the part of the State to determine whether religious beliefs or the means used to express such beliefs are legitimate',[225] the ECtHR concluded that national legislation has been utilized 'to impose rigid, or indeed prohibitive, conditions on practice of religious beliefs by certain non-Orthodox movements, in particular Jehovah's Witnesses'.[226] Finally, it found that the conviction of the applicants was neither proportionate to the legitimate aim pursued, nor necessary in a democratic society, and therefore there had been a violation of the right to religious freedom.[227] It would appear that the Court is less inclined to accord wide discretion when a state interferes with the autonomy of a religious organization, in particular with matters of liturgy and the appointment of religious leaders.[228]

The situation becomes more complex however (as we shall see) when the state is faced with a conflict between the right of a church to self-organize and the rights of others, and in such cases must act to protect the rights of the latter. When, for example, a church's interpretations of religion result in regulations that impair the very substance of an employee's human rights, it becomes clear

---

[223] *Svyato-Mykhaylivska Parafiya v. Ukraine*, para. 114.

[224] *Manoussakis and Others v. Greece*, Application no. 18748/91, Judgment of 26 September 1996, para. 44.

[225] In *Hasan and Chaush*, it qualifies this statement by introducing the phrase 'but for very exceptional cases'. *Hasan and Chaush v. Bulgaria*, Application no. 30985/96, Judgment of 26 October 2000, para. 78.

[226] *Manoussakis and Others v. Greece*, para. 48.

[227] *Manoussakis and Others v. Greece*, para. 53.

[228] See *Hasan and Chaush v. Bulgaria*, Application no. 30985/96, Judgment of 26 October 2000.

that a state's inaction is unjustified. We shall argue that the best defence against interventionism by secular courts in matters of religious interpretation is for religious organizations themselves to acknowledge their human rights obligations and interpret religion accordingly. To support this assertion, the next section will show that the jurisprudence of the ECtHR asserts positive obligations for states, from which one can discern the obligations of religious organizations under the ECHR.

2. Positive state obligations and the responsibilities of religious organizations

In a number of cases, mostly but not exclusively related to employment matters, the EComHR and the ECtHR have been asked to clarify the limits of church autonomy. These cases centre on conflicts between the right to autonomy of religious organizations and the human rights of others. Ian Leigh explains the stakes involved in the following terms:

Claims that the collective interests of the religious body should take priority in these cases are often represented in contemporary public debate as 'special pleading' or exceptionalism, with the organization cast in the role of the human rights oppressor. However, this is to over-simplify since the collective right of the organization in these cases can also be seen as an aggregation of the rights of its individual members to compose themselves into a like-minded association. From this perspective denial of the ability for religious organizations, for example, to exclude those who do not share their beliefs or values diminishes the freedom of the individual members who do subscribe to the beliefs or values in question. Of course this does not entail that the group's interests should always prevail but it does mean that human rights arguments must be counted on both sides of the legal equation...[229]

The approach of the Strasbourg mechanisms was to establish the positive obligations of states in cases where the right to religious autonomy conflicted with the rights of others. These state obligations disclose that procedural and substantive limitations[230] apply to religious autonomy, which in turn help to reveal the responsibilities of religious organizations themselves under the ECHR.

This section focuses first on the early case law of the EComHR on church autonomy. Subsequently, this will be contrasted to recent jurisprudence of the ECtHR, to emphasize the evolution of the Strasbourg's mechanisms' understanding of the limitations applicable to the right to church autonomy. Cases where procedural and substantive limitations of church autonomy have been asserted will be examined, to clarify the state's obligations and the duties of churches and other religious non-state actors.

---

[229] Leigh, 'Balancing Religious Autonomy and Other Human Rights under the European Convention', at 110–111.

[230] This typology is proposed in Evans and Hood, 'Religious Autonomy and Labour Law: A Comparison of the Jurisprudence of the United States and the European Court of Human Rights', at 19 and 21.

2.1. *The principle of voluntariness as the sole limitation to church autonomy in the early case law of the EComHR*

Based on the early jurisprudence of the EComHR, the Council of Europe's guide to the implementation of article 9 as authored by Jim Murdoch states:

An 'interference' with an individual's rights will normally involve the taking of a measure by a state authority; it can, where a positive obligation on the part of state authorities is recognised, also involve the failure to take some necessary action.... For the purposes of Article 9, though, it is crucial that the challenged [interference] involves a state rather than an ecclesiastical body. Thus where a dispute over a matter such as use of the liturgy, state responsibility will not be engaged since such involves a challenge to a matter of internal church administration taken by a body that is not a governmental agency. This is so even where the religious body involved is recognised by domestic law as enjoying the particular status of an established church.[231]

Murdoch contends that the action of a church, even an established church, cannot be attributed to the state and thereby it does not give rise to direct responsibility under the ECHR;[232] however, he does not proclaim the absence of states' positive obligations to protect the right of others (specifically here under article 9) when a conflict with religious autonomy occurs. Liturgy is expressly mentioned in the above citation, because it belongs to the sphere of internal administration, and one can imagine situations where members of a church would oppose certain liturgical practices sanctioned by the church: Would they enjoy the right to freedom of religion vis-à-vis the religious organization? Would the state have any positive obligations towards them? Would the church incur any duties under the ECHR? Employment matters are surely central to the autonomy of a church or religious organization: Could a religious organization impose duties upon its employees that are in violation of their rights to freedom of religion, expression, privacy, or assembly? Not least, could a school run by a religious organization, and therefore within the sphere of church autonomy, set discriminatory admission criteria based on racial grounds?

The aim of the remainder of this chapter is to offer answers to these questions. We will demonstrate that in their jurisprudence regarding articles 6, 8, 9, 10 and 11, the Convention mechanisms have set limits to church autonomy. In the early case law, these were guided by the principle of voluntariness, essentially recognizing the right of individuals to join, as well as exit, a church or religious organization.[233] Later on, procedural and substantive limitations[234] were developed. Throughout the period, nonetheless, obligations for religious organizations arise.

---

[231] J. Murdoch, *Freedom of Thought, Conscience and Religion. A guide to the implementation of Article 9 of the European Convention on Human Rights*, (Council of Europe Human Rights Handbooks No. 9, 2007), at 20. (Citations omitted).

[232] See also *Clapham, Human Rights Obligations of Non-State Actors*, at 82.

[233] This term is used by Ian Leigh in Leigh, 'Balancing Religious Autonomy and Other Human Rights under the European Convention', at 116.

[234] To recall, the notions are proposed by Carolyn Evans and Anna Hood in Evans and Hood, 'Religious Autonomy and Labour Law: A Comparison of the Jurisprudence of the United States and the European Court of Human Rights', at 19–21.

2.1.1. *X v. Denmark* and *Hautaniemi v. Sweden*

At this point, it is appropriate to examine more closely the two cases of the EComHR which prompted Murdoch's assertion cited earlier. In *X v. Denmark*,[235] a minister of the state Church of Denmark had required parents to attend five religious lessons before their children could be baptised. The Church Ministry considered that the cleric had no right to impose such a condition and advised him to abandon the practice or present his resignation. On his refusal, the Ministry set up a consistory court of an advisory character. In the view of the public prosecutor's office, the case was disciplinary in character, with no criminal law implication, and the clergyman's request for public proceedings before a consistory court with judicial authority was therefore denied. Following this, the minister filed an application before the EComHR complaining that his freedom of conscience had been violated under article 9 as had his right to a fair trial under article 6.1. In finding that the complaint did not fall within the scope either of article 9 or article 6.1, the EComHR held:

> A church is an organised religious community based on identical or at least substantially similar views. Through the rights granted to its members under Art. 9, the church itself is protected in its right to manifest its religion, to organise and carry out worship, teaching practice and observance, and it is free to act out and enforce uniformity in these matters. Further, in a State church system its servants are employed for the purpose of applying and teaching a specific religion. Their individual freedom of thought, conscience or religion is exercised at the moment they accept or refuse employment as clergymen, and their right to leave the church guarantees their freedom of religion in case they oppose its teachings. In other words, the church is not obliged to provide religious freedom to its servants and members, as is the State as such for everyone within its jurisdiction.[236]

The EComHR considered that, since the individual had chosen to join the church and serve as its minister, the principle of voluntariness justified the church's wide sphere of discretion in relation to him. In the view of the EComHR, the right to leave the church therefore becomes a sufficient guarantee of the minister's religious freedom in the context of church autonomy. As Leigh asserts, this 'exit/surrender principle' risks undervaluing 'what may be the high costs for those involved of exercising it'[237] and as such it essentially minimizes the scope of individual religious freedom. In *Siebenhaar v. Germany*, a case decided in 2011 which similarly involved the religious freedom of an employee of a religious organization, the exit principle was no longer regarded as sufficient to secure the right to freedom of religion.[238] Nonetheless, even such a minimalist approach to religious freedom assumes that the state has certain positive obligations: to secure the right, a state would have to take action to ensure that any minister, or other individual, would not be prevented from leaving the church. For example, the rights of such individuals would

---

[235] *X v. Denmark*, Application No. 7374/76, Decision of 8 March 1976.

[236] *X v. Denmark*, at 158.

[237] Leigh, 'Balancing Religious Autonomy and Other Human Rights under the European Convention', at 116.

[238] *Siebenhaar c. Allemagne*, Requête no 18136/02, Arrêt du 3 février 2011.

not be effectively secured in the absence of legislation exempting those who leave the church from church tax. At the same time, the right of the cleric (in the case at hand) and adherents in general to leave the church represents a limitation of the church's autonomy. The church itself would have an obligation not to prevent its members from leaving, implicitly recognizing the rights of individuals to change their religion. From this perspective, the approach of the EComHR appears less minimalist.

The second case on which Murdoch draws, *Hautaniemi v. Sweden*,[239] concerns an application filed by a parish of the State Church of Sweden. The applicant alleged that the Church of Sweden had violated the parish's right to freedom of religion when it prohibited the parish from using the Finnish Evangelical-Lutheran Church liturgy. In finding that there was no violation of article 9, the EComHR held that the applicant parish did not establish that it would have been prevented from leaving the Church of Sweden.[240] The EComHR again applied the principle of voluntariness as an exit option. The right to leave the church (on this occasion for the parish) can be seen as a limitation of the church's autonomy. The church would be required not to prevent what it would essentially regard as a schism. When viewed from the perspective of the church, this limitation of church autonomy is remarkable. As a consequence, the church might prefer to take into consideration the right of its parish to freedom of religion, if the alternative to doing so was a schism. A number of positive obligations may arise for the state, in the light of this case. The state would have to ensure that a parish that decided to leave the church was not effectively prevented from doing so, and authorities would therefore need to take steps, for example, to register the group's new statutes and grant it legal status.[241]

There is admittedly a curious dimension to the Commission's decision in *Hautaniemi v. Sweden*. The EComHR observed that, although the Church of Sweden was a public law entity, it did not exercise governmental functions and as a result Sweden could not be held responsible for the alleged violation of the parish's right to freedom of religion resulting from the decision of the Church.[242] As observed in section II.1 of this chapter, the legal argumentation in this decision is limited. One must therefore assume that the EComHR could not have intended to disregard its earlier case law on positive obligations of states in issues related to church autonomy,[243] or the ECtHR findings on positive obligations in many other cases.[244] It is suggested that the EComHR intended to assert that 'the "publicness"

---

[239] *Finska församlingen i Stockholm and Teuvo Hautaniemi v. Sweden*, Application No. 24019/94, Decision of 11 April 1996, EComHR, Decisions and Reports, vol. 62.

[240] *Finska församlingen i Stockholm and Teuvo Hautaniemi v. Sweden*, at 97.

[241] See for example *Svyato-Mykhaylivska Parafiya v. Ukraine*, Application no. 77703/01, Judgment of 14 June 2007.

[242] *Finska församlingen i Stockholm and Teuvo Hautaniemi v. Sweden*, at 97.

[243] *Maximilian Rommelfanger v. Federal Republic of Germany*, Application No. 12242/86, Decision of 26 June 1986, EComHR, Decisions and Reports, vol. 62.

[244] See *Case "Relating to Certain Aspects of the Laws on the Use of Languages in Education in Belgium" v. Belgium (Merits)*, Application no 1474/62; 1677/62; 1691/62; 1769/63; 1994/63; 2126/64,

of the public law corporation is not enough to bar it from bringing an application, and is not enough to imply direct state responsibility under the Convention'.[245] This interpretation by no means negates the theory of positive obligations, which rests on the principle that a human rights violation by a *non-state actor* may engage the responsibility of a state, if the latter fails to prevent or punish the violation.

2.1.2. Early alternative approaches
What is perhaps most curious in the EComHR's practice concerning the limits of church autonomy is that it developed an understanding early on that the voluntariness principle is not sufficiently satisfactory and therefore made use of this principle in an inconsistent manner, appealing time and again to alternative approaches.

In *Maximilian Rommelfanger v. the Federal Republic of Germany*,[246] the Commission explicitly recognized that positive obligations of the state arise in the context of a conflict between church autonomy and the freedom of expression of an individual employee. A doctor employed in a hospital run by a Catholic foundation was dismissed for having expressed an opinion on abortion in the press that was not in conformity with the position of the Catholic Church. The EComHR acknowledged that, under article 1 of the ECHR, the state is under an obligation to secure the Convention rights of an individual, which in turn may require the authorities to take positive steps.[247] The EComHR went to great length to show that access to remedies existed for the doctor to challenge his dismissal and that the competent state courts weighed his interests, including freedom of expression, against those of his employer. It concluded:

> It is true that particular weight was finally given to the views of the church concerning the duties of loyalty of church employees. According to the Federal Constitutional Court this was necessary in order to safeguard the constitutional right of the church to regulate its internal affairs. Nevertheless the Federal Constitutional Court held that there were limits to the right of the church to impose its views on its employees. In particular the State courts were competent to ensure that no unreasonable demands of loyalty were made.[248]

In *Maximilian Rommelfanger*, the EComHR regarded the autonomy of a religious organization as qualified, even though it acknowledged that the latter could not function effectively without imposing certain duties of loyalty on its employees, in accordance with its convictions and value judgments. However, the duty of loyalty imposed by the church or the religious association through a contract could not be unreasonable and 'strike at the very substance of the freedom of expression'.[249] Concurrently, the state has a positive obligation to ensure that procedural

---

Judgment of 23 July 1968; *Hokkanen v. Finland*, Application No. 19823/92, Judgment of 24 August 1994; *López-Ostra v. Spain*, Application No. 16798/90, Judgment of 9 December 1994.

[245] Clapham, *Human Rights Obligations of Non-State Actors*, at 82.

[246] See *Maximilian Rommelfanger v. Federal Republic of Germany*, Application No. 12242/86, Decision of 26 June 1986, EComHR, Decisions and Reports, vol. 62.

[247] *Maximilian Rommelfanger v. Federal Republic of Germany*, at 160.

[248] *Maximilian Rommelfanger v. Federal Republic of Germany*, at 161.

[249] *Maximilian Rommelfanger v. Federal Republic of Germany*, at 161.

safeguards are in place to assure that the religious freedom of a church employee is not annulled by the right to church autonomy.[250]

It is evident that *Maximilian Rommelfanger* was adjudicated under article 10 of the ECHR. Jean-François Akandji-Kombe observed in 2007 that the ECtHR showed itself reluctant to establish positive obligations for states in the context of article 9 jurisprudence and instead 'preferred to class as interference what might have been seen as a failure to act'.[251] However, as the scholar notes, there is no reason why the reasoning in article 10 could not be transposed to article 9 jurisprudence, 'in particular as regards infringements of freedom of thought, conscience and religion by a private individual, in the professional framework, for example'.[252] *Siebenhaar v. Germany*, as mentioned earlier and discussed in detail later, proves him right.

The case of *Tyler v. the United Kingdom*[253] can also be seen to depart from the voluntariness principle. An applicant priest, disciplined by an ecclesiastical court for adultery, 'contended that the Church of England has been prosecution, judge and jury in the proceedings against him, in breach of Article 6 para. 1 of the Convention'.[254] The EComHR analysed whether a civil right was at stake in order for article 6 to be applicable, and pointed to the loss of the applicant's income, his pension rights, and free accommodation. It proceeded from the assumption that a civil right may have been at stake[255] and concluded that 'the fact that members of the disciplining body participate in the exercise of disciplinary jurisdiction over other members cannot suffice to bear out a charge of bias, even where Article 6 is applicable'.[256] After examining in detail the ecclesiastical court system of the Church of England, which had the jurisdiction to hear Tyler's case, the EComHR concluded that they were independent and impartial in the sense of article 6.1 and dismissed the application as manifestly ill-founded. What needs to be remembered

---

[250] 'As regards employers such as the Catholic foundation which employed the applicant in its hospital, the law in any event ensures that there is a reasonable relationship between the measures affecting freedom of expression and the nature of the employment as well as the importance of the issue for the employer. In this way it protects an employee against compulsion in matters of freedom of expression which would strike at the very substance of this freedom (cf. a contrario *Young, James and Webster* judgment, loc. cit., p. 23 para. 55). The Commission considers that Article 10 (Art. 10) of the Convention does not, in cases like the present one, impose a positive obligation on the State to provide protection *beyond this standard*. It follows that there has been no State interference with the applicant's right to freedom of expression as guaranteed in Article 10 para. 1 (Art. 10.1) of the Convention, nor a failure to comply with positive obligations resulting from this provision.' *Maximilian Rommelfanger v. Federal Republic of Germany*, at 161 (Emphasis added).

[251] Akandji-Kombe, *Positive Obligations under the European Convention on Human Rights*, at 50–51.

[252] See note 251, at 51.

[253] *Tyler v. the United Kingdom*, Application No. 21283/9, Decision of 5 April 1994.

[254] *Tyler v. the United Kingdom*.

[255] In two more recent cases involving termination of ministers' employment, the Court was less generous in making such assumptions about the existence of a civil right and therefore dismissed the applications as falling outside the scope of article 6. *Ahtinen v. Finland*, Application no. 48907/99, Judgment of 23 Septembre 2008; *Duda and Dudová v. the Czech Republic*, Application no. 40224/98, ECtHR, Third Section, Decision of 30 January 2001. Termination *as such* in the context of church employment appears not to give rise to a civil right in the eyes of the Court. One scholar notes that 'these decisions show the Court acknowledging the religious autonomy interests inherent in religious adjudication'. Leigh, 'Balancing Religious Autonomy and Other Human Rights under the European Convention', at 118.

[256] *Tyler v. the United Kingdom*.

is that the Court did not dismiss the case based on the principle of voluntariness, along the lines of *X v. Denmark*; it analysed whether the Church of England court system had upheld fairness standards, demonstrating therefore that ecclesiastical courts have an obligation to respect fair trial guarantees.

2.2. *The procedural and substantive limitations to church autonomy in recent case law of the ECtHR*

Recent jurisprudence of the ECtHR suggests that it has abandoned the principle of voluntariness as the fundamental guarantee of the rights of others when these conflict with church autonomy. The new approach of the Court is seen by Carolyn Evans and Anna Hood as a move away from 'the traditional European jurisdictional approach to religious autonomy'.[257] Judicial authorities across Europe have traditionally declared that they lack the power to review decisions of religious organizations, and the processes underpinning those decisions, because these entities enjoyed religious autonomy.

When invoking the jurisdictional approach, courts neither approve nor disapprove of employment decisions made by religious institutions—they say that they have no jurisdiction with respect to them and thus leave the outcomes to be determined by the religious employer.[258]

It could be argued that the traditional jurisdictional approach to church autonomy is justified to a certain extent by the ECtHR's cautioning that the role of state authorities should not be to assess the legitimacy of religious beliefs or the means by which those beliefs are expressed.[259] States may be wary that, should they assess the boundaries of church autonomy, they risk assessing the legitimacy of religious interpretations.[260] From a logical point of view, this justification of the traditional jurisdictional approach is weak; if judicial authorities are competent to assess the limits of an individual's freedom to manifest religion, why would they be less competent to assess the limits of the collective manifestation of religion? To assume jurisdiction in the first situation and deny it in the second situation, would mean that collective rights, merely because of their collective dimension, deserve higher protection.

In Chapter 1 it was argued that individuals are *often* in the best position to define what represents a manifestation of their religious belief and courts should therefore be inclined to accept these interpretations as legitimate, while performing

---

[257] Evans and Hood, 'Religious Autonomy and Labour Law: A Comparison of the Jurisprudence of the United States and the European Court of Human Rights', at 15.

[258] See note 257.

[259] See *Hasan and Chaush v. Bulgaria*, Application no. 30985/96, Judgment of 26 October 2000, para. 78; *Leyla Şahin v. Turkey*, para. 107; *Refah Partisi (the Welfare Party) and Others v. Turkey*, Application Nos. 41340/98, 41342/98, 41343/98 and 41344/98, Grand Chamber, Judgment of 13 February 2003, para. 91.

[260] See for example, *Sindicatul 'Păstorul cel Bun' v. Romania*, Application no. 2330/09, Judgment of 31 January 2012, para. 49.

their judicial function *mostly* under the second limb of article 9.[261] The same view is taken here with regard to the capacity of religious organizations to better interpret religion and therefore articulate which religious manifestations are central to their functioning. It would seem that the ECtHR is of a similar opinion and generally also follows this approach.[262] The important caveat is that neither religious interpretations, nor their effect on the rights of others, should be immune from judicial review: States are not relieved from their obligations to secure the rights of others under the ECHR and, perhaps more importantly, religious bodies may themselves incur responsibilities under the ECHR. It follows that, where conflict arises between the right of religious organizations to self-administration and the rights of others, the state must have in place a system that secures the rights of both categories. By placing supervision of the limitations on church autonomy outside the jurisdiction of domestic courts, states would effectively treat religious autonomy as limitless, sometimes at the expense of securing the rights of others affected by the decisions of religious organizations. It is in this area that recent ECtHR case law clarifies the issues.

2.2.1. *Pellegrini v. Italy*: a new approach to church autonomy

One shortcoming of the principle of voluntariness is that it is difficult to apply outside of the church employment context. The ECtHR was faced with providing an alternative approach in *Pellegrini v. Italy*[263] and introduced a procedural limitation to church autonomy. Ms Pellegrini married Mr Gigliozzi in a religious ceremony that was valid under civil Italian law; in 1987 she petitioned and obtained a judicial separation from her husband in a civil court. In the meantime, Ms Pellegrini was summoned to appear before an ecclesiastical court in Rome 'to answer questions in the matrimonial case of Gigliozzi-Pellegrini'.[264] She was informed on the day of the hearing that her husband had petitioned the ecclesiastical court for an annulment of their marriage on the ground of consanguinity. She was asked during the hearing whether she had obtained the required special licence for such cases, but could not reply. She received notice that a decree nullifying her marriage had been issued in expedited proceedings, but no explanation was provided of the grounds on which the decision had been made. Her appeal to the Tribunal of the Roman Rota alleging breaches of her defence rights, because the adversarial principle had not been respected, and she had not been assisted by a lawyer, was dismissed. Italian courts authorized the enforcement of the judgment of the ecclesiastical tribunals, and rejected Ms Pellegrini's objections, noting that:

[T]he opportunity given to the applicant on 1 December 1987 to answer questions had been sufficient to ensure that the adversarial principle had been complied with and that,

---

[261] See Chapter 1, III.2.
[262] See *Leyla Şahin v. Turkey*, para. 107; Wadham, et al., *Blackstone's Guide to the Human Rights Act 1998*, 4th ed., paras. 8.457 and 8.462.
[263] *Pellegrini v. Italy*, Application no. 30882/96, Judgment of 20 July 2001, para. 6.
[264] *Pellegrini v. Italy*, para. 14.

moreover, she had freely chosen to bring the proceedings before the Rota and had been able to exercise her defence rights in those proceedings 'irrespective of the special features of proceedings under canon law'.[265]

Ms Pellegrini complained before the ECtHR that her rights under article 6 of the ECHR had been violated. The Italian courts' approach invited the European judges to acknowledge that the applicant had addressed the appeal to the ecclesiastical tribunal voluntarily, suggesting that the principle of voluntariness would be applicable to the case. The ECtHR did not adopt this reasoning, however; it carefully explained that, since 'the Vatican has not ratified the Convention', its task was not to review whether the proceedings before the ecclesiastical courts complied with article 6 of the ECHR, 'but whether the Italian courts, before authorising enforcement of the decision annulling the marriage, duly satisfied themselves that the relevant proceedings fulfilled the guarantees of Article 6'.[266] The European judges held that the Italian courts had 'breached their duty' to ensure that procedural safeguards were in place in ecclesiastical courts to effectively protect the due process rights of the applicant.[267]

This case is particularly interesting. Although the ECtHR could not take a position on proceedings before ecclesiastical courts at the Vatican, its judgment reveals what the scope of article 6 obligations would be if the Holy See became a party to the ECHR. To uphold the principle of adversarial debate, ecclesiastical tribunals should have given the defendant an opportunity to examine all the evidence and observations in the file.[268] A second obligation under article 6 is expressed in surprisingly direct terms:

In the Court's opinion, given that the applicant had been summoned to appear before the Ecclesiastical Court without knowing what the case was about, that court had a duty to inform her that she could seek the assistance of a lawyer before she attended for questioning.[269]

Article 6 of the ECHR and its standards can be seen to underpin the protection of all other substantive rights of the Convention; as such, *Pellegrini v. Italy* which centred on article 6, may be regarded as the case where the procedural approach to church autonomy emerged.

It should be also noted that the position expressed in the case accords with the position of the HRC in General Comment 32.[270] The treaty body held that, under the ICCPR, states have an obligation to ensure that religious courts cannot give binding judgments unless the proceedings in question are minor civil and criminal matters; meet fair trial requirements; and their judgments are validated by state courts and can be challenged by the concerned parties in a procedure that satisfies fair trial guarantees. Only in such circumstances, it asserted, should a state recognize

---

[265] *Pellegrini v. Italy*, para. 26.
[266] *Pellegrini v. Italy*, para. 40.
[267] *Pellegrini v. Italy*, para. 47.
[268] *Pellegrini v. Italy*, para. 44.
[269] *Pellegrini v. Italy*, para. 46.
[270] HRC, *General Comment No. 32*, para. 24.

their decisions.[271] The obligations of state parties outlined here essentially disclose the scope of the responsibilities of religious courts under the ICCPR.

2.2.2. *Lombardi Vallauri v. Italy*: the assertion of procedural limitations

In *Lombardi Vallauri v. Italy*[272] the ECtHR embarked on a new course in its articulation of the procedural limits to church autonomy. The facts of the case were that the lecturer Lombardi Vallauri was prevented from participating in a competition to renew his contract with a Catholic university. Having received no explanation for the university's decision, having been offered no possibility of administrative appeal, and having been denied an appeal in Italian courts—which embraced the traditional jurisdictional approach to church autonomy—Mr Lombardi Vallauri filed an application under articles 9, 10, and 6.1 of the ECHR. The ECtHR ruled that a violation of freedom of expression, of the right to access a court, and the right to an adversarial debate had occurred. While it considered that it was unnecessary to treat the issue under article 9, it did not exclude that a violation of religious freedom may have occurred as well.[273]

In its assessment, the ECtHR specifically addressed the tension between the right of churches to religious autonomy and the human rights of others. The Court's reasoning is significant for the argument made in this chapter and will therefore be cited at length:

En ce qui concerne…l'efficacité du contrôle juridictionnel de la procédure administrative, la Cour rappelle d'emblée que l'appréciation par les Etats de la légitimité des convictions religieuses ou des modalités d'expression de telles convictions doit en principe être exclue…Dans le cas présent, la Cour estime qu'il n'appartenait pas aux autorités nationales d'examiner la substance de la décision émanant de la Congrégation.

51. Toutefois, elle relève que les juridictions administratives internes ont limité leur examen de la légitimité de la décision litigieuse au fait que le Conseil de faculté avait constaté l'existence du refus d'agrément.

52. Ainsi, les juges nationaux ont refusé d'examiner le fait que le Conseil de faculté n'avait pas indiqué au requérant quelles étaient les opinions qui lui étaient reprochées. Or la communication de ces éléments n'aurait nullement impliqué un jugement de la part des autorités judiciaires quant à la compatibilité entre les positions du requérant et la doctrine catholique. En revanche, elle aurait permis à l'intéressé de connaître et, dès lors, de pouvoir contester l'incompatibilité alléguée entre lesdites opinions et son activité d'enseignant à l'Université catholique.

53. Au demeurant, la Cour observe que, même si l'article 10 de l'Accord et l'article 45 du Statut n'imposaient aucune obligation d'indiquer les raisons pour lesquelles la candidature du requérant était écartée, l'opportunité d'une telle information a cependant été envisagée à l'époque des faits: lors de la réunion du Conseil de faculté, l'un des professeurs, appuyé par trois autres, a proposé au Conseil de « demander à la Congrégation d'indiquer les raisons de la mesure prise à l'encontre du professeur Lombardi Vallauri », estimant que « cette demande se justifi[ait] par l'intérêt, pour les enseignants de la faculté, de recevoir des

---

[271] HRC, *General Comment No. 32*, para. 24.
[272] *Lombardi Vallauri c. Italie*, Requête no. 39128/05, Arrêt du 20 octobre 2009.
[273] *Lombardi Vallauri v. Italy*, paras. 55–56, 71–72, and 58.

indications concernant les aspects des études et des enseignements du professeur Lombardi Vallauri qui [avaient] été jugés incompatibles avec l'inspiration catholique de la faculté ». Cette proposition a été mise aux voix et rejetée par une courte majorité: douze voix contre dix, avec une abstention....

54. De plus, la Cour relève que l'impossibilité pour le requérant de connaître les raisons précises de la perte de son agrément l'a définitivement empêché de se défendre dans le cadre d'un débat contradictoire; or ce point n'a pas non plus fait l'objet d'un examen de la part des tribunaux internes. De l'avis de la Cour, le contrôle juridictionnel de l'application de la mesure litigieuse n'a donc été pas adéquat en l'espèce.[274]

The ECtHR spells out the state's positive obligation to ensure procedural guarantees aimed at securing the human rights of individuals in cases where religious organizations exercise their right to self-administration. In this particular case, the ECtHR held that the refusal of Italian courts to hear the case effectively nullified the applicant's procedural guarantees. It would appear that civil courts cannot simply defer to ecclesiastic instances under the traditional jurisdictional approach on church autonomy, but are under an obligation to review the procedural guarantees in place in order to ensure that the rights of third parties are respected.

It is clear that the *Lombardi Vallauri* judgment has important implications for religious organizations. The ECtHR's approach is remarkable in that, in paragraph 53, it appears to directly address the obligations of the Catholic university. It clarifies that the organization failed to uphold certain procedural guarantees. It suggests that, on terminating the contract of an employee, a religious organization must ensure minimal fair process guarantees which serve to protect the human rights of the employee. Even in the absence of a specific provision to that effect

---

[274] *Lombardi Vallauri c. Italy*, paras. 50–54. (This author's translation: Concerning...the effectiveness of the judicial review of the administrative proceedings, the Court recalls at the outset that an assessment by States of the legitimacy of religious beliefs or the means used to express such beliefs should in principle be excluded...In this case, the Court considers that it was not for the national authorities to examine the substance of the Congregations' decision. 51. However, it notes that the domestic administrative courts have limited their examination of the legitimacy of the contested decision to the mere finding of the Faculty Council which had noted the existence of a decision [of the Congregation] not to grant approval. 52. Thus, national courts have refused to consider the fact that the Faculty Council had not informed the applicant what the opinions which he was accused of holding were. The communication of these elements would have in no way involved a judgment on the part of the judicial authorities as to the compatibility between the opinions of the applicant and Catholic doctrine. However, it would have allowed the applicant to know and therefore to be able to challenge the alleged inconsistency between his opinions and his teaching activity at the Catholic University. 53. Moreover, the Court notes that, even if Article 10 of the Agreement and Article 45 of the Statute did not impose any obligation to inform the reasons why the applicant's application was rejected, the desirability of such communication was considered, at the time: during the meeting of the Faculty Council, one of the professors, supported by three others, proposed to the Council to 'ask the Congregation to give reasons for the measures taken against Professor Lombardi Vallauri', arguing that 'this demand [was] warranted by the interest of the faculty to receive information on aspects of lecturing and the teachings of Professor Lombardi Vallauri who [had] been deemed incompatible with the Catholic values of the faculty.' This proposal was put to vote and rejected by a narrow majority of twelve votes against ten, with one abstention.... 54. In addition, the Court notes that the impossibility for the applicant to know the precise reasons for the loss of his contract has categorically prevented him from defending himself in the context of an adversarial debate, yet this was not the subject of a review by the national courts. In the opinion of the Court, the judicial review of the contested measure has, in this case, been inadequate.)

in domestic law, the Catholic university should have inquired with the Holy See's Congregation for Catholic Education what the reason for the termination was and should have informed the applicant, so that he could challenge these reasons in a genuine adversarial debate.

2.2.3. Church employment cases: the emergence of substantive limitations

Three recent German cases decided by the ECtHR,[275] each of which concerns employment issues in the context of church autonomy, go a step further than earlier decisions and assert that in addition to procedural limitations substantive limitations apply to religious autonomy. The substantive limitations derive from balancing the right of a religious organization to self-administration against the human rights of others. In these cases, the ECtHR appears to effectively establish an obligation of review on civil courts when the rights of others are at stake.

The German cases are very similar in the problem that they posed to the ECtHR and the reasoning which the Court put forward in response. The facts of the first case are as follows: Bernhard Josef Schüth, an organist and choirmaster in a Catholic parish, separated from his wife and started to live with another woman with whom he was expecting a child; he was dismissed by his religious employer on the grounds that he had violated the duty of loyalty toward the sanctity of marriage as a fundamental principle of the Catholic Church. When a German court confirmed his dismissal, he filed an application under article 8 of the ECHR.[276] Second, in *Obst v. Germany*, the applicant was the former director of public relations for Europe of the Mormon Church. He relied on the right to private and family life under the ECHR to complain against the refusal of German courts to overturn the termination of his employment, which occurred after he confided to his pastor that he had had an extramarital affair.[277] In a third case, Astrid Siebenhaar invoked her right to freedom of religion under the ECHR to complain of her dismissal, also confirmed by German courts; a Catholic, she was first employed by a Protestant parish as a kindergarten educator and later to manage a kindergarten run by another Protestant parish. Her contract was terminated after it became known that she had been active as a member of the Universal Church/Brotherhood of Humanity and was offering initiation lessons in the religious teachings of that community.[278] In these cases, the ECtHR clearly spelled out that articles 8 and 9 give rise to both negative and positive obligations on the state in the context of church autonomy.[279] Importantly, in *Siebenhaar* it held: 'Ces obligations peuvent nécessiter l'adoption de mesures visant au respect de la liberté de religion jusque dans les relations des individus entre eux'.[280] This represents

---

[275] *Obst c. Allemagne*, Requête no 425/03, Arrêt du 23 septembre 2010; *Schüth v. Germany*, Application no 1620/03, Judgment of 23 of September 2010; *Siebenhaar c. Allemagne*, Requête no 18136/02, Arrêt du 3 février 2011.

[276] *Schüth v. Germany*, paras. 1–3.

[277] *Obst c. Allemagne*, para. 9.

[278] *Siebenhaar c. Allemagne*, paras. 7–12.

[279] *Obst c. Allemagne*, para. 41; *Schüth v. Germany*, para. 55.

[280] *Siebenhaar c. Allemagne*, para. 38. (This author's translation: These obligations may require the adoption of measures aimed at the respect of freedom of religion including in the relationship between individuals themselves.)

an acknowledgment that religious organizations have a duty to respect the religious freedom of their employees.

The question which the ECtHR identifies as fundamental is whether Germany realized its positive obligations by securing the right to private and family life of Schüth and Obst, and the right to the religious freedom of Siebenhaar, in the context of their dismissal by the Catholic, Mormon, and Protestant churches respectively.[281] While judicial organs are encouraged to accept the religious organization's interpretation of the significance of failures of employee conduct which led to dismissal, they are also expected to weigh these arguments against the human rights of the employees in question.[282]

Accordingly, the Court, by examining how the German employment tribunals balanced the applicant's right with the Catholic Church's right under Articles 9 and 11, will have to ascertain whether or not a sufficient degree of protection was afforded to the applicant.[283]

Unlike in *Obst* and *Siebenhaar*, in *Schüth* the Court found a violation of the European Convention. Mr Schüth had signed a contract that imposed a duty of loyalty towards the Catholic Church. In the ECtHR's view this cannot be seen as an unequivocal personal agreement to live a life of abstinence in case of separation or divorce.[284] In this particular case, it ruled that German courts had not sufficiently taken into consideration the right to private and family life of the applicant, including his slim prospects of employment given the restrictive policies of other churches about employing organists of other denominations than their own. Domestic courts had given overwhelming importance to church autonomy, which in the view of the ECtHR resulted in an unsatisfactory balance which justified their finding of a violation of article 8.[285]

Sindicatul 'Păstorul cel Bun' v. Romania,[286] a fourth case of employment in the context of religious autonomy, seems prima facie similar to the previously discussed judgments. Thirty-five priests and lay personnel of the Romanian Orthodox Church decided to form a trade union; in conformity with domestic legislation, they sought to provide the union with a legal personality and to register it in the state's trade union register. The Church opposed recognition by the authorities of the union, arguing that the Statute of the Romanian Orthodox Church forbade any form of association without the prior agreement of the bishop. The tribunal sided with the unionists, and the appeals court reversed its decision. Before the ECtHR, the Păstorul cel Bun union claimed that the refusal of the authorities

---

[281] *Obst c. Allemagne*, para. 43; *Schüth v. Germany*, para. 57; *Siebenhaar c. Allemagne*, para. 40.

[282] Evans and Hood, 'Religious Autonomy and Labour Law: A Comparison of the Jurisprudence of the United States and the European Court of Human Rights', at 103.

[283] *Schüth v. Germany*, para. 57. Mutatis mutandis *Obst c. Allemagne*, para. 43; *Siebenhaar c. Allemagne*, para. 57.

[284] *Schüth v. Germany*, para. 71.

[285] *Schüth v. Germany*, para 74.

[286] *Sindicatul 'Păstorul cel Bun' v. Romania*, Application no 2330/09, Judgment of 31 January 2012.

to register it as a union was in violation of its members' right to unionize. The ECtHR found a violation of article 11 of the Convention.

In *Sindicatul 'Păstorul cel Bun'* the ECtHR remained consistent in affirming the application of procedural and substantive limitations on the right of a church to administer itself and the corresponding obligations of state authorities. As such, it held:

78. The County Court did not examine the repercussions of the employment contract on the employer-employee relationship, the distinction between members of the clergy and lay employees of the Church or the compatibility of the ecclesiastical rules prohibiting union membership with the domestic and international regulations enshrining the right of employees to belong to a trade union. In the Court's opinion, however, such questions were of particular importance in the present case and, on that account, should have been explicitly addressed and taken into consideration in weighing up the interests at stake...

79. The Court accepts that under the Convention, an employer whose ethos is based on religion may impose special duties of loyalty on its employees. It also acknowledges that when signing their employment contract, employees bound by such a duty of loyalty may accept a certain restriction of some of their rights...

80. However, it reiterates that a civil court reviewing a penalty imposed following a breach of such duties cannot, on the basis of the employer's autonomy, refrain from carrying out a proper balancing exercise between the interests at stake in accordance with the principle of proportionality...[287]

The decision of the Court was reversed by the Grand Chamber with 11 votes to 6. The Grand Chamber's reasoning hinged on the fact that the applicants failed to formally request permission from the bishop to form the trade union as required by the Statute of the Church. In the view of the judges, given this failure, domestic courts were correct not to register the union, thereby respecting church proceedings and ultimately religious autonomy.[288] Be that as it may, of great relevance for the current analysis and the wider argument that alongside states, non-state actors have the capacity to incur responsibilities under the European Convention is the Grand Chamber's assertion:

[A] mere allegation by a religious community that there is an actual or potential threat to its autonomy is not sufficient to render any interference with its members' trade-union rights compatible with the requirements of Article 11 of the Convention. *It must also show*, in the light of the circumstances of the individual case, that the risk alleged is real and substantial and that the impugned interference with freedom of association does not go beyond what is necessary to eliminate that risk and does not serve any other purpose unrelated to the exercise of the religious community's autonomy. The national courts must ensure that these conditions are satisfied, by conducting an in-depth examination of the circumstances of the case and a thorough balancing exercise between the competing interests at stake.[289]

---

[287] *Sindicatul 'Păstorul cel Bun' v. Romania*, paras. 77–80 (references omitted).
[288] *Sindicatul 'Păstorul cel Bun' v. Romania*, Application no 2330/09, Grand Chamber, Judgment of 9 July 2013, in particular paras. 167–170.
[289] *Sindicatul 'Păstorul cel Bun' v. Romania*, Grand Chamber, para. 159. (Emphasis added).

The Grand Chamber seems to have gone one step further than the Court in the *Lombardi Vallauri* judgment and places the onus on the church itself to show that it respects the human rights of its employees, while the duty to review such demonstration lies with domestic courts.

From a more practical point of view, one may wonder how much consideration religious organizations must give to the human rights of third parties: Are they merely expected to consider carefully the human rights of their employees, students, and members, or to perform comprehensive assessments as they would do if they were human rights bodies? For example, in *R (Begum) v. Governors of Denbigh High School*,[290] the UK Court of Appeal considered that the school (which had prohibited Ms Begum from attending classes dressed in a jilbab, rather than the school uniform that was specifically designed to accommodate the requirements of Muslim girls for modest dress) should have performed a rather elaborate test.

1. Has the claimant established that she has a relevant Convention right which qualifies for protection under article 9(1)? 2. Subject to any justification that is established under article 9.2, has the Convention right been violated? 3. Was the interference with her Convention right prescribed by law in the Convention sense of that expression? 4. Did the interference have a legitimate aim? 5. What are the considerations that need to be balanced against each other when determining whether the interference was necessary in a democratic society for the purpose of achieving that aim? 6. Was the interference justified under article 9.2?[291]

Lord Bingham's comment on this method is instructive. 'The Court of Appeal's decision-making prescription would be admirable guidance to a lower court or legal tribunal, but cannot be required of a head teacher and governors, even with a solicitor to help them.'[292] This author agrees that such a test may be ideal, but seems excessive when its performance is demanded of a religious organization.

To conclude, based on the ECtHR's findings, one can infer that what is expected from religious organizations is to acknowledge their human rights responsibilities. They are expected to consider the rights of others to the best of their efforts and weigh them against their own interest in good faith, while ensuring due process guarantees. While they are entitled to require their employees to show loyalty to the tenets of their religion, this duty of loyalty cannot infringe on the substance of the employees' human rights. By associating with a church, individuals accept certain restrictions in conformity with the requirements of the church, but they do not relinquish their human rights.

Another conclusion that can be drawn from the four employment cases presented in this section is that the state has a positive obligation to ensure that procedural measures are in place which safeguard the rights of others in the context of church autonomy; *and* that sufficient consideration is given to their interests, balanced against the right of religious organizations to autonomy. It appears that, when the decisions of ecclesiastical tribunals are contested, civil courts have an

---

[290] *Begum v. Denbigh High School* [2005] EWCA Civ 199
[291] *Begum v. Denbigh High School*, para. 66.
[292] *R (on the application of Begum (by her litigation friend, Rahman)) (Respondent) v. Headteacher and Governors of Denbigh High School (Appellants)* [2006] UKHL 15, para. 31.

obligation to review those decisions. Would this in turn mean that provisions of church statutes that deny the competence of civil courts to review decisions of ecclesiastical tribunals in matters of internal administration are a priori invalid?

Let us examine, for instance, the Statute of the Romanian Orthodox Church, which was adopted by the Holy Synod of that Church in November 2007, and recognized by the Romanian Government in decision no. 53 of 16 January 2008. It stipulates:

By virtue of the autonomy of religious cults provided by law and their specific competences, the instances of church judgment decide matters related to internal discipline, and their rulings at all levels cannot be challenged in civil jurisdictions.[293]

Article 26, paragraphs 1–3 of Law 489/2006, stipulates that religious communities may establish ecclesiastical tribunals in conformity with their own statutes, which are to be applied exclusively in matters of internal discipline, and provides that the existence of these courts does 'not remove the application of legislation concerning civil offences and crimes'.[294]

When asked to review the decision of the courts of the Romanian Orthodox Church concerning the defrocking of a priest, two very different approaches were taken by the tribunal[295] and the appeals court of Constanța.[296] The former priest asked to be reinstated and to retroactively receive his salary benefits. He alleged that he refused to involve his parish in political activities, including during the elections, and as a consequence the church authorities proceeded to defrock him. Before that decision, he had resigned but the resignation was not taken into consideration in ecclesiastical courts. He claimed to have been subjected to degrading physical and psychological pressure, and to have been removed by force from the church which he served, and where some of his possessions were left behind.

The defendant church argued that the applicable law was the Statute of the Romanian Orthodox Church and law no. 489/2006, rather than labour legislation, and that the tribunal therefore lacked competence to hear the case. The tribunal contended that it would deny the complainant access to justice were it to decide that a civil court could not review the case. It went on to argue:

The fact that the jurisdictional review stops at the level of the Holy Synod of the Romanian Orthodox Church, denying the possibility of courts of general jurisdiction to express their legal opinion (whereby criminal offences committed by clerics are of the competence of penal courts) amounts to a situation of discrimination concerning the free access to justice

---

[293] An English version of the Statute of the Romanian Orthodox Church is available on its official website. However, the quality of the translation of this particular article is doubtful. Therefore the author's translation is preferred. It reflects as closely as possible the original Romanian text and English usage. Statutul pentru organizarea şi funcţionare Bisericii Ortodoxe Române, Noiembrie 2007, HG no. 53, 16 ianuarie 2008, accessed March 2014, http://patriarhia.ro/images/documente/statutul_bor.pdf, art. 156.6 (own translation).

[294] Legea nr. 489/2006 privind libertatea religioasă şi regimul general al cultelor, publicată în Monitorul oficial Partea I, nr. 11/8.01.2007, art. 25.1–3 (own translation).

[295] Tribunalul Constanţa, sentinţa civilă nr.1625/13 octombrie 2010, Dosar nr. 12028/118/2009.

[296] Curtea de Apel Constanţa, Decizia civilă nr. 176/CM/19.04.2011, Dosar nr. 12028/118/2009.

of clerics who are made the subject of final decisions of ecclesiastical courts, a situation which in turn creates a parallel system of canonical justice.[297]

The tribunal insisted that, because the priest had a work contract with the church, the applicable law was ecclesiastical law as well as domestic labour legislation, thereby contradicting a contrary submission by the government. In the opinion of the judge, the resignation should have resulted in termination of the labour relation between the priest and the church, but not the loss of his right to exercise his ministry. The subsequent proceedings of ecclesiastical courts, which resulted in the defrocking, were annulled and the priest reinstated.[298]

This decision was reversed on appeal.[299] In support of the reversal, the appeals court relied on the Romanian Constitutional Court's finding that paragraphs 1–3 of article 26 of Law 489/2006 were constitutional,[300] and therefore did not infringe a priest's right of access to justice. The appeal court also relied on the decision of the EComHR in the case *(Thomas) Tyler v. the United Kingdom* (which it cited incorrectly as the 'Tyler Tomson' case and attributed incorrectly to the ECtHR). Unlike the EComHR in *Tyler,*[301] the appeals court simply invoked the provisions of the Statute of the Romanian Orthodox Church to proclaim the independence and impartiality of the ecclesiastical court system in general. The court did not specifically inquire into whether procedural safeguards were in place to secure the rights of the complainant in the context of church autonomy, nor did it seek to balance his rights (of which freedom of religion, the right not to be subjected to degrading treatment, and the right to property had been invoked) against those of the church to autonomy. The court gave considerable weight to the church's argument that resignation amounted to apostasy under the doctrine of the Romanian Orthodox Church, and did not consider the principle of voluntariness; as a result it considered the ecclesiastical proceedings after the resignation to be legitimate. In the end, the court agreed that it lacked the competence to review decisions of the ecclesiastical tribunals and dismissed the case.

It appears to this author that the decision of the court of appeals of Constanța, dating from 2011, would fail to meet the standards set by the ECtHR in recent cases on employment in the context of church autonomy. Whether the review of procedural guarantees provided by ecclesiastical courts was sufficient is a point of debate. Certainly, the exercise of weighing the rights of the petitioner against those of the church to autonomy was deficient. Finally, there was no recognition by the court that the most basic guarantee of religious freedom in the context of church autonomy, the exit opinion (or principle of voluntariness), had been denied to the cleric.

---

[297] Tribunalul Constanța, Sentința civilă nr.1625/13 octombrie 2010, Dosar nr. 12028/118/2009 (own translation).

[298] Tribunalul Constanța, Sentința civilă nr.1625/13.

[299] Curtea de Apel Constanța, Decizia civilă nr. 176/CM/19.04.2011, Dosar nr. 12028/118/2009.

[300] See Curtea Constituționala, Decizia 448 din 7 aprilie 2011, No. 448/2011, M. Of. 424/2011.

[301] See III.2.1 in this chapter, and *Tyler v. the United Kingdom*, Application No. 21283/9, Decision of 5 April 1994.

The two decisions of Romanian courts have been discussed here because they portray the difficulties in reconciling religious autonomy with the rights of others, when the former is interpreted in a maximalist way by denying the jurisdiction of civil courts to review any decisions relating to internal church matters. It may well be that such maximalist claims of church autonomy are no longer sustainable; this is so, because the state is under an obligation to ensure that procedural measures are in place to safeguard the rights of others in the context of church autonomy *and* ensure that sufficient consideration is given to their interests, while weighing these against the right of religious organizations to autonomy.

To sum up, one can see an evolution in the Strasbourg mechanism's approach to limitations on church autonomy. From applying a voluntariness principle, as an exit strategy for church employees or members who felt their rights had been infringed by their institutions, they have developed procedural limitations that require religious organizations to uphold fair trial guarantees in their relationships with third parties, and have finally adopted substantive limitations that delineate the duty of these organizations to respect the rights of third parties.

2.2.4. Assessing the legitimacy of religious interpretations

Despite apparent similarities with the German cases discussed earlier, the reasoning of the ECtHR in *Sindicatul 'Păstorul cel Bun'* departs from its previous case law in certain respects.[302] The most important departure that needs to be addressed here is the readiness of the Court to assess the legitimacy of the religious interpretation of the Romanian Orthodox Church in denying the right of its employees to unionize. After undertaking a succinct analysis, the ECtHR concluded that:

The Court observes that the applicant union's constitution did not contain any passages that were critical of the faith or of the Church.... In the present case the Court observes that the applicant union's demands related exclusively to defending the economic, social and cultural rights and interests of salaried employees of the Church. Recognition of the

---

[302] For instance, the European judges considered the refusal of the authorities to register the union as pursuing a legitimate aim: that of protecting public order 'which encompasses the freedom and autonomy of religious communities'. *Sindicatul 'Păstorul cel Bun' v. Romania*, Application no 2330/09, Judgment of 31 January 2012, para. 67. The Court's approach in the *Schüth* case was to balance the right of the applicant against the right of a religious organization to autonomy. *Schüth v. Germany*, Application no 1620/03, Judgment of 23 September 2010, para. 56. Given that church autonomy derives from the collective right of individuals to freedom of religion, one is hard pressed to see why the protection of church autonomy would be regarded as a legitimate aim under the heading of public order, as opposed to the rights of others. As the two dissenting judges argued, it would have seemed more logical and in keeping with its own jurisprudence for the Court to balance the competing interests of the trade union under article 11 against those of the church to autonomy under article 9. Joint Dissenting Opinions of Judges Ziemele and Tsotsoria, *Sindicatul 'Păstorul cel Bun' v. Romania*, Application no 2330/09, Judgment of 31 January 2012, para. 6. See also the Grand Chamber's take on the issue, *Sindicatul 'Păstorul cel Bun' v. Romania*, Application no 2330/09, Grand Chamber, Judgment of 9 July 2013, para. 158. Some commentators argue that the consequences of substituting public order for the rights of others as a legitimate ground for interference permitted the Court to apply more strict criteria for the interference, in respect to article 11. See G. Puppinck, A. Popescu, *Critica hotărârii CEDO cu privire la Sindicatul Păstorul cel bun Impotriva României* (nr. 2330/09), European Centre for Law and Justice, accessed May 2012, http://strasbourgconsortium. org/document.php?DocumentID=5866, at 3–4.

union would therefore not have undermined either the legitimacy of religious beliefs or the means used to express them.[303]

One commentator went so far as to hold that, through this assessment, 'the Court was usurping the statutory law and organization integrity of the Orthodox Church in contradiction to its long held position of neutrality towards religious beliefs and internal church structure'.[304] Whether such vehemence is justified by the ECtHR's finding is doubtful, nonetheless, it is clear that, in making the quoted statement, the Court was declaring that it felt competent to understand and evaluate the doctrine of the Romanian Orthodox Church. The two dissenting judges in the case claimed that it was not appropriate for the Court to place itself in this position.[305] The most curious aspect perhaps is the fact that while reversing the judgment, the Grand Chamber also undertakes an assessment of the legitimacy of the religious interpretations of both the clerical union and the Orthodox Church.[306]

Another analytical angle may explain the Court's decision to disregard its own cautionary advice ('but for very exceptional cases, . . . the Convention excludes any discretion on the part of the State to determine whether religious beliefs or the means used to express such beliefs are legitimate'[307]), and to question the legitimacy of the interpretation of religion offered by the Romanian Orthodox Church in this specific case. One senses that, in the *Sindicatul 'Păstorul cel Bun'*, the main issue was not how to balance correctly the rights of its employees to unionize and the right of the church to self-administration, it was the legitimacy of the Church's religious interpretation that was problematic. In none of the previous employment cases which addressed church autonomy was the ECtHR confronted with a church document that explicitly denied a human right. Certainly, restrictions on the right to privacy and on freedom of religion could be inferred from the work contracts in the German cases, yet the difference in this case is evident. Article 123.8 in the Statute of the Romanian Orthodox Church is unequivocal:

The priests, deacons and monks are not allowed to set up, be members of or take part in associations, foundations or organisations of any sort, without having the blessing of the Diocesan Bishop.[308]

As a consequence of this provision, setting up a union without the agreement of the bishop (i.e. higher official) is excluded. Indeed, one is hard-pressed to

---

[303] *Sindicatul 'Păstorul cel Bun' v. Romania,* Application no 2330/09, Judgment of 31 January 2012, paras. 73 and 75.

[304] R. Kiska, *The Question of Church Autonomy in Affaire Sindicatul Pastorul cel bun c. Roumanie, Alliance Defense Fund,* accessed May 2012, http://strasbourgconsortium.org/document.php?DocumentID=5848.

[305] Joint Dissenting Opinion of Judges Ziemele and Tsotsoria, *Sindicatul 'Păstorul cel Bun' v. Romania,* Application no.2330/09, Judgment of 31 January 2012, para. 5.

[306] *Sindicatul 'Păstorul cel Bun' v. Romania,* Application no. 2330/09, Grand Chamber, Judgment of 9 July 2013, paras. 161–162 and 164.

[307] *Hasan and Chaush v. Bulgaria,* Application no. 30985/96, Judgment of 26 October 2000, para. 78.

[308] The Statutes for the Organisation and Functioning of the Romanian Orthodox Church. General Stipulations, November 2007, HG no. 53, 16 January 2008, English translation, accessed March 2014, http://patriarhia.deveu.com/_upload/documente/121438488425759490.pdf, art. 123.8.

understand what protection of the right to unionize remains under article 11 if establishing a union is made dependent on the express agreement of superiors.[309] In the words of the Freedom of Association Committee of the Governing Body of the International Labour Organization: 'The principle of freedom of association would often remain a dead letter if workers and employers were required to obtain any kind of previous authorization to enable them to establish an organization'.[310] It is rather unfortunate and indeed erroneous that the Grand Chamber had failed to grasp this crucial aspect.[311] Article 123.8 of the church statute also reveals its full impact on issues of privacy when one realizes that a priest would be prevented from becoming a member of a tennis club if the bishop disagreed with his hobby.[312] If the heart of the issue is indeed religious interpretation, the Court seems to have treated this case as 'exceptional' and assessed the legitimacy of the Church's opinion.

Contrast *Sindicatul 'Păstorul cel Bun'* with the judgment of the Supreme Court of the United Kingdom in *R v The Governing Body of JFS and the Admissions Appeal Panel of JFS and others*.[313] This case concerned the refusal of JFS (formerly Jewish Free School) to admit E's son M to the school. M was a practising Masorti Jew, his mother, of Italian and Catholic origin, had converted to Judaism under the auspices of a non-Orthodox synagogue. This procedure of conversion was not recognized by the Office of the Chief Rabbi of the United Hebrew Congregation of the Commonwealth (OCR). The OCR recognizes a person as Jewish if that person is either descended in the matrilineal line from a woman whom the OCR would recognize as Jewish, or has undertaken a qualifying course of Orthodox conversion.[314]

---

[309] See Freedom of Association and Protection of the Right to Organize Convention, 1948 (No. 87), art. 2; Right to Organize and Collective Bargaining Convention, 1949 (No. 98), art. 2.1.

[310] Digest of Decisions and Principles of the Freedom of Association Committee of the Governing Body of the ILO, 5th (revised) edition, (Geneva: ILO, 2006), para. 272. Contrast with the Grand Chambers' statement that the Statute of the Romanian Orthodox Church does not provide for 'an absolute ban' on clergy to form a trade union. *Sindicatul 'Păstorul cel Bun' v. Romania*, Application no 2330/09, Grand Chamber, Judgment of 9 July 2013, para. 170.

[311] In this author's view the Grand Chamber's interpretation that 'there is nothing to stop' the applicant's members from forming a union that respects church doctrine or joining an existing one is incorrect. Due to the prior authorization requirement entailed by the Statute the hierarchical superior is entitled to interpret what conforms to church doctrine and can stop the forming or joining of a union by the applicant's members at any time.

[312] The cited article 123.8 is not unique in restricting the human rights of priests to the point of annulment. Article 50.e. for example touches upon the core of the right to access a court and the right to private and family life. 'Similarly, the clergy of parishes, by virtue of the oath of subordination towards the Diocesan Bishop sworn in at the ordination, and monks by virtue of the monastic vote of obedience, can appear in court only with the previous written consent of the Diocesan Bishop including in cases concerning personal matters.' Statutul pentru organizarea şi funcţionare Bisericii Ortodoxe Române, art. 50.e. An English translation of this article can be found in the English version of the Statute, available on the official website of the Romanian Orthodox Church, http://patriarhia. deveu.com/_upload/documente/121438488425759490.pdf, but the translation appears imperfect to this author. The author's translation has therefore been preferred.

[313] *R (on the application of E) (Respondent) v. The Governing Body of JFS and the Admissions Appeal Panel of JFS and others (Appelants)* [2009] UKSC 15.

[314] See *R (on the application of E) (Respondent) v The Governing Body of JFS and the Admissions Appeal Panel of JFS and others (Appellants)* [2009] UKSC 15, Press Summary, 16 December 2009, accessed May 2012, http://www.supremecourt.gov.uk/docs/uksc_2009_0136_ps.pdf.

As the school was over-subscribed, it was the policy of JFS to give precedence in admission to those children recognized as Jewish by the OCR, and M's application for admission to JFS was therefore rejected. It should be noted here that religious discrimination in school admissions is prohibited under the Equality Act 2006, but that designated faith schools, such as JFS, are exempted and can therefore utilize religiously discriminatory criteria for admission purposes.[315] In this context, E wanted to show that his son suffered discrimination, not on grounds of religion but on grounds of ethnicity under the Race Relations Act 1976. The case reached the Supreme Court after the claim had been rejected by the High Court and admitted on appeal. A split Supreme Court decided by five to four that JFS had directly discriminated against M on grounds of his ethnic origin.

It is clear that the case was decided on the Race Relations Act 1976 and not on the Human Rights Act 1998 and involved a juridical analysis of direct and indirect discrimination under the former instrument.[316] Some authors have explored the intricacies of the case and imagined what its outcome would have been had it been brought under the Human Rights Act 1998.[317] What is central for the current study is the question of what 'being Jewish' means and how the Supreme Court tackled this question. Christopher McCrudden, junior counsel for JFS in the case, explains that JFS sought to distinguish the two ways in which someone may be regarded as Jewish: in terms of ethnicity, and religion.[318] JFS recognized that M was ethnically Jewish according to an anthropological definition, because M self-identified himself as Jewish, was involved in the Jewish community, and was recognized to be part of it. JFS did not, however, recognize M as religiously Jewish under the Orthodox interpretation of Jewish law embraced by OCR.[319]

Lord Brown—as part of the majority—accepted that the decision as to who qualifies as a Jew, as a matter of Jewish law, is a religious one; descent is therefore employed as a means of determining a religious question. He nonetheless cautioned:

But, when the answer to that religious question has consequences in the civil law sphere, its legality falls to be examined. If the decision has consequences that are not permitted under

---

[315] McCrudden, 'Multiculturalism, Freedom of Religion, Equality, and the British Constitution: The JFS Case Considered', at 209.

[316] The Race Relations Act 1976 is understood to address both direct and indirect discrimination. Race Relations Act 1976, s.1 and s.1(1A). The difference is that direct discrimination cannot be justified. The Supreme Court proceeded to determine whether the victim's ethnic origins as 'factual criteria' determined the decision made by the discriminator. The intention of JFS to discriminate or not was irrelevant. Indirect discrimination, on the other hand, is measured by whether the means adopted to pursue a legitimate aim are proportionate to the effects on the discriminated individual. *R(E) v Governing Body of JFS*, paras. 13–21 and 93–103.

[317] See McCrudden, 'Multiculturalism, Freedom of Religion, Equality, and the British Constitution: The JFS Case Considered', at 215 ff. See also Kiviorg, 'Collective Religious Autonomy under the European Convention on Human Rights: the UK Jewish Free School Case in International Perspective', at 9–14.

[318] McCrudden, 'Multiculturalism, Freedom of Religion, Equality, and the British Constitution: The JFS Case Considered', at 210–212. One should note here that the claim that Israel is not a religious state similarly relies on this distinction. See Goldstein, 'Israel: A Secular or a Religious State?'; Temperman, *State-Religion Relationships and Human Rights Law: Towards a Right to Religiously Neutral Governance*, at 25–28.

[319] McCrudden, 'Multiculturalism, Freedom of Religion, Equality, and the British Constitution: The JFS Case Considered', at 211.

the law, the fact that it was taken for a religious purpose will not save it from the condition of illegality.[320]

In Lord Brown's view, the fact that the decision to reject M's application to the JFS was based 'on the determination of a religious issue cannot, of itself, insulate it from the charge of discrimination on racial grounds'.[321] To extrapolate Lord Brown's point, religious decisions made by a religious organization should not escape the test of legality merely because the decision is a religious one and the organization making it enjoys a special legitimacy: indeed, this is precisely what this study aims to demonstrate throughout its various chapters.

The objection in this case is that the religious decision does not mask racial, but religious, discrimination and in the UK religious discrimination is permitted for admission purposes in a designated faith school. The justices in minority under-lined that race was not the basis of the religious decision made by JFS. Lord Roger's parallel with the Dutch Reformed Church of South Africa is instructive:

The discrimination there was plainly against blacks and in favour of whites—self-evidently, therefore, on the ground of race and irredeemable by reference to the Church's underly-ing religious motive. Ethnic Jews and Jews recognised as members of the religion, distin-guishable as groups though they are, clearly overlap. Not so blacks and whites. What I am suggesting here is that it is quite unrealistic, given that those being treated less favourably and those being treated more favourably by JFS's policy are all (save, of course, for those who have no connection with Judaism whatsoever) in the same ethnic group, to regard the policy as discriminatory on racial rather than religious grounds. I recognise, of course, that under section 3(2) of the 1976 Act a particular racial group within a wider racial group still enjoys protection under the Act. The point I am making, however, is that the differential treatment between Jews recognised by the OCR and those not so recognised within the wider group of ethnic Jews (no less obviously than the differential treatment between the former and those with no connection whatever to Judaism) is plainly on the ground of religion rather than race.[322]

The dispute among the different Jewish denominations is not whether membership in the Jewish religion should or should not be defined by descent and conversion, there is agreement on that. The debate concerns the rules applied to conversion, whereby Orthodox Jews require that it be recognized by the OCR, while Masorti, Reform, and Liberal Jews apply less demanding criteria for conversion.[323] Joseph Weiler therefore takes the argument of the majority further and points to its logi-cal, troubling, yet unstated conclusion: if JFS is racially discriminatory because it relies on descent and conversion to define who is Jewish for purposes of admission, than all Jewish denominations are equally discriminatory because they similarly rely on descent and conversion.[324] In Weiler's view, the majority judges projected

---

[320] *R(E) v Governing Body of JFS*, para. 119.
[321] *R(E) v Governing Body of JFS*, para. 120.
[322] *R(E) v Governing Body of JFS*, para. 245.
[323] J. H. H. Weiler, 'Discrimination and Identity in London: The Jewish Free School Case', *Jewish Review of Books* 1 (2010).
[324] See note 323.

their Christian understanding of membership in a religion—that it is essentially a 'matter of doctrinal conviction', whereby one is a Christian because one believes in Christ—onto the definition of Jewishness in this case.

What is troubling about the Majority is its sheer incomprehension and consequent intolerance of a religion whose self-understanding is different than that of Christianity. Their anthropological reading of ethnicity is suitable in the circumstances for which the Race Relations Act was intended. But when the law makes an exception for religion and the religion in question is Judaism, it should be understood on its own terms, not on Christian (or, more precisely, Protestant) terms.... [T]he most troubling discrimination I see here is the one against Jewish institutions applying religious criteria of membership.[325]

This case is revealing because it portrays how a highly respected and competent judicial instance, despite undertaking a thorough analysis, had difficulties in understanding and therefore evaluating the legitimacy of a religious belief, and thereby arguably infringed upon the right to church autonomy. The rather ironic result is that, while holding that the admission criterion (arguably one based on grounds of ethnic origin) adopted by JFS was racially discriminatory, the Court went out of its way to insist that neither JFS, nor the Chief Rabbi, should be seen as racists 'in the popular way'.[326] It is interesting that Lord Mance, of the majority, who was the only judge to acknowledge the right to religious autonomy and also pointed to its limitations, apparently dismissed their usefulness to the case. It is suggested that it would have been a better approach to focus on the limitations of church autonomy, rather than the legitimacy of the descent and conversion criteria applied by JFS and the OCR. The former option would have engaged the court in assessing whether the interpretation given by the JFS and OCR to what 'being Jewish' means had a *disproportionately discriminatory impact* on M, as opposed to whether the claimed definition of Jewishness in itself was discriminatory. The former option was readily available to the Supreme Court: it would have essentially determined the Lords to ask whether indirect discrimination was at stake.[327] This would have allowed for a proportionality test and would have potentially better served the Court.[328] When a court focuses on limiting the impact of the manifestations of religious organizations on the rights of others, it runs less risk of becoming entangled with the religious interpretations themselves, in particular such fundamental matters as the criteria stipulating who belongs to a religion.

This section cannot conclude however that the preferred option is always to limit the effects of a religious belief by applying a proportionality test, rather than

---

[325] See note 323.

[326] *R(E) v Governing Body of JFS*, paras. 9, 54, 156, 184. See also what appears to be a disclaimer in *R (on the application of E) (Respondent) v The Governing Body of JFS and the Admissions Appeal Panel of JFS and others (Appellants)* [2009] UKSC 15, Press Summary, 16 December 2009, accessed May 2012, http://www.supremecourt.gov.uk/docs/uksc_2009_0136_ps.pdf.

[327] This is precisely what Lord Hope and Lord Walker did.

[328] See generally McCrudden, who discusses the mutations of the meaning of direct and indirect discrimination in the context of changing world views on multiculturalism and equality, and how these may have had an impact on the case. McCrudden, 'Multiculturalism, Freedom of Religion, Equality, and the British Constitution: The JFS Case Considered', 200–229.

addressing the legitimacy of the religious belief itself. Fundamentally, one cannot accept a racist religion, not because of its impact, but because the belief *itself* fails the legality test. One cannot accept a religious interpretation that expressly denies, to the point of extinction, the rights of an organization's employees, not because of its actual or potential impact but because the interpretation *itself* fails to uphold the law. The refutation of a religious interpretation is unquestionably legitimate where religious organizations advocate national, racial, or religious hatred which constitutes incitement to discrimination, hostility or violence.[329] It is true that registration and recognition requirements usually provide authorities with the possibility to make an initial assessment of the fundamental principles of a religious organization. This has been found to serve:

> the legitimate aim of allowing the Government to ensure that the religious organisations aspiring to their official recognition by the State were acting in accordance with the law, did not present any danger for a democratic society and did not carry out any activity directed against the interests of public safety, public order, health, morals or the rights and freedoms of others.[330]

Even against this background, it must be admitted that religious organizations may move away from the initial religious principles set out in their registration document. Societies and their interests may evolve in the same way. It seems undesirable to *always* deny a court's capacity to assess the legitimacy of beliefs, while certainly such undertaking should be seen an a means of last resort.

To conclude, what becomes clear is that the best defence for religious organizations seeking to shield their interpretations of religion from the review of secular courts—and thereby protect their right to religious autonomy—is to uphold human rights by assuming their human rights responsibilities, the contours of which are emerging, as we have seen, in recent case law of the ECtHR. In practice, this means that it is not enough for a church to consider its religious law when deciding a termination of employment or setting up admission criteria for a faith school, religious organizations must also take into consideration the human rights of their employees, their potential students, and other third parties.

IV. Conclusion

This chapter has demonstrated that religious organizations can enjoy and claim rights under the ECHR in a similar fashion to their non-religious peers. Churches and other organizations with religious or philosophical aims have successfully invoked the rights to fair trial and to effective remedies, freedom of expression, freedom of association and assembly, and rights to property under article 1 of Protocol 1. Serious doubts have been expressed about the existence of a right of

---

[329] See discussion at II.2.3 in this chapter.

[330] *Cârmuirea Spirituală a Musulmanilor din Republica Moldova*, Application no. 12282/02, Decision of 14 June 2005, para. 1.

religious organizations—and their non-religious peers—not to have their religious feelings offended. Religious organizations do not enjoy parental rights under article 2 of Protocol 1. It has been established that among legal entities only organizations with religious or philosophical objects can invoke article 9. The analysis has shown that this different treatment is not to be explained by the religious legitimacy of the latter, which would translate into a different legality regime: rather, religious legal entities enjoy religious freedom as a right that derives from the right of individuals to collectively manifest religion. In the absence of such a derived link, non-religious legal entities cannot invoke article 9. It is in this context that church autonomy, as the exclusive right of religious organizations, should be understood. The analysis has further focused on identifying the limits of the right to religious autonomy when it conflicts with the human rights of third parties. It has identified an evolution in the ECtHR's practice, from the voluntariness principle as an exit strategy for church employees and members who felt that their rights had been infringed by the religious entity, to the adoption of procedural limitations requiring religious organizations to uphold fair trial guarantees in their relationship with third parties, and finally the application of substantive limitations on church autonomy which affirm the duty of these organizations to consider the human rights of third parties.

To conclude, it seems appropriate to offer some arguments for suggesting why religious organizations might be willing to assume human rights obligations. Some scholars have pointed out that religious organizations may find such an exercise 'irksome', because human rights are not internal to their laws and practices, or their autonomy.[331] On the contrary, we posit that human rights obligations are internal to religious entities, and upholding them is the best means to protect against state interference in a democratic society. The first claim draws on the roots of church autonomy itself (that is, the collective right of individuals to manifest religion), protected by article 9.1 of ECHR and limited by article 9.2. Therefore, church autonomy as a human right, and its limitations giving rise to human rights responsibilities, are internal to religious organizations. It would be irreconcilable from a legal viewpoint for a religious organization to assume the right, while negating the limitations on the right and therefore its responsibilities.

The second claim is inspired by the philosophical concept of relational autonomy. Marina Oshana developed the notion of relational autonomy as an autonomy constructed by a person's relations with other individuals. The individual is not 'an island of independence', but exists in the context of relations with others. In this context, the autonomous individual has the freedom to oversee 'states of affairs and events vital to the administration of one's life', as well as alter significant relations in one's life.[332] It is evident that Oshana's concept was not describing church, but personal autonomy, the analogy is nevertheless interesting. Church autonomy exists,

---

[331] Evans and Hood, 'Religious Autonomy and Labour Law: A Comparison of the Jurisprudence of the United States and the European Court of Human Rights', at 22.

[332] M. Oshana, *Personal Autonomy in Society*, (Aldershot: Ashgate 2006), at 158–159. See also W. W. Cao, 'Review: Personal Autonomy in Society', 3 *In-Spire Journal of Law, Politics and Societies* 2 (2008), 171–173.

as various domestic legislative texts prove, in relation to the state: in this sense, it is a relational autonomy. Therefore, religious autonomy cannot mean complete insulation from the state, but freedom of self-administration, including the evaluation of how relationships with the state should change or be maintained. In this context, a religious organization may wish to assume human rights responsibilities, not because these have been imposed in a paternalist manner by the state, but because it makes a deliberate move to define its relationship with the state in a way that minimizes interference.[333] In a democratic society, state interference with the right to religious autonomy will be minimized when religious organizations themselves ensure procedural safeguards and maintain a balance between their religious interpretations and the human rights of others. In conclusion, we submit that human rights responsibilities are internal to religious organizations, and assuming them will strategically advance respect of church autonomy by state authorities.

---

[333] Our proposition echoes Theo van Boven's assertion: 'The responsibility of Non-State Actors and their duties to respect and to comply with international law, must be regarded as inherently linked with the claim that they qualify as acceptable parties in national and international society'. At the same time we go further, to suggest that acknowledging these responsibilities is in the interest of religious organizations themselves. T. van Boven, 'Non-State Actors; Introductory Comments [1997]', in F. Coomans, et al. (eds.), *Human Rights from Exclusion to Inclusion; Principles and Practice: An Anthology from the Work of Theo van Boven*, (The Hague: Kluwer, 2000), 363–369, at 501.

4

The Holy See-Vatican State-Like Construct

'The older I get... the more convinced I am that we must only work on ourselves, to grow in grace.'

—Dorothy Day[1]

I. Introduction

Let us assume that the international community accepted the Obama Administration as a UN permanent observer *state*, not for the benefit of the United States population that it governs, but by virtue of the important mission which the Obama Administration fulfils as governing body of the Universal Healthcare-Reform Organization. If one were to substitute the Holy See[2] for the Obama Administration, the population at the Vatican for US citizens, and the Roman Catholic Church for the Universal Healthcare-Reform Organization, this admittedly wild hypothetical situation would shed some of its triviality.

This unusual and imperfect parallel offers some initial insights into why and how the Holy See religious actor was granted access to an arena traditionally limited to states. With respect to the why, historical circumstances and the religious legitimacy of the Holy See appear to make the difference between a ludicrous hypothesis and a legal fact. With respect to the how, it appears that the resemblance to a state,[3] resulting from the provisions of the Lateran Treaty—which 'recognizes

---

[1] E. Elssberg (ed.), *The Selected Letters of Dorothy Day* (Milwaukee, WI: Marquette University Press, 2010), at 326.

[2] The term Holy See is used interchangably with Apostolic See; it includes the Pope, the Secretariat of State, the Congregation for the Doctrine of the Faith and other congregations, tribunals, and other institutions of the Roman Curia. The Holy See is the central government of the Catholic Church and acts as the government of the Vatican City State. Code of Canon Law (CIC) 1983, can. 361; CRC Committee, Initial Report to the Committee on the Rights of the Child on the Optional Protocol on the Sale of Children, Child Prostitution and Child Pornography, Holy See, UN Doc. CRC/C/OPSC/VAT/1, para. 4.b; G. Westdickenberg, 'Holy See', in R. Wolfrum (ed.), *MPEPIL*, (Online edition: Oxford University Press, 2006), para. 1. See also IV.3 in this chapter.

[3] When describing the Holy See-Vatican construct this study uses the phrases 'resemblance of statehood', 'resemblance to a state', 'akin to a state', as opposed to 'statehood', to underline the peculiar features of this actor. See part IV in this chapter.

the full ownership and the exclusive and absolute power and jurisdiction of the Holy See over the Vatican…creating in this manner Vatican City'[4]—facilitated the access. Sir Hersch Lauterpacht summarized the situation masterfully:

We are thus confronted with the phenomenon of a spiritual purpose, utterly different from that normally represented by States in the international arena, clothing itself with the formal attributes of statehood and recognized as such by the other members of the international community. The formal requirements of statehood still constitute a condition of representation of that new type of interest. But it is a condition reduced to formality.[5]

Nonetheless, as we shall see, arguing, based on the effectiveness criteria of statehood, that the Holy See or the Vatican are a state is similar to fitting a square peg into a round hole. But 'the lawyer cannot afford to ignore entities which maintain some sort of existence on the international legal plane in spite of their anomalous character'.[6] Therefore jurists often attempt to accommodate the Holy See as an entity sui generis.[7] Antonio Cassese defined this class of entities as exhibiting three characteristics; they:

(1) have come to acquire a legal status on account of specific *historic circumstances*; (2)…*do not possess any distinct territory* or, if they do use a territory, this belongs to another entity; (3) have a *very limited international personality*, not different, *in practice* from that of…diminutive States (which however in theory are vested with all the rights and powers belonging to sovereign States).[8]

The above characteristics suggest that the Holy See has acquired international legal status by virtue of tradition, resulting from the religious legitimacy of the Holy See as the government of the Catholic Church; that the Vatican territory is deprived of sovereignty for it is subjected to the supremacy of the Holy See and as such it is the Holy See that enjoys a limited international personality which confers certain rights that are akin to those of states.[9] But, as the saying goes, *le bon Dieu est dans le détail*. First, in interpreting the practice of states, early doctrine had different views on the first element in Cassese's definition, specifically on whether the Holy See continued to enjoy international personality in the absence of its territories, after their annexation by Italy in 1870. Scholars today debate the second and third aspects, in other words whether the Vatican is a state and therefore whether statehood gives rise to a separate international personality for the Vatican City State, alongside that of the Holy See. Second, what are the implications of the personality variants for the obligations of the entity/entities? At times, one has the impression

---

[4] Conciliation Treaty between the Holy See and Italy (signed 11 February 1929, ratified 7 June 1929), English version accessed January 2012, http://www.vaticanstate.va/content/dam/vaticanstate/documenti/leggi-e-decreti/Normative-Penali-e-Amministrative/LateranTreaty.pdf, art. 3 (hereafter Lateran Treaty).

[5] Lauterpacht, 'General Rules of the Law of Peace', at 306.

[6] Brownlie, *Principles of Public International Law*, 7th ed., at 61.

[7] Brownlie, *Principles of Public International Law*, 7th ed., at 64; Cassese, *International Law*, 2nd ed., at 131.

[8] Cassese, *International Law*, 2nd ed., at 131. (Emphasis in the original).

[9] See note 8.

that the personality question has become a controversy in itself and is treated as an abstract issue, divorced of its implications in terms of the rights *and* obligations that flow from each of the different personality variants.

In the context of this study's general endeavour to demonstrate that religious actors do not form an autonomous legal category in international law, this chapter will show that the Holy See and the Vatican together form a construct with a single personality grounded in two sources: international custom recognizing the religious legitimacy of the Holy See, and the Lateran Treaty which confers upon the construct the resemblance of statehood. It will be argued that this state-like construct enjoys the rights and incurs the responsibilities of a state. The present chapter departs from the predominantly jurisprudential analysis of Chapter 3, by also relying on legal positivism, the examination of diplomatic practice, and insights from social constructivism.

As to the outline, the chapter starts by identifying the three personality variants articulated by doctrine, focusing on the dual personality scenario and the legal challenges it poses. It introduces the Holy See-Vatican construct with one international personality as a solution to these challenges (II). An examination of the post-1870 legal status of the Holy See then establishes whether its personality ceased to exist because of the loss of its territories to Italy (III). The fourth part analyses the provisions of the Lateran Treaty in the light of the effectiveness criteria for statehood, in an effort to distinguish whether the law offers support to the dual personality scenario or, on the contrary, to the Holy See-Vatican state-like construct (IV). The logic behind the Holy See's self-perception as a dual person is discussed in the fifth part (V). The sixth part marks the transition from law and rhetoric to practice. The diplomatic practice of states and the jurisprudence of their courts are largely compatible with the construct proposal, whereby the Holy See enjoys privileges of statehood no different from any other state. It is argued that the participation of the Holy See and the Vatican in international organizations, and as a party to treaties, is explainable by appeal to the resemblance of statehood conferred upon the construct. Lastly, this part examines the obligations of the Holy See under human rights law, in particular the Convention on the Rights of the Child (CRC), in the context of child sexual abuse by Catholic clerics. It is submitted that these obligations are not different in nature from the obligations of other states, although their extraterritorial applicability may well be of greater significance than in the case of other states (VI). The chapter ends with some concluding remarks on the discrepancy between the self-perception of the Holy See, on one hand, and law and state practice, on the other (VII).

II. Some Preliminary Observations on the Personality Question

Three variants of international personality can be distilled from legal literature: the Vatican City State as the only international legal person; the Holy See as the sole international legal person, which also controls the Vatican territory; the Holy See and the Vatican City State as two distinct legal personae, whereby the Holy See also functions as the government of the state.[10] Accordingly, a seemingly straight-forward exercise, pinpointing the international personality of an actor, promises to be a complicated analysis. The personality question is far from being an academic or semantic debate. The question of whether there exist one or two personalities, and what rights and obligations each have, is of utmost importance given the different legal implications in practice.

As we shall see, the variant that envisages only the personality of the Vatican City State is difficult to reconcile with history and the provisions of the Lateran Treaty, which both point to the existence of a personality of the Holy See;[11] at the same time, practice appears to assume the resemblance of statehood, and therefore the territoriality of the Vatican becomes relevant. In the absence of the resemblance of statehood it would be difficult to understand the participation of the Holy See as a member or observer *state* in inter-governmental organizations[12] and international treaties[13] restricted to states, as well as the commencement of bilateral

[10] See J. Crawford, *The Creation of States in International Law*, 2nd ed., (Oxford: Oxford University Press, 2006), at 226–227. See also Kurt Martens who offers a similar typology, discerned from the writings of some canon lawyers. K. Martens, 'The Position of the Holy See and Vatican City State in International Relations', 83 *University of Detroit Mercy Law Review* (2005), 729–760, at 754.

[11] See III and IV in this chapter.

[12] The Holy See enjoys the status of permanent observer state of the UN, see VI.3.2 in this chapter. The Holy See is a member of the United Nations Conference on Trade and Development; the World Intellectual Property Organization; the International Atomic Energy Agency; the Organization for the Prohibition of Chemical Weapons; the International Organization of Supreme Audit Institutions; the Organization for Security and Co-operation in Europe (participating state); and is a member of the Executive Committee of the UN High Commissioner for Refugees. It is an observer to the United Nations Food and Agriculture Organization; the International Labour Organization; the World Health Organization; the United Nations Educational, Scientific and Cultural Organization; the United Nations Industrial Development Organization; the International Fund for Agricultural Development; the World Tourist Organization; the World Meteorological Organization; the United Nations Development Program; the United Nations Centre for Human Settlements; the United Nations Environment Programme; the World Food Programme; the World Trade Organization; the International Organization for Migration; the Council of Europe; and the Organization of American States; and is a non-member accredited state of the African Union. *Bilateral and Multilateral Relations of the Holy See*, Secretariat of State, 22 October 2009, accessed February 2012, http://www.vatican.va/roman_curia/secretariat_state/documents/rc_seg-st_20010123_holy-see-relations_en.html; Holy See Press Office, *Bilateral and Multilateral Relations of the Holy See*, Secretariat of State, 1 February 2001, accessed February 2012, http://www.vatican.va/news_services/press/documentazione/documents/corpo-diplomatico/corpo-diplomatico_ internazionali_elenco_en.html.

[13] The Holy See is party to several multilateral treaties, including the 1961 Vienna Convention on Diplomatic Relations (ratified 17 April 1964); the 1963 Vienna Convention on Consular Relations (ratified 8 October 1970); and the 1969 Vienna Convention on the Law of Treaties (ratified 25 February 1977). It has ratified or acceded to the following human rights conventions: the 1966 International Convention on the Elimination of All Forms of Racial Discrimination (ratified 1 May 1969); the 1984 Convention against Torture and Other Cruel, Inhuman or Degrading Treatment or Punishment (acceded 26 June 2002); the 1989 Convention on the Rights of the Child (ratified 20 April 1990); the 2000 Optional Protocol to the Convention on the Rights of the Child on the Involvement of Children in Armed Conflict and the Optional Protocol on the Sale of Children, Child Prostitution and Child Pornography (ratified 24 October 2001). It has ratified or acceded to the following humanitarian, refugee and disarmament treaties: the Four Geneva Conventions of 1949 (ratified 22 February 1951); Additional Protocol I relating to the Protection of Victims of International Armed Conflicts and II relating to the Protection of Victims of Non-International Armed Conflicts of 8 June 1977 (ratified 21 November 1985); the 1951 Convention relating to the Status of Refugees (ratified 15 March 1956) and its 1967 Protocol (acceded 8 June 1967); the 1968 Treaty on the

diplomatic relations with certain states.[14] Lastly, the membership of the Vatican City State in inter-governmental organizations[15] and its participation in international treaties[16] would seem to exclude the variant which presents the Holy See as the single international personality.

These preliminary observations on the three variants of personality would suggest that the dual personality scenario, the third variant proposed by doctrine, which corresponds to the self-perception of the Holy See,[17] is the most viable. This chapter disagrees and will demonstrate that this scenario is not supported by the Lateran Treaty or by most instances of practice.

Moreover, the dual personality scenario causes legal tensions that are difficult to resolve. Logic would suggest that acts by the Holy See in its capacity as the government of the Vatican are to be seen as state acts, and under certain conditions these could trigger the international responsibility of the state;[18] at the same time the Holy See would enjoy state immunity from trial in foreign courts for these acts, subject to certain exceptions.[19] Whereas, other acts of the Holy See that are attributed to the

Non-Proliferation of Nuclear Weapons (acceded 25 February 1971); the 1980 Convention on Prohibitions or Restrictions on the Use of Certain Conventional Weapons which may be deemed to be Excessively Injurious or to have Indiscriminate Effects (acceded 22 July 1997); the 1992 Convention on the Prohibition of the Development, Production, Stockpiling and Use of Chemical Weapons and on their Destruction (ratified 12 May 1999); the 1996 Comprehensive Nuclear-Test-Ban Treaty (ratified 18 July 2001); the 1997 Convention on the Prohibition of the Use, Stockpiling, Production and Transfer of Anti-Personnel Mines and on their Destruction (ratified 17 February 1998); and the 2008 Convention on Cluster Munitions (ratified 3 December 2010). It has ratified or acceded to the following conventions against terrorism and organized crime: the International Convention for the Suppression of Counterfeiting Currency of 1929 (acceded 1 March 1965); the 1988 UN Convention against Illicit Traffic in Narcotic Drugs and Psychotropic Substances (ratified 25 January 2012); the 1999 International Convention for the Suppression of the Financing of Terrorism (acceded 25 January 2012); and the 2000 United Nations Convention against Transnational Organized Crime (acceded 25 January 2012). In the realm of environmental law, it has acceded to the Vienna Convention for the Protection of the Ozone Layer of 1985 and its Montreal Protocol of 1987 (5 June 2008). It has ratified or acceded to the following copyright and cultural property conventions: the 1954 Convention and Protocol for the Protection of Cultural Property in the event of armed conflict (acceded 24 February 1958); Convention for the Protection of Producers of Phonograms against Unauthorized Duplication of their Phonograms of 1971 (ratified 4 April 1977); the Universal Copyrights Convention as revised in 1972 (ratified 6 February 1980).

[14] See VI.1 in this chapter.

[15] The Vatican is listed as member of the Universal Postal Union (UPU); the International Telecommunication Union (ITU); the International Grains Council (IGC); the International Telecommunications Satellite Organization (ITSO); the European Telecommunication Satellite Organization; the European Conference of Postal and Telecommunications; the International Institute of Administrative Sciences. See *Bilateral and Multilateral Relations of the Holy See*, Secretariat of State, 22 October 2009. However, a 2001 Note by the Secretariat of States attributes to the Holy See the membership 'also in the name and on behalf of the Vatican City State' in the above enumerated organizations. See Holy See Press Office, *Bilateral and Multilateral Relations of the Holy See*, Secretariat of State, 1 February 2001. See discussion VI.3 in this chapter.

[16] The Vatican has ratified a number of treaties among which are the Convention on the Recovery Abroad of Maintenance (ratified 5 October 1954); the International Wheat Agreement (ratified 9 July 1956); and the Statute of the International Atomic Energy Agency (ratified 20 August 1957).

[17] See V in this chapter.

[18] See ILC, Articles on Responsibility of States for Internationally Wrongful Acts, UN Doc. A/56/10 (2001), arts. 1 and 2, at 32–36.

[19] The principle *par in parem non habet imperium* is seen as the foundation of state immunity in the post-Westphalian system in which states are sovereign equals, and as such one state's court

second international personality not stemming from statehood could not engage state responsibility;[20] conversely, when the Holy See acts as the government of the Catholic Church it would not enjoy state immunity from trial in foreign courts.[21] One may argue, therefore, that political acts performed by the Holy See as the government of the Vatican are state acts, whereas acts performed by the Holy See in the spiritual field are acts of the government of the Roman Catholic Church which are not attributable to the state under the rules of state responsibility. This distinction, sound in theory, does not hold true in practice.

The issue of sexual abuse of children by Catholic clerics showcases the legal challenges posed by the dual personality scenario and the inadequacy of the political/spiritual criterion of differentiation between the two personae. In United States courts, the Holy See has invoked state immunity from civil claims over the Catholic Church's handling of clerics accused of child sexual abuse. According to the political/spiritual distinction, the handling of clerics would certainly fall within the remit of spiritual matters, for which the Holy See as the government of the Roman Catholic Church is responsible, and should therefore not be covered by state immunity. However, US judges have not differentiated between the two personalities based on the political/spiritual criterion, but have accorded to the Holy See, as a construct akin to a state, the privileges of state immunity from trial.[22] In turn, the Holy See's reporting to the CRC Committee illustrates that it does not assume its obligations under the Convention on the Rights of the Child as a state, but portrays them as moral obligations drawing on its personality as the government of the Catholic Church.[23] Other instances confirm this approach by the Holy See, which amounts to a *shifting of personalities* according to its needs. For example, the Special Representative of the Secretary-General on human rights defenders, Hina Jilani, sent a communication to the Holy See concerning a priest who was arguably removed from his position partly because of his participation in a 'gay pride' march in defence of the human rights of homosexual persons.[24] The

---

cannot sit in judgment of another state's acts. As a consequence of the evolution from the general principle of absolute state immunity to that of a relative state immunity, today a distinction needs to be made between *actae iure imperii* and *actae iure gestionis*. While acts performed by a state in its capacity as a sovereign are immune from foreign jurisdiction, state immunity does not extend to commercial transactions. The territorial tort exception should also be mentioned here. State immunity is excluded in cases concerning pecuniary compensation for personal injuries or damage to property if the act or omission causing the injuries took place in the territory of the forum state. Cassese, *International Law*, 2nd ed., at 100–101; P.-T. Stoll, 'State Immunity', in R. Wolfrum (ed.), *MPEPIL*, (Online edition: Oxford University Press, 2011), paras. 37–40. See also United Nations Convention on Jurisdictional Immunities of States and Their Property, 2004 (not entered into force), arts. 10–17.

[20] Certainly, the entity would still be bound by customary international law. However, *state* responsibility would not be an issue.

[21] This claim has been made by the plaintiffs in *O'Bryan v. Holy See*, 490 F. Supp. 2d 826 (W.D. Ky. 2005), at 828. See VI.2.3 in this chapter.

[22] See VI.2.3 in this chapter.

[23] See VI.4 in this chapter.

[24] Report submitted by the Special Representative of the Secretary-General on human rights defenders, Hina Jilani, Addendum, Compilation of developments in the area of human rights defenders, UN Doc. E/CN.4/2006/95/Add.5, 6 March 2006, para. 713.

Holy See responded to the communication by stressing that the measures taken against the cleric were not related to his participation in a 'gay pride' march and 'were an expression of the self-organizing capacity proper to every religious community and recognized by the Declaration on the Elimination of All Forms of Intolerance and Discrimination Based on Religion or Belief'.[25] The emphasis is clearly on the right to church autonomy and the human rights obligations of the Holy See qua government of a state do not seem to be taken into account.

Even if the dual personality scenario is accepted as valid—which this study contests—the assumption that solely moral obligations bind the Holy See is problematic, since the Holy See's personality qua church would be bound by human rights obligations of a customary nature. Indeed, this is the risk of the dual personality scenario: it opens the door to legal uncertainty. The major underlying problem is that the shifting of personalities creates a situation in which the Holy See may legitimately avail itself of the rights of a state, and at the same time not comply with the obligations deriving from statehood.

It is submitted that the *sui generis* definition as proposed by Antonio Cassese is very much applicable to the Holy See, with a further refinement. The proposed refinement echoes Malcolm Shaw's observation that 'the Vatican City is closely linked with the Holy See and they are essentially part of the same construct'.[26] The submission of this chapter—which has not previously been developed in literature—is that the Holy See and the Vatican form a construct and thereby share a single international personality, which nevertheless derives from two different sources: historic recognition of the religious legitimacy of the Holy See; *and* the state-like resemblance conferred upon the construct by the Lateran Treaty in 1929. It will be argued that this variant reflects history, is supported by the Lateran Treaty, domestic jurisprudence and international monitoring of human rights bodies, and makes sense of an otherwise erratic practice of states.

Conceiving of the Holy See-Vatican as a construct would resolve most of the legal difficulties identified earlier in relation to the other three personality variants. First, the membership of international organizations and participation in treaties by either the Holy See or the Vatican would not raise objections provided they are considered as parts of a construct akin to a state. Second, the acts of the construct would need to be considered as state acts that enjoy immunity from foreign courts' jurisdiction; however, as with 'normal' states, the distinction between *actae jure imperii* and *actae jure gestionis* would apply, as would the exception for certain tortious acts to limit immunity. Third, the corollary must be that the Holy See, as a construct, incurs international obligations under both treaty law and customary law, the non-performance of which may engage the state's international responsibility.

Promising as the Holy See-Vatican state-like construct may be at a theoretical level, it must be sanctioned by positive law and the practice of states and jurisprudence—this is what this chapter sets out to verify. To inform such analysis an

[25] See note 24.
[26] M. N. Shaw, *International Law*, 5th ed., (Cambridge: Cambridge University Press, 2003), at 219.

account of the post-1870 international status of the Holy See as revealed by legal doctrine is necessary at this stage.

III. The Post-1870 International Status of the Holy See

As a first step in this chapter's quest to settle the personality question and with it the rights and obligations which attach to the Holy See and the Vatican, this part will examine whether the Holy See's international personality ceased to exist when it lost its territories to Italy in 1870.

The Holy See is the government of the Catholic Church and is composed of the Pope,[27] the Secretariat of State, the Congregation for the Doctrine of the Faith, and other congregations, tribunals, and institutions of the Roman Curia.[28] Concomitantly, from the eighth century, when the Papal States were gradually created and guaranteed by the Carolingian dynasty, the Pope accumulated both spiritual and temporal powers.[29] It should be noted that the Holy See is credited with playing an important role in the emergence of modern international relations among sovereign states.[30] The first apostolic nunciature set up in Venice around 1500 was the blueprint of today's permanent diplomatic missions.[31] Moreover, the Holy See concluded treaties with states on temporal matters, as well as concordats regulating the treatment of Catholics and Catholic institutions by other states.[32] Before 1870 the involvement of the Holy See in international affairs was associated with the government of the Papal States and no inconsistencies arose in practice in relation to its legal status.[33] It was only after the annexation of the Papal States by the Kingdom of Italy and the loss of 'normal territorial sovereignty'[34] that the question arose—'jusque-là latente et dissimulée'[35]—as to the status of the Holy

---

[27] The terms Pope, Supreme Pontiff, and Sovereign Pontiff are used interchangeably throughout the chapter.

[28] Code of Canon Law (CIC) 1983, can. 361. See also G. Westdickenberg, 'Holy See' in *MPEPIL* (2006), para. 1.

[29] Crawford, *The Creation of States in International Law*, 2nd ed., at 220; P. Daillier, et al., *Droit international public*, 8ème ed., (Paris: L.G.D.J, 2009), at 505. For a concise history of the Papal States over the centuries, see J. Duursma, *Fragmentation and the International Relations of Micro-states: Self-determination and Statehood*, (Cambridge: Cambridge University Press, 1996), at 375–376. For a more lengthy account, including the brief interruptions of territoriality between 1793–1801 and 1809–1814, see R. J. Araujo, 'The International Personality and Sovereignty of the Holy See', 50 *Cath. U. L. Rev.* (2001), 291–360, at 294–320.

[30] H. F. Köck, 'Holy See', in R. Bernhardt (ed.), *Encyclopedia of Public International Law*, vol. II, (Amsterdam: Elsevier, 1995), 866–869, at 867.

[31] See note 30. For an insider's perspective of the Holy See's diplomacy, see I. Cardinale, *Le Saint-Siège et la diplomatie*, (Paris: Desclée, 1962). For leading Vatican historians focusing on diplomatic relations between the Holy See and particular countries, see P. C. Kent and J. F. Pollard, *Papal Diplomacy in the Modern Age*, (Westport, Connecticut: Praeger, 1994).

[32] Cassese, *International Law*, 2nd ed., at 131.

[33] Crawford, *The Creation of States in International Law*, 2nd ed., at 226.

[34] Shaw, *International Law*, 5th ed., at 218.

[35] P. Fauchille, *Traité de Droit International Public*, 8ème ed., entièrement refondue, complétée et mise au courant du Manuel de droit international public de M. Henry Bonfils ed., vol. I, (Paris: Rousseau & Co., 1922), at 748. (Own translation: hitherto latent and concealed.)

See in international law. In this context, there appears to be consensus on one matter among legal scholars: in 1870 the Papal States ceased to exist and the Holy See lost its claim to statehood.[36] Beyond this glimmer of clarity, a hundred years of literature describe disagreement about the international personality of the Holy See. Charles G. Fenwick offered an account of the variety of opinions held by early writers:

The great majority of publicists agreed that upon the showing of facts the Papacy could not be regarded as possessing full legal international personality. Many went so far as to say that the Papacy had since 1870 lost all international character whatever. Notably was this the case with writers of the positive school whose determination of questions of international law was based upon the facts of international intercourse rather than upon abstract theories. In sharp contrast certain Latin writers saw in the minimum territory left to the Pope by the Law of Guarantees and in the world-wide spiritual authority exercised by the Pope over those professing the Roman Catholic religion a sufficient basis for a claim of sovereignty in the technical sense. The middle position was represented by Oppenheim who held that by custom, by tacit consent of the members of the family of nations, the Holy See had a "quasi-international" position, which did not however make it a subject of international law. Fauchille (elaborating Bonfils), while denying to the Papacy sovereignty in the ordinary sense of the word, recognized in it a "special", "particular" sovereignty, and consequently a juridical personality of its own, different from that of other states but nevertheless international in character.[37]

This overview of early writings reveals several interesting points. First, one can observe two opposing positions: the extinction of the international legal personality of the Holy See together with the loss of its territories versus a remaining, although limited, international status. Joseph Kunz argued that the 'pseudo-positivistic prejudice' which equated international personality with statehood was responsible for the negation of even a limited personality of the Holy See after 1870.[38] Similarly, Patrick Daillier et al. note:

La controverse a peut-être été artificiellement entretenue par l'absence d'alternative au statut étatique: on a trop longtemps pensé que la personnalité juridique internationale du Saint-Siège, à moins d'être niée complètement—ce qui serait très contestable—, supposait la qualité d'Etat.[39]

Today, doctrinal developments clarify that the circle of international legal personae comprises other entities beyond states.[40] Accordingly, it can be concluded that the

---

[36] See for example Daillier, et al., *Droit international public*, 8ème ed., at 505; J. L. Kunz, 'The Status of the Holy See in International Law', 46 *AJIL* 2 (1952), 308–314, at 311.

[37] C. G. Fenwick, 'The New City of the Vatican', 23 *AJIL* 2 (1929), 371–374, at 371.

[38] J. L. Kunz, 'The Status of the Holy See in International Law', at 309.

[39] Daillier, et al., *Droit international public*, 8ème ed., at 507. (This author's translation: The controversy may have been artificially mantained by the absence of an alternative to statehood: for too long we have thought that the international legal personality of the Holy See, unless denied completely—which would be highly questionable—had to assume statehood).

[40] The Advisory Opinion of the ICJ in the *Reparation for injuries* case could be considered as a doctrinal turning point towards acceptance of a wider circle of international legal personae. See ICJ, *Reparation for injuries suffered in the service of the United Nations*, Advisory Opinion, ICJ Reports 1949, p. 174, at 178.

opinion that the international personality of the Holy See ceased when it lost its territories in 1870 is obsolete.

A second aspect emphasized by Fenwick's description of early doctrine refers to the source of the personality of the Holy See after 1870. The Italian Law of Guarantees of 1871 was seen by some writers as constitutive in nature, thereby conferring on the Holy See a personality vulnerable to unilateral revocation by Italy.[41] Others regarded the law as merely declarative in nature.[42] This early point of contention is particularly interesting if read in the context of modern literature on the topic. There appears to be a dominant opinion among jurists of our time, which asserts that the maintenance of diplomatic relations and continued activity in international affairs post-1870[43] is evidence of 'a degree of international personality' of the Holy See.[44] Yet these are precisely some of the prerogatives guaranteed by the 1871 Law of Guarantees.[45] In consequence, if credence is given to the early strand of doctrine which argued that the Law of Guarantees had constitutive force, the evidence for continued international personality is actually evidence of the implementation of an Italian municipal law. The alternative view is that the international personality of the Holy See after 1870 was supported by custom and the acquiescence of states.[46] It is important to mention here a speech in 1929 by the dean of the diplomatic corps at the Vatican, the Brazilian Ambassador Charles Maghalaès de Azeredo, during a ceremony celebrating the conclusion of the Lateran Pacts.

---

[41] G. Ireland, 'The State of the City of the Vatican', 27 *AJIL* (1933), 271–289, at 271; J. Westlake, *International Law. Peace*, 1st ed., vol. 1, (Cambridge: Cambridge University Press, 1904), at 38. See also discussion in F. Seyersted, *Common Law of International Organizations*, (Leiden: Martinus Nijhoff, 2008), at 387–388.

[42] See discussion in Fauchille, *Traité de droit international public*, 8ème ed., entièrement refondue, complétée et mise au courant du Manuel de droit international public de M. Henry Bonfils ed., at 749–750; Seyersted, *Common Law of International Organizations*, at 387–388.

[43] Robert John Araujo discusses the involvement of the Holy See in international mediation and arbitration post-annexation and relies on numerous authors to show that new diplomatic missions, including missions of non-Catholic states, were established after 1870. Araujo, 'The International Personality and Sovereignty of the Holy See', at 302–303. Josef Kunz made a case for considering concordats as international treaties, as opposed to domestic legislation of states. Kunz, 'The Status of the Holy See in International Law', at 310. See also P. Petkoff, 'Legal Perspectives and Religious Perspectives of Religious Rights under International Law in the Vatican Concordats (1963–2004)', 158 *Law & Justice—The Christian Law Review* (2007), 30–53.

[44] Representative is Crawford, *The Creation of States in International Law*, 2nd ed., at 226. See also N. Dias, 'Roman Catholic Church & International Law', 13 *Sri Lanka Journal of International Law* (2001), 107–135, at 112. For early scholars making the same claim see the excellent exposé of Fauchille, *Traité de droit international public*, 8ème ed., entièrement refondue, complétée et mise au courant du Manuel de droit international public de M. Henry Bonfils ed., at 732–755.

[45] The Law of Guarantees of 1871 recognizes the inviolability of the Pope's person, and the assimilation to the King of Italy in respect to honours, immunities, and penal protection; the right to maintain an armed force; freedom of correspondence; the right to pursue diplomatic relations, and the guarantee of immunity for diplomatic envoys accredited to the Holy See residing on Italian territory. Daillier, et al., *Droit International Public*, 8ème ed., at 506; L. Oppenheim, *International Law: A Treatise*, 1st ed., vol. 1, (London: Longmans, Green, and Co, 1905), at 150–151; U. Benigni, 'Law of Guarantees', *The Catholic Encyclopedia* (New York: Robert Appleton Company), accessed October 2011, http://www.newadvent.org/cathen/07048a.htm.

[46] This would be Oppenheim's explanation for what he called the 'quasi international position' of the Holy See. Oppenheim, *International Law: A Treatise*, 1st ed., at 153.

Tandis que des juristes, des journalistes, des amateurs de politique internationale, discutaient l'essence et même l'existence de la souveraineté des Papes, et que d'aucuns en identifiaient le caractère *sui generis* avec une implicite négation d'elle-même... notre présence ici attestait tranquillement, silencieusement, en face de l'univers entier, que les Papes (le problème du territoire à restituer restant debout en vertu de leurs protestations réitérées contre le fait accompli) continuaient à être souverains, comme autrefois, puisque les Puissances n'eussent pas délégué à leurs ambassadeurs et à leurs ministres la mission de plaider leurs intérêts auprès d'une personne non qualifiée pour les recevoir, c'est-à-dire ne possédant pas les attributs essentiels de la souveraineté.[47]

Even before 1870, the position of the Popes was 'due not alone to their being monarchs of a State, but to their being the head of the Roman Catholic Church',[48] 'le lieutenant et le représentant de Dieu sur la terre'.[49] According to Kunz, the status of the Holy See in international law is to be explained by appeal to the medieval Christian community and the role of the Holy See within it:

During the European Middle Ages the Holy See was the spiritual leader of the communitas Christiana of Europe. Our modern international community developed historically by way of decentralization of the medieval Christian community of Europe. Historically, the original members of our international community were only the Christian states of Europe and the Holy See. It is this historical development which explains the unique position in international law of the Holy See as the Supreme Head of the Catholic Church.[50]

In 1905, Lassa Oppenheim underlined in similar terms the importance of religious legitimacy in what he called the 'anomalous' international status of the Holy See before and after the loss of the Papal States;[51] which in turn would suggest that the municipal legislation passed by the Italian Parliament in May 1871 merely confirmed the previous status, and did not create it.

Subsequent Popes have considered themselves 'prisoners in the Vatican' to show their rejection of the juridical solution proposed by Italy to the 'Roman Question', which arose in 1870 following the annexation of Rome by the Kingdom of Italy.[52] It could indeed be argued that the constant Papal refusal to accept the juridical

---

[47] As quoted in Y. de la Brière, 'La condition juridique de la cité du Vatican', 33 *Recueil des Cours de l'Académie de droit international de la Haye* (1930) 113–165, at 160. (This author's translation: While lawyers, journalists, observers of international politics, discussing the essence and even the existence of the sovereignty of the Popes, and while some identified in the sui generis character an implied negation of the sovereign character itself... our presence here attested calmly, silently, in front of the whole universe, that the Popes (the problem of territory still standing given the repeated protests against the fait accompli) continued to be sovereign, as before, since the Powers would not have entrusted their ambassadors and ministers with the mission to advocate for their interests in front of a person who was unqualified to receive them, that is to say, not possessing the essential attributes of sovereignty).

[48] Oppenheim, *International Law: A Treatise*, 1st ed., at 150.

[49] Fauchille, *Traité de droit international public*, 8ème ed., entièrement refondue, complétée et mise au courant du Manuel de droit international public de M. Henry Bonfils ed., at 728. (Own translation: lieutenant and the representative of God on earth).

[50] Kunz, 'The Status of the Holy See in International Law', at 309.

[51] Oppenheim, *International Law: A Treatise*, 1st ed., at 150.

[52] J. Duursma, *Fragmentation and the International Relations of Micro-states: Self-determination and Statehood*, at 376; D. I. Kertzer, *Prisoner of the Vatican: The Popes' Secret Plot to Capture Rome from the New Italian State*, (Boston, New York: Houghton Mifflin, 2004), at 85–88.

situation affirmed in the Law of Guarantees amounted to a protest in international law.[53] The main legal function of the protest, as a unilateral act of international law, was the preservation of rights ante-1870, and the denial of Italy's claim that it could resolve the situation through legislation at municipal level after its project for an international conference had failed.[54] It is important to note that only subjects of international law are accepted as parties to a protest.[55] Therefore by equating the refusal of Pope Pius IX and his successors to a protest in international law a degree of international personality is implicitly recognized.

When they have attempted to make sense of the continued diplomatic relations and involvement in international affairs of the Holy See after the loss of the Papal States, contemporary scholars have benefited from the knowledge that the Holy See regained some of its temporal powers in 1929 through the Lateran Treaty. It comes as no surprise that early writings on the practice of states in the post-1870 period were read in a way that assured coherence with the events that followed, and therefore the declarative strand which identified customs and acquiescence as the source of the Holy See's international personality was preferred. An opposing view, one that takes the Law of Guarantees as constitutive of the Holy See's (national) personality, would be inconsistent with the signing of the Lateran Treaty by two international persons.[56] Arguing on these lines, Giorgio Balladore-Pallieri noted:

La convenzione fu infatti conchiusa dallo Stato italiano non con lo Stato della Città del Vaticano, allora inesistente e di cui solo si prevedeva il sorgere, ma con la Santa Sede quale somma autorità della Chiesa Cattolica, e il fatto che tra questi due enti sia stato conchiuso un trattato produttivo, come nessuno dubita, di diritti e di doveri internazionali fra le Parti, e pienamente valido, come parimenti nessuno dubita, secondo l'ordine internazionale, sta a dimostrare che entrambi gli enti che lo conchiusero, e in specie la Santa Sede, avevano capacità di conchiudere convezioni internazionali ed erano quindi soggetti internazionali.[57]

If it is accepted that the Holy See enjoyed 'a degree of' international legal personality[58] in the absence of its territories, and that custom and tacit consent were the source of

---

[53] See *Ubi Nos* of 15 May 1871; Benedictus XV, *Inscrutabili Dei consilio* on the evils of society of 21 April 1878; Benedictus XV, *Ad beatissimi Apostolorum Principis*, November 1914; Pius XI, *Ubi arcano Dei consilio*, December 1922, in Martens, 'The Position of the Holy See and Vatican City State in International Relations', at 733–739. For the characteristics of protest, see C. Eick, 'Protest', in R. Wolfrum (ed.), *MPEPIL*, (Online ed.: Oxford University Press, 2006), paras. 1–14; I. MacGibbon, 'Some Observations on the Part of Protest in International Law', 30 *BYBIL* (1953), 293–319.

[54] See K. Martens, 'The Position of the Holy See and Vatican City State in International Relations', at 732–739.

[55] MacGibbon, 'Some Observations on the Part of Protest in International Law', at 294.

[56] See G. Balladore-Pallieri, *Diritto internazionale pubblico*, (Milano: A. Giuffrè, 1962), at 122.

[57] See note 56. (This author's translation: The Convention was concluded by the Italian State not with the Vatican City State, which did not exist at that time and the emergence of which one could only envisage, but with the Holy See as the highest authority of the Catholic Church; the fact that an agreement could be reached which undoubtedly gave rise to rights and obligations between the parties and that the validity of such agreement was not contested by the international order demonstrates that the entities, and in particular the Holy See had the capacity to conclude international treaties and therefore was a subject of international law.)

[58] The expression is used by Crawford to define the personality of the Holy See in terms of the legal rights and duties that it retained after the loss of statehood. Crawford, *The Creation of States in International Law*, 2nd ed., at 226.

this personality, which could therefore not be revoked by an Italian municipal law, why was there a need for the 1929 Lateran Treaty? Robert John Araujo's discourse is instructive in this context. While arguing that the Papal States 'never proved to be essential in preserving the sovereignty of universal spiritual leadership',[59] in the same passage he admitted that these territories 'enabled the Holy See to resemble other temporal powers'.[60] Writing in 1922, Paul Fauchille observed that the temporal power was considered to guarantee the freedom and independence of the spiritual power: 'Il était censé mettre le Chef de l'Eglise à l'abri des influences et des pressions exercées par les souverains des divers Etats.'[61] Heribert Franz Köck also noted that the Holy See sought, 'for practical reasons', to regain some of its temporal powers to provide clear evidence of its independence from other states.[62]

It is submitted that statehood or the resemblance to a state remained an important interest of the Holy See in the post-1870 era, not so much as a proof of its international legal personality, but as an *unequivocal* guarantee of the rights, or rather privileges,[63] which attach to statehood. What Köck, in an understatement, terms 'practical reasons' are in fact claims to the privileges of statehood as a corollary to sovereign equality: the principle of territorial integrity; the inviolability of internal affairs; the right of a sovereign to freely participate in international affairs including in international organizations, and enjoy full treaty-making and ratification capacity;[64] immunity from trial in foreign courts;[65] and the immunity of state officials.[66] It should be underscored here that the principle of sovereign equality affirmed in article 2 of the UN Charter and further detailed in

[59] Araujo, 'The International Personality and Sovereignty of the Holy See', at 296.

[60] See note 59.

[61] (This author's translation: It was intended to safeguard the Head of the Church from influence and pressure from the sovereigns of various states). Fauchille doubts, however, whether the protective function of territoriality has actually worked in the past as envisaged, and exposes a more complex reality. He argues that it was often the Popes that had to step in and defend the temporal power which was threatened or attacked and in doing so they relied on armies or on means which they had at their disposal as the spiritual power. Fauchille, *Traité de droit international public*, 8ème ed., entièrement refondue, complétée et mise au courant du Manuel de droit international public de M. Henry Bonfils ed., at 730.

[62] Köck, 'Holy See', *MPEPIL* (1995), at 868.

[63] Andrea Bianchi asserts that, for instance, '[i]mmunity is a privilege granted by international law to states to prevent abuses from being perpetrated against them.' A. Bianchi, 'Overcoming the Hurdle of State Immunity in the Domestic Enforcement of Human Rights', in B. Conforti and F. Francioni (eds.), *Enforcing International Human Rights in Domestic Courts*, (The Hague: Martinus Nijhoff, 1997), 405–440, at 410. The idea that international law attaches privileges rather than rights to states is an important one, which does not stem from *droit-de-l'hommisme*, but from the need to preserve the international law system itself. The ICJ appears to have either missed or refuted as irrelevant this argument in its *Jurisdictional Immunities* case. *Jurisdictional Immunities of the State (Germany v. Italy: Greece Intervening)*, Judgment, ICJ Reports 2012, p. 99.

[64] See UN Charter, art. 2; Declaration on Principles of International Law concerning Friendly Relations and Co-operation among States in Accordance with the Charter of the United Nations, GA res. 2625 (XXV) of 24 October 1970; A. Verdross and B. Simma, *Universelles Völkerrecht. Theorie und Praxis*, 3rd ed., (Berlin: Duncker & Humblot, 1984), at 272ff.

[65] See notes 19 and 63.

[66] There are two different categories of immunities from foreign jurisdiction: so-called functional, organic or immunities *ratione materiae* are enjoyed by any state official for acts that they perform in their official capacity; personal immunities or *ratione personae*, and with regard to diplomatic agents diplomatic immunities, cover any act that some classes of state officials (heads of states or government, foreign

the Declaration on Friendly Relations sets out the rights of states and also their obligations towards other states.[67]

As will be demonstrated throughout this chapter, the 'practical reasons' which prompted the Holy See to conclude the Lateran Treaty had the significant effect of allowing it, as a construct, to join the privileged circle of states and to acquire a general rather than limited personality. By contrast, one can observe that in the absence of a Lateran Treaty of its own, the Military Sovereign Order of Malta remains a religious entity with an international personality limited to states which recognize it.[68] As such, in the absence of territoriality, the Order exchanges envoys with several states and has the status of non-state observer in the UN General Assembly; it does not however have treaty-making capacities and cannot participate as a full member in international organizations.[69] A special Papal Tribunal described the international status of the Order as 'functional, that is to say, intended to assure the fulfillment of the scope of activities of the Order and its development throughout the world'.[70] James Crawford also denies a general international personality to the Order and comments that 'under the Geneva Conventions of 1949 its status is merely that of a "relief society"'.[71]

In summary, it is clear today that the circle of international legal subjects includes entities other than states, and therefore that the Holy See did not require the existence of the Vatican City State to enjoy an international personality; however, the prerogatives of statehood continue to be attractive, not least for the Holy See. The conclusion of the Lateran Treaty is evidence of this point. Read in this light, the continuing controversy on personalities is, in certain respects, constructed by the Holy See itself.

IV. The Personality Question Read in the Light of the Lateran Treaty

The Conciliation Treaty between the Holy See and Italy, referred to as the Lateran Treaty, signed by Cardinal Pietro Gasparri on behalf of Pope Pius XI and by the fascist Prime Minister of Italy, Benito Mussolini, is part of the Lateran Pacts of

---

ministers, diplomats) perform while in office. Contemporary doctrine and practice do not allow state officials to claim functional immunity for international crimes; moreover, after they leave office, senior state officials and diplomats may be prosecuted for international crimes. See A. Cassese, 'When May Senior State Officials Be Tried for International Crimes? Some Comments on the *Congo v. Belgium* Case', 13 *EJIL* 4 (2002), 853–875, at 864–866; Cassese, *International Law*, 2nd ed., at 113 and 119–120. See also P. Gaeta, 'Ratione Materiae Immunities of Former Heads of State and International Crimes: The Hissène Habré Case', 1 *Journal of International Criminal Justice* (2003), 186–196; S. Zappalà, 'Do Heads of State in Office Enjoy Immunity from Jurisdiction for International Crimes? The Ghaddafi Case Before the French Cour de Cassation', 12 *EJIL* 3 (2001), 595–612.

[67] UN Charter, art. 2; Declaration on Principles of International Law concerning Friendly Relations and Co-operation among States in Accordance with the Charter of the United Nations, GA res. 2625 (XXV) of 24 October 1970.

[68] Crawford, *The Creation of States in International Law*, 2nd ed., at 233.

[69] See F. Gazzoni, 'Malta, Order of', *MPEPIL*, (Online ed.: Oxford University Press, 2009).

[70] As quoted in Crawford, *The Creation of States in International Law*, 2nd ed., at 232.

[71] Crawford, *The Creation of States in International Law*, 2nd ed., at 233.

1929, alongside the Financial Convention and the Concordat.[72] The Treaty purports to assure 'to the Holy See in a permanent manner a position in fact and in law which guarantees it absolute independence for the fulfilment of its exalted mission in the world [and] permits the Holy See to consider as finally and irrevocably settled the "Roman Question" '.[73] It is beyond doubt that the aim of the Lateran Treaty was to provide the final clarification of the international legal status of the Holy See; it is an ironic twist of history that legal literature today continues to be divided precisely on the point of personality.

This section examines whether the Lateran Treaty offers legal evidence for the dual personality scenario (the Holy See and the Vatican as two distinct personae) or, on the contrary, lends support to a Holy See-Vatican construct with one international personality. The analysis of the relevant provisions of the Lateran Treaty will be guided by the general rules of interpretation stipulated in article 31 of the Vienna Convention on the Law of Treaties (VCLT), which reflects customary international law.[74] As such, the ordinary meaning of terms will be sought in their context and in the light of the object and purpose of the treaty; subsequent agreements, practice, and any relevant rules will be used for interpretation purposes.[75]

The Lateran Treaty enunciates its object and purpose in a preambular clause:

Since, in order to assure the absolute and visible independence of the Holy See, it is required that it be guaranteed an indisputable sovereignty even in the international realm, it has been found necessary to create *under special conditions* Vatican City, recognizing the full ownership and the exclusive and absolute power and sovereign jurisdiction of the Holy See over the same.[76]

The conditionality provision 'under special conditions' is key to a textual reading of the instrument. The Treaty reveals that 'special conditions' refers to the fact that the resemblance of statehood has been conferred for the benefit of the Holy See and its mission in the world.[77] In article 2, Italy recognizes the sovereignty of the

---

[72] The Financial Convention settled the claims of the Holy See after the loss of its territories. The Concordat, which addressed ecclesiastical relations with Italy, was amended by an Agreement between the Holy See and the Italian Republic modifying the Lateran Concordat, 24 *ILM* 1589 (1985), entered into force on 3 June 1985. The latter agreement is said to have 'loosened the ties between Italy and the Holy See, most importantly by disestablishing the Roman Catholic Church from the Republic of Italy'. Temperman, *State-Religion Relationships and Human Rights Law: Towards a Right to Religiously Neutral Governance*, at 17.

[73] Lateran Treaty, preamble.

[74] The Holy See ratified the the Vienna Convention on the Law of Treaties on 25 February 1977. The instrument does not, strictly speaking, apply to the Lateran Treaty because this would mean that the Convention would apply retroactively. *A contrario* Vienna Convention on the Law of Treaties, (done on 23 May 1969, entered into force on 27 January 1980), (1155 UNTS 331), art. 4 (Hereafter VCLT). However, in that article 31 represents a codification of custom, its applicability in the present case is sound. For the customary nature of article 31, see *Arbitral Award of 31 July 1989 (Guinea-Bissau v. Senegal)*, Judgment, ICJ Report 1991, p. 53, para. 48.

[75] VCLT, art. 31.

[76] Lateran Treaty, preamble (emphasis added). In addition, article 3 reads 'creating in this manner Vatican City for the special purposes and under the conditions given in this Treaty'.

[77] As Jorri Duursma puts it, 'the Vatican City is subordinated to the existence of the Holy See'. Duursma, *Fragmentation and the International Relations of Micro-states: Self-determination and Statehood*, at 385.

Holy See 'as an attribute inherent in its nature in conformity with its tradition and the requirements of its mission in the world'.[78] The Lateran Treaty does not contain any similar provision stipulating the international personality of the Vatican City per se: quite the opposite—article 3 proclaims the full ownership, exclusive power and jurisdiction of the Holy See over the Vatican.[79] Article 4 pulls together the provisions mentioned so far in a reassertion of the Holy See's sovereignty over the Vatican City:

The sovereignty and exclusive jurisdiction over Vatican City which Italy recognizes as pertaining to the Holy See means that within the same City there cannot be any interference on the part of the Italian Government and that there is no other authority there than that of the Holy See.[80]

The final provision in article 26, in which Italy recognizes the Vatican City State 'under the Sovereign Pontiff',[81] should therefore also be read in association with the previous stipulations. Moreover, an Agreement between the Italian Republic and the Holy See that was signed in 1984, to amend the Concordat that was part of the Lateran Pacts, does not sanction a separate international personality for the Vatican City.[82]

The remainder of this part will show that a reading of the Lateran Treaty, in the light of relevant rules of international law applicable in the relations between parties,[83] reveals that the resemblance of statehood has been conferred by Italy upon the Holy See and the Vatican City as a construct. It will also be shown that, if considered apart, the Holy See and the Vatican do not meet the effectiveness test of statehood.[84] Article 1 of the Montevideo Convention contains the provisions that are traditionally cited as the 'basic' criteria for statehood: a defined territory, a permanent population, a government, and the capacity to enter into relations

---

[78] Lateran Treaty, art. 2.　　　[79] Lateran Treaty, art. 3.

[80] Lateran Treaty, art. 4.　　　[81] Lateran Treaty, art 26.

[82] Article 1 reads: 'The Italian Republic and the Holy See reaffirm that the State and the Catholic Church are, each in its own order, independent and sovereign...' It is clear that the term State refers to the Italian State. In fact the formulation is retained from article 7(2) of the Italian Constitution, cited in the preamble of the Agreement referring to 'relations between the State and the Catholic Church'. Agreement between the Holy See and the Italian Republic modifying the Lateran Concordat, entered into force 3 June 1985.

[83] VCLT, art. 31.3.c. Art. 31.3.c. includes treaty law and international custom. International Law Commission, *Fragmentation of International Law: Difficulties Arising from the Diversification and Expansion of International Law*, Report of the Study Group of the International Law Commission finalized by Martti Koskenniemi, UN Doc. A/CN.4/L.682, 13 April 2006, para. 426.b. The Montevideo Convention is said to have codified in 1933 existing customary international law. It can thus be inferred that, when the Lateran Treaty was concluded in 1929, the same criteria for statehood were considered relevant, based on customary law. See T. D. Grant, 'Defining Statehood: The Montevideo Convention and Its Discontents', 37 *Columbia Journal of Transnational Law* (1998) 403–457, at 414–418.

[84] According to Christakis, the effectiveness test refers to the principle based upon which an entity which meets the constitutive elements of a state (population, a determined territory and an effective and stable government) accedes to statehood and enjoys the protection of international law which flow from this status. T. Christakis, 'The State as a 'Primary Fact': Some Thoughts on the Principle of Effectiveness', in M. Kohen (ed.), *Secession: International Law Perspectives*, (Cambridge: Cambridge University Press, 2006), at 140 and 143.

with other states.[85] The fourth criterion, the capacity to enter into relations with other states is not an exclusive attribute of states.[86] The 'essence' of this criterion is said to be the independence requirement[87] and it is on this that the study will focus on here.

1. Territory

The Vatican City covers a territory of 0.44 square kilometres ceded by Italy in the Lateran Treaty.[88] Partly surrounded by walls, the territory stretches into Saint Peter's Square, which is usually open to the public.[89] As its official website notes, 'because Vatican City is so small', several departments and offices which belong to the Holy See are situated in buildings around Rome.[90] Article 15 of the Lateran Treaty conferred on these buildings the immunities granted by international law to the headquarters of the diplomatic agents of foreign states.[91] The premises of these buildings are therefore inviolable, immune from search, requisition, attachment, or execution.[92] Commenting on the size of the territory of the Vatican City, Hersch Lauterpacht noted that comparatively 'Andorra and San Marino constitute veritable empires'.[93] Nonetheless, doctrine has not considered territorial exiguity to preclude the status of the Vatican City as a state.[94] Jorri Duursma also emphasizes that:

Italy and the Holy See were convinced that the Vatican territory was a necessary and sufficient element in order to fulfil the territorial criterion for statehood in international law, while no third State has ever made a reservation concerning the territorial element of the State of the Vatican.[95]

---

[85] Montevideo Convention on the Rights and Duties of States (1933), 165 LNTS 19, accessed January 2012, art. 1 (see http://avalon.law.yale.edu/20th_century/intam03.asp). It should be noted that the effectiveness criteria are considered to be basic, but in themselves insufficient for the acceptance of a new state in the community of states in current times. Other elements must be taken into consideration, including the principles of non-intervention and non-use of force. See I. Cismas, 'Secession in Theory and Practice: The Case of Kosovo and Beyond', 2 *Goettingen Journal of International Law* 2 (2010) 531–587, at 551; M. Kohen, 'La création d'Etats en Droit International Contemporain', 6 *Cursos Euromediterráneos Bancaja de Derecho Internacional* (2002), 546–635, at 629–631; O. C. Okafor, *Re-defining Legitimate Statehood: International Law and State Fragmentation in Africa*, (The Hague: Martinus Nijhoff Publishers, 2000), at 65ff.

[86] For example, international organizations are also able to enter into relations with states. D. Raič, *Statehood and the Law of Self-determination*, (The Hague: Kluwer Law International, 2002), at 74.

[87] See note 86.

[88] Lateran Treaty, art. 3.

[89] Vatican City State Geography, accessed January 2012, http://www.vaticanstate.va/EN/State_and_Government/General_informations/Geography.htm.

[90] See note 89.

[91] Lateran Treaty, art. 15.

[92] Vienna Convention on Diplomatic Relations, 500 UNTS 95 (signed on 18 April 1961, entered into force 28 April 1964), art. 22.3 (hereafter VCDR).

[93] Lauterpacht, 'General Rules of the Law of Peace', at 306.

[94] See for example Duursma, *Fragmentation and the International Relations of Micro-states: Self-determination and Statehood*, at 441; M. H. Mendelson, 'Diminutive States in the United Nations', 21 *ICLQ* 4 (1972) 609–630, at 21.

[95] Duursma, *Fragmentation and the International Relations of Micro-states: Self-determination and Statehood*, at 411.

2. Permanent population

As to the population at the Vatican City, article 9 of the Lateran Treaty is instructive. It stipulates that 'all persons having permanent residence within Vatican City are subject to the sovereignty of the Holy See'.[96] It should thus be underlined that the sovereignty in question is that of the Holy See, not the Vatican City.

Some 800 individuals have permission to reside at the Vatican either temporarily or permanently; of these, around 450 are citizens, half of whom are part of the diplomatic corps of the Holy See and therefore live in a different country.[97] The majority of the population is formed of dignitaries, officials, and staff who by the virtue of their office are 'celibate clergy and nuns'.[98]

Various legal writers have questioned whether the population living on the territory of the Vatican City fulfils the permanence requirement. For Maurice Mendelsohn a permanent population must have the capacity 'of maintaining and reproducing itself'.[99] Anecdotal evidence is put forward to portray the non-self-propagation of this population: 14 people are said to have been born at the Vatican City between 1929 and 1980.[100] For Yasmin Abdullah the functional character of the population residing at the Vatican denotes its non-permanence.[101] Indeed, the basis of citizenship at the Vatican is neither *jus soli* nor *jus sanguinis*, but rather *jus officii*, 'where the status arises from the person's office'.[102] The new Law on Citizenship, Residence and Access to the Vatican, which was promulgated by Pope Benedict XVI and entered into force on 1 March 2011, clarifies that citizens are: the Cardinals residing at the Vatican or in Rome; diplomats of the Holy See; and those who are 'kept' at the Vatican for reasons of duty or service.[103] Cardinals lose their citizenship when they cease to reside at the Vatican or in Rome; the other categories must give up citizenship when they are no longer in the service of the Holy See or the Vatican; and '[i] figli di un cittadino vaticano, al compimento del 18° anno di età perdono la cittadinanza vaticana . . .'[104]

---

[96] Lateran Treaty, art. 9.

[97] Vatican City State, Population, accessed January 2012, http://www.vaticanstate.va/EN/State_and_Government/General_informations/Population.htm.

[98] Y. Abdullah, 'The Holy See at United Nations Conferences: State or Church?', 96 *Col. LR* 7 (1996) 1835–1875, at 1862; See also Mendelson, 'Diminutive States in the United Nations', at 612.

[99] Mendelson, 'Diminutive States in the United Nations', at 612.

[100] M.J. Walsh, *Vatican City State* (Oxford: Clio Press, 1983) in Y. Abdullah, 'The Holy See at United Nations Conferences: State or Church?', at 1862.

[101] Abdullah, 'The Holy See at United Nations Conferences: State or Church?', at 1861–1863.

[102] M. N. Bathon, 'The Atypical International Status of the Holy See', 34 *Vanderbilt Journal of Transnational Law* (2001) 597–632, at 610.

[103] Legge sulla cittadinanza, residenza e l'acceso, L. CXXXI, 22 febbraio 2011, accessed January 2012, http://www.vaticanstate.va/NR/rdonlyres/FBFEA0E8-B43A-452A-AAA0-1AF49590F658/3550/Leggesullacittadinanzalaresidenzaelaccesso.pdf, art. 1. For a comparative discussion of the 1929 Law on citizenship and sojourn and the 2011 law see 'New law on citizenship residence and access to the Vatican', *L'Osservatore Romano*, 2 March 2011.

[104] (This author's translation: The children of a Vatican citizen lose their citizenship when they reach the age of 18 . . .). Legge sulla cittadinanza, residenza e l'acceso (2011), art. 3.

In the view of some,[105] the provisions of the Lateran Treaty are themselves the most obvious indication of the non-permanence of the population residing at the Vatican. It states: '[o]n ceasing to be subject to the sovereignty of the Holy See, the persons [who] are not to be considered as possessing another citizenship, will be regarded in Italy as certainly being Italian citizens'.[106] The default to Italian citizenship is certainly unusual. It serves to illustrate yet again that the attributes of statehood are not conferred for the sake of a Vatican human community 'to whose presence [a] distinctive value for the governmental structure' is attached, but are intended to benefit the Holy See and its religious mission.[107]

It becomes clear that the population residing at the Vatican is not permanent in the traditional sense of the term, that of a 'stable society united in a territory'.[108] The Vatican does not conform to the traditional understanding that '[l]'état agit pour un ensemble d'individus qui lui sont attribués'.[109] However, as long as the Holy See continues to exist, it confers to the population at the Vatican an institutional permanence, assuring 'a sort of' human continuity on the Vatican territory. The institutional permanence of the population *at* the Vatican—as opposed to *of* the Vatican—represents an important qualification of the population criterion of statehood; as such, it is more appropriate to use the term 'resemblance of statehood' rather than 'statehood'.

In conclusion, even if it were to be accepted that a permanent population existed on the territory of the Vatican, its permanent attachment would be to the Holy See, as the texts of the Lateran Treaty and subsequent domestic legislation clearly indicate. It can be said that the existence of a permanent population is therefore dependent upon the acknowledgment that the Holy See and the Vatican build a construct. In the absence of this acknowledgment, the Vatican does not fulfil the permanent population criterion of statehood.

3. Government

The criterion of government entails two dimensions: the existence of a government in the sense of an institutionalized 'machinery for the purpose of regulating the relations in the community and with the task of upholding these rules', and the existence of an effective government, meaning that this machinery should 'exercise state authority over the claimed territory and the people residing in that

---

[105] See Duursma, *Fragmentation and the International Relations of Micro-states: Self-determination and Statehood*, at 412.

[106] Lateran Treaty, art. 9.

[107] Duursma, *Fragmentation and the International Relations of Micro-states: Self-determination and Statehood*, at 412. James Crawford regards the population residing at the Vatican, not as a 'distinct society but an annex or apanage of the Papacy'. Crawford, *The Creation of States in International Law*, 2nd ed., at 223.

[108] Duursma, *Fragmentation and the International Relations of Micro-states: Self-determination and Statehood*, at 412.

[109] P. Guggenheim, *Les principes de droit international public*, Collected Courses of the Hague Academy of International Law (Online ed.: Martinus Nijhoff 1952), at 82. (Author's translation: the state acts for a community of individuals who are assigned to it.)

territory'.[110] In the case of the Holy See and the Vatican, before evaluating whether government is effective, it should be asked who the government is. The debate between Jorri Duursma and James Crawford is particularly interesting in this respect, since the former author questions the widely held position that the Holy See is the government of the Vatican.[111] Based on canon law, Duursma argues that:

The Sovereign Pontiff and the Secretary of State are positions which the Holy See and the worldly governmental institutions of the Vatican City have in common. Neither the Pontifical Commission, the 'Consulta', the State General Counselor, nor the secular judicial organs which have been separated from the ecclesiastical tribunals since 1987, can be considered as part of the Holy See as they are not incorporated in the Roman Curia by special law and do not belong to the Holy See through natural law or the context due to their exclusively secular tasks.... The Vatican City possesses a governmental organization which is proper to itself and which juridically speaking cannot be identified with the Holy See.[112]

Crawford dismisses this argument rather sharply, because it would appear to:

confuse the issue under Canon Law of organization of the Church with the identification under international law of the Government of the Vatican City... The means by which that sovereignty is exercised in terms of the legal system of the Vatican City is a matter of indifference to international law...[113]

To start with the latter assertion, it is accurate that, as a matter of international law, the Holy See may choose whatever governmental institutions it considers right to run the affairs of the Vatican, nonetheless, the source of governmental authority of these institutions must always remain the Holy See, as stipulated in the Lateran Treaty which created the Vatican 'under special conditions'.[114] This provision excludes the possibility that a Vatican government could exist in the absence of the Holy See's authority over it. It is the compulsory authority of the Holy See over the Vatican which prompts an examination of Duursma's proposition that the government of Vatican City is a separate entity from the Holy See.

The observation that the governmental institutions of the Vatican do not correspond *in toto* with those of the Holy See is also correct. This does not however refute the fact that it is the Holy See which exercises control over the population on the Vatican territory, or (as we shall see) that, as a matter of positive law, only the Holy See has the capacity to enter into external relations. Indeed, these are the internal and external governmental capacities which are required for statehood.

Absolute governmental power is vested in the Pope, the pre-eminent constituent of the Holy See:[115] this is the crux of the matter. The Fundamental Law of the

[110] Raič, *Statehood and the Law of Self-determination*, at 62.
[111] Bathon, 'The Atypical International Status of the Holy See', at 612; Crawford, *The Creation of States in International Law*, 2nd ed., at 230.
[112] Duursma, *Fragmentation and the International Relations of Micro-states: Self-determination and Statehood*, at 387 and 413.
[113] Crawford, *The Creation of States in International Law*, 2nd ed., at 230.
[114] Lateran Treaty, preamble, arts. 3 and 4.
[115] Fundamental Law of the Vatican City State, 26 November 2000, accessed January 2012, http://www.vaticanstate.va/NR/rdonlyres/3F574885-EAD5-47E9-A547-C3717005E861/2522/

Vatican City State of 2000, reiterating the provisions of the 1929 Fundamental Law, stipulates that the 'Supreme Pontiff, Sovereign of Vatican City State, has the fullness of legislative, executive and judicial powers':[116] as such, the governmental institutions of the Vatican have been created by the will of the Pope,[117] who delegated his authority.[118] The absolute right which the Pope possesses to delegate authority also implies the right to reverse that delegation, and its possible, if not probable, exercise. As will be illustrated in the following paragraphs, the Pope retains the means to influence, directly and indirectly, the conduct of legislative, executive, and judicial affairs.

The members of the Pontifical Commission are all named by the Pope for a five-year mandate.[119] The Commission exercises legislative power 'except for those cases which the Supreme Pontiff intends to reserve to himself or to other subjects',[120] and does so within the limits of the Law concerning the Sources of Law.[121] This latter law confirms the indissoluble link between the Vatican and the Holy See on legislative matters, in stipulating that '[l]'ordinamento giuridico vaticano riconosce nell'ordinamento canonico la prima fonte normativa e il primo criterio di riferimento interpretativo'.[122] To reiterate, canon law refers to the rules which govern the public order of the Catholic Church and provide individual regulations for church discipline.[123] This provision, which stipulates that canon law is the primary source of law at the Vatican, serves to show that the legal order of the Vatican is derived from that of the Catholic Church.

The exercise of 'executive power' is entrusted to the Cardinal President of the Pontifical Commission, who thereby assumes the title of President of the Governorate.[124] The Governorate is formed of the totality of organs entrusted to exercise executive power within the limits imposed by their 'specifica condizione giuridica' and solely within the areas referred to in articles 15 and 16 of the Lateran Treaty.[125] It thus counts among its departments the administration of museums, the departments of accounting, pontifical villas, telecommunications, the florist subordinated

---

FundamentalLaw1.pdf, art. 1.1. As Duursma herself points out: 'It is the Pope, as the Head of the Roman Catholic Church and the Head of the Vatican Government, who decides on the hierarchical relation between the Holy See and the Vatican Government. Given the fact that the Vatican City is at the service of the Holy See, the supremacy of the authority of the Holy See over the Vatican Government cannot be affected.' Duursma, *Fragmentation and the International Relations of Micro-states: Self-determination and Statehood*, at 387.

[116] Fundamental Law of the Vatican City State (2000), art.1.1.
[117] Fundamental Law of the Vatican City State (2000), preamble and the given clause.
[118] Fundamental Law of the Vatican City State (2000), arts. 2, 3, 15.
[119] Fundamental Law of the Vatican City State (2000), art. 3.1.
[120] Fundamental Law of the Vatican City State (2000), art. 3.1.
[121] Fundamental Law of the Vatican City State (2000), art. 4.1.
[122] Legge sulle fonti del diritto (2008), art.1.1. (This author's translation : the legal order of the Vatican recognizes canon law as the primary source of law and the main criteria of interpretation).
[123] See J. A. Coriden, *An Introduction to Canon Law*, (Mahwah, NJ: Paulist Press, 2004), at 4.
[124] Fundamental Law of the Vatican City State (2000), art. 5.1.
[125] Legge sul governo dello Stato della Città del Vaticano, N. CCCLXXXIV, 16 luglio 2002, AAS Suppl. 73, (2002), 35–49, art. 1. (This author's translation: specific legal status.)

to the General Services Administration, the service that manages security and public order together with the Pontifical Swiss Guard (this latter an institution of the Holy See), and general offices such as the judicial and personnel offices.[126] Given its restricted area of competence,[127] it becomes evident that the 'executive' attributions of the President of the Governorate are administrative in nature. A suitable parallel would be with the attributions of a mayor of an Italian city, as opposed to those of the head of the government of a state.[128] To underline this, Article 6 of the Fundamental Law stipulates that 'matters of greater importance' are dealt with together with the Secretariat of State, an organ of the Holy See.[129]

In this context, one matter considered of great importance by the Holy See—and concomitantly of relevance for the mere existence of a state—is the capacity to enter into foreign relations. In article 12 of the Lateran Treaty, Italy recognizes the right of the *Holy See* to active and passive legation.[130] Echoing this provision, the Fundamental Law of the Vatican City State reserves:

the representation of the State in relations with foreign states and with other subjects of international law, for the purpose of diplomatic relations and the conclusion of treaties . . . to the Supreme Pontiff, who exercises it by means of the Secretariat of State.[131]

Canons 362–367, which follow the 1969 *Motu Propriu Sollicitudo omnium ecclesiarum* of Paul VI,[132] regulate the diplomatic corps of the Holy See.[133] It is the Pope's 'innate and independent right to appoint, send, transfer and recall his own legates either to particular churches . . . or to states and public authorities', whereas the norms of international law ought to be respected in relation to legates to states.[134] Canon 364 stipulates that 'the principal function' of a nuncio is 'to make stronger and more effective the bonds of unity which exist between the

---

[126]   Legge sul governo dello Stato della Città del Vaticano, arts. 11–26. See also http://www.vaticanstate.va/EN/State_and_Government/Structure_Governorate/Administrations_and_Central_Offices.htm.

[127]   See Lateran Treaty, arts. 15 and 16.

[128]   S. E. Young and A. Shea, 'Separating State from Church: A Research Guide to the Law of the Vatican City State', 99 *Law Library Journal* 3 (2007), 589–610, at 597.

[129]   Fundamental Law of the Vatican City State (2000), art. 6.

[130]   As to the right of passive legation, the Treaty stipulates that '[e]nvoys of foreign Governments to the Holy See continue to enjoy [within Italy], all the prerogatives and immunities enjoyed by diplomatic agents under International Law, and their headquarters may continue to remain within Italian territory enjoying the immunities due to them under International Law, even if their States do not have diplomatic relations with Italy'. As to the right of active legation, 'the diplomats of the Holy See and the diplomatic couriers dispatched in the name of the Supreme Pontiff enjoy within Italian territory, even in time of war, the same treatment as that enjoyed by diplomatic personages and official couriers of other foreign Governments, according to the provisions of International Law.' Lateran Treaty, art. 12.

[131]   Fundamental Law of the Vatican City State (2000), art. 2.

[132]   Lettera Apostolica in forma di Motu Proprio, *Sollicitudo omnium ecclesiarum*, Paul VI, L'ufficio dei rappresentanti del Pontefice Romano, 24 June 1969, accessed January 2012, http://www.vatican.va/holy_father/paul_vi/motu_proprio/documents/hf_p-vi_motu-proprio_19690624_sollicitudo-omnium-ecclesiarum_it.html.

[133]   J. P. Beal, J. A. Coriden and T. J. Green, *New Commentary on the Code of Canon Law*, (Mahwah, NJ: Paulist Press, 2002), at 490.

[134]   Canon 363, in *New Commentary on the Code of Canon Law* at 490.

Apostolic See and particular churches', while canon 365 provides that 'the special function' of the nuncio is 'to promote and foster relations between the Apostolic See and the authorities of the State' and 'to deal with questions which pertain to the relations between Church and state'.[135] The mandate of the nuncios is a compound of ecclesiastical and diplomatic functions anchored in 'papal diplomacy'.[136]

As will be shown in section VI.1, this composite function of the diplomatic corps of the Holy See poses challenges when interpreting the practice of other states in respect to recognition. Another puzzling element examined later in this study refers to the involvement of both the Holy See and the Vatican in international affairs, which, at least at a first glance, appears to contradict the provisions of the Lateran Treaty and the Fundamental Law.[137] Setting practice aside for the moment, if based exclusively on positive law, the conclusion can be drawn that the Vatican City lacks its own capacity to entertain international relations. Consequently, only in association with the Holy See can the Vatican fulfil the effectiveness criterion that requires a state to have the capacity to enter into foreign relations.

As to judicial power, which is exercised in the name of the Sovereign Pontiff,[138] the Pope retains the right in any civil or penal case to defer the 'instruction and the decision to a particular subject (*istanza*), even with the faculty of pronouncing a decision according to equity and with the exclusion of any further recourse (*gravamen)*'.[139] The Pope nominates the *giudice unico*, the judges of the *tribunale* and the *corte d'appello*.[140] As Stephen E. Young and Alison Shea point out, despite the 1987 reform of the judicial system,[141] the Vatican judiciary showcases the Vatican's dependence on the Holy See.

Most of the judges on the *Corte d'Appello* are also judges on the Roman Rota which is responsible for governing the ecclesiastical side of the house...From the perspective of a common law jurisdiction that strongly adheres to the doctrine of the separation of church

---

[135] Canons 364 and 365, in *New Commentary on the Code of Canon Law* at 493 and 496. The legates of the Supreme Pontiff referred to in canons 362–367 comprise the nuncio, the inter-nuncio, and the apostolic delegate. The nuncio has the rank of ambassador and generally fulfils the role of head of the Holy See mission, while the inter-nuncio acts as nuncio in the absence of the latter. According to article 16.3 of the VCDR, provided the receiving State accepts the practice, the nuncio enjoys the prerogatives of the deanship of the diplomatic corps from the moment it presents his credential letters. The apostolic delegate is in charge solely of ecclesiastical affairs and does not fulfil any diplomatic functions. As the Holy See has established diplomatic relations with over 170 states and nuncios have been appointed, the number of apostolic delegates has decreased considerably. *New Commentary on the Code of Canon Law* at 492. See also Duursma, *Fragmentation and the International Relations of Micro-states: Self-determination and Statehood*, at 390; VCDR, art. 16.3.

[136] H. Cardinale, *The Holy See and the International Order*, (London: Colin Smythe, 1976), at 37.

[137] See VI.3 in this chapter.

[138] Fundamental Law of the Vatican City State (2000), art. 15.1; Legge che approva l'ordinamento giudiziario dello Stato della Città del Vaticano, N. CXI X, 21 novembre 1987, AAS Suppl. 58 (1987), 45–50 art. 1.

[139] Fundamental Law of the Vatican City State (2000), art. 16.

[140] Legge che approva l'ordinamento giudiziario dello Stato della Città del Vaticano, arts. 7 and 12.

[141] Reference is made to the Legge che approva l'ordinamento giudiziario dello Stato della Città del Vaticano.

and state, it is interesting to examine a modern day state in which a high ranking church official serves on its supreme court. This is the case in the *Corte di Cassazione*, where the president is also the prefect of the Apostolic Signatura, the highest canon law court in the Catholic Church. The two other judges who serve on the VCS's [Vatican City State's] highest court are also cardinals and members of the Apostolic Signatura.... The VCS does not have its own dedicated body of lawyers designated to temporal courts, instead it relies on canon lawyers.[142]

It becomes clear that in its most essential governmental attributions—be they legislative, executive, including external representation, or judicial—the Vatican is *de jure* and *de facto* dependent on the institutions of the Holy See, even if not all the governmental institutions of the Holy See overlap with those of the Vatican.[143]

Against this backdrop, one question remains to be answered: Is the Holy See effective as the government of the Vatican, in the sense that it exercises authority over the territory and the population at the Vatican?

Reflecting the actual circumstance of the Vatican, which is essentially an enclave of Rome, the text of the Lateran Treaty stipulates that Italy will provide the Vatican with a number of public services, including water provision and railway connection.[144] Charles Rousseau considered that these provisions demonstrate that the governmental authorities at the Vatican cannot be said to be effective.

Plus qu'un territoire et qu'une population l'Etat moderne est avant tout un ensemble de services publics organisés et coordonnés. Ce sont ces services publics qui forment l'armature véritable de l'Etat. Or la Cité du Vatican ne possède pas l'autonomie de ses services publics, aussi bien en ce qui touche leur aménagement que leur fonctionnement.[145]

If read in the light of the wave of privatizations of public services during the last decades—including sectors such as water, electricity, transport, education, health, social security, public security, and even military functions in many states—the above observations denying the effective authority of the Holy See over the Vatican do not seem convincing. It is evident that a state does not lose its statehood because services are privatized to another state.[146]

---

[142] S. E. Young and A. Shea, 'Separating State from Church: A Research Guide to the Law of the Vatican City State', 99 *Law Library Journal* 3, at 600–602.

[143] Along similar lines, Kurt Martens notes that while the Vatican City State has its own flag, coat of arms and seal, and a national anthem (the Papal Hymn), 'these are only external signs of sovereignty, but not determining elements for obtaining juridical personality under international law'. Martens, 'The Position of the Holy See and Vatican City State in International Relations', at 752–753.

[144] Lateran Treaty, art. 6.

[145] C. Rousseau, *Droit international public*, vol. II, Les sujets de droit, (Paris: Editions Sirey, 1974), at 377. (This author's translation: More than a territory and a population, the modern State is primarily a set of organized and coordinated public services. It is these public services which form the true backbone of the State. But the Vatican has no autonomy of its public services, both in what regards their development and their operation.)

[146] The fact that UN treaty bodies have continued to stress the obligations of states vis-à-vis individuals in the context of privatization supports this statement. See for instance, CESCR, *General Comment No. 19: The right to social security (art. 9)*, 4 February 2008, UN Doc. E/C.12/GC/19, para. 5. See, more generally, K. Feyter and F. G. Isa (eds.), *Privatisation and Human Rights in the Age of Globalisation*, (Antwerp: Intersentia, 2005).

A more important objection to the governmental effectiveness of the Holy See is revealed by article 3 of the 1929 Law on the Sources of Law, which provided for Italian legislation to be applied at the Vatican as a secondary source of law, as long as its application does not conflict with pontifical or canon law.[147] The revised Law on the Sources of Law of 2008 stipulates a systematic review of the compatibility of Italian legislation with canon law before its adoption as a source of law at the Vatican.[148] This legislative reform serves to prove beyond doubt that the option to default to Italian legislation can be reversed at any time and replaced unilaterally by a 'proper Vatican' rule.[149] In the view of this author, the dependence of certain public services and the voluntary reliance on Italian legislation and the judiciary do not cause the Holy See government to lack effective authority over the Vatican territory.[150]

To buttress this assertion, a parallel could be made with the effectiveness requirement applied to governments in the course of decolonization. In this respect, David Raič proposes a distinction between juridical and empirical statehood, between 'a right or title to exercise authority and the actual or effective exercise of that authority'.[151] He goes on to argue that many of the former colonies that have found seats at the table of states have primarily done so by virtue of fulfilling the juridical statehood test and much less by the effective exercise of authority over their territory.[152] To reiterate, articles 3 and 4 of the Lateran Treaty represent a clear recognition by Italy of the right of the Holy See to exercise authority over the Vatican. While the principle of self-determination outweighed the insufficient effectiveness of governments of former colonies,[153] in the case of the Holy See its religious legitimacy appears to compensate for its 'imperfect' control over such issues as water provision and railway services.

Up to this point, a contextual reading of the Lateran Treaty has revealed that the only criterion that the Vatican itself undoubtedly brings into the statehood equation is territory. If the population residing at the Vatican could be described as permanent, its permanent attachment is not to the Vatican, but to the Holy See. Based on the Lateran Treaty and domestic legislation, the government of the Vatican—in its legislative, judicial, and executive functions, including in respect to international relations—depends on the Holy See.

The last question that will need to be settled is how the Vatican's dependence on the Holy See with respect to governmental capacity bears upon the independence requirement of a state?

---

[147] See Lateran Treaty, arts. 9 and 22; Legge sulle fonti del diritto N. II, 7 giugno 1929, AAS Suppl. 1 (1929), 5–13.

[148] Legge sulle fonti del diritto (2008), art 3. See also 'Vatican ends automatic adoption of Italian law', *Reuters*, 31 December 2008 and S. Young and A. Shea, 'Update: Researching the Law of the Vatican City State', *GlobaLex* (2009).

[149] See also Duursma, *Fragmentation and the International Relations of Micro-states: Self-determination and Statehood*, at 394.

[150] For a similar line of argumentation see Duursma, *Fragmentation and the International Relations of Micro-states: Self-determination and Statehood*, at 416.

[151] Raič, *Statehood and the Law of Self-determination*, at 408.

[152] See note 151.

[153] R. Higgins, *The Development of International Law through the Political Organs of the United Nations*, (London: Oxford University Press 1963), at 20–24.

4. Independence

The concept of independence is embodied by the Montevideo requirement that states should have the capacity to enter into relations with other states, and is stressed by many jurists as the key criterion of statehood.[154] It denotes the 'status of a state which controls its own external relations without dictation from other states'.[155] Krystyna Marek explains this criterion by appealing to the nature of international law, which is 'a legal order governing relations between independent States, that is to say between separate and distinct entities'.[156] In the absence of a clear delimitation of its subjects, which must therefore be 'endowed with separate personality', international law would not be conceivable: 'the independence of States forms the necessary prerequisite of international law, a condition which the latter cannot renounce, without at the same time renouncing its own *raison d'être*'.[157] Indeed it would be difficult to distinguish the obligations of one state from those of another—or, as we shall argue here, from those of another international person—if the two entities were not separate and independent. It would be equally difficult to attribute responsibility for a breach of obligations.

It is important at this stage to recall the words of J.L. Brierly: ' "independence" does not mean freedom from law, but merely freedom from control by other states'.[158] In effect, two elements are involved: legal and 'actual' independence.[159] A state is *de jure* independent 'when it is directly subordinated to international law' and when it possesses 'a basic norm of its own which is neither derived from nor shared with any other State'.[160] Actual or *de facto* independence refers to the capacity of a state to be 'free from subjection to any other State or group of States'.[161]

---

[154] Brownlie, *Principles of Public International Law*, 7th ed., at 71; Crawford, The *Creation of States in International Law*, 2nd ed., at 62.

[155] Clapham, *Brierly's Law of Nations*, 7th ed., at 143.

[156] K. Marek, *Identity and Continuity of States in Public International Law*, (Geneva: Librairie Droz, 1968), at 162–163.

[157] Marek, *Identity and Continuity of States in Public International Law*, at 163.

[158] J. L. Brierly, *The Law of Nations: an Introduction to the International Law of Peace*, (Oxford: Clarendon Press, 1949), at 115. See also Clapham, *Brierly's Law of Nations*, 7th ed., at 145. Hans Kelsen explained the condition of independence as follows. 'The community thus constituted must be independent, i.e., it must not be under the legal control of another community, equally qualified as a state. It is not incompatible with this requirement that the community, acting as a subject of international law, is under the legal control of an international community, in so far as it belongs to a union of states which has an international character, such as the League of Nations. The community of states constituted by general international law is itself such a community to the legal control of which all states are subjected. The state, in an international law sense, is a legal community which is subject only to general or particular international law but not to the law of any other state.' H. Kelsen, 'Recognition in International Law: Theoretical Observations', 35 *AJIL* 4 (1941), 605–617, at 608.

[159] Brownlie, *Principles of Public International Law*, 7th ed., at 72; Marek, *Identity and Continuity of States in Public International Law*, at 162.

[160] Marek, *Identity and Continuity of States in Public International Law*, at 168 and 180.

[161] See note 160, at 180.

4.1. Independence from a state versus independence from an international person

In the case at hand, these assertions translate into a simple question and an intricate problem. Let us start with the simple question: is the Vatican legally and actually independent from another state? Given its history and territorial proximity, Italy is certainly the state on which the Vatican is most likely to depend. Arguments which highlight a relation of dependency have focused on effective governmental authority over issues such as railway services and water provision, and the reliance on Italian legislation and judiciary.[162] Such arguments have been dismissed in this chapter and in any event do not prove that the Holy See (as the government of the Vatican) would be prevented from entering into foreign relations independent of Italian influence. Italy has recognized the sovereignty and exclusive jurisdiction of the Holy See over the Vatican City, and the Lateran Treaty stipulates that Italy will not interfere in those matters.[163] There are no indicia to support the claim of dependency on Italy in foreign relations.

The complex problem, of course, is not whether the Vatican is independent of Italy or any other state, but its relation with the Holy See and the implications of this relationship for the independence requirement. First, let us recall that the earlier definitions of legal and actual independence take as their reference the relation of one putative state to another state. The Holy See is not a state (at least not on its own account),[164] however, as already emphasized in this chapter, the Holy See enjoys international legal personality. It is submitted that, while understandable, restricting the definition of independence of a putative state solely to its relation with another state—as opposed to its relation with another international person—is artificial. It is understandable because the territorial logic has dominated international law and international relations since the peace of Westphalia.[165] Most definitions of independence therefore reflect this domination.[166] It is artificial, however, at least since the Advisory Opinion in the *Reparation for injuries case*, when the International Court of Justice (ICJ) clarified that international legal personality is not an exclusive attribute of statehood and that entities enjoying legal personality have certain rights

---

[162] See IV.3 in this chapter.

[163] Lateran Treaty, art. 4.

[164] For Duursma, the fact that the Holy See is 'neither a State nor a territorial entity' disqualifies prima facie the influence of the Holy See on the Vatican as an objection to the independence criterion. Duursma, *Fragmentation and the International Relations of Micro-states: Self-determination and Statehood*, at 413.

[165] The rise of the territorial state at the Peace of Westphalia is considered to be 'one of the most significant "revolutions"' in the evolution of the concept of sovereignty. C. Rudolph, 'Sovereignty and Territorial Borders in a Global Age', 7 *International Studies Review* 1 (2005) 1–20, at 4–5.

[166] The dominance of the territorial logic in international law is also highlighted in the context of the principle of self-determination. According to Marcelo Kohen, 'c'est le territoire qui définit le peuple et non le contraire'; when it recognizes the right of a people to self-determination, UN practice is to rely on territorial entities having a historical or administrative background. Kohen, 'La création d'Etats en droit international contemporain', at 585. See also G. Alfredsson, 'The Right of Self-determination and Indigenous Peoples', in C. Tomuschat (ed.), *Modern Law of Self-Determination*, (Dordrecht: Martinus Nijhoff Publishers, 1993), 41–54, at 41 and 46.

and obligations under international law.[167] The independence criterion should therefore aim to distinguish the rights and obligations under international law of a putative state, from those of another international person, regardless of whether the latter is a state or not. It would seem only consistent with the ICJ's findings to acknowledge that an actor possessing international personality may have the capacity to control another entity in its conduct of international relations to a point at which the independence requirement is not met. As Ian Brownlie put it: 'the question is that of foreign *control* overbearing the decision-making of the entity concerned on a wide range of matters of high policy and doing so systematically and on a permanent basis';[168] it is not whether the control is exercised by a state or by an entity possessing international personality. When he asserted that 'interference by [state] legal orders, or by an *international agency,* must be based on a title of international law', Brownlie expressly provided for the possibility that other entities, not just states, may wield foreign control.[169]

For instance, considering Kosovo's capacity to enter into international relations after its unilateral declaration of independence on 17 February 2008, some authors argue that:

[A]s so many of Kosovo's institutions rely on the foreign presence, its ability to independently commit itself to any undertakings in its international relations is, at best, partial. Furthermore, even in this context, Kosovo's constitution recognizes the final authority of the head of the international military presence and the international civilian representative in military and civilian issues respectively.[170]

While the situation in the case of Kosovo is rather complex,[171] what should be retained is that these scholars do not see any objection to analyzing the dependency

---

[167] *Reparation for injuries suffered in the service of the United Nations,* Advisory Opinion, ICJ Reports 1949, p. 174, at 178.

[168] Brownlie, *Principles of Public International Law,* 7th ed., at 72.

[169] See note 168.

[170] Z. Nevo and T. Megiddo, 'Lessons from Kosovo: The Law of Statehood and Palestinian Unilateral Independence,' 5 *Journal of International Law and International Relations* 2 (2009) 89–115, at 100. See also Constitution of the Republic of Kosovo, accessed January 2012, http://www.kushtetutakosoves.info/repository/docs/Constitution.of.the.Republic.of.Kosovo.pdf, arts. 146, 147 and 153.

[171] The case of Kosovo is not the object of this study. However, it serves to show how important context is in determining whether an entity fulfils the criterion of independence (in this case as an initial qualification for statehood). The contentious point is whether the international presences in Kosovo are based on a title of international law; if so, the independence requirement could be fulfilled. An example is the international military presence. The Comprehensive Proposal for the Kosovo Status Settlement (the Ahtisaari Plan) stipulates that an International Military Presence is to operate under the authority, and subject to the direction and political control of, the North Atlantic Council through the NATO chain of command. See Letter dated 26 March 2007 from the Secretary-General addressed to the President of the Security Council, Addendum, *Comprehensive Proposal for the Kosovo Status Settlement,* UN Doc. S/2007/168/Add.1, 26 March 2007. However, it is well-known that the Ahtisaari Plan has not been endorsed in a resolution by the UN Security Council, nor did it secure the agreement of Belgrade. In practice, following the unilateral declaration of independence of Kosovo, a downsized NATO-led Kosovo Force (KFOR) based its continued mission in Kosovo on UN Security Council resolution (UNSCR) 1244. See NATO, *Bucharest Summit Declaration,* 3 April 2008, accessed January 2012, http://www.nato.int/cps/en/natolive/official_texts_8443.htm; UN Security Council resolution 1244 of 10 June 1999, Annex, art. 4. Moreover, according to NATO, 'the Advisory Opinion of the Court on the legality of Kosovo's unilateral declaration of independence is that it did not violate international law, nor the UNSCR 1244' and hence did not affect the

of an entity claiming to be a state on actors which are not states, including NATO and the European Union.

4.2. *The relation between the Holy See and the Vatican and its implications for statehood*

The relation between the Holy See and the Vatican is therefore relevant to establish whether the Vatican meets the independence criterion for statehood. According to Ian Brownlie, absence of statehood is observable where an entity is 'subordinated to a state so completely as to be within its control and the origin of the subordination does not establish agency or representation'.[172]

4.2.1. The Lateran Treaty subordinates the Vatican to the Holy See

To assess the level of control that the Holy See wields over the Vatican, this section will appeal to the two non-cumulative instances of control that, according to James Crawford, derogate from formal independence. The first describes the existence of 'a special claim of right to exercise governmental authority over the putative state' as a matter of international law, irrespective of the consent of this entity.[173] The second refers to 'discretionary authority to intervene in the international affairs of the putative state';[174] it is clear that intervention could occur in the absence of consent by the putative state.

Let us therefore apply these theoretical instances to the actual relation between the Vatican and the Holy See. First, it can be substantiated through the provisions of the Lateran Treaty that the Holy See has 'a special claim of right to exercise governmental authority'[175] over the Vatican territory. A recapitulation of previous findings may be helpful at this stage: the Pope has the right and the effective capacity to influence directly and indirectly the conduct of legislative, executive, and judicial affairs of the Vatican; canon law, defined as the rules that govern the public order of the Roman Catholic Church, is the primary source of law at the Vatican; and the capacity to enter into foreign relations is entrusted to the Holy See. These stipulations of domestic legislation of the Vatican rely on article 3 of the Lateran Treaty, which proclaims that 'the Holy See has the full ownership and the exclusive and

---

KFOR mandate. See NATO, *NATO's role in Kosovo*, accessed January 2012, http://www.nato.int/cps/en/natolive/topics_48818.htm. On the other hand, some authors strongly disagree with the Court's opinion, in particular with its findings concerning UNSCR 1244 which would in their view uphold the territorial integrity of the Former Yugoslav Republic and thus invalidate the unilateral declaration of independence of Kosovo. See in particular M. G. Kohen and K. Del Mar, 'The Kosovo Advisory Opinion and UNSCR 1244 (1999): A Declaration of 'Independence from International Law'?', 24 *Leiden J Intl L* 1 (2011), 109–126.

[172] Brownlie, *Principles of Public International Law*, 7th ed., at 73. Again, the fact that Brownlie's definition refers to the subordination to a 'state' should not distract from the problem under discussion, because the same argument is valid when subordination is to an international person that is not a state.

[173] Crawford, *The Creation of States in International Law*, 2nd ed., at 71–72. See also Duursma, *Fragmentation and the International Relations of Micro-states: Self-determination and Statehood*, at 123.

[174] Crawford, *The Creation of States in International Law*, 2nd ed., at 71–72.

[175] Lateran Treaty, art. 3.

absolute power and jurisdiction over the Vatican as it is presently constituted...creating in this manner Vatican City'.[176] This provision of the Lateran Treaty affirms the Holy See's special claim of right to exercise governmental authority over the Vatican, irrespective of the latter's consent. The text of the treaty is straightforward in explaining the context of this special claim: the Vatican has been created to assure to the Holy See 'an indisputable sovereignty even in the international realm'.[177] The second situation that precluded formal independence, in Crawford's judgment, occurs when an actor claims discretionary authority to intervene in the international affairs' of the putative state.[178] This situation is in fact surpassed by the arrangements made in the Lateran Treaty, under which the Holy See is *the* authority carrying out the international relations of the Vatican. The Vatican has no distinct authority to consent, therefore consent is clearly not an issue.

4.2.2. The Lateran Treaty does not establish agency or representation

The Lateran Treaty proclaims the sovereignty of the Holy See over the Vatican.[179] The fact that in the conduct of its international affairs the Holy See sometimes acts 'on behalf and in the name of the Vatican'[180] cannot be compatible with the requirement that a Vatican state must genuinely represent an independent interest. No such independent interest is retained by the Lateran Treaty.[181] Any action of the Holy See in the name of the Vatican is not undertaken on behalf of the Vatican population—in itself a problematic term, as discussed earlier—but to advance the mission of the Holy See. For instance, the postal services at the Vatican are not intended to serve the needs of a permanent human community to communicate with the outside world, but are meant to serve the 'population of functionaries' supporting the works of the Holy See.

Moreover, the subordination arrangement is not transitory or provisional, but has been sought as a permanent means of showcasing the independence of the Holy See from Italy and to fortify the legal status of the Holy See in the international realm.[182] For comparative purposes, Robert Jennings' analysis of the situation in Germany, when it was occupied by Allied Forces after World War II, may be edifying.

The view that the German state has ceased to exist rests very largely on the—it is submitted mistaken—assumption that the Allies have in fact vested themselves with full sovereignty over Germany in the ordinary sense of that term. The Berlin Declaration is obviously a carefully drafted document and it is significant that, far from declaring that the occupying Powers have assumed the sovereignty over Germany, it studiously avoids any reference to sovereignty. It speaks only of an assumption of 'supreme authority' (*l'autorité*

---

[176] Crawford, *The Creation of States in International Law*, 2nd ed., at 71–72.
[177] Lateran Treaty, preamble.
[178] Crawford, *The Creation of States in International Law*, 2nd ed., at 72.
[179] Lateran Treaty, art. 4.
[180] See VI.3 in this chapter.
[181] Hyginus Eugene Cardinale contends that 'the Vatican City State was not established with an autonomous purpose but as a means to support a religious body'. Cardinale, *The Holy See and the International Order*, at 101.
[182] Lateran Treaty, preamble.

suprême: oberste Regierungsgewalt), which is not necessarily the same thing. For the 'supreme authority' assumed by the occupying Powers is not without qualification: it is assumed for certain stated purposes; it is 'without prejudice to any subsequent decisions that may be taken respecting Germany'; it is a provisional regime to provide for 'the period when Germany is carrying out the basic requirements of unconditional surrender'; furthermore, it is specifically stated that 'the assumption, for the purposes stated above, of the said authority and powers does not effect the annexation of Germany'.[183]

Against this background, it must be observed that there is no provision in the Lateran Treaty which resembles the qualifications of Allied Powers' 'supreme authority' in the Berlin Declaration. Quite the opposite is true: the creation of the Vatican is qualified by the sovereignty of the Holy See over it.

Moreover, it would be inaccurate to regard the Vatican either as a vassal state of the Holy See or as state under its protectorate.[184] These arrangements have been best explained by Hersch Lauterpacht.[185] Suzerainty, as distinct from sovereignty, implies that the suzerain represents to a lesser or greater extent the vassal state on the international plane, while the internal affairs remain the domain of the former.[186] As such, the vassal state would be a 'half sovereign state', without or with a limited international personality,[187] yet the Holy See is the *sovereign* of the Vatican in the international and internal realm. As to the protectorate arrangement, the ICJ found that under the 1912 Treaty of Fez, Morocco 'remained a sovereign State' regardless of the arrangement it undertook with France, whereby the latter was to exercise certain powers in the name and on behalf of Morocco, including conducting Morocco's international relations.[188] In the end, these relational arrangements, which describe 'a kind of international guardianship',[189] are built on the premise that the guarded entity is a state, albeit not an independent one.[190] The

---

[183] R. Y. Jennings, 'Government in Commission', 23 *BYBIL* (1946) 112–141, at 121.

[184] Alfred Verdross contended that, while the legal order of the Vatican is not self-standing but derived from the order of the Church, Vatican City is nonetheless a state: 'da es sich um eine räumliche Herrschaftsordnung handelt, die von den geistigen Funktionen der Kirche verschieden ist. Dieser Staat ist aber kein souveräner Staat, also ein Vasallenstaat der katholischen Kirche'. A. Verdross, *Völkerrecht*, (Berlin: Julius Springer, 1937), at 59. Whether the Pontifical Commission and the Governorate, which are directly and indirectly subordinated to the Pope, and must conduct the more important affairs of the Vatican together with the Holy See's Secretariat of State, can be seen as the governmental authority of the territory of Vatican, has been questioned by this study. See IV.3 in this chapter. See also Crawford, *The Creation of States in International Law*, 2nd ed., 230.

[185] H. Lauterpacht (ed.), *Oppenheim's International Law*, 8th ed., vol. I, (London: Longman, Green and Co, 1955), at 188–196. Robert Jennings and Arthur Watts generally confirmed Lauterpacht's earlier analysis while noting that the term vassal state and suzerainty are little used today (solely in relation to the Tibet-China relations). They list Andorra as the only contemporary protectorate in Europe. R. Jennings and A. Watts (eds.), *Oppenheim's International Law*, 9th ed., vol. I, (London: Longman, 1996), at 266–274.

[186] Lauterpacht (ed.), *Oppenheim's International Law*, 8th ed., at 189–191.

[187] See note 186.

[188] *Case concerning rights of nationals of the United States of America in Morocco*, Judgment of 27 August 1952, ICJ Reports 1952, p. 176, at 188.

[189] Lauterpacht (ed.), *Oppenheim's International Law*, 8th ed., at 192.

[190] See T. Poulose, 'India as an Anomalous International Person (1919–1947)', 44 *BYBIL* (1970) 201–212, at 202–203.

same premise applies in the case of personal and real unions, respectively.[191] But the Vatican on its own cannot make pretensions to statehood: it does not possess a population of its own, it lacks the internal and governmental capacity in the absence of the Holy See, and its legal order is derived from that of the Church.

The Vatican fails the independence test of statehood, however, and this is the crucial caveat, this is so only if the Holy See is a personality external to the Vatican. To turn the argument on its head, if the Holy See and the Vatican form a construct, then the control exercised by the Holy See over the Vatican would not pose any problems in terms of independence. Such control would amount to the control of a government over its territory.

Some concluding remarks on the personality question, as it was revisited in the light of the Lateran Treaty and the domestic legislation of the Vatican, are in order at this stage. First, it has become evident from part III of this chapter that, following the extinction of the Papal States, the international personality of the Holy See—but not as a state—continued to be recognized as customary by virtue of the latter's religious legitimacy. Second, as a result of the Lateran Treaty, the resemblance of statehood was granted to, we argued, the Holy See-Vatican construct. Third, it would seem to us that if the resemblance of statehood were to disappear (for example, after loss of the Vatican territory) the personality of the Holy See would continue to exist—not as a state—but grounded in its primary source, its religious legitimacy. The alternative is not valid however. If the Holy See were to cease to exist, the Vatican would vanish. It would have no government or population and would be only a territory, with no pretence to statehood or claim to international personality. It can therefore be asserted that the Vatican as a distinct entity is merely a territory, not a state, and has on its own no basis to claim a distinct international legal personality.

Understanding the situation in this way clarifies that the dual personality scenario is legally unsustainable. Only as a construct with the Vatican, and due to its territoriality, can the Holy See 'clothe' itself with the cloak of statehood. That, however, means that the Holy See's claim to have a distinct international personality external to the construct invalidates the resemblance to statehood, because the requirement of independence would not be fulfilled. Let us recall Marek's argument, according to which the criterion of independence for statehood originates from and is a prerequisite for the nature and functioning of international law.[192] The attribution of rights and obligations, and the consequences of a breach of international law, all require the existence of separate, distinct international

---

[191] A personal union is characterized by the existence of *two sovereign states* and separate international persons that are linked together through the 'accidental' fact that they have the same monarch. The real union is defined by *two sovereign states* coming together by virtue of an international treaty recognized by other states in a permanent union with one international personality. Lauterpacht (ed.), *Oppenheim's International Law*, 8th ed., at 170–171. The 9th edition of *Oppenheim's International Law* reasserts the two definitions. Jennings and Watts observed that a personal union may exist between the UK and 'those other independent members of the Commonwealth, such as Canada and Australia, of which Queen Elizabeth II is also Head of State'. No real union exists to date. Jennings and Watts (eds.), *Oppenheim's International Law*, 9th ed., at 245–246.

[192] Marek, *Identity and Continuity of States in Public International Law*, at 162 ff.

personae. As such, a situation in which an international person is the government of a state and at the same time is an external and distinct personality appears legally untenable.

These findings suggest that the only sustainable possibility is one in which the Holy See forms together with the Vatican a construct with a single international personality. The origin of this personality is nonetheless twofold, as history and the Lateran treaty attest: custom recognizes the religious legitimacy of the Holy See, and the Lateran Treaty confers the resemblance of statehood. Together, as a construct, the Holy See and the Vatican are akin to a state and therefore acquire the rights and incur the responsibilities of a state.

This preliminary conclusion, based on an analysis of the Lateran Treaty and subsequent domestic legislation interpreted in the light of the Montevideo criteria of statehood, ought to be verified against the recognition of states and the jurisprudence of domestic courts. Before subjecting the findings to the test of practice, it is necessary to address the self-perception of the Holy See, in an effort to understand the logic behind its insistence on the dual personality scenario.

V. Self-Perception of the Holy See and the Logic Behind the Dual Personality Scenario

A deconstruction of the self-perception of the Holy See informs the subsequent legal analysis of state practice. This section will therefore attempt to sketch the logic behind the dual personality scenario which the Holy See presents as valid.

The 1999 report to the Committee monitoring the implementation of the International Convention on the Elimination of All Forms of Racial Discrimination (CERD) portrays the Holy See's claim of its dual personality as follows:

(a) In international law, the Holy See is a sovereign subject having an original, non-derived legal personality independent of any authority or jurisdiction....

(d) Historically, the international personality of the Holy See has never been confused with that of the territories over which it has exercised State sovereignty, e.g. the Patrimony of St. Peter (or Church States) from 754 to 1870 and Vatican City since 1929.

(e) The international personality of the Holy See takes precedence over any territorial personality, as is borne out, for example, by the years 1870–1929 which lay between the loss of the traditional Church States and the establishment of the State of Vatican City. During those sixty years the Holy See continued to act as a subject of international law by concluding concordats and international treaties with a great number of States, participating in international conferences, conducting mediation and arbitration missions, and maintaining both active and passive diplomatic relations.[193]

While it will be demonstrated in part VI of this chapter that there is no uniform state practice in the post-Lateran period which supports the claim in point (d), for

---

[193] CERD Committee, Thirteenth, fourteenth and fifteenth periodic report (consolidated), Holy See, Committee on the Elimination of Racial Discrimination, UN Doc CERD/C/338/Add.11, 26 May 2000, para. 4.

the purpose of this section the above statement is instructive in that it exemplifies the one major concern of the Holy See: the continuity of its international legal personality regardless of territoriality. History, the claim of divine origin, and the facilitation of diplomatic relations may well explain the firm resolve to differentiate the Holy See personality from that of the Vatican. These aspects will be examined in more detail in the coming paragraphs.

First, to the Holy See's awareness of its own history. As was discussed earlier, the loss of the Papal States in 1870 was not without controversy for the continuation of the personality of the Holy See: indeed, in the absence of statehood, several scholars of the period denied the personality of the Holy See altogether. Some jurists considered that the treaty-making and diplomatic activity of the Holy See was merely permitted by the Italian Law of Guarantees and did not reflect an international legal personality. It must be acknowledged that contemporary legal scholars have interpreted the practice of the Holy See with the benefit of hindsight. The benefit of hindsight refers here to international law's move away from strict territoriality as the basis of international personality, and the admission of other entities than states to the status of international subjects. It also refers to the knowledge that the Lateran Treaty had recognized in 1929 the international personality of the Holy See. The point here is not to re-open a debate on whether the personality of the Holy See continued or was extinguished when it lost its territories, it is to underline that the loss of territories represented a lesson for the future. Rooted in precisely this lesson of history, the Holy See's insistence on delinking its personality from that of the Vatican territory appears to be only sensible. Whether awareness of history represents a sufficient legal ground for the two entities to be considered distinct as a matter of law is, however, doubtful.

Second, the Catholic Church and the Holy See claim a divine origin.[194] This divine origin may represent an important reason for the perseverance in distinguishing the Holy See's legal personality from that of the Vatican, the latter being a construct of worldly law. Since the primary role of the Catholic Church in the world is 'the preaching of the Gospel and the salvation of souls',[195] one may justifiably ask how this can be compatible with the Holy See's involvement in international politics. Even in the dual personality scenario, it has been challenging to reconcile papal diplomacy—understood as a system that governs, in conformity with the rules of ecclesiastical and international law, the relations between the Catholic Church and states with the aim of 'ensuring their harmony and co-operation and thus promoting lasting goodwill, understanding, and peace among all peoples'[196]—with the divine

---

[194] According to canon 113, para. 1, the Catholic Church and the Apostolic See are said to have 'the character of a moral person by divine ordinance'. Canonists assert that the 'classification as moral persons distinguishes the Catholic Church and the Apostolic See from juridic persons which are creations of ecclesiastical authority, and affirmation of the divine origin of the Catholic Church and the Apostolic See distinguishes them from other moral persons, such as associations of the faithful, or funds, which are of human origin.' See Beal, Coriden and Green, *New Commentary on the Code of Canon Law*, at 154–155.

[195] Cardinale, *The Holy See and the International Order*, at 23.

[196] See note 195, at 37.

origin and a strictly religious understanding of the role of the Church. As Hyginus Eugene Cardinale, an outspoken defender of papal diplomacy,[197] admitted:

Papal diplomacy has always been a controversial issue.... It is seen by some as a powerful means, by which the papacy is able to wield a beneficial influence over the course of world politics. But it is also considered by others as anachronistic and even unworthy of a Church, that claims divine origin and should therefore refuse to speak the language of the world.[198]

While underlining that the Church 'does not place her trust in the privileges offered by civil authority' and that she 'will even give up the exercise of certain rights which have been legitimately acquired, if it becomes clear that their use raises doubt about the sincerity of her witness or that new ways of life demand new methods',[199] the Second Vatican Council is said to support not only the concern with world politics but the involvement of the Holy See therein as a consequence of its spiritual and religious mission.[200]

Despite objections and challenges from within, as well as outside, the Catholic Church,[201] the Holy See does pursue papal diplomacy, the main instruments of which are the papal nuncios. The mandate of the papal nuncio is best described as a compound of ecclesiastical and political functions. The political function should raise at least the same objections as would a Holy See-Vatican construct without separate international personalities for its two entities. Yet, Cardinale proposed a number of pragmatic arguments in support of the composite role of the nuncios. He underlines the unnecessary multiplication of personnel, the overt publicity of the right to external legation of the Pope, and past experience that testifies to the 'non-expediency' of differentiating the roles.

Furthermore, the ambassadorial function requires professional training and special skill and experience for the kind of problems nuncios are likely to be confronted with. A local ecclesiastic, who is an outsider to the diplomatic service is not always equipped with those qualities. Even more, he would lack the protection of diplomatic status, since as a national, he would remain within the jurisdiction of the law of the land: as a result the State could intervene in different ways to paralyse his action.[202]

If these pragmatic arguments are considered solid enough to overcome criticisms based on the Church's divine origin in the case of the nuncios, one may ask if legal arguments may not have a similar effect with respect to the personality question.

---

[197] Cardinale had a long career in the service of the Holy See, inter alia as nuncio to Belgium and Luxemburg (1969–1983) and to the European Community (1970–1983).

[198] Cardinale, *The Holy See and the International Order*, at xv.

[199] Pastoral Constitution on the Church in the Modern World, *Gaudium et Spes*, promulgated by Pope Paul VI, 7 December 1965, para. 76.

[200] R. J. Araujo and J. A. Lucal, *Papal Diplomacy and the Quest for Peace: The Vatican and International Organizations from the Early Years to the League of Nations*, (Naples, FL: Sapientia Press, 2005), at 11.

[201] Cardinale enumerated a number of theological, juridical, structural, ethical, historical, and ecumenical objections to papal diplomacy stemming from inside the Catholic Church. His work is an effort to rebut these challenges. Cardinale, *The Holy See and the International Order*, at 47–58. For a scholarly critique see Abdullah, 'The Holy See at United Nations Conferences: State or Church?'. For an NGO perspective, see See Change, *The Catholic Church at the United Nations: Church or State?* accessed March 2012, http://www.seechange.org/PDF/See%20Change%20Briefing%20Paper.pdf.

[202] Cardinale, *The Holy See and the International Order*, at 51–52.

Third, perhaps in an interactionist account, the self-perception of the Holy See as a dual personality may be seen as a response to the perceptions of certain states.[203] The constitutions of some states require a strict separation of state and church relations,[204] while other states have an assumed religious character: the Holy See may be prompted to claim a second personality, separate from the one which derives from its religious legitimacy, precisely to facilitate its diplomatic relations with these two different categories of states.[205] Giovanni Lajolo, the former President of the Vatican City State explains that the sovereignty of the Holy See in the international arena as an attribute of her religious mission is a sufficient reason for many states to enter into diplomatic relations with it; he goes on to note that:

Other States, however, prefer to make exclusive reference to the territorial reality of Vatican City State, which corresponds to their own nature; Vatican City is internationally recognized as a State visibly independent from any other, a State which as such guarantees the Holy See inalienable sovereignty in the international arena. The motivation for the attitude of these other States can vary; for some it might be their own non-denominational nature, which prevents them from recognizing the specifically religious aspect of the Holy See (I am thinking especially of Islamic States), but for others it might be their pronounced secular character, which does not recognize any active role for religions on the international stage.[206]

This line of argumentation in support of the dual personality scenario may appear to some as opportunistic. Be that as it may, it remains to be seen whether the practice of states, their courts, and of international organizations supports the two personae or, on the contrary, confirms the construct variant.

VI. On Practice

This part will discuss the bilateral diplomatic relations of the Holy See, instances of jurisprudence in relation to the actor, and the participation of the Holy See and the Vatican in international organizations and international treaties. It will be argued that the resemblance of statehood conferred upon the Holy See and the Vatican as a construct allows it to enjoy the privileges of a state—including limited sovereign immunity from trial in foreign courts—and participation rights in the UN General Assembly and related international conferences as a state. The

---

[203] The term interactionist is understood here in the context of Herbert Blumer's theory of society as symbolic interactionism, where individuals define each other's actions instead of merely reacting to them. H. Blumer, *Symbolic Interactionism: Perspective and Method*, (Berkley: University of California Press, 1986), at 78–79.

[204] See, for instance, the diplomatic relations between the Holy See and the United States examined later in this chapter at VI.1.1.

[205] *Lecture on Vatican/Holy See Diplomacy*, Speech by His Excellence Giovanni Lajolo, President, State of Vatican City, Sophia University, Tokyo, 10 May 2007, accessed March 2012, http://www.vaticanstate.va/EN/State_and_Government/Structure_Governorate/Presidency/President/2007/10_May_2007--p--1.htm.

[206] See note 205.

resemblance of statehood also facilitates the construct's access to international conventions which are restricted to participation of states. The corollary is that the construct incurs international obligations, including under human rights treaties, which are equivalent to the obligations of any other state. An analysis of clerical child sexual abuse in Ireland in the context of the CRC will serve to portray these international obligations of the Holy See-Vatican.

1. The personality question and bilateral diplomatic relations

The general view among scholars is that, in the case of the Holy See and the Vatican, recognition by states is of crucial importance for the indication or confirmation of their international status.[207] Beyond the traditional complications that arise from the dispute between the declaratory and constitutive schools,[208] recognition in the case at hand is particularly convoluted. In the dual personality scenario proposed by the Holy See itself, it becomes unmanageable to understand who is being recognized as a result of the diplomatic relations which the Holy See has entered into with over 170 states:[209] is it the Holy See, the Vatican, or both? Or has the personality of the construct that the two entities built together driven recognition of the Holy See in the post 1929 period? A full grasp of the meaning of bilateral diplomatic relations between the Holy See and a state would require a substantive historical analysis in respect of every single bilateral relation. For example, a state that entered into diplomatic relations with the Holy See after 1870 has thereby recognized the international personality of the latter. Can it be assumed that as of 1929 the state's recognition was extended to the Vatican as a separate international personality? Surely this cannot be a valid assumption. In the absence of a practice under which the state recognizes both personalities, the dual personality of the Holy See cannot be inferred.[210]

---

[207] Observing that '[s]ome jurists regard the Vatican City as a state, although its special functions make this doubtful', Brownlie contended that 'its personality seems to rest partly on its approximation to a state function..., and partly on acquiescence and recognition by existing legal persons'. He also noted that 'more difficult to solve is the question of the personality of the Holy See as a religious organ apart from its territorial base in the Vatican City. It would seem that the personality of political and religious institutions of this type can only be relative to those states prepared to enter into relationships with such institutions on the international plane'. Brownlie, *Principles of Public International Law*, 7th ed., at 64. See also Shaw, *International Law*, 5th ed., at 219.

[208] For an analysis of declarative versus constitutive conceptions, see Crawford, *The Creation of States in International Law*, 2nd ed., at 19–26; and Daillier, et al., *Droit international public*, 8ème ed., at 621–622.

[209] See *Bilateral and Multilateral Relations of the Holy See*, Secretariat of State, 22 October 2009.

[210] Referencing Yves de la Brière, Paul Guggenheim observed that collective recognition of the 'effectiveness of the new state' took place on 9 March 1929, during a ceremonial reception by Pope Pius XI of the diplomatic corps to the Holy See. P. Guggenheim, *Lehrbuch des Völkerrechts*, vol. I, (Basel: Verlag für Recht und Gessellschaft AG, 1948), at 202. De la Brière cited a speech by the dean of the diplomatic corps at the Holy See, the Brazilian Ambassador Charles Maghalaès de Azeredo, which insists on the continued personality of the Holy See post-1870 and does not refer explicitly to the dual personality of the Holy See. In the view of this author, the Ambassador's remarks would not put in question the single personality of the Holy See-Vatican construct. De la Brière, 'La condition juridique de la cité du Vatican', at 159–160.

An extensive analysis of the practice of every single state that entered into diplomatic relations with the Holy See is, of course, beyond the scope and capacity of this study. We are in a position to highlight certain examples which illustrate the different conclusions that could be drawn, based on diplomatic practice, with regard to the personality question. It would be too easy to dismiss this practice of states as erratic. The argument made is that the dual personality is rarely recognized as such and that, even when it is recognized, national courts tend to treat the Holy See and the Vatican as a construct with a single personality. It is therefore submitted that the personality question, and ultimately the rights and obligations of the Holy See and the Vatican respectively, can be discerned only in the context of the jurisprudence of domestic courts.

To exemplify the variety of interpretations that states give to the personality question, three categories of diplomatic practice will be proposed. For instance, Spain under Franco recognized the dual personality of the Holy See and the Vatican respectively in its 1953 concordat with the Holy See.[211] Such explicit acknowledgment of the dual personality is rare. Other states—mostly, but not exclusively then communist states—have stressed in their diplomatic relations with the Holy See the latter's duty of non-interference in their internal affairs as codified in article 41 of the Vienna Convention on Diplomatic Relations.[212] At times, diplomatic conflict degenerated to the point that local authorities expelled the Holy See's nuncios. This occurred in 1931 in Lithuania, in 1947 in Albania, in 1950 in Romania, in 1951 in China, and in 1952 in the S.F.R. Yugoslavia.[213] Similarly, influenced by a French doctrine that forbade all direct communications between the nuncio and national Catholic clergy, the interference of the papal nuncio in the internal affairs of France was a constant source of tension.[214] Lastly, as canon lawyers point out:

History is replete with attempts on the part of civil authorities to circumscribe, either totally or partially, the rights of the Roman Pontiff regarding his legates. These have included attempts to limit them to merely diplomatic or political functions, in order to control the

---

[211] 'El Estado español reconoce la personalidad jurídica internacional de la Santa Sede y del Estado de la Ciudad del Vaticano', Concordato entre La Santa Sede y España, 27 August 1953, accessed March 2012, http://www.vatican.va/roman_curia/secretariat_state/archivio/documents/rc_seg-st_19530827_concordato-spagna_sp.html. Some authors present this concordat as an 'imprimatur' by the Holy See, helping the Franco regime to escape diplomatic isolation. E. J. Heubel, 'Church and State in Spain: Transition toward Independence and Liberty', 30 *The Western Political Quarterly* 1 (1977), 125–139, at 129.

[212] Rousseau, *Droit international public*, at 360; VCDR, art. 41.1.

[213] Rousseau, *Droit international public*, at 362–363.

[214] In the eyes of Charles Rousseau, diplomatic conflict is the unfortunate but logical outcome of the twofold mission of nuncios—diplomatic and ecclesiastical—which in turn is rooted in the international status of the Holy See, whereby the Catholic Church 'agit sous le couvert d'un Etat—réel jusqu'à 1870, fictif depuis 1929' (This author's own translation: acts under the guise of a state—real until 1870, fictional since 1929). Rousseau, *Droit international public*, at 360 and 362.

Church and to hinder contacts, whether on the part of the hierarchy or on the part of the lay faithful, between particular churches and the Apostolic See.[215]

Indeed, these states seem not to have acknowledged the dual personality of the Holy See and to have insisted on the latter's obligations under international law as a state. They required the Holy See to respect the obligation of non-interference in internal affairs, as they would have in the case of other states. A recent example from Ireland is perhaps even more revelatory: here, it appears as if Ireland, a Catholic state, regards the Holy See-Vatican as a construct while imposing on it the obligations of a state. In 2011, the principal chamber of the Irish parliament debated the disclosure of a report into clerical sexual abuse in Ireland. Several of the deputies deplored the 'intervention' of the Holy See, which in their view had contributed to undermining the child protection frameworks and guidelines of the Irish state and the Irish bishops.[216] A member of parliament also underlined that the issue of child sexual abuse by clerics in Ireland engaged the international obligations of the Holy See as a state-like construct.

As a candidate country for the United Nations Human Rights Council and one struggling to deal with the legacies of generations of abuse, Ireland should be able to show leadership on the international stage by calling on the Vatican to stop acting like a rogue state and live up to the commitments it has made by signing and ratifying binding international human rights treaties. As a Catholic, it is my strong belief that my church should not be a reluctant convert to the protection of human rights and children. Surely it should be in the global vanguard in respect of these issues. That it is not saddens and offends. This must change.[217]

1.1. The US-Holy See relations: recognition of a state or a church?

The United States provides one of the most interesting examples of confusing state practice in relation to the personality question. Having acknowledged the dual personality of the Holy See and the Vatican, the US government chose explicitly to enter into diplomatic relations solely with the Holy See as the government of the Vatican.

The Establishment Clause in the First Amendment of the US Constitution stipulates that 'Congress shall make no law respecting an establishment of religion...'.[218] It requires the government to display neutrality between religions and between religion and non-religion, and in consequence the government may not take action that has the purpose or effect of advancing or inhibiting religion.[219]

---

[215] Beal, Coriden and Green, *New Commentary on the Code of Canon Law*, at 491.

[216] Dáil Éireann, Commission of Investigation Report in the Catholic Diocese of Cloyne: Motion, 20 July 2011, accessed March 2012 http://debates.oireachtas.ie/dail/2011/07/20/00013.asp.

[217] Deputy Caoimhghín Ó Caoláin, in Commission of Investigation Report in the Catholic Diocese of Cloyne: Motion, 20 July 2011.

[218] First Amendment to the Constitution of the United States of America (1791).

[219] See *Epperson v. Arkansas*, 393 U. S. 97, 104 (1968); *Everson v. Board of Education of Ewing*, 330 U. S. 1, 15–16 (1947); *McCreary County v. American Civil Liberties Union of Kentucky*, 545 U.S. 844 (2005). For current developments, see T. B. Colby, 'A Constitutional Hierarchy of Religions—Justice Scalia, the Ten Commandments, and the Future of the Establishment Clause', 100 *Northwestern University Law Review* (2006) 1097–1140.

Read in this light, formal diplomatic relations with the Holy See have proved constitutionally problematic for the United States for a long period of time.[220] In 1984, when the United States formally established diplomatic relations with the Holy See, the dual personality scenario, despite or because of the confusion it generates, was found convenient.[221] While expressly recognizing the dual personality of the Holy See and the Vatican respectively, the US government specifically chose to enter into diplomatic relations with the Holy See as government of the Vatican. The 1984 press briefing by John Hughes, Assistant Secretary of State for Public Affairs, discloses the superficial basis in law—and indeed in logic—of the dual personality scenario and the opportunistic 'pick-and-choose-a-personality' strategy which it facilitates. It will, therefore, be cited at length:

Q How do you respond to protests from the American Jewish Congress and other religious groups that this is a violation of the separation of church and state?
A Well, it isn't.
Q Why isn't it?
A It's not a violation of church and state because for a long time, we recognized the Holy See as having an international personality distinct from the Roman Catholic Church. This relationship will be with the Holy See. The Holy See is distinct from the Catholic Church.
Q Could you parse that a little bit? What is the distinction?
A I think the Pope has responsibilities and a leadership role in the Roman Catholic Church, as he has in the Holy See, which is responsible for the Vatican, which is a sovereign city-state. The two roles, as I understand it, are separate.
Q Does that mean the relationship will be between the Government of the United States—
A —And of the Holy See.
Q —and of the Government of the Vatican City-State, and not with the Catholic Church?
A With the Holy See, that's correct. With the Holy See.
Q Not with the Catholic Church?
A Correct.
…
Q Sir, you said that the Vatican has an international personality distinct from the Catholic Church—
A Yes.
Q —and that's how you get around the church-state thing. Could you—
A Well, it's not a "getting around it". It's a recognition of the fact.

---

[220] Samuel W. Bettwy classifies the US-Holy See relations as follows: 1797–1895, consular; 1848–1868, non-reciprocal diplomatic; 1893–1984, unofficial; 1984–, full diplomatic relations. S. W. Bettwy, 'United States-Vatican Recognition: Background and Issues', 29 *Catholic Lawyer* (1984), 225–265, at 241–244. For a brief background to US-Holy See relations through the eyes of the court, see *Americans United for Separation of Church and State et al. v. Ronald Reagan, et al.*, 607 F.Supp. 747 (E.D. PA, 1985), at 750.
[221] The Italian journalist, Massimo Franco, discusses the context that prompted the United States and Holy See to establish diplomatic relations in 1984. He points inter alia to the strong stance against communism of Pope John Paul II and the context of the US elections, in which President Reagan sought political gains among conservative Catholics. M. Franco, *Parallel Empires: the Vatican and the United States—Two Centuries of Alliance and Conflict*, (New York: Doubleday, 2008).

Q Could you explain what is that international personality that makes it distinctive and different from the Catholic Church?

A Well, the Holy See is a government of a sovereign city-state and operates as such, and is recognized as such by most of the nations of the world.

Q What does that government do, sir, besides administer 100-some acres?

A Well, I think it's involved in treaties, and it's involved in negotiations, and a variety of other activities, but I don't think I ought to be speaking for the Holy See. I think you ought to talk to them.

Q Would it be accurate for us to report, then, that the relationship will deal not with matters relating to the Catholic Church but only with treaties and—

A I don't think it will be accurate to report that. I think it will be accurate to make a point that there is separation—constitutional, legal separation between the Holy See and the Catholic Church, and that it is not a conflict between church and state for the United States, nor indeed, for the other countries.[222]

The 'pick-and-choose-a-personality' strategy embraced by the US Government, which allowed it to recognize the Holy See while upholding the religious neutrality clause of its Constitution, was not found convincing by everyone in the United States.[223] In *Americans United for Separation of Church and State v. Reagan,* a group of 20 religious organizations and other individual members of clergy of various denominations initiated a class action suit against the commencement of diplomatic relations with the Holy See.[224] The plaintiffs challenged the constitutionality of establishing diplomatic relations with the Holy See, since in their view:

Congress has violated the First Amendment because the arrangement (a) establishes a formal official relationship with a church, (b) amounts to a preference of one church over all other churches, (c) provides special benefits to one church to the detriment of all others, (d) produces excessive entanglement of the government in church affairs and vice-versa, and (e) creates religious divisiveness.[225]

---

[222] Department of State, Daily Press Briefing, Tuesday, January 10, 1984, 11:48 A.M., Addendum in *James H. O'Bryan et al. v. the Holy See,* Final Brief for the United States as Intervenor and Amicus Curiae Supporting the Defendant, US Court of Appeals, 6th Cir., Nos. 07-5078, 07-5163. See also M. N. Leich, 'Contemporary Practice of the United States Relating to International Law', 78 *AJIL* 2 (1984) 427–440, at 427.

[223] For an account contrasting opposition in the 1950s by Protestant, Baptist and Jewish and secular groups to US diplomatic relations with the Holy See to opposition in the 1980s, see M. Gayte, '"I Told the White House If They Give One to the Pope, I May Ask for One": The American Reception to the Establishment of Diplomatic Relations between the United States and the Vatican in 1984', 54 *Journal of Church and State* 1 (2012), 33–56. For court cases see *Americans United for Separation of Church and State et al. v. Ronald Reagan, et al.,* 607 F.Supp. 747 (E.D. PA, 1985); *Americans United for Separation of Church and State v. Ronald Reagan,* 3rd Cir., 786 F.2d 194 (1986); *Phelps v. Ronald Reagan,* 10th Cir., No. 85-2279 (1987).

[224] *Americans United for Separation of Church and State et al. v. Ronald Reagan, et al.,* 607 F.Supp. 747 (E.D. PA, 1985), at 749.

[225] The plaintiffs brought three additional claims: '2. The President has exceeded his Article II powers, since the Holy See is a church, not a state; moreover, the President's actions contravene the First Amendment, for the reasons mentioned above. 3. The arrangement violates the Equal Protection Clause of the Fifth Amendment. 4. The defendants have violated the Constitution in various specific ways, including (a) supporting the Catholic Church, to the detriment of all others, (b) spending tax dollars for the benefit of the Catholic Church and its prelates, (c) supporting the Catholic Church in its efforts to counteract and nullify the influence of foreign missionaries allied with other churches,

The Court did not address the case on its merits, but summarily dismissed it on grounds of standing and non-justiciability given the political question involved.[226] The plaintiffs' arguments that they had standing as taxpayers, citizens and voters, and were victims of stigmatization, were described by the district judge as 'nothing more than a statement of some of the reasons why the separation of church and state is a good idea'.[227] The judge went on to assert the non-justiciablity of the case by holding that 'in no area of governmental activity is judicial intervention less likely to be permissible than in the President's conduct of foreign policy'.[228] In brief, procedural barriers were erected that prevented the Court from evaluating the dual personality scenario proclaimed by the Holy See and embraced by the US.

While upholding the District Court's findings on lack of standing and subject-matter, the Court of Appeals made a rather interesting statement, which on the one hand downplays the Holy See as a *sui generis* entity in international law, and on the other underlines the crucial role played by territoriality in the recognition of the Holy See by states such as the US.[229]

We start with two palpable facts pleaded in the complaint. The State of the City of the Vatican is a territorial sovereignty, however small its size and population. The head of the Roman Catholic Church controls the government of that sovereign territory. No other religious organization that is a plaintiff, or in which individual plaintiffs are members, is similarly situated....

It may be true, as plaintiffs allege, that as a result of opening diplomatic relations with the Vatican the Vatican's diplomatic representatives will enjoy the benefit of certain federal statutes and of the Treaty of Vienna. And it is true that plaintiffs' church representatives do not enjoy the same benefits. However, the benefits that may be available to the Vatican's representatives are available only because, unlike the plaintiffs' church organizations, the

---

and (d) cooperating with the Catholic Church in investigating other United States religious organizations.' *Americans United for Separation of Church and State et al. v. Ronald Reagan, et al.*, note 224, at 749–750.

[226] Standing and the political question doctrine are two procedural barriers covered by the concept of justiciability, deriving from article III of the US Constitution. A litigant must prove that she has suffered or is threatened with legal injury. Only then will she have standing to seek judicial remedy. The political question doctrine is a consequence of the tripartite allocation of powers in the US constitutional system, whereby federal courts are not to intrude into areas of other governmental branches. *Americans United for Separation of Church and State et al. v. Ronald Reagan, et al.*, note 224, at 750 ff; see also M. L. Hekker, 'Constitutional Issues Raised by Diplomatic Relations Between the United States and the Holy See', 15 *Hastings Constitutional Law Quarterly* (1987) 101–124, at 108 ff.

[227] *Americans United for Separation of Church and State et al. v. Ronald Reagan, et al.*, note 224, at 750.

[228] *Americans United for Separation of Church and State et al. v. Ronald Reagan, et al.*, note 224, at 751.

[229] In particular, unaccounted for are the historical circumstances which led to the recognition of the Holy See as a subject of international law in contrast to its re-gained territoriality through the Lateran Treaty. As James A. Coriden comments: 'The court would seem to imply that if the Dal[a]i Lama or the Patriarch of Constantinople or the General Secretary of the American Baptist Churches only had an enclave which enjoyed territorial autonomy then they too could be accorded diplomatic recognition'. J. A. Coriden, 'Diplomatic Relations Between the United States and the Holy See', 19 *Case W. Res. J. Int'l L.* (1987), 361–373, at 368.

Vatican exercises territorial sovereignty over a small geographical area. It is this fact that accounts for the disparity of treatment of which the plaintiffs complain.[230]

According to Judge Gibbons' reasoning, territoriality is what makes the difference between the Catholic Church and the plaintiffs' organizations, and it is this which prompted, and seemingly justified, US recognition of the Holy See. Consequently, in his view, it becomes irrelevant to dwell on the two personalities (of the Holy See and Vatican respectively) or to ask whether a separation of the two exists or not.[231] What he seems to suggest is that the Holy See, regardless of its preferred formula of personality, will enjoy the privileges of states because of its sovereignty over the Vatican territory and the resemblance to statehood which that confers. While Judge Gibbons' reasoning fails to account for the historical circumstances which have placed the Holy See as a legal person on the international plane, and over-emphasizes the territorial aspect gained via the 1929 Lateran Treaty, it does delineate the contours of the Holy See-Vatican construct.

2. The personality question in domestic jurisprudence

Compared to diplomatic practice, the jurisprudence of domestic courts is certainly clearer on the personality question. Courts generally treat the Holy See and the Vatican as a construct, implicitly if not explicitly, and afford it the rights and impose on it the obligations of states.

2.1. Contrasting Banque du Gothard and Marcinkus and Others

Two cases, *Banque du Gothard v. Chambre des recours en matière pénale du Tribunal d'appel du canton du Tessin*, decided by the Swiss Federal Tribunal in 1987, and *Marcinkus, Mennini and De Strobel*, decided by the Italian Court of Cassation in the same year, offer contrasting views of the rights and corresponding obligations of the Holy See and the Vatican under international law. The two cases are related to proceedings instituted in 1982 by Italian authorities against various individuals

---

[230] *Americans United for Separation of Church and State v. Ronald Reagan*, 3rd Cir., 786 F.2d 194 (1986), paras. 13 and 27.

[231] In their petition for a writ of certiorari to the Supreme Court made by the plaintiffs in 1986 (which was subsequently denied), the dual personality scenario again takes centre stage: 'The error in the Third Circuit's analysis of this issue lies in the fact that it failed to accept as true the allegations that the relations established were not with a foreign state to which article II powers relate, but rather with a church. The Third Circuit began its discussion with the statement, "Because the Vatican [is a territorial sovereignty], the question of whether the President may constitutionally establish diplomatic relations with a church *qua* church is not presented in this action." Yet this is precisely the issue that is raised by the allegations of the complaint.... What is not committed to the President by the Constitution... is the power to establish diplomatic relations with a church. That is the action alleged in the complaint to have been taken by the President. That is the question the courts are asked to decide in this case. It is a threshold question that must be resolved before the political question doctrine is even implicated. It is a question the courts have the power and the duty to answer in order to uphold the constitutional rights of the petitioners'. As quoted in Coriden, 'Diplomatic Relations Between the United States and the Holy See', at 370.

suspected of being involved in the illegal dealings of the Banco Ambrosiano, which had been declared insolvent by the Tribunal of Milan.[232] Closely concerned with the proceedings were the Institute for the Works of Religion (known under its Italian abbreviation IOR), located in Vatican City, and some of its officials, including its President at the time, Monsignor Paul Marcinkus.[233] It is submitted that contrasting views on the rights and obligations of the Holy See ensue from the different approach of the two courts towards the personality question.

In 1983, the Italian authorities requested legal assistance with obtaining documents relating to IOR bank accounts at the Banque du Gothard. Swiss courts granted the seizure of documents and upheld the decision on appeal.[234] Subsequently, the Banque du Gothard entered an administrative law appeal before the Swiss Federal Tribunal, arguing that administrators of the IOR enjoyed diplomatic immunity and were subject to the exclusive jurisdiction of the Pope, and that therefore the assets of the IOR enjoyed immunity from execution.[235] The Federal Tribunal distinguished between the status of IOR officials named in the inquiry in the requested state (Switzerland) and in the requesting state (Italy). It concluded that IOR officials did not 'enjoy any diplomatic status' in Switzerland and that the request for mutual assistance must be acceded to by the Swiss authorities.[236]

Moreover, and we shall see this represents a crucial point of difference from the Court of Cassation's approach in *Marcinkus and Others*, the Federal Tribunal insisted that:

[T]he assets at issue, the bank accounts which are the subject of the enquiry directed to the Banque du Gothard..., have never been designated or attributed by the Pontifical State for activities governed by *jus imperii* or for the furtherance of activities directly aimed at the performance of State functions...On the contrary the deposits in question are governed by *jus gestionis* and are comparable to those which a State or a bank of a foreign State could make in Switzerland...[237]

It is clear that the Federal Tribunal applied to the Holy See the principle of limited sovereign immunity, explicitly recalling its past practice in the case of other foreign states.[238] As such, the Federal Tribunal held that the Holy See does not enjoy

[232] *Banque du Gothard v. Chambre des recours en matière pénale du Tribunal d'appel du canton du Tessin*, Federal Tribunal, Switzerland, 15 April 1987, 82 ILR, 50 (1990), at 50; *Re Marcinkus, Mennini and De Strobel, Court of Cassation* (criminal division), Italy, 17 July 1987, 87 ILR, 48 (1992), at 48.

[233] *Banque du Gothard v. Chambre des recours*, at 50; *Marcinkus and Others*, at 48.

[234] *Banque du Gothard v. Chambre des recours*, at 50–51.

[235] *Banque du Gothard v. Chambre des recours*, at 52.

[236] It argued that whether Marcinkus and the others enjoyed diplomatic immunity in Italy was a matter to be decided by the Italian judge who had jurisdiction over the case, and that an examination of its merits was not required to answer the request before it, which concerned legal assistance under the European Convention on Mutual Assistance in Criminal Matters. *Banque du Gothard v. Chambre des recours*, at 52.

[237] *Banque du Gothard v. Chambre des recours*, at 52. (Citations omitted).

[238] The Tribunal quotes, inter alia, *Socialist Libyan Arab Popular Jamahiriya v. Libyan American Oil Company (LIAMCO)*, Federal Supreme Court, First Public Law Department, Switzerland, 19 June 1980, 62 ILR, 228 (1982), at 235. 'According to a general rule of international law, the sovereignty of every State is limited by the immunity of the other States, particularly in court and enforcement

immunity for acts governed by *jus gestionis*, but that the Court would not have had jurisdiction if the acts had been performed *jure imperii*. In finding that the IOR's transactions fell squarely in the category of commercial acts, the court seems to have been unimpressed either by the Holy See's qualification of the IOR as a central organ of the Catholic Church, or by its purpose of supporting the religious mission of the Holy See in the world. Perhaps the reasoning of the Tribunal is best understood in three stages. First, the court accepted without objection that the Holy See-Vatican is a *sui generis* entity by virtue of its religious legitimacy, which enjoys rights akin to a state, i.e. sovereign immunity. Second, it therefore applied the test of private versus sovereign acts, exactly as it would apply it to any other state. Third, in assessing the acts performed *jure imperii* it did not consider the special character of the Holy See and its religious mission. In other words, while historical circumstance and religious legitimacy were the reason why the Holy See attained a status akin to a state and thus differed from other religious organizations, its *sui generis* status was not assumed to blur the lines between private and sovereign acts. In an attempt to extrapolate, this decision may well indicate that, when it is recognized that the Holy See enjoys the rights of a state, it is also recognized to have the obligations of a state.

In Italy, *Marcinkus and Others* reached the Court of Cassation after the Tribunal of Milan had dismissed the appeal against an arrest warrants issued in the name of IOR officials.[239] The Court of Cassation held that Italian courts had no jurisdiction over the case and that the arrest warrants should therefore be annulled.[240] Before examining the different approach of the Italian Court, compared to the Federal Tribunal in the related case, it is important to first address the different ground that IOR officials invoked to bar the jurisdiction of Italian courts. They did not claim diplomatic immunity, as in the Swiss case, but invoked Article 11 of the Lateran Treaty,[241] which reads:

The central entities of the Catholic Church are exempt from any interference on the part of the Italian State (except as provided by Italian law in regard to acquisitions made by corporate persons) and from conversion with regard to real estate.[242]

It is evident that state immunity could have been a ground for challenging the jurisdiction of Italian courts, however, invoking state immunity would necessarily have triggered the test which distinguishes between states acts governed by *jus imperii* and those governed by *jus gestionis*. This suggests that the choice made by the IOR officials, to lodge their appeal under article 11 of the Lateran Treaty, was in fact a choice of international persona. The Holy See suggested to the court

---

proceedings. A State can therefore in principle not be called before domestic courts and authorities in another state . . . While this rule was applied without exception in the past, this has no longer been the case in recent years. . . . In their practice, most States today observe the principle of limited immunity and they do this because they are convinced that they are obliged by international law to do so . . . [T]he Federal Court has accepted the theory of limited immunity of foreign States and has confirmed this decision repeatedly thereafter . . . '

[239] *Marcinkus and Others*, at 48–49.   [240] *Marcinkus and Others*, at 48 and 52.
[241] *Marcinkus and Others*, at 48–49.   [242] Lateran Treaty, art. 11.

that at stake was its personality qua church. Between the case in Switzerland and the one in Italy, the Holy See effectively shifted its personality to benefit from a stronger defence than that provided by the doctrine of limited sovereign immunity. It should be noted here that no state would have access to such an option.

The Italian Court of Cassation clarified forcefully that:

> To examine the reasons and historical background of the Holy See's present status within the international legal system is irrelevant to the case at issue. It is therefore of no consequence whether or not the Holy See is the supreme organ of the so-called *societas perfectas* (the Catholic Church), whether or not the Holy See is autonomous, and whether it is a separate entity from the State of Vatican City, or strictly connected with it....The conclusive and determinant factor in this case is that the Holy See is undisputedly and decisively a subject of international law.[243]

By refusing to analyse the circumstances of the Holy See's current status, the Court missed the chance to acknowledge that the Holy See is a subject of international law as an entity *sui generis*, given its specific historical circumstance *and* its resemblance to a state: it focused instead solely on the personality of the Holy See as the government of the Catholic Church. Perhaps also compelled by a turbulent shared history, the Italian Court interpreted the provisions of article 11 very broadly: 'Italy is not to invade the sovereign sphere of its other contracting party, which is regarded as an organizational and active network of central bodies and institutions'.[244] It did not address the issue of whether Italy's 'duty of non-interference' (which it read from the expression 'exemption of interference' in article 11) applied solely to acts of the Holy See governed by *jus imperii*, but assumed implicitly that all acts of the Holy See are covered by immunity from jurisdiction. In the view of the Italian Court of Cassation, the Holy See enjoyed absolute immunity because it is the government of the Catholic Church—this is a privilege denied to 'normal' states.[245] What this implies, in the end, is that the Holy See's practice of shifting personalities was accommodated by the Court and facilitated the granting of absolute immunity.

In the light of more recent case law of the European Court of Human Rights (ECtHR), the Italian's court approach is problematic. From ECtHR jurisprudence, one can infer that Italy's duty to avoid interference with the central entities of the Catholic Church is qualified, beyond the exemption expressly stipulated in the Lateran Treaty. For instance, in *Pellegrini v. Italy*[246] the Court was faced with an ecclesiastical court of the Rome Vicariate that had annulled the applicant's marriage and with the Florence Court of Appeal judgment that such decision was enforceable.[247] The European Court concluded that Italy was in violation of article 6.1 of the

---

[243] *Marcinkus and Others*, at 50.

[244] *Marcinkus and Others*, at 50.

[245] Read in the light of other recent decisions by Italian courts on sovereign immunity, the granting of absolute immunity to the Holy See appears even more surprising. See *Ferrini v. Federal Republic of Germany*, Decision No. 5044/2004, 128 ILR, 658 (2006). See also *Jurisdictional Immunities of the State (Germany v. Italy: Greece Intervening)*, Judgment, ICJ Reports 2012, p. 99.

[246] See *Pellegrini v. Italy*, Application no. 30882/96, Judgment of 20 July 2001. See Chapter 3, III.2.2.1.

[247] *Pellegrini v. Italy*, paras. 11–29.

European Convention on Human Rights (ECHR), given that 'the Italian Courts breached their duty of satisfying themselves, before authorizing enforcement of the Roman Rota's judgment, that the applicant had had a fair trial in the proceedings under canon law'.[248] This decision emphasizes that Italy has an obligation to protect the rights of the individuals within its jurisdiction, implying that interference with the decisions of central entities of the Holy See may be required, where those decisions are subjected to enforcement by Italian authorities. The acceptance of interference is limited however: it may not refer to the substance of the decisions, but must ensure that procedural rights were respected.[249] Conversely, one scholar argues that such judgments may give rise to 'indirect' obligations for the Holy See. Although the Holy See is not party to the ECHR, it would have an obligation to respect the provisions of the Convention when its actions affect the rights of individuals in Italy.[250]

In conclusion, if the Court of Cassation had acknowledged in the first place that the international personality of the Holy See is that of a state-like construct, it would have had to analyse the jurisdictional immunity of the Holy See in the light of the limited sovereign immunity principle. In this context, Article 11 of the Lateran Treaty and the characterization of the IOR as a central entity (as invoked by the Holy See) would have been elements in the analysis, but not final determinants of the case. If the Court had examined whether the IOR (even as a central entity of the Church) had acted *jure gestionis* as opposed to *jure imperii*, the Court might have reached different conclusions.

2.2. *Holy See v. Starbright Sales Enterprises*

In *Holy See v. Starbright Sales Enterprises*, the Supreme Court of the Philippines followed the approach of the Swiss Federal Tribunal in so far as it rejected the dual personality option[251] and essentially portrayed the Holy See and the Vatican as a construct with one international personality. The petition arose from a controversy over three lots of land registered in the name of the Holy See and sold to Starbright Sales Enterprises.[252] In 1990, the company filed a case against the Holy See requesting the annulment of the sale and damages. The Holy See moved to dismiss the case for lack of jurisdiction based on

---

[248] *Pellegrini v. Italy*, para. 47. See also the discussion of *Lombardi Vallauri v. Italy* case in Chapter 3, III.2.2.2.

[249] *Lombardi Vallauri c. Italie*, Requête no. 39128/05, Arrêt du 20 octobre 2009, paras. 50–55.

[250] N. Leyns, 'The Holy See: Sovereign Power Internationally Recognized. Does the Authority the Holy See Exercises within the International Community go along with a Responsibility for Human Rights Violations?', E.MA Thesis, European Inter-University Centre for Human Rights and Democratization, 2011, at 40–58.

[251] For a different reading of this decision see R. Portmann, *Legal Personality in International Law*, (New York: Cambridge University Press, 2010), at 118.

[252] *The Holy See v. Starbright Sales Enterprises, Inc.*, Philippines Supreme Court, 102 ILR, 163 (1995), at 164–167.

sovereign immunity from trial in courts in the Philippines.[253] In 1991 the trial court denied the Holy See's motion to dismiss after finding that it 'shed off [its] sovereign immunity by entering into the business contract in question'; the Holy See then took the matter to the Supreme Court of the Philippines.[254] The Supreme Court found it necessary to assess the status of the Holy See in international law before it answered the jurisdictional question, which underlines the fact that the two personalities may trigger different consequences in terms of rights and obligations. Three passages from the Court's decision are important to understand the choice it made to set the dual personality scenario aside in favour of a single international person, the Holy See, which enjoys rights and obligations akin to a state by virtue of its interdependence with the Vatican. In other words, the Philippines Supreme Court adopted the theory of a construct.

In view of the wordings of the Lateran Treaty, it is difficult to determine whether the statehood is vested in the Holy See or in the Vatican City. Some writers even suggested that the treaty created two international persons—the Holy See and Vatican City...

The Vatican City fits into none of the established categories of states, and the attribution to it of 'sovereignty' must be made in a sense different from that in which it is applied to other states...In a community of national states, the Vatican City represents an entity organized not for political but for ecclesiastical purposes and international objects. Despite its size and object, the Vatican City has an independent government of its own, with the Pope, who is also head of the Roman Catholic Church, as the Holy See or Head of State, in conformity with its traditions, and the demands of its mission in the world. Indeed, the world-wide interests and activities of the Vatican City are such as to make it in a sense an 'international state'...

Inasmuch as the Pope prefers to conduct foreign relations and enter into transactions as the Holy See and not in the name of the Vatican City, one can conclude that in the Pope's own view, it is the Holy See that is the international person.[255]

While establishing that the Holy See enjoyed sovereign immunity, the Court also found that the restrictive theory of sovereign immunity was a general principle of international law, and that by virtue of article II.2 of the Philippine Constitution it was incorporated in municipal law.[256] Consequently, the immunity of the Holy See covered only acts *jure imperii*, while private and commercial acts were not exempt from the Court's jurisdiction.[257] Since the Holy See acquired the land for its apostolic nunciature and did not sell it with the aim of obtaining profit,[258] the Court

---

[253] The land was initially sold to Ramon Licup, who later assigned his rights to the sale to Starbright Sales Enterprises. Individuals squatting the land refused to vacate the lots and a dispute arose as to which of the parties had the responsibility to evict them and clear the land. *The Holy See v. Starbright Sales Enterprises, Inc.*, at 165–166.

[254] *The Holy See v. Starbright Sales Enterprises, Inc.*, at 166.

[255] *The Holy See v. Starbright Sales Enterprises, Inc.*, at 169. (Citations omitted).

[256] *The Holy See v. Starbright Sales Enterprises, Inc.*, at 170–173.

[257] *The Holy See v. Starbright Sales Enterprises, Inc.*, at 170–173.

[258] The Holy See claimed that it sold the land because it did not manage to make use of it, because of the individuals squatting there.

concluded that the land transaction was not an act *jure gestionis* and was therefore covered by sovereign immunity.[259] The Supreme Court's decision underlines, as the Swiss Federal Tribunal's decision did, that while the Holy See enjoys rights akin to a state, these rights do not go beyond those of a state.

2.3. *The personality question and clerical child sexual abuse in US courts*

Clergy child sexual abuse litigation in US courts tests the issue of the Holy See's personality. As one scholar explains, the 'sheer number' of sexual abuse allegations in the United States, and the perception that the Catholic Church had not provided an appropriate response, led to a 'plethora of litigation' against local dioceses, religious orders and their superiors, with legal settlements amounting to more than 840 million US dollars.[260] The Holy See itself was rarely named as a defendant because sovereign immunity acted as a disincentive.[261] The US Foreign Sovereign Immunity Act (FSIA) stipulates in paragraph 1604 that 'a foreign state shall be immune from the jurisdiction of the courts of the United States except as provided in sections 1605 to 1607 of this chapter'.[262] The principal exceptions covered are: the explicit or implicit waiving of immunity by the foreign state; commercial activity including property disputes; tortious act; and acts of terrorism (under the 1996 amendment of the FSIA).[263]

A number of pragmatic reasons have prompted judicial claims to be brought against the Holy See itself in recent years.[264] In addition, there is a sense that the Catholic Church should be made accountable at the highest level for the perceived inaction or mismanagement of clerical child sexual abuse in the US. One victim summarized his decision to name the Holy See as defendant as follows: 'I would just like to see the Catholic Church changed'.[265]

---

[259] *The Holy See v. Starbright Sales Enterprises, Inc.*, at 170–173.

[260] J. Fantau, 'Rethinking the Sovereign Status of the Holy See: Towards a Greater Equality of States and Greater Protection of Citizens in United States Courts', 19 *Cardozo Journal of International & Comparative Law* (2011), 487–487, at 488. For cases against dioceses, religious orders and their superiors, see *John Doe No. 23 v. Archdiocese of Miami, Inc.*, 965 So. 2d 1186, 1187 (Fla. Dist. Ct. App. 2007); and *Rigazio v. Archdiocese of Louisville*, 853 S.W.2d 295, 296 (Ky. Ct. App. 1993).

[261] In *Doe v. Holy See (State of Vatican City)*, 793 N.Y.S.2d 565, 569 (N.Y. Appeal Division 2005), the appeal was denied, based on a statute of limitations and jurisdictional grounds. In *English v. Thorne*, 676 F. Supp. 761, 762 (S.D. Miss. 1987), the court dismissed the complaint on subject matter jurisdiction. See also W. B. Mason, 'A New Call for Reform: Sex Abuse and the Foreign Sovereign Immunities Act', 33 *Brooklyn Journal of International Law* (2007), 655–683, at 664–665.

[262] Foreign Sovereign Immunities Act of 1976, Pub. L. 94-583, 90 Stat. 2891, 28 U.S.C., sec. 1604. (Hereafter FSIA).

[263] FSIA., sec. 1605.a.1-5. For a discussion of the degree to which the 1996 amendment concerning acts of terrorism creates opportunites to litigate human rights violations in US civil courts, see A. Bellal, *Immunités et violations graves des droits humains. Vers une évolution structurelle de l'ordre juridique international?* (Bruxelles: Bruylant, 2011), at 57–58.

[264] Often priests have taken a vow of poverty, and several dioceses have filed for bankruptcy in response to clerical abuse lawsuits. In such cases, the only way to obtain financial redress is by filing a civil case suit against the Holy See itself. Mason, 'A New Call for Reform: Sex Abuse and the Foreign Sovereign Immunities Act', at 208.

[265] Mason, 'A New Call for Reform: Sex Abuse and the Foreign Sovereign Immunities Act', at 676; see also J. R. Formicola, 'Catholic Clerical Sexual Abuse: Effects on Vatican Sovereignty and Papal Power', 53 *Journal of Church and State* 4 (2011), 479–502, at 480ff.

This section emphasizes that, in cases where allegations were brought specifically against the Holy See, US Courts have not differentiated between its two claimed international personalities (the government of a state, and the government of the Church), but have regarded the construct as qualifying for state immunity under section 1604 of the FSIA. On the other hand, it will be shown that the territorial tort exception to the FSIA can be used—albeit in a highly qualified manner—as a means to hold the Holy See accountable for violations of child rights in the context of clerical sexual abuse.

John V. Doe v. the Holy See[266] is cited as the first case where a suit was allowed to proceed with claiming damages from the Holy See for clerical sexual abuse of children.[267] *O'Bryan v. the Holy See*[268] presents a similar analysis to *John V. Doe v. the Holy See* in respect to the sovereign status and the territorial tort exception. This section focuses on the former case and highlights where there are discrepancies in the reasoning of the courts in the two cases. In *O'Bryan v. the Holy See,* the three plaintiffs filed a putative class action on behalf of all victims of clerical sexual abuse in the United States, alleging that the Holy See was liable under the doctrine of *respondeat superior,* and for violation of the customary international law of human rights, negligence, breach of fiduciary duty, infliction of emotional distress, deceit, and misrepresentation.[269] The lawsuit was brought against the 'Holy See in its Capacity as a Foreign State (State of the Vatican City), and its Capacity as an Unincorporated Association and Head of an International Religious Organization'.[270] This intended distinction between the two claimed personalities of the Holy See, served the purpose of arguing that the FSIA did not apply to the Holy See in its capacity as a church, but only in its capacity as the government of the Vatican City State.[271] However, as we have seen, when diplomatic relations were established, the US authorities emphasized strongly the fact that it was establishing relations with the latter. The district court dismissed the argument as follows:

---

[266] In the *John V. Doe* case, it is alleged that M. Ronan, who was employed as a priest in Ireland in the 1950s, molested a minor and admitted to doing so to the order to which he belonged. He was later removed and placed in employment at the St. Philip's High School in Chicago, where he is said to have molested at least three male students, and when confronted, admitted to the abuse. The plaintiff asserts that Ronan asked his superiors in Chicago to explain why he had been assigned to work with the private counselling office, where he had both the opportunity and the temptation to molest children. Ronan was then transferred to a parish church in Oregon where allegedly he molested the plaintiff who was then 15 or 16. Doe asserted three causes of action against the Holy See: *respondeat superior,* negligence, and fraud. The Holy See invoked sovereign immunity under FSIA. *John V. Doe v. Holy See et al.,* No. CV 02-430-MO, 434 F. Supp. 2d 925, LEXIS (Dist. Oregon, 2006).

[267] *John V. Doe v. the Holy See* was filed first, but it was delayed and the judge often cites *O'Bryan v. Holy See,* which had already been concluded. L. C. Martinez Jr, 'Sovereign Impunity: Does the Foreign Sovereign Immunities Act Bar Lawsuits Against Holy See in Clerical Sexual Abuse Cases?', 44 *Texas International Law Journal* (2008), 123–155, at 142.

[268] *O'Bryan v. Holy See,* 490 F. Supp. 2d 826 (W.D. Ky. 2005).

[269] *O'Bryan v. Holy See,* at 828. See also Martinez Jr, 'Sovereign Impunity: Does the Foreign Sovereign Immunities Act Bar Lawsuits Against Holy See in Clerical Sexual Abuse Cases', at 136.

[270] *O'Bryan v. Holy See,* 490 F. Supp. 2d 826 (W.D. Ky. 2005), at 828.

[271] Lucian C. Martinez Jr comments that 'the plaintiffs may have deliberately confused the two entities in order to create an artificial distinction'. Martinez Jr, 'Sovereign Impunity: Does the Foreign Sovereign Immunities Act Bar Lawsuits Against Holy See in Clerical Sexual Abuse Cases', at 139.

Plaintiffs cite no authority for the proposition that the Holy See may be sued in a separate, non-sovereign function as an unincorporated association and as head of an international religious organization. They can point to no instance in which any sovereign's status has been disregarded on these grounds.[272]

The Court of Appeals upheld this finding.[273] In other words, given the absence of a precedent concerning the two claimed personalities of the Holy See, in order to claim the benefit of jurisdictional immunity under FSIA they are to be treated essentially as a construct, having one personality akin to a state. In effect, the dual personality scenario, which the government had employed to explain the establishment of diplomatic relations with the Holy See and secure compatibility with the Establishment Clause of the US Constitution, was discarded.[274] In the realm of adjudication, it is the construct which is credited as enjoying the rights of the state. Perhaps the most powerful argument portraying the desuetude of the dual personality scenario comes from the Holy See itself.

As Defendant rightly notes, under Plaintiffs' argument, potential claimants would be permitted to skirt the requirements of the FSIA merely by claiming that a sovereign was not acting as a sovereign, in the 'context' of a particular case, but rather was acting in some other 'capacity'.[275]

While this point will be developed later on, it should be noted here that if the shifting of personalities cannot be used to deny the privilege of state immunity applying to the Holy See, then it should similarly not be used to decline obligations which the Holy See incurs as a state party to human rights treaties. The shifting of its two claimed personalities is exactly what the Holy See attempted in *O'Bryan*, after it argued successfully that it should enjoy state immunity under the FSIA. Specifically, the Holy See asserted that the freedom of religion clause of the First Amendment would bar the plaintiffs' claims.[276] The judge rejected again the dual personality scenario, stating that foreign sovereigns do not enjoy rights derived from the US Constitution: 'Defendant Holy See cannot simultaneously seek the protections of the FSIA and the United States Constitution.'[277]

---

[272] *O'Bryan v. Holy See*, 490 F. Supp. 2d 826 (W.D. Ky. 2005), at 830.

[273] *O'Bryan v. the Holy See*, US Court of Appeals, 6th Cir., Nos. 07-5078, 07-5163 (2009), at 9–10.

[274] Roger Alford comments in this context: 'It is worth pondering the essential conclusion of the Court: every religion in the world except the Catholic Church can be sued for illegal supervision of religious leaders who engage in sexual abuse of children. The head of the Catholic Church—the Holy See—stands alone, immune from suit because it is a sovereign entity protected by the FSIA. The Holy See can only be liable if one of the FSIA exceptions applies.' R. Alford, 'Clergy Sexual Abuse, the Holy See, and the FSIA', *OpinioJuris*, accessed March 2012, http://opiniojuris.org/2009/02/24/clergy-sexual-abuse-the-holy-see-and-the-fsia/.

[275] *O'Bryan v. Holy See*, 490 F. Supp. 2d 826 (W.D. Ky. 2005), at 830.

[276] *O'Bryan v. Holy See*, 471 F.Supp.2d 784 (W.D. Ky. 2007), at 794. It should be noted that, in clergy sexual abuse cases, local churches that were named as defendants have invoked the First Amendment in their defence. See K. W. G. Clark, K. S. Roggendorf and P. B. Janci, 'Of Compelling Interest: The Intersection of Religious Freedom and Civil Liability in the Portland Priest Sex Abuse Cases', 85 *Oregon Law Review* (2006), 481–538.

[277] *O'Bryan v. Holy See*, 471 F.Supp.2d 784 (W.D. Ky. 2007), at 794.

One exception to the sovereign immunity rule, which the plaintiffs argued applied to the case at hand,[278] concerns territorial tortious acts.[279] Unlike the commercial activities exception, this exception does not require a distinction to be made between acts governed by *jus imperii* and those performed *jure gestionis*.[280] The plaintiffs did not have to show that the Holy See's alleged policy of keeping 'all allegations of childhood sexual abuse... under a cloak of complete secrecy'— as arguably required by the 1962 *Crimen sollicitationis*—was governed by *jus gestionis*.[281] Before addressing the application of the territorial tort exception to this case, some words on the *Crimen sollicitationis* may be helpful at this point, as this instruction has been a point of the contention.

The Instruction on the Manner of Proceeding in Causes of Solicitation (*Crimen sollicitationis*) was issued on 16 March 1962 by the Sacred Congregation of the Holy See and approved by the Pope John XXIII. It succeeded a similar document of 1922 and set out procedures for dealing with 'delicts' of solicitation in the confessional. By extension it therefore covered child sexual abuse by priests.[282] The instruction was superseded in 2001 by the Norms of the *Motu Proprio Sacramentorum sanctitatis tutela*, which were further amended in 2010 following adoption of the *Normae de gravioribus delictis*.[283] Canon lawyer John P. Beal explains that the *Crimen sollicitationis* stipulated the 'reservation of delicts' to the

---

[278] The district court dismissed the plaintiffs' arguments, based on the implicit waiver of immunity and the commercial exception. See Martinez Jr, 'Sovereign Impunity: Does the Foreign Sovereign Immunities Act Bar Lawsuits Against Holy See in Clerical Sexual Abuse Cases', at 139–140.

[279] A foreign state is not to be considered immune from jurisdiction in US courts in cases 'in which money damages are sought against a foreign state for personal injury or death, or damage to or loss of property, occurring in the United States and caused by the tortious act or omission of that foreign state or of any official or employee of that foreign state while acting within the scope of his office or employment'. FSIA, sec. 1605(a)(5).

[280] Bellal, *Immunités et violations graves des droits humains. Vers une évolution structurelle de l'ordre juridique international?*, at 56. See also Stoll, 'State Immunity', in *MPEPIL* (2011), para. 37.

[281] The plaintiffs argued that *Crimen sollicitationis* imposed 'the highest level of secrecy on the handling of clergy sexual abuse matters' and that the policies of the Holy See, as set out in *Crimen* and other documents, 'require bishops in the United States to, among other things, refuse to report childhood sexual abuse committed by priests to criminal or civil authorities, even where such failure to report would itself be a criminal offense'. *O'Bryan v. the Holy See*, US Court of Appeals, 6th Cir., Nos. 07-5078, 07-5163 (2009), at 2–3. Jeffrey S. Lena, Counsel for the Holy See, summed up the counter-arguments as follows: 'First,... *Crimen* was *itself* the first "reporting statute." That is to say, long before any civil jurisdiction in either Civil Law or Common Law countries had even contemplated imposing a duty to report such crimes, *Crimen* articulated specific procedures... Second, *Crimen* obviously could not have been designed to prevent reporting under civil law reporting statutes because there were no civil reporting statutes in existence when *Crimen* first appeared in 1922 [nor] by 1962, when *Crimen* was reprinted with minor modifications... Finally, *Crimen* dealt with *canonical* obligations, not civil obligations, and did not bar the reporting of incidents of sexual abuse to civil authorities, whether before or after civil reporting statutes came into force.' Statement of Jeffrey S. Lena Regarding *John Doe 16 v. Holy See, et al.*, accessed March 2012, http://vaticaninsider.lastampa.it/fileadmin/user_upload/mondo/Statement_of_Jeffrey_S._Lena_re_John_Doe_16_v_Holy_See.pdf.

[282] J. P. Beal, 'The 1962 Instruction *Crimen sollicitationis*: Caught Red-handed or Handed a Red Herring?', 41 *Studia canonica* (2007) 199–236, at 199–201.

[283] The *Crimen sollicitationis* (1962), Norms of the *Motu Proprio Sacramentorum sanctitatis tutela* (2001) and *Normae de gravioribus delictis* (2010) can be found on the website of the Holy See, accessed May 2012, http://www.vatican.va/resources/index_en.htm.

Congregation for the Doctrine of the Faith, which meant that the Congregation had the right to receive such complaints directly and to prosecute them itself; established an 'obligation of local authorities to inform the Congregation of their receipt of a denunciation for one of these reserved delicts and to keep it apprised of the development of the case until its conclusion'; stipulated further that the Congregation was exclusively competent to hear appeals against decisions of lower ecclesiastical tribunals; and provided that 'all officials involved in investigating and prosecuting these delicts are bound by "pontifical secret"'.[284] The 1962 instruction was to be sent to all bishops and was to be kept secret; it appears, from inquiries concerning child sexual abuse by clerics in two Irish dioceses, that very few people were aware of its existence.[285]

Returning to the *O'Bryan* case, application of the tort exception—in the case at hand and more generally in human rights cases that are brought against foreign states in US courts—is subject to restrictions. The act must have occurred in the United States, and must be caused by an act or omission of the foreign state in question, or any official or employee of that foreign state while acting within the scope of his office or employment.[286] Moreover, two exceptions apply to the exception itself: the discretionary function, and the origin of the tortious act in misrepresentation, deceit, or other grounds.[287] The analysis here will focus on the courts' examination of territorial limitation and on whether the status of Catholic clergy in the US can be described as officials or employees of the Holy See.

Following *Amerada Hess*, the district and appeal courts in *O'Bryan* applied the territorial test in a restrictive manner, requiring that the 'entire tort' had to occur in the US; a tortious act that caused a 'direct effect' in the US was not found sufficient.[288] On these grounds the court found that 'the claims against the Holy See specifically (i.e. as opposed to via its officials or employees) cannot be sustained because these actions or omissions occurred outside of the United States.'[289] It seems cynical to observe that, had the Pope issued the *Crimen sollicitationis* while visiting the US, the territorial test might have been satisfied. *O'Bryan v. Holy See* primarily concerned the responsibility of

---

[284] Beal, 'The 1962 Instruction *Crimen sollicitationis*: Caught Red-handed or Handed a Red Herring?', at 202–203. The term 'local authorities' and 'officials' in the quotation refer to clerical authorities.

[285] Commission of Investigation, Report into the Catholic Archdiocese of Dublin, July 2009, accessed March 2012, http://www.dacoi.ie/, paras. 4.21 and 4.26 (hereafter Report into the Catholic Archdiocese of Dublin); Commission of Investigation, Report into the Catholic Diocese of Cloyne, December 2010, accessed March 2012, http://www.dacoi.ie/, para. 4.6, (hereafter Report into the Catholic Archdiocese of Cloyne).

[286] FSIA, sec. 1605(a)(5).

[287] The exceptions do not apply to (a) any claim based upon the exercise or performance or the failure to exercise or perform a discretionary function regardless of whether the discretion be abused; or (b) any claim arising out of malicious prosecution, abuse of process, libel, slander, misrepresentation, deceit, or interference with contract rights. FSIA, sec.1605(a)(5).

[288] *O'Bryan v. Holy See*, 471 F.Supp.2d 784 (W.D. Ky. 2007), at 789–790; *O'Bryan v. the Holy See*, US Court of Appeals, 6th Cir., Nos. 07-5078, 07-5163 (2009), at 13–14. See also *Argentine Republic v. Amerada Hess Shipping Corporation et al.*, 488 U.S. 428 (1989), at 441.

[289] *O'Bryan v. Holy See*, 471 F.Supp.2d 784 (W.D. Ky. 2007), at 792.

the Holy See as the principal authority that determined the response to sexual abuse cases in the US. The strict territorial lens of the courts concerning jurisdiction therefore affected the heart of the case.

In this instance, the territorial test appears to be divorced from the declaration of purpose of the FSIA, which proclaims that the role of the courts in determining claims of sovereign immunity is 'to serve the interests of justice and [to] protect the rights of both foreign states and litigants in United States courts'.[290] In keeping with this declaration of purpose, one important issue that the court should have considered—when it balanced the interest to protect the right of the Holy See as a sovereign against those of victims of child sexual abuse in the US—is whether the right to fair trial is upheld under canon law norms and procedures.[291]

In the view of this author, a number of essential fair trial guarantees may not be respected by canonical norms and procedures that deal with clerical child sexual abuse;[292] one of these guarantees refers to the right to equality before the courts. One has to observe in this context, as Thomas P. Doyle and Stephen C. Rubino do, that most clerical sexual abuse victims have first approached Church authorities for assistance and redress, but have found the 'Church's internal system unwilling or unable to provide the relief sought. Further, in many cases, the official Church reaction amounted to a re-victimization, whereby the victims were

---

[290] This declaration of purpose in FSIA, sec. 1602 suggests a balancing of the interests of foreign states against those of litigants in US courts. As a topic for another study, surely one could ask how the ICJ finding in the *Jurisdictional Immunities* case regarding the lack of any relationship between state immunity and the existence of alternative means of securing redress can be reconciled with the US approach to state immunity in FSIA, and whether the latter is in fact evidence for such a nexus which the Court just failed to acknowledge. See also A. Bianchi, 'On Certainty', *EJIL:Talk!*, accessed March 2012, http://www.ejiltalk.org/author/abianchi/; and *Jurisdictional Immunities of the State (Germany v. Italy: Greece Intervening)*, Judgment, ICJ Reports 2012, p. 99, para. 101.

[291] It should be emphasized here that the United States is bound by the ICCPR, which it ratified on 9 June 1992. Patrick Robinson also points to the customary character of the right to fair trial. P. Robinson, 'The Right to a Fair Trial in International Law, with Specific Reference to the Work of the ICTY', 3 *Berkeley Journal of International Law Publicist* (2009) 1–11, art. 1. General Comment 32 of the HRC clarifies that the concept of 'suit at law' in article 14 refers inter alia to judicial procedures that seek to determine rights and obligations pertaining to torts in the area of private law. HRC, *General Comment No. 32: Article 14: Right to equality before courts and tribunals and to a fair trial*, 23 August 2007, UN Doc. CCPR/C/GC/32, para. 16.

[292] Current canon law norms and procedures relevant for the Holy See's handling of clerical child sexual abuse cases are to be found in the *Normae de gravioribus delictis* approved by Pope Benedict XVI on 21 May 2010, and canons 1717–1719 of the Code of Canon Law, 1983. Currently, bishops are responsible for dealing with cases of sexual abuse of minors. If an accusation 'has the semblance of truth', they must carry out a preliminary investigation in accord with canon 1717. After completion of the preliminary investigation, they are to communicate the matter to the Congregation for the Doctrine of the Faith, which will then direct the bishops how to proceed. Alternatively, the case may be referred directly to the Congregation for the Doctrine of the Faith, which will itself undertake the preliminary investigation. The Congregation for the Doctrine of the Faith is the Supreme Apostolic Tribunal for 'delicts' of child sexual abuse by clerics. See Congregation for the Doctrine of the Faith, *Circular Letter to Assist Episcopal Conference in Developing Guidelines for Dealing with Cases of Sexual Abuses of Minors Perpetrated by Clerics*, Rome, 3 May 2011, accessed June 2012, http://www.vatican.va/roman_curia/congregations/cfaith/documents/rc_con_cfaith_doc_20110503_abuso-minori_en.html. See also *Normae de gravioribus delictis* (2001), arts. 1, 16 and 17. For a spirited critique of canon law norms and procedures concerning fair trial guarantees, see G. Robertson, *The Case of the Pope: Vatican Accountability for Human Rights Abuse*, (London: Penguin Books, 2010), at 42–62.

treated as an enemy force.'[293] This is what led them to seek redress through the US civil court system. It seems fitting to recall the findings of the Human Rights Committee (HRC) in *Angel Oló Bahamonde v. Equatorial Guinea*: 'the notion of equality before the courts and tribunals encompasses the very access to the courts' and 'a situation in which an individual's attempts to seize the competent jurisdictions of his/her grievances are systematically frustrated runs counter to the guarantees' provided by the right to a fair trial.[294]

A second guarantee that may not be upheld by the Congregation for the Doctrine for the Faith and lower ecclesiastical tribunals refers to the independence and impartiality principles. The Congregation accumulates executive and judicial functions.[295] The HRC has found that situations where the competencies and functions of the judiciary and the executive are not clearly distinguishable are 'incompatible with the notion of an independent tribunal'.[296] Victims of clerical sexual abuse seeking redress directly from the Holy See would necessarily face ecclesiastic courts in which, essentially, clerics sit in judgment of clerics. Fears that these courts lack independence and impartiality could be 'objectively justified'.[297] One would imagine that the finding of the African Commission on Human and Peoples' Rights according to which 'everyone should have the right to be tried by a secular court if they wish'[298] would have an important echo in the US, in the context of the First Amendment and the neutrality culture that it established.

Thirdly, the requirement to hold hearings in public is certainly not met by ecclesiastical courts. Article 30 of the *Normae de gravioribus delictis* provides that cases concerning clerical child sexual abuse 'are subject to the pontifical secret'.[299] A hearing in camera is the exception in human rights law and must be justified on a case-by-case basis on grounds of morals, public order or national security in a democratic society, or in the interest of the parties' private lives, or where

---

[293] T. P. Doyle and S. C. Rubino, 'Catholic Clergy Sexual Abuse Meets the Civil Law', 31 *Fordham Urban Law Journal* (2003) 549–616, at 550. See also J. Berry, G. Renner, 'Sex-related case blocked in Vatican', *National Catholic Reporter*, 7 December 2001, accessed March 2012, http://natcath.org/NCR_Online/archives2/2001d/120701/120701g.htm.

[294] *Angel N Oló Bahamonde v. Equatorial Guinea*, UN Doc. CCPR/C/49/D/468/1991 (1993), para. 9.4.

[295] Apostolic Constitution *Pastor Bonus*, John Paul, Bishop Servant of the Servants of God for an Everlasting Memorial, English-language translation by F. C.C.F. Kelly, J. H. Provost, M. Thériault, accessed March 2012, http://www.vatican.va/holy_father/john_paul_ii/apost_constitutions/documents/hf_jp-ii_apc_19880628_pastor-bonus-index_en.html, arts. 48–55.

[296] HRC, *General Comment No. 32*, para. 19.

[297] The ECtHR has found such an 'objectively justified' fear and therefore a violation of the right to an independent and impartial tribunal in *Çiraklar v. Turkey*. In this case, one of three judges trying a civilian student was a military judge belonging to the army and subject to military discipline and assessment reports. *Çiraklar v. Turkey*, Application no. 24246/94, Judgment of 28 October 1998. It is submitted that the situation of victims of child sexual abuse by Catholic clerics is similar to *Çiraklar v. Turkey*, and dissimilar from *Tyler v. the United Kingdom*, Application No. 21283/9, Decision of 5 April 1994. For a discussion of the latter case see Chapter 3, III.2.1.2.

[298] *Amnesty International, Comité Loosli Bachelard, Lawyers Committee for Human Rights, Association of Members of the Episcopal Conference of East Sudan v. Sudan*, Communication nos. 48/90-50/91-52/91-89/93 (1999), para. 73.

[299] *Normae de gravioribus delictis*, art. 30.

the interest of justice so requires.[300] Judgments must be made public unless very exceptional circumstances demand the contrary.[301] Secrecy as a rule, as opposed to justified exception, covering the entire process of a trial *including* the judgment, as provided for in the *Normae,* is starkly in conflict with the public hearing guarantees provided by human rights law.

In the absence of alternative means to seek redress from the Holy See in secular courts, and given the possible shortcomings of clerical courts with respect to fair trial guarantees, it could be argued that US courts should move towards relaxing the territorial tort test so as to acknowledge the rights of litigants in addition to those of foreign states, as the FSIA declaration of purpose requires.

What is remarkable in the view of this study is the district judge's application of the territorial requirement in *John V. Doe*. His approach was based on the considerations in *Olsen* that 'requiring every aspect of the tortious conduct to occur in the United States,…would encourage foreign states to allege that some tortious conduct occurred outside the United States' and thus to 'diminish the rights of injured persons seeking recovery'; Judge Mosman proceeded by inquiring whether 'at least one entire' tort occurred in the United States.[302] His analysis is mindful of how geography may indeed be a relative concept when applied to the case at hand.

The Holy See's alleged failures could be said to have occurred inside the Vatican where investigation would have occurred, or where warnings could have been issued. On the other hand, it is also possible to situate a failure to warn at the location where such warning would have been heard—Portland, Oregon.[303]

Not least it should be mentioned that, following *Amerada Hess* (which held that the FSIA provided the only means for US courts to establish jurisdiction over a foreign state),[304] the geographical requirement of the tort exception—as applied in *O'Bryan*—would bar cases brought by an alien under the Alien Tort Statute (ATS), against the Holy See or its instrumentalities, for an alleged act 'in violation of the law of nations or a treaty of the United States' that took place outside the United States.[305]

---

[300] ICCPR, art. 14.1. See OHCHR, *Human Rights in the Administration of Justice: A Manual on Human Rights for Judges, Prosecutors and Lawyers* (Geneva, 2003) at 262–266 and HRC, *General Comment No. 32*, para. 29.

[301] Under the ICCPR these circumstances refer to the interest of juvenile persons or judgements concerning matrimonial disputes or the guardianship of children. HRC, *General Comment No. 32*, para. 29.

[302] *John V. Doe v. Holy See et al.*, No. CV 02-430-MO, 434 F. Supp. 2d 925, LEXIS (Dist. Oregon, 2006), at 23–24.

[303] *John V. Doe v. Holy See*, at 24–25.

[304] *Argentine Republic v. Amerada Hess Shipping Corporation et al.*, 488 U.S. 428 (1989), at 434.

[305] The Alien Tort Statute (ATS) was enacted by the US Congress in 1789 and reads: 'The district courts shall have original jurisdiction of any civil action by an alien for a tort only, committed in violation of the law of nations or a treaty of the United States'. Alien Tort Statute, 28 U.S.C. sec. 1350. Recently, a clerical sexual abuse case was brought under the ATS by a Mexican national against the American national Cardinal Roger Mahoney, the Roman Catholic Archdiocese of Los Angeles, the Mexican nationals Cardinal Norberto Rivera and Fr. Nicholas Aguilar Rivera, and the Diocese of Tehuacan. The plaintiff alleged that he was abused by Fr. Aguilar Rivera when he was 12 years old in

Turning to the second point of focus, the district and appeals courts had to grapple with the question of whether Catholic clergy in the US can be considered officials or employees of the Holy See for the purpose of applying the tort exception to state immunity. In the absence of a general definition of the term 'employee' under the FSIA, the district court applied the law of the state of Kentucky. 'Under Kentucky law the right to control is considered to be the most critical element in determining whether an agency relationship exists.'[306] Following the plaintiffs' claim that the Holy See has 'absolute and unqualified power and control' over archbishops, priests, brothers, sisters, dioceses, and archdioceses, the court found it prima facie sufficient to fulfil the Kentucky test of control.

The Holy See has declined to provide such evidence at this time, and therefore the Court concludes at this time that the Holy See does exercise control substantial enough to justify a conclusion that those persons are 'employees' of the Holy See for the purposes of FSIA.[307]

Clearly there is an element of oddity in calling an archbishop an employee of the Holy See, as the inverted commas used by Judge Heyburn symbolically emphasize. The judge further found it necessary to explain that the archdiocese of Kentucky is not an instrumentality of the Holy See—which would have made it immune from court proceedings in the US—even though the archbishop was the latter's employee.[308] The judge compared the situation of the archdiocese to that of a foreign bank that is fully owned by a foreign state and has a business entity incorporated in the US. For the purpose of FSIA the business entity is not part of the foreign state. He further compared the situation of the archbishop to that of the president of the bank's entity, who may still be effectively an employee of the foreign state, taking direction from the foreign government and following polices laid down by its leaders.[309]

Mexico because the defendants conspired to conceal the previous widespread sexual abuse of children committed by Fr. Aguilar. The defendants argued that the Court lacked jurisdiction because: the claims were barred by the ATS's statute of limitations; the Archdiocese of Los Angeles could not be held liable under the ATS because it is a corporation; the plaintiff was not a victim of a crime under international law; the plaintiff had not exhausted remedies under Mexican law; and the plaintiff could not bring an ATS claim against Cardinal Mahony under a conspiracy theory. Judge Staton Tucker analysed and dismissed the statute of limitations and exhaustion arguments, as the 'only arguments that potentially address jurisdiction' and found that the court had subject-matter jurisdiction. It should be noted that the defendants did not invoke sovereign immunity as an agency or instrumentality of the Holy See and therefore application of the FSIA did not arise. *Juan Doe I v. Cardinal Roger Mahony et al.*, Case No. CV 10-02902-JST (JEMx), (Cal. Central District, Dist. Ct. 2011).

[306] *O'Bryan v. Holy See*, 471 F.Supp.2d 784 (W.D. Ky. 2007), at 790. See also *Grant v. Bill Walker Pontiac-GMC, Inc.*,523 F.2d 1301, 1305 (6th Cir.1975), at 1305.

[307] *O'Bryan v. Holy See*, 471 F.Supp.2d 784 (W.D. Ky. 2007), at 791.

[308] An 'agency or instrumentality' of a foreign state which would benefit from sovereign immunity under FSIA is defined as an entity which is, inter alia, 'neither a citizen of a State of the United States...nor created under the laws of any third country'. FSIA, sec. 1603(b)(3). The Archdiocese of Louisville, which is a citizen of Kentucky and is organized as a Kentucky corporation, was found on these grounds not to be an agency or instrumentality of the Holy See. *O'Bryan v. Holy See*, at 791 and footnote 3.

[309] *O'Bryan v. Holy See*, at 791.

In *Joe V. Doe v. the Holy See*, the district and circuit judges also held that the plaintiffs had sufficiently proved that the alleged perpetrator of the child sexual abuse, Father Ronan, was 'an employee of the Holy See acting within the "scope of his employment" under Oregon law', and that Ronan's acts could therefore be attributed to the Holy See for jurisdictional purposes under the Holy See's *respondeat superior* liability doctrine.[310] It should be stressed that canon law appears to support the courts' conclusion, which was based on acknowledgment of the Holy See's substantive authority over the Roman Catholic Church. Canon 331 provides that the Pope:

is the head of the College of Bishops, the Vicar of Christ, and the Pastor of the universal Church here on earth. Consequently, by virtue of his office, he has supreme, full, immediate and universal ordinary power in the Church, and he can always freely exercise this power.[311]

In as much as the Pope is the head of the College of Bishops and has the capacity to act without the consent of the College, while the latter does not, canon 336[312] does not relativize or restrain the absolute power of the Sovereign Pontiff. In fact, as canon lawyers explain, without its head the college of bishops 'does not bear supreme power over the entire Church'.[313] It is often asserted that geographic distance, and the number of clergy that would have to be under the control of the Pope, should be factored into the control equation.[314] It suffices to mention here that canon law affirms the capacity of the Holy See to exercise authority over clerics, irrespective of their geographic location. More important, this authority has been used effectively in the past.[315] In this light, and for the purpose of tort claims brought in US courts, it would seem that the conclusion of Lucian C. Martinez is justified. 'Once there was credible evidence of a systemic problem with the handling of clergy and members of religious order accused of abuse,... the inaction of the Holy See... may have been negligent.'[316]

---

[310] *John V. Doe v. Holy See et al.*, US Court of Appeals for the 9th Cir. Oregon, No. 06-35563, D.C. No.v. CV-02-00430-MWM, No. 06-35587, D.C. No.v.CV-02-00430- MWM (2009), at 2548.

[311] Canon 331 in Beal, Coriden and Green, *New Commentary on the Code of Canon Law*, at 431.

[312] 'The college of bishops, whose head is the Supreme Pontiff and whose members are bishops by virtue of sacramental consecration and hierarchical communion with the head and members of the college and in which the apostolic body continues, together with its head and never without this head, is also the subject of supreme and full power over the universal Church.' Canon 336 in Beal, Coriden and Green, *New Commentary on the Code of Canon Law*, at 443.

[313] Beal, Coriden and Green, *New Commentary on the Code of Canon Law*, at 432 and 444–446. The historian and Jesuit priest Jean-Blaise Fellay asserts that bishops must sign a declaration 'promettant de ne s'opposer en rien au saint-père. Cela leur enlève toute autorité.' (Author's own translation: promising not to oppose in any respect the Holy Father. This removes all their authority.)'La révolte des catholiques progressistes', *Le Temps*, 23 mars 2012.

[314] See Martinez Jr, 'Sovereign Impunity: Does the Foreign Sovereign Immunities Act Bar Lawsuits Against Holy See in Clerical Sexual Abuse Cases', at 151.

[315] See note 314, at 150–151.

[316] See note 314, at 151.

As a result of *O'Bryan*, and *John V. Doe*, US archbishops and priests are—if one accepts the parallel—*sui generis* employees, as the Holy See is a *sui generis* entity akin to a state in international law. The veil of state immunity in cases of child sexual abuse has been pierced in US courts, based on the territorial tort exception; and, in general, the Holy See enjoys in foreign courts the same privilege of sovereign immunity that is granted to other states, no more or less. The question to be answered in the following section is whether the Holy See assumes the obligations of states in addition to enjoying their privileges.

3. Participation in international organizations and multilateral conventions

When maintaining that both the Holy See and the Vatican City are separate international personae, scholars tend to point to the fact that both the Holy See and the Vatican are members or observers of international organizations and specialized agencies, and that both have signed international treaties.[317] Yet, as we recall, article 12 of the Lateran Treaty and article 2 of the Fundamental Law of the Vatican City stipulate that the Holy See represents the Vatican externally. Concluding, based on this, that the Holy See and the Vatican acted in contradiction to the Lateran Treaty and the Vatican's own Fundamental Law would be hasty, and just as premature as it would be to infer a dual personality from the practice of the Holy See and the Vatican concerning participation in international organizations and treaty-making.

To make sense of a confusing practice, some authors have attempted to find patterns of action. It has been suggested, for example, that the Vatican City State seeks participation in international organizations that are relevant to its territorial existence and worldly matters, and becomes a party to functional or technical treaties on similar grounds, while the Holy See focuses on political treaties and organizations that are relevant to the pursuit of its religious mission.[318] The invariable conclusion has been that this distinction does not stand the test of practice. Samuel W. Bettwy observes that:

Both titles [the Holy See and the Vatican City State] have been used consistently since 1929. In fact, with respect to treaty-making, both titles have been used in conventions dealing with topics ranging from the highly political to the highly technical, in the same fields of international law, by the same person on separate occasions in conference activities, and to indicate membership in international organizations.[319]

---

[317] See Crawford, *The Creation of States in International Law*, 2nd ed., at 227–228. A list of the international organizations and specialized agencies of which the Holy See is a member state or observer can be found in footnote 12. For a list of the treaties to which the Holy See is party see footnote 13. For the Vatican's membership in international organizations see footnote 15. For the Vatican's participation in international treaties see footnote 16.

[318] Bettwy, 'United States-Vatican Recognition: Background and Issues', at 233; Crawford, *The Creation of States in International Law*, 2nd ed., at 227–228.

[319] Bettwy, 'United States-Vatican Recognition: Background and Issues', at 233.

3.1. *The Universal Postal Union: erratic practice of two personalities or the practice of a construct?*

One cannot simply discard the practice of the Holy See and the Vatican in the conduct of international relations as erratic, not least because of the serious implications it entails. Bettwy's use of the notion 'both titles' rather than 'both entities' is particularly appropriate in this context. One could understand that one entity (that is, the construct) has two titles. Let us therefore take one of the principal examples, based on which some authors infer the dual personality of the Vatican and the Holy See—the Vatican's membership of the Universal Postal Union (UPU)—and analyse treaty-making activities related to this organization.[320] On 1 June 1929, the Vatican City State joined the UPU by becoming party to the Stockholm Postal Convention of 1924.[321] The Vatican City State signed[322] and ratified the Universal Postal Convention of 1952,[323] alongside a number of other agreements on different postal issues.[324] The Universal Postal Convention of 1964 was signed by the Vatican City State[325] but ratified by the Holy See,[326] as was the case with a series of agreements on various postal matters[327] and more importantly the UPU Constitution.[328] The Vatican City State ratified and became a party to the 1974 Universal Postal Convention,[329] whereas the 1979 Convention was ratified by the Holy See; it is the Holy See which is listed as a party.[330] The 1989 Universal Postal Convention was signed and ratified by the Vatican City State.[331] Lastly, a press information note by the Secretariat of State declares that the Holy See is a member of the UPU, 'also in the name and on behalf of the Vatican City State'.[332]

There is only one acceptable reading of this practice: the 'two titles' form a state-like construct with one international personality. Any other interpretation would mean that two separate international personae were constantly replacing each other as members of the UPU, and when signing and ratifying UPU conventions, while eluding norms on state succession or continuity.[333] The absence of protest from states and their acquiescence can only be interpreted in the same terms: they understand the Holy See and the Vatican to be a construct. Any other

---

[320] The UPU is a specialized agency of the UN.

[321] Duursma, *Fragmentation and the International Relations of Micro-states: Self-determination and Statehood*, at 401.

[322] 169 UNTS 3.   [323] 186 UNTS 356.

[324] See S. W. Bettwy and M. K. Sheehan, 'United States Recognition Policy: The State of Vatican City', 11 *Cal. W. Int'l L.J* (1981), 1–31, at 26.

[325] 611 UNTS 105.   [326] 639 UNTS 368.

[327] See Bettwy and Sheehan, 'United States Recognition Policy: The State of Vatican City', at 27.

[328] 611 UNTS 7 and 639 UNTS 368.   [329] 1005 UNTS 72.

[330] 1326 UNTS 352.   [331] 1687 UNTS 181.

[332] Holy See Press Office, *Bilateral and Multilateral Relations of the Holy See*, Secretariat of State, 1 February 2001.

[333] For state succession see Brownlie, *Principles of Public International Law*, 7th ed., at 80; Vienna Convention on Succession of States in respect of Treaties (done on 23 August 1978, entered into force 6 November 1996).

explanation, which proposes the perpetual exchange of two distinct personalities in respect to the same international organization, would simply be inconsistent with the systems of state continuity and succession, respectively. It is submitted that the construct formula has also been accepted by states in the case of other international organizations and international treaties, and this is why there is quiet acceptance of the Holy See and Vatican practice of interchangeability.

Jorri Duursma describes a similar practice in the case of the International Telecommunication Union and its predecessor organizations, the International Wheat Council, the World Intellectual Property Organization (WIPO), and the International Atomic Energy Agency (IAEA).[334] In relation to the latter two organizations she notes:

It is noticeable that the Holy See became a member of the IAEA and WIPO without being subjected to a vote by a general conference and that no other Member State has raised the legal objection that the Holy See is not a 'State' and cannot therefore be admitted as a 'State Member' under either the WIPO Convention or the Statute of the IAEA. For at least the purposes of these international organizations the Holy See has been assimilated to a State with the same rights and duties.[335]

She then goes on to conclude that:

The State of the Vatican City was smoothly replaced by the Holy See without international objections. The international community appeared to admit that the State of the Vatican City was created at the service of the Holy See with which it could be identified, despite its separate international legal status.[336]

Duursma's description of practice is correct. In our view, however, the author errs by taking the dual personality scenario as a premise—accepting thereby the discourse of the Holy See—and as a result reads the practice of states through the dual personality lens. Had she taken state practice as her premise, she would have reached the same conclusion, but importantly would not have added the qualification 'despite its separate legal status'. This would have revealed that state practice is in fact evidence of the existence of one single international personality, a construct of the Holy See and the Vatican.

3.2. *The Holy See and its permanent observer state status at the UN*

An important support for the construct formula, as opposed to the dual personality scenario, is the fact that the personality of the Holy See, qua government of the Church, would not have been accepted as eligible to be a member or observer *state* in an international organization. The UN is a case in point.

In 1944, Pope Pius XI inquired into the conditions on which the *Holy See* could join the United Nations.[337] In asserting that 'it would seem undesirable that the

---

[334] Duursma, *Fragmentation and the International Relations of Micro-states: Self-determination and Statehood*, at 400–402, 403, 416.
[335] See note 334, at 403.
[336] See note 334, at 416.
[337] See note 334, at 406.

question of membership of the *Vatican State* be raised now', the US Secretary of State, Cordell Hull, pointed out a number of difficulties, such as its status as a diminutive state and its neutrality, which in his view would have prevented the Vatican from fulfilling all the responsibilities of UN membership.[338] More importantly, it is clear that in Hull's understanding an eventual application could not have been made by the Holy See as the government of the Catholic Church, as in his assessment, the resemblance to statehood was essential.

In 1964, it was the Holy See which informed the UN Secretary General that it had appointed a permanent observer in New York. This marked the commencement of the non-member permanent observer state status of the Holy See at the UN.[339] To understand that at stake was the observer status of the Holy See as part of a construct akin to a state, and not the international personality of the Holy See as the government of the Church, one has to understand the practice of granting UN observer status. Writing back in the 1960s, A. Glenn Mower Jr explained that:

Observer status is an institution which the United Nations has acquired through historical accident and usage rather than through planning. It is also a relationship which a *country* enters through somewhat loose procedures established by practice, not by nicely defined steps according to a legal prescription for the role.[340]

When accepting observers to the UN, Secretary Generals have followed a line of action characterized by whether '*the country* in question is recognized diplomatically in this form or that form by a majority of UN members'.[341] One could of course examine whether the number of states which had entered into bilateral diplomatic relations with the Holy See in 1964 was sufficient,[342] or whether the recognition which the Holy See received from specialized agencies was satisfactory.[343] Be that as it may, it is clear that, had it not resembled a state, the Holy See's persona as government of the Church would not have qualified it to obtain

---

[338] As cited in Crawford, *The Creation of States in International Law*, 2nd ed., at 224–225. (Emphasis added). We should recall that according to the UN Charter, membership in the Organization is open to 'all . . . peace-loving states which accept the obligations contained in the present Charter and, in the judgment of the Organization, are able and willing to carry out these obligations'. UN Charter, art. 4. Hull also added that 'original members not maintaining diplomatic relations with the Vatican State would in some instances probably oppose its admission'. As cited in Duursma, *Fragmentation and the International Relations of Micro-states: Self-determination and Statehood*, at 406.

[339] Duursma, *Fragmentation and the International Relations of Micro-states: Self-determination and Statehood*, at 404; J. Lucien-Brun, 'Le Saint-Siège et les Institutions internationales', *Annuaire français de droit international* (1964) 536–542, at 536 and 539.

[340] A. G. Mower, 'Observer Countries: Quasi Members of the United Nations', 20 *International Organization* 2 (1966), 266–283, at 270–271. (Emphasis added).

[341] As cited in Mower, 'Observer Countries: Quasi Members of the United Nations', at 273. (Emphasis added).

[342] According to the See Change Campaign in 1958, only 14 of the 82 members of the UN had formal diplomatic relations with the Holy See. See Change, *The Catholic Church at the United Nations: Church or State?*, accessed March 2012, http://www.seechange.org/PDF/See%20Change%20Briefing%20Paper.pdf, at 2.

[343] According to Ian Brownlie, collective recognition may be inferred from membership of an international organization such as the UN, while membership of the specialized agencies of the United Nations is not necessarily an attestation of statehood. Brownlie, *Principles of Public International Law*, 7th ed., at 93–94.

the permanent status of an observer state at the UN.[344] This leaves us with only one legally sustainable conclusion, that the Holy See and the Vatican obtained UN observer status as a construct with one international personality. The simplistic representation of Judge Gibbons in *Americans United for Separation of Church and State v. Ronald Reagan*, who identified territoriality as the major advantage of the Holy See over other religious entities, appears to make the big difference in this case, enabling it to enjoy the right to participate alongside states in the work of the UN. The construct formula explains why the Holy See enjoys observer *state* status, while the Sovereign Order of Malta, which lacks a territorial base, is an observer entity.[345]

Several scholars have identified one important privilege that the Holy See's UN observer state status brings with it. Yasmin Abdullah explains:

Because UN conferences generally are open to all 'states', the Holy See, by virtue of its Non-Member state status, is automatically considered to be a 'state' for the purpose of the conference. As a result of its statehood status, the Holy See is permitted to participate on the same level as UN Member states at UN conferences: '[The] Holy See attends...as a full participant, rather than as an observer'. Consequently, the Holy See has full voting rights at the conferences.[346]

The consensus-based process underpinning these conferences means that the Holy See wields 'significant decision-making power regarding the wording of the documents adopted and thus also [in relation to] setting international human rights standards'.[347] The ability to participate or prevent the formation of consensus, which derives from its statehood attribute, represents the major difference to non-state entities, such the Sovereign Order of Malta[348] or the International Committee of the Red Cross,[349] both of which have received a standing invitation to participate as observers in the sessions and work of the UN General Assembly (GA) and may attend UN conferences, but lack the right to vote in the latter.[350]

---

[344] In the past, Austria, Finland, Italy, Japan, and Switzerland have belonged to the category of non-member state permanent observers. All these states subsequently became UN members. See http://www.un.org/en/members/aboutpermobservers.shtml, June 2012.

[345] See Observer status for the Sovereign Military Order of Malta in the General Assembly, GA resolution 48/265 of 24 August 1994.

[346] Abdullah, 'The Holy See at United Nations Conferences: State or Church?', at 1844. (Citations omitted). The author discusses the participation of the Holy See as a state in the International Conference on Population and Development (Cairo, 1994), and in the Fourth World Conference on Women (Beijing, 1995). See also M. Pentikäinen, 'The Right to Speak for the Women's Cause: May Also Women Participate?', in J. Petman and J. Klabbers (eds.), *Nordic Cosmopolitanism. Essays in International Law for Martti Koskenniemi*, (Leiden: Martinus Nijhoff Publishers, 2003), 141–154, at 143; and R. G. Sybesma-Knol, *The Status of Observers in the United Nations*, (Brussel: Centrum voor de Studie van het Recht van de Verenigde Naties en de Gespecialiseerde Organisaties, 1981), at 69–77. See also discussion in Chapter 2, III.1.

[347] Pentikäinen, 'The Right to Speak for the Women's Cause: May Also Women Participate?', at 143.

[348] See Observer status for the Sovereign Military Order of Malta in the General Assembly, GA resolution 48/265 of 24 August 1994.

[349] See GA resolution 45/6 of 16 October 1990.

[350] See notes 348 and 349.

Indeed, this is a privilege which the Holy See, as an observer state, has, but that Palestine, for a long period a UN observer 'entity', did not have.[351]

Civil society organizations and scholars[352] have questioned in recent years the status of the Holy See at the UN. In 1995, Catholics for a Free Choice initiated a petition asking the Secretary General to review the UN observer state status of the Holy See, calling into question the 'appropriateness of allowing the Holy See, a religious entity, to act on a par with states'.[353] Four years later the *See Change Campaign* argued:

The Roman Catholic Church has made significant contributions to the well-being of Catholics and non-Catholics throughout the world through its emphasis on social and economic justice. [But] at the same time, its actions have been detrimental to many women and men.[354]

As discussed in Chapter 2, in support of their claim the petitioners asserted that, at the Beijing World Conference, the Holy See had managed to prevent the inclusion of safe, legal abortion in the list of basic reproductive rights for women and that it sought to block international policy decisions that would make condom education and use a major tool in the prevention of HIV/AIDS.[355] The petitioners argued that 'while the Holy See has the right to a voice at the United Nations, that voice should only be as loud as those of the world's other religions'; and that it should not enjoy the privileges and influence that states enjoy at the UN.[356]

The UN GA provided a reply in 2004. In its resolution 58/314 entitled *Participation of the Holy See in the work of the United Nations*, the GA stated that it:

[a]cknowledges that the Holy See, in its capacity as an *Observer State*, shall be accorded the rights and privileges of participation in the sessions and work of the General Assembly and

---

[351] Palestine became a member of UNESCO in 2011. Admission of Palestine as a Member of UNESCO, Resolution adopted at the 11th plenary meeting, on 31 October 2011, 36 C/30 Add. However, according to Brownlie, that would not have been sufficient to attest Palestine's statehood. Brownlie, *Principles of Public International Law*, 7th ed., at 93–94. Palestine applied for UN member state status on 23 September 2011. Application of Palestine for admission to membership in the United Nations, UN Doc. A/66/371–S/2011/592, 23 September 2011. The Committee on the Admission of New Members 'was unable to make a unanimous recommendation to the Security Council' and the Security Council is said to be deadlocked on the issue of Palestine's membership. Report of the Committee on the Admission of New Members concerning the application of Palestine for admission to membership in the United Nations, UN Doc. S/2011/705, 11 November 2011, para. 21. On 29 November 2012, the General Assembly upgraded Palestine to 'non-member observer State status in the United Nations' through resolution 67/19.

[352] See Abdullah, 'The Holy See at United Nations Conferences: State or Church?', 1835–1875; and Pentikäinen, 'The Right to Speak for the Women's Cause: May Also Women Participate?', 141–154.

[353] Hundreds of NGOs and 2,000 individuals at the Fourth World Conference on Women in Beijing and the NGO Forum are said to have signed the petition. See Change, FAQ, accessed March 2012, http://www.seechange.org/faq.htm.

[354] The campaign was endorsed by a significant number of women's, religious, and reproductive rights organizations. See Change, *The Catholic Church at the United Nations: Church or State?*, at 5.

[355] See Change, *The Catholic Church at the United Nations: Church or State?*, at 5–6.

[356] See Change, *The Catholic Church at the United Nations: Church or State?*, at 6.

the international conferences convened under the auspices of the Assembly or other organs of the United Nations, as well as in United Nations conferences as set out in the annex to the present resolution.[357]

In the annex mentioned the Holy See is accorded the following rights: the right to participate in the general debate of the GA; the right of inscription on the list of speakers under agenda items at any plenary meeting of the GA, after the last member state inscribed on the list; the right to make interventions; the right of reply; the right to have its communications relating to the work of the GA and relating to international conference convened under the auspices of the UN issued and circulated directly, and without intermediary, as official documents of the Assembly; the right to raise points of order relating to any proceedings involving the Holy See, provided that the right to raise such a point of order shall not include the right to challenge the decision of the presiding officer; and the right to co-sponsor draft resolutions and decisions that make reference to the Holy See. Seating for the Holy See is to be arranged immediately after member states and before the other observers. Finally, the annex stipulates that the Holy See does not enjoy the right to vote in the GA or to put forward candidates.[358]

It may be appropriate to note that Palestine's rights as an observer entity were only marginally different to those of the Holy See as observer state.[359] It is nonetheless clear that Palestine's considerations in submitting an application for observer state status to the General Assembly were not driven by the desire to gain those few procedural rights which the Holy See as a state enjoys. It was the confirmation of statehood which derives from this status that it sought, and the legal consequences it entails: the right to territorial integrity; the right to self-defence if attacked; full treaty-making and treaty ratification capacity; participation in other international organizations as a member; and state immunity and immunities for state officials.[360] At the same time, the UN Conference on the Arms Trade Treaty (convened in New York in July 2012) illustrates how much the Holy See cherishes its observer state status. Palestine submitted its credentials to participate as a state in the diplomatic conference; this was opposed by some states, which delayed the start of negotiations. The solution found by the President of the conference was to reseat Palestine between the Holy See and Afghanistan at the front of the meeting room.[361] It was reported that in response the Holy See took the floor to complain

---

[357] Participation of the Holy See in the work of the United Nations, GA resolution 58/314 of 1 July 2004.

[358] Participation of the Holy See in the work of the United Nations, GA resolution 58/314, Annex, paras. 1–10.

[359] See J. Cerone, 'The UN and the Status of Palestine—Disentangling the Legal Issue', 15 *Insights* 26 (2011). See also GA resolution 43/160 of 9 December 1988; GA resolution 52/250 of 13 July 1998; Participation of the Holy See in the work of the United Nations, GA resolution 58/314 of 1 July 2004.

[360] See Amnesty International, *Q&A: Human rights implications of the Palestinian bid for UN membership*, 26 September 2011, accessed June 2012, http://www.amnesty.org/en/news-and-update s/q-and-human-rights-implications-palestinian-bid-un-membership-2011-09-26; J. Cerone, 'The UN and the Status of Palestine—Disentangling the Legal Issue'.

[361] See Geneva Academy of International Humanitarian Law and Human Rights, Arms Trade Treaty Legal Blog, 'The End of the Beginning', 4 July 2012, accessed July 2012, http://armstrade-treaty.blogspot.ch/2012/07/end-of-beginning.html.

'that they had been downgraded from their status of participating state, which was a "flagrant disregard of the principles and practices of the organization". "In no way" was this a precedent for future conferences'.[362]

In conclusion, as a result of the GA resolution of 2004, the UN observer state status of the Holy See, an arrangement initially left to the discretion of the Secretary General, became legitimate and increasingly difficult to challenge. One can certainly argue that by virtue of this resolution the collective recognition of the Holy See has been achieved. Yet, it should be emphasized again that the Holy See is expressly addressed by the UN GA as a state, not as the government of a church; only the construct with its single personality is recognized or can be. Moreover, the rights it was granted are the rights of a state. For this reason, the obligations of the Holy See in the UN system must not be less than those of its non-religious state peers. This understanding is verified in the next section, which examines international human rights instruments.

4. International human rights treaties and the Holy See's obligations

As highlighted by the Universal Postal Union example discussed earlier, the construct formula, with its resemblance to statehood, has allowed the Holy See and the Vatican to become party to a number of international treaties which are open exclusively to states. In the realm of human rights, the Holy See is party to the 1966 International Convention on the Elimination of All Forms of Racial Discrimination (ratified 1 May 1969), the 1984 Convention against Torture and Other Cruel, Inhuman or Degrading Treatment or Punishment (acceded 26 June 2002), the 1989 Convention on the Rights of the Child (ratified 20 April 1990), the 2000 Optional Protocol to the Convention on the Rights of the Child on the Involvement of Children in armed conflict and the Optional Protocol on the Sale of Children, Child Prostitution and Child Pornography (OPSC), both ratified on 24 October 2001.[363]

As the resemblance to statehood of the Holy See-Vatican construct had been considered sufficient for it to be able to accede to these human rights conventions, one must logically hold that the obligations it incurs in becoming party to these instruments are the obligations of a state. To test this conclusion, the Apostolic See's understanding of its obligations under the Convention on the Rights of the Child (CRC) will be explored, as well as the response of the CRC Committee. An 'intermezzo' on the perception of its obligations under the International Convention on the Elimination of All Forms of Racial Discrimination (CERD) and the stance of the CERD Committee will also be presented. The last segment of analysis will focus on the Holy See's handling of clerical sexual abuse in Ireland and beyond, while taking account of obligations that flow from the CRC and the OPSC.

---

[362] See note 361.
[363] The Holy See is an observer state to the Council of Europe. It has not ratified the ECHR.

4.1. *The Holy See's reservations to the Convention on the Rights of the Child*

Upon ratifying the CRC in 1990 the Holy See made three reservations and one declaration. It is important to dwell on these four reserving instruments, which gave rise to a heated debate in 1995 during the review of its initial state report to the CRC Committee, because they reveal the Holy See's understanding of its international obligations under the Convention.

Of the three reservations which the Holy See entered to the CRC, only the first is specific. It refers to the interpretation of family planning in article 24.2. The Holy See interprets the term to refer only to those methods of family planning which it considers 'morally acceptable, that is, the natural methods of family planning'.[364] In 1968, Pope Paul VI declared that the 'first principles of a human and Christian doctrine of marriage' mean that:

[T]he direct interruption of the generative process already begun and, above all, all direct abortion, even for therapeutic reasons, are to be absolutely excluded as lawful means of regulating the number of children. Equally to be condemned . . . is direct sterilization, whether of the man or of the woman, whether permanent or temporary. Similarly excluded is any action which either before, at the moment of, or after sexual intercourse, is specifically intended to prevent procreation—whether as an end or as a means.[365]

The position of the Holy See has not changed since, but a specific prohibition has been added, on the 'use of condoms, either as a family planning measure or in HIV/AIDS prevention programmes'.[366] The Holy See's first reservation to the CRC reflects this position and excludes contraception and abortion, because in the Holy See's view the right to life starts at the moment of conception.[367] This definition of the right to life was explicitly excluded from the Convention as confirmed

---

[364] Reservations and Declaration of the Holy See to the CRC, para. a, accessed March 2012, UNTC, Online Database, Chapter IV: Human Rights, Convention on the Rights of the Child.

[365] Encyclical Letter *Humanae Vitae* of the Supreme Pontiff Paul VI to his venerable brothers the patriarchs, archbishops, bishops and other local ordinaries in peace and communion with the Apostolic See, to the clergy and faithful of the whole Catholic world, and to all men of good will, on the regulation of birth, 25 July 1968, accessed June 2012, http://www.vatican.va/holy_father/paul_vi/encyclicals/documents/hf_p-vi_enc_25071968_humanae-vitae_en.html. (Citations omitted).

[366] Statement of the Holy See in Explanation of Its Position on the Resolution 'Women, the girl child and HIV/AIDS' (E/CN.6/2011/L.3), 55th session of the Commission on the Status of Women of the ECOSOC, New York, 4 March 2011.

[367] In the declaration entered to the CRC, the Holy See proclaims that 'the Convention represents an enactment of principles previously adopted by the United Nations, and once effective as a ratified instrument, will safeguard the rights of the child *before* as well as after birth, as expressly affirmed in the "Declaration of the Rights of the Child" [Res. 136 (XIV)] and restated in the ninth preambular paragraph of the Convention. The Holy See remains confident that the ninth preambular paragraph will serve as the perspective through which the rest of the Convention will be interpreted, in conformity with article 31 of the Vienna Convention on the Law of Treaties of 23 May 1969.' Reservations and Declaration of the Holy See to the CRC. (Emphasis added). See also Second Report to the Committee on the Rights of the Child on the Convention on the Rights of the Child, Holy See, UN Doc. CRC/C/VAT/2, at 20(a) and (i).

in the *travaux préparatoires*.[368] During its 1995 review of the Holy See, the CRC Committee clearly did not endorse the Holy See's understanding of the right to life from conception. One member stressed that natural methods of family planning are not viable and information about alternatives needs to be provided to women.[369]

The second reservation of the Holy See is of a general nature. It interprets all the articles of the Convention, and specifically articles 13, 14, 15, 16, and 28 'in a way which safeguards the primary and inalienable rights of parents'.[370] How does this reservation fare with article 51.2 of the Convention, which stipulates that a reservation incompatible with the object and purpose of the CRC is not permitted?[371] The International Law Commissions (ILC) Guide to Practice on Reservations to Treaties states that, when assessing the compatibility of a reservation that contains numerous interdependent rights and obligations with the object and purpose of a treaty, there need to be taken into account the importance of the reserved provisions for the 'general tenour' of the treaty and the impact of the reservation on the treaty.[372] It does appear as if all the rights of the child, and in particular the rights to freedom of expression, education, religion, association, and privacy, are, in the view of the Holy See, subordinated to those of parents, so that the child becomes 'seulement une personne que la société ou la famille se doit de protéger'.[373] Clearly, the general character of the treaty—its 'tenour' (in the words of the ILC)—is intended to emphasize the personhood of the child as such, and is frustrated if the child is treated as anything less than a subject of rights. The impact is similarly incalculable. The CRC Committee pointedly questioned the compatibility of this reservation with the Convention's purpose, and argued for the recognition of the child as a full subject of rights.[374]

The third reservation is even wider in scope, certainly in its potential impact:

[The Holy See declares] that the application of the Convention be compatible in practice with the particular nature of the Vatican City State and of the sources of its objective law

---

[368] Philip Alston, who makes this comment, also notes that the compromise entailed by the text of the Convention was seen as allowing individual states ratifying 'to adopt whatever position they prefer with respect to the rights of the unborn child, provided that they act in conformity with other applicable provisions of international human rights law'. P. Alston, 'The Unborn Child and Abortion under the Draft Convention on the Rights of the Child', 12 *HRQ* 1 (1990) 156–178, specifically 157, and 163–167 for the Holy See's involvement in the drafting process.

[369] Swithun Mombeshora, CRC Committee, Summary Record of the 256th Meeting, Consideration of Reports of State Parties: Holy See (continued), UN Doc. CRC/C/SR.256, 17 November 1995, para. 26.

[370] Reservations and Declaration of the Holy See to the CRC, para. b.

[371] CRC, art. 51.2. See also VCLT, art. 19.c.

[372] ILC, Guide to Practice on Reservations to Treaties, UN Doc. A/66/10 (2011), para. 3.1.5.6 (Hereafter ILC, Guide to Practice on Reservations).

[373] Yuri Kolosov, CRC Committee, Compte rendu analytique de la 255ème seance, Examen des rapports présentés par les Etats parties: Rapport initial du Saint-Siège, UN Doc. CRC/C/SR.255, 24 novembre 1995, para. 12. (This author's translation: Merely a person recipient of protection from society or the family).

[374] CRC Committee, Concluding observations of the Committee on the Rights of the Child: Holy See, UN Doc. CRC/C/15/Add.46, 27 November 1995, para. 7. See also CRC/C/SR.255, paras. 11, 12, 32, 37; CRC/C/SR.256, para. 37.

(art. 1, Law of 7 June 1929, n. 11) and, in consideration of its limited extent, with its legislation in the matters of citizenship, access and residence.[375]

The declaration is of a similarly all-encompassing character:

By acceding to the Convention on the Rights of the Child, the Holy See intends to give renewed expression to its constant concern for the well-being of children and families. In consideration of its singular nature and position, the Holy See, in acceding to this Convention, does not intend to prescind in any way from its specific mission which is of a religious and moral character.[376]

In as far as it seeks to exclude or modify the legal effect of certain provisions of the CRC in their application to the Holy See, this declaration is subject to the rules applicable to reservations.[377]

According to the last two reserving instruments, the Holy See subjects the implementation of the CRC to its compatibility with the Catholic religion generally, and in particular to its domestic legislation. The Holy See makes clear that it intends to implement only those provisions that are compatible with canon law, apostolic constitutions, and the legislation emanating from the Vatican authorities as stipulated by article 1 of the 1929 Law on the Source of Law.[378]

According to the ILC, reservations relying on internal law 'in order to preserve the integrity of specific rules' are permissible only insofar as they do not affect an essential element of the treaty or its general tenor.[379] In this light, one could accept that the reservation of the Holy See would be permissible to the extent that it should be compatible with its legislation concerning citizenship, access, and residence—even so, as will be shown further, this would not detract from the extraterritoriality of the Holy See's international obligations. It is impossible however to qualify the 'nature' of the Holy See, the Catholic religion in its entirety, and the Vatican's entire body of legislation as 'specific rules' which this reservation intends to preserve. As shown previously, because the Holy See may not always regard the child as a subject of rights, these two reserving instruments may indeed affect the general tenor of the Convention.

Moreover, the Holy See appears to suggest that its particular nature may prevent it from fulfilling the CRC. In 1962, when defining the term 'treaties', the ILC held that the term covered international agreements concluded, inter alia, by the Holy See 'which enters into treaties on the same basis as States'.[380] This clarifies that international treaties give rise to the same obligations of performance for the Holy See as they do for any other state. The suggestion that the Holy See's particular nature might cause it not to fulfil the CRC, or fulfil it only partly, is

---

[375] Reservations and Declaration of the Holy See to the CRC, para c. It should be noted that reference is made to the Law on the Sources of Law of 7 June 1929 and that no.11 referenced in the text should read Roman no. II.

[376] Reservations and Declaration of the Holy See to the CRC, declaration.

[377] ILC, Guide to Practice on Reservations, paras. 1.4(1) and 1.4(2).

[378] Legge sulle fonti del diritto N. II, 7 giugno 1929, AAS Suppl. 1 (1929), 5–13, art. 1. The 1929 Law on the Sources of Law has been superseded by the 2008 Legge sulle fonti del diritto (2008).

[379] ILC, Guide to Practice on Reservations, para. 3.1.5.5.

[380] Report of the International Law Commission on the work of its 14th session, *Yearbook of the International Law Commission*, Vol. II, 1962, at 162.

incomprehensible in the light of a long history of concordats and international conventions successfully performed by the Holy See. It should also be emphasized that the Holy See did not enter similar reservations to the CERD.[381]

It is peculiar that not one single state has objected to the general form of the Holy See's reservations and declaration, or their incompatibility of substance with the object and purpose of the CRC. Many states have objected to reservations by Muslim states, similar in both form and substance to those entered by the Holy See, because they were considered to infringe the *bona fide* and certainty principles (see Chapter 5). In certain cases, states have even adhered to the severability doctrine, deeming that these impermissible reservations did not exclude or modify the legal effect of the treaty's provisions.[382] Essentially, the Holy See clauses are the perfect equivalent of Islamic reservations[383] and could be legitimately termed as Catholic reservations. One has to ask, therefore, whether double standards are at play. It is only appropriate to note that the Holy See justifies the compatibility of its reservations to the CRC by pointing to the absence of objections from other state parties.[384] In this sense, the recognition of the competence of treaty bodies to assess the permissibility of reservations is a welcome development.[385]

This brings us to the final point. There are reasons to claim that, in the view of the CRC Committee, the second and third reservations and the declaration entered by the Holy See are impermissible on grounds of incompatibility with the object and purpose of the Convention, and therefore have no effect on changing the treaty obligations of the state party.[386] First, this view can be discerned from the review process itself, which proceeded as if the Holy See's reservations had not affected its obligations under the Convention. Interestingly, the Committee felt that the Holy See's reservations might be replicated by other (Catholic) states given

---

[381] However, the declaration it entered to the CAT is similar to the CRC one, and states: 'The Holy See, in becoming a party to the Convention on behalf of the Vatican City State, undertakes to apply it insofar as it is compatible, in practice, with the peculiar nature of that State.' Declaration of the Holy See to the CAT, UNTC, Online Database, Chapter IV: Human Rights, Convention against Torture and Other Cruel, Inhuman or Degrading Treatment or Punishment.

[382] The severability doctrine refers to the severance of a state's impermissible reservation to a treaty, while maintaining the ratification and hence the obligations that flow from it intact. See, for example, the objection of Italy to the reservation of Iran (CRC), the objections of Denmark to the reservations of Brunei Darussalam and Saudi Arabia (CRC), accessed June 2012, UNTC, Online Database, Chapter IV: Human Rights, Convention on the Rights of the Child. For a discussion, see Chapter 5, IV.1.1.3.

[383] See on this point also W. Schabas, 'Reservations to the Convention on the Rights of the Child', 18 *HRQ* 2 (1996) 472–491, at 478–479.

[384] 'The Holy See contends that the said Reservations and Interpretative Declaration are not "contrary to the object and purpose" of the CRC but rather in conformity with art. 51 (2) of the Convention. In addition, no State Party has raised an objection to the reservations as being incompatible with the object and purpose of the present Convention...'. Second Report to the Committee on the Rights of the Child on the Convention on the Rights of the Child, Holy See, UN Doc. CRC/C/VAT/2, para. 12. See also CRC/C/SR.255, at 47.

[385] See ILC, Guide to Practice on Reservations, para. 3.2.1.

[386] CRC Committee, Concluding observations of the Committee on the Rights of the Child: Holy See, UN Doc. CRC/C/15/Add.46, 27 November 1995, para. 7. See also CRC/C/SR.255, paras. 11, 12, 32, 37; CRC/C/SR.256, para. 37. According to the ILC Guide to Practice on Reservations , para. 3.2.1(1), '[a] treaty monitoring body may, for the purpose of discharging the functions entrusted to it, assess the permissibility of reservations formulated by a State or an international organization'.

the religious legitimacy of the Holy See. Consequently, the treaty body found it necessary to 'draw attention to the fact that the reservations by the Holy See should not be used as justification for reservations by other States parties'.[387] Second, this submission is supported by the treaty body's concluding observations. Under the heading 'principal subjects of concern', the Committee expressed its concern with the Holy See's reservations, 'in particular with respect to the full recognition of the child as a subject of rights'.[388] It encouraged 'the State party to consider reviewing its reservations to the Convention with a view to withdrawing them'.[389] It must be admitted, nonetheless, that the expression 'invalid reservations' does not appear either in the review process, or in the concluding observations. Forthcoming reviews of the Holy See (on the CRC, OPSC, and the OPAC) should further clarify the Committee's position on the Holy See's reservations.

4.2. *Challenging the Holy See's understanding of its obligations under the Convention on the Rights of the Child*

Requiring the CRC to be compatible with canon law, and the saving clause regarding the Holy See's special nature, tie into the Holy See's understanding of its obligations under the Convention. This understanding is best emphasized by the dialogue between the Holy See's officials and the CRC Committee during the 1995 review of the state party.

Three stages can be carved out from the dialogue: the insistence of the Holy See on its *moral* obligations deriving from the Convention; the challenge of a Committee member as to the status of the Holy See as a state party to the CRC given that it considers itself to have solely moral responsibilities; and the view of the Holy See that it is as a state and as such it has the right to be a party to the CRC.

To start with, the Holy See's delegate asserted that, through the worldwide promotion of a 'child rights culture' via the structures of the Roman Catholic Church, the Holy See is fulfilling its mission and 'est convaincu…de s'acquitter simultanément et pleinement des obligations dérivant de son adhésion à la Convention'.[390] Moreover, Vincenzo Buonomo, (representing the Holy See) suggested that, given that the citizens of the Holy See are citizens *jus officii*, there are no children on the Vatican territory and, therefore, the jurisdiction of the Holy See is a 'moral jurisdiction':

[l]e Saint-Siège n'en a pas moins ratifié la Convention relative aux droits de l'enfant parce qu'il exerce une juridiction *morale* et—même si les enfants sont soumis aux lois du pays dans lequel ils résident—il fait œuvre d'éducation des consciences.[391]

---

[387] CRC/C/SR.256, para. 47.

[388] CRC Committee, Concluding observations of the Committee on the Rights of the Child: Holy See, UN Doc. CRC/C/15/Add.46, 27 November 1995, para. 7.

[389] CRC Committee, Concluding observations of the Committee on the Rights of the Child: Holy See, para. 10.

[390] CRC/C/SR.255, para. 4. (Author's translation: is convinced to fulfil simulatnously and fully its obligations stemming from its adherence to the Convention).

[391] CRC/C/SR.255, para. 19. (Author's translation: [t]he Holy See has nevertheless ratified the Convention on the Rights of the Child because it exercises a moral jurisdiction and—even if

In response, a member of the Committee underlined the inequality between the Holy See and other state parties if the Holy See were to incur solely moral obligations under the CRC:

Pour ce qui est des responsabilités internationales des Etats parties à la Convention, M. Kolosov constate que les responsabilités du Saint-Siège sont de nature purement morales alors que les autres Etats parties ont des devoirs plus concrets. Ainsi, le Saint-Siège peut reprocher à un Etat partie de ne pas prendre les mesures législatives et administratives requises pour donner effet aux dispositions de la Convention, mais cet Etat partie ne peut en faire autant vis-à-vis du Saint-Siège. De même, un Etat partie peut faire référence à la position du Saint-Siège ou aux réserves qu'il a formulées lors de son adhésion à la Convention pour justifier sa propre position ou le dépôt de réserves. Cette inégalité risque de rendre plus difficile la tâche du Comité. Tout en reconnaissant l'importance des activités menées par le Saint-Siège, M. Kolosov se demande s'il ne serait pas plus utile que l'Etat du Vatican ait un statut d'observateur.[392]

In reply, Vincenzo Buonomo made, on the one hand, what could be viewed as a relative concession in respect to the international obligations that result from the Holy See's adherence to a treaty. In his analysis, the jurisdiction of the Holy See under the CRC is portrayed as moral, however, given that this jurisdiction 's'applique à des personnes..., l'action d'un évêque ou d'un établissement scolaire engage la responsabilité de l'Eglise'.[393] On the other hand, he asserted the Holy See's right *as a state* to adhere to treaties and thereby to formulate reservations on their provisions.

A propos des réserves formulées par le Saint-Siège, il y a lieu de signaler que l'article 47 de la Convention stipule que cet instrument est ouvert à tous les Etats. Or selon la définition retenue par l'Organisation des Nations Unies le Saint-Siège en est un. A ce titre, il est habilité à émettre des réserves.[394]

The Holy See's understanding concerning its obligations under the CRC is distorted by a fundamental error: it confuses the nature of its obligations with the means by which these obligations are discharged. This error is entertained by the

the children are subject to the laws of the country in which they reside—it works to educate their conscience.)

[392] CRC/C/SR.255, para. 32. (Author's translation: In what concerns the international responsibility of States parties to the Convention, Mr Kolosov notes that the responsibilities of the Holy See are purely moral while other States parties have more concrete duties. Thus, the Holy See can point to a State party for not taking the legislative and administrative measures necessary to give effect to the provisions of the Convention, whereas the State party cannot do the same in relation to the Holy See. Similarly, a State party may refer to the position of the Holy See or to reservations made upon accession to the Convention to justify its own position or the entering of reservations. This inequality risks making the [monitoring] task of the Committee more difficult. While recognizing the importance of the activities of the Holy See, M. Kolosov questions whether it would not be more useful if the Vatican State had the status of observer.)

[393] CRC/C/SR.255, para. 46. (Author's translation: applies to people..., the action of a bishop or a school engages the responsibility of the Church').

[394] CRC/C/SR.255, para. 47. (Author's translation: In what concerns the reservations made by the Holy See, it should be noted that Article 47 of the Convention stipulates that the Convention is open to all states. And, according to the definition adopted by the United Nations the Holy See is one. As such, it is entitled to make reservations.)

dual personality scenario—the personality variant claimed by the Holy See—which is legally unsustainable and only marginally sanctioned by practice, and which allows for the two personalities to be shifted at will.

The obligations that the Holy See incurs under any treaty, and under international custom and general principles of international law, are legal in nature. As we have seen, courts, such as the Swiss Federal Tribunal and the Philippines Supreme Court, have underlined that the general principle of limited sovereign immunity is applicable to the Holy See, as it is to any other state. In respect to treaties, the *pacta sunt servanda* principle dictates that 'every treaty in force is binding upon the parties to it and must be performed by them in good faith'.[395] An interpretation that confines the obligations of the Holy See solely to the moral realm is disingenuous.[396] It would mean that the Holy See acknowledges its resemblance to a state only in as far as it avails itself of the legal rights of a state, yet denies the corresponding obligations. The particular nature of the Holy See is what allowed it to acquire the rights of a state: this particular nature is that of a construct formed by a *sui generis* entity recognized historically for its religious legitimacy *and* by its resemblance to a state as a result of the Lateran Treaty. As has been stressed on numerous occasions in this chapter, and as Mr Buonomo appears to admit, it is doubtful that, in the absence of the state resemblance afforded by its minimal territoriality, the Holy See would have been able to join international organizations or become party to multilateral treaties restricted to states. Surely, this same particular nature cannot be used as an excuse to dismiss or disregard the legal obligations flowing from ratified treaty law.

In this context, the self-proclaimed moral jurisdiction of the Holy See, which is taken as evidence of the non-existence of legal obligations under the CRC, ought to be discussed. The argument of the Holy See appears to be that, because of the reduced territory of the Vatican, the Holy See has only moral jurisdiction and thus no legal obligation to apply the Convention.[397] To start with, moral jurisdiction is not a term in human rights law. Jurisdiction refers to the space within which a state exercises its legislative, judicial, and executive functions, and is therefore generally understood to be territorial.[398]

The question, with particular relevance to the case of the Holy See, is whether a state is bound by human rights treaty law when acting outside its state borders.

---

[395] VCLT, art. 26.

[396] According to William Schabas, the reservations and declarations entered by the Holy See support this point. 'It would appear...that the Holy See does not really expect the Convention to apply to the Vatican City territory. Rather, its cynical purpose in ratifying seems to be to enhance its credibility in insisting upon an antiabortion interpretation of Article 6 of the Convention. Ratification also permits the Holy See, which has an international legal personality but which is not a "state," to participate (at no real cost) as a "state party" in designating members of the Committee on the Rights of the Child'. Schabas, 'Reservations to the Convention on the Rights of the Child', at 478–479. (Emphasis omitted).

[397] Article 2.1 of the CRC stipulates that 'States Parties shall respect and ensure the rights set forth in the present Convention to each child within their jurisdiction'.

[398] F. Hampson, 'The Scope of the Extra-territorial Applicability of International Human Rights Law', in G. Gilbert, F. Hampson and C. Sandoval (eds.), *The Delivery of Human Rights: Essays in Honour of Professor Sir Nigel Rodley*, (Abingdon: Routledge, 2011), 157–182, at 166. But see, for exceptions, *Al-Skeini and Others v. the United Kingdom*, Application no. 55721/07, Grand Chamber, Judgment of 7 July 2011, paras. 133–140.

The reply of the ECtHR in *Bankovic*[399] provoked a flurry of sometimes divergent reactions, from scholars and practitioners alike,[400] and this chapter cannot do justice to a topic which is itself the object of doctoral theses.[401] What will be underlined here is a largely shared opinion in the literature that the judges in *Bankovic* confused 'the lawfulness of an exercise of jurisdiction with the fact of it'.[402] Subsequent case law departed from the confusion of normativity with facticity in determining the applicability of the ECHR when a state acts outside its territory.[403] The point made by many scholars, in keeping with the findings of the Human Rights Committee and UN Special Procedures, is that, when acting outside its territory, a state makes an assertion of its executive jurisdiction whether or not it has international authority for its action in the other state.[404] Martin Scheinin similarly insists that 'facticity creates normativity', not vice versa, and that the notion of jurisdiction in fact describes the relation of the state to the individual.[405] In Francoise Hampson's analysis, the applicability of human rights law extraterritorially depends on the control exercised by the state over the alleged harm inflicted on the individual, whereas the scope of the state's responsibility depends on the 'degree of control exercised by the state over the conduct alleged to constitute a violation of human rights'.[406] Interestingly, the interpretation of

---

[399] The applicants, all citizens of the Federal Republic of Yugoslavia and family members of persons deceased, including an injured survivor, complained about the bombing of the Radio Televizije Srbije (RTS) building on 23 April 1999 by NATO forces. They invoked article 2 (the right to life), article 10 (freedom of expression), and article 13 (the right to an effective remedy) of the European Convention. *Bankovic and Others v. Belgium and Others*, Application no. 52207/99, Grand Chamber Decision of 12 December 2001.

[400] Marko Milanović, for instance, asserts that the interpretation of the Court in *Bankovic*, according to which 'the application of human rights treaties depends on the rights of states to regulate certain types of conduct by their domestic law is nothing else than a category error'. M. Milanović, *Extraterritorial Application of Human Rights Treaties: Law, Principles, and Policy*, (Oxford: Oxford University Press, 2011), at 40. Contrast the chapters by Rick Lawson and Martin Scheinin with Dominic McGoldrick's chapter in F. Coomans and M. T. Kamminga (eds.), *Extraterritorial Application of Human Rights Treaties*, (Antwerp: Intersentia, 2004).

[401] See K. Oliviera Da Costa, *The Extraterritorial Application of Selected Human Rights Treaties*, (PhD Thesis, Geneva: IHEID, 2011).

[402] Hampson, 'The Scope of the Extra-territorial Applicability of International Human Rights Law', at 177. In Martin Happold's view: 'Regardless of whether a Contracting Party is exercising a legal or an illegal extra-territorial jurisdiction, the situation of the individual affected is the same: he or she is subject to the State's authority and control. It seems excessively formal to determine whether the Convention applies or not on the basis of the legality rather than the fact of the State's behaviour.' M. Happold, '*Bankovic v. Belgium* and the Territorial Scope of the European Convention on Human Rights', 3 *Human Rights Law Review* (2003), 77–90, at 89.

[403] *Issa and Others v. Turkey*, Application no. 31821/96, Judgment of 16 November 2004, para. 71.

[404] Hampson, 'The Scope of the Extra-territorial Applicability of International Human Rights Law', at 161–165; M. Scheinin, 'Extraterritorial Effect of the International Covenant on Civil and Political Rights', in F. Coomans and M. T. Kamminga (eds.), *Extraterritorial Application of Human Rights Treaties*, (Antwerp: Intersentia, 2004), 73–82. See also *Celiberti de Casariego v. Uruguay*, Communication No. 56/1979, UN Doc. CCPR/C/OP/1 (1984), para. 12.3; *Lopez Burgos v. Uruguay*, communication no. 52/1979, U.N. Doc. Supp. No. 40 (A/36/40) (1981), para. 10.3.

[405] Scheinin, 'Extraterritorial Effect of the International Covenant on Civil and Political Rights', at 80.

[406] Hampson, 'The Scope of the Extra-territorial Applicability of International Human Rights Law', at 182.

the ECtHR in one of its most recent cases, *Al-Skeini v. the United Kingdom*, seems to allow for a personal notion of jurisdiction, as suggested by Hampson.[407]

Against these doctrinal and jurisprudential developments in the area of extraterritoriality, even if it were to be accepted that due to its particular nature no children live on the Vatican territory,[408] this would only mean that the Holy See would discharge its international legal obligations under the CRC in a somewhat different way. The jurisdiction of the Holy See under the CRC cannot be portrayed as moral, because the Holy See exercises authority over dioceses, parishes and their priests, over schools and other facilities and their employees, and children are invariably within its jurisdiction.[409] It has been emphasized that, for jurisdiction to be established, the acts of the Holy See need not be lawful. However, in many states, as a result of concordats, the authority of the Holy See over Catholic school facilities, for instance, is in fact recognized by the forum state. In this light, the Holy See's position, that its jurisdiction is merely moral, becomes even less comprehensible. As *Lombardi Vallauri* and *Pellegrini* show, the authority of the Holy See exists not merely at a moral level and its impact on the rights of individuals is certainly real (see Chapter 3, sections III.2.2.1. and 2.2.2.). The Holy See may well be a unique case—a state in which the extraterritorial discharge of its obligations is more significant than the performance of its obligations on the territory of the Vatican.[410] This fact, however, does not make the international obligations of the Holy See under the CRC, or under other human rights instruments that it has ratified, any less legal or less binding.

The Holy See's understanding that its international responsibilities under the CRC are merely moral has not found a positive echo among the members of the CRC Committee.[411] In addition to the previously discussed intervention of Yuri

---

[407] The Court however qualifies its progressive interpretation by pointing to the 'exceptional circumstances' of the case pertaining to the UK's exercise of certain 'public powers' of a governmental character in Basra. *Al-Skeini and Others v. the United Kingdom*, Application no. 55721/07, Grand Chamber, Judgment of 7 July 2011, paras. 137 and 149. See also M. Milanovic, 'Al-Skeini and Al-Jedda in Strasbourg', 23 *EJIL* 1 (2012) 121–139, at 129–130.

[408] As of February 2008, 14 citizens at the Vatican were less than 14 years of age; 17 were less than 18 years of age. CRC Committee, Initial Report to the Committee on the Rights of the Child on the Optional Protocol on the Sale of Children, Child Prostitution and Child Pornography, Holy See, UN Doc. CRC/C/OPSC/VAT/1, para. 59.

[409] In its Second Report to the CRC, the Holy See asserts that it: 'promotes and encourages the system of Catholic schools, which are not State institutions but nonetheless have a public function. The educational activities are carried out in accordance with the Catholic school's own authority and responsibility under canon law, and pursuant to the laws of the respective States in which they operate.' As of December 2008, the Holy See estimated that there are approximately 195,397 Catholic schools in the world, attended by 54,662,553 students of different religious backgrounds. Second Report to the Committee on the Rights of the Child on the Convention on the Rights of the Child, Holy See, UN Doc. CRC/C/VAT/2, paras. 29–30.

[410] The CRC expressly includes extraterritorial obligations. Examples of explicit clauses are CRC, arts. 7.2, 11.2, 17.b, 21.e, 22.2, 23.4, 24.4, 27.4, 28.3, 34 and 35. See also CRC Committee, *General Comment No. 5: General measures of implementation of the Convention on the Rights of the Child*, UN Doc. CRC/GC/2003/5, 27 November 2003, paras. 7 and 60.

[411] It should be noted that the 'particular nature' argument has been accommodated by the CRC in as far as the report submitted did not observe precisely the guidelines of the Committee. In the view of this author, the insistence of the Holy See on its special character has been accommodated more fully

Kolosov, other members of the Committee have clarified that the obligations at issue are *legal*. For instance, it is recommended that the Holy See takes the CRC into account when it concludes concordats with various governments,[412] that it reviews instruments that are not in accordance with the Convention,[413] that the teaching methods in Catholic schools should reflect the 'spirit and philosophy of the Convention' and the aims of education laid down by the CRC,[414] that adequate training should be given to professionals and voluntary workers involved in the education and protection of children in Catholic institutions,[415] and that:

the principles of non-discrimination, of the best interests of the child and of respect for the views of the child, be fully taken into account in the conduct of all the activities of the Holy See and of the various Church institutions and organizations dealing with the rights of the child.[416]

Whether the Holy See incurs moral responsibility, in addition to the international legal obligations flowing from a human rights treaty, is a separate issue which treaties do not regulate. It would seem that some members of the CRC Committee correctly acknowledge the religious legitimacy and great influence which the Holy See enjoys in the world, which, though they do not in any respect lessen or loosen its legal obligations under the CRC, may enable the Holy See to uphold the CRC and influence other states to do the same.[417]

4.3. An 'intermezzo' on the practice of the Committee on the Elimination of Racial Discrimination

Some insights into the practice of the CERD Committee, concerning the review process of the Holy See's implementation of the Convention, are useful at this stage. The Holy See became a party to the CERD in 1969 and has been reviewed by the monitoring body on 11 occasions. By analysing the process of review and concluding observations of the treaty body, one can see that the CERD Committee initially nurtured the Holy See's understanding and portrayal of its obligations as moral; but that, gradually and in a non-linear manner, the Committee became increasingly unwilling to accommodate these.

Let us start with the 1973 dialogue between the treaty body and the Holy See's representatives. Some members of the Committee emphasized that:

[T]he Holy See was a State sui generis and that special criteria must be applied in considering its reports. Unlike other States, its reports were expected to emphasize not legislative,

---

by certain members of the Committee, while others have treated the Holy See like other state parties. The 1995 concluding observations of the CRC seem to represent a compromise between the two positions. CRC Committee, Concluding observations of the Committee on the Rights of the Child: Holy See, UN Doc. CRC/C/15/Add.46, 27 November 1995.

[412] CRC/C/SR.255, para. 25.   [413] CRC/C/SR.255, paras. 15 and 43.

[414] CRC Committee, Concluding observations of the Committee on the Rights of the Child: Holy See, UN Doc. CRC/C/15/Add.46, 27 November 1995, para. 12.

[415] CRC/C/15/Add.46, para. 12.   [416] CRC/C/15/Add.46, para. 14.

[417] CRC/C/15/Add.46, para. 14.

judicial or administrative measures but educational measures, indicative of the essentially moral and spiritual role which it played; and the Committee, in considering the reports of the Holy See, would naturally look for information about the role which it played in the struggle against racial discrimination on the international plane.[418]

This view was largely shared in 1975.[419] In 1977, however, some members of the treaty body took a radically different approach:

[I]t was not for the Committee to decide what provisions of the Convention were applicable to a State, but it was for that State to describe how it had applied the provisions of a Convention to which it was a party; and it was recalled that the Holy See had not made any reservations, when it ratified the Convention, regarding the limited applicability of some of its provisions.[420]

The positioning of the cited paragraph within the summary dialogue on the Holy See's report is relevant. It is part of the introduction and follows immediately after other members of the Committee had stated that the Holy See 'was not expected to fulfil all the obligations laid down in the convention'.[421] It is evident that certain members of the treaty body were reluctant to accommodate the special nature argument of Holy See. The mention of reservations, and the Holy See's decision not to enter any, is also interesting, because, as we know, it did formulate reservations when it acceded to the CRC. At the same time, by pointing out the right to make reservations in a human rights treaty, the Committee's members underlined their belief that they saw the Holy See as no different from other states parties to the Convention.

In 1981, the representative of the Apostolic See 'reminded' the Committee of the 'particular nature of the Holy See which, although it had an international legal status, was not a State and therefore occupied a unique position in the community of nations'.[422] This assertion may be contrasted to the one made during the CRC review, when the Holy See insisted that *as a state* it had the right to formulate reservations.[423] Taken together, these instances portray again the Holy See's appetence for shifting its personalities according to context. The Holy See's 'unique nature' was stressed in subsequent review years, as the Committee increasingly engaged in a constructive dialogue on practical implementation of the Convention. Issues it considered included the position of the Holy See on apartheid in the early 1980s, liberation theology in Latin America, and the links of certain individuals in the Church with right-wing movements.[424] It recognized the important role of the Church's advocacy on disarmament and poverty reduction and the strong position

[418] CERD Committee, Consideration of State party reports: Holy See, CERD 28th, No. 18 UN Doc. A/9018, 1973, para. 158. (Underlined in the original.)

[419] CERD Committee, Consideration of State party reports: Holy See, CERD 30th, No. 18 UN Doc. A/10018, 1975, para. 110.

[420] CERD Committee, Consideration of State party reports: Holy See, UN Doc. A/32/18, 1977, para. 210.

[421] A/32/18, 1977, para. 210.

[422] CERD Committee, Consideration of State party reports: Holy See, UN Doc. A/36/18, 1981, para. 294.

[423] CRC/C/SR.255, para. 47.

[424] See CERD Committee, Consideration of State party reports: Holy See, UN Doc. A/36/18, 1981; CERD Committee, Consideration of State party reports: Holy See, UN Doc. A/37/18, 1982;

adopted by Pope John Paul II in the late 1980s against apartheid.[425] During this period, the reviews of the Committee suggest a limited accommodation of the Holy See's 'special' or 'unique' nature, and in this context it was accepted that some obligations were not relevant for the Holy See while others were emphasized as significant.

A definitive turning point in the treaty body's understanding of the Holy See's obligations under the CERD occurred in 1993. The Committee appears to have rejected the assumption that the Holy See incurred obligations of a moral character under the Convention. Instead it acknowledged that, because of the nature of the 'State party', 'the directness of the measures it could take to implement fully the provisions of the Convention' was limited.[426] In other words, while the obligations are legal, a different approach to their implementation may be required. In 2000, the CERD Committee recommended 'that the State party implement, as appropriate, the Convention' and invited it to provide information on canon law and the implementation of article 4 which requires states to take legislative measures to penalize the incitement to racial hatred and discrimination and to prohibit organizations which engage in such activity.[427] Perhaps the clearest sign that the Committee currently regards the obligations of the Holy See as legally binding and enforceable, is the request it made in its concluding observations that the Holy See should consider making a declaration under article 14, recognizing the competence of the treaty body to receive individual communications.[428]

In conclusion, there has been a shift from embracing the position that the Holy See is a bearer of moral duties under the CERD, to one acknowledging that it incurs legal obligations, the extraterritorial discharge of which is more relevant than in the case of other states. This is a similar line of reasoning to that of the CRC Committee, as shown earlier.

4.4. *The Holy See's obligations under the CRC concerning clerical child sexual abuse in the Irish context*

The extraterritorial reach of the legal obligations of the Holy See under the CRC and the OPSC is of particular importance in the case of child sexual abuse perpetrated by Catholic clergy in other states. This section is structured in two parts. First, the situation of clerical abuse of children in Ireland is briefly introduced, focusing on the 1997 letter by the Apostolic Nuncio Luciano Storero. Second, some

---

CERD Committee, Consideration of State party reports: Holy See, UN Doc. A/40/18, 1985; CERD Committee, Consideration of State party reports: Holy See, UN Doc. A/42/18, 1987; CERD Committee, Consideration of State party reports: Holy See, UN Doc. A/45/18, 1990.

[425] See note 424.

[426] CERD Committee, Consideration of State party reports: Holy See, UN Doc. A/48/18, 1993, para. 299.

[427] CERD Committee, Consideration of State party reports: Holy See, UN Doc. A/55/18, 2000, para. 397.

[428] A/55/18, 2000, para. 400.

of the legal obligations of the Holy See under the CRC and the OPSC, which are of particular relevance in the context of child sexual abuse by Catholic clergy, are discussed in an attempt to show that an understanding of these obligations as legal and binding upon the Holy See would have contributed to a different course of action in the Irish context and beyond.

Two reports sponsored by the Irish government focused on the issue of clerical child sexual abuse in the Catholic Archdiocese of Dublin between 1975 and 2004, and in the Catholic Diocese of Cloyne between 1996 and 2009. They were published in 2009 and 2010 respectively, by a Commission of Investigation led by Judge Yvonne Murphy. The reports followed a more general document by the Commission to Inquire into Child Abuse, which had found that clerical sexual abuse of children was widespread during the decades covered by the inquiry.[429] The Dublin report investigated 102 priests, many of whom admitted to sexual abuse. One priest admitted to having sexually abused over 100 children, while another 'accepted that he had abused on a fortnightly basis during the currency of his ministry which lasted for over 25 years'.[430] The Commission concluded:

The Commission has no doubt that clerical child sexual abuse was covered up by the Archdiocese of Dublin and other Church authorities over much of the period covered by the Commission's remit. The structures and rules of the Catholic Church facilitated that cover-up. The State authorities facilitated the cover up by not fulfilling their responsibilities to ensure that the law was applied equally to all and allowing the Church institutions to be beyond the reach of the normal law enforcement processes. The welfare of children, which should have been the first priority, was not even a factor to be considered in the early stages. Instead the focus was on the avoidance of scandal and the preservation of the good name, status and assets of the institution, and of what the institution regarded as its most important members—the priests. In the mid 1990s, a light began to be shone on the scandal and the cover up. Gradually, the story has unfolded. It is the responsibility of the State to ensure that no similar institutional immunity is ever allowed to occur again. This can be ensured only if all institutions are open to scrutiny and not accorded an exempted status by any organs of the State.[431]

The findings of the Cloyne report covered a period when clerical sexual abuse of children was already in the limelight, and after the Advisory Committee of the Irish Bishops' Conference had adopted a Framework Document which established structures and procedures to deal with cases of sexual abuse (including mandatory reporting to Irish authorities). The Cloyne report concluded:

The reaction of the Vatican to the *Framework Document* was entirely unhelpful to any bishop who wanted to implement the agreed procedures ... This effectively gave individual Irish bishops the freedom to ignore the procedures which they had agreed and gave comfort and support to those who ... dissented from the stated official Irish Church policy. The effect was to strengthen the position of those who dissented ...[432]

---

[429] Commission to Inquire into Child Abuse, *Report*, May 2009, accessed March 2012, http://www.childabusecommission.com/rpt/index.php, ch. 11-57.
[430] Report into the Catholic Archdiocese of Dublin, paras. 1.8 and 1.9.
[431] Report into the Catholic Archdiocese of Dublin, para. 1.113.
[432] Report into the Catholic Diocese of Cloyne, paras. 1.18 and 1.76.

The Cloyne report refers to a 1997 letter which the Apostolic Nuncio Luciano Storero sent to the Bishops of Ireland. The letter observes that the procedures and dispositions of the Framework Document, and in particular the 'mandatory reporting' to civil authorities give rise to 'serious reservations of both a moral and a canonical nature'.[433] It further states that the nuncio was:

directed to inform the individual Bishops of Ireland...that in the sad cases of accusations of sexual abuse by clerics, the procedures established by the Code of Canon Law must be meticulously followed under pain of invalidity of the acts involved if the priest so punished were to make hierarchical recourse against his Bishop.[434]

Arguably the letter can be construed to forbid reporting or to encourage clerics not to cooperate with Irish authorities and disobey Irish civil law.[435] This construction was suggested by the Irish prime minister Enda Kenny,[436] and strongly denied by the Holy See.[437] In this study the angle from which the situation is regarded is that of cooperation for the prevention and punishment of clerical child sexual abuse. The aim here is to show that the Holy See's handling of child sexual abuse in this particular context constitutes a breach of its own international obligations under the CRC to prevent child sexual abuse.[438] In 1997, when the nuncio's letter was sent to the Irish Bishops, the Holy See was a party to the CRC and as a result was legally bound to respect the stipulations of the Convention.

International law experts recently adopted a document on the extraterritorial obligations of states which asserted that these take two forms: obligations concerning acts and omissions of a State, within or beyond its territory, that have effects on the enjoyment of human rights outside that State's territory; and obligations of a global character, that are set out in the Charter of the United Nations and human rights instruments, to take action separately and jointly, through international cooperation, to realize human rights universally.[439] Article 34 of the CRC would

---

[433] Apostolic Nunciature in Ireland, N. 808/97, Strictly Confidential, Dublin, 31 January 1997, accessed January 2012, http://graphics8.nytimes.com/packages/pdf/world/Ireland-Catholic-Abuse.pdf; see also L. Goodstein, 'Vatican Letter Warned Bishops on Abuse Policy', *The New York Times*, 18 January 2011.

[434] Apostolic Nunciature in Ireland, N. 808/97, Strictly Confidential, Dublin, 31 January 1997.

[435] Civil law is to be understood here as secular law, in opposition to canon law.

[436] '[F]or the first time in Ireland, a report into child sexual-abuse exposes an attempt by the Holy See, to frustrate an Inquiry in a sovereign, democratic republic as little as three years ago, not three decades ago. And in doing so, the Cloyne Report excavates the dysfunction, disconnection, elitism....the narcissism that dominate the culture of the Vatican to this day. The rape and torture of children were downplayed or "managed" to uphold instead, the primacy of the institution, its power, standing and "reputation".' Enda Kenny's speech on Cloyne Report in the Dáil Éireann on the Commission of Investigation into the Catholic Diocese of Cloyne, accessed March 2012, http://www.rte.ie/news/2011/0720/cloyne1.html.

[437] Response of the Holy See to the Government of Ireland regarding the Report of the Commission of Investigation in to the Catholic Diocese of Cloyne, 3 September 2011, at 12.

[438] As is well known, '[t]here is a breach of an international obligation by a State when an act of that State is not in conformity with what is required of it by that obligation, regardless of its origin or character'. ILC, Articles on Responsibility of States for Internationally Wrongful Acts, UN Doc. A/56/10 (2001), art. 12, at 26.

[439] The focus of the Principles is on economic, social, and cultural rights, yet the experts do not exclude their applicability to civil and political rights and certainly the above classification appears to refer to both 'categories' of rights. Maastricht Principles on Extraterritorial Obligations of States in the

seem to conform to the second form and certainly has an embedded extraterritorial reach.[440] It reads:

States Parties undertake to protect the child from all forms of sexual exploitation and sexual abuse. For these purposes, States Parties shall in particular take *all appropriate national, bilateral and multilateral measures to prevent*:

(a) The inducement or coercion of a child to engage in any unlawful sexual activity;
(b) The exploitative use of children in prostitution or other unlawful sexual practices;
(c) The exploitative use of children in pornographic performances and materials.[441]

Article 34 can be understood fully only in the context of article 19 which defines the notion of 'all appropriate measures'. Article 19 stipulates:

1. States Parties shall take all appropriate legislative, administrative, social and educational measures to protect the child from…sexual abuse, while in the care of parent(s), legal guardian(s) or any other person who has the care of the child.
2. Such protective measures should, as appropriate, include effective procedures for the establishment of social programmes to provide necessary support for the child and for those who have the care of the child, as well as for other *forms of prevention and for identification, reporting, referral, investigation, treatment and follow-up of instances of child maltreatment described heretofore, and, as appropriate, for judicial involvement*.[442]

The above clause generates an obligation on the Holy See to cooperate with the Irish authorities to prevent child sexual abuse by Catholic clergy, by taking all appropriate legislative measures to protect the child from sexual abuse, and by identifying and reporting abuse to civil authorities. It may be relevant to remember that in *Bosnia v. Serbia*,[443] the ICJ set out the obligation to prevent genocide that is enshrined in the Genocide Convention; clearly, as the Court itself noted, it did not purport 'to establish a general jurisprudence applicable to all cases where a treaty instrument, or other binding legal norm, includes an obligation for States to prevent certain acts.'[444] Nonetheless, one certainly cannot see an objection in applying the *principle* which the Court identified, under which the obligation 'to prevent' is one of conduct and not one of result.[445] In the case at hand, this would imply that a state is not under an obligation under the CRC to succeed in preventing child sexual abuse. However, responsibility under the CRC may be incurred when a state 'manifestly failed to take all measures'[446] to prevent child sexual abuse which 'were within its power, and which might have contributed to preventing'[447] sexual abuse.

---

area of Economic, Social and Cultural Rights, 28 September 2011, accessed March 2012, http://www.icj.org/dwn/database/Maastricht %20ETO%20Principles%20-%20FINAL.pdf, para. 8.

[440] CRC Committee, *General Comment No. 5*, para. 60 and footnote 16.
[441] CRC, art. 34. (Emphasis added).   [442] CRC, art. 19. (Emphasis added).
[443] *Application of the Convention on the Prevention and Punishment of the Crime of Genocide* (*Bosnia and Herzegovina v. Serbia and Montenegro*), Judgment, ICJ Reports 2007, p. 43.
[444] *Bosnia and Herzegovina v. Serbia and Montenegro*, para. 429.
[445] *Bosnia and Herzegovina v. Serbia and Montenegro*, para. 430.
[446] *Bosnia and Herzegovina v. Serbia and Montenegro*, para. 430.
[447] *Bosnia and Herzegovina v. Serbia and Montenegro*, para. 430.

It should be reiterated at this point that the Pope has 'immediate and universal ordinary power in the Church'.[448] Notwithstanding this clear provision, it would seem appropriate to look for evidence of the Holy See's practical authority over the Irish bishops with regard to specific cases of child sexual abuse by clerics in Ireland. Clearly, as the subsequent adoption of norms and procedures attest,[449] the Holy See had the authority to take measures to address child sexual abuse in a uniform manner throughout the Catholic Church, including in Ireland. In this sense, the letter of the Apostolic Nuncio exemplifies the Holy See's failure to discharge its obligation to cooperate with the Irish authorities to prevent clerical sexual abuse of children[450]- as the Cloyne report shows, the influence of the Holy See's position on individual Irish bishops in this particular circumstance was considerable, to the point that the nuncio's letter effectively authorized them to ignore the Framework Document.[451]

The situation could be compared—while acknowledging the differences of context and applicable law—with that of *McCann v. the United Kingdom*.[452] That case concerned the killing of three terrorist suspects in Gibraltar by members of the Special Air Service (SAS) of the United Kingdom. The ECtHR found the United Kingdom in violation of article 2 of the ECHR. The central argument in the Court's finding was that the government had not acted to prevent the terrorist suspects from travelling to Gibraltar, although they had the opportunity to do so.[453] It is clear from the *McCann* case that the failure to prevent resulted in the death of the terrorists. This casual link cannot be asserted with the same strength in the case of the failure of the Holy See to cooperate with Irish authorities to prevent clerical child sexual abuse simply because a contextual analysis of the instances of abuse would be required that goes beyond the scope of this chapter. The focus here is not on attribution, but on the legal obligations that an actor incurs as a result of adhering to the CRC, and how those obligations should be implemented in the context of clerical child sexual abuse.

In the 1997 letter of the Apostolic Nuncio, the Holy See suggested that mandatory reporting to the Irish authorities was incompatible with canon law. The correct discharge of obligations, in the light of article 19 and 34 of the CRC, would have been to amend canon law so as to make it compatible with the provisions of

---

[448] Canon 331 in Beal, Coriden and Green, *New Commentary on the Code of Canon Law*, at 431.

[449] *Normae de gravioribus delictis* (2010); The Norms of the *Motu Proprio Sacramentorum Sanctitatis Tutela* (2001), Historical Introduction, accessed March 2012, http://www.vatican.va/resources/resources_introd-storica_en.html.

[450] See also Amnesty International, *In Plain Sight: Responding to the Ferns, Ryan, Murphy and Cloyne Reports*, September 2011, accessed March 2012, http://www.amnesty.ie/content/plain-sight, at 127–128.

[451] Report into the Catholic Diocese of Cloyne, para. 1.18.

[452] *McCann and Others v. the United Kingdom*, Application no. 18984/91, Grand Chamber, Judgment of 27 September 1995.

[453] '[T]he danger to the population of Gibraltar—which is at the heart of the Government's submissions in this case—in not preventing their entry must be considered to outweigh the possible consequences of having insufficient evidence to warrant their detention and trial. In its view, either the authorities knew that there was no bomb in the car—which the Court has already discounted...—or there was a serious miscalculation by those responsible for controlling the operation. As a result, the scene was set in which the fatal shooting, given the intelligence assessments which had been made, was a foreseeable possibility if not a likelihood.' *McCann and Others v. the United Kingdom*, paras. 205 and 213.

the Convention, which therefore would have allowed certain reporting procedures to be included. One could argue that the reservation which made the Holy See's implementation of the CRC's provisions subject to their compatibility with canon law may have excluded the application of article 19 and 34 in the case at hand. As pointed out previously, there are reasons to consider this reservation impermissible, not least in the opinion of the CRC Committee.[454] In this case, it has no effect on the obligations of the Holy See under the Convention.

The fact that canon law can be amended and interpreted[455] is evidenced by the modifications to the norms and procedures concerning child sexual abuse which have been made by Pope John Paul II in 2001 and Pope Benedict XVI in 2010.[456] Nonetheless, it is important to note that even these modifications seem to fall short of what is required by the CRC. As such, non-governmental organizations and some legal practitioners have persistently doubted whether the amended norms permit cases of sexual abuse to be reported to civil authorities.[457] A circular letter from the Congregation for the Doctrine of the Faith addressed to all bishops interprets the norms as follows:

Sexual abuse of minors is not just a canonical delict but also a crime prosecuted by civil law. Although relations with civil authority will differ in various countries, nevertheless it is important to cooperate with such authority within their responsibilities. Specifically, *without prejudice to the sacramental internal forum, the prescriptions of civil law regarding the reporting of such crimes to the designated authority should always be followed.* This collaboration, moreover, not only concerns cases of abuse committed by clerics, but also those cases which involve religious or lay persons who function in ecclesiastical structures.[458]

The non-binding recommendation of the Congregation falls short of mandatory reporting. It explicitly excludes the reporting by clergy of cases of child sexual abuse revealed to them during confession, and it is unclear whether abuse should be reported in the absence of specific prescriptions in the law of the forum state. Evidence that canon law can be interpreted to promote human rights was recently provided by the Holy See in its second periodic report to

---

[454] See VI.4.4.

[455] Canon law encompasses three bodies of law: divine, ecclesiastical, and civil law. The second and third bodies are amendable. According to the Dublin report 'ecclesiastical law ... is human in origin and can be created, reformed and abolished by competent legislative authorities of the Church.' We submit that divine law can and should be interpreted in such a way so as not to conflict with the human rights obligations of the Holy See. Report into the Catholic Archdiocese of Dublin, paras. 4.4 and 4.5.

[456] See for the process of amendment of the Holy See's instructions concerning child sexual abuse http://www.vatican.va/resources/resources_introd-storica_en.html, accessed March 2012.

[457] As a consequence of art. 30, as soon as a bishop starts his preliminary investigation into an allegation of sexual abuse he would be bound by pontifical secret and would therefore be prevented from informing local authorities. Some argue that all those involved in the investigation, including the victim and witnesses are sworn to secrecy. See Robertson, *The Case of the Pope: Vatican Accountability for Human Rights Abuse*, at 57–62, 116; V. Mosen, *Römisch-katholische Kirche und Kinderrechtskonvention in der Bundesrepublik Deutschland*, (Initiative Kirche von unten, KirchenVolksBewegung Wir sind Kirchen, Catholics for a Free Choice, September 2003), accessed March 2012, http://kirche-von-unten. org/html/archiv/ikvu/missbrauch/un-bericht.pdf, at 8.

[458] Congregation for the Doctrine of the Faith, Circular Letter to Assist Episcopal Conference in Developing Guidelines for Dealing with Cases of Sexual Abuses of Minors Perpetrated by Clerics, Rome, 3 May 2011, para. I.e. (Emphasis added).

the CRC Committee. It cites as good practice the document *Our Children, Our Church* adopted by the Irish Bishops Conference in 2005. Ironically, this latter paper largely follows the procedures for dealing with allegations of child abuse that were set out in the Framework Document (including mandatory reporting of alleged abusers) and which were refuted as inappropriate by the 1997 letter of the Apostolic Nuncio.[459]

The OPSC was ratified by the Holy See without reservations in 2001, thus occuring after the 1997 letter of the Apostolic Nuncio in Ireland, and is therefore not applicable to the analysis of that letter. However, the Protocol includes a number of provisions that should have guided the Holy See's handling of child sexual abuse by clergy since the ratification in 2001. Based on the OPSC one can conclude that where, in the course of abuse, the threat of shaming or the promise of absolution or other forms of consideration are used, and the child is used in sexual activities by force, clerical child sexual abuse could be considered as a form of child prostitution.[460] Furthermore, OPSC binds every state party to address child prostitution in its penal law, 'whether it is committed domestically or transnationally or on an individual or organized basis'.[461] The Holy See has not incorporated this provision in canon law. Article 3 of the Protocol further stipulates that '[e]ach State Party shall make such offences punishable by appropriate penalties that take into account their grave nature'.[462] The most severe penalties for child sexual abuse that priests face under canon law are dismissal or deposition.[463] Without minimizing the significance of dismissal or deposition for a Catholic priest, these punishments contrast sharply with the text of the Optional Protocol and the intention of its drafters. This is where we understand the tremendous difference between canon and civil law and the fact that canon law cannot be a substitute or an alternative for the latter. In its Initial Report submitted to the CRC Committee on the Optional Protocol, the Holy See notes under the heading Limitations of canon law: '[t]he fact that a given act may also be treated as a religious offense under penal canon law does not preclude prosecution according to the criminal law and procedures of any State'.[464] It then goes on to suggest—in the dual personality scenario, which the report adopts—that the Vatican City State, whose first source of law is canon law, would rely in respect to codification and prosecution of child prostitution on 'supplementary' Italian legislation.[465] It is important that the Holy See realizes that, in the Vatican territory, it cannot rely on canon law

---

[459] See Second Report to the Committee on the Rights of the Child on the Convention on the Rights of the Child, Holy See, UN Doc. CRC/C/VAT/2, para. 79.e.

[460] See Optional Protocol to the Convention on the Rights of the Child on the sale of children, child prostitution and child pornography, 2171 UNTS 227 (adopted 25 May 2000, entered into force 18 January 2002), art. 2.2 (hereafter OPSC).

[461] OPSC art. 3.1.b.

[462] OPSC, para. 3.3.

[463] *Normae de gravioribus delictis*, art. 3.2.

[464] CRC Committee, Initial Report to the Committee on the Rights of the Child on the Optional Protocol on the Sale of Children, Child Prostitution and Child Pornography, Holy See, UN Doc. CRC/C/OPSC/VAT/1, para. 57.

[465] CRC/C/OPSC/VAT/1, paras. 60–61.

when dealing with perpetrators of child sex abuse and must appeal to Italian law: what better argument can be made for introducing a mandatory reporting scheme in canon law to avoid confusion among bishops in other countries?

It appears again from the report on the OPSC that the Holy See does not grasp, or refuses to acknowledge, that this instrument applies extraterritorially. Again the error is rooted in its claimed dual personality, under which it presents the activities of the Holy See outside the borders of the Vatican as those of the Church and thereby not legally bound by the provisions of human rights treaty law. As this chapter has shown, this interpretation is flawed. The Holy See is bound to give effect to the provisions of human rights treaty law in canon law, which affects individuals worldwide. A correct understanding of its obligations under the CRC and the Optional Protocol would require the Holy See to criminalize and prosecute clerical abusers of children in the Vatican territory (perhaps by deferring to Italy); to ensure that canon law does not preclude the prosecution of accused priests by civil authorities in other states; and to actively cooperate internationally towards that end.[466] None of these obligations are fully reflected in the *Normae de gravioribus delictis*. In this light, Pope Benedict's acknowledgement that 'a misplaced concern for the reputation of the Church and the avoidance of scandals'[467] had resulted in the 'failure to apply existing canonical penalties and to safeguard the dignity of every person'[468] represented a start, but is insufficient to fulfil the construct's obligations under human rights law.

VII. Conclusion

Even the most ardent critics commence their critique of the Holy See's positions— on clerical child sexual abuse, on contraception, on the rights of homosexual persons—by acknowledging the significant contributions made by this actor to the well-being of Catholics and non-Catholics worldwide. To point out the international legal obligations of the Holy See does not imply denying its religious legitimacy. Rather, these legal obligations need to be assumed alongside its religious legitimacy. This chapter has offered evidence that the dual personality scenario claimed by the Holy See is an obstacle to acknowledgment and implementation of its international obligations. The dual personality scenario creates a situation where the international personae of the Holy See, qua state and qua government of the Roman Catholic Church, can be shifted at will according to need. In turn, this allows the Holy See to avail itself of the privileges restricted to states, while denying that it has the corresponding obligations of states. It has been illustrated that neither law nor practice lends sufficient support to the dual personality variant.

---

[466] OPSC, art. 5.5 (prosecute or extradite rule), art. 6, and art. 10.

[467] Pastoral Letter of the Holy Father, Benedict XVI, to the Catholics of Ireland, 19 March 2010, accessed March 2012, http://www.vatican.va/holy_father/benedict_xvi/letters/2010/documents/hf_ben-xvi_let_20100319_church-ireland_en.html.

[468] See Amnesty International, *Annual Report 2011, Vatican*, accessed March 2012, http://www.amnesty.org/en/region/vatican/report-2011.

The chapter responds to the personality question by postulating the notion of a construct, according to which the Holy See and the Vatican share a single international personality that derives from two sources: specific historical circumstances which led to recognition of the religious legitimacy of the Holy See; *and* the state-like resemblance conferred on the construct by the Lateran Treaty in 1929. The analysis reveals that the Holy See had a degree of personality after 1870, as a *sui generis* entity by virtue of historical circumstances drawing on its religious legitimacy. Nonetheless, its personality was essentially restricted to recognizing states. In the absence of the Lateran Treaty it would have remained an international person similar to the Sovereign Order of Malta, with limited rights and obligations under international law. It further shows that the construct personality reflects history, is supported by the Lateran Treaty and general international law, domestic jurisprudence and international monitoring of human rights bodies, and makes sense of what otherwise would be erratic state practice. As a construct, the Holy See enjoys the privileges of statehood: the guarantee of territorial integrity; the inviolability of its internal affairs; the right of a sovereign to freely participate in international affairs, including in international organizations and to enjoy full treaty-making and ratification capacity; state immunity from trial in foreign courts; and immunities of its state officials. Acceptance into the privileged circle of states, however, comes with the obligation to respect the rights of other states and of individuals under customary and treaty law. Human rights treaties to which the Holy See is a party give rise to legal obligations for the construct and the extraterritorial applicability of these conventions may well be of greater significance than is the case for other states. In the context of clerical child sexual abuse, the Holy See fails to meet its obligations under the CRC and the OPSC. This failure is traceable to the success of its own dual personality rhetoric. If it recognized itself as a construct, the Holy See would find it easier to both understand and implement its human rights obligations.

The Holy See is an actor that enjoys tremendous 'special' or religious legitimacy. The common thread which runs through this study is the proposition that religious legitimacy does not translate into a special form of legality for religious actors. The analysis of the Holy See's rights and obligations in law, diplomatic practice, the jurisprudence of domestic courts, and the monitoring of treaty bodies has upheld this hypothesis. However, it should be acknowledged that some states and certainly the treaty bodies have only recently recognized that the human rights obligations of the Holy See are legal, not merely moral. The analysis shows, in a side argument, that (il)legality may affect the legitimacy of a religious actor when egregious abuse provokes deep feelings in society, as it has done in the case of child sexual abuse by Catholic clerics.

5

The Organization of
Islamic Cooperation as Interpreter
of Human Rights in the
Context of Islam

'[T]here is no other way except by understanding and putting into practice every human right for all mankind, irrespective of race, gender, faith, nationality or social status. In anticipation of that day.'

—Shirin Ebadi[1]

I. Introduction

One cannot close the circle of religious actors to be operationalized in this study without examining the Organization of Islamic Cooperation (OIC), formerly known as the Organization of the Islamic Conference[2] as this is the sole inter-governmental actor to display religious contours and to claim the role of interpreter of human rights in the context of Islam. Of particular interest is the work of the OIC in the development of three instruments: the Cairo Declaration on Human Rights in Islam (CDHRI), the Covenant of the Rights of the Child in Islam (CRCI), and the Statute of the OIC Independent Permanent Human Rights Commission (IPHRC)—which sets up a human rights body for the Organization.

This chapter finds a theoretical anchor for analysing the three instruments in the work on fragmentation of the International Law Commission (ILC). This work provides for two forms of regionalism in the area of human rights: cultural relativism which creates exceptions to universal norms, or a regionalism that provides context-sensitive approaches to the interpretation and application of shared standards.[3] The submission is that while the Cairo Declaration puts forward an

---

[1] S. Ebadi, *Nobel Lecture*, 10 December 2003, http://www.nobelprize.org/nobel_prizes/peace/laureates/2003/ebadi-lecture-e.html.
[2] The change in title of the Organization was decided by the OIC Council of Foreign Ministers in June 2011. OIC Astana Declaration: Peace, Cooperation and Development, adopted by the Thirty-eighth Session of the OIC Council of Foreign Ministers, Astana, 30 June 2011, art. 2.
[3] ILC, Fragmentation of International Law: Difficulties Arising from the Diversification and Expansion of International Law, Report of the Study Group of the International Law Commission

interpretation of human rights subject to sharia law, the two more recent instruments have the potential to interpret human rights in the context of the 'Muslim world'[4] in a manner that is more in resonance with the practice of other regional human rights systems. Underpinning this development is a dialectic between the various OIC member state's obligations under international human rights treaties, and the aim of the Organization to assert itself as the 'collective voice of the Muslim world'.[5]

In terms of structure, this chapter examines the OIC's attributes as a religious actor and sheds light on the diversity which characterizes its membership (II). The chapter then discusses regionalism in the context of the fragmentation of international law, and cultural relativism in its various guises, in an attempt to understand what drives the codification of human rights in the framework of the OIC (III). Finally, it analyses the provisions of the Cairo Declaration against the background of members' obligations under international human rights treaties and the reservations they have entered to them, while also discussing the Cairo Declaration's influence in guiding member states in the area of human rights and the accountability of the OIC in this context. The substantive provisions of the CRCI will be examined in an attempt to emphasize departures from the OIC's own Cairo Declaration and its particularities compared to the UN Convention on the Rights of the Child (CRC). The mandate, composition, and functioning of the OIC Independent Permanent Human Rights Commission is analysed to reflect upon its potential to provide a context-sensitive interpretation of universal human rights (IV). The conclusion draws together the findings of the analysis and evaluates the OIC's performance as an interpreter of human rights in the context of Islam, exploring the shapes that its regionalism can take in the future (V).

II. The OIC as an Actor with Religious Contours and its Internal Diversity

The main assumption that has been made in the introductory paragraphs needs careful examination before going further. Does the OIC have the contours of a religious actor, as defined in this study? Let us recall that in Chapter 2 different approaches were proposed for identifying a religious actor.[6] First, the empirical approach suggested that certain observable characteristics differentiate religious actors from non-religious ones: in particular, the perception of them, by their members or the outside public, may be relevant. Turkey's position on the character of the OIC at its inception is interesting in this context. In 1969, while attending the inaugural Rabat summit, Turkey insisted on characterizing the OIC

---

finalized by Martti Koskenniemi, UN Doc. A/CN.4/L.682, 13 April 2006, para. 216. (Hereafter ILC, Fragmentation Report, 2006).

[4] The expression is used here to echo the OIC's own description.
[5] See 'About the OIC', accessed May 2011, http://www.oic-oci.org/page_detail.asp?p_id=52.
[6] See Chapter 2, II.

as a political entity, rather than stressing its obvious religious aspects. It has been observed that Turkey's position, juggling between its own constitutional secularism and adherence to an organization whose title declares its religious identity,[7] was designed to secure political gains in the Arab world.[8] Beyond this, Turkey's understanding of the OIC reveals that the Organization's structure combines politics with religious identity. This duality is further evident when the founding of the OIC is considered: the arson attack on the Al-Aqsa Mosque, the third holiest Shrine of Islam which was at the heart of the birth of the OIC as an international organization, can also be read through the lenses of the Israel-Palestinian conflict and the attachment of the OIC to Palestinian statehood.[9] While its title, the reason it was created, and its activity over time (not least within the UN system),[10] place the OIC among religious actors, the Organization has a complex character, where the role of religion is intertwined with political goals.

Second, a legal approach to identifying religious actors focuses on an organization's founding instruments. The constitutive Charter of 1972 stresses common belief as 'a strong factor for rapprochement and solidarity among Islamic people'.[11] The important place of religion in the ideological architecture of the OIC is also evident in the revised Charter of 2008. The Charter opens symbolically with the words 'In the name of Allah, the most Compassionate, the most Merciful' and stipulates that the objectives of the Charter are to be pursued in accordance to 'the noble Islamic teachings and values'.[12] The 20 objectives listed in article 1 of the OIC Charter span a wide range of issues, from protection of the right to self-determination, sovereignty, and territorial integrity, to strengthening cooperation in trade, science, culture, humanitarian emergencies, combating terrorism, ensuring active participation, and defending a 'unified position on issues of common interest in the international fora'.[13] The objectives also contain some religious-specific clauses:

To disseminate, promote and preserve the Islamic teachings and values based on moderation and tolerance, promote Islamic culture and safeguard Islamic heritage;
    To protect and defend the true image of Islam, to combat defamation of Islam and encourage dialogue among civilisations and religions.[14]

Not least, the OIC undertakes to 'promote and to protect human rights and fundamental freedoms including the rights of women, children, youth, elderly and people with special needs as well as the preservation of Islamic family values'.[15]

---

[7] Charter of the Islamic Conference (1972); Charter of the Organization of the Islamic Conference (adopted 14 March 2008). (Hereafter OIC Charter (2008)). See also S. Mahmoudi, 'Organization of the Islamic Conference (OIC)', in R. Wolfrum (ed.), *MPEPIL*, (Online edition: Oxford University Press, 2009), para. 1.

[8] M. B. Aykan, 'The Palestinian Question in Turkish Foreign Policy from the 1950s to the 1990s', 25 *International Journal of Middle East Studies* 1 (February 1993) 91–110, at 95.

[9] See 'About the OIC'. See also OIC Charter (2008), art. 1.8.

[10] See notably the 'defamation of religions' agenda promoted by the OIC at the UN Human Rights Council. See Chapter 2, III.2.

[11] Charter of the Islamic Conference (1972), preamble.

[12] OIC Charter (2008), art. 2.   [13] OIC Charter (2008), art.1.

[14] OIC Charter (2008), arts. 1.11 and 1.12.   [15] OIC Charter (2008), art. 1.14.

Certainly, the most important formal indication of the attachment to religion in the Charter is the criterion that restricts membership of the OIC to 'member[s] of the United Nations, having Muslim majority'.[16] At the time of writing, the Organization brings together 57 member states from Africa, Asia, Europe and Latin America[17] and describes itself as 'the collective voice of the Muslim world'.[18]

Having shown that the OIC has the features of a religious actor for the purpose of this study, notwithstanding its political features, a clarification needs to be made: the OIC does not attempt to unite Muslim nations into a single state. The Islamic concept of *umma* mentioned by OIC documents,[19] which might suggest such an undertaking, signifies the community of believers where solidarity and unity are best expressed.[20] Despite emphasizing the unity of believers, the overarching goal of the OIC is not to achieve a Muslim nation; there is, it is asserted, no higher ambition to trespass across state borders.[21] The prominence of the principles of sovereignty, independence, and territorial integrity in the constitutive Charter,[22] reinforced by the 2008 Charter,[23] led scholars to conclude that the existence of the OIC per se 'rejects the core legal doctrine defining the dar al-islam, namely, that *universal Islamic law* [binds] all Muslims, including their rulers'.[24] Yet, while they deny that the OIC is 'a resurrection of juridical notions of the dar al-islam, or even an attempt to accommodate modern realities to pre-modern Islamic theories of the relations among Muslim States', scholars draw attention to the ambivalence of contemporary Muslim states, between their Islamic heritage, on one hand, and modern international law on the other.[25] As Mohammad Fadel explains:

Whether to continue to legitimize the State in Islamic (or quasi-Islamic) terms or only on nationalist grounds was vigorously debated in post-World War I Egypt... This same debate

---

[16] OIC Charter (2008), art. 3.2. In this context a peculiarity should be noted. The two OIC member states from Latin America, Guyana and Suriname, as well as some African members such as Cameroon, Mozambique, Togo and Uganda, do not have Muslim majorities.

[17] The member states of the OIC (as listed on the Organization's website in June 2012) are: Afghanistan, Albania, Algeria, Azerbaijan, Bahrain, Bangladesh, Benin, Brunei Darussalam, Burkina Faso, Cameroon, Chad, Comoros, Côte d'Ivoire, Djibouti, Egypt, Gabon, Gambia, Guinea, Guinea-Bissau, Guyana, Indonesia, Iran (Islamic Rep.), Iraq, Jordan, Kazakhstan, Kuwait, Kyrgyzstan, Lebanon, Libyan Arab Jamahiriya, Malaysia, Maldives, Mali, Mauritania, Morocco, Mozambique, Niger, Nigeria, Oman, Pakistan, Palestine, Qatar, Saudi Arabia, Senegal, Sierra Leone, Somalia, Sudan, Suriname, Syrian Arab Republic, Tajikistan, Togo, Tunisia, Turkey, Turkmenistan, Uganda, United Arab Emirates, Uzbekistan, and Yemen. See http://www.oic-oci.org/member_states. asp, accessed December 2011. Note that the OIC lists Palestine as a member state.

[18] See 'About the OIC'.

[19] Including by the revised OIC Charter (2008), arts. 7, 9, 10.3 and 27.

[20] Mahmoudi, 'Organization of the Islamic Conference (OIC)', *MPEPIL* (2009), para. 5.

[21] See note 20.   [22] Charter of the Islamic Conference (1972), art. II.B.

[23] OIC Charter (2008), preamble, arts. 1.3, 2.2 and 2.4.

[24] M. Fadel, 'International Law, Regional Developments: Islam', in R. Wolfrum (ed.), *MPEPIL*, (Online edition: Oxford University Press, 2009), para. 56. (Emphasis added); see also H. Moinuddin, *The Charter of the Islamic Conference and Legal Framework of Economic Co-operation Among Its Member States: A Study of the Charter, the General Agreement for Economic, Technical, and Commercial Co-operation and the Agreement for Promotion, Protection, and Guarantee of Investments Among Member States of the OIC*, (Oxford: Clarendon Press, 1987), at 84–85.

[25] Fadel, 'International Law, Regional Developments: Islam', *MPEPIL* (2009), para. 56; see also M. Khadduri, 'Islam and the Modern Law of Nations', 50 *AJIL* 2 (1956) 358–372, at 369–372; Mahmoudi, 'Organization of the Islamic Conference (OIC)', *MPEPIL* (2009), para. 5.

occurred in other Muslim countries with the result that contemporary Muslim countries are committed both to general international norms as well as a vague set of weak and idiosyncratic international commitments arising out of vague sentiments of Islamic solidarity.[26]

Therefore, while the OIC is undoubtedly an inter-governmental organization formed of sovereign states, and is not an enterprise that aims to reshape borders based on a common religion, the Organization and some of its members communicate the ambivalence described above between adherence to norms of international law and their Islamic heritage.

It is against this background that the OIC's role of interpreter of human rights and Islam crystallizes. The performance of this role is complicated however by the rich diversity of its membership. To start with, it is important to recall that the OIC is formed of countries that embrace one of the two major branches of Islam, Sunni and Shia, that some states have Sufi minorities, and indeed minorities of other denominations. The Sunni and Shia branches are further divided into various schools of legal thought.[27]

The religion-state relationship in the constitutional architecture of these states varies considerably, and there is also important variation concerning the role of sharia law[28] as a source of legislation. In a comparative analysis, Nisrine Abiad identifies states in which Islamic law is not a source of legislation (such as Turkey, to which we could add Albania and Tajikistan); is the sole source of law (Iran, Pakistan, Saudi Arabia); is an important but not exclusive source (Egypt, Yemen); or in which Islam is the state religion (Libya, Malaysia, Morocco).[29] In the last two categories, personal status and family code are most usually governed by sharia law. One can further differentiate between states in which the legislature adopts the family code (Egypt, Morocco) and ones in which religious authorities are responsible for personal status law (Lebanon, and partly in Bahrain).[30] The substance of sharia law (or Islamic law) can take 'the form of positive law or prescriptive norms and moral exhortations' that are 'derived from a methodological interpretation of the Quran and the Sunnah'.[31] It can be codified or not.

---

[26] Fadel, 'International Law, Regional Developments: Islam', *MPEPIL* (2009), para. 54.

[27] There are four schools of jurisprudence for Sunni Islam and three for Shia. See A. M. Emon, 'Conceiving Islamic Law in a Pluralist Society: History, Politics and Multicultural Jurisprudence', *Singapore Journal of Legal Studies* (2006), 331–355, at 335; B. Gartner, *Der religionsrechtliche Status islamischer und islamistischer Gemeinschaften*, (Wien, New York: Springer, 2011), at 8–17.

[28] If not part of a citation, the forms 'sharia' and 'Quran' will be used throughout the paper.

[29] Abiad, *Sharia, Muslim States and International Human Rights Treaty Obligations: A Comparative Study*, at 5–19. See also Stahnke and Blitt, 'The Religion-State Relationship and the Right to Freedom of Religion or Belief: A Comparative Textual Analysis of the Constitutions of Predominantly Muslim Countries', at 958–961.

[30] Abiad, *Sharia, Muslim States and International Human Rights Treaty Obligations: A Comparative Study*, at 32–58. See also Stahnke and Blitt, 'The Religion-State Relationship and the Right to Freedom of Religion or Belief: A Comparative Textual Analysis of the Constitutions of Predominantly Muslim Countries', at 958–961.

[31] Abiad, *Sharia, Muslim States and International Human Rights Treaty Obligations: A Comparative Study*, at xviii; M. A. Baderin, 'Islamic Law and the Interpretation of International Human Rights Law: A Case Study of the International Covenant on Civil and Political Rights', in M. A. Baderin and M. Ssenyonjo (eds.), *International Human Rights Law: Six Decades after the UDHR and Beyond*, (Aldershot: Ashgate 2010), 337–359, at 340–341.

Cultural and political differences—in terms of both systems and priorities—among OIC member states are as much a feature of the Organization as religious identity. Perhaps this point cannot be emphasized enough. Tensions between Iran and Saudi Arabia, for example, are driven by a combination of factors, including differences associated with the different branches of Islam, *Realpolitik*, and ambitions for political influence in the region. As the recent conflict in Syria shows, the Syrian government apparently has more in common with China and Russia than with many of the OIC's members. The efforts involved in passing 'defamation of religions' resolutions, as discussed in Chapter 2, have been shouldered by few states, while other OIC members, had reservations, if not vocal ones. There is, in summary, a remarkable diversity within the Organization. A recurrent theme of this chapter is that it would be more precise for the OIC to attempt to articulate human rights in Muslim *contexts* rather than in *the* Muslim context.

III. Regionalism and Cultural Relativism

The OIC is not *stricto sensu* a regional organization, since, as pointed out, it is not geography which is the binding element but Muslim identity. To explain the interest of this chapter in regionalism, within the fragmentation framework, and in cultural relativism as a possible expression of regionalism, we will draw on Malcolm D. Evans' observation concerning the OIC (and the Western Europe and Others Group):

In terms of the diplomacy of international human rights protection these groupings...are of major significance and comprise elements of what might be best termed as 'regionalism of ideas' rather than a regionalism based on geography and which is all the more potent for that. One might pause to ponder how elements of the international human rights community might react to the creation of an 'Islamic Court of Human Rights'. Such an entity would be a regional human rights court, after a fashion.[32]

Indeed, this part will first show that regional human rights systems after a 'fashion' are accommodated by international law, while their norms are subjected to few but important conditions. There is also a pull towards a coherent interpretation of their various norms with general norms. The OIC's attempt to interpret, codify, and apply human rights is not a peculiarity per se. Second, regionalism appearing under the guise of cultural relativism will be discussed, in an attempt to understand the extent to which the OIC's interpretation of human rights in the context of Islam has the effect of creating exceptions to universality or applying universal norms in a context-sensitive manner.

---

[32] M. D. Evans, 'The Future(s) of Regional Courts of Human Rights', in A. Cassese (ed.), *Realizing Utopia: The Future of International Law*, (Oxford: Oxford University Press, 2012) 261–274, at 271. It should be mentioned in this context that the OIC Charter provides for an Islamic International Court of Justice, which is not functional however at the time of writing. OIC Charter (2008), art. 14.

1. The fragmentation framework and regionalism

Theories on the fragmentation of international law draw on a narrative that links globalization to the expansion of legal activity into a multitude of new fields. The globalized world is characterized not only by interconnectivity, but also by the advent of relatively autonomous, specialized rules and rule-systems, complexes or regimes.[33] Georges Abi-Saab appeals to a norm of legal physics to explain the phenomenon: 'To each level of normative density, there corresponds a level of institutional density necessary to sustain the norms.'[34] Mirroring this development, fragmentation has become a buzzword in the legal field, if not a paradigm of international law. Fragmentation has been identified in the context of trade, environment, and human rights law and various special regimes have been analysed with a focus on their fragmentation potential.[35] The pervasive concern is that:

specialized law-making and institution-building tends to take place with relative ignorance of legislative and institutional activities in the adjoining fields and of the general principles and practices of international law. The result is conflicts between rules or rule-systems, deviating institutional practices and, possibly, the loss of an overall perspective on the law.[36]

The ILC report on fragmentation notes that 'when…deviations become general and frequent, the unity of the law suffers'.[37] At the same time, the great strength of this report lies in its insistence that there is nothing entirely new, or predestined to be disastrous, in the fragmentation of international law: it is mainly states, international bodies, and legal professionals who contribute to fragmentation and they too manage the process by solving, via legal techniques and reasoning, conflicts that arise between special regimes and between the latter and general law.[38] Both fragmentation, and efforts to recreate a coherent system, appear as deconstruction and reconstruction processes. The ILC itself becomes an actor in this process, in as far as it strips 'self-contained regimes' of their autarchy and rebrands them as 'special regimes'.[39] The reason for this move lies in the inappropriateness of the term

---

[33] ILC, Fragmentation Report, 2006, paras. 7–9.

[34] G. Abi-Saab, 'Fragmentation or Unification: Some Concluding Remarks', 31 *NYU J.L. & Pol.* (1999), 919–933, at 925.

[35] See for example A. Fischer-Lescano and G. Teubner, 'Regime-collisions: the Vain Search for Legal Unity in the Fragmentation of Global Law', 25 *Mich. J. Int'l L.* (2004), 999–1046; G. Hafner, 'Pros and Cons Ensuing from Fragmentation of International Law', 25 *Mich. J. Int'l L.* (2004), 849–863; M. Koskenniemi and P. Leino, 'Fragmentation of International Law? Postmodern Anxieties', 15 *Leiden J Int'l L* 3 (2002), 553–579; A. Lindroos and M. Mehling, 'Dispelling the Chimera of Self-Contained Regimes: International Law and the WTO', 16 *EJIL* 5 (2005), 857–877; H. Van Asselt, F. Sindico and M. A. Mehling, 'Global Climate Change and the Fragmentation of International Law', 30 *Law & Policy* 4 (2008), 423–449.

[36] ILC, Fragmentation Report, 2006, para. 8. [37] ILC, Fragmentation Report, 2006, para. 15.

[38] ILC, Fragmentation Report, 2006, para. 222. See also J. Pauwelyn, *Conflict of Norms in Public International Law: How WTO Law Relates to Other Rules of International Law*, (Cambridge: Cambridge University Press, 2003); A. Sadat-Akhavi, *Methods of Resolving Conflicts between Treaties*, (Leiden Bosten: Martinus Nijhoff, 2003); B. Simma and D. Pulkowski, 'Of Planets and the Universe: Self-contained Regimes in International Law', 17 *EJIL* 3 (2006), 483–529; Singh, 'The Potential of International Law: Fragmentation and Ethics', 23–43.

[39] ILC, Fragmentation Report, 2006, paras. 152.1 and 152.5.

'self-contained', because there is little support for the proposition that general law would be fully excluded from any regime.[40]

Continuing with this argument it could be said that applying, modifying, updating, or setting aside general law through *lex specialis* is possible. Nonetheless, a number of limitations apply to derogations by way of special laws. These cannot occur in the case of: a *jus cogens* norm;[41] law that benefits third parties (including individuals and non-state entities); obligations of general law that are of an integral or interdependent nature, have an *erga omnes* character or where practice has created a legitimate expectation of non-derogation; treaties that have a public law nature and constituent instruments of international organizations.[42] Specifically in relation to conflicts between human rights norms, in joining doctrine the ILC asserts that 'the one that is more favourable to the protected interest is usually held overriding. At least derogation to the detriment of the beneficiaries would seem precluded'.[43] There is also the pull towards harmonization or systemic integration, under the influence of article 31.3.c of the Vienna Convention on the Law of Treaties (VCLT), under which international obligations are interpreted by reference to the normative system, meaning by appeal to any relevant rules of international law applicable in the relations between the parties.[44]

The ILC discusses regionalism in the context of fragmentation. The caveat, stressed from the beginning, is that regionalism may have lost its autonomy as a legal concept.[45] The post-World War II process of uniformization of international law and the increased importance of functional differentiation, combined with the doctrinal and economic divisions and the diminishing significance of regional demarcations, have transformed the concept of regionalism into 'nothing more than an intermediate and undefined level between national and universal levels'.[46] It is worth noting that the VCLT does not include the concept of regional treaty law. In relation to custom, Mathias Forteau shows that, beyond international customary law, any custom (regional, local, or bilateral) is consensual in nature and

---

[40] ILC, Fragmentation Report, 2006, para. 152.5.

[41] The HRC enumerates, as norms of *jus cogens*, the prohibition of arbitrary deprivation of life; the prohibition of torture and cruel, inhuman or degrading treatment or punishment; the prohibition of taking of hostages; the non-imposition of collective punishments; the prohibition on arbitrary deprivations of liberty; and the fundamental principles of fair trial, including the presumption of innocence. HRC, *General Comment No. 29: States of Emergency (article 4)*, 31 July 2001, UN Doc. CCPR/C/21/Rev.1/Add.10, para. 11. The ILC lists: the prohibitions of aggression, genocide, slavery, racial discrimination, crimes against humanity, torture, the right to self-determination. ILC, Articles on Responsibility of States for Internationally Wrongful Acts, UN Doc. A/56/10 (2001), at 85. See also Clapham, *Human Rights Obligations of Non-State Actors*, at 87–91.

[42] ILC, Fragmentation Report, 2006, para. 109. See also para. 154 in relation to special regimes.

[43] ILC, Fragmentation Report, 2006, para. 108. See also W. Karl, 'Treaties, Conflicts between', *Encyclopaedia of Public International Law*, vol. I, (Amsterdam: Elsevier, 2000), at 939; S. A. Sadat-Akhavi, *Methods of Resolving Conflicts between Treaties* (Leiden: Martinus Nijhoff, 2003), at 213–231.

[44] ILC, Fragmentation Report, 2006, paras. 410–432.

[45] ILC, Fragmentation Report, 2006, para. 195.

[46] M. Forteau, 'Regional International Law', in R. Wolfrum (ed.), *MPEPIL*, (Online edition: Oxford University Press, 2006), para. 16; see also ILC, Fragmentation Report, 2006, para. 204. For the decline in importance of regional divisions see also C. Schreuer, 'Regionalism v. Universalism', 6 *EJIL* (1995) 477–499, at 498.

must be proven to be applied constantly and uniformly by all concerned states.[47] Arguably this has been the position taken by the International Court of Justice (ICJ) in the *Asylum* case. Colombia invoked the customary character of the right of a state in Latin America granting diplomatic asylum to qualify the nature of the offence of the asylum seeker by a unilateral and definitive decision, which in this case was to be binding on Peru. The ICJ asserted:

> But even if it could be supposed that such a custom existed between certain Latin American States only, it could not be invoked against Peru which, far from having by its attitude adhered to it, has, on the contrary, repudiated it...[48]

One aspect of regionalism that retained the attention of the ILC for its continued actuality in the context of fragmentation, refers to the question of universalism and regionalism in human rights law.[49] The ILC suggested two variants of it: first, cultural relativism that generates exceptions from universal human rights norms—which would be challenging to the extent that derogations that are to the detriment of beneficiaries of human rights are prohibited; and second, cultural relativism that applies universal human rights standards in a context-sensitive manner.[50] This second interpretation 'would fall under the more general question of the relationship between general and special law, no different from the general problem of the applicability and limits of *lex specialis*'.[51] In this sense, Christina Cerna asserts that 'there are no regional human rights norms; there are only regional arrangements which supervise compliance with international standards'.[52]

In conclusion, nothing prevents the OIC from adopting legal instruments, including in the area of human rights, or from setting up mechanisms for their monitoring or adjudication. What applies to other regional organizations applies to the OIC, regardless of its religious contours. However, OIC instruments—like those of non-religious peers—are subject to limits: they may not derogate from *jus cogens* or treaty law benefitting third parties. In this regard, the Vienna Declaration of the World Conference on Human Rights encourages the establishment of regional arrangements for the promotion and protection of human rights where they do not exist, and the strengthening of those that do; it is clear that the aim of these arrangements should not be to carve out exceptions from human rights law by means of regional law but to 'reinforce universal human rights standards, as contained in international human rights instruments and their protection'.[53] The

---

[47] Forteau, 'Regional International Law', para. 20.

[48] *Colombian-Peruvian Asylum Case*, Judgment, ICJ Reports 1950, p. 266, at 277–278. See also *Case concerning Right of Passage over Indian Territory (Merits)*, Judgment, ICJ Reports 1960, p. 6, at 40.

[49] The other aspect refers to regional organizations in the context of collective security. ILC, Fragmentation Report, 2006, paras. 216, 217.

[50] ILC, Fragmentation Report, 2006, para. 216.

[51] ILC, Fragmentation Report, 2006, para. 216.

[52] C. M. Cerna, 'Universality of Human Rights and Cultural Diversity: Implementation of Human Rights in Different Socio-cultural Contexts', 16 *HRQ* (1994), 740–752, at 752.

[53] Vienna Declaration and Programme of Action, 25 June 1993, UN Doc. A/CONF.157/23, para. 37. See also Cerna, 'Universality of Human Rights and Cultural Diversity: Implementation of Human Rights in Different Socio-cultural Contexts', at 752.

issue of consistency arises for the OIC too: its member states are party to several human rights treaties and are under an obligation to perform them in good faith; all Muslim states are bound by human rights norms that have a customary character; and, the OIC itself, as will be argued in this chapter, is bound by human rights obligations.[54]

In consequence, this study needs to answer several questions: What forms of regionalism does the OIC apply in the field of human rights? Does the OIC strive to create exceptions to human rights norms or to apply universal human rights in ways that are sensitive to context? If the latter, what does a 'sensitive' application mean in Muslim contexts? Before these questions can be answered (by analysing the CDHRI, the CRCI and the Statute of the OIC IPHRC in part III), it is important to appreciate how cultural relativism has been understood in anthropology and human rights law. It is submitted that insights from anthropology may be helpful in understanding the potential role of the OIC as interpreter of human rights in the context of Islam.

2. Cultural relativism: from challenging the universality of human rights to forging their legitimacy

When drafting of the Universal Declaration of Human Rights (UDHR) began, anthropologists were requested to provide their input. As Ellen Messer explains, American cultural anthropologists recognized that all societies have some basis for evaluating and enforcing correct or permissible human behaviour and that both individuals and societies 'refer to some superhuman or legal authority (national constitution or international treaty) as the basis for behavioral norms':[55] yet this was not the input they provided to the drafters of the UDHR. Franz Boas and Melville Herskovitis, alongside other cultural relativists, were challenging ethnocentrism and imperialism and were preoccupied by the violations of the rights of tribal people, who the Western world judged to be 'primitive' with backward and inferior cultures and customs.[56] Against this background, the American Anthropological Association (AAA) pronounced itself in 1947 *against* formulations of universal human rights and *for* cultural tolerance. In its Statement, it declared:

> Standards and values are relative to the culture from which they derive so that any attempt to formulate postulates that grow out of beliefs or moral codes of one culture must to that extent detract from the applicability of any Declaration of Human Rights to mankind as a whole.[57]

---

[54] See IV.1.2. in this chapter.

[55] E. Messer, 'Anthropology, Human Rights, and Social Transformation', in M. Goodale (ed.), *Human Rights: an Anthropological Reader*, (Oxford: Wiley-Blackwell, 2009) 103–134, at 109.

[56] American Anthropological Association, 'Statement on Human Rights', 49 *American Anthropologist* 4 (1947), 539–543; Messer, 'Anthropology, Human Rights, and Social Transformation', at 109–110.

[57] American Anthropological Association, 'Statement on Human Rights', at 542.

Since then, the aspect emphasized by those inside and outside the discipline is that tolerance of culture must have limits; criticism of political systems must be appropriate in some circumstances. Were this not so, for example, the conduct of the Nazi government in Germany would have to be tolerated without interference or criticism.[58] The 'embarrassment' caused by the AAA Statement to the discipline of anthropology is said to have plagued it for the past half century.[59] As Karen Engle explains, contemporary anthropologists are embarrassed by cultural relativism to the extent that it is associated with failure to condemn human rights violations; however, when it represents anti-racist or anti-colonial views, 'it would seem to be redeemed'.[60] It would appear that the challenge for pro-rights anthropologists, as well as for human rights scholars and practitioners, is to separate the two strands of relativism.[61] In 1999, the AAA went on to adopt a Declaration of Anthropology on Human Rights. It asserts that:

People and groups have a generic right to realize their capacity for culture, and to produce, reproduce and change the conditions and forms of their physical, personal and social existence, *so long as such activities do not diminish the same capacities of others*.[62]

The AAA grounds its approach to human rights in international legal instruments, but does not limit it to existing law, recognizing that human rights are evolving.[63] The realization that has been achieved is that it is acceptable to limit cultural tolerance in the name of universal human rights in certain conditions and that it is not acceptable to carve out exceptions to human rights law on grounds of culture.

A comparison of developments in the field of anthropology and in international human rights diplomacy is revealing. In the 1990s, as anthropologists came to engage more positively with human rights whilst reassessing cultural relativism in

---

[58] It should be noted that one paragraph of the AAA Statement, described as the 'Nazi Germany paragraph', is in a sense a safeguard, because it addresses the differences within culture and accepts that political systems may not be representative, and that therefore some limiting of tolerance must be acceptable. American Anthropological Association, 'Statement on Human Rights', at 543. K. Engle, 'From Skepticism to Embrace: Human Rights and the American Anthropological Association from 1947–1999', 23 *HRQ* 3 (2001), 536–559, at 542.

[59] Interestingly, initially the AAA Statement was found to be embarrassing because it acknowledged that there must be limits to tolerance. Later the discipline was embarrassed because those limits were not asserted forcefully enough. Engle, 'From Skepticism to Embrace: Human Rights and the American Anthropological Association from 1947–1999', at 536 ff.

[60] Engle, 'From Skepticism to Embrace: Human Rights and the American Anthropological Association from 1947–1999', at 551.

[61] In an attempt to separate the two strands of relativism, Alison Dundes Renteln embarked on a project to examine how universal rights resonate in different cultures. She argued that, essentially, relativism and universality need not be contradictory concepts in relation to human rights; but misrepresentations of relativism can lead to perceptions of incompatibility. See A. Dundes Renteln, 'Relativism and the Search for Human Rights', 90 *American Anthropologist* 1 (1988), 56–72. See also A. Dundes Renteln, *International Human Rights: Universalism versus Relativism*, (Newbury Park, California: Sage Publications, 1990); Engle, 'From Skepticism to Embrace: Human Rights and the American Anthropological Association from 1947–1999', at 551.

[62] American Anthropological Association, Committee for Human Rights, *Declaration on Anthropology and Human Rights*, 1999, accessed June 2012, http://www.aaanet.org/about/Policies/statements/Declaration-on-Anthropology-and-Human-Rights.cfm.

[63] See note 62.

their discipline, some states started to challenge the universality of human rights under the same cultural relativist banner. At the 1993 World Conference on Human Rights in Vienna, a group of states, including Asian and Islamic states, sought to 'redefine the content of the term "human rights"' as 'the principles enshrined in the Universal Declaration reflect Western values and not their own'. They claimed that, '[b]ecause of social and cultural differences in their countries...they should not be held to the same standards'.[64] Human rights scholars and practitioners put forward two main counter-claims against the charge of non-representativeness of human rights and for their universality. The first refers to the important contribution that a number of non-Western drafters made to the UDHR.[65] The second argues that the UDHR and 1966 Covenants represent a 'distillation' of the interaction of many cultures over time, and these texts cannot consequently be said to reflect only one stream of thought.[66] The Vienna Declaration on Human Rights, adopted by consensus, reaffirms the principle of universality 'again and again, almost to the point of redundancy'.[67]

The lesson some legal scholars took from Vienna is that it is not entirely helpful to dismiss all questions concerning the universality of human rights as revisionist. This is because human rights are meaningful when they are recognized to be legitimate.[68] In the absence of such recognition individuals in day-to-day situations suffer, regardless of the Vienna consensus. It is interesting, therefore, that human rights scholars and anthropologists have the same persistent preoccupation: they need human rights instruments to be convincing and meaningful for individuals and groups in particular cultural contexts. A second common feature is the need 'to rethink, not just relativism, but "its underlying assumption of 'culture' as a homogenous, integral, coherent unity"'.[69] This preoccupation acknowledges that

---

[64] Cerna, 'Universality of Human Rights and Cultural Diversity: Implementation of Human Rights in Different Socio-cultural Contexts', at 740.

[65] Charles Habib Malik of Lebanon, Peng-chun Chang of China, and Hansa Mehta from India are said to have made essential contributions during drafting of the UDHR. See M. A. Glendon, *The Forum and the Tower: How Scholars and Politicians Have Imagined the World, from Plato to Eleanor Roosevelt*, (New York: Oxford University Press, 2011), in particular 206–207 and 215. A rather important objection to the 'Western birth defect' of the UDHR is made by Christian Tomuschat, who acknowledges the presence and influence of the socialist states in the Human Rights Commission and General Assembly. C. Tomuschat, *Human Rights: Between Idealism and Realism*, (Oxford: Oxford University Press, 2003), at 63. Contrast with A.A. An-Na'im, 'Problems of Universal Cultural Legitimacy for Human Rights', in A.A. An-Na'im and F. M. Deng (eds.), *Human Rights in Africa: Cross-cultural Perspectives*, (Washington D.C.: Brookings Institution Press, 1990), 331–367, at 346–352.

[66] B. G. Ramcharan, 'The Universality of Human Rights', *Review—International Commission of Jurists* (1997), 105–117, at 105; Statement by Mary Robinson, United Nations High Commissioner for Human Rights, *The Universality of Human Rights*. Conference, Bonn, 11 November 1999.

[67] Cerna, 'Universality of Human Rights and Cultural Diversity: Implementation of Human Rights in Different Socio-cultural Contexts', at 742. See Vienna Declaration and Programme of Action, 25 June 1993, UN Doc. A/CONF.157/23, paras. 1, 5, 6, 8, 10,18, 32, 37.

[68] Cerna, 'Universality of Human Rights and Cultural Diversity: Implementation of Human Rights in Different Socio-cultural Contexts', at 752; Marks and Clapham, *International Human Rights Lexicon*, at 388.

[69] A.-B. S. Preis, 'Human Rights as Cultural Practice: An Anthropological Critique', 18 *HRQ* (1996), 286–315, at 288–289. As quoted in Engle, 'From Skepticism to Embrace: Human Rights and the American Anthropological Association from 1947–1999', at 558.

no culture exists in a pure form: cultures are constructed from the interactions that occur within them and with other cultures.

Lila Abu-Lughod illustrates this point. In an article on intervention in Afghanistan and 'the need to save Muslim women', the author emphasizes both 'the dangers of reifying culture, apparent in the tendencies to plaster neat cultural icons like the Muslim woman over messy historical and political dynamics' and the limits of cultural relativism.[70] In Abu-Lughod's words:

> Cultural relativism is certainly an improvement on ethnocentrism and the racism, cultural imperialism, and imperiousness that underlie it; the problem is that it is too late not to interfere. The forms of lives we find around the world are already products of long histories of interactions.[71]

In other words, the reality we see is not a pure state of culture (with religion understood as part of it), but a process constructed not only by actors inside the culture but by a constant interaction with outside influences. In the past, colonialism certainly had its share in this construction, as globalization does today. So, when states defend culture from outside interference, they defend a construct that already reflects the interaction between multiple selves and multiple others. Abu-Lughod's reflections are echoed by other scholars, who have considered Muslim contexts in particular:

> The contentious nature of Sharia's interpretation of individual rights and its arguable incompatibilities with modern paradigms of human rights law nevertheless have to take into account the historic inequities within which Islamic societies have operated. In the imperialistic and colonial struggles, Islamic communities found themselves overpowered and dominated by others, who were more strategic, manipulative and powerful. *Not only were indigenous Islamic laws disturbed or displaced by the misfortunes of colonialism, the Sharia as a legal system was not allowed a natural growth.* . . . In the urgency to build nation-States and to repress ethnic, cultural and religious identities, Islam and the Sharia were frequently used to repress pluralism and the rule of law.[72]

The conclusion is that, while it is unacceptable to create exceptions to human rights law in the name of culture, context-sensitive application of universal human rights should be permitted. But context-sensitive application should mean more than adoption of a margin of appreciation doctrine, based on the European model.[73] It should mean that, where the cultural legitimacy of universal human rights is felt to be lacking, this must be addressed, notably by recognizing that culture is constructed and can therefore be reconstructed or transformed. The dynamic approach suggested by Abdullahi Ahmed An-Na'im in the context of

---

[70] L. Abu-Lughod, 'Do Muslim Women Really Need Saving? Anthropological Reflections on Cultural Relativism and its Others', 104 *American Anthropologist* 3 (2002), 783–790, at 783.

[71] Abu-Lughod, 'Do Muslim Women Really Need Saving? Anthropological Reflections on Cultural Relativism and its Others', at 786–787.

[72] J. Rehman and S. Breau, 'Introductory Reflections', in J. Rehman and S. Breau (eds.), *Religion, Human Rights and International Law*, (Leiden: Martinus Nijhoff Publishers, 2007) 3–22, at 14. (Emphasis added).

[73] See IV.3.1. in this chapter.

Islam—which resonates beyond Muslim contexts—starts from the premise that 'scholars and activists should neither underestimate the challenges of relativism to the universality of human rights nor concede too much to its claims.'[74] His approach:

seeks to explore the possibilities of cultural reinterpretation and reconstruction through *internal cultural discourse and cross-cultural dialogue* [elsewhere termed critique], as a means to enhancing the universal legitimacy of human rights. This approach does not assume that sufficient cultural support for the full range of human rights is either completely present or completely lacking in any cultural tradition.[75]

This assumed-constructivist endeavour[76] starts from the premise that culture influences individual, collective, and institutional behaviour.[77] In turn, actors can shape culture. The aim of the approach is not to revise international human rights standards, and not particularly to undo a wrong of the past—the lack of representation of colonized people in the early days of the human rights movement.[78] The goal is to forge universal cultural legitimacy and, through 'enlightened interpretations of cultural norms',[79] increase the extent to which existing and also emerging human rights standards are perceived to be justified, proper, and appropriate. The result would be improved protection of human rights in practice.

If the above framework is applied, a discussion of sharia law and human rights law is not reduced to the dichotomy harmony-conflict, but focuses on the potential for change. At this point it is essential to make a clarification, necessary even though it has been made by many other writers before. It is a tenet of Islam that God communicated his will through revelations to the Prophet Muhammad, which are contained in the Quran; Muslim believers are expected to seek to understand God's will and to organize their life accordingly. However, as scholars note, the Quran does not include rules for all human interactions and, even where rules exist to address a situation, their implementation requires interpretation.[80] Sharia law 'is not really divine law in the sense that all its specific principles and detailed rules were directly revealed by God to the Prophet Muhammad.... Shari'a was constructed by the early Muslim jurists out of the fundamental sources of Islam,

---

[74] A.A. An-Na'im, 'Introduction', in A.A. An-Na'im (ed.), *Human Rights in Cross-Cultural Perspectives: A Quest for Consensus*, (Philadelphia, PA: University of Pennsylvania Press, 1992) 1–18, at 3.

[75] See note 74. (Emphasis in the original).

[76] See A.A. An-Na'im, 'Human Rights in the Muslim World: Socio-Political Conditions and Scriptural Imperatives—A Preliminary Inquiry', 3 *Harv. Hum. Rts. J.* (1990), 13–52, at 17.

[77] An-Na'im, 'Introduction', at 4.

[78] An-Na'im, 'Problems of Universal Cultural Legitimacy for Human Rights', at 347–352; An-Na'im, 'Toward a Cross-Cultural Approach to Defining International Standards of Human Rights: The Meaning of Cruel, Inhuman or Degrading Treatment or Punishment', at 21.

[79] An-Na'im, 'Toward a Cross-Cultural Approach to Defining International Standards of Human Rights: The Meaning of Cruel, Inhuman or Degrading Treatment or Punishment', at 20–21; see also Marks and Clapham, *International Human Rights Lexicon*, at 394–396.

[80] Krivenko Yahyaoui, *Women, Islam and International Law: within the context of the Convention on the Elimination of All Forms of Discrimination against Women* (Leiden: Martinus Nijhoff Publishers, 2009), at 46–48.

namely the Qur'an and Sunna' and other traditions.[81] *Fiqh* represents the developing jurisprudence of sharia, i.e. the reasoned reflections of Muslim scholars and jurists 'concerning what they consider the Shari'a to require of Muslims in the particular time and locality they find themselves', as well as the method of deducing such opinions.[82] The potential for change is embedded in sharia law:

[B]ecause Shari'a is always the product of human interpretation of divine sources, any interpretation of it will reflect the human limitations of those who are interpreting it, despite the divinity of the sources they are working with. From this perspective Shari'a will always remain open to reinterpretation and evolution, in response to the constantly changing needs of Islamic societies and communities in different times and places.[83]

To conclude this section on regionalism and cultural relativism, some observations concerning the role of the OIC as interpreter of human rights in the context of Islam can be made. Were the OIC to embrace a context-sensitive application of universal human rights, it would have to ensure that its human rights instruments do not derogate from human rights law benefitting individuals and groups. In addition, it would seem that its most important role could be to forge cultural legitimacy for human rights standards by promoting interpretations of sharia which reinforce protection of human rights.

IV. The OIC: Between 'Religionalism' and Regionalism

This part first portrays the OIC as proposing, through the Cairo Declaration, a 'religionalism'. It will be shown that the CDHRI subjects universal human rights standards to sharia law by means of limitation clauses based on sharia and by declaring that Islamic law is the sole principle of interpretation of this non-binding instrument. At the same time, a detailed analysis of the reservations of Muslim states to international human rights treaties, if read in association with treaty body reviews and dialogues with objecting states, reveals that the majority of OIC states take a different position on the universality of human rights than the Cairo Declaration. They perceive sharia as amendable and acknowledge that reform within the framework of sharia is necessary if they are to comply fully with their international obligations. The influence of the CDHRI on OIC membership is explored, alongside the OIC's accountability and its obligation not to put obstacles to human rights compliance in the path of its member states. Second, the substantive provisions of

---

[81] A. A. An-Na'im, *Toward an Islamic Reformation: Civil Liberties, Human Rights and International Law*, (Syracuse: Syracuse University Press, 1990), at 11–33.

[82] R. Ahdar and N. Aroney, 'The Topography of Shari'a in the Western Political Landscape', in R. Ahdar and N. Aroney (eds.), *Shari'a in the West*, (Oxford: Oxford University Press, 2010), 1–31, at 3–4; see also L. A. Khan, 'Jurodynamics of Islamic Law', 61 *Rutgers Law Review* (2008), 231–293, at footnote 4.

[83] A.A. An-Na'im, *Islam and the Secular State: Negotiating the Future of Shari'a*, (Cambridge, MA: Harvard University Press, 2008), at 282–283. For a discussion on orthodox v. reform/liberal scholarship and how these schools define sharia, see Ahdar and Aroney, 'The Topography of Shari'a in the Western Political Landscape', at 4–6.

the CRCI—a legally binding document, not yet in force—are analysed, focusing on its religious particularities, as well as the stipulations that appear to strengthen human rights standards while responding to regional contexts. Finally, it examines the mandate, composition, and functioning of the OIC IPHRC and suggests how this body could positively influence human right situations in the OIC region.

1. The Cairo Declaration on Human Rights in Islam

The OIC Islamic Conference of Foreign Ministers, one of the main decision-making bodies of the Organization adopted the CDHRI on 5 August 1990. The intended aim of the Cairo Declaration was to 'serve as a general guidance for Member States in the field of human rights'.[84] The CDHRI was presented as the contribution of the OIC to the World Conference on Human Rights in Vienna.[85]

It is important to emphasize from the start that the Cairo Declaration is a non-binding legal instrument. As such, it does not have the legal capacity to either derogate or set aside human rights law. Moreover, as this section will demonstrate, there is no evidence that the Declaration or parts of it may have attained a customary character. Therefore, when the following analysis mentions 'deviations' or 'departures' from human rights standards, it is not being suggested that the legal effect of the Declaration is to derogate or set aside human rights norms. The aim of the section is, first, to show how some of the (non-binding) provisions of the Cairo Declaration differ from those in the UDHR and human rights treaties to which OIC member states are party and, second, to discuss what influence the instrument has had on Muslim states and whether it can report any success in promoting and protecting human rights.

1.1. Human rights law 'in accordance with Islamic Shari'ah'

The Cairo Declaration does not reject human rights standards outright; however, three features of the Declaration deserve careful attention: the silence concerning certain rights which are well established and enshrined in human rights instruments to which Muslim states are party; limitations based on sharia attached to other rights and the general limitation clause based on sharia; and a clause that stipulates that sharia is the only source of interpretation of the Declaration.

1.1.1. The missing rights
To begin with the first feature, the Cairo Declaration does not include provisions on certain rights that are well established in human rights treaty law. Notably, the rights to freedom of assembly and association are absent from the Cairo Declaration. This

---

[84] OIC, Resolution No. 49/19-P, Nineteenth Islamic Conference of Foreign Ministers, Cairo, 5 August 1990, art. 1. The Cairo Declaration on Human Rights in Islam, hereafter CDHRI, was annexed to the resolution.
[85] Conférence mondiale sur les droits de l'homme, Comité préparatoire, Quatrième session, Genève, 19 avril-7 mai 1993, UN Doc. A/CONF.157/PC/62/Add.18.

silence on the part of the CDHRI contrasts with the protection afforded to these rights by the UDHR,[86] the International Covenant on Civil and Political Rights (ICCPR),[87] the International Covenant on Economic, Social and Cultural Rights (ICESCR),[88] African, European and Inter-American treaties on human rights,[89] and a number of International Labour Organization conventions that affirm the rights of workers to organize and bargain through trade unions[90]—to all of which several OIC member states are party. There is no religious explanation for the absence of the right to freedom of assembly or association. This has led Ann Elizabeth Meyer to suggest that the silence of the Declaration in respect to these rights is better explained by the fact that some OIC member states have a history of restricting the freedoms of assembly and association and suppressing protest and advocacy.[91]

Importantly, the Cairo Declaration does not sanction the right to freedom of religion, beyond some vague and controversial provisions on religious education (in article 9) and coerced religious conversion (in article 10). Article 9.a. states:

The State shall ensure the availability of ways and means to acquire education and shall guarantee educational diversity in the interest of society so as to enable man to be acquainted with the religion of Islam and the facts of the Universe for the benefit of mankind.[92]

It is unclear whether this guarantee to educational diversity includes religious education beyond Islam. It would seem that the first part of the sentence is qualified by the second. While proclaiming Islam as 'the religion of unspoiled nature', article 10 stipulates that it is 'prohibited to exercise any form of compulsion on man or to exploit his poverty or ignorance in order to convert him to another religion or to atheism'.[93] Since, apparently, compulsion and exploitation are prohibited by the CDHRI only when they are 'employed to convert a Muslim to another faith or atheism, not when [they are] used to make someone adopt Islam', one scholar interprets this ban on proselytism by coercion as one-sided and distortive of the principle set forth in article 18.2 of the ICCPR.[94]

The issue of forced conversion, persecution, harassment, and denial of the right to manifest religion of non-Muslims from Southern Sudan was invoked in *Amnesty International and Others v. Sudan*.[95] The African Commission on Human and Peoples' Rights (AComHPR) found the state party to be in violation of its

---

[86] UDHR, arts. 20 and 23.4.   [87] ICCPR, arts. 21 and 22.
[88] ICESCR, art. 8.   [89] ACHPR, arts. 10 and 11; ECHR, art. 11; ACHR, arts. 15 and 16.
[90] ILO Convention 87—Freedom of Association and Protection of the Right to Organise Convention (1948); ILO Convention 98—Right to Organise and Collective Bargaining Convention (1949); ILO Convention 135 (1978); ILO Convention 151 (1987). See also Human Rights Education Associates, Freedom of assembly and association, accessed November 2011, http://www.hrea.org/index.php?doc_id=406#instruments.
[91] A. E. Mayer, 'Universal versus Islamic Human Rights: A Clash of Cultures or Clash with a Construct', 15 *Mich. J. Int'l L.* 2 (1994), 307–404, at 337.
[92] CDHRI, art. 9.   [93] CDHRI, art. 10.
[94] Mayer, 'Universal versus Islamic Human Rights: A Clash of Cultures or Clash with a Construct', at 334–335.
[95] *Amnesty International, Comité Loosli Bachelard, Lawyers Committee for Human Rights, Association of Members of the Episcopal Conference of East Sudan v. Sudan*, Communication nos. 48/90-50/91-52/91-89/93 (1999), paras. 20 and 76.

obligation concerning religious freedom and put forward a number of important findings concerning the subjection of non-Muslims *and* Muslims to sharia tribunals.

When Sudanese tribunals apply Shari'a, they must do so in accordance with the other obligations undertaken by the State of Sudan. Trials must always accord with international fair-trial standards. Also, it is fundamentally unjust that religious laws should be applied against non-adherents of the religion. Tribunals that apply only Shari'a are thus not competent to judge non-Muslims, and everyone should have the right to be tried by a secular court if they wish.[96]

In so far as it held that an individual has an explicit right to choose a secular court over a religious tribunal if she so wishes, the AComHPR buttresses and enhances the scope of the right to equality before the courts, as interpreted by the Human Rights Committee (HRC) in its General Comment 32.[97] The right to choose a secular court appears to stem, in the AComHPR's reasoning, from the individual's right to religious freedom. It presupposes that states that use a religious court system provide alternatives not only for individuals of different faiths, but also for those who share the religion according to which the court hands down its rulings.

Returning to the Cairo Declaration, it must be observed that the few stipulations on the *forum externum* and *internum* of freedom of religion fall short of the UDHR and the ICCPR standards, and also those of the African Charter on Human and Peoples' Rights (ACHPR).[98]

As discussed in Chapter 1 of this study, change of religion has been the subject of controversy during the drafting of international human rights instruments.[99] The *travaux préparatoires* of the UDHR and ICCPR show that some Muslim states opposed the inclusion of change of religion in those instruments. Often cited is an amendment by Saudi Arabia which sought to exclude change of religion from article 18 of the UDHR, motivated by the need to 'prevent missionaries from abusing the right based on political motivations'.[100] It should be mentioned at this stage that apostasy is considered a crime of *hudud*, which, according to certain interpretations of sharia, triggers the death sentence.[101] Natan Lerner suggests

---

[96] *Amnesty International, Comité Loosli Bachelard, Lawyers Committee for Human Rights, Association of Members of the Episcopal Conference of East Sudan v. Sudan*, para. 72.

[97] The HRC held that religious courts should not hand down binding judgments recognized by states unless the proceedings deal with minor civil and criminal matters, meet fair trial requirements, and their judgments are validated by state courts and can be challenged by the parties concerned in a procedure meeting fair trial requirements under the ICCPR. HRC, *General Comment No. 32*, para. 24.

[98] Contrast CDHRI, arts. 9, 10 to UDHR, art 18; ICCPR, art. 18; and ACHPR, art. 8.

[99] See Chapter 1, III.

[100] In the end, Saudi Arabia was the only Muslim state to abstain when the UDHR was approved; Egypt, Lebanon, Iran, and Pakistan voted in favour. Lerner, 'Proselytism, Change of Religion, and International Human Rights', at 502–503.

[101] Crimes of *hudud* are explicitly identified in the Quran and the Sunnah. They are defined as violations of the claims of God and their penalization (under certain interpretations of sharia) is said to be aimed at protecting public interest in Muslim society. The crimes are: theft, punishable by amputation of a hand; rebellion/armed robbery, requiring death, crucifixion, cross-amputation of the hand and foot or banishment; adultery and extra-marital sex, requiring 100 lashes; false accusation of adultery or extra-marital sex, requiring 80 lashes; apostasy, punishable by death; intoxication, punishable by

that this explains the opposition to the language on change of religion that Saudi Arabia and other Muslim states proposed, particularly those states where sharia was part of the positive law.[102] In contrast, Thomas Franck emphasizes the following argument put forward by the Pakistani delegate in favour of the Saudi amendment:

Sir Zafrullah Khan, admitted that 'the problem. . . involved the honour of Islam.' He added, however, that 'the Moslem religion had unequivocally proclaimed the right to freedom of conscience and had declared itself against any kind of compulsion in matters of faith or religious practice.' Ambassador Khan quoted the Koran: 'Let he who chooses to believe, believe, and he who chooses to disbelieve, disbelieve'.[103]

The Pakistani representative's declaration seems to suggest that while the change of religion is opposed as a matter of 'honour', within Islam, religious interpretations can be found which accommodate confessional conversion.

Be that as it may, most Muslim states have ratified the ICCPR, which avoids the explicit stipulation 'to change' but retains the expression 'to adopt a religion' in article 18.[104] It is noteworthy that the majority of these states have not entered reservations to this article.[105] The Declaration on the Elimination of All Forms of Intolerance and of Discrimination Based on Religion or Belief of 1981 portrays a further inconsistent practice of Muslim states. While insisting that language stipulating either 'change of' or 'adoption of' religion is not inserted in the Declaration, OIC member states agreed to article 8 which provides that 'nothing in the present Declaration shall be construed as restricting or derogating from any right defined in the Universal Declaration of Human Rights and the International Covenants on Human Rights'.[106] According to Roger S. Clark, the importance of article 8 cannot be overstated, given that it 'allays any fears that the Declaration is a retrograde rather than a progressive step'.[107]

---

flogging (40 or 80 lashes). See Abiad, *Sharia, Muslim States and International Human Rights Treaty Obligations: A Comparative Study*, at 5; E. Peiffer, 'The Death Penalty in Traditional Islamic Law and as Interpreted in Saudi Arabia and Nigeria', 11 *William and Mary Journal of Women and the Law* (2004), 507–539, at 511–515.

[102] Lerner, 'Proselytism, Change of Religion, and International Human Rights', at 503.

[103] As cited in T. M. Franck, 'Is Personal Freedom a Western Value', 91 *AJIL* (1997), 593–627, at 601.

[104] ICCPR, art. 18. The inclusion in the UDHR of the term 'to adopt a religion' rather than the term 'change' is said to have been 'a concession of the West' to Muslim states. R. S. Clark, 'The United Nations Declaration on the Elimination of All Forms of Intolerance and Discrimination Based on Religion or Belief', 31 *Chitty's Law Journal* (1983), 23–39, at 37–38.

[105] Bahrain, the Maldives, and Mauritania have formulated explicit reservations to freedom of religion, limiting the application of article 18 of the ICCPR and requiring the compatibility with Islamic sharia or as in the case of the Maldives with its Constitution, which in turn stipulates sharia as source of legislation. See UNTC, Online Database, Chapter IV: Human Rights, International Covenant on Civil and Political Rights, accessed June 2012.

[106] Declaration on the Elimination of All Forms of Intolerance and of Discrimination Based on Religion or Belief, art. 8.

[107] Clark, 'The United Nations Declaration on the Elimination of All Forms of Intolerance and Discrimination Based on Religion or Belief', at. 28.

Overall, it would appear that there is no consistent practice of the OIC member states concerning freedom of religion. Even if it were to be accepted that, in relation to the right to change one's religion, several Muslim states have been persistent objectors, not all OIC member states could make that claim. Nor can the persistent objection argument—a doctrine the validity of which is questioned[108]—extend to the right to freedom of religion in its entirety (that is, internal and external fora). Based on the discussion as laid out here, the silence of the Cairo Declaration, drafted as guidance in the realm of human rights for all Muslim states, does not reflect the practice of all Muslim states; it raises questions however for all OIC member states, if one accepts that freedom of religion has acquired the status of international custom and is therefore generally binding.[109] In any event, the OIC members that are state parties to the ICCPR are bound to uphold international legal obligations that flow from article 18 of the ICCPR, which cannot be derogated from.[110]

1.1.2. Sharia limitation clauses

The Islamic limitation clauses certainly distinguish the Cairo Declaration from other human rights instruments. The CDHRI puts forward rights in a discreetly altered form, which may involve significant alterations of substance. Rights and freedoms in the CDHRI are qualified, and thus limited by provisions such as 'except for' or 'without a Shari'ah prescribed reason'; 'as would not be contrary to the principles of the Shari'ah'; 'in accordance with ethical values', the 'tenets', the 'principles' or the 'provisions of the Shari'ah'; and 'within the framework of the Shari'ah'.[111] Article 2 on the right to life, article 7 on the rights of the child, article 12 on freedom of movement, article 16 on property rights, article 19 on aspects of criminal justice, article 22 on freedom of expression, and article 23 on democratic freedoms are subjected to such religious limitations.[112] However, these qualifications would have been unnecessary in the face of the sweeping Islamic limitation clause in article 24 which provides that '[a]ll the rights and freedoms stipulated in this Declaration are subject to the Islamic Shari'ah.'[113]

It is uncontested that states have the right to use limitation clauses in international human rights instruments to lawfully restrict the free exercise of some human rights. A proper understanding of human rights requires an acknowledgement of the permanent balance that needs to be negotiated between the interests of the individual and those of society.[114] Nonetheless, the same human rights logic requires that the relation between a right and a restriction, and between a norm

---

[108] Patrick Dumberry shows that there is very weak judicial recognition of the theory of persistent objector and no actual State practice: '[t]here are no instances where such a claimed special status actually prevented the application of customary rule to the dissenting State.' See P. Dumberry, 'Incoherent and Ineffective: the Concept of Persistent Objector Revisited', 59 *ICLQ* 3, 779–802.

[109] See Chapter 1, III.4.   [110] See Chapter 1, III.1.

[111] CDHRI, arts. 2, 7, 12, 16, 19, 22, and 23.

[112] CDHRI, arts. 2, 7, 12, 16, 19, 22, and 23.   [113] CDHRI, art. 24.

[114] See M. E. Badar, 'Basic Principles Governing Limitations on Individual Rights and Freedoms in Human Rights Instruments', 7 *The International Journal of Human Rights* 4 (2004), 63–92, at 63.

and exceptions to it, may not be reversed to empty the right of its substantive protection.[115] Accordingly, jurisprudence at regional and international level shows a restrictive reading of limitations. As an example, the doctrine of implied or inherent limitations on rights that are already defined and qualified in a convention has fallen into desuetude.[116]

While general limitation clauses are present in the UDHR[117] and the ICESCR,[118] express restrictions on rights are the norm in more recent human rights treaties. This evolution from general limitation clauses to specific restrictions on rights is considered a 'significant element in the development' of human rights instruments.[119] In this context, the closest provision to the wide limitation clause in article 24 of the Cairo Declaration is a clawback clause[120] of the ACHPR, which is nonetheless far less wide-reaching in nature. It reads: 'The rights and freedoms of each individual shall be exercised with due regard to the rights of others, collective security, morality and common interest'.[121] The African Commission interpreted this clause to accord the maximum protection to the individual and, to use Inger Österdahl's graphic remark, gave it the 'death-blow':[122]

The reasons for possible limitations must be founded in a legitimate state interest and the evils of limitations of rights must be strictly proportionate with and absolutely necessary for the advantages which are to be obtained....Even more important, a limitation may never have as a consequence that the right itself becomes illusory.[123]

Regardless of whether they are general or specific, limitation clauses in human rights instruments follow an established form which serves as a procedural

---

[115] See HRC, *General Comment 34*, para. 21.

[116] See for example *The Word 'Laws' in Article 30 of the American Convention on Human Rights*, Advisory Opinion OC-6/86, May 9, 1986, Inter-Am. Ct. H.R. (Ser. A) No. 6 (1986), paras. 14 and 18. See also discussion of the turning point represented by the *Golder* case in European jurisprudence in J. G. Merrills, *The Development of International Law by the European Court of Human Rights*, (Manchester: Manchester University Press, 1995), at 88–90 and 115.

[117] UDHR, art. 29.2.

[118] ICESCR, art. 4.

[119] Badar, 'Basic Principles Governing Limitations on Individual Rights and Freedoms in Human Rights Instruments', at 63.

[120] In the context of the ACHPR, Richard Gittleman defines clawback clauses as those 'that entitle a State to restrict the granted rights to the extent permitted by domestic law' and observes that these clauses render the protection of rights 'substantively questionable'. R. Gittleman, 'The African Charter on Human and Peoples' Rights: A Legal Analysis', 22 *Virginia Journal of International Law* (1981), 667–714, at 691. See also Report of the International Law Commission on the work of its 52 session, Yearbook of the International Law Commission, Vol. I, 2000, UN Doc. A/CN.4/SER.A/2000, at 165.

[121] ACHPR, art. 27.2.

[122] I. Österdahl, 'The Surprising Originality of the African Charter on Human Rights and Peoples' Rights', in J. Petman and J. Klabbers (eds.), *Nordic Cosmopolitanism: Essays in International Law for Martti Koskenniemi*, (Leiden: Martinus Nijhoff Publishing, 2003), 5–32, at 13.

[123] *Media Rights Agenda and Constitutional Rights Project vs. Nigeria*, Communications 105/93, 128/94, 130/94, 152/96, Twelfth Activity Report 1998-1999, Annex V, paras. 69–70. See also M. Evans and R. Murray, *The African Charter on Human and Peoples' Rights: The System in Practice 1986-2006*, 2nd ed., (Cambridge: Cambridge University Press, 2008), at 26–28; F. Ouguergouz, *The African Charter on Human and Peoples' Rights: A Comprehensive Agenda for Human Dignity and Sustainable Democracy in Africa*, (Leiden: Martinus Nijhoff, 2003), at 430–437.

guarantee that the rights at stake are not emptied of their meaning. Such clauses usually provide that restrictions on rights must be prescribed by law, must pursue a legitimate aim, and must be necessary in a democratic society.[124] The formulation of article 24 of the CDHRI and other sharia restrictions on specific rights do not follow this model, nonetheless how do they fare in terms of ensuring legality, necessity and proportionality?.

The 'prescribed by law' requirement may prove insurmountable from a legal and practical point of view in those countries where sharia is not codified. The ambiguity, lack of precision and accessibility which characterize unwritten religious rules, and the unforeseeable outcome when rights are adjudicated under such rules, has caused the HRC to declare that restrictions on freedom of religion enshrined in traditional and religious law are incompatible with the 'prescribed by law' condition of the ICCPR.[125] In Nigeria, for example, which uses a tripartite legal system (common law, customary law, and sharia law), the family and personal status law under sharia that is applicable in the North of the country is not codified. In both 2004 and 2008, the concluding observations on Nigeria's implementation of the Convention on the Elimination of All Forms of Discrimination against Women (CEDAW) noted the inconsistencies and ambiguities resulting from this system. The Committee specifically highlighted:

discriminatory provisions within these sources of law with regard to marriage, divorce, custody of children and inheritance. Recalling its previous concluding observations of 2004, the Committee reiterates that the tripartite legal system results in a lack of compliance by the State party with its obligations under the Convention and leads to continuing discrimination against women.[126]

Similarly, in the case of Saudi Arabia personal status matters are governed by sharia, which is not yet codified. This shifts decisions on limitations of rights vigorously away from articulate standards of the principle of legality to ad hoc interpretation by judges and the Council of Senior Religious Scholars appointed by the king. The Special Rapporteur on violence against women, Yakin Ertürk, observed that: '[t]here is an overall consensus that judges have significant discretionary

---

[124] See *Media Rights Agenda and Constitutional Rights Project vs. Nigeria*, paras. 65–70; UN Commission on Human Rights, Siracusa Principles on the Limitation and Derogation of Provisions in the International Covenant on Civil and Political Rights, UN Doc E/CN.4/1984/4 and Annex (1984); *The Word 'Laws' in Article 30 of the American Convention on Human Rights*, Advisory Opinion OC-6/86, May 9, 1986, Inter-Am. Ct. H.R. (Ser. A) No. 6 (1986), para. 18. See also the analysis in Badar, 'Basic Principles Governing Limitations on Individual Rights and Freedoms in Human Rights Instruments', at 63–92.

[125] HRC, *General Comment 34*, para. 24. In the European system the *Sunday Times* test applies, under which law shall be 'clear, accessible, precise and foreseeable'. *Sunday Times v. The United Kingdom*, Application no. 6538/7, Judgment of 26 April 1979, para. 49.

[126] CEDAW Committee, Concluding observations of the Committee on the Elimination of Discrimination against Women, Nigeria, UN Doc. CEDAW/C/NGA/CO/6, 8 July 2008, para. 17. See also UN Doc. A/59/38, 2004, para. 295.

power in adjudicating cases. Sentences can thus differ from court to court or even case to case.'[127] The case of Bahrain is also noteworthy. In 2008 the CEDAW Committee expressed deep concern at the lack of a codified family law.[128] A year later Bahrain adopted family legislation, in what could be seen as the outcome of a successful dialogue between treaty bodies and state parties: however, the family code is applicable only to the Sunni Muslim minority, reportedly because of opposition to the codification by Shia religious leaders.[129] Another example is that of the United Arab Emirates. In 2003, the CRC Committee recommended that the state party should conduct a comprehensive review of its domestic laws, including uncodified sharia law, and bring them into conformity with human rights standards. It emphasized the need to ensure that 'laws are sufficiently clear and precise, are published, and are accessible to the public'.[130] The concern expressed was that unwritten sharia rules resulted in irregularities and discrepancies in judicial outcomes. Interestingly, while invoking 'the universal values of equality and tolerance inherent in Islam', the treaty body observed that the 'State party's narrow interpretations of Islamic texts, particularly in areas relating to personal status law, may impede the enjoyment of some human rights protected under the Convention'.[131] The United Arab Emirates adopted a Personal Status Law governed by sharia in 2005. While codification was generally seen to be positive because it brings predictability in the act of adjudication,[132] a CEDAW Committee review in 2010 demonstrated that previously uncodified discriminatory practices with regard to marriage, divorce, property relations, custody, and inheritance had been integrated into written law.[133] This brings us to the next challenge posed by sharia limitations.

Most instruments, as we have seen in Chapter 1, provide an exhaustive list of legitimate aims that a state must pursue when restricting the enjoyment of human rights. These are: public order, public health, public morals, national security, public safety, and rights and freedoms of others.[134] Imagine a situation in which a state limits a right, based on interpretations of sharia, and argues that its aim is to protect public morals. For the purpose of the ICCPR, to which it should be reiterated most OIC member states are party, the HRC has considered that 'the

---

[127] Report of the Special Rapporteur on violence against women, its causes and consequences, Yakin Ertürk, UN Doc. A/HRC/11/6/Add.3, 14 July 2009, para. 75.

[128] CEDAW Committee, Concluding observations of the Committee on the Elimination of Discrimination against Women, Bahrain, UN Doc. CEDAWCEDAW/C/BHR/CO/2, 14 November 2008, para. 38.

[129] See Social Institutions and Gender Index, Bahrain, accessed June 2012, http://genderindex.org/country/bahrain.

[130] CRC Committee, Concluding observations of the Committee on the Rights of the Child, United Arab Emirates, UN Doc. CRC/C/118, 2002, para. 374.c.

[131] CRC/C/118, para. 370.

[132] See Social Institutions and Gender Index, United Arab Emirates, accessed June 2012, http://genderindex.org/country/united-arab-emirates.

[133] CEDAW Committee, Concluding observations of the Committee on the Elimination of Discrimination against Women, United Arab Emirates, UN Doc. CEDAW/C/ARE/CO/1, 5 Febarury 2010, para. 47.

[134] See for example the Siracusa Principles on the Limitation and Derogation of Provisions in the International Covenant on Civil and Political Rights, art. 27.

concept of morals derives from many social, philosophical and religious traditions; consequently, limitations... for the purpose of protecting morals must be based on principles not deriving exclusively from a single tradition'.[135] Moreover, the burden of proof would lie on the state to prove that the limitation in question is 'essential to the maintenance of respect for fundamental values of the community'.[136] The provision 'necessary in a democratic society' requires that a reasonable relationship of proportionality must exist between the means employed and the aim in mind. The ECtHR takes the view that any instance of interference should strike 'a "fair balance" between the demands of the general interest of the community and the requirements of the protection of the individual's fundamental rights'.[137]

In this context the case *Doebbler v. Sudan*,[138] decided by the AComHPR in 2003, is interesting because of the position the Commission took (or rather refused to take) on the issue of proportionality when it considered the preservation of public order as the justification for flogging. A group of students held a picnic in Khartoum and were arrested by security agents and policemen for having violated public order, contrary to article 152 of the criminal code which stipulates that indecent acts and obscene outfits 'shall be punished with flogging which may not exceed forty lashes or with fine or with both', where the 'standard of the person's religion' is taken to indicate whether an act is indecent and an outfit obscene.[139] The complaint claimed that the 'offences comprised of girls kissing, wearing trousers, dancing with men, crossing legs with men, sitting with boys and sitting and talking with boys'[140] and that these students had been sentenced by a public order court to fines and/or lashes. The formulation of the complaint is interesting, since neither the legitimate aim of the punishment, nor the punishment per se was challenged, but its disproportional character. The complainant submitted that:

[A]ccording to Islamic law the penalty of lashings may be meted out for some serious crimes. For example, *hadd* offenses may be punished with lashes under *Shari'a* because they are considered grave offences and strict requirements of proof apply. Minor offenses, however, cannot be punished as *hadd* because the *Qur'an* does not expressly prohibit them with a prescribed penalty. The acts committed by the students were minor acts of friendship between boys and girls at a party.[141]

---

[135] HRC, *General Comment No. 22*, para. 8. See also HRC, *General Comment 34*, para. 32.

[136] Siracusa Principles on the Limitation and Derogation of Provisions in the International Covenant on Civil and Political Rights, art. 27.

[137] *Tre Traktörer Aktiebolag v. Sweden*, Application no. 10873/84, Judgment of 7 July 1989, para. 46.

[138] *Francis Doebbler v. Sudan*, Communication No. 236/2000 (2003).

[139] The full text of article 152 of the Memorandum to the Sudanese Penal Code 1991 can be found in Amnesty International, *Sudan: Amnesty International calls on government to repeal law penalizing women for wearing trousers*, Press Release, 4 September 2009, accessed January 2012, http://www.amnesty.org/en/for-media/press-releases/sudan-amnesty-international-calls-government-repeal-law-penalizing-women.

[140] *Francis Doebbler v. Sudan*, para. 3.

[141] *Francis Doebbler v. Sudan*, para. 40. In this chapter, we use the form *hudud* instead of *hadd*.

The Commission however refused to engage in an interpretation of sharia law or assess whether the punishment was or was not disproportionate to the offence sanctioned by the latter. It addressed the lashes penalty as follows:

There is no right for individuals, and particularly the government of a country to apply physical violence to individuals for offences. Such a right would be tantamount to sanctioning State sponsored torture under the Charter and contrary to the very nature of this human rights treaty.[142]

The AComHPR further held that article 152 of the criminal code was in 'clear incompatibility with international human rights law',[143] and requested that Sudan immediately amend the law and abolish the penalty of lashes. Note that the AComHPR not only found that lashing amounted to inhuman and degrading treatment under the Convention, but also appears to suggest that this was so irrespective of whether a state or non-state actor applied the penalty.

If we return to the text of the Cairo Declaration, article 19.d states: 'There shall be no crime or punishment except as provided for in the Shari'ah'.[144] Certainly, this sharia limitation clause cannot mean that the Cairo Declaration requires OIC states to impose lashes as punishment (to take the above example). To reiterate, in any event this instrument does not carry binding force. However, the Cairo Declaration does accommodate *interpretations* of sharia, like the one in Sudan, which do impose lashing or other corporal punishments for certain crimes. Against this background, it should be stressed that some OIC member states follow interpretations of sharia that sanction flogging for intoxication, lashing or in certain circumstances death by stoning for extra-marital sex, and the amputation of the right hand for theft.[145] At the same time, it is evident that flogging, amputation, and stoning are irreconcilable with the provisions of the UDHR, the ICCPR, or the CAT on the prohibition of torture and cruel, inhuman and degrading treatment; moreover, the prohibition of torture is a peremptory norm.[146] As Nigel Rodley, the former UN Special Rapporteur on torture and other cruel, inhuman or degrading treatment or punishment put it:

As there is no exception envisaged in international human rights or humanitarian law for torturous acts that may be part of a scheme of corporal punishment, the Special Rapporteur

---

[142] *Francis Doebbler v. Sudan*, para. 42.   [143] *Francis Doebbler v. Sudan*, para. 44.

[144] CDHRI, art. 19.d.

[145] See Abiad, *Sharia, Muslim States and International Human Rights Treaty Obligations: A Comparative Study*, at 22–26. States that apply sharia in the criminal code are: Libya, Iran, Saudi Arabia, Sudan, Yemen, Pakistan, and Northern Nigeria. See Baderin, 'Islamic Law and the Interpretation of International Human Rights Law: A Case Study of the International Covenant on Civil and Political Rights', at 340.

[146] UDHR, art. 5; ICCPR, art. 7; CAT, art. 1; see also *Prosecutor v. Furundžija* (Case IT-95-17/1-T), Judgement of the International Criminal Tribunal for the former Yugoslavia, 10 December 1998, para. 156. Some scholars argue that article 1 of the CAT excludes pain or suffering arising from lawful sanctions from the scope of the definition of torture. J. H. Langbein, *Torture and the Law of Proof: Europe and England in the ancien régime*, (Chicago: University of Chicago Press, 2006), at 3; S. Reza, 'Torture and Islamic law', 8 *Chicago Journal of International Law* (2007), 21–41, at 23. Nigel Rodley disagreed with this interpretation. Report of the Special Rapporteur, Mr Nigel S. Rodley, submitted pursuant to Commission on Human Rights resolution 1995/37 B, UN Doc. E/CN.4/1997/7, 10 January 1997, paras. 6–8.

must consider that those States applying religious law are bound to do so in such a way as to avoid the application of pain-inducing acts of corporal punishment in practice.[147]

As was emphasized in a previous section, because sharia law is a construct of human interpretation, the potential for change is unquestionable. Even *hudud* crimes (theft, apostasy, rebellion/armed robbery, extra-marital sex, intoxication), which are crimes expressly identified in the Quran and the Sunnah and defined as violations of the will of God, can be interpreted in such a way so as to render the application of their required punishment (which can amount to torture) effectively impossible.[148] It may be unacceptable for many observers that Islamic law sanctions amputation or stoning, just as many other observers find unacceptable the practice of capital punishment in the United States: yet, if the premise is that the true value of human rights lies in the protection that they offer in practice, and that forging legitimacy for human rights in various cultural contexts requires cross-cultural critique and internal dialogue as opposed to imposition of values which may be perceived as alien, then one may have to accept that a moratorium-like scheme on the application of corporal punishment for *hudud* crimes may be the best outcome achievable at this point in history.

It is useful to return to the Sudan and the imposition of flogging for offences against public order, to observe whether, after the decision of the AComHPR, any changes could be detected in the interpretation of sharia law. In 2007, the HRC reviewed Sudan's implementation of its obligations under the ICCPR. The Committee underscored that flogging, amputation, and death by stoning were punishments incompatible with the provisions of the Covenant.[149] A representative of Sudan observed in this context that '[a]lthough certain provisions of Sudanese legislation certainly required review, there were no substantive inconsistencies with the Covenant. Flagellation and whipping, for example, were lawful forms of punishment in the Sudan and as such not incompatible with the Covenant.'[150] One can surely object to the interpretation offered by the Sudanese official, that the legality of a punishment in a given legal system guarantees the legality of the latter under human rights law. It is clear that flogging is in violation of article 7. Yet a second point that should be emphasized is the acknowledgment by the official that sharia law can be changed. This was made even clearer during the review process when a state official declared:

---

[147] Report of the Special Rapporteur, Mr Nigel S. Rodley, submitted pursuant to Commission on Human Rights resolution 1995/37 B, UN Doc. E/CN.4/1997/7, 10 January 1997, para. 10.

[148] See An-Na'im, 'Toward a Cross-Cultural Approach to Defining International Standards of Human Rights: The Meaning of Cruel, Inhuman or Degrading Treatment or Punishment', at 32–37.

[149] HRC, Summary Record of the 2459th meeting: Sudan, UN Doc. CCPR/C/SR.2459, 31 July 2007, para. 34; HRC, Summary Record of the 2460th meeting: Sudan, UN Doc. CCPR/C/SR.2460, 13 October 2008, para. 7. In its Concluding observations the HRC noted 'with concern the scale of values applied to punishment in the State party's legislation. It considers that corporal punishment including flogging and amputation is inhuman and degrading.... The State party should abolish all forms of punishment that are in breach of articles 7 and 10 of the Covenant.' HRC, Concluding observations of the Human Rights Committee: Sudan, UN Doc. CCPR/C/SDN/CO/3, 29 August 2007, para. 10.

[150] HRC, Summary Record of the 2459th meeting: Sudan, UN Doc. CCPR/C/SR.2459, 31 July 2007, para. 37.

As to apostasy, the punishment of which was alleged to be incompatible with article 18, it should be borne in mind that there were several Islamic schools and that in the Sudan itself the interpretation of the Koran had evolved over time. In any event, laws passed subsequent to the 2005 Constitution could be reviewed and amended.[151]

Essentially, the Sudanese authorities placed the ball firmly in their own court. This is clear evidence that changing sharia law so that flogging and other corporal punishments are rendered inapplicable is as much a question of political will as religious interpretation.

It is important to note that interpretations of sharia law may conflict with international standards in other areas, for example with respect to the equality of women, freedom of religion, freedom of expression, freedom of assembly and association, democratic freedoms, criminal justice, and provisions on states of emergency.[152] These interpretations, however, are not a given and other formulations can be promoted.

To conclude, sharia law limitations on specific rights in the Cairo Declaration and the general limitation clause of article 24 mark a departure from the usual architecture of human rights instruments, whether these are binding or non-binding. The CDHRI does not as such sanction violations of human rights, however, sharia law is not a body of fixed, precise, and codified laws, and certainly interpretations exist that are at odds with human rights standards. By subjecting human rights to sharia law the Declaration can be read to accommodate those interpretations and therefore to open the door widely to human rights violations.

1.1.3. Islamic reservations to human rights treaties

The sharia limitations on rights in the Cairo Declaration are strikingly similar to what have come to be known as 'Islamic' or 'sharia' reservations to international human rights treaties. As we shall see, the general Islamic reservations echo article 24, while specific reservations on rights present similarities to specific limitations on rights in the Cairo Declaration. It is important to note, at the same time, that Muslim states do not hold the monopoly on religious reservations. While they are not the subjects of this chapter, both the Holy See and Israel have formulated wide-ranging reservations which prioritize religious law over the international human rights treaty provisions.[153]

---

[151] HRC, Summary Record of the 2460th meeting: Sudan, UN Doc. CCPR/C/SR.2460, 13 October 2008, para. 68.

[152] See notably Abiad, *Sharia, Muslim States and International Human Rights Treaty Obligations: A Comparative Study*, at 21–32; An-Na'im, 'Human Rights in the Muslim World: Socio-Political Conditions and Scriptural Imperatives-A Preliminary Inquiry', at 37–44; H. Bielefeldt, '"Western" versus "Islamic" Human Rights Conceptions? A Critique of Cultural Essentialism in the Discussion on Human Rights', 28 *Political Theory* 1 (2000), 90–121, at 105–106; E. Brems, *Human Rights: Universality and Diversity*, (The Hague: Martinus Nijhoff Publishers, 2001), at 259–267; Mayer, 'Universal versus Islamic Human Rights: A Clash of Cultures or Clash with a Construct', at 308–349; A. Quraishi, 'Her Honor: An Islamic Critique of the Rape Laws of Pakistan from a Woman-Sensitive Perspective', 18 *Mich. J. Int'l L.* (1996), 287–320; J. Rehman, *International Human Rights Law*, 2nd ed., (Essex: Pearson Education, 2010), at 367–370.

[153] Reservation of Israel to the ICCPR, accessed June 2012, UNTC, Online Database, Chapter IV: Human Rights, International Covenant on Civil and Political Rights; Reservations and Declaration of the Holy See to the CRC, accessed March 2012, UNTC, Online Database, Chapter IV: Human Rights, Convention on the Rights of the Child. See also Chapter 4, VI.4.1.

Given the similarity between Islamic reservations and the CDHRI limitation clauses, an examination of the reservations which OIC states have entered to human rights treaties, and of how they have been dealt with by states and treaty bodies, may shed some light on how the limitation clauses of the Cairo Declaration should be understood.

Upon signature or ratification of international human rights treaties, general or specific Islamic reservations have been introduced by some, but not all Muslim states that are members of the OIC. Even among the states which have entered Islamic reservations, no consistent practice can be observed. By way of example, only a few states have reserved provisions of the ICCPR on grounds of sharia law or domestic legislation applying Islamic law.[154] The largest number of general and specific reservations, based on sharia law, Islam or domestic laws that apply sharia law, relate to the CEDAW and the CRC. More recent human rights instruments are distinguished by the lack of Islamic reservations. Iran stands out among Muslim states parties to the Convention on the Rights of Persons with Disabilities (CRPD) for having introduced a veiled Islamic reservation.[155]

The example of Mauritania is illustrative of the form that Islamic reservations take, but also of the inconsistency in introducing them in all international human rights treaties. Mauritania entered two specific Islamic reservations to article 18 and 23.4 of the ICCPR, which read:

The Mauritanian Government, while accepting the provisions set out in article 18 concerning freedom of thought, conscience and religion, declares that their application shall be without prejudice to the Islamic Shariah.... The Mauritanian Government interprets the provisions of article 23, paragraph 4, on the rights and responsibilities of spouses as to marriage as not affecting in any way the prescriptions of the Islamic Shariah.[156]

Upon accession to the CEDAW, Mauritania declared that it approved the instrument 'in each and every one of its parts which are not contrary to Islamic Sharia and are in accordance with our Constitution'.[157] This is the model of a general Islamic reservation. The reservation entered to the CRC has a similarly general

---

[154] Specific or general Islamic reservation clauses have notably been formulated by Algeria, Bahrain, Kuwait, the Maldives, Mauritania, and Pakistan. See accessed June 2012, UNTC, Online Database, Chapter IV: Human Rights, International Covenant on Civil and Political Rights.

[155] The reservation is described as 'veiled' because Iran called its reservation a declaration, and did not explicitly require compatibility with sharia but with domestic legislation, which is based on sharia. The 'declaration' reads '... with regard to Article 46, the Islamic Republic of Iran declares that it does not consider itself bound by any provisions of the Convention, which may be incompatible with its applicable rules'. Austria, Belgium, the Czech Republic, France, Germany, Latvia, Mexico, Portugal, and Slovakia, in their respective objections, considered the declaration to be a reservation because its purpose was to modify or exclude provisions of the Convention. The declaration of Iran to the CRPD, and the objections of other states are available at UNTC, Online Database, Chapter IV: Human Rights, Convention on the Rights of Persons with Disabilities, accessed June 2012.

[156] Reservation of Mauritania to the ICCPR, accessed June 2012, UNTC, Online Database, Chapter IV: Human Rights, International Covenant on Civil and Political Rights.

[157] Reservation of Mauritania to the CEDAW, accessed June 2012, UNTC, Online Database, Chapter IV: Human Rights, Convention on the Elimination of All Form of Discrimination Against Women.

nature. 'In signing this important Convention, the Islamic Republic of Mauritania is making reservations to articles or provisions which may be contrary to the beliefs and values of Islam, the religion of the Mauritania People and State.'[158] Yet, Mauritania has entered no reservations to the CRPD. It should be mentioned in this context that article 23 of the CRPD echoes article 23.4 of the ICCPR and several provisions of the CRC.[159]

Reservations have been on the agenda of the ILC since it began its work on legal codification and progressive development, in the early 1950s.[160] In the 1960s, it reversed the unanimity rule in favour of flexibility. In other words, at signature, ratification, accession or acceptance, a state may formulate reservations on any matter that is not forbidden by the convention, provided it 'shall have regard to the compatibility of the reservation with the object and purpose of the treaty.'[161] The VCLT framework for reservations[162] describes a relation of a contractual and recip-rocal nature between states based on the premise that formulating reservations is an established right of states, justified by the need to ensure universal acceptance of international instruments; the practice of entering objections to reservations reflects the need to ensure the integrity of the treaty. Part of the work of the ILC in recent years has been to accommodate in this framework the mindset of human rights treaties that provide rights to individuals rather than states.[163] The aim of this section is certainly not to review the work of the ILC in the last 60 years, it is rather to take note of the most recent developments while discussing the practice of Islamic reservations, objections by states to such Islamic reservations, and the approach of monitoring bodies.

States that have objected to Islamic reservations have raised three interre-lated issues, which may be illustrated by the objection of Denmark to Brunei Darussalam's reservation to the CRC. This reservation contains a self-proclaimed general reserving clause and clauses attached to specific articles. It reads:

[The Government of Brunei Darussalam] expresses its reservations on the provisions of the said Convention which may be contrary to the Constitution of Brunei Darussalam and to

---

[158] Reservation of Mauritania to the CRC, accessed June 2012, UNTC, Online Database, Chapter IV: Human Rights, Convention on the Rights of the Child.

[159] See CRPD, art. 23; ICCPR, art. 23.4; CRC, art. 18.

[160] Reservations to Multilateral Conventions, Mr J.L. Brierly, Special Rapporteur, UN Doc. A/CN.4/41, 1951.

[161] First Report on the Law of Treaties by Sir Humphrey Waldock, UN Doc. A/CN.4/144 and Add.1, 1962, paras. 2–4.

[162] VCLT, arts. 19–23.

[163] See Report of the International Law Commission on the work of its 47th session, UN GAOR 50th Sess., Supp. No. 10, UN Doc. A/50/10, 1995, para. 481. The outcome of the ILC work on reservations is the ILC Guide to Practice on Reservations to Treaties, UN Doc. A/66/10 (2011) (hereafter ILC Guide to Practice on Reservations). The following articles engage with the 'human rights mindset' in the context of the VCLT: D. N. Hylton, 'Default Breakdown: The Vienna Convention on the Law of Treaties' Inadequate Framework on Reservations', 27 *Vanderbilt Journal of Transnational Law* (1994), 419–452; R. Moloney, 'Incompatible Reservations to Human Rights Treaties: Severability and the Problem of State Consent', 5 *Melbourne Journal of International Law* (2004), 155–168. See also HRC, *General Comment No. 24.*

the beliefs and principles of Islam, the State, religion, and *without prejudice to the generality of the said reservations*, in particular expresses its reservation on articles 14, 20 and 21 of the Convention.[164]

Denmark's objection reads:

The Government of Denmark finds that the general reservation with reference to the Constitution of Brunei Darussalam and to the beliefs and principles of Islamic law is of *unlimited scope and undefined character*. Consequently, the Government of Denmark considers the said reservation as being *incompatible with the object and purposes of the Convention* and accordingly inadmissible and without effect under international law. Furthermore, it is a general principle of international law that *national law may not be invoked as justification for failure to perform treaty obligations*. The Convention remains in force in its entirety between Brunei Darussalam and Denmark. It is the opinion of the Government of Denmark, that no time limit applies to objections against reservations, which are inadmissible under international law. The Government of Denmark recommends the Government of Brunei Darussalam to reconsider its reservation to the Convention on the Rights of the Child.[165]

First, objecting states underline that the principles of certainty and *bona fide* are endangered by a general reservation of a broad scope which appeals to a fluid, dynamic concept like sharia to limit the application of treaty provisions.[166] It becomes problematic for states to identify which parts of the treaty the reserving state intends not to apply and, in a logic of contract, this makes it impossible to determine 'the extent of their treaty relations with the reserving State'.[167] The HRC explained that it is not only states that require 'specific and transparent' reservations; the Committee itself and those under the jurisdiction of the reserving state also need to understand what obligations have or have not been assumed under the treaty.[168] Good faith, a fundamental principle of international law that has left imprints on every aspect of the system,[169] is difficult to reconcile with general Islamic reservations, which create uncertainty and doubt about the reserving state's intention to implement any of the provisions of the treaty. As the ILC Guide to Practice on Reservations to Treaties notes: 'a reservation shall be worded in such a way as to allow its meaning to be understood, in order to assess in particular its compatibility with the object and purpose of the treaty'.[170] The commentary to the

---

[164] Reservation of Brunei Darussalam to the CRC, accessed June 2012, UNTC, Online Database, Chapter IV: Human Rights, Convention on the Rights of the Child (Emphasis added).

[165] Objection of Denmark to the reservation of Brunei Darussalam (CRC), accessed June 2012, UNTC, Online Database, Chapter IV: Human Rights, Convention on the Rights of the Child. (Emphases added).

[166] Abiad, *Sharia, Muslim States and International Human Rights Treaty Obligations: A Comparative Study*, at 68–69.

[167] This precise formulation is used by Ireland in its objection to the general Islamic reservation of Iran to the CRC, accessed June 2012, UNTC, Online Database, Chapter IV: Human Rights, Convention on the Rights of the Child.

[168] HRC, *General Comment No. 24*, para. 19.

[169] See M. Virally, 'Review Essay: Good Faith in Public International Law', 77 *AJIL* 1 (1983), 130–134.

[170] ILC, Guide to Practice on Reservations, para. 3.1.5.2.

Guide points out that it cannot be maintained that general reservations are invalid *ipso iure*; rather, in the eyes of the ILC, such reservations are particularly prone to criticism because they make it impossible to assess whether they satisfy the permissibility conditions.[171]

This is indeed the second point of contention made by the objecting states. Given the vagueness of general Islamic reservations, it is difficult to assess whether they defeat the object and purpose of a treaty, contrary to the provisions of article 19.c of the VCLT or specific permissibility clauses contained by treaties.[172] One scholar goes so far as to argue that general Islamic reservations 'cheat' the compatibility test of article 19.c. of the VCLT.[173] The concluding observations of the CRC Committee on the review of Brunei in 2003 noted that 'the broad and imprecise nature of the State party's general reservation potentially negates many of the provisions and principles of the Convention [and raises concerns] as to its compatibility with the object and purpose of the Convention, as well as the overall implementation of the Convention'.[174] The Committee strongly recommended that the state party withdraw its reservations.[175] In this context, it should be stressed that, in the ILC's opinion, where it is impossible to assess the compatibility of general reservations with the object and purpose of a treaty *in abstracto*, a 'reservations dialogue'[176] between states and monitoring bodies is particularly necessary.[177]

Third, states that object to general Islamic reservations, or to specific treaty provisions requiring compatibility with sharia law or domestic legislation, invoke the customary norm of treaty interpretation, codified in article 27 of the VCLT. This prohibits states from relying upon provisions of domestic law to justify a failure to perform their treaty obligations.[178] According to the ILC, this is an erroneous interpretation of article 27, because the assumption is made that the state is already bound by treaty obligations when it is not.[179] A state that is either incapable, or at least at the moment of ratification unable, to amend its internal legislation, enters

---

[171] Report of the International Law Commission on the work of the sixty-third session, UN Doc. A/66/10/Add.1, 2011, at 368. (Hereafter ILC, A/66/10/Add.1).

[172] Objection of Austria to Saudi Arabia's reservation (CRC), accessed June 2012, UNTC, Online Database, Chapter IV: Human Rights, Convention on the Rights of the Child.

[173] B. Clark, 'The Vienna Convention Reservations Regime and the Convention on Discrimination Against Women', 85 *AJIL* 2 (1991) 281–321, at 311.

[174] CRC Committee, Concluding observations of the Committee on the Rights of the Child: Brunei Darussalam, UN Doc. CRC/C/133, 31 December 2003, para. 4.

[175] See note 174, para. 5.

[176] The 'reservations dialogue' envisaged by the ILC has several aspects. States and monitoring bodies should explain to the reserving states the reasons for their concerns about the reservation and request clarifications. They should encourage the withdrawal of reservations, the reconsideration of the need for a reservation or the gradual reduction of the scope of a reservation through partial withdrawals. The reserving state should address the concerns and reactions and take them into account 'to the extent possible with a view to reconsidering, modifying or withdrawing a reservation'. ILC, Guide to Practice on Reservations, Annex, Conclusions on the reservations dialogue, paras. 6–8.

[177] ILC, A/66/10/Add.1, at 368.

[178] VCLT, art. 27.

[179] ILC, A/66/10/Add.1, at 381–382.

the reservation precisely so as not to be bound by the provision.[180] In 1987, for example, on accession to the CEDAW, Malawi (which it should be noted is not a member of the OIC), entered the following reservation:

Owing to the deep-rooted nature of some traditional customs and practices of Malawians, the Government of the Republic of Malawi shall not, *for the time being*, consider itself bound by such of the provisions of the Convention as require *immediate* eradication of such traditional customs and practices.[181]

Note that the reservation appears to be time-bound, and that it indicates an intention to remove the discriminatory customs and practices in the future. In 1991, Malawi notified the Secretary General of its decision to withdraw its reservation to the CEDAW.

It follows thus that a reservation that seeks to exclude the application of certain provisions of the treaty, in order to preserve the integrity of specific rules of the reserving state, is not prohibited as such, however such a reservation 'may be formulated only insofar as it does not affect an essential element of the treaty nor its general tenour'.[182] In this context, it is necessary to differentiate between general and specific Islamic reservations because, as shown earlier, general Islamic reservations make an assessment of their permissibility impossible and do not attempt to preserve a specific rule but a system of internal rules. Under these circumstances, a state which enters a general Islamic reservation may well join a treaty not with the aim of assuming new international obligations, but to preserve its internal law, traditions, and customs intact, in spite of the treaty's aim to change such laws and practices.[183] As a result, general Islamic reservations do not appear to be 'a proper exercise of a legitimate right, but rather an . . . *abus de droit*'.[184] One should note in this context that it is not the religious nature of the domestic law which is objectionable, but the wide scope of a reservation. In 1995, for example, when the HRC reviewed the United States' performance of its obligations under the ICCPR, its concluding observations expressed regret at the 'extent of the State party's reservations, declarations and understandings to the Covenant. It believes that, taken together, they intended to ensure that the United States has accepted only what is already the law of the United States.'[185]

Even specific Islamic reservations must be compatible with the object and purpose of the treaty. When the aim of the treaty is to remove *de jure* and *de facto* discrimination, as is the case with the CEDAW, specific reservations that seek to preserve sharia law by not implementing provisions that require

---

[180] ILC, A/66/10/Add.1, at 381–382.

[181] Reservation of Malawi to the CEDAW (withdrawn), accessed June 2012, UNTC, Online Database, Chapter IV: Human Rights, Convention on the Elimination of All Form of Discrimination Against Women.

[182] ILC, Guide to Practice on Reservations, para. 3.1.5.5.

[183] See note 182.

[184] Abiad, *Sharia, Muslim States and International Human Rights Treaty Obligations: A Comparative Study*, at 71.

[185] HRC, Concluding observations of the Human Rights Committee: United States of America, UN Doc. A/50/40, 1995, para. 279.

legislative reform may not be permissible. An example would be Niger's instrument which 'expresses reservations with regard to article 2, paragraphs (d) and (f), concerning the taking of all appropriate measures to abolish all customs and practices which constitute discrimination against women, particularly in respect of succession.'[186] Note that in contrast to Malawi's reservation cited earlier, here there is no element of time, nor an expressed intention to take any action in the future.[187]

Several states have effectively applied the severability doctrine in their objections to Islamic reservations.[188] In other words, they severed what they regarded to be impermissible reservations, while retaining ratification, and the obligations that flow from it intact. Denmark's objection to Brunei's reservation to the CRC (cited earlier) is an example: Denmark considered that the treaty remained in force in its entirety between the parties. In another example, Estonia objected to Syria's Islamic reservations to the CRC, and held that '[t]he Convention will thus become operative between the two States without the Syrian Arab Republic benefiting from its reservations'.[189] Similar examples are available in the context of the ICCPR, where Canada objected to the Islamic reservations of Pakistan and considered that the objection did not preclude the entry into force of the entire Covenant between the parties.[190] The Czech Republic held that Iran's reservation to the CRPD was null and void and that the Convention had entered into force between the parties without Iran 'benefiting from its reservation'.[191] It should be noted that most objecting states explain the reasons for their objections and some encourage the reserving states to clarify or withdraw them.[192] This approach may be interpreted as evidence of state practice that sets aside the logic of contract, when addressing reservations that are deemed impermissible, and centres instead on individuals as the subjects of human rights treaties.

---

[186] Reservation of Niger to CEDAW, accessed June 2012, UNTC, Online Database, Chapter IV: Human Rights, Convention on the Elimination of All Form of Discrimination Against Women.

[187] See also CEDAW Committee, Concluding comments of the Committee on the Elimination of Discrimination against Women: Niger, UN Doc. CEDAW/C/NER/CO/2, 11 June 2007, para. 9.

[188] However, it should be noted that the practice of entering objections to Islamic reservations is not consistent. See for example J. Riddle, 'Making CEDAW Universal: A Critique of CEDAW's Reservation Regime Under Article 28 and the Effectiveness of the Reporting Process', 34 *Geo. Wash. Int'l L. Rev.* (2002), 605–638, at 625.

[189] Objection of Estonia to the reservation of Syria (CRC), accessed June 2012, UNTC, Online Database, Chapter IV: Human Rights, Convention on the Rights of the Child.

[190] Objection of Canada to the reservation of Pakistan (ICCPR), accessed June 2012, UNTC, Online Database, Chapter IV: Human Rights, International Covenant on Civil and Political Rights.

[191] Objection of the Czech Republic to the reservation of Iran (CRPD), accessed June 2012, UNTC, Online Database, Chapter IV: Human Rights, Convention on the Rights of Persons with Disabilities.

[192] In the context of CEDAW, Austria held that it 'cannot consider the reservation made by the Government of the Islamic Republic of Pakistan as admissible unless the Government of the Islamic Republic of Pakistan, by providing additional information or through subsequent practice, ensures that the reservation is compatible with the provisions essential for the implementation of the object and purpose of the Convention'. Objection of Austria to the reservation of Pakistan (CEDAW), accessed June 2012, UNTC, Online Database, Chapter IV: Human Rights, Convention on the Elimination of All Form of Discrimination Against Women. For a state encouraging the withdrawal of a reservation, see also the Communication of Finland to the modfied reservation of the Maldives (CEDAW), UNTC, Online Database, Chapter IV: Human Rights, Convention on the Elimination of All Form of Discrimination Against Women.

Reading together the jurisprudence of the European Court on Human Rights (ECtHR),[193] General Comment 24 of the HRC,[194] and scholarly proposals on how courts and monitoring bodies' can objectify the compatibility test,[195] it is clear that a purely contractual approach to human rights treaties is unsatisfactory. The ILC Guide to Practice on Reservations to Treaties seems to have acknowledged this, in that it concedes that dispute settlement bodies and treaty monitoring bodies may assess the permissibility of reservations to a treaty formulated by a state.[196] Moreover, the Commission asserts that '[u]nless the author of the invalid reservation has expressed a contrary intention or such an intention is otherwise established, it is considered a contracting State or a contracting organization without the benefit of the reservation'.[197]

Accordingly, treaty bodies have proceeded to review several Muslim states which have formulated reservations deemed invalid as if the reservations in question were non-existent. Treaty bodies generally aim to encourage states to withdraw their reservations. By way of example, the CRC Committee adopted a constructive approach by noting Mauritania's willingness to consider reviewing its general Islamic reservation and recommending that it 'seek[s] inspiration from other countries which have either withdrawn similar reservations or not entered any reservations to the Convention'.[198] In the early 1990s, confronted with an increasing number of reservations to the CEDAW, the Committee recommended that states 'should resolutely discourage any notions of inequality of women and men which are affirmed by laws, or by religious or private law or by custom, and progress to the stage where reservations, particularly to article 16, will be withdrawn'.[199] Pakistan's example in the context of the CRC[200] shows that sweeping reservation clauses, echoing article 24 of the CDHRI, can be withdrawn.

---

[193] The *Belilos* and *Weber* cases before the ECtHR are examples of the severability practice. The Court found that Switzerland's interpretative declaration to Article 6(1) of the European Convention—a reservation in disguise—was invalid and that therefore the article in question applied in its entirety. In the well-known *Loizidou* case against Turkey, the Court proceeded in a similar fashion. See *Belilos v. Switzerland*, Application No. 10328/83, Judgment of 29 April 1988, para. 60; *Weber v. Switzerland*, Application no. 11034/84, Judgment of 22 May 1990, para. 38; *Loizidou v. Turkey* (Preliminary Objections), Application No. 40/1993/435/514, Judgment of 23 March 1995, para. 97.

[194] HRC, *General Comment No. 24*. See also Moloney, 'Incompatible Reservations to Human Rights Treaties: Severability and the Problem of State Consent', 155–168.

[195] See for example R. Baratta, 'Should Invalid Reservations to Human Rights Treaties be Disregarded?', 11 *EJIL* 2 (2000), 413–425; R. Goodman, 'Human Rights Treaties, Invalid Reservations, and State Consent', 96 *AJIL* (2002), 531–559; Schabas, 'Reservations to the Convention on the Rights of the Child', 479–491; I. Ziemele, *Reservations to Human Rights Treaties and the Vienna Convention Regime: Conflict, Harmony or Reconciliation*, (Leiden: Martinus Nijhoff, 2004).

[196] ILC, Guide to Practice on Reservations, paras. 3.2., 3.2.2., 3.2.3.

[197] ILC, Guide to Practice on Reservations, para. 4.5.3(2).

[198] CRC Committee, Concluding observations of the Committee on the Rights of the Child: Mauritania, CRC/C/MRT/CO/2, 17 June 2009, paras. 9–10.

[199] CEDAW Committee, *General Recommendation No. 21*. See also http://www.un.org/womenwatch/daw/cedaw/reservations.htm.

[200] CRC Committee, Consideration of Reports Submitted by State Parties under Article 44 of the Convention, Concluding observations: Pakistan, UN Doc CRC/C/15/Add.217, 27 October 2003, para. 3.

Withdrawing reservations based on the fundamental and most sacred values of a religion may reflect the preference for a new interpretation of that religion so as to terminate potential conflict with human rights standards. Such interpretations should certainly be encouraged, whether through what the ILC calls 'reservations dialogue' or what An-Na'im terms cross-cultural critique and internal dialogue. Such withdrawals may however indicate—as scholars observe—the disingenuousness of the initial interpretation, erroneously promoted as permissible and legitimized by appeal to religion.[201]

Be that as it may, a study by Ekaterina Yahyaoui Krivenko of Islamic reservations to the CEDAW formulated by 20 Muslim states, all members of the OIC, suggests that the majority of these states intend to progress towards full implementation of the Convention.[202] Yahyaoui Krivenko analyses state reports, the process of review, and concluding observations of the CEDAW Committee; based on these, she concludes that, in most cases, Islamic reservations—whether general or specific—should not be read as an expression of the respective governments' unwillingness to perform the treaty or assume new obligations. Rather, they mask 'areas of concern', which in most cases relate to the personal status of women (marriage, divorce, custody of children) in societies where forces promoting modernist interpretations of sharia law are battling conservative views.[203] This is a reminder that sharia is a construct and that its interpretative evolution must be driven by political will but must also accord with changes in social attitudes. Such an approach subjects the full performance of a treaty to the variable of time, which, as the author admits, may result in the 'freezing of reservations'.[204] At the same time, this approach takes account of reality in the complex shapes it actually assumes, stresses the role that states and social actors (including religious leaders and non-governmental organizations) play in prompting changes of religious interpretation, and notes the important contribution of treaty bodies. What is paramount however is the willingness of Muslim states to fully assume their obligations by accepting prima facie that sharia law may be interpreted in different ways. The following extract from Saudi Arabia's 2007 report to CEDAW speaks to this point:

To talk about the philosophy of domestic and international law and the application thereof in the Kingdom of Saudi Arabia in isolation from the Islamic Shariah is inconceivable. Lawmaking in an Islamic state proceeds from the Islamic Shariah and this is the case in the Kingdom...As such, the country's laws cannot transgress the framework of the Islamic Shariah and, consequently, may not be changed or developed by the legislative authority in the Kingdom in a

---

[201] See Abiad, *Sharia, Muslim States and International Human Rights Treaty Obligations: A Comparative Study*, at 90.

[202] Krivenko Yahyaoui, *Women, Islam and International Law: within the context of the Convention on the Elimination of All Forms of Discrimination against Women*, at 130–177. This opinion appears to be evident also in the context of the ICCPR. See Baderin, 'Islamic Law and the Interpretation of International Human Rights Law: A Case Study of the International Covenant on Civil and Political Rights' 337–359.

[203] Krivenko Yahyaoui, *Women, Islam and International Law: within the context of the Convention on the Elimination of All Forms of Discrimination against Women*, at 175.

[204] See note 203.

manner which would lead to the creation of new principles, inconsistent with the bases of the Islamic Shariah, in letter and spirit. [T]he legislative authority in the Kingdom is obliged to adhere to the totality of the sources of the Islamic Shariah... This is what is made clear, albeit in condensed form, by the Kingdom's explanatory reservation to the provisions of the Convention, being a reservation relating to the application of the Convention within a framework which does not conflict with the principles of the Islamic Shariah.[205]

In this statement, little if any space is allowed for interpretations of sharia law that would challenge patriarchal and discriminatory practices in Saudi Arabia. Its argument appears to play into the hands of those who consider that human rights law and sharia law are unavoidably in conflict. As argued by this author and more importantly by many Islamic scholars, this need not be the case. It has to be reiterated that different or less strict interpretations of sharia law are possible in Islam and ultimately the decision on whether or not to consider them is a political one.

Nisrine Abiad shows in her analysis how reservations based on sharia, formulated by 10 Muslim states, facilitated their accession to human rights treaties.[206] She also reveals a more complex dynamic, suggesting that, despite sweeping reservation clauses, there is a real potential for Muslim states to:

reform their laws such that they appeal to both human rights norms whilst remaining within the framework of Sharia. The added effect of these reforms is not only the realization of human rights norms within the written law, but the actualization of human rights norms within such religiously conscious societies.[207]

Abiad also stresses the importance of the political will to fully implement human rights. In her words again:

Sharia is merely one factor among many which influences human rights practices, and... its effects on human rights practices, whether positive or negative, largely depends on how it is used and by whom.[208]

What lessons can be learnt for the OIC's Cairo Declaration from this review of Islamic reservations and objections to them? A first point to underline is that sharia law limitation clauses in the Cairo Declaration are not representative of the views and approaches of all OIC member states. The practice of Muslim states shows that not all OIC states enter Islamic reservations to human rights treaties. Those that do enter sharia reservations are not consistent in their practice. And, as the analyses of Yahyaoui Krivenko and Abiad reveal, the reservations of numerous Muslim states mask their understanding that discriminatory patterns within sharia law exist,

---

[205] CEDAW Committee, Combined initial and second periodic reports of Saudi Arabia, UN Doc. CEDAW/C/SAU/2, 29 March 2007, at 10–11. Cited also in Krivenko Yahyaoui, *Women, Islam and International Law: within the context of the Convention on the Elimination of All Forms of Discrimination against Women*, at 169.

[206] The reservations of 10 states to the ICCPR, ICESCR, CERD, CEDAW, CAT, and the CRC are considered. Abiad, *Sharia, Muslim States and International Human Rights Treaty Obligations: A Comparative Study*, at xvii–xxi.

[207] Abiad, *Sharia, Muslim States and International Human Rights Treaty Obligations: A Comparative Study*, at 137.

[208] See note 207, at xv.

mostly in respect to marriage, divorce and custody of children, and that these must be addressed; but that this is possible only over time and in step with changes in social attitudes. From this perspective, the limitation clause in article 19.d of the Cairo Declaration ('There shall be no crime or punishment except as provided for in the Shari'ah') appears to be opportunistically designed to accommodate the few states that follow conservative interpretations of sharia law and retain corporal punishment in their criminal codes. By contrast, many Muslim states which enter general or specific reservations appear willing to work towards the full implementation of human rights norms enshrined in treaties they have signed or ratified; this implies an openness to review their reservations with the ultimate aim of withdrawing them.

On these grounds, a second point that should be emphasized is that the incorporation of sharia limitations within the Declaration diminishes the incentive for Muslim states to work towards removing potential conflicts stemming from interpretations of sharia. Dialogues with monitoring bodies and peer states encouraged states to reconsider their reservations to human rights treaties; these discussed why and how interpretations of sharia that accord with international human rights standards should be preferred. The regime of limitations in the text of the CDHRI is different. Limitations cannot be removed unilaterally. While an argument can be made that they should not be used, and the new OIC IPHRC may interpret them, the 'excuse' for non-action readily provided by the Cairo Declaration cannot be overlooked.

In brief, the CDHRI projects a static understanding of sharia law, and disregards the variety of contexts of OIC member states. Its effect can therefore be twofold. At best, those states that feel unrepresented by the CDHRI provisions will disregard them. At worst, states that adopt interpretations of sharia which are discriminatory or fail to uphold human rights will feel legitimized. We return to this point later in this chapter.

A third point revealed by the analysis is that states which object to general Islamic reservations do so because the reservations create uncertainty about the commitment of Muslim states to implement their obligations under human rights treaties. In a similar manner, article 24 of the CDHRI casts doubt on the commitment of OIC member states to alter interpretations of sharia that conflict with human rights standards. This engenders a *mala fide* bias against OIC states, which in most cases is undeserved. From this angle, it could be argued that the Cairo Declaration, instead of acting as a guide for OIC states in the area of human rights, tends rather to undermine their standing as members of an international community that seek to work towards fulfilment of human rights.

1.1.4. Sharia as the interpretative principle of the Cairo Declaration

The three concerns just discussed—that the Cairo Declaration is not representative of OIC member states, that it discourages a critical engagement with existing interpretations of sharia, and creates the risk of a *male fide* bias against OIC states—are only heightened by article 25 of the Declaration, which reads: 'The Islamic Shari'ah is the only source of reference for the explanation or clarification of any of the articles of this Declaration'.[209]

---

[209] CDHRI, art. 25.

From the outset, the Cairo Declaration's drafters appear to have ignored the considerable variety of legal systems among OIC member states and therefore disregarded the fact that in certain countries sharia is not a source of law, or is only a source in certain respects or in relation to part of the population. In addition, the clause may play into the hands of conservative forces in society and disadvantage those that propose different interpretations that are in accord with human rights standards by relying on the argument that change is required by the international obligations assumed by the state. Finally, the clause supports a view that it is permissible to introduce exceptions to human rights standards if the latter are not in accord with sharia law. This is unfortunate, as we have seen, because it does not represent the view of the majority of Muslim states.

In the remainder of this section, an 'if/then' exercise is proposed, to underline the effects of article 25 *if* the Cairo Declaration *were* binding. Article 25 of the Cairo Declaration received relatively little attention precisely because the instrument is non-binding; however, if such a clause were to be replicated in a binding treaty it could have significant effects. Article 25 proposes sharia as the exclusive rule of interpretation of the Cairo Declaration: were it to be legally binding, it would be a claim against the customary rules codified by the VCLT in article 31.3.c which stipulates the principle of systemic integration. Article 31.3.c. provides that, when interpreting a treaty, there shall be taken into account 'any relevant rules of international law applicable in the relations between the parties'.[210] The ILC has clarified that the provision is a mandatory element of the treaty interpretation process.[211] The relevant rules to which the article refers cover all sources of international law, including customary law, general principles, and, where applicable, treaties.[212] If the CDHRI were a convention, then article 25 would seem to exclude customary law and international and regional human rights treaties to which OIC members are party, insofar as their provisions are inconsistent with sharia law. This situation would create something that the ILC considers could not exist: a self-contained, as opposed to a special regime. In symbolic terms this would not be a regionalism but rather a 'religionalism'. In light of the general attitudes of Muslim states during their reviews by the various treaty bodies, it is doubtful that the majority would ever enter into a binding agreement that was likely to cause them to renege on their international human rights obligations. In reality, as will be shown in the next part, member states have little attachment to the Cairo Declaration.

1.2. *The Cairo Declaration's influence and the accountability of the OIC*

In the introductory paragraphs of this chapter, it was argued that there is a dialectic process between the international human rights obligations of OIC member states and the Organization's desire to assert itself as the voice of the Muslim

---

[210] VCLT, art. 31.3.c.   [211] ILC, Fragmentation Report, 2006, para. 425.
[212] ILC, Fragmentation Report, 2006, para. 427.b.

world. As pointed out earlier in this study, the Cairo Declaration appears to fail to reflect the variety of legal systems that OIC members embrace, or the human rights commitments of these states. Despite the general Islamic reservation clauses that some Muslim states have formulated, many OIC states seem to acknowledge that reinterpretations of sharia are possible and necessary for them to fully uphold their human rights obligations. The aim of this analytical section is to examine the influence exerted by the CDHRI on OIC member states and to engage with questions pertaining to the OIC's accountability in relation to the Cairo Declaration.

As noted previously, the aim of the Cairo Declaration is to provide general guidance for OIC member states in the field of human rights. Having reviewed some of its provisions, it is therefore important to see what influence the CDHRI has had on the state practice of members of the Organization. To measure this, an analysis was undertaken of the reports that OIC member states produced between 1990 and 2012 as part of the process of review of their implementation of the ICCPR, the CEDAW, and the CRC. Among the 56 member states of the OIC which were eligible to be party to these conventions,[213] 50 are party to the ICCPR, 53 to the CEDAW, and all to the CRC.[214] Both core documents and state reports have been examined.[215] In these reports, state parties are required to present the general legal framework for the protection and promotion of human rights. As such, states list the respective conventions to which they are party as well as declarations that they support. They often use declarations to explain the understanding they have of their commitments under the treaty in question and their implementation of its various provisions. One may legitimately assume that the CDHRI, as the guide for OIC member states in the area of human rights, would have been listed in the general legal framework alongside other non-binding legal instruments; or that Muslim states would have used the Cairo Declaration to justify general or specific Islamic reservations, given that, as we have seen, these present similarities with the general limitation clause of article 24 and specific limitations on rights in the Declaration.

The research showed that the Cairo Declaration was mentioned in total on three occasions. In the core report it submitted in 2007, Afghanistan recalled its history within the OIC and that '[i]n 1990, when the Cairo Declaration was approved,

---

[213] Palestine, the 57th member of the OIC, could not previously accede to treaties, but see discussion in Chapter 4, VI.3.2.

[214] The UNTC Database, accessed online June 2012.

[215] Core documents are intended as background for the use of all treaty bodies and provide information on land, people, general legal framework, statistics, institutions and others. Some states never produced a core report or their report is outdated. Therefore, many state parties tend to provide information about their legal framework in the state report. Over the years the reporting guidelines of the treaty bodies have changed. However, the requirement to provide an overview of the legal framework has remained. See Compilation of guidelines on the form and content of reports to be submitted by states parties to the international human rights treaties, HRI/GEN/2/Rev.2, 7 May 2004; Harmonized guidelines on reporting under the international human rights treaties, including guidelines on a core document and treaty-specific documents, Extract from HRI/GEN/2/Rev.6, 10 May 2006.

some of the leaders of *Jehadi* parties attended the Conference and took part in the discussions and finalization of the Declaration'.[216] The (amended) 1992 state report of Egypt on the implementation of the ICCPR noted that Egypt has 'played an effective role in the adoption of the African Charter on Human and Peoples' Rights, the Cairo Declaration on Human Rights in Islam, as well as in the current preparation for the adoption of the Arab Charter on Human Rights'.[217] It is perhaps symbolically relevant that this reference was in a corrigendum to paragraph 168 of Egypt's report which had initially omitted to mention the Cairo Declaration.[218] Finally, in its initial report to the CRC Committee, Saudi Arabia explained that it had 'ratified' the CDHRI 'to reaffirm its deep-rooted faith in human rights and dignity as prescribed in Islam'.[219] Concerning the measures of implementation of religious freedom (art. 12, CRC), Saudi Arabia cited article 7(b) of the CDHRI, according to which 'parents or legal guardians have the right to choose the form of upbringing they want for their children in a manner consistent with their interests and their future in the light of moral values and the regulations of Islamic law'.[220]

A related reference should be mentioned here. During the periodic review of Iran's implementation of the ICCPR in 1994, the HRC member Bertil Wennergren asked the Iranian delegation whether the state party supported the CDHRI, which, in his view, 'imposed considerable restrictions vis-à-vis the Covenant'.[221] Iran has not provided an answer to this question.

A second means for evaluating the influence or impact of the Cairo Declaration was suggested by Abdullah al-Ahsan. The author analysed, in an article, how successful the Declaration had been 'in guiding and ensuring human dignity and rights' in Muslim countries, and to what extent the OIC had promoted human rights in accordance with Islam.[222] It should be noted that al-Ahsan did not primarily set out to question the form or validity of the provisions of the CDHRI. His aim was to examine the implementation of the Cairo Declaration by certain OIC member states, including Algeria, Egypt, and Turkey, and the role played by the OIC itself. He noted that, during the conflict between Islamists and the military in Algeria, which started in the 1990s and resulted in many deaths and scores of disappearances, the 'OIC never raised any question with the Algerian authorities';

---

[216] Core documents forming part of the reports of state parties: Afghanistan, UN Doc. HRI/CORE/AFG/2007, 27 April 2007, para. 129. (Emphasis in the original).

[217] Second periodic report, Egypt, Corrigendum, UN Doc. CCPR/C/51/Add.7/Corr.1, 19 July 1993.

[218] Contrast Second periodic report, Egypt, Corrigendum, UN Doc. CCPR/C/51/Add.7/Corr.1, 19 July 1993 with Second periodic report, Egypt, UN Doc. CCPR/C/51/Add.7, 2 September 1992, para. 168.

[219] First periodic report, Saudi Arabia, Committee on the Rights of the Child, UN Doc. CRC/C/61/Add.2, 1998, para. 15.

[220] CRC/C/61/Add.2, 1998, para. 121.

[221] HRC, Summary Record of the 1252 Meeting: Iran (Islamic Republic of), UN Doc CCPR/C/SR.1252, 27 June 1994, para. 33.

[222] A. al-Ahsan, 'Law, Religion and Human Dignity in the Muslim World Today: An Examination of OIC's Cairo Declaration of Human Rights', 24 *J.L. & Relig.* (2008), 569–597, at 571.

in his view, an inquiry into the military's conduct was required by the CDHRI, which proclaims that '[l]ife is a God given gift and the right to life is guaranteed to every human being..., it is prohibited to take away life except for a *shari'ah* prescribed reason.'[223] In regard to Egypt's human rights record during the Mubarak era, al-Ahsan observes that the Cairo Declaration raises a number of questions:

Were the Egyptian emergency laws enacted in accordance with *shari'ah*? Has the state authority ensured citizens safety from physical injuries? Was the torture...conducted in accordance with *shari'ah*? Does the *shari'ah* approve torture under custody? Who decides whether government actions were based on the teachings of *shari'ah*?...Neither any of the OIC-based institutions, nor traditional Egyptian Islamic institutions such as al-Azhar even raised any such question.[224]

Given that Egypt was a leading supporter of the adoption by the OIC of the Declaration, al-Ahsan suggests that different conduct would have been expected from both Egypt and the OIC.[225] Similarly, al-Ahsan found that the Cairo Declaration and the OIC had little relevance for Turkey. He suggests that Turkey's (relative) openness to human rights groups and dialogue in recent years was due to changes of legislation which the state made in preparation for EU membership rather than a commitment to the CDHRI and the OIC.[226] In conclusion, the scholar suggests that the Cairo Declaration merely served as an apology for non-action in the area of human rights. It did not promote reinterpretation of sharia or uphold universal human rights, and was largely ineffective.[227]

Following this review of state practice, which confirms how little the Cairo Declaration has been used, a final reference should be recorded. Considering the provisions of the Revised Arab Charter on Human Rights of 2004, Mervat Rishmawi submits that the instrument is devoid of cultural relativist clauses and that its preamble makes reference to human rights standards enshrined in various international conventions, but also to the Cairo Declaration.[228] While some of the Charter's provisions appear to reflect the 'conservatism' of the Cairo Declaration, the scholar observes that this is 'perplexing, when one notes that Arab States do not have a uniform position on some of these issues'.[229]

Based on the previous paragraphs, the attachment of the OIC member states to the Cairo Declaration appears to have been minimal, at least when these were acting in UN fora. It is remarkable that only three states considered it necessary to mention the CDHRI among the legal instruments to which they adhere, or use to interpret human rights. On the evidence, furthermore, the OIC has not acted in the past as the voice of the Muslim world when advocacy to protect and promote

---

[223] See note 222, at 579.
[224] See note 222, at 584. al-Ahsan comments that Egypt, as a signatory of the CDHRI would have been 'under an obligation to follow the teachings of *shari'ah*'. However, this author disagrees with this interpretation because the Cairo Declaration is not a legally binding instrument.
[225] See note 222, at 589.　　　[226] See note 222, at 596–597.
[227] See note 222, at 594ff.
[228] Rishmawi, 'The Revised Arab Charter on Human Rights: A Step Forward?', at 367.
[229] See note 228, at 367.

human rights in the OIC region has been required. The OIC has been rather silent. Both these assertions raise questions about the accountability of the OIC, and it is to this that we turn in the remainder of this part.

Ige F. Dekker summarizes the efforts of doctrine concerning the accountability of international organizations and contends that 'international organizations should "account" for their performance in a much broader way than only on the basis of clear violations of their obligations established under international law'.[230] What is proposed is a broader concept that incorporates, but is not limited to, the traditional notion of responsibility of international organizations for international wrongful acts. The 2004 Report of the International Law Association (ILA) Committee on the Accountability of International Organizations identified three interrelated levels of accountability which can be summarized as follows:

1. Internal and external scrutiny and monitoring, irrespective of potential and subsequent liability and/or responsibility;

2. Tortious liability for acts or omissions not involving a breach of any rule of international and/or institutional law;

3. Responsibility arising out of acts or omissions which constitute a breach of a rule of international and/or institutional law. [231]

It is submitted that this comprehensive accountability framework—as opposed to the sole focus on responsibility in its traditional sense—resonates with the concept of international legal personality, grounded in a theory of justice, embraced by this study.[232] The 'novel' level 1 deserves particular attention in an environment where levels 2 and 3 are rather difficult to pursue, given the reluctance of national courts to remove immunity and the absence of an international court with general jurisdiction over international organizations.[233] The added value of level 1 lies also, of course, in its preventive force. It requires an international organization to be transparent in decision-making and implementation, to be inclusive and foster participation, for example by holding periodic and organized fora where non-governmental organizations can present their views on its work, and to develop an efficient civil service.[234] Aspects related to level 1 accountability will be discussed in connection with the newly established OIC IPHRC.

The second level of accountability proposed by the ILA Committee is perhaps best introduced by a citation from the Final Report: 'There is no reason in principle why primary rules of international law should not apply to collective enterprises undertaken by states in the framework of IO-s [international organizations]'.[235]

---

[230] Dekker, 'Accountability of International Organisations: An Evolving Concept?', at 22–23. See also V. Gowlland-Debbas, *The Security Council and Issues of Responsibility under International Law*, Collected Courses of the Hague Academy of International Law vol. 353, (Online ed.: Martinus Nijhoff, 2012).

[231] International Law Association, Accountability of International Organizations: Final Report, Berlin Conference, 2004, at 5 (Hereafter ILA, Accountability Report).

[232] See Chapter 2, IV.2.

[233] See Dekker, 'Accountability of International Organisations: An Evolving Concept?', at 22–23.

[234] ILA, Accountability Report at 8–17.

[235] See note 234, at 18.

As the ICJ convincingly argued, international organizations are not 'some form of "super-State[s]"'.[236] International organizations, including the OIC, are bound by customary international law of human rights[237] and by norms that have achieved *jus cogens* status.[238] Where the possibility exists, they can acquire obligations by acceding to human rights treaties.[239] In addition, some authors have explored whether human rights treaties concluded by member states could, by succession or substitution, become a source of human rights obligations for international organizations, and have concluded that the difficulties of applying these theories mean there are only few opportunities for this in practice.[240] More interesting, perhaps, are cases where international organizations appear to be willing themselves to accept obligations arising from treaty or soft law.[241]

The preceding paragraphs disclose a salient feature: the human rights accountability of an international organization cannot be surgically separated from the responsibility of its member states with regard to human rights. What prompts this conclusion is the dictum according to which states cannot escape their obligations under international law merely by acting collectively through inter-governmental organizations. Ignaz Seidl-Hohenveldern regarded this principle as unequivocal, at least since the *Attilio Regolo Award* of 1945.[242] In two back-to-back judgments, the ECtHR confirmed that the human rights obligations of states persist when they act as members of international organizations:

[W]here States establish international organisations in order to pursue or strengthen their cooperation in certain fields of activities, and where they attribute to these organisations certain competences and accord them immunities, there may be implications as to the protection of fundamental rights. It would be incompatible with the purpose and object of the

---

[236] *Interpretation of the Agreement of 25 March 1951 between the WHO and Egypt*, Advisory Opinion, ICJ Reports 1980, p. 73, para. 37; *Reparation for injuries suffered in the service of the United Nations*, Advisory Opinion, ICJ Reports 1949, p. 174, at 179.

[237] A. Reinisch, 'Securing the Accountability of International Organizations', 7 *Global Governance* (2001), 131–150, at 133, 135–136; B. Simma and P. Alston, 'The Sources of Human Rights Law: Custom, Jus Cogens, and General Principles', 12 *Australian Yearbook of International Law* (1988), 82–108, at 101 ff; J. Wouters, et al., 'Accountability for Human Rights Violations by International Organisations: Introductory Remarks', in J. Wouters, et al. (eds.), *Accountability for Human Rights Violations by International Organisations*, (Antwerp: Intersentia, 2010), 1–20, at 6–8.

[238] ILC, Articles on the Responsibility of International Organizations, UN Doc. A/66/10 (2011), art. 26, at 120ff.; Wouters, et al., 'Accountability for Human Rights Violations by International Organisations: Introductory Remarks', at 6–7.

[239] At the time of writing, the only case refers to the European Union, which has become party to the CRPD in accordance with article 41.1 of the Convention. See UNTC, Online Database, Chapter IV: Human Rights, Convention on the Rights of Persons with Disabilities, accessed June 2012.

[240] O. De Schutter, 'Human Rights and the Rights of International Organisations: The Logic of Sliding Scales in the Law of International Responsibility', in J. Wouters, et al. (eds.), *Accountability for Human Rights Violations by International Organisations*, (Antwerp: Intersentia, 2010), 51–128, at 58–66; F. Naert, 'Binding International Organisations to Member State Treaties or Responsibility of Member States for their Own Actions in the Framework of International Organizations', in J. Wouters, et al. (eds.), *Accountability for Human Rights Violations by International Organisations*, (Antwerp: Intersentia, 2010), 129–168, at 129–155.

[241] See the examples provided in Clapham, *Human Rights Obligations of Non-State Actors*, at 137.

[242] I. Seidl-Hohenveldern, *Corporations in and under International Law*, (Cambridge: Grotius Publications, 1987), at 121.

Convention, however, if the Contracting States were thereby absolved from their responsibility under the Convention in relation to the field of activity covered by such attribution.[243]

And:

The Convention does not exclude the transfer of competences to international organisations provided that Convention rights continue to be 'secured'. Member States' responsibility therefore continues even after such a transfer.[244]

Related to this, there appears to be agreement that an international organization is under an obligation not to create obstacles that prevent its member states from complying with their pre-existing human rights obligations.[245] Member states of the OIC can therefore not derogate from these obligations simply by joining the Organization, nor should the OIC create obstacles that impede member states from complying with human rights obligations they have assumed under international instruments, or have as a matter of custom.

Did the OIC, by adopting the Cairo Declaration, create such an 'obstacle'? It would be sensible to answer this question by assessing the extent to which the Cairo Declaration deviates from human rights standards. It became clear in the earlier analysis that the CDHRI deviates from human rights standards in two main ways: by not providing in the text for certain rights, such as religious freedom and the rights to freedom of association and assembly, and by limiting rights (via specific limitation clauses and the general clause in article 24) to the point that in certain instances interpretations of sharia may void some human rights of their substantive content. In this context, a member of the HRC remarked that as:

sharia was the supreme standard, and took precedence over all international treaties or instruments... it would be materially impossible for a State party which gave priority to the principles set out in the Cairo Declaration to implement the Covenant to the full.[246]

On the one hand, the Cairo Declaration, which does not carry binding force, cannot derogate from human rights standards enshrined in international treaty law. It does not function as *lex specialis* and a state adhering to the principles of the CDHRI would still have to realize its obligations, under the ICCPR for example. It is highly unlikely that the CDHRI or parts of it reflect regional custom. This would presuppose not only settled state practice, but also the conviction that the Declaration or parts of it legally bind OIC member states.[247] In light of the

---

[243] *Waite and Kennedy v. Germany*, Application no. 26083/94, Judgment of 18 February 1999, para. 67.

[244] *Matthews v. the United Kingdom*, Application no. 24833/94, Judgment of 18 February 1999, para. 32. See also S. Peers, 'Fundamental Rights or Political Whim: WTO Law and the European Court of Justice', in G. De Burca and J. Scott (eds.), *The EU and the WTO: Legal and Constitutional Issues*, (Oxford: Hart, 2001) 111–130, at 127.

[245] De Schutter, 'Human Rights and the Rights of International Organisations: The Logic of Sliding Scales in the Law of International Responsibility', at 58–62.

[246] Bertil Wennergren, HRC, Summary Record of the 1252 Meeting: Iran (Islamic Republic of), UN Doc CCPR/C/SR.1252, 27 June 1994, paras. 32–33.

[247] It is well known that 'extensive and virtually uniform' state practice and *opinio juris* are the two elements of international custom. *North Sea Continental Shelf*, Judgment, ICJ Reports 1969, p. 3, para. 74. See also Cassese, *International Law*, 2nd ed., at 157–160.

discussion earlier on the lack of influence of the Cairo Declaration—OIC member states have not used it in their international practice, nor have they expressed a conviction that parts of it or the entire Declaration are binding on them—there is no evidence to support a claim that the Declaration or parts of it are regional customary law. Even the 'stronger' test case, opposition to the right to freedom of religion due to possible conflicts with interpretations of sharia law, fails. State practice in the OIC region on this matter is not consistent, as has been shown.

On the other hand, what the HRC member was probably questioning is the subordination of human rights norms to sharia in the Cairo Declaration. In this sense, while the Cairo Declaration is not a legal obstacle per se to the compliance of member states with their binding human rights obligations, it may inhibit states that interpret sharia law in a manner which collides with human rights norms from harmonizing national with international standards. In this case we are considering the legitimation of conduct contrary to international human rights obligations, rather than legality. And while only few states seem to have made use of such legitimation, the potential of use, or misuse, certainly exists.

It remains to be seen if level 3 of the accountability framework, referring to the liability of international organizations for international wrongful acts applies to the case at hand. In the context of the previous discussion of corporal punishments provided by the penal codes of some OIC member states, one may recall the concluding observations of the HRC on the third periodic report submitted by Iran under article 40 of the ICCPR:

The Committee is concerned about the continued imposition of corporal punishment by judicial and administrative authorities, in particular amputations and flogging for a range of crimes, including theft, enmity against God (mohareb) and certain sexual acts.... The State party should amend the Penal Code to abolish the imposition of corporal punishment by judicial and administrative authorities.[248]

As has been emphasized before, amputations and flogging are in breach of article 7 of the ICCPR, which prohibits torture and cruel, inhuman, or degrading treatment or punishment; while amputation is certainly covered by the *jus cogens* prohibition against torture. In other words, the imposition of amputation and flogging by judicial and administrative authorities in Iran may be characterized as internationally wrongful acts which entail the international responsibility of Iran.[249] At the same time, article 17.2 of the Articles on the Responsibility of International Organizations adopted by the ILC in 2011 states:

An international organization incurs international responsibility if it circumvents one of its international obligations by authorizing member States or international organizations to

---

[248] HRC, Concluding observations of the Human Rights Committee: Islamic Republic of Iran, UN Doc. CCPR/C/IRN/CO/3, 29 November 2011, para. 16.

[249] It could further be argued that the continued application of amputation by Iranian authorities may amount to a serious breach by Iran under the *jus cogens* prohibition against torture. ILC, Articles on Responsibility of States for Internationally Wrongful Acts, UN Doc. A/56/10 (2001), arts. 1–3, and 40.

commit an act that would be internationally wrongful if committed by the former organization and the act in question is committed because of that authorization.[250]

It is clear that the peremptory norm on the prohibition against torture binds the OIC and that, if amputation were to be committed by the Organization, this would be internationally wrongful. It should be remembered that article 19.d of the Cairo Declaration's stipulates that '[t]here shall be no crime or punishment except as provided for in the Shari'ah'.[251] However, sharia is not defined throughout the Declaration, which permits states to interpret sharia as they see fit. In these terms, Iran's interpretation of sharia, that allows amputations, seems to be accommodated by the CDHRI. This does not, nevertheless, amount to an authorization by the OIC for Iran to use corporal penalties, but can certainly be seen as a very questionable legitimation of such conduct.

What conclusions can be drawn from the analysis of the Cairo Declaration? The CDHRI seeks to provide general guidance on human rights for OIC member states, however, it distinguishes itself rather as a 'major compromise on human rights'.[252] This is not because it rejects human rights standards outright, but because it accommodates interpretations of sharia by OIC member states that may collide with such standards. Furthermore, while it is not a binding instrument, it might legitimize human rights abuse in those states which interpret sharia in a manner that falls short of universal human rights standards. The CDHRI is also found to have had little impact on the practice of OIC member states. This was perhaps the most striking evidence of the failure of the Cairo Declaration to provide general guidance and of the OIC to speak for the Muslim world on human rights. Instead of building a regionalism that strengthens the human rights protection accorded by member states, the OIC built a form of 'religionalism', which subjects human rights to sharia. This development may reflect the legal systems and approach of a minority of OIC member states, but does not reflect those of the majority. States that do not use sharia as part of their domestic law can make little use of the CDHRI. Moreover, the 'reservations dialogues' with states and monitoring bodies suggest that most states, even those in which sharia law governs personal status laws, take the view that Islamic law is dynamic and that change will be necessary if they are to fully uphold their international human rights obligations. The CDHRI is disconnected from the intentions of these states. Indeed, in the view of this author, this is the main problem of the Cairo Declaration: it does not encourage states to promote reform of sharia law, but accommodates the status quo. Ultimately, if the intention of the OIC is to construct cultural legitimacy for international human rights in Muslim societies, the Cairo Declaration does not reflect such an intention. The reported statement of the OIC Secretary General at the opening session of the OIC IPHRC, when he asked the human rights body 'to

---

[250] ILC, Articles on Responsibility of International Organizations, UN Doc. A/66/10 (2011), art. 17.2.
[251] CDHRI, art. 19.d.
[252] Rishmawi, 'The Revised Arab Charter on Human Rights: A Step Forward?', at 367.

review and update OIC instruments, including the Cairo Declaration'[253] should perhaps be read with this conclusion in mind.

2. The Covenant on the Rights of the Child in Islam

The CRCI is a legally binding instrument approved by the 32nd Islamic Conference of Foreign Ministers in Sana'a in June 2005.[254] It was drafted by the Intergovernmental Expert Group as a follow up to the Cairo Declaration on Human Rights in Islam and finalized during the 2004 meeting of that forum.[255] The instrument has not entered into force.[256] It follows a number of previous resolutions that marked the rights of children as an area of key interest to the Organization.[257] It should be recalled that 56 members of the OIC are party to the UN CRC.[258]

This part will analyse the substantive provisions of the CRCI in order to understand the protection it affords to the rights of the child by comparison with the CRC. The interest lies in examining whether the Covenant strengthens the human rights protection of children while seeking to respond to the contexts of the Muslim world, or whether it embarks on a cultural relativist challenge to universal standards in the field of child rights.

2.1. The missing right: religious freedom

One of the particularities of the CRCI is its silence concerning the right of the child to freedom of thought, conscience, and religion. It would seem that the pattern set by the Cairo Declaration has been replicated in the Covenant. Can it be inferred that OIC member states generally object to the right to freedom of religion and that the CRCI merely reflects this objection? It is submitted that the reservations to article 14 of the UN CRC reveal a more complex picture. Of the 56 OIC states party to the UN instrument, 11 states have formulated specific

---

[253] As cited in Turan Kayaoğlu, 'It's Time to Revise The Cairo Declaration of Human Rights in Islam', Brookings Doha Center, 23 April 2012.

[254] OIC, Resolution on Legal Affairs No. 1/32-LEG, adopted by the 32nd session of the Islamic Conference of Foreign Ministers, Sana'a, 21–23 June 2005, para. 14.

[255] See note 254.

[256] According to article 23, the Covenant enters into force after 30 days pursuant to the ratification of the 20th member state of the OIC. Covenant on the Rights of the Child in Islam (2005), IC/9-IGGE/HRI/2004/Rep.Final, annexed to the Resolution on Legal Affairs No. 1/32-LEG, adopted by the 32nd session of the Islamic Conference of Foreign Ministers, Sana'a, 21–23 June 2005, art. 23. (Hereafter CRCI). See also I. Brownlie and G. S. Goodwin-Gill, *Brownlie's Documents on Human Rights. Additional Materials—Part 5*, 6th ed., (Oxford: Oxford University Press, 2010).

[257] OIC, Resolution No.14/31-S&T on Global cooperation in polio eradication programme among OIC member states, 31st session of the Islamic Conference on Foreign Ministers, 2004; OIC, Resolution No. 13/30-C on Child Care and Protection in the Islamic World, 13th Session of the Islamic Conference of Foreign Ministers, 2004; OIC, Resolution on Child Care and Protection in the Islamic World, 10th Session of the Islamic Summit Conference, 17 October 2003.

[258] As mentioned previously, Palestine, which is considered the 57th member state of the OIC, could not join this treaty in the past.

reservations on article 14; they are: Algeria, Bangladesh, Brunei Darussalam, Iraq, Jordan, Malaysia, Maldives, Oman, Qatar, Syria, and the United Arab Emirates.[259] Another four states—Iran, Kuwait, Mauritania, and Saudi Arabia—have entered general Islamic reservations that may reserve the provisions of article 14.[260] It is noteworthy that Djibouti, Indonesia, and Pakistan withdrew their general Islamic reservations and that Morocco withdrew its specific reservation to article 14.[261] Even such a purely quantitative analysis demonstrates that the majority of OIC member states have not formulated reserving instruments and have formally assumed an obligation to uphold the right to freedom of religion of the child under the UN CRC. Furthermore, the specific reservations disclose that reserving states mainly object, first to the right to change one's religion; and second to the clause affirming that parents have the right to educate their children in accordance with their religious belief, in the sense that several states understand this provision to be an exclusive right of the father.[262] While these are very problematic aspects—one denying the child's capacity to change religion, the other sanctioning gender discrimination—they do not amount to a total rejection of *forum internum* freedoms, and even less of *forum externum* rights. Interestingly, Lawrence LeBlanc explains that article 14 of the UN CRC does not guarantee the right of the child to choose or change his or her religion, precisely because of the successful opposition of some Muslim states during the CRC's drafting.[263] On this reading, the provision merely imposes on states the obligation to respect the right of the child to religious freedom, while qualifying it by the rights and duties of parents to provide direction to the child in the exercise of the right.[264]

As pointed out earlier, the HRC judges that 'article 18 [of the ICCPR] does not permit any limitations whatsoever on the freedom of thought and conscience or on the freedom to have or adopt a religion or belief of one's choice'.[265] In General Comment 24 it further asserted that reservations denying the right to freedom of thought, conscience, and religion would not be permitted.[266] The CRC Committee has encouraged Muslim states that reserved article 14 of the

---

[259] UNTC Database, accessed online June 2012.

[260] See note 259.   [261] See note 259.

[262] By way of example, Iraq's reservation states: 'The Government of Iraq has seen fit to accept [the Convention] . . . subject to a reservation in respect to article 14, paragraph 1, concerning the child's freedom of religion, as allowing a child to change his or her religion runs counter to the provisions of the *Islamic Shariah*.' Reservation of Iraq to the CRC, accessed June 2012, UNTC, Online Database, Chapter IV: Human Rights, Convention on the Rights of the Child. See also in the same database the Reservation of Algeria to the CRC and Reservation of Oman to the CRC.

[263] L. J. LeBlanc, 'Reservations to the Convention on the Rights of the Child: A Macroscopic View of State Practice', 4 *International Journal of Children's Rights* (1996), 357–381, at 368. See also M. Baderin, 'A Macroscopic Analysis of the Practice of Muslim State Parties to International Human Rights Treaties: Conflict of Congruence', 1 *Human Rights Law Review* 2 (2001), 265–303, at 298.

[264] LeBlanc, 'Reservations to the Convention on the Rights of the Child: A Macroscopic View of State Practice', at 368. Several states, including Belgium and the Netherlands, formulated interpretative declarations asserting that in their understanding article 14 includes the rights to change and adopt a religion. See Declaration of the Netherlands to the CRC, and Interpretative declaration of Belgium to the CRC, UNTC, Online Database, Chapter IV: Human Rights, Convention on the Rights of the Child, accessed June 2012.

[265] HRC, *General Comment No. 22*, para. 3.

[266] HRC, *General Comment No. 24*, para. 8.

Convention to review their reservation in the light of these general comments of the HRC, with a view to withdrawing them.[267] These exchanges portray the interdependence of the international law system which seeks coherence as opposed to fragmentation. It is likely, therefore, that OIC states which become party to the CRCI and are at the same time party to the ICCPR[268] and the CRC will continue to have international obligations to protect religious freedom, irrespective of the silence of the OIC instrument. In this context the absence of protection from the CRCI is rather anachronistic and of little legal significance. It would have been more sensible for the drafters of the Covenant to include the right in the text, because states that objected to specific aspects of it could have formulated reservations. This would also have been the more representative option, which would have taken into account the view of the majority of OIC members that do not formally deny religious freedom.

2.2. Religious limitations and clawback clauses

As the title of the Covenant indicates Islam retains an important place in the text of the instrument. As one of the objectives of the CRCI, article 2.2 stipulates:

To ensure a balanced and safe childhood and ensure the raising of generations of Muslim children who believe in their creator, adhere to their faith, are loyal to their country, committed to the principles of truth and goodness in thoughts and in deeds, and to the sense of belonging to the Islamic civilization.[269]

It should be emphasized that the CRCI does not entail an equivalent to the general limitation clause in article 24 of the CDHRI. When compared to the Cairo Declaration, the CRCI has fewer clauses which limit specific rights by appeal to sharia, however, some still appear. For instance, one is inserted in article 9.1 on freedom of information and expression.[270] When read in connection with article 17.4, which requires the state to protect the child from 'cultural, ideological, information and communication invasion which contradicts the Islamic Shari'a or the national interest of state parties',[271] the child's freedoms of information and expression appear vulnerable to state interference.

---

[267] CRC Committee, Concluding observations of the Committee on the Rights of the Child: Oman, UN Doc. CRC/C/111, 2001, para. 157.b; CRC Committee, Concluding observations of the Committee on the Rights of the Child: Syria, UN Doc. CRC/C/SYR/CO/3-4, 9 February 2012, paras. 10, 11, and 45.

[268] 50 members of the OIC are party to the ICCPR. Note that only the Maldives and Mauritania entered specific reservations on article 18. UNTC, Online Database, accessed June 2012.

[269] CRCI, art. 2.2. The other objectives entailed in article 2 stipulate: care for the family and the strengthening of capabilities in order to 'habilitate the husband and wife to endure their fulfillment of their role of raising children'; care for the child and the adolescent; free, compulsory primary and secondary education; opportunities for the child to discover his/her talents and importance in society and encouragement to participate in the cultural life of society; necessary care for children with special needs and those living in difficult situations while addressing the root causes of the latter's conditions; assistance and support for Muslim children worldwide.

[270] CRCI, art. 9.1.   [271] CRCI, art 17.4.

Of the two provisions on education and culture which are qualified by appeal to religion,[272] article 12.2.iv is of particular interest. It stipulates '[t]he right of every child to wear clothes "compatible with *her* beliefs" while complying with Islamic Sharia, public etiquette and modesty'.[273] Significantly, this provision declares that wearing clothing with religious connotations, presumably at school or in public, is a freedom, not an obligation. The limitation clause is what makes the difference between this right stipulated in the CRCI, and the right to manifest one's religion by wearing religious dress which receives protection under the CRC and ICCPR.[274] In the CRC and ICCPR, the right is subject only to limitations that are prescribed by law and are necessary to protect public safety, order, health or morals, or the fundamental rights and freedoms of others.[275] In the CRCI, sharia, public etiquette, and modesty may restrict the right. As noted throughout the chapter, interpretations of sharia differ across the OIC region and ultimately, as a result, states will determine the scope of this right. Nonetheless, in the view of this author, the fact that article 12.2.iv is formulated as a right and not an obligation may not be construed to mean that a child must wear religious clothes, rather that she may do so if she wishes. That an obligation to wear religious dress would be contrary to human rights standards has been emphasized by the UN Special Rapporteur on freedom of religion and belief, Asma Jahangir.[276] In conclusion, article 12.2.iv raises difficulties both for states that impose on women religious dress, and for those that prohibit it. The fact that the limitations on these rights do not include the habitual legitimate aims—in particular public order and the rights of others—would make it difficult for states like Turkey to justify their interference with the right in the name of secularism.[277]

Article 13.3 dealing with rest and activity times provides that 'parents or the one legally responsible for the child, have the right to oversee the child while exercising the activities he desires in accordance to this Article in the framework of education, moral and religious control'.[278] Seemingly, this provision counterbalances article 14.5 which guarantees mandatory measures for the child to compel her or his parents, under sharia law, to offer her or him support according to their abilities.[279] Shaheen Sardar Ali explains that the balance between the rights of parents and those of children assumes a central role in contemporary Muslim states: 'Children are ordered to obey their parents, *wali* or guardian . . . , this duty of obedience has

---

[272] The other article under the heading education and culture reads: 'The provisions of this article and article 11 immediately preceding it shall not be in conflict with the freedom of the Muslim child to joint private educational institutions, provided that such institutions respect the provisions of the Islamic Shari'a and that the education given in such institutions observe the rules laid down by the State.' CRCI, art 12.4.

[273] CRCI, art. 12.2.iv. (Emphasis added).   [274] See HRC, *General Comment No. 22,* para. 4.

[275] CRC, art. 14.3; ICCPR, art. 18.3.

[276] Report of the Special Rapporteur on freedom of religion or belief, Asma Jahangir, UN Doc. E/CN.4/2006/5, 9 January 2006, para. 38.

[277] In the *Leyla Şahin case,* public order and the rights of others were the legitimate aims that Turkey invoked when it prohibited the veil in universities. See *Leyla Şahin v. Turkey,* Application no. 44774/98, Grand Chamber, Judgment of 10 November 2005.

[278] CRCI, art.13.3.   [279] CRCI, art. 14.5; see also art. 20.

been balanced however by strict injunctions of the Quran of duties parents owe children.'[280] There exists an understanding that the child is the subject of rights and protections vis-à-vis his or her parents and the state. However, the best interest of the child, which is of paramount importance in Islamic law, is often qualified by religious interpretation.[281] For example, the practice to accord legal guardian-ship to the father, and custody to the mother only up to a certain age, does not stem from the Quran itself but is a conservative interpretation of a statement by the Prophet Muhammad, that 'the child belongs to him or her on whose bed it is born'.[282] In a patriarchal set up where men are seen as the breadwinners and the ones with the duty to provide household effects, the bed is considered to literally belong to the men.[283]

While the use of religious limitations on rights is less evident in the CRCI, the instrument does include a number of provisions that require compatibility with domestic law. Clawback clauses that allow a state to restrict a right stipulated in an international instrument by appeal to domestic legislation often render the protec-tion of rights 'substantively questionable'.[284] The insertion of clawback clauses in international human rights instruments questions the logic underpinning these instruments. Their *raison d'être* to improve human rights protection necessarily presupposes that national legislation should be introduced, amended, or abrogated in accordance with international standards. In the context of the CRCI clawback clauses may permit Islamic sharia, via the backdoor, to limit rights in those OIC states in which sharia is a source of legislation, often in the area of family law and in some cases in criminal justice matters.

Article 4.1, which provides that states shall respect and take the necessary steps to enforce the Covenant 'in accordance with their domestic legislation', is illus-trative of a clawback clause.[285] Its negative effects may be mitigated to a certain extent by provision 4.3 which requires the '[e]nd of action based on customs, traditions or practices that are in conflict with the rights and duties stipulated in this Covenant.'[286]

The non-discrimination provision in article 5 guarantees 'equality of all children *as required by law* to enjoy their rights and freedoms... regardless of sex, birth, race, religion, language, political affiliation, or any other considerations affecting the right of the child, the family, or his/her representative under the law or Shari'a'.[287] If the provision 'as required by law' is taken to mean domestic law, and the latter is discriminatory with regard to gender, religion, or in other areas, then the equal-ity clause is rendered useless. Specifically in respect to equality, clawback clauses

---

[280] S. S. Ali, 'A Comparative Perspective of the Convention on the Rights of the Child and the Principles of Islamic Law Law Reform and Children's Rights in Muslim Jurisdictions', in UNICEF (ed.), *Protecting the World's Children: Impact of the Rights of the Child in Diverse Legal Systems*, (New York: Cambridge University Press, 2007), 142–208, at 152.

[281] See note 280, at 142–208.   [282] See note 280, at 158.   [283] See note 280, at 158.

[284] Gittleman, 'The African Charter on Human and Peoples' Rights: A Legal Analysis', at 691; V. O. O. Nmehielle, *The African Human Rights System: Its Laws, Practice, and Institutions*, (The Hague: Martinus Nijhoff, 2001), at 165–167.

[285] CRCI, art. 4.1.   [286] CRCI, art. 4.3.

[287] CRCI, art. 5. (Emphasis added).

question the object or purpose of a treaty that is intended to remove discrimination, including by means of domestic legislative reform.

A last important veiled limitation appears in the definition of the child. Article 1 of the CRCI reads: 'a child means every human being who, *according to the law applicable to him/her*, has not attained maturity'.[288] The provision defers the responsibility for setting the upper age limit of childhood to each OIC member state.[289] By contrast, the UN Convention defines the child as 'every human being below the age of eighteen years unless under the law applicable to the child, majority is attained earlier'.[290] While clearly setting an upper limit to legal childhood, the UN CRC would seem to accommodate domestic laws that stipulate the age of majority lower than 18. By comparison the African Charter on the Rights and Welfare of the Child allows no margin of appreciation to the state and defines the child to be any human being below the age of 18 years.[291]

In a number of areas, and particularly in respect to early marriage and juvenile criminal responsibility, article 1 of the CRCI could prove to have serious implications and increase the vulnerability of children. For example, a Human Rights Watch report emphasizes the devastating and long lasting effects of child marriage in Yemen, where the laws do not stipulate a minimum age for marriage.[292] The education of girls is forcibly cut short; their potential to provide for themselves is greatly reduced; they find themselves trapped in paternalistic relationships, unable to control how many children they have or when they have them; and they are often exposed to gender-based violence, including domestic abuse and sexual violence.[293] Since the overwhelming majority of OIC states are party to the CRC, and the CEDAW, the provisions of article 1 of the CRCI should be interpreted in the light of the recommendations provided by monitoring bodies of these treaties. The CRC Committee has encouraged states to adopt the 18 years limit for majority and to increase protection for children under 18, notably those in early childhood (defined as below 8 years old).[294] Considering the example of Yemen, the CRC Committee said in 2005 that it was 'concerned about the legislative inconsistency concerning the definition of a child and in particular the difference between age of majority, 18 years, and age of maturity, 15 years', as well as the lack of law enforcement to prevent the marriage of girls as young as 12.[295] The Committee

---

[288] CRCI, art. 1. (Emphasis added).

[289] Aphrodite Smagadi regards the definition of the child as one of the weaknesses of the CRCI. A. Smagadi, *A Sourcebook on International Human Rights Materials*, (London: BIICL, 2008), at 74.

[290] CRC, art. 1.

[291] African Charter on the Rights and Welfare of the Child, OAU Doc. CAB/LEG/24.9/49 (1990) (adopted 11 July 1990, entered into force 29 November 1999), art. 1. The majority of African members of the OIC are party to this treaty.

[292] Human Rights Watch, *'How Come You Allow Little Girls to Get Married?'—Child Marriage in Yemen, December 2011*, accessed December 2011, http://www.hrw.org/print/reports/2011/12/08/how-come-you-allow-little-girls-get-married.

[293] See note 292.

[294] See CRC Committee, *General Comment No. 7: Implementing child rights in early childhood*, UN Doc. CRC/C/GC/7/Rev.1, 20 September 2006.

[295] CRC Committee, Concluding observations of the Committee on the Rights of the Child: Yemen, UN Doc. CRC/C/15/Add.267, 21 September 2005, paras. 30–31.

recommended that all persons below the age of 18 receive the same protection under the Convention.[296] In this context it is relevant to revist article 16.2 of the CEDAW:

The betrothal and the marriage of a child shall have no legal effect, and all necessary action, including legislation, shall be taken to specify a minimum age for marriage and to make the registration of marriages in an official registry compulsory.[297]

The CEDAW Committee emphasized in its General Recommendation that states should understand this provision as requiring the minimum age for marriage to be set at 18 years for both men and women.[298]

The CRC Committee has taken a clear stance in respect to juvenile justice and requires it to be applied to 'every person under the age of 18 years at the time of the alleged commission of an offence'.[299] Furthermore, it commends states that set the limit of criminal responsibility at 19 or even 21 years, either as a general rule or in exceptional cases.[300] Nisrine Abiad and Farkhanda Mansoo observe that Muslim jurists hold various opinions on the minimum age for attaining criminal responsibility, ranging from 7 to 19 years of age.[301] In an OIC state where sharia is a source of legislation and *hudud* crimes are punishable by death, executions of children and juveniles can therefore not be excluded.[302] However, scholars suggest that a correct implementation of the CRCI—taking into consideration its other provisions that protect the rights of juvenile offenders, and promote their rehabilitation and reintegration[303]—would not be compatible with either execution or corporal punishment.[304]

2.3. General convergence with the Convention on the Rights of the Child and the potential for increased protection

It is important to underline that the protection offered to the majority of the rights enshrined in the CRCI echoes that offered by the UN Convention. A significant point of convergence with the UN CRC is that the OIC Covenant upholds the principle of the interdependence of human rights and includes economic, social, and cultural as well as civil and political rights.

The protection offered to some economic, social, and cultural rights by the instrument would seem to be more elaborate than that granted under the CRC.

---

[296] See note 295.　　[297] CEDAW, art. 16.2.

[298] CEDAW Committee, *General Recommendation No. 21*, para. 36.

[299] CRC Committee, *General Comment No. 10: Children's rights in juvenile justice*, UN Doc. CRC/C/GC/10, 25 April 2007, paras. 36–39.

[300] CRC Committee, *General Comment No. 10: Children's rights in juvenile justice*, paras. 36–39.

[301] Abiad and Mansoor, *Criminal Law and the Rights of the Child in Muslim States: A Comparative and Analytical Perspective*, at 81.

[302] See for example CRC Committee, Consideration of Reports Submitted by State Parties under Article 44 of the Convention, Concluding observations: Nigeria, UN Doc. CRC/C/NGA/CO/3-4, 11 June 2010, paras. 32–33.

[303] CRCI, art. 19.

[304] Abiad and Mansoor, *Criminal Law and the Rights of the Child in Muslim States: A Comparative and Analytical Perspective*, at 81, see also 49–51.

Article 12.2.ii and vi, concerning secondary education and the education of out-standing and gifted students, might be regarded as an advance in relation to the stipulations of the CRC and ICESCR.[305] Of particular interest is article 12.3, which provides for 'the right of the child approaching puberty to receive proper sex education distinguishing between the lawful and unlawful'.[306] The inclusion of this provision in the CRCI is laudable and responds to a call by both the CRC and the CEDAW treaty bodies.[307] A comparative analysis of the child rights situation in states in Middle East and North Africa identifies that the right of children and adolescents to sexual and reproductive health care services and information is one where 'very little progress has been achieved'.[308] The report on the analysis further argues that it is important to take measures in the field of sexual education, given that indicators show that the prevalence of HIV/AIDS, although currently rela-tively low in Arab countries, is expected to rise unless preventive measures are put in place.[309] The merit of article 12.3 of the CRCI may however depend in certain countries on the interpretation of 'proper', 'lawful', and 'unlawful', which qualify the right to sexual education. It should be observed that under certain interpreta-tions of sharia *zina*, extra-marital sex, is considered unlawful and triggers severe criminal punishments.[310] The curriculum on sexual education in some countries may therefore take the form of commands to abstain from sexual activity, while in others it may include preventive measures against sexual diseases and insist on action to address unlawful practices such as rape, sexual abuse, and child prostitu-tion. What is certain is that the provision does not directly prohibit and cannot be construed to prohibit extra-marital sex between consenting adults. Article 12.3 of the CRCI may indicate an increased willingness to confront the issue of child sexual abuse and exploitation, discussion of which has long been a social taboo in many OIC states.[311]

The CRCI appears to take a comprehensive approach to the well-being of the child by underscoring that the vulnerability of the child is associated with the vul-nerability of the mother. Under the right to health, it requires the provision of care for the mother 'from the onset of pregnancy and during natural nursing either by

---

[305] Contrast art. 12.2.ii with CRC, art. 28.1.b; ICESCR, art. 13.2.b.

[306] CRCI, art. 12.3.

[307] See OHCHR, *Girls, Women and Sexuality Education—The Link to Achieving the MDGs*, accessed December 2011, http://www.un.org/en/events/women/iwd/2011/pdfs/Infonote_Women_and_the_right_to_sexual_education.pdf.

[308] Y. Abdul-Hamid, *Child Rights Situation Analysis for the Middle East and North Africa Region*, (Save the Children Sweden: August 2011), accessed December 2011, http://mena.savethechildren.se/PageFiles/2867/Regional%20MENA%20CRSA.pdf.

[309] See note 308.

[310] In an analysis of rape laws of Pakistan which fall under *zina*, Asifa Quraishi demonstrates how cultural patriarchy has determined the application of certain Islamic laws, 'resulting in the very injus-tice which the Quran so forcefully condemns'. Quraishi, 'Her Honor: An Islamic Critique of the Rape Laws of Pakistan from a Woman-Sensitive Perspective', at 288–290.

[311] For specific initiatives by OIC states, see UNICEF, *Investing in the Children of the Islamic World*, New York, 2005, accessed June 2012, http://www.unicef.org/publications/files/Investing_Children_Islamic_World_full_E.pdf, at 19.

the mother or someone else if the mother is unable to suckle the baby';[312] it also provides for preventive medical care, and malnutrition control for both the child and the mother.[313] In a similar fashion, article 15.2. states that sharia and other judicial rules should be interpreted in favour of the mother.[314] Given that for certain *hudud* crimes some interpretations of sharia require the death penalty, article 15.2 would require the postponement of the death sentence until the pregnant woman has delivered her child and nursed it.[315] One has to note however that such an accommodation of the needs of the child and the mother is insufficient in light of the abolitionist developments of recent decades, or the provisions of the Second Optional Protocol of the ICCPR.[316]

In keeping with the comprehensive approach, it would appear that the drafters of the CRCI consider the interests of women also in article 6. The provision on the right to life of the child, which is more elaborate than its equivalent in the CRC reads:

[t]he child shall have the right to life from when he is a fetus in his/her mother's womb or in the case of his/her mother's death; abortion should be prohibited except under necessity warranted by the interests of the mother, the fetus, or both of them.[317]

Accordingly, abortion is lawful before the embryo reaches the foetal stage and, depending on the meaning attributed to 'necessity warranted by the interests of the mother, the fetus, or both' also after the end of the eighth week of pregnancy.[318] Donna Lee Bowen asserts that sharia jurisprudence is divided over termination of pregnancy: the majority opinion either forbids or strongly discourages abortion in the first four months of pregnancy, in the absence of a 'strong reason', while a minority of schools of Islamic law permits abortion before the embryo reaches the foetal stage (120 days, or four months) and prohibits it thereafter.[319] Article 6 appears to adopt the more liberal features of both opinions by not forbidding the termination of pregnancy during the first 120 days and allowing for exceptions based on necessity thereafter. It should be observed here that, alongside France and Luxembourg, Tunisia entered the following declaration to the CRC on the scope of article 6 concerning the right to life of the child:

The Government of the Republic of Tunisia declares that the Preamble to and the provisions of the Convention, in particular article 6, shall not be interpreted in such a way

---

[312] CRCI, art. 15.1. It is unclear whether this applies if the mother is unwilling to breastfeed.

[313] CRCI, art. 15.7.   [314] CRCI, art. 15.2.

[315] Abiad, *Sharia, Muslim States and International Human Rights Treaty Obligations: A Comparative Study*, at 23.

[316] See W. Schabas, *The Abolition of the Death Penalty in International Law*, 3rd ed., (Cambridge: Cambridge University Press, 2002); Second Optional Protocol to the International Covenant on Civil and Political Rights, aiming at the abolition of the death penalty, 1642 UNTS 414 (1989).

[317] CRCI, art. 6.

[318] Contrast to article 4.1 of the ACHR which protects the right to life 'from conception'. See Rehman, *International Human Rights Law*, 2nd ed., at 372.

[319] D. Lee Bowen, 'Contemporary Muslim Ethics of Abortion', in J. E. Brockopp (ed.), *Islamic Ethics of Life: Abortion, War, and Euthanasia*, (Columbia, South Carolina: University of South Carolina Press, 2003), 51–81, at 51–52.

as to impede the application of Tunisian legislation concerning voluntary termination of pregnancy.[320]

Article 15.5 which stipulates the right of the male child to circumcision,[321] and article 15.6 that requires non-interference by parents or others in 'medically altering the shape, features or sex of the fetus except for medical necessities',[322] are unique in the landscape of binding human rights law provisions. An equivalent to the latter provision appears in a resolution on prenatal sex-selection of the Committee on Equal Opportunities for Women and Men of the Council of Europe's Parliamentary Assembly.[323] However, research from the field strongly suggests that such legal prohibitions do little to change societal preferences for sons rather than daughters. They tend rather to interfere with the rights of women to privacy and health and further victimize them.[324] It is suggested that comprehensive and deep societal reforms are needed to establish that men and women are equal in value in order to address what has come to be known as gendercide.

2.4. Coherence with the system of international law

The CRCI departs most clearly from the Cairo Declaration in not including an equivalent to article 25. It should be remembered here that article 25 stipulates that Islamic sharia is the only source of interpretation of the provisions of the Cairo Declaration. Given that the CRCI is a binding document (which will enter into force on ratification by 20 states), the non-inclusion of such a clause is commendable. The CRCI does not attempt to isolate itself from the system of international law, and implicitly recognizes that its provisions must be interpreted in accordance with principles established by the VCLT, including the systemic integration principle of article 31.3.c. Interpretation of the CRCI, therefore, will have to take into account 'any relevant rules of international law applicable in the relations between the parties',[325] including those of the CRC, CEDAW, ICCPR, ICESCR, and others treaties and customary norms that address the rights of the child. On these grounds, the term 'religionalism', used to describe the full subjection of human rights to sharia in the OIC's Cairo Declaration, can be replaced by the proper term of 'regionalism' when describing the CRCI's relationship to the system of international law.

---

[320] Declaration of Tunisia to the CRC, accessed March 2012, UNTC, Online Database, Chapter IV: Human Rights, Convention on the Rights of the Child. On the issue of abortion during the drafting of the CRC, see Alston, 'The Unborn Child and Abortion under the Draft Convention on the Rights of the Child', 156–178.

[321] CRCI, art. 15.5. See also Rehman, *International Human Rights Law*, 2nd ed., at 372.

[322] CRCI, art. 15.6.

[323] Resolution on prenatal sex selection, Committee on Equal Opportunities for Women and Men, Parliamentary Assembly, Council of Europe, 9 September 2011.

[324] M. Kaur, 'Lessons from Punjab's "Missing Girls": Toward a Global Feminist Perspective on "Choice" in Abortion', 97 *California Law Journal* 3 (2009) 905–942; S. W. Tiefenbrun and C. J. Edwards, 'Gendercide and the Cultural Context of Sex Trafficking in China', 32 *Fordham International Law Journal* 3 (2009) 731–780. See also J. Westeson, 'Rights-based approach to sex-selection', accessed January 2012, http://www.intlawgrrls.com/2012/01/rights-based-approach-to-sex-selection.html.

[325] VCLT, art. 31.3.c.

It should be noted in this context that the CRCI does advance the principle that the provisions of sharia and the domestic legislation of member states should be respected.[326] However, neither the wording of these references nor their position in the architecture of the Covenant suggest that the rights of the child are subject to Islamic sharia or attempt to insulate OIC regionalism from treaty and customary human rights norms. The drafters linked the CRCI into the web of international agreements, noting in the preamble that the document is 'proceeding from Islamic efforts on issues of childhood, which contributed to the development of the 1989 United Nations Convention on the Rights of the Child' and that it is 'cognizant of... international conventions signed by its member states'.[327] This amounts to recognition of the continued international human rights obligations of states when acting as members of the OIC and parties to OIC human rights instruments.

Before concluding this section on the CRCI, some words on the mechanism charged with supervising the instrument are in order. Article 24 of the CRCI provides for the establishment of an Islamic Committee on the Rights of the Child, composed of representatives of all state parties to the instrument, which is 'to examine the progress made in the implementation of the Covenant'.[328] Unfortunately, the mandate of this Islamic Committee remains undefined, particularly in relation to monitoring and enforcement functions aimed at ensuring compliance with the Covenant.[329] Also disappointing is the fact that the drafters of the CRCI opted—contrary to international practice—for an inter-governmental mechanism to monitor implementation, as opposed to one formed of independent experts that could have better guaranteed the independence of the evaluations, whatever form these take.

A summary of the findings of our examination of the CRCI is in order at this stage. The most important point that should be retained is that the CRCI does not subject the rights of the child to a general sharia limitation clause or propose that sharia provides the interpretative principle of the instrument. The Covenant does provide for international legal anchors, which would require it to be interpreted in accord with universal standards on the rights of the child. Some provisions of the Covenant, moreover, may be regarded as advances on the UN CRC and other international human rights instruments. Certainly, the OIC Covenant has its particularities: Islam retains an important place; and more disappointing are the absence of the right to freedom of religion, the Islamic limitations on specific rights, and the clawback clauses. However, the limitations on rights are less extensive and important than those in the Cairo Declaration, and they do not weaken

---

[326] The other principles which ought to be followed in order to achieve the objectives in article 2 are: respect for the objectives and principles of the OIC; 'high priority to the rights, interest, protection, and development of children'; equality in care, rights, and duties; non-interference in the internal affairs of states; the cultural and civilization 'constants of the Islamic Ummah'. CRCI, art. 3.

[327] CRCI, preamble.   [328] CRCI, art. 24.

[329] Abiad and Mansoor, *Criminal Law and the Rights of the Child in Muslim States: A Comparative and Analytical Perspective*, at 49.

the protection of the rights of the child if they are interpreted in the light of the obligations of states under the CRC and other international instruments. It is possible to interpret the CRCI in manner that is consistent with the CRC. In this context, the establishment of the OIC Independent Permanent Human Rights Commission, as a mechanism potentially charged with the interpretation of the CRCI, is of great relevance.

3. The OIC Independent Permanent Human Rights Commission

In 2008 the revised OIC Charter set up the OIC Independent Permanent Human Rights Commission (IPHRC) as a permanent body to promote human rights in member states.[330] In June 2011 the OIC Council of Foreign Ministers adopted the Statute of the IPHRC.[331] According to the then OIC Secretary General the Statute attempts 'to strike a delicate balance' between Islamic human rights instruments, notably the Cairo Declaration and the CRCI, and international human rights instruments.[332] Indeed, the architecture of the Commission embeds this balancing act; the preamble of the IPHRC Statute recalls article 15 of the OIC Charter, which stipulates that the body:

shall promote civil, political, social and economic rights enshrined in the organisation's covenants and declarations and in universally agreed human rights instruments, in conformity with Islamic values.[333]

The preamble further '[recalls] the Cairo Declaration on Human Rights in Islam adopted in 1990' and stipulates that OIC member states' agreement on the Statute is 'pursuant to relevant international instruments, charters and conventions'.[334] This acknowledgement of the continued obligations under international human rights treaty law of OIC member states appears to set the Commission on the course of context-sensitive application of universal human rights standards.[335]

The importance of the OIC IPHRC should be understood against the scarcity of expert human rights mechanisms in the Asian region and the Middle East. Its establishment was greeted with a mixture of skepticism and moderate enthusiasm in both diplomatic circles and civil society. While the potential of the IPHRC can be grasped, it is also clear that the mandate of the Commission, and its procedural

---

[330] OIC Charter (2008), arts. 5 and 15. See also, Ten-Year Programme of Action to Meet the Challenges Facing the Muslim Ummah in the 21st Century, Third Extraordinary Session of the Islamic Summit Conference, Makkah al Mukarramah, 7–8 December 2005, art. VIII.2.

[331] OIC, Resolution on Legal Affairs No. 2/38-LEG, adopted by the 38th session of the Council of Foreign Ministers, Astana, 28–30 June 2011.

[332] 'OIC leader circles globe to represent voice of Muslim world', *Hürriyet Daily News*, 16 July 2010.

[333] Statute of the OIC Independent Permanent Human Rights Commission, Resolution on Legal Affairs No. 2/38-LEG, adopted by the 38th session of the Council of Foreign Ministers, Astana, 28–30 June 2011, preamble.(Hereafter OIC IPHRC Statute).

[334] OIC IPHRC Statute, preamble.

[335] This part of the chapter expands upon I. Cismas, 'Introductory Note to the Statute of the OIC Independent Permanent Human Rights Commission', 50 *ILM* 6 (2011) 1148–1160.

arrangements, will have a bearing on the legitimacy of the new body and the effectiveness of its work.[336]

3.1. Mandate of the OIC IPHRC

Article 12 of the Statute lays out the mandate as follows: 'The Commission shall carry out consultative tasks for the Council and submit recommendations to it. It shall also carry out other tasks as may be assigned to it by the Summit or the Council.'[337] Specifically, the Commission is allocated the task of supporting the OIC in issues of human rights at international level; consolidating cooperation among member states; providing technical cooperation and awareness-raising in the field of human rights; and undertaking studies and research.[338] In what appears to be a pull towards the coherence of the international system, article 15, gives the Commission the task of enhancing cooperation 'between the Organization and other international and regional human rights organizations'.[339] The IPHRC may want to read this stipulation as an encouragement to link its methods of work, research and interpretation to those of other regional and international human rights mechanisms and to draw upon their experience.

When compared to other human rights mechanisms at regional and international level, it becomes apparent that most monitoring attributes, and functions related to complaint procedures, are absent from the OIC IPHRC Statute.[340] The Statute does not empower the OIC IPHRC to review periodic state reports on the situation of human rights in OIC member states. Interestingly, the term 'monitoring' appears only once in the Statute, where the IPHRC is allocated the task of monitoring 'the observance of the human rights of Muslim communities and minorities'.[341] It should be recalled that, to be a member of the OIC, a state must have a Muslim majority. It must therefore be assumed that article 10 refers to states that are not OIC members. The notion 'Muslim communities and minorities' is often used in resolutions of the OIC Council of Foreign Ministers to mean communities in states that do not belong to the OIC.[342] Thus, the Commission is entrusted with an *ex parte* task, to monitor the obligations (towards Muslim minorities) of states which are not members of the OIC.[343] The Statute also does

---

[336] See Statement by Bacre Waly Ndiaye, Director, Human Rights Council and Treaties Division, Office of the United Nations High Commissioner for Human Rights to the 38th Session of the Council of Foreign Ministers, Organization of Islamic Conference, Astana, 28–30 June 2011.

[337] OIC IPHRC Statute, art. 12.

[338] OIC IPHRC Statute, arts. 9, 10, 13, 14 and 16.

[339] OIC IPHRC Statute, art. 15.

[340] For the mandate of the Inter-American Commission on Human Rights see ACHR, VII. For the African Commission on Human and Peoples' Rights see ACHPR, II. For an example at international level, see the mandate of the Human Rights Committee in part IV of the ICCPR.

[341] OIC IPHRC Statute, art. 10.

[342] See, for example, Resolutions on Communities and Minorities in Non-OIC Member States, adopted by the 37th session of the Council of Foreign Ministers, Dushanbe, 18–20 May 2010, OIC/CFM-37/2010/MM/RES/FINAL.

[343] This is confirmed by the Rules of Procedure of the Independent Permanent Human Rights Commission of the Organization of Islamic Cooperation, adopted by the 39th session of the Council

not make provision for the Commission to receive individual and inter-state complaints of human rights violations. If it was hoped that the IPHRC would represent an access to justice mechanism for individuals victims of human rights violations in the OIC region, this may well remain a distant wish.

It would appear that the IPHRC was conceived, not as a monitoring body but rather as a consultative one or a think tank of the OIC Council of Foreign Ministers. The relationship between the OIC Council of Foreign Ministers and the IPHRC resembles that between the UN Human Rights Council and its Advisory Committee, yet the competences attributed to the IPHRC surpass those of the Advisory Committee. As an example, the Advisory Committee lacks the right of initiative to choose the studies it undertakes, and is dependent upon an express mandate from the Human Rights Council and the latter's priorities.[344] Moreover, the Committee cannot offer advice or consultancy on human rights issues directly to states, whereas the IPHRC Statute makes provision for such services where OIC member states approve of or request them.[345] This optional clause may seriously limit the effectiveness of the Commission's work if it is interpreted to mean that governments may exclude the human rights situation in their states from the consultative tasks of the IPHRC. This would sharply contrast with the affirmation of independence contained in its title, and would raise questions about the Commission's substantive independence and its capacity to fulfil its tasks.

Nonetheless, nothing in the mandate prevents the commissioners from exploring a variety of working methods, drawing on the example of the UN Special Procedures,[346] as opposed to the much less ambitious Advisory Committee of the Human Rights Council. The varied and efficient working methods which UN Special Rapporteurs, Independent Experts, and Working Groups have developed over the past three decades are partly responsible for the reputation of the UN Special Procedures, as the 'crown jewel' of the UN human rights system.[347] As such, in addition to drafting thematic reports, the IPHRC commissioners could undertake country missions to observe the human rights situation in OIC countries. Such visits would enable them to benefit from on-site input from civil society[348] and the authorities, examine legislation, and advise on legislative and administrative

of Foreign Ministers, November 2012, Djibouti, OIC/IPHRC/ROP/FINAL, Rule 2.2 (Hereafter OIC IPHRC Rules of Procedure).

[344] See Human Rights Council, Resolution 5/1 of 18 June 2007, Institution-building of the United Nations Human Rights Council, Annex, para. 75.

[345] OIC IPHRC Statute, arts. 14 and 17.

[346] See Manual of Operations of the Special Procedures of the Human Rights Council, August 2008. See also Golay, Mahon and Cismas, 'The Impact of the UN Special Procedures on the Development and Implementation of Economic, Social and Cultural Rights', 299–318; J. Gutter, 'Special Procedures and the Human Rights Council: Achievements and Challenges Ahead', 7 *Human Rights Law Review* 1 (2007) 93–107; B. G. Ramcharan, *The Protection Roles of UN Human Rights Special Procedures*, (The Hague: Martinus Nijhoff, 2009).

[347] K. Annan, Statement: 'Urging End to Impunity, Annan sets forth ideas to bolster UN efforts', UN Doc. SG/SM/10788, 8 Dec. 2006.

[348] It should be noted that, under article 15, the Commission is mandated to provide support to 'Member State-accredited national institutions and civil society organizations active in the area of human rights'. OIC IPHRC Statute, art. 15.

reform. The Rules of Procedure adopted by the IPHRC in August 2012 and sub-sequently approved by the Council of Foreign Ministers provide the possibility for commissioners to undertake, upon receipt of consent of the state in question, 'needs assessments missions' and 'election observance missions'.[349] These can certainly be tailored in practice to resemble the model of the country missions of UN Special Procedures. Although individual complaints were not included in the mandate of the IPHRC, nothing prevents the commissioners from making use of diplomatic channels to address various human rights violations.

Alongside thematic studies, article 17 holds the greatest potential in respect to the balancing act embedded in the Statute as it sets out the IPHRC's interpretation role: the Commission may submit recommendations designed to refine OIC human rights declarations and covenants.[350] This could put the IPHRC in a situation similar to that of UN treaty bodies, which adopt general comments interpreting the various provi-sions of the conventions they monitor. Interestingly, the former OIC Secretary General had already recommended to the commissioners during the opening session that they should review OIC human rights instruments, including the Cairo Declaration.[351] It is disappointing to note that the Rules of Procedure of the Commission appear less ambitious in relation to its interpretation role than the Statute's provision would allow, and fail to elaborate extensively on this role—however they also do not pose restrictions.[352]

In an optimistic account, the balancing act embedded in the OIC IPHRC Statute could thus have at least two types of effects on OIC regionalism. First, through the activity of the Commission, the OIC may move away from claiming that rights are subject to sharia towards a margin of appreciation doctrine guided by the maxim *in dubio pro libertate* which allows for a context-sensitive application of universal human rights. The caveat, of course, is that the IPHRC—which is not a judicial body—must be willing to systematically adopt that approach in its thematic reports and interpre-tation of OIC human rights instruments, and use a variety of working methods, as suggested earlier.

A digression towards the previous discussion on cultural relativism is necessary at this point. Some legal scholars consider that relativism, rooted in contextuality as opposed to exceptionalism, is essential for the human rights movement. 'Human rights are not just abstract', they argue, since human rights acquire value in their application, and they must therefore be made meaningful in particular social conditions.[353] The Committee on Economic, Social and Cultural Rights and various UN Special Rapporteurs often stress the need to address issues of cultural acceptability when promoting the rights

---

[349] OIC IPHRC Rules of Procedure, Rules 64 and 65.

[350] OIC IPHRC Statute, art. 17.

[351] As cited in Turan Kayaoğlu, 'It's Time to Revise The Cairo Declaration of Human Rights in Islam', Brookings Doha Center, 23 April 2012.

[352] See OIC IPHRC Rules of Procedure, Rule 56.

[353] Marks and Clapham, *International Human Rights Lexicon*, at 388. For another point of view, see E. Benvenisti, 'Margin of Appreciation, Consensus, and Universal Standards', 31 *NYU J.L. & Pol.* (1998) 843–854.

to food, health, education, and sanitation, for instance.[354] In another example, the ECtHR has acknowledged that profound questions concerning the fundamental right to life are raised by the freezing of embryos, which may be answered in different ways by different countries of Europe,[355] dispelling the myth of a monolithic Judeo-Christian *espace juridique européen*. At the same time, the Inter-American Court of Human Rights is said to have rejected the margin of appreciation doctrine based on a 'deep distrust of domestic governments'.[356] The IACtHR identified as dangerous the fact that discourses of cultural relativism are often rooted in arbitrariness and not in contextuality, as in the context-sensitive application of human rights.[357] Similarly, Farida Shaheed, the Independent Expert in the field of cultural rights, notes that recognizing the importance of culture for the realization of human rights does not imply that 'all cultural practices can be considered as protected in international human rights law'; challenging cultural practices represents, at times, the only way to realize human rights.[358]

Against this background, a margin of appreciation doctrine should not embrace forms of cultural relativism that are used rhetorically by authorities to shield their domination from internal and external review, or by societies to perpetuate discriminatory, patriarchal, and oppressive patterns. Martti Koskenniemi summarized disagreements regarding the role and application of 'pragmatic directives which on the whole would seem to give the most satisfactory solution', to which the margin of appreciation certainly belongs, as follows:

---

[354] The normative content of socio-economic rights is often described in terms of the 4As schema: availability, accessibility (physical and economic), acceptability (cultural and gender), and adequacy or quality. See Annual report of the Special Rapporteur on the right to education, Katarina Tomasevski, UN doc E/CN.4/1999/49, 13 January 1999, paras. 51–74; CESCR, *General Comment No. 12: Right to adequate food*, UN Doc. E/C.12/1999/5, paras. 7–13; CESCR, *General Comment No. 14: The right to the highest attainable standard of health (art. 12)*, 11 August 2000, UN Doc. E/C.12/2000/4, para. 12; Report of the independent expert on the issue of human rights obligations related to access to safe drinking water and sanitation, Catarina de Albuquerque, Un doc A/HRC/12/24, 1 July 2009, paras. 70–80.

[355] In the case in question, Ms Evans complained to the ECtHR that requiring the father's consent for the continued storage and implantation of her fertilized eggs was in breach of her rights under Articles 8 (right to respect for her private and family life) and 14 (non-discrimination clause) of the Convention and the rights of the embryos, under Article 2 (right to life). *Evans v. the United Kingdom*, Application no. 6339/05, Grand Chamber, Judgment of 10 April 2007; *Evans v. the United Kingdom*, Application no. 6339/05, Judgment of 7 March 2006. See also Clapham, *Human Rights: A Very Short Introduction*, at 47.

[356] X. Fuentes, 'International Law-making in the Field of Sustainable Development: the Unequal Competition between Development and the Environment', in N. Schrijver and F. Weiss (eds.), *International Law and Sustainable Development: Principles and Practice*, (Leiden: Martinus Nijhoff, 2004), 7–38, at 32.

[357] See also Adamantia Pollis' masterful contrast of Japan and East Asian countries, depicting the fine line between legitimate cultural differences and relativism employed to shield domination from critique. A. Pollis, 'Cultural Relativism Revisited: Through a State Prism', 18 *HRQ* (1996), 316–344, at 332–338. See also S. A. James, 'Reconciling International Human Rights and Cultural Relativism: the Case of Female Circumcision', 8 *Bioethics* 1 (1994), 1–26.

[358] Report of the independent expert in the field of cultural rights, Ms Farida Shaheed, submitted pursuant to the resolution 10/23 of the Human Rights Council, UN Doc. A/HRC/14/36, 22 March 2010, para. 34. See also CEDAW Committee, *General Recommendation No. 3*, 6th session, 1987; CEDAW Committee, *General Recommendation No. 19: Violence against women*, 11th session, 1992; CEDAW Committee, *General Recommendation No. 21*.

These disagreements reflect the twin concern of modern lawyers: Their use should not be such as to allow States complete freedom (apologism). But they should neither lead into solutions which are not responsive to the social context (utopism).[359]

Along these lines, should the OIC IPHRC embrace a margin of appreciation doctrine, then this must conform strictly to the maxim *in dubio pro libertate* and be characterized by the following cluster of elements:[360]

1. In response to cases where states may lawfully reach different decisions on the application of an international norm, given that the rule is open-ended or unsettled;

2. The Commission should review:

   i. that the decision concerning the modality of execution of a state's international obligation was the outcome of a democratic decision-making process, inclusive of civil society, minorities, and the specifically affected groups;

   ii. that the manner chosen by the state to execute its international obligation is in accord with the object and purpose of the norm;

   iii. that the interference with a human right conforms to international procedural standards is prescribed by law, pursues a legitimate aim, is necessary in a democratic society, and is proportional.

   iv. that the domestic court which reviewed the interference fulfilled international fair-trial standards, and in the case of religious courts whether secular alternatives were readily available;

3. Following such review, the Commission could allow a certain degree of discretion to national authorities on the manner they choose to execute their international obligations.

Following on from this, the interpretation of Islamic law may become a main task of the IPHRC. Certainly, limitation clauses based on sharia and clawback clauses would fall within the ambit of the Commission's general comments on OIC human rights instruments. As has been stressed throughout this chapter, conflict between sharia and human rights is not inevitable, but it can occur when sharia is interpreted in particular ways. The IPHRC will be in a unique position to develop the capacity of sharia to respond constructively to changing circumstances by proposing interpretations of Islamic law which promote human rights and uphold the existing international obligations of OIC member states. Its status as the OIC's human rights mechanism gives it the advantage of being able to draw on comparative uses and interpretations of sharia and to forge cultural legitimacy for human rights standards in various Muslim

---

[359] M. Koskenniemi, *From Apology to Utopia: The Structure of International Legal Argument*, (Cambridge: Cambridge University Press, 2005), at 41.

[360] I am drawing on the analysis of limitations based on sharia in this chapter; on the discussion in Chapter 1, III.1 in this volume concerning the pitfalls of the margin of appreciation doctrine as utilized by the European Court; and also on lessons from Brems, *Human Rights: Universality and Diversity*, at 357–421; I. de la Rasilla del Moral, 'The Increasingly Marginal Appreciation of the Margin-of-Appreciation Doctrine', 7 *German Law Review* 6 (2006), 611–623; Y. Shany, 'Toward a General Margin of Appreciation Doctrine in International Law?', 16 *EJIL* 5 (2005), 907–940.

contexts. It is significant to note that, during the inaugural session, the IPHRC set itself a number of priorities, which included the rights of women and issues related to the rights of the child, such as education.[361] Given that personal status laws governed by sharia in several OIC member states concern precisely the rights of women and children, the IPHRC's list of priorities is encouraging.

3.2. Procedural aspects

The Statute includes a number of provisions on the composition and functioning of the IPHRC.[362] The Commission is composed of 18 members, nominated by OIC governments from 'among experts of established distinction in the area of human rights', who are elected by the OIC Council of Foreign Ministers for a three-year period, renewable once.[363] While it encourages gender and geographic balance,[364] the Statute lacks explicit provisions requiring the commissioners to be independent and impartial. The requirement of independence of the commissioners is provided for in the Commission's Rules of Procedures, however these fail to explicitly point to conflicts of interest or to request that members do not serve in governmental functions.[365] The composition of the Commission is divided by region, with six seats each for Asian, African, and Middle Eastern members. Neither the Statute, nor the Rules of Procedure provide for a transparent mechanism for the selection of candidates which ensures information to the interested public.[366]

It should be noted that only four of the 18 members of the current Commission are women, however one of the four is the President of the body.[367] One commentator notes that the Commission appears to be a rather interesting mix of lawyers, human rights practitioners, academics, and diplomats.[368]

The provisions on participation of civil society appear extraordinarily cumbersome and raise questions about the transparency of the IPHRC's future work. The Commission may invite guests, including non-governmental organizations and national human rights institutions, to attend its meetings, however, their participation is conditioned on the host country's consent (thus giving the headquarter country a potential *de facto* veto power over attendance requests),[369] on receiving the approval of all members of the Commission, and on the OIC's willingness to

---

[361] *OIC Journal*, No. 20, January–March 2012, accessed June 2012, http://www.oic-oci.org/journal.asp.

[362] OIC IPHRC Statute, arts. 3–7 and 18–24.   [363] OIC IPHRC Statute, art. 3.

[364] OIC IPHRC Statute, arts. 6 and 7.

[365] OIC IPHRC Rules of Procedure, Rule 6.

[366] The establishment of such a mechanism forms part of the recommendations put forward by a group of experts, including this author, see Recommendations to the Organization of Islamic Cooperation's Independent Permanent Human Rights Commission, *Todays Zaman*, October 2013, accessed November 2013, http://www.todayszaman.com/newsDetail_getNewsById.action;jsessionid=799552C30986D4C20CDC36DB39A4B611?newsId=330895.

[367] OIC Journal, No. 20, January-March 2012, at 28.

[368] M. Juul Petersen, 'Islamic or Universal Human Rights? The OIC's Independent Permanent Human Rights Commission', Danish Institute for International Studies, 2012, at 23.

[369] There appears to have been a heated debate over which country will serve as headquarters of the OIC Commission. Both Saudi Arabia and Indonesia were major contenders. The resolution of the OIC

accredit such organizations.[370] As they appear now, these conditions may fall short of ensuring wide participation, transparency and ultimately the accountability of the OIC and its Commission for their decisions and omissions on human rights issues. In its Final Report on the Accountability of International Organizations, the ILA Committee recommended that bodies like the IPHRC should regularly organize briefings with representatives of non-governmental organizations and provide the latter with opportunities to offer input, information, and expertise, in this case, on human rights issues and situations.[371] The experience of UN treaty bodies, UN Special Procedures, and the Universal Periodic Review of the Human Rights Council demonstrates that an institutionalized relation with non-governmental organizations is vital for the effective functioning of these mechanisms and for holding international organizations accountable for their conduct. In this light, it is important that the OIC establishes clear, transparent, and non-restrictive criteria for accreditation of non-governmental organizations and does not devolve accreditation decisions to national authorities, which may be inclined to screen some out on political grounds. The OIC Commission should institutionalize regular consultations with human rights defenders and non-governmental organizations. The IPHRC could thereby offer a voice to civil society across the OIC region, while benefiting from its insights and expertise on human rights issues.

The Rules of Procedure of the Commission which could have ironed out some of the deficiencies in relation to participation of civil society organizations remove only the express approval of all members of the Commission, while keeping in place the other restrictions (host country approval and OIC accreditation).[372] Rule 45, which stipulates that the 'Commission may invite an individual, organization or other relevant entities whose aims and purposes are in conformity with the spirit, objectives and principles of Charter to facilitate exchange of views on any specific issue under consideration'[373] could, nonetheless, prove useful in bypassing the outlined restrictive conditions. This remains an ad-hoc solution however, as opposed to institutionalized cooperation with non-governmental organization and other individuals.

In its first years of operation, the IPHRC will reveal the degree to which it is eager to advance the protection of human rights in the OIC region, and able to do so in a context-sensitive manner. In the end it can be argued that the OIC IPHRC's

---

Council of Foreign Ministers of 2011 foresaw that the General Secretariat of the OIC in Jeddah would host the IPHRC's first session. OIC, Resolution on Legal Affairs No. 2/38-LEG, adopted by the 38th session of the Council of Foreign Ministers, Astana, 28–30 June 2011, para. 3. In fact, Jakarta hosted the event, on 20–24 February 2012. See *OIC Journal*, No. 20, January–March 2012, at 28.

[370] OIC IPHRC Statute, art. 21. Article 15 also restricts the support that the Commission could give only to 'Member State-accredited national institutions and civil society organizations active in the area of human rights'. See also 'Human Rights Defenders Call for Inclusion in OIC Human Rights Body', 22 June 2011, accessed December 2011, http://oichumanrights.wordpress.com/2011/07/14/human-rights-defenders-call-for-inclusion-in-oic-human-rights-body/.

[371] International Law Association, Accountability of International Organizations: Final Report, Berlin Conference, 2004, at 16–17.

[372] OIC IPHRC Rules of Procedure, Rule 44.2.

[373] OIC IPHRC Rules of Procedure, Rule 45.

Statute is flawed because it does not include monitoring and an individual communications procedure, and because it fails to fully guarantee independence, transparency, and participation. And while the Rules of Procedures could provide some fixes, they essentially remain open for interpretation. Be that as it may, the adoption of the Statute of the OIC Commission, with all its imperfections, reflects the balancing act that is to be achieved by the IPHRC between Muslim contexts and the respect for international human rights standards. In this sense, the OIC IPHRC promises, but does not yet deliver, a regionalism that understands the need to build legitimacy for international human rights in the Muslim world.

V. Conclusion

If the Cairo Declaration is taken as a measure of success, the OIC's performance as interpreter of human rights in Islam is disappointing, at the very least. The Cairo Declaration chooses a cultural relativism that subjects universal human rights to local interpretations of sharia law. For those Muslim states which rely on interpretations of sharia that conflict with human rights standards, it provides a disincentive to reform Islamic law. However, the real measure of the failure of the Cairo Declaration to guide OIC states in the area of human rights in Islam is its demonstrated lack of influence on OIC members. This is so, on one hand, because this instrument which proclaims sharia as the source of its provisions cannot be reconciled with legal systems that do not use sharia or use Islamic law for only certain areas of their legislation; and because the CDHRI does not seem to represent the position of the majority of Muslim states. The majority acknowledge that reforms within sharia are necessary if they are to comply with their international human rights obligations. The Cairo Declaration seems to be the foundation of a 'religionalism' that fails to reflect the interests of its own members.

With the adoption of the CRCI and the Statute of the OIC IPHRC, the OIC has made a step towards a regionalism that can potentially provide a context-sensitive application of universal human rights. There are certainly particularities in the CRCI, such as potentially dangerous sharia limitations on specific rights and clawback clauses that may accommodate interpretations of Islamic law which do not uphold international standards; not least, the text is silent on the protection of religious freedom, whereas OIC member states are bound by international obligations to respect this right. Based on these shortcomings, some would see plenty of opportunities for state abuse, if the CRCI is to enter into force. However, provided a coherent interpretation of the CRCI with the CRC and other international human rights instruments is sought systematically, acceding OIC member states would not be hampered in their efforts to achieve compliance with their international obligations. It is suggested that the regional and international instruments could be mutually supportive provided that clauses identified as problematic in the CRCI are read in the light of provisions of international human rights treaties.

Finally, the OIC IPHRC represents a promise. Its mandate is not as elaborate as that of peer bodies. In particular, it cannot receive individual communications and certain procedural issues need to be ironed out through practice, such as the restrictive participation of civil society organizations in its work. It does nonetheless have the potential to adopt general comments after the model of the UN treaty bodies, to propose modifications of existing OIC human rights instruments, and adopt working methods inspired by those of UN Special Procedures. By these means, it could legitimately address the human rights situations in OIC member states. The task is on the shoulders of the commissioners to prove cynics wrong.

The OIC is in a particularly favourable position to make use of its 'special' legitimacy as an organization with religious contours, of its Muslim but not uniform membership, and its activity in various fora, to construct universal appreciation for human rights by means of an enlightened interpretation of Islam. In a context in which Islamic principles constitute a prime legitimating factor for legal norms in many parts of the Muslim world,[374] instruments on human rights in Islam can play a vital role. The scope and shape of these instruments will vary, reflecting members' and the OIC's political agendas. A crucial element in influencing the agendas of states will be the success of cross-cultural dialogues, within and between OIC member states and with external actors such as other states and treaty bodies, and non-state actors, not least those emerging from the 'Arab Spring'. If the OIC's instruments are to have an influence on the human rights records of Muslim states they need to represent the variety of contexts that exist, and should not be restrictive, or reflect the views and position of a conservative minority. In the end, in a reiterative manner, the validity of OIC regionalism will acquire legitimacy if it is firmly grounded in the system of international law, of which universal human rights standards are an important component. In the words of Robert Jennings: 'Universality does not mean uniformity. It does mean, however, that such a regional international law, however variant, is part of the system as a whole, and not a separate system, and it ultimately derives its validity from the system as a whole'.[375]

---

[374] Baderin, 'A Macroscopic Analysis of the Practice of Muslim State Parties to International Human Rights Treaties: Conflict of Congruence', at 266.

[375] R. Y. Jennings, 'Universal International Law in a Multicultural World', in B. Marten and I. Brownlie (eds.), *Liber Amicorum for Lord Wilberforce* (Oxford: Calderon Press, 1987), 39–51, at 42.

Conclusions
Accountability and Legitimacy

'If I live three more days, I would want to see that the world has cleared.'

—Elisabeta Rizea[1]

I. Do Religious Actors Form an Autonomous Legal Category?

Premised on the understanding that religious actors are engaging with international law and contributing to its construction, either through the promotion of human rights standards or the hindrance of their development, this project proposed a shift in focus from religion to religious actors. To that end, it employed the analytical category of religious actors comprised of non-state entities, states, and international organizations which assume the role of interpreting religion and claim a 'special' legitimacy anchored foremost in tradition or charisma. The study, thus, outlined the contours of a new narrative which is not primarily concerned with the (in)compatibility of religion with international law but with the accountability of religious actors under international law for the interpretations they choose to put forward. The analytical category of religious actors served as a heuristic device in the démarche to demonstrate that these actors do not form an autonomous legal category in international law and their special legitimacy does not frustrate the international legality regime. Three challenging case studies were chosen to verify two central arguments: whether religious actors enjoy special or exclusive rights compared to their non-religious peers; and whether religious actors have the same legal obligations as their respective non-religious peers.

The aim of the first case study was to illustrate that religious organizations acquire rights under the European Convention on Human Rights (ECHR) in a similar fashion to non-religious legal entities, and that the scope of their obligations can be discerned from states' positive obligations to prevent and punish human rights violations by non-state actors. Like their non-religious peers, religious organizations have successfully claimed a number of rights under the ECHR.

---

[1] In original: 'Trei zile dacă mai trăiesc, dar vreau să știu că s-a limpezit lumea'. I. Nicolau and T. Nițu (eds.), *Povestea Elisabetei Rizea din Nucșoara urmată de mărturia lui Cornel Drăgoi*, 2nd ed., (București: Humanitas, 2010) at 23.

Unlike their peers however, religious organizations have benefitted from protection under article 9 of the Convention, which guarantees the right to freedom of thought, conscience, and religion. At first sight, this exclusivity seems to invalidate one of the two central arguments of this book, the proposition that religious actors do not enjoy special or exclusive rights in relation to their non-religious peers. The study shows however that the right of religious organizations to freedom of religion was derived by the Strasbourg mechanisms from the right of individuals to collectively manifest religion. Thus, the comparative category is not non-religious legal entities, but individuals, who as we know, receive protection for their manifestations of belief under the Convention on an equal footing. Simply put, what appears to be a difference in treatment between legal entities stems from the fact that some individuals *choose* to express this right in an institutionalized religious form (through churches and religious organizations with philosophical objects) while others do not.

The second part of the analysis, focusing on the limits to church autonomy, clarified that religious organizations are not cocooned or isolated from legal obligations under the ECHR. The European Court of Human Rights (ECtHR) has specifically anchored religious autonomy in the right of individuals to manifest their religion collectively and in freedom of association provisions. While cautioning states that assessing the legitimacy of religious beliefs and their expression is generally incompatible with their obligations under the Convention, the Strasbourg mechanisms have gradually developed limitations to church autonomy in an attempt to account for the realization of the rights of others. The ECHR mechanisms began by affirming a principle of voluntariness, which provided an exit strategy for church employees or members who felt that their rights had been breached by a church, subsequently they adopted procedural limitations which set out the duties of religious organizations to provide due process guarantees, and recently introduced substantive limitations. The later restrictions reflect the effects of balancing the right of a religious organization to administer itself and the human rights of those affected by the decisions or commands of religious institutions. As such, the ECtHR affirmed that states have a positive obligation to ensure sufficient consideration is given to employees' rights to privacy, freedom of religion, and freedom of association, balanced against the right of religious organizations to autonomy. In turn, the Court's judgments can be read to imply obligations for the religious bodies themselves: in their decisions, they must consider the rights of third parties. It is evident that while religious organizations are entitled to require loyalty and obedience from their employees, in accordance with their interpretations of religion, this duty of loyalty cannot remove the substance of their employees' human rights. This is a remarkable evolution in the Strasbourg court's thinking: from church autonomy interpreted as a quasi-untouchable regime to a portrayal of religious organizations as rights-holders *and* duty-bearers under the ECHR. It is our conclusion that religious organizations do not belong to an autonomous legal category in international law.

Here, another tale emerges. The legitimacy of religious organizations' actions and interpretations appears to be correlated to their legality under the ECHR. It was

claimed in this study that, for religious organizations which seek to shield their interpretations of religion from review by courts in a democratic society, the best defence
is to assume their human rights responsibilities, the contours of which have emerged
in Strasbourg jurisprudence. Going forward, religious bodies should not rely only
on the duty of obedience of their employees and adherents to their interpretation of
religion, when they manage church governance, employment relations, and membership issues. Churches must also embrace human rights standards if they wish to
operate in a way that is fully legitimate in society and under international law.

The second case study focused on the Holy See and the Vatican. It was proposed
that the Holy See and the Vatican form a construct with one single personality
anchored in two different sources: international custom recognizing the religious
legitimacy of the Holy See, and the resemblance of statehood conferred on the
construct by the Lateran Treaty. This state-like construct challenged the dual personality scenario which posits the existence of two distinct legal personae—the
Holy See and the Vatican City State. It also challenged the practice of the Holy
See, that shifts its personalities according to context and assumes the privileges of
statehood while denying the corresponding obligations.

The research demonstrated that the state-like construct proposal is supported
by reading the provisions of the Lateran Treaty in the light of the effectiveness
criteria for statehood (territory, population, government, and independence). It
is unquestionable today that, after the extinction of the Papal States, the international personality of the Holy See (but not as a state) continued to be recognized
as customary by virtue of the latter's religious legitimacy. As a result of the Lateran
Treaty, a resemblance of statehood was granted to the Holy See-Vatican construct,
not to the Holy See, nor to the Vatican on its own. Only as a construct with the
Vatican (and thanks to the latter's territoriality) can the Holy See 'clothe' itself
with the resemblance of statehood. The Holy See's claim to an external, distinct
international personality invalidates the resemblance of statehood, mainly because
the requirement of independence would not be fulfilled. Furthermore, the Vatican
is essentially a territory and has *on its own* no legal basis to support the claim for
a distinct international legal personality. The dual personality scenario is therefore
legally untenable.

An analysis of diplomatic practice and the jurisprudence of national courts generally upheld the construct proposal. The research also revealed that the right of the
two 'titles' to become members of inter-governmental organizations and parties to
international treaties exclusively open for signature to states is difficult to reconcile
with a dual personality scenario; circumstances support the construct formula.
Thus, while collective recognition of the Holy See has been achieved through its
participation at the UN as non-member observer state, it is the construct with
its single personality which has been recognized. Importantly, the rights it was
granted are those of a state. For that reason, the obligations of the Holy See in the
UN system would have to be not less than those of other states. Having established
that the Holy See-Vatican construct enjoys the rights of a state and has *formally*
incurred the obligations of a state through its adherence to international treaties,
including human rights treaties, it can be confirmed that the standing of the Holy

See-Vatican in international law is no different than that of other states. It should be emphasized at this point that, despite advances made to hold non-state actors accountable, the strongest accountability framework today remains that addressed to states. In this sense, our conclusion that the Holy See-Vatican construct incurs legal responsibilities on a par with other states results in strengthening its accountability under human rights law.

When we take a step back from positive law, the above conclusion is not refuted but appears relativized. No other state claims that its obligations under international human rights treaty law are moral by invoking its 'unique' and 'special' nature. More relevant, perhaps, it is doubtful that any other state's similar claims would have been nurtured as the Holy See's have been. Reading through the early reports of the Committee on the Elimination of Racial Discrimination, one gets the strong impression that the Holy See was regarded as a special actor, which joined the circle of states with the sole purpose of lending its tremendous legitimacy to human rights standards. In recent years, however, treaty bodies strike a very different tone. At present praise continues for the Holy See's 'universal mission'; but treaty bodies also insist that the Holy See incurs legal obligations and that a different approach to their discharge, with a strong focus on extraterritoriality, is required.

In the end, this study must conclude that while the religious legitimacy of the Holy See is acknowledged, this does not translate into a different legality regime. In the context of clerical child sexual abuse in Ireland and discussion of the Holy See's responsibility for handling the prevention and reporting of such cases, claims that the state party should fulfil its obligations under the Convention on the Rights of the Child (CRC) have become increasingly vocal. One is left with a sense that, this time around, human rights standards and their acknowledgment could lend legitimacy to the Holy See. This is a tale to which we shall return.

The third case study examined the Organization of Islamic Cooperation (OIC), an actor which bases its membership on Muslim identity and pursues religious as well as political objectives. The aim of the analysis was to flesh out how far, and in what ways, the OIC has succeeded in fulfilling its assumed mission of being the voice of the Muslim world in the area of human rights. The study started by asserting the right of the OIC to set up regional human rights instruments and mechanisms for their supervision, in a similar fashion to its non-religious regional peers. At the same time, it emphasized that regionalism in the area of human rights can take two forms: a highly problematic cultural relativism that creates exceptions from international standards, and a context-sensitive application of universal human rights.

An examination of the non-binding Cairo Declaration on Human Rights in Islam revealed the contours of a 'religionalism' which made human rights standards subject to Islamic law. The drafters of the Cairo Declaration undertook to limit the application of the rights it affirmed by appeal to sharia law, and proclaimed that the latter was the sole principle for interpretation of the instrument. The approach accommodates, on an equal footing, local interpretations of sharia that sanction corporal penalties such as flogging and amputation and interpretations that strive for greater equality between women and men.

Perhaps the most interesting conclusion was that the Cairo Declaration, far from matching its intention to provide 'general guidance' for OIC member states in the field of human rights, has had little influence. How can this be explained? The research demonstrates that the Cairo Declaration failed to take account of the variety of legal systems of OIC member states. In some states, sharia plays no role, whereas in others it is a source of law among others. Moreover, the cultural relativist challenge of the Cairo Declaration appears not to reflect the views expressed by many OIC member states when their implementation of international human rights treaty obligations is reviewed. Many OIC states appear to accept that certain interpretations of sharia law need to (and can) be reformed, to enable them to fully realize their international treaty obligations. Importantly, other states and treaty bodies consider that OIC states which use sharia have the same international obligations as their non-religious peers. Taken together, these facts may explain why most Muslim states do not make use of the Cairo Declaration either to guide their conduct in the area of human rights or to excuse imperfect performance of their treaty obligations.

The binding Covenant on the Rights of the Child in Islam (CRCI), which 10 years after its drafting has not entered into force, demonstrates a departure from the Cairo Declaration. Islam and sharia law continue to play a role in this instrument, but it is much reduced. Disappointingly, clawback clauses and Islamic limitations on some specific rights may still accommodate local interpretations of sharia law that fail international standards. It should be emphasized however that the CRCI does not attempt to contract out from the system of international law, and its provisions should therefore be read in conjunction with those of the UN Convention on the Rights of the Child and other international human rights treaties to which OIC member states are party. The Covenant also provides some interesting normative additions to the canon of international standards, which may strengthen the protection of human rights in Muslim contexts. The newly established OIC Independent Permanent Human Rights Commission, while clearly not designed as an access to justice mechanism for victims of human rights violations across the OIC region, has a certain potential to set the OIC on the path towards a regionalism that could promote the context-sensitive application of universal human rights.

Over two decades, the codification process of the OIC in the area of human rights has shown both faces of cultural relativism, one which challenges universal standards, and one which timidly promises context-sensitive application of human rights. Throughout the period, other states and international judicial mechanisms have shown no sign that they will allow the OIC and its member states to assert special rights or obligations because of their claim to legitimacy in the context of Islam. Most striking is that the special legality regime proposed by the Cairo Declaration has been, albeit implicitly, contested by OIC member states themselves. Chapter 5 therefore revealed that neither the OIC, nor Muslim states, belong to an autonomous legal category. What it did suggest is that the international legality framework is a guarantee for universal human rights standards because regional arrangements are legitimated based on the coherence of their norms with general norms. At the same time, the study suggests that the OIC, with its Muslim but

varied membership, is in a particularly favourable position to forge cultural legitimacy for universal human rights standards in Muslim contexts. A tale of mutual
need, for legitimation of both the religious actor and the law, emerges again.

What answer does the study provide to its principal question: Are religious
actors an autonomous legal category in international law? Based on the cases analysed here, the answer must be negative. Some religious actors surely pose certain
challenges, to which the international system must respond; however, the response
has not been to propose a different legality regime. The framework of rights and
obligations applicable to religious actors appears to be the same one that is applicable to non-religious states, international organizations, and non-state legal entities.

This brings us back to Ms Lubna Hussein on the opening page of this volume.
Six years before Ms Hussein was arrested in Khartoum for committing an indecent act, by wearing trousers, the African Commission of Human and Peoples'
Rights found that Sudan had violated its obligations under the African Charter.
Based on article 152 of the Sudanese criminal code, the authorities had detained,
sentenced, and imposed the penalty of flogging on university students who held
a picnic beside a river and were deemed to have committed indecent acts.[2] In the
most critical terms, the Commission condemned the flogging as cruel, inhuman,
and degrading treatment and the physical violence imposed for the offences as
state-sponsored torture. It requested the state party to:

a) **Immediately amend** the Criminal Law of 1991, in conformity with its obligations
   under the African Charter and other relevant international human rights instruments;
b) **Abolish** the penalty of lashes...[3]

Sudan, which interprets Islam in enacting its laws, was held *accountable* because its
interpretation of sharia law was in conflict with its international legal obligations.
In 2009, the same article 152, under the same criminal code, was used to apply the
same penalty of flogging on 10 of Ms Hussein's 'co-offenders'. This could be taken
as evidence of the limited operational effect of the approach taken in this study.
A court may recognize the agency of a religious actor in promoting interpretations
which are in conflict with human rights standards; it may hold the actor legally
accountable under the framework, in the same way as a non-religious peer. In practice, nevertheless, this may have little relevance if it does not result in strengthening
the human rights protection of individuals at risk.

It is submitted that this does not invalidate the approach taken in this project: rather, it is a reminder that, outside the confines of positive law, we face
a complex reality. In this reality, change *may* be slow, incremental and in some
cases non-existent. That should not prevent monitoring and judicial bodies, states,
and the various other actors of the international legal system, from engaging
with religious actors. Not engaging would make it certain that change *will* be
slow, incremental, or would not exist at all. This confirms that assertions of legal
accountability in relation to religious actors whose practices, based on religious

---

[2] *Francis Doebbler v. Sudan*, Communication No. 236/2000 (2003), paras. 37–39 and 42.
[3] *Francis Doebbler v. Sudan* (Emphases in the original).

interpretation, conflict with international human rights standards need to also be supported by the perception that those standards have legitimacy. A tale of legitimacy ensues.

II. A Tale of Legitimacy...

This research project, concerned foremost with the law, has unearthed some important findings on legitimacy.

Religious actors, whether states or non-state entities, have come to need the legitimacy of international law to strengthen the legitimacy of their authority to interpret religion. This is the case for the Holy See, which is attempting to deal with clerical child sexual abuse and is perceived, in certain circles, as an adversary of sexual and reproductive rights. This is also true of the OIC, which seeks to establish a regionally sensitive understanding of international human rights, while grappling with the tensions posed by its diverse membership, and of religious organizations that seek to protect their autonomy from state interference. This study's observation is that the interpretations of religion that are proposed by these actors are perceived to be legitimate, or not, by reference not only to their religious integrity but also in terms of human rights standards. In the Weberian paradigm, tradition or charisma alone will no longer be sufficient to underpin the legitimacy of religious interpretation. Religious actors will need to provide evidence for the legality of their religious interpretations.

But this tale of legitimacy is two-sided. There is a growing understanding among scholars, certain courts, and treaty bodies, that international law, and in particular human rights law, may also benefit if religious actors forge their legitimacy in different cultural contexts and do so in a manner that strengthens the protection afforded. Treaty bodies have frequently recognized the Holy See's legitimating influence in certain areas. We have argued in this study that the OIC has a similar, albeit unfulfilled potential. Unquestionably, the potential for complementary legitimation exists and has sometimes materialized in the work of religious organizations, which are often of intimate value to individuals and their needs. How should we understand this side of the tale of legitimacy? It surely cannot mean that the legitimacy of human rights law, or international law for that matter, should depend on religious interpretation. It is certainly not our intention to propose that international law should renounce its rational-legal roots of legitimation. What is suggested here is another way of understanding the process of legitimation of international law.

Let us recall Thomas Franck's view:

The real power of law to secure systematic compliance does not rest, primarily, on police enforcement—not even in police states, surely not in ordinary societies, and especially not in the society of nations—but, rather, on the general belief of those to whom the law is addressed that they have a stake in the rule of law itself: that law is binding because it is the law.[4]

---

[4] T. M. Franck, 'The Power of Legitimacy and the Legitimacy of Power: International Law in an Age of Power Disequilibrium', 100 *AJIL* (2006), 88–106, at 91.

In earlier paragraphs of these Conclusions, we emphasized that international law, and in particular human rights law, needs to be perceived as legitimate by religious actors if they are to comply with its norms. It seems to us that, to conquer the hearts of religious actors, international law needs to emphasize forms of legitimation that foster ownership. We join other scholars who have concluded that new approaches are necessary to address the legitimacy of international law, which currently suffers from a divorce between theory and practice:

> The actors, structures, and processes identified and theorized as determinative by the dominant approaches to the study of international law and organization have ceased to be of singular importance.[5]

In our view, mainstream perspectives need to take account, not only of actors, structures, and processes, but their configurations. One configuration is constructed by the place that actors grant to religion. In this sense we should reconceive the legitimation process of international law. Such an exercise has been proposed by Jutta Brunnée and Stephen J. Toope. Their interactional framework posits that legitimate international law depends on three dimensions: the construction of 'social legitimacy' through the emergence of shared understandings; the creation of 'legal legitimacy' which requires that legality criteria are substantially met; and continuous interaction to reinforce shared understandings.[6]

This approach, which benefits from social constructivist insights, is interesting in the context of this study's observation that religious actors might help to forge the legitimacy of international law in general, and human rights law in particular. While Brunnée and Toope's framework does not change the priority of legitimation sources in Weberian terms (charisma and tradition do not become the main legitimation sources of international law), the interactional approach does challenge the convention that legitimate rules emerge purely as a result of state consent and claims that they are rather constructed by 'communities of practice'.[7] This definitely accords a greater role to values and principles. The approach also challenges a static view of law creation and adherence, by suggesting that a continuous negotiation of meanings is necessary to achieve and reinforce the shared understandings that underpin law and adherence to it. These two aspects—attaching importance to values and principles and ongoing interaction to achieve shared understandings—do not imply a challenge to the rational-legal character of international law, but reinforce it. In other words, 'belief in the legality of enacted rules' is what persuades actors to follow international law norms. The interactional approach, however, supposes a different process for enacting these rules: inclusive and dynamic. This process can therefore provide space for religious actors to play their part in forging law's legitimacy.

---

[5] Cutler, 'Critical Reflections on the Westphalian Assumptions of International Law and Organization: a Crisis of Legitimacy', at 133.

[6] J. Brunnée and S. J. Toope, *Legitimacy and Legality in International Law: an Interactional Account*, (Cambridge: Cambridge University Press, 2010), at 53–54.

[7] See note 6, at 53–54.

Does an interactional framework bring us back to the narratives on the relation between religion and international law—a relation that can be beneficial, but also dangerous in circumstances where law might replicate patterns that are oppressive? In a narrow sense, it does. At the same time, it must be acknowledged that religion *on its own* plays little role in the continuous negotiation of meanings, because the actors who interpret it take centre-stage in the process of legitimating law. And here is the caveat: religious actors need to reach shared understandings, and in this process their own interpretations are confronted by human rights standards and the interpretations of other actors and therefore re-shaped. Will this interaction transform the slow, incremental process of change that Ms Hussein's archetypal case illustrates? Probably not, but it indicates again how complex the world is that international law has to 'clear', and portrays a more honest foundation on which states, courts, scholars, non-governmental organizations, and religious actors can build their efforts to achieve change.

Bibliography

Abbott, K. W. and D. Snidal, (1998), 'Why States Act through Formal International Organizations' 42 *The Journal of Conflict Resolution* 1, 3–32.

Abdul-Hamid, Y. (2011), *Child Rights Situation Analysis for the Middle East and North Africa Region*, (Save the Children Sweden), http://mena.savethechildren.se/PageFiles/2867/Regional%20MENA%20CRSA.pdf.

Abdullah, Y. (1996), 'The Holy See at United Nations Conferences: State or Church?' 96 *Col. LR* 7, 1835–1875.

Abi-Saab, G. (1999), 'Fragmentation or Unification: Some Concluding Remarks' 31 *NYU J.L. & Pol.*, 919–933.

Abiad, N. (2008), *Sharia, Muslim States and International Human Rights Treaty Obligations: A Comparative Study*, (London: British Institute of International and Comparative Law).

Abiad, N. and F. Mansoor (2010) *Criminal Law and the Rights of the Child in Muslim States: A Comparative and Analytical Perspective* (London: British Institute of International and Comparative Law).

Abu-Lughod, L. (2002), 'Do Muslim Women Really Need Saving? Anthropological Reflections on Cultural Relativism and its Others' 104 *American Anthropologist* 3, 783–790.

Addo, M. K. (1999), 'The Corporation as a Victim of Human Rights Violations', in M. K. Addo (ed.), *Human Rights Standards and the Responsibility of Transnational Corporations* (The Hague: Kluwer Law), 187–196.

Ahdar, R. and N. Aroney (2010), 'The Topography of Shari'a in the Western Political Landscape', in R. Ahdar and N. Aroney (eds.) *Shari'a in the West*, (Oxford: Oxford University Press), 1–31.

Akandji-Kombe, J.-F. (2007), *Positive Obligations under the European Convention on Human Rights* (Council of Europe: Human Rights Handbook no. 7).

Al-Ahsan, A. (2008) 'Law, Religion and Human Dignity in the Muslim World Today: An Examination of OIC's Cairo Declaration of Human Rights' 24 *J.L. & Relig.*, 569–597.

Aldeeb Abu-Sahlieh, S. A. (1997), 'Conflits entre droit religieux et droit étatique chez les musulmans dans les pays musulmans et en Europe' 49 *Revue internationale de droit comparè* 4, 813–834.

Alfredsson, G. (1993), 'The Right of Self-determination and Indigenous Peoples', in C. Tomuschat (ed.) *Modern Law of Self-Determination* (Dordrecht: Martinus Nijhoff Publishers), 41–54.

Ali, S. S. (2000), *Gender and Human Rights in Islam and International Law: Equal Before Allah, Unequal Before Man?* (The Hague: Kluwer Law International).

Ali, S. S., (2007), 'A Comparative Perspective of the Convention on the Rights of the Child and the Principles of Islamic Law Law Reform and Children's Rights in Muslim Jurisdictions', in UNICEF (ed.), *Protecting the World's Children: Impact of the Rights of the Child in Diverse Legal Systems*, (New York: Cambridge University Press), 142–20.

Annan, K (2006) 'Urging End to Impunity, Annan Sets Forth Ideas to Bolster UN Efforts', UN Doc. SG/SM/10788.

Alston, P. (1990), 'The Unborn Child and Abortion under the Draft Convention on the Rights of the Child' 12 *HRQ* 1, 156–178.

Alston, P. (2005), 'The "Not-a-Cat" Syndrome: Can the International Human Rights Regime Accommodate Non-State Actors?', in P. Alston (ed.) *Non-state Actors and Human Rights*, (New York: Oxford University Press), 3–36.

American Anthropological Association (1947), 'Statement on Human Rights', 49 *American Anthropologist* 4, 539–543.

American Anthropological Association (1999), Committee for Human Rights, *Declaration on Anthropology and Human Rights*, http://www.aaanet.org/about/Policies/statements/Declaration-on-Anthropology-and-Human-Rights.cfm.

Amnesty International (2011), *Annual Report 2011, Vatican*, http://www.amnesty.org/en/region/vatican/report-2011.

Amnesty International (2011), *In Plain Sight: Responding to the Ferns, Ryan, Murphy and Cloyne Reports*, http://www.amnesty.ie/content/plain-sight.

Amnesty International (2011), *Q&A: Human rights implications of the Palestinian bid for UN membership*, http://www.amnesty.org/en/news-and-updates/q-and-human-rights-implications-palestinian-bid-un-membership-2011-09-26.

Amnesty International (2009), *Sudan: Amnesty International calls on government to repeal law penalizing women for wearing trousers*, Press Release, 4 September 2009, http://www.amnesty.org/en/for-media/press-releases/sudan-amnesty-international-calls-government-repeal-law-penalizing-women.

An-Na'im, A. A. (1990), 'Human Rights in the Muslim World: Socio-Political Conditions and Scriptural Imperatives-A Preliminary Inquiry' 3 *Harv. Hum. Rts. J.*, 13–52.

An-Na'im, A. A. (1990), 'Problems of Universal Cultural Legitimacy for Human Rights', in A.A. An-Na'im and F. M. Deng (eds.) *Human Rights in Africa: Cross-cultural Perspectives* (Washington D.C.: Brookings Institution Press), 331–367.

An-Na'im, A. A. (1990), *Toward an Islamic Reformation: Civil Liberties, Human Rights and International Law* (Syracuse: Syracuse University Press).

An-Na'im, A. A. (1992), 'Introduction', in A.A. An-Na'im (ed.), *Human Rights in Cross-Cultural Perspectives: A Quest for Consensus* (Philadelphia, PA: University of Pennsylvania Press), 1–18.

An-Na'im, A. A. (1992), 'Toward a Cross-Cultural Approach to Defining International Standards of Human Rights: The Meaning of Cruel, Inhuman or Degrading Treatment or Punishment', in A.A. An-Na'im (ed.), *Human Rights in Cross-Cultural Perspectives: A Quest for Consensus* (Philadelphia, PA: University of Pennsylvania Press), 19–43.

An-Na'im, A. A. (2003), 'The Synergy and Interdependence of Human Rights, Religion and Secularism', in J. Runzo, M. N. Martin, and A. Sharma (eds.), *Human Rights and Responsibilities in the World Religions* (Oxford: Oneworld Publications), 27–50.

An-Na'im, A. A. (2008), *Islam and the Secular State: Negotiating the Future of Shari'a* (Cambridge, MA: Harvard University Press).

Anderson, L. (2011) 'Demystifying the Arab Spring: Parsing the Differences Between Tunisia, Egypt, and Libya', 90 *Foreign Affairs* 3, 2–7.

Angeletti, S. (2008), *Libertà religiosa e patto internazionale sui diritti civili e politici: La prassi del comitato per i diritti umani delle Nazioni Unite*, (Torino: G.Giappichelli Editore).

Antoun, R. T. and M. E. Hegland (eds.) (1987), *Religious Resurgence: Contemporary Cases in Islam, Christianity, and Judaism*, (New York: Syracuse University Press).

Apostolic Nunciature in Ireland (1997), N. 808/97, Strictly Confidential, Dublin, http://graphics8.nytimes.com/packages/pdf/world/Ireland-Catholic-Abuse.pdf.

Araujo, R. J. (1999), 'International Tribunals and Rules of Evidence: The Case for Respecting and Preserving the Priest-Penitent Privilege under International Law' 15 *Am. U. Int'l L. Rev.*, 639–666.

Araujo, R. J. (2001), 'The International Personality and Sovereignty of the Holy See' 50 *Cath. U. L. Rev.*, 291–360.

Araujo, R. J. and J. A. Lucal (2005), *Papal Diplomacy and the Quest for Peace: The Vatican and International Organizations from the Early Years to the League of Nations* (Naples, FL: Sapientia Press).

Arendt, H. (1958) *The Human Condition* (Chicago: University of Chicago Press).

Arjomand, S. A. (1989), 'Constitution-Making in Islamic Iran: The Impact of Theocracy on the Legal Order of a Nation-State', in J. Starr and J. Collier Fishburne (eds.), *History and Power in the Study of Law: New Directions in Legal Anthropology* (New York: Cornell University Press).

Asociaţia pentru Apărarea Drepturilor Omului în România—Comitetul Helsinki (2008), *Stat şi religii în România: O relaţie transparentă?*, Bucureşti.

Aykan, M. B. (1993), 'The Palestinian Question in Turkish Foreign Policy from the 1950s to the 1990s', 25 *International Journal of Middle East Studies* 1, 91–110.

Badar, M. E. (2004), 'Basic Principles Governing Limitations on Individual Rights and Freedoms in Human Rights Instruments' 7 *The International Journal of Human Rights* 4, 63–92.

Baderin, M. (2001), 'A Macroscopic Analysis of the Practice of Muslim State Parties to International Human Rights Treaties: Conflict of Congruence' 1 *Human Rights Law Review* 2, 265–303.

Baderin, M. A. (2009), 'Religion and International Law: Friends or Foes?' 5 *European Human Rights Law Review*, 637–658.

Baderin, M. A. (2010), 'Islamic Law and the Interpretation of International Human Rights Law: A Case Study of the International Covenant on Civil and Political Rights', in A.M. Baderin and M. Ssenyonjo (eds.) *International Human Rights Law: Six Decades after the UDHR and Beyond* (Aldershot: Ashgate), 337–359.

Badr, G. M. (1999), 'A Survey of Islamic International Law', in M.W. Janis and C. Evans (eds.), *Religion and International Law* (The Hague: Martinus Nijhoff).

Balladore-Pallieri, G. (1962) *Diritto internazionale pubblico*, (Milano: A. Giuffrè).

Bantekas, I. (2007), 'Religion as a Source of International Law', in J. Rehman and S. Breau (eds.), *Religion, Human Rights and International Law* (Leiden: Martinus Nijhoff Publishers), 115–136.

Baratta, R. (2000) 'Should Invalid Reservations to Human Rights Treaties be Disregarded?' 11 *EJIL* 2, 413–425.

Barberini, G. (2003), 'Religious Freedom in the Process of Democratization of Central and Eastern European States', in S. Ferrari, C. W. Durham, and E. A. Sewell (eds.) *Law and Religion in Post-Communist Europe* (Leuven: Peeters), 7–22.

Bathon, M. N. (2001), 'The Atypical International Status of the Holy See' 34 *Vanderbilt Journal of Transnational Law*, 597–632.

Beal, J. P. (2007), 'The 1962 Instruction *Crimen Sollicitationis*: Caught Red-handed or Handed a Red Herring?' 41 *Studia canonica*, 199–236.

Beal, J. P., J. A. Coriden, and T. J. Green (2002), *New Commentary on the Code of Canon Law* (Mahwah, NJ: Paulist Press).

Bellal, A. (2011), *Immunités et violations graves des droits humains. Vers une évolution structurelle de l'ordre juridique international?* (Bruxelles: Bruylant).

Belnap, A. G. (2010) 'Defamation of Religions: A Vague and Overbroad Theory that Threatens Basic Human Rights' 2010 *BYU L. Rev.*, 635–685.

Benvenisti, E. (1998), 'Margin of Appreciation, Consensus, and Universal Standards' 31 *NYU J.L. & Pol.*, 843–854.

Berger, P. L. (1999), 'Introduction', in P. L. Berger (ed.), *The Desecularization of the World: Resurgent Religion and World Politics* (Washington D.C.: Wm. B. Eerdmans Publishing), 1–18.

Bettwy, S. W. (1984), 'United States-Vatican Recognition: Background and Issues', 29 *Catholic Lawyer*, 225–265.

Bettwy, S. W. and M. K. Sheehan (1981), 'United States Recognition Policy: The State of Vatican City', 11 *Cal. W. Int'l L.J.*, 1–31.

Bianchi, A. (1997), 'Globalization of Human Rights: The Role of Non-state Actors' in G. Teubner (ed.) *Global Law Without a State* (Aldershot: Dartmouth), 179–211.

Bianchi, A. (1997), 'Overcoming the Hurdle of State Immunity in the Domestic Enforcement of Human Rights', in B. Conforti and F. Francioni (eds.) *Enforcing International Human Rights in Domestic Courts* (The Hague: Martinus Nijhoff), 405–440.

Bianchi, A. (2009), 'Introduction: Relativizing the Subjects or Subjectivizing the Actors: Is That the Question?', in A. Bianchi (ed.) *Non-state Actors and International Law* (Dartmouth: Ashgate Publishing), xi–xxx.

Bianchi, A. (2011), 'The Fight for Inclusion: Non-state Actors and International Law', in U. Fastenrath et al. (eds.) *From Bilateralism to Community Interest: Essays in Honour of Judge Bruno Simma* (Oxford: Oxford University Press), 39–57.

Bickford, L. (2007), 'Unofficial Truth Projects' 29 *HRQ* 4, 994–1035.

Bielefeldt, H. (2000), '"Western" versus "Islamic" Human Rights Conceptions?: A Critique of Cultural Essentialism in the Discussion on Human Rights' 28 *Political Theory* 1, 90–121.

Bjarnason, T. and M. R. Welch (2004), 'Father Knows Best: Parishes, Priests, and American Catholic Parishioners' Attitudes Toward Capital Punishment' 43 *Journal for the Scientific Study of Religion* 1, 103–118.

Blitt, R.C. (2011), 'Russia's Orthodox Foreign Policy: The Growing Influence of the Russian Orthodox Church in Shaping Russia's Policies Abroad' 33 *U. Pa. J. Int'l L.* 2, 364–460.

Blumer, H. (1986) *Symbolic Interactionism: Perspective and Method*, (Berkley: University of California Press).

Boesenecker A. P., and L. Vinjamuri (2011), 'Lost in Translation? Civil Society, Faith-based Organizations and the Negotiation of International Norms' 5 *International Journal of Transitional Justice* 3, 345–365.

Borer, T.A. (2004), 'Reconciling South Africa or South Africans? Cautionary Notes from the TRC', 8 *African Studies Quarterly* 1, 20–38.

Brems, E. (2001), *Human Rights: Universality and Diversity* (The Hague: Martinus Nijhoff).

Brierly, J. L. (1949), *The Law of Nations: An Introduction to the International Law of Peace* (Oxford: Clarendon Press).

Brownlie, I. (2008), *Principles of Public International Law*, 7th ed. (Oxford: Oxford University Press).

Brownlie, I. and G. S. Goodwin-Gill (2010), *Brownlie's Documents on Human Rights. Additional Materials—Part 5*, 6th ed. (Oxford: Oxford University Press).

Brugger, W. (2007), 'On the Relationship between Structural Norms and Constitutional Rights in Church-State-Relations', in W. Brugger and M. Karayanni (eds.) *Religion in the Public Sphere: A Comparative Analysis of German, Israeli, American and International Law*, (Berlin: Springer Verlag), 21–86.

Brunnée, J. and S. J. Toope (2010), *Legitimacy and Legality in International Law: an Interactional Account* (Cambridge: Cambridge University Press).

Bryan, I (1999), 'Suffering Offence: The Place, Function and Future of the Blasphemy Laws Revisited' 4 *JCL*, 332–362.

Buss D., and D. Herman (2003), *Globalizing Family Values. The Christian Rights in International Politics* (Minneapolis, MN: University of Minnesota Press).

Cameron, L. (2006), 'Private Military Companies: Their Status under International Humanitarian Law and its Impact on their Regulation' 88 *International Review of the Red Cross* 863, 573–598.

Cao, W. W. (2008), 'Review: Personal Autonomy in Society' 3 *In-Spire Journal of Law Politics and Societies* 2, 171–173.

Cardinale, H. (1976), *The Holy See and the International Order* (London: Colin Smythe).

Cardinale, I. (1962), *Le Saint-Siège et la diplomatie* (Paris: Desclée).

Carty, A. (2005), 'Review Essay: International Legal Personality and the End of the Subject: Natural Law and Phenomenological Responses to New Approaches to International Law' 6 *Melbourne Journal of International Law* 2, 534–552.

Cassese, A. (2002), 'When May Senior State Officials Be Tried for International Crimes? Some Comments on the Congo v. Belgium Case' 13 *EJIL* 4, 853–875.

Cassese, A. (2005), *International Law*, 2nd ed. (Oxford: Oxford University Press).

Center for Inquiry-International (CFI) (2009), 'The European Court of Human Rights and the interpretation of "advocacy of religious hatred that constitutes incitement to discrimination, hostility or violence"', Written Statement, UN Human Rights Council, 10th Session, http://www.centerforinquiry.net/uploads/attachments/CFI_statement_on_advocacy_of_religious_hatred.pdf.

Ceretti, A. (2009), 'Collective Violence and International Crime', in A. Cassese (ed.), *The Oxford Companion to International Criminal Justice* (Oxford: Oxford University Press), 5–15.

Cerna, C. M. (1994), 'Universality of Human Rights and Cultural Diversity: Implementation of Human Rights in Different Socio-cultural Contexts' 16 *HRQ*, 740–752.

Cerone, J. (2011), 'The UN and the Status of Palestine—Disentangling the Legal Issue' 15 *Insights* 26.

Chapman A. R., and P. Ball (2001), 'The Truth of Truth Commissions: Comparative Lessons from Haiti, South Africa, and Guatemala' 23 *HRQ* 1, 1–43.

Charlesworth, H. (2012), 'Law-making and Sources', in J. Crawford and M. Koskenniemi (eds.) *The Cambridge Companion to International Law* (Cambridge: Cambridge University Press), 187–202.

Charlesworth, H. and C. Chinkin (2000), *The Boundaries of International Law: A Feminist Analysis* (Manchester: Manchester University Press).

Charlesworth, H., C. Chinkin and S. Wright (1991), 'Feminist Approaches to International Law' 85 *AJIL* 4, 613–645.

Christakis, T. (2006), 'The State as a 'Primary Fact': Some Thoughts on the Principle of Effectiveness', in M. Kohen (ed.), *Secession: International Law Perspectives* (Cambridge: Cambridge University Press), 138–170.

Cismas, I. (2010), 'Secession in Theory and Practice: The Case of Kosovo and Beyond' 2 *Goettingen Journal of International Law* 2, 531–587.

Cismas, I. (2011), 'Introductory Note to the Statute of the OIC Independent Permanent Human Rights Commission' 50 *ILM* 6, 1148–1160.

Clapham A. (1993), *Human Rights in the Private Sphere* (Oxford: Oxford University Press).

Clapham, A. (2006), *Human Rights Obligations of Non-State Actors* (Oxford: Oxford University Press).

Clapham, A. (2006), 'Human Rights Obligations of Non-state Actors in Conflict Situation' 88 *International Review of the Red Cross* 863, 491–523.

Clapham, A. (2007), *Human Rights: A Very Short Introduction* (Oxford: Oxford University Press).

Clapham, A. (2008), 'Extending International Criminal Law Beyond the Individual to Corporations and Armed Opposition Groups' 6 *Journal of International Criminal Justice* 5, 899–926.

Clapham, A. (2012), *Brierly's Law of Nations*, 7th ed. (Oxford: Oxford University Press).

Clark, B. (1991), 'The Vienna Convention Reservations Regime and the Convention on Discrimination Against Women' 85 *AJIL* 2, 281–321.

Clark, K. W. G., K. S. Roggendorf and P. B. Janci (2006), 'Of Compelling Interest: The Intersection of Religious Freedom and Civil Liability in the Portland Priest Sex Abuse Cases' 85 *Oregon Law Review*, 481–538.

Clark, R. S. (1978) 'The United Nations and Religious Freedom' 11 *Journal of International Law and Politics*, 197–226.

Clark, R. S. (1983), 'The United Nations Declaration on the Elimination of All Forms of Intolerance and Discrimination Based on Religion or Belief' 31 *Chitty's Law Journal*, 23–39.

Cockayne, J. (2002), 'Islam and International Humanitarian Law: From a Clash to a Conversation Between Civilizations' 84 *International Review of the Red Cross* 847, 597–626.

Cohen, S. A. (1999), 'From Integration to Segregation The Role of Religion in the IDF' 25 *Armed Forces & Society* 3, 387–405.

Cohen, S. A. (2007), 'The Re-Discovery of Orthodox Jewish Laws Relating to the Military and War (Hilkhot Tzavah U-Milchamah) in Contemporary Israel: Trends and Implications' 12 *Israel Studies* 2, 1–28.

Colby, T. B., (2006), 'A Constitutional Hierarchy of Religions-Justice Scalia, the Ten Commandments, and the Future of the Establishment Clause' 100 *Northwestern University Law Review*, 1097–1140.

Conte, A. and R. Burchill (2009), *Defining Civil and Political Rights: the Jurisprudence of the United Nations Human Rights Committee*, 2nd ed., (Aldershot: Ashgate).

Coomans, F. and M. T. Kamminga (eds.) (2004), *Extraterritorial Application of Human Rights Treaties* (Antwerp: Intersentia).

Commission of Investigation (2009), *Report into the Catholic Archdiocese of Dublin*.

Commission of Investigation (2010), *Report into the Catholic Diocese of Cloyne*.

Commission to Inquire into Child Abuse (2009), *Report*.

Coriden, J. A. (1987), 'Diplomatic Relations Between the United States and the Holy See' 19 *Case W. Res. J. Int'l L.w*, 361–373.

Coriden, J. A. (2004), *An Introduction to Canon Law* (Mahwah, NJ: Paulist Press).

Cosnard, M. (2005), 'Avant-propos', in *Le sujet en droit international: Colloque du Mans* (Paris: Editions A. Pedone), 13–54.

Crawford, J. (2006), *The Creation of States in International Law*, 2nd ed. (Oxford: Oxford University Press).

Cutler, A. C. (2001), 'Critical Reflections on the Westphalian Assumptions of International Law and Organization: a Crisis of Legitimacy' 27 *Review of International Studies* 2, 133–150.

d'Aspremont, J. (2011), 'Inclusive Law-Making and Law-Enforcement for an Exclusive International Legal System', in J. d'Aspremont (ed.) *Participants in the International Legal System: Multiple Perspectives on Non-State Actors in International Law* (London: Routledge), 425–439.

Daillier, P. et al. (2009), *Droit international public*, 8ème ed., (Paris: L.G.D.J.).

Danchin, P. G. (2011), 'Islam in the Secular Nomos of the European Court of Human Rights' 32 *Mich. J. Int'l L.*, 663–747.

Davies, M. (2008), 'Pluralism in Law and Religion', in P. Cane, C. Evans, and Z. Robinson (eds.), *Law and Religion in Theoretical and Historical Context* (Cambridge: Cambridge University Press), 72–99.

de Beauvoir, S. (1999), *The Mandarins*, 2 ed., (New York: W.W. Norton & Company).

de Jong, C. D. (2000), *The Freedom of Thought, Conscience and Religion or Belief in the United Nations (1946-1992)* (Antwerpen: Intersentia).

de Jong, D. (2007), 'Freedom of Religion and Belief in the Light of Recent Challenges: Needs, Clashes and Solutions', in N. Ghanea, A. Stephens, and R. Walden (eds.) *Does God Believe in Human Rights? Essays on Religion and Human Rights* (Leiden: Martinus Nijhoff Publishers), 181–206.

de la Brière, Y. (1930) 'La condition juridique de la cité du Vatican' 33 *Recueil des Cours de l'Académie de droit international de la Haye*, 113–165.

de la Rasilla del Moral, I. (2006), 'The Increasingly Marginal Appreciation of the Margin-of-Appreciation Doctrine' 7 *German Law Review* 6, 611–623.

de Schutter, O. (2010), 'Human Rights and the Rights of International Organisations: The Logic of Sliding Scales in the Law of International Responsibility', in J. Wouters et al. (eds.) *Accountability for Human Rights Violations by International Organisations* (Antwerp: Intersentia), 51–128.

Dekker, I. F. (2010), 'Accountability of International Organisations: An Evolving Concept?', in J. Wouters et al. (eds.) *Accountability for Human Rights Violations by International Organisations* (Antwerp: Intersentia), 21–36.

Detrick, S., J. Doek and N. Cantwell (1992), *The United Nations Convention on the Rights of the Child: A Guide to the 'Travaux Préparatoires'* (Dordrecht: Martinus Nijhoff Publishers).

Dias, N. (2001), 'Roman Catholic Church & International Law' 13 *Sri Lanka Journal of International Law*, 107–135.

Dickson, B. (1995), 'The United Nations and Freedom of Religion' 44 *ICLQ* 2, 327–357.

Dinstein, Y. (1986), 'International Law as a Primitive Legal System' 19 *NYU J.L. & Pol.* 1, 1–32.

Dobras, R. J. (2009), 'Is the United Nations Endorsing Human Rights Violations: An Analysis of the United Nations' Combating Defamation of Religions Resolutions and Pakistan's Blasphemy Laws' 37 *Ga. J. Int'l & Comp. L.*, 341–380.

Doe, N. (2011), *Law and Religion in Europe: A Comparative Introduction*, (Oxford: Oxford University Press).

Dogan, M. (2004), 'Conceptions of Legitimacy', in M. Hawkesworth and M. Kogan (eds.), *Encyclopedia of Government and Politics*, 2 ed., vol. I (London: Routledge).

Domb, F. (1995), 'The Gaza and Jericho Autonomy and Human Rights' 25 *Israel Yearbook on Human Rights*, 21–49.

Doswald-Beck, L. (2011) *Human Rights in Times of Conflict and Terrorism* (Oxford: Oxford University Press).

Doyle, T. P. and S. C. Rubino (2003), 'Catholic Clergy Sexual Abuse Meets the Civil Law' 31 *Fordham Urban Law Journal*, 549–616.

Dreisbach, D. L. (1991), 'A New Perspective on Jefferson's Views on Church-State Relations: The Virginia Statute for Establishing Religious Freedom in Its Legislative Context' 35 *The American Journal of Legal History* 2, 172–204.

Dumberry, P. (2010), 'Incoherent and Ineffective: the Concept of Persistent Objector Revisited' 59 *ICLQ*, 779–802.

Dundes Renteln, A. (1988), 'Relativism and the Search for Human Rights' 90 *American Anthropologist* 1, 56–72.

Dundes Renteln, A. (1990) *International Human Rights: Universalism versus Relativism* (Newbury Park, California: Sage Publications).

Durrant, R. (2006), 'Where There's Smoke, There's Fire (and Brimstone): Is It Time to Abandon the Clergy-Penitent Privilege', 39 *Loyola of Los Angeles Law Review*, 1339–1368.

Duursma, J. (1996), *Fragmentation and the International Relations of Micro-states: Self-determination and Statehood* (Cambridge: Cambridge University Press).

Edge, P. W. (2006), *Religion and Law: An Introduction* (Aldershot: Ashgate Publishing).

Edge, P. W. (2008), 'The European Court of Human Rights and Religious Rights' 47 *ICLQ* 3, 680–687.

Eick, C., 'Protest' (2006), in R. Wolfrum (ed.), *MPEPIL* (Online ed.: Oxford University Press).

Eide, A. and G. Alfredsson (1999), 'Introduction', in G. Alfredsson and A. Eide (eds.) *The Universal Declaration of Human Rights: A Common Standard of Achievement* (The Hague: Martinus Nijhoff Publishers), xxv–xxxv.

Emberland, M. (2006), *The Human Rights of Companies: Exploring the Structure of ECHR Protection* (Oxford: Oxford University Press).

Emon, A. M. (2006), 'Conceiving Islamic Law in a Pluralist Society: History, Politics and Multicultural Jurisprudence' 2006 *Singapore Journal of Legal Studies*, 331–355.

Engle, K. (2001), 'From Skepticism to Embrace: Human Rights and the American Anthropological Association from 1947-1999' 23 *HRQ* 3, 536–559.

Edrei, A. (2006), 'Divine Spirit and Physical Power: Rabbi Shlomo Goren and the Military Ethic of the Israel Defense Forces' 7 *Theoretical Inquiries in Law* 1, 257–300.

Evans, C. (2001), *Freedom of Religion under the European Convention on Human Rights*, (Oxford: Oxford University Press).

Evans, C. (2005), 'The Double-Edged Sword: Religious Influences on International Humanitarian Law' 6 *Melbourne Journal of International Law* 1, 1–31.

Evans, C. (2008), 'Introduction', in P. Cane, C. Evans, and Z. Robinson (eds.) *Law and Religion in Theoretical and Historical Context* (Cambridge: Cambridge University Press).

Evans, C. and A. Hood (2012), 'Religious Autonomy and Labour Law: A Comparison of the Jurisprudence of the United States and the European Court of Human Rights' 1 *Oxford J.L. & Relig.*, 1–27.

Evans, C. and C. Thomas (2006) 'Church-State Relations in the European Court of Human Rights', 2006 *BYU L. Rev.*, 699–725.

Evans, M. and R. Murray, (2008), *The African Charter on Human and Peoples' Rights: The System in Practice* 1986–2006, 2nd ed. (Cambridge: Cambridge University Press).

Evans, M. D. (1997), *Religious Liberty and International Law in Europe* (Cambridge: Cambridge University Press).

Evans, M. D. (2000), 'The United Nations and Freedom of Religion: The Work of the Human Rights Committee', in R.J. Ahdar (ed.), *Law and Religion* (Aldershot: Ashgate), 35–62.

Evans, M. D. (2012), 'The Future(s) of Regional Courts of Human Rights', in A. Cassese (ed.), *Realizing Utopia: The Future of International Law*, (Oxford: Oxford University Press), 261–274.

Fadel, M. (2009), 'International Law, Regional Developments: Islam', in R. Wolfrum (ed.) *MPEPIL* (Online edition: Oxford University Press).

Fadel, M. (2009), 'Islamic Politics and Secular Politics: Can They Co-Exist?', 25 *J.L. & Relig.* 1, 101–118.

Fantau, J. (2011), 'Rethinking the Sovereign Status of the Holy See: Towards a Greater Equality of States and Greater Protection of Citizens in United States Courts' 19 *Cardozo Journal of International & Comparative Law*, 487–524.

Fauchille, P. (1922), *Traité de droit international public*, 8ème ed., entièrement refondue, complétée et mise au courant du Manuel de droit international public de M. Henry Bonfils ed. vol. I (Paris: Rousseau & Co).

Feldman, D. (2009), 'Standards of Review and Human Rights in English Law', in *Oxford Principles of English Law: English Public Law*, 2nd ed. (Oxford: Oxford University Press), 317–378.

Fenwick, C. G. (1929), 'The New City of the Vatican' 23 *AJIL* 2, 371–374.

Feyter, K. and F. G. Isa (eds.) (2005), *Privatisation and Human Rights in the Age of Globalisation* (Antwerp: Intersentia).

Fischer-Lescano, A. and G. Teubner (2004), 'Regime-collisions: the Vain Search for Legal Unity in the Fragmentation of Global Law' 25 *Mich. J. Int'l L.*, 999–1946.

Formicola, J. R. (2011), 'Catholic Clerical Sexual Abuse: Effects on Vatican Sovereignty and Papal Power' 53 *Journal of Church and State* 4, 479–502.

Forteau, M. (2006), 'Regional International Law', in R. Wolfrum (ed.) *MPEPIL* (Online edition: Oxford University Press).

Franck, T. M. (1988) 'Legitimacy in the International System' 82 *AJIL* 4, 705–759.

Franck, T. M. (1990) *The Power of Legitimacy Among Nations* (New York: Oxford University Press).

Franck, T. M. (1997), 'Is Personal Freedom a Western Value' 91 *AJIL*, 593–627.

Franck, T. M. (2006), 'The Power of Legitimacy and the Legitimacy of Power: International Law in an Age of Power Disequilibrium' 100 *AJIL*, 88–106.

Franco, M. (2008), *Parallel Empires: the Vatican and the United States—Two Centuries of Alliance and Conflict* (New York: Doubleday).

Fuentes, X. (2004), 'International Law-making in the Field of Sustainable Development: the Unequal Competition between Development and the Environment', in N. Schrijver and F. Weiss (eds.), *International Law and Sustainable Development: Principles and Practice* (Leiden: Martinus Nijhoff), 7–38.

Gaeta, P. (2003), 'Ratione Materiae Immunities of Former Heads of State and International Crimes: The Hissène Habré Case' 1 *Journal of International Criminal Justice*, 186–196.

Gartner, B. (2011), *Der religionsrechtliche Status islamischer und islamistischer Gemeinschaften* (Wien, New York: Springer).

Gayte, M. (2012), ' "I Told the White House If They Give One to the Pope, I May Ask for One": The American Reception to the Establishment of Diplomatic Relations between the United States and the Vatican in 1984' 54 *Journal of Church and State* 1, 33–56.

Gazzoni, F. (2009), 'Malta, Order of', in *MPEPIL* (Online ed.: Oxford University Press).

Gerth H. H. and C. Wright Mills (eds.) (1975), *From Max Weber: Essays in Sociology* (New York: Oxford University Press).

Ghanea N. (ed) (2010), *Religion and Human Rights*, vol. I, vol. II, vol. III, vol. IV (New York: Routledge).

Ghanea, N., A. Stephens and R. Walden (eds.) (2007), *Does God Believe in Human Rights? Essays on Religion and Human Rights* (Leiden: Martinus Nijhoff Publishers).

Gittleman, R. (1981), 'The African Charter on Human and Peoples' Rights: A Legal Analysis' 22 *Virginia Journal of International Law*, 667–714.

Glendon, M. A. (2011), *The Forum and the Tower: How Scholars and Politicians Have Imagined the World, from Plato to Eleanor Roosevelt* (Oxford: Oxford University Press).

Golay, C., C. Mahon and I. Cismas (2011), 'The Impact of the UN Special Procedures on the Development and Implementation of Economic, Social and Cultural Rights', 15 *The International Journal of Human Rights* 2, 299–318.

Gowlland-Debbas, V. (2012), *The Security Council and Issues of Responsibility under International Law*, Collected Courses of the Hague Academy of International Law vol. 353, (Online ed.: Martinus Nijhoff).

Goldstein, S. (1991), 'Israel: A Secular or a Religious State?', 36 *St. Louis U. L.J.* 1, 143–161.

Goodman, R. (2002) 'Human Rights Treaties, Invalid Reservations, and State Consent' 96 *AJIL*, 531–559.

Graham, L. B. (2009), 'Defamation of Religions: The End of Pluralism' 23 *Emory Int'l L. Rev.*, 69–84.

Grant, T. D. (1998), 'Defining Statehood: The Montevideo Convention and Its Discontents' 37 *Columbia Journal of Transnational Law*, 403–457.

Greer, S. C. (2006), *The European Convention on Human Rights: Achievements, Problems and Prospects* (Cambridge: Cambridge University Press).

Guggenheim, P. (1948), *Lehrbuch des Völkerrechts*, vol. I, (Basel: Verlag für Recht und Gessellschaft AG).

Guggenheim, P. (1952), *Les principes de droit international public*, Collected Courses of the Hague Academy of International Law (Online ed.: Martinus Nijhoff).

Gutter, J. (2007), 'Special Procedures and the Human Rights Council: Achievements and Challenges Ahead', 7 *Human Rights Law Review* 1, 93–107.

Habermas, J. (2008), 'Secularism's Crisis of Faith: Notes on Post-Secular Society' 25 *New Perspectives Quarterly* 4, 17–29.

Hafner, G. (2004) 'Pros and Cons Ensuing from Fragmentation of International Law' 25 *Mich. J. Int'l L.*, 849–863.

Hammond, P. E., L. Salinas and D. Sloane (1978), 'Types of Clergy Authority: their Measurement, Location, and Effects' 17 *Journal for the Scientific Study of Religion*, 241–253.

Hampson, F. (2011), 'The Scope of the Extra-territorial Applicability of International Human Rights Law', in G. Gilbert, F. Hampson, and C. Sandoval (eds.) *The Delivery of Human Rights: Essays in Honour of Professor Sir Nigel Rodley* (Abingdon: Routledge), 157–182.

Happold, M. (2003), 'Bankovic v. Belgium and the Territorial Scope of the European Convention on Human Rights' 3 *Human Rights Law Review*, 77–90.

Hawkesworth M. (1997), 'Confounding Gender' 22 *Signs* 3, 649–685.

Hekker, M. L. (1987), 'Constitutional Issues Raised by Diplomatic Relations Between the United States and the Holy See' 15 *Hastings Constitutional Law Quarterly*, 101–124.

Henckaerts, J. M. and L. Doswald-Beck (2009) *Customary International Humanitarian Law: Rules*, vol. I (Cambridge: Cambridge University Press).

Henckaerts, J. M. and L. Doswald-Beck (2009), *Customary International Humanitarian Law: Practice*, vol. II (Cambridge: Cambridge University Press).

Heschel, S. (1998), *Abraham Geiger and the Jewish Jesus* (Chicago: Chicago University Press).

Heubel, E. J. (1977), 'Church and State in Spain: Transition toward Independence and Liberty' 30 *The Western Political Quarterly* 1, 125–139.

Heynes, J. (2012), *Religious Transnational Actors and Soft Power* (Aldershot: Ashgate).

Heynes, J. (2013), *Faith-based Organisations at the United Nations*, European University Institute Working Papers, RSCAS 2013/70.

Heynes, J. and Hennig, A. (eds.) (2011), *Religious Actors in the Public Sphere: Means, Objectives, and Effects* (London: Routledge).

Higgins, R. (1963), *The Development of International Law through the Political Organs of the United Nations* (London: Oxford University Press).

Higgins, R. (1995), *Problems and Process: International Law and How We Use It* (Oxford: Oxford University Press).

Hill, M. (2011), 'Church Autonomy in the United Kingdom', in G. Robbers (ed.), *Church Autonomy: A Comparative Survey* (Frankfurt am Main: Peter Land), 267–283.

Hill, M. (2005), 'The Permissible Scope of the Legal Limitations on the Freedom of Religion or Belief in the United Kingdom' 19 *Emory Int'l L. Rev.*, 1129–1185.

Hill, M. (2007), *Interpreting the European Convention on Human Rights in the United Kingdom Courts: The Impact for Religious Organisations*, European Consortium for Church and State Research, Cyprus.

Hill, M. (2011), R. Sandberg and N. Doe, *Religion and Law in the United Kingdom* (Alphen an den Rijn: Kluwer Law International).

Holden, A. (2002), *Jehovah's Witnesses: Portrait of a Contemporary Religious Movement* (London: Routeledge).

The Holy Bible. King James Version (2008), 7th ed., (Peabody, MA: Hendrickson Publishers).

Holy See (2011), Response to the Government of Ireland regarding the Report of the Commission of Investigation in to the Catholic Diocese of Cloyne.

Howland, C. W. (ed.) (2001), *Religious Fundamentalisms and the Human Rights of Women* (New York: Palgrave Macmillan).

Human Rights Watch (2011), 'How Come You Allow Little Girls to Get Married?'—*Child Marriage in Yemen*, http://www.hrw.org/print/reports/2011/12/08/how-come-you-allow-little-girls-get-married.

Huntington, S.P. (1993), 'The Clash of Civilizations?' 72 *Foreign Affairs* 3, 22–49.

Huntington, S. P. (2003), *The Clash of Civilizations and the Remaking of World Order* (New York: Simon & Schuster).

Hylton, D. N. (1994) 'Default breakdown: The Vienna Convention on the Law of Treaties' Inadequate Framework on Reservations', 27 *Vanderbilt Journal of Transnational Law*, 419–452.

Ignatieff M. (A. Gutmann ed.) (2001), *Human Rights as Politics and Idolatry* (Princeton: Princeton University Press).

International Law Association (2004), Accountability of International Organizations: Final Report, Berlin Conference.

International Law Association (2014), Committee on Islamic Law and International Law, Draft Conference Report Washington.

Ireland, G. (1993), 'The State of the City of the Vatican' 27 *AJIL*, 271–289.

Jackson Preece, J. (2001), 'Minority Rights in Europe: from Westphalia to Helsinki' 23 *Review of International Studies* 1, 75–92.

Jain, S. C. (2003), 'Jainism, War and International Law' 43 *Indian Journal of International Law* 4, 75–92.

James, S. A. (1994), 'Reconciling International Human Rights and Cultural Relativism: the Case of Female Circumcision' 8 *Bioethics* 1, 1–26.

Janis, M. W. (1999), 'Introduction', in M.W. Janis and C. Evans (eds.), *Religion and International Law* (The Hague: Martinus Nijhoff Publishers), xi–xiii.

Janis, M. W. and C. Evans (eds.) (1999), *Religion and International Law*, (The Hague: Martinus Nijhoff Publishers).

Jennings, R. and A. Watts (eds.) (1996), *Oppenheim's International Law*, 9th ed., vol. I (London: Longman).

Jennings, R. Y. (1946), 'Government in Commission' 23 *BYBIL*, 112–141.

Jennings, R. Y. (1987), 'Universal International Law in a Multicultural World', in B. Marten and I. Brownlie (eds.) *Liber Amicorum for Lord Wilberforce* (Oxford: Calderon Press), 39–51.

Jochnick, C. (1999), 'Confronting the Impunity of Non-state Actors: New Fields for the Promotion of Human Rights' 21 *HRQ*, 56–79.

Johnston, D. M. (2008), *The Historical Foundations of World Order: the Tower and the Arena* (Leiden: Martinus Nijhoff Publishers).

Juul Petersen, M. (2010), 'International Religious NGOs at The United Nations: A Study of a Group of Religious Organizations', *The Journal of Humanitarian Assistance*, available at https://sites.tufts.edu/jha/archives/847.

Juul Petersen, M. (2012), *Islamic or Universal human rights? The OIC's Independent Permanent Human Rights Commission*, Danish Institute for International Studies.

Jussim, L. (2012), *Social Perception and Social Reality: Why Accuracy Dominates Bias and Self-Fulfilling Prophecy* (Oxford: Oxford University Press).

Karl, W. (2000), 'Treaties, Conflicts between', in *Encyclopaedia of Public International Law*, vol. I (Amsterdam: Elsevier).

Kaur, M. (2009), 'Lessons from Punjab's "Missing Girls": Toward a Global Feminist Perspective on "Choice" in Abortion' 97 *California Law Journal* 3, 905–942.

Kayaoğlu, T. (2012), 'It's Time to Revise The Cairo Declaration of Human Rights in Islam', Brookings Doha Center.

Kayaoğlu, T (2014, forthcoming), 'Giving an Inch only to Lose a Mile: Muslim States, Liberalism, and Human Rights in the UN' 36 *HRQ* 1.

Kearns, P. (2008), 'The End of Blasphemy Law' 76 *Amicus Curiae: Journal for the Society for Advanced Legal Studies*, 25–27.

Kelsen, H. (1941), 'Recognition in International Law: Theoretical Observations' 35 *AJIL* 4, 605–617.

Kennedy, D. (1999), 'Images of Religion in International Legal History', in M.W. Janis and C. Evans (eds.), *Religion and International Law* (The Hague: Martinus Nijhoff Publishers), 145–153.

Kent, P. C. and J. F. Pollard (1994), *Papal Diplomacy in the Modern Age* (Westport, Connecticut: Praeger).

Kertzer, D. I. (2004), *Prisoner of the Vatican: The Popes' Secret Plot to Capture Rome from the New Italian State*, (Boston: Houghton Mifflin).

Khadduri, M. (1956), 'Islam and the Modern Law of Nations' 50 *AJIL* 2, 358–372.

Khan, L. A. (2008), 'Jurodynamics of Islamic Law' 61 *Rutgers Law Review*, 231–293.

Kiviorg, M. (2009), 'Religious Autonomy in the ECHR', IV *Derecho y Religión,* 131–144.

Kiviorg, M. (2010), 'Collective Religious Autonomy under the European Convention on Human Rights: the UK Jewish Free School Case in International Perspective' 40 *EUI Working Paper*, 1–14.

Klabbers, J. (2003), '(I Can't Get No) Recognition: Subjects Doctrine and the Emergence of Non-State Actors', in J. Petman and J. Klabbers (eds.) *Nordic Cosmopolitanism. Essays in International Law for Martti Koskenniemi* (Leiden: Martinus Nijhoff), 351–369.

Klabbers, J. (2009) *An Introduction to International Institutional Law*, 2nd ed. (Cambridge: Cambridge University Press).

Köck, H. F. (1995), 'Holy See', in R. Bernhardt (ed.), *Encyclopedia of Public International Law*, vol. II (Amsterdam: Elsevier, 1995), 866–869.

Kohen, M. (2002), 'La création d'Etats en droit international contemporain' 6 *Cursos Euromediterráneos Bancaja de Derecho Internacional*, 546–635.

Kohen, M. G. and K. Del Mar (2011), 'The Kosovo Advisory Opinion and UNSCR 1244 (1999): A Declaration of 'Independence from International Law'?' 24 *Leiden J Intl L* 1, 109–126.

Koskenniemi, M. (2005), *From Apology to Utopia: The Structure of International Legal Argument* (Cambridge: Cambridge University Press).

Koskenniemi, M. (2007), 'The Fate of Public International Law: Between Technique and Politics' 70 *Modern Law Review* 1, 1–30.

Koskenniemi, M. and P. Leino (2002), 'Fragmentation of International Law? Postmodern Anxieties' 15 *Leiden J Intl L* 3, 553–579.

Krishnaswami, A. (1978), 'Study of Discrimination in the Matter of Religious Rights and Practices, UN Document (1960)(reprinted)' 11 *NYU J.L. & Pol.*, 227–298.

Krivenko Yahyaoui, E. (2009), *Women, Islam and International Law: Within the Context of the Convention on the Elimination of All Forms of Discrimination against Women* (Leiden: Martinus Nijhoff Publishers).

Lajolo, G. (2007), *Lecture on Vatican/Holy See Diplomacy*, Speech by His Excellency President, State of Vatican City, Sophia University, Tokyo.

Kunz, J. L. (1952), 'The Status of the Holy See in International Law' 46 *AJIL* 2, 308–314.

Lakatos, I (1970), 'Falsification and the Methodology of Scientific Research Programmes' in I. Lakatos and A. Musgrave (eds.) *Criticism and the Growth of Knowledge* (Cambridge, Cambridge University Press), 91–196.

Langbein, J. H. (2006), *Torture and the Law of Proof: Europe and England in the* Ancien Régime (Chicago: University of Chicago Press).

Langer, L. (2010), 'The Rise (and Fall?) of Defamation of Religions' 35 *Yale Journal of International Law*, 257–263.

Laplante, L.J. (2009), 'Outlawing Amnesty: The Return of Criminal Justice in Transitional Justice Schemes' 50 *Virginia Journal of International Law* 1, 915–984.

Lauterpacht, H. (ed.) (1955), *Oppenheim's International Law*, 8th ed., vol. I (London: Longman, Green and Co).

Lauterpacht, H. (1970), 'General Rules of the Law of Peace', in E. Lauterpacht (ed.), *International Law Being the Collected Papers of Hersch Lauterpacht*, vol. I, The General Works (Cambridge: Cambridge University Press).

Laycock, D. (2009), '"The Things that are not Caesar's: Religious Organizations as a Check on the Authoritarian Pretensions of the State": Church Autonomy Revisited' 7 *Georgetown Journal of Law and Public Policy*, 253–278.

Leathley, C. (2007), 'An Institutional Hierarchy to Combat the Fragmentation of International Law: Has the ILC Missed an Opportunity?' 40 *NYU J.L. & Pol.* 1, 259–306.

LeBlanc, L. J. (1996), 'Reservations to the Convention on the Rights of the Child: A Macroscopic View of State Practice' 4 *International Journal of Children's Rights*, 357–381.

Lecomte, J.-P. (2005), *Sociologie politique*, (Paris: Gualino éditeur).

Lee Bowen, D. (2003), 'Contemporary Muslim Ethics of Abortion', in J.E. Brockopp (ed.), *Islamic Ethics of Life: Abortion, War, and Euthanasia* (Columbia, South Carolina: University of South Carolina Press), 51–81.

Leich, M. N. (1984), 'Contemporary Practice of the United States Relating to International Law' 78 *AJIL* 2, 427–440.

Leigh, I. (2012), 'Balancing Religious Autonomy and Other Human Rights under the European Convention' 1 *Oxford J.L. & Relig.* 1, 109–125.

Leith, J. B. (2007), 'A More Constructive Encounter: A Bahá'í View of Religion and Human Rights', in N. Ghanea, A. Stephens, and R. Walden (eds.) *Does God Believe in Human Rights? Essays on Religion and Human Rights* (Leiden: Martinus Nijhoff Publishers), 121–147.

Lerner, N. (1996), 'Religious Human Rights under the United Nations', in J. Witte Jr and J. D. Van der Vyver (eds.) *Religious Human Rights in Global Perspective: Religious Perspectives* (The Hague: Martinus Nijhoff Publishers), 79–134.

Lerner, N. (1998), 'Proselytism, Change of Religion, and International Human Rights' 12 *Emory Int'l L. Rev.*, 477–561.

Lerner, N. (2000), *Religion, Beliefs, and International Human Rights* (Maryknoll, New York: Orbis Books).

Lewis, J. R. (2003), *Legitimating New Religions*, (New Jersey: Rutgers University Press, 2003).

Leyns, N. (2011), *The Holy See: Sovereign Power Internationally Recognized. Does the Authority the Holy See Exercises within the International Community go along with a Responsibility for Human Rights Violations?*, E.MA Thesis, European Inter-University Centre for Human Rights and Democratization.

Lindroos, A. and M. Mehling (2005), 'Dispelling the Chimera of Self-Contained Regimes: International Law and the WTO' 16 *EJIL* 5, 857–877.

Lucien-Brun, J. (1964) 'Le Saint-Siège et les Institutions internationales', 10 *Annuaire français de droit international*, 536–542.

Lunze, S. (2004), 'Serving God and Caesar: Religious Personnel and their Protection in Armed Conflict' 86 *International Review of the Red Cross* 853, 69–91.

MacGibbon, I. (1953), 'Some Observations on the Part of Protest in International Law' 30 *BYBIL*, 293–319.

Madeley, J. (2003), 'European Liberal Democracy and the Principle of State Religious Neutrality' 26 *West European Politics* 1, 1–22.

Mahmoudi, S. (2009), 'Organization of the Islamic Conference (OIC)', in R. Wolfrum (ed.) *MPEPIL* (Online edition: Oxford University Press).

Marek, K. (1968), *Identity and Continuity of States in Public International Law*, (Geneva: Librairie Droz).

Marks, S. R. and A. Clapham (2005), *International Human Rights Lexicon* (Oxford: Oxford University Press).

Martens, K. (2005), 'The Position of the Holy See and Vatican City State in International Relations' 83 *University of Detroit Mercy Law Review*, 729–760.

Martin, F. (2009), 'The Notion of 'Protected Group' in the Genocide Convention and its Application', in P. Gaeta (ed.) *The UN Genocide Convention: A Commentary* (Oxford: Oxford University Press), 112–127.

Martinez, L. C. Jr (2008), 'Sovereign Impunity: Does the Foreign Sovereign Immunities Act Bar Lawsuits Against Holy See in Clerical Sexual Abuse Cases' 44 *Texas International Law Journal*, 123–155.

Mason, P. W. (1993), 'Pilgrimage to Religious Shrines: An Essential Element in the Human Right to Freedom of Thought, Conscience, and Religion' 25 *Case W. Res. J. Int'l L.*, 619–652.

Mason, W. B. (2007), 'A New Call for Reform: Sex Abuse and the Foreign Sovereign Immunities Act' 33 *Brooklyn Journal of International Law*, 655–683.

Massis, T. and C. Pettiti (eds.) (2004), *La liberté religieuse et la Convention européenne des droits de l'homme* (Bruxelles: Bruylant).

Maastricht Principles on Extraterritorial Obligations of States in the area of Economic, Social and Cultural Rights, 28 September 2011, http://www.lse.ac.uk/humanRights/articlesAndTranscripts/2011/MaastrichtEcoSoc.pdf.

Matheson, C. (1987), 'Weber and the Classification of Forms of Legitimacy' 38 *The British Journal of Sociology* 2, 199–215.

Mayer, A. E. (1994) 'Universal versus Islamic Human Rights: A Clash of Cultures or Clash with a Construct' 15 *Mich. J. Int'l L.* 2, 307–404.

McCrudden, C. (2011), 'Multiculturalism, Freedom of Religion, Equality, and the British Constitution: The JFS Case Considered' 9 *International Journal of Constitutional Law* 1, 200–229.

McGoldrick, D. (2006), *Human Rights and Religion: The Islamic Headscarf Debate in Europe* (Portland, OR: Hart).

Mendelson, M. H. (1972), 'Diminutive States in the United Nations' 21 *ICLQ* 4, 609–630.

Merin, Y. (2004), 'The Right to Family Life and Civil Marriage Under International Law and Its Implementation in the State of Israel' *bepress Legal Series* 275, 1–51.

Merrills, J. G. (1995), *The Development of International Law by the European Court of Human Rights*, (Manchester: Manchester University Press).

Messer, E. (2009), 'Anthropology, Human Rights, and Social Transformation', in M. Goodale (ed.) *Human Rights: an Anthropological Reader* (Oxford: Wiley-Blackwell), 103–134.

Meyerson, D. (2008), 'Why Religion Belongs in the Private Sphere, not the Public Square', in P. Cane, C. Evans, and Z. Robinson (eds.) *Law and Religion in Theoretical and Historical Context* (Cambridge: Cambridge University Press), 44–71.

Milanović, M. (2011), *Extraterritorial Application of Human Rights Treaties: Law, Principles, and Policy* (Oxford: Oxford University Press).

Milanović, M. (2012), 'Al-Skeini and Al-Jedda in Strasbourg' 23 *EJIL* 1, 121–139.

Moinuddin, H. (1987), *The Charter of the Islamic Conference and Legal Framework of Economic Co-operation Among Its Member States: A Study of the Charter, the General Agreement for Economic, Technical, and Commercial Co-operation and the Agreement for Promotion, Protection, and Guarantee of Investments Among Member States of the OIC* (Oxford: Clarendon Press).

Moloney, R. (2004), 'Incompatible Reservations to Human Rights Treaties: Severability and the Problem of State Consent' 5 *Melbourne Journal of International Law*, 155–168.

Mosen, V. (2003), *Römisch-katholische Kirche und Kinderrechtskonvention in der Bundesrepublik Deutschland*, (Initiative Kirche von unten, KirchenVolksBewegung Wir sind Kirchen, Catholics for a Free Choice), http://kirche-von-unten.org/html/archiv/ikvu/missbrauch/un-bericht.pdf.

Mower, A. G. (1966), 'Observer Countries: Quasi Members of the United Nations' 20 *International Organization* 2, 266–283.

Mungiu-Pippidi, A. and D. Mindruta (2002), 'Was Huntington Right? Testing Cultural Legacies and the Civilization Border' 39 *International Politics* 2, 193–213.

Murdoch, J. (2007), *Freedom of Thought, Conscience and Religion. A guide to the implementation of Article 9 of the European Convention on Human Rights* (Council of Europe Human Rights Handbooks no. 9).

Murphy, P. and L. Baddour (2010), 'International Criminal Law and Common Law: Rules of Evidence', in K. Khan, C. Buisman, and C. Gosnell (eds.) *Principles of Evidence in International Criminal Justice* (New York: Oxford University Press), 96–156.

Naert, F. (2010), 'Binding International Organisations to Member State Treaties or Responsibility of Member States for their Own Actions in the Framework of International Organizations', in J. Wouters et al. (eds.) *Accountability for Human Rights Violations by International Organisations* (Antwerp: Intersentia), 129–168.

Nafziger, J. A. R. (1999), 'The Functions of Religion in the International Legal System', in M.W. Janis and C. Evans (eds.) *Religion and International Law* (The Hague: Martinus Nijhoff Publishers), 155–176.

Naldi, G. J. (2001), 'Limitation of Rights under the African Charter on Human and Peoples' Rights: The Contribution of the African Commission on Human and Peoples' Rights' 17 *South African Journal on Human Rights*, 109–118.

Nanda, V. P. (1999), 'International Law in Ancient Hindu India', in M.W. Janis and C. Evans (eds.), *Religion and International Law* (The Hague: Martinus Nijhoff Publishers), 51–62.

Ndiaye, B.W. (2011), Statement, Director, Human Rights Council and Treaties Division, Office of the United Nations High Commissioner for Human Rights to the 38th Session of the Council of Foreign Ministers, Organization of Islamic Conference, Astana.

Nersessian, D. L. (2003), 'The Razor's Edge: Defining and Protecting Human Groups under the Genocide Convention' 36 *Cornell International Law Journal*, 293–327.

Nevo, Z. and T. Megiddo (2009), 'Lessons from Kosovo: The Law of Statehood and Palestinian Unilateral Independence' 5 *Journal of International Law and International Relations* 2, 89–115.

Nieuwenhuis, A. (2005), 'European Court of Human Rights: State and Religion, Schools and Scarves. An Analysis of the Margin of Appreciation as Used in the Case of Leyla Sahin v. Turkey, Decision of 29 June 2004, Application Number 44774/98' 1 *European Constitutional Law Review* 3, 495–510.

Nijman, J. E. (2004), *The Concept of International Legal Personality: An Inquiry into the History and Theory of International Law* (The Hague: TMC Asser Press).

Nijman, J. E. (2004), 'Leibniz's Theory of Relative Sovereignty and International Legal Personality: Justice and Stability or the Last Great Defence of the Holy Roman Empire', *IILJ Working Paper no. 2004/2*.

Nijman, J. E. (2007), 'Paul Ricoeur and International Law: Beyond 'The End of the Subject'. Towards a Reconceptualization of International Legal Personality', 20 *Leiden J Intl L* 1, 25–64.

Nmehielle, V. O. O. (2001), *The African Human Rights System: Its Laws, Practice, and Institutions* (The Hague: Martinus Nijhoff).

Norwegian Agency for Development Cooperation (2013), *Lobbying for Faith and Family: A Study of Religious NGOs at the United Nations*, NORAD Report 7/2013.

Nowak, M. (2005), *UN Covenant on Civil and Political Rights. CCPR Commentary* 2nd ed. (Kehl: N.P. Engel).

OHCHR (not dated), *Girls, Women and Sexuality Education—The Link to Achieving the MDGs*, http://www.ohchr.org/Documents/Issues/Women/WRGS/IntlDay2011/Infonote_Women_and_the_right_to_sexual_education.pdf.

OHCHR (2002), *Human Rights in the Administration of Justice: A Manual on Human Rights for Judges, Prosecutors and Lawyers*, Geneva.

OHCHR (2004), Compilation of guidelines on the form and content of reports to be submitted by states parties to the international human rights treaties, HRI/GEN/2/Rev.2.

OHCHR (2006), Harmonized guidelines on reporting under the international human rights treaties, including guidelines on a core document and treaty-specific documents, Extract from HRI/GEN/2/Rev.6.

OHCHR (2008), Manual of Operations of the Special Procedures of the Human Rights Council.

OHCHR (2008), *Study of the United Nations High Commissioner for Human Rights compiling existing legislations and jurisprudence concerning defamation of and contempt for religions*, UN Doc. A/HRC/9/25.

OHCHR (2013), Report of the United Nations High Commissioner for Human Rights on the expert workshops on the prohibition of incitement to national, racial or religious hatred, Annex, Rabat Plan of Action on the prohibition of advocacy of national, racial or religious hatred that constitutes incitement to discrimination, hostility or violence, UN Doc. A/HRC/22/17/Add.4.

Okafor, O. C. (2000), *Re-defining Legitimate Statehood: International Law and State Fragmentation in Africa* (The Hague: Martinus Nijhoff Publishers).

Olaniyan, K. (2008), 'Civil and Political Rights in the African Charter: Articles 8–14', in M.D. Evans and R. Murray (eds.), *The African Charter on Human and Peoples' Rights: The System in Practice, 1986-2006* (Cambridge: Cambridge University Press), 213–243.

Oliver, D. and J. Fedtke (eds.) (2007), *Human Rights and the Private Sphere: A Comparative Study*, (New York: Routledge).

Oliviera Da Costa, K. (2011) *The Extraterritorial Application of Selected Human Rights Treaties*, (PhD Thesis, Geneva: IHEID).

Oppenheim, L. (1905), *International Law: A Treatise*, 1st ed., vol. 1 (London: Longmans, Green, and Co).

Örsy, L. M. (2002), 'Theology and Canon Law', in J.P. Beal, J. A. Coriden, and T. J. Green (eds.), *New Commentary on the Code of Canon Law* (Mahwah, NJ: Paulist Press), 1–10.

Oshana, M. (2006), *Personal Autonomy in Society*, (Aldershot: Ashgate).

Österdahl, I. (2003), 'The Surprising Originality of the African Charter on Human Rights and Peoples' Rights', in J. Petman and J. Klabbers (eds.), *Nordic Cosmopolitanism: Essays in International Law for Martti Koskenniemi* (Leiden: Martinus Nijhoff Publishing), 5–32.

Otis, P. (2008), 'Armed with the Power of Religion: Not Just a War of Ideas', in J.H. Norwitz (ed.), Armed Groups: Studies in National Security, Counterterrorism, and Counterinsurgency, (Newport, RI: Naval War College Press).

Ouguergouz, F. (2003), *The African Charter on Human and Peoples' Rights: A Comprehensive Agenda for Human Dignity and Sustainable Democracy in Africa* (Leiden: Martinus Nijhoff).

Palmer, S. (2007), 'Public, Private and the Human Rights Act 1998: An Ideological Divide' 66 *Cambridge Law Journal* 3, 559–573.

Pauwelyn, J. (2003), *Conflict of Norms in Public International Law: How WTO Law Relates to Other Rules of International Law* (Cambridge: Cambridge University Press).

Peers, S. (2001), 'Fundamental Rights or Political Whim: WTO Law and the European Court of Justice', in G. De Burca and J. Scott (eds.) *The EU and the WTO: Legal and Constitutional issues* (Oxford: Hart), 111–130.

Peiffer, E. (2004), 'The Death Penalty in Traditional Islamic Law and as Interpreted in Saudi Arabia and Nigeria' 11 *William and Mary Journal of Women and the Law*, 507–539.

Pentikäinen, M. (2003), 'The Right to Speak for the Women's Cause: May Also Women Participate?', in J. Petman and J. Klabbers (eds.) *Nordic Cosmopolitanism. Essays in International Law for Martti Koskenniemi* (Leiden: Martinus Nijhoff Publishers), 141–154.

Petkoff, P. (2007), 'Legal Perspectives and Religious Perspectives of Religious Rights under International Law in the Vatican Concordats (1963-2004)' 158 *Law & Justice—The Christian Law Review*, 30–53.

Philpott, D (2009), 'When Faith Meets History: the Influence of Religion on Transitional Justice', in T. Brudholm and T. Cushman (eds.) *The Religious in Response to Mass Atrocity: Interdisciplinary Perspectives*, (Cambridge: Cambridge University Press), 174–212.

Pinzon, D. R. (2000), 'The Victim Requirement, the Fourth Instance Formula and the Notion of Person in the Individual Complaint Procedure of the Inter-American Human Rights System' 7 *ILSA Journal of International & Comparative Law* 1, 369–386.

Pollis, A. (1996), 'Cultural Relativism Revisited: Through a State Prism' 18 *HRQ* 316–344.

Popovski, V., G. M. Reichberg and N. Turner (eds.) (2009) *World Religions and Norms of War* (New York: United Nations University Press).

Portmann, R. (2010), *Legal Personality in International Law*, (New York: Cambridge University Press).

Poulose, T. (1970), 'India as an Anomalous International Person (1919-1947)', 44 *BYBIL*, 201–212.

Preis, A.-B. S. (1996), 'Human Rights as Cultural Practice: An Anthropological Critique' 18 *HRQ*, 286–315.

Pronto, A.N. (2008), 'Some Thoughts on the Making of International Law' 19 *EJIL* 3, 611–616.

Quraishi, A. (1996), 'Her Honor: An Islamic Critique of the Rape Laws of Pakistan from a Woman-Sensitive Perspective' 18 *Mich. J. Int'l L.*, 287–320.

Raday, F. (2003), 'Culture, Religion, and Gender' 1 *International Journal of Constitutional Law* 4, 663–715.

Raday, F. (2007), 'Culture, Religion, and CEDAW's Article 5 (a)', in H. Schöpp-Schilling and C. Flinterman (eds.) *Circle of Empowerment: Twenty-Five Years of the UN Committee on the Elimination of Discrimination against Women*, (New York: Feminist Press), 68–85.

Raič, D. (2002), *Statehood and the Law of Self-determination* (The Hague: Kluwer Law International).

Ramcharan, B. G. (1997), 'The Universality of Human Rights' 58–59 *Review—International Commission of Jurists*, 105–117.

Ramcharan, B. G. (2009), *The Protection Roles of UN Human Rights Special Procedures* (The Hague: Martinus Nijhoff).

Ratner, S. (2001), 'Corporations and Human Rights: a Theory of Legal Responsibility', 111 *Yale Law Journal*, 443–546.

Rehman, J. (2010), *International Human Rights Law*, 2nd ed., (Harlow: Pearson Education).

Rehman, J. and S. Breau (2007), 'Introductory Reflections', in J. Rehman and S. Breau (eds.) *Religion, Human Rights and International Law* (Leiden: Martinus Nijhoff Publishers), 3–22.

Rehman, J. and S. E. Berry (2012), 'Is "Defamation of Religions" Passé? The United Nations, Organisation of Islamic Cooperation, and Islamic State Practices: Lessons from Pakistan' 44 *Geo. Wash. Int'l L. Rev.*, 3–22.

Reinisch, A. (2001), 'Securing the Accountability of International Organizations' 7 *Global Governance*, 131–150.

Report of the Secretary-General, *Combating Defamation of Religions*, 12 September 2006, UN Doc. A/61/325.

Reuter, A. (2007), 'Säkularität und Religionsfreiheit: ein doppeltes Dilemma' 35 *Leviathan* 2, 178–192.

Reza, S. (2007), 'Torture and Islamic law', 8 *Chicago Journal of International Law* 21–41.

Riddle, J. (2002), 'Making CEDAW Universal: A Critique of CEDAW's Reservation Regime Under Article 28 and the Effectiveness of the Reporting Process', 34 *Geo. Wash. Int'l L. Rev.*, 605–638.

Riedel, E. (2002), 'Article 55(c)', in B. Simma (ed.) *The Charter of the United Nations: A Commentary*, 2nd ed., vol. 2 (Oxford: Oxford University Press), 917–941.

Riley P. (ed.) (1988), *Leibniz: Political Writings*, 2nd ed. (Cambridge: Cambridge University Press).

Rishmawi, M. (2005), 'The Revised Arab Charter on Human Rights: A Step Forward?' 5 *Human Rights Law Review* 2, 361–376.

Rishmawi, M. (2010) 'The Arab Charter on Human Rights and the League of Arab States: An Update' 10 *Human Rights Law Review* 1, 169–178.

Robertson, G. (2010), *The Case of the Pope: Vatican Accountability for Human Rights Abuse* (London: Penguin Books).

Robinson, Mary (1999), Statement, United Nations High Commissioner for Human Rights, *The Universality of Human Rights*, Conference, Bonn.

Robinson, P. (2009), 'The Right to a Fair Trial in International Law, with Specific Reference to the Work of the ICTY' 3 *Berkeley Journal of International Law Publicist*, 1–11.

Rousseau, C. (1974), *Droit international public*, vol. II, Les sujets de droit (Paris: Editions Sirey).

Rudolph, C. (2005), 'Sovereignty and Territorial Borders in a Global Age' 7 *International Studies Review* 1, 1–20.

Ruiz Fabri, H. (2005), 'Les catégories de sujets du droit international', in *Le sujet en droit international: Colloque du Mans* (Paris: Editions A. Pedone), 55–71.

Runzo, J., M. N. Martin and A. Sharma (eds.) (2003), *Human Rights and Responsibilities in the World Religions* (Oxford: Oneworld Publications).

Sadat-Akhavi, S. A. (2003), *Methods of Resolving Conflicts between Treaties* (Leiden: Martinus Nijhoff).

Satow, R. L. (1975), 'Value-Rational Authority and Professional Organizations: Weber's Missing Type', 20 *Administrative Science Quarterly* 4, 526–531.

Schabas, W. (1996), 'Reservations to the Convention on the Rights of the Child' 18 *HRQ* 2, 472–491.

Schabas, W. (2000), *Genocide in International Law: The Crime of Crimes* (Cambridge: Cambridge University Press).

Schabas, W. (2000), *The Abolition of the Death Penalty in International Law*, 3rd ed. (Cambridge: Cambridge University Press).

Scheinin, M. (1999), 'Article 18', in G. Alfredsson and A. Eide (eds.) *The Universal Declaration of Human Rights: A Common Standard of Achievement* (The Hague: Martinus Nijhoff Publishers), 379–392.

Scheinin, M. (2004), 'Extraterritorial Effect of the International Covenant on Civil and Political Rights', in F. Coomans and M. T. Kamminga (eds.) *Extraterritorial Application of Human Rights Treaties* (Antwerp: Intersentia), 73–82.

Schreuer, C. (1995), 'Regionalism v. Universalism' 6 *EJIL*, 477–499.

Seidl-Hohenveldern, I. (1987), *Corporations in and under International Law* (Cambridge: Grotius Publications).

Sen, A. (2008), 'Violence, Identity and Poverty', 45 *Journal of Peace Research* 1, 5–15.

Seyersted, F. (2008), *Common Law of International Organizations* (Leiden: Martinus Nijhoff).

Shabtai, R. (1999), 'The Influence of Judaism on the Development of International Law— An Assessment', in M.W. Janis and C. Evans (eds.) *Religion and International Law* (The Hague: Martinus Nijhoff Publishers), 63–92.

Shani, G. (2011), 'Transnational Religious Actors and International Relations', in J. Heynes (ed.), *Routledge Handbook of Religion and Politics* (New York: Routledge), 308–322.

Shany, Y. (2005), 'Toward a General Margin of Appreciation Doctrine in International Law?' 16 *EJIL* 5, 907–940.

Shaw, M. N. (2003), *International Law*, 5th ed. (Cambridge: Cambridge University Press).

Simma, B. and P. Alston (1988) 'The Sources of Human Rights Law: Custom, Jus Cogens, and General Principles' 12 *Australian Yearbook of International Law*, 82–108.

Simma, B. and D. Pulkowski (2006) 'Of Planets and the Universe: Self-contained Regimes in International Law' 17 *EJIL* 3, 483–529.

Singh, S. (2011) 'The Potential of International Law: Fragmentation and Ethics' 24 *Leiden J Int L*, 123–143.

Sinha, M. K. (2005), 'Hinduism and International Humanitarian Law' 87 *International Review of the Red Cross* 858, 285–294.

Smagadi, A. (2008), *A Sourcebook on International Human Rights Materials* (London: BIICL).

Smith, C. (2008), 'A Very English Affair: Establishment and Human Rights in an Organic Constitution', in P. Cane, C. Evans, and Z. Robinson (eds.) *Law and Religion in Theoretical and Historical Context* (Cambridge: Cambridge University Press), 157–185.

Spencer, M. E. (1970), 'Weber on Legitimate Norms and Authority' 21 *The British Journal of Sociology* 2, 123–134.

Spielmann, D. (1998), 'Obligations positives et effet horizontal des dispositions de la Convention', in F. Sudre (ed.) *L'interprétation de la Convention Européenne des droits de l'homme* (Bruxelles: Bruylant), 133–174.

Stahnke, T. and R. C. Blitt (2005) 'The Religion-State Relationship and the Right to Freedom of Religion or Belief: A Comparative Textual Analysis of the Constitutions of Predominantly Muslim Countries' 36 *Georgetown Journal of International Law*, 947–1078.

Stan, L. and L. Turcescu (2000), 'The Romanian Orthodox Church and Post-Communist Democratisation' 52 *Europe-Asia Studies* 8, 1467–1488.

Stanton, T. and H. Stanton Blatch (eds.) (1922), *Elizabeth Cady Stanton as Revealed in Her Letters, Diary and Reminiscences*, vol. 2 (New York: Harper & brothers, http://archive.org/stream/elizabethcadyst00blatgoog#page/n11/mode/2up).

Steuerkonferenz SSK (2009), *Kirchensteuern. Stand der Gesetzgebung: 1. Januar 2009*, Abteilung Grundlagen/ESTV Bern.

Stoll, P.-T. (2011), 'State Immunity', in R. Wolfrum (ed.) *MPEPIL* (Online edition: Oxford University Press).

Sullivan, D. J. (1988), 'Advancing the Freedom of Religion or Belief through the UN Declaration on the Elimination of Religious Intolerance and Discrimination' 82 *AJIL* 3, 487–520.

Sybesma-Knol, R. G. (1981), *The Status of Observers in the United Nations*, (Brussel: Centrum voor de Studie van het Recht van de Verenigde Naties en de Gespecialiseerde Organisaties).

Tahzib, B. (1996), *Freedom of Religion or Belief: Ensuring Effective International Legal Protection* (Dordrecht: Martinus Nijhoff Publishers).

Tahzib-Lie, B. G. (2001), 'Women's Equal Right to Freedom of Religion or Belief: An Important but Neglected Subject', in C.W. Howland (ed.) *Religious Fundamentalisms and the Human Rights of Women* (New York: Palgrave Macmillan), 117–128.

Taylor, P. M. (2005), *Freedom of Religion: UN and European Human Rights Law and Practice* (Cambridge: Cambridge University Press).

Temperman, J. (2008), 'Blasphemy, Defamation of Religions and Human Rights Law' 26 *Netherlands Quarterly of Human Rights* 4, 517–545.

Temperman, J. (2009), 'The Emerging Counter-defamation of Religion Discourse: a Critical Analysis' 4 *Droit et Religions: Annuaire*, 553–559.

Temperman, J. (2010), *State-Religion Relationships and Human Rights Law: Towards a Right to Religiously Neutral Governance* (Leiden: Martinus Nijhoff Publishers).

Temperman, J. (2011), 'Freedom of Expression and Religious Sensitivities in Pluralist Societies: Facing the Challenge of Extreme Speech' *BYU L. Rev.*, 729–757.

Temperman, J. (ed.) (2012), *The Lautsi Papers: Multidisciplinary Reflections on Religious Symbols in the Public School Classroom* (Leiden: Martinus Nijhoff Publishers).

Thomas, S. (1999), 'The Global Resurgence of Religion, International Law and International Society', in M. W. Janis and C. Evans (eds.), *Religion and International Law* (The Hague: Martinus Nijhoff Publishers), 321–338.

Thürer, D. (2008), *International Humanitarian Law: Theory, Practice, Context*, Collected Courses of the Hague Academy of International Law vol. 338, (Online ed.: Martinus Nijhoff).

Tiefenbrun, S. W. and C. J. Edwards (2009), 'Gendercide and the Cultural Context of Sex Trafficking in China', 32 *Fordham International Law Journal* 3, 731–780.

Tomasevski, K. (2003), *Education Denied: Costs and Remedies* (London: Zed Books).

Tomuschat, C. (2003), *Human Rights: Between Idealism and Realism* (Oxford: Oxford University Press).

Tse-shyang Che, F. (1999), 'The Confucian View of World Order', in M.W. Janis and C. Evans (eds.), *Religion and International Law*, (The Hague: Martinus Nijhoff Publishers).

Uitz, R. (2007), *Freedom of Religion in European Constitutional and International Case Law* (Strasbourg: Council of Europe Publishing), 27–50.

UNICEF (2005), *Investing in the Children of the Islamic World*, New York.

van Asselt, H., F. Sindico and M. A. Mehling (2008), 'Global Climate Change and the Fragmentation of International Law' 30 *Law & Policy* 4, 423–449.

van Boven, T. (2000), 'Non-State Actors; Introductory Comments [1997]', in F. Coomans et al. (eds.), *Human Rights from Exclusion to Inclusion; Principles and Practice: An Anthology from the Work of Theo van Boven* (The Hague: Kluwer), 363–369.

van Bueren, G. (1998), *The International Law on the Rights of the Child* (The Hague: Martinus Nijhoff Publishers).

van Dijk, P. and G. J. H. van Hoof (1998), *Theory and Practice of the European Convention on Human Rights*, 3rd ed. (The Hague: Kluwer Law International).

Verdross, A. (1937), *Völkerrecht* (Berlin: Julius Springer).

Verdross, A. and B. Simma (1984), *Universelles Völkerrecht. Theorie und Praxis*, 3rd ed. (Berlin: Duncker & Humblot).

Virally, M. (1960), *La pensée juridique*, (Paris: LGDJ).

Virally, M. (1983), 'Review Essay: Good Faith in Public International Law' 77 *AJIL* 1, 130–134.

Voll, J., P. Mandaville, S. Kull and A. Arieff (2012), 'Political Islam in the Arab Awakening: Who Are the Major Players?' 19 *Middle East Policy* 2, 10–35.

Wadham, J., et al. (2007), *Blackstone's Guide to the Human Rights Act 1998*, 4th ed. (Oxford: Oxford University Press).

Walter, C. (2008), 'Religion or Belief, Freedom of, International Protection', in R. Wolfrum (ed.) *MPEPIL* (Online edition: Oxford University Press).

Walters, P. (1993), 'A Survey of Soviet Religious Policy', in S.P. Ramet (ed.), *Religious Policy in the Soviet Union* (Cambridge: Cambridge University Press), 3–30.

Weber, M. (1978), *Economy and Society (G. Roth and C. Wittich eds.)* (Berkeley: University of California Press).

Weddle, D. A. (2006), 'Jehovah's Witnesses', in E. V. Gallagher and W. Michael Ashcraft (eds.), *Introduction to New and Alternative Religions in America*, vol. 2 (Westport, Connecticut: Greenwood), 62–66.

Weeramantry, C. (2004), *Universalising International Law* (Leiden: Martinus Nijhoff Publishers).

Weil, P. (1992), 'Le droit international en quête de son identité: Cours général de droit international public' 237 *Recueil des Cours de l'Académie de droit international de la Haye*, 9–370.

Weiler, J. H. H. (2010), 'Discrimination and Identity in London: The Jewish Free School Case', *Jewish Review of Books* 1, available at https://jewishreviewofbooks.com/articles/97/discrimination-and-identity-in-london-the-jewish-free-school-case/.

Weiler, J. H. H. (2010), 'Lautsi: Crucifix in the Classroom Redux' 21 *EJIL* 1, 1–6.

Westdickenberg, G. (2006), 'Holy See', in R. Wolfrum (ed.), *MPEPIL* (Online edition: Oxford University Press).

Westerlund, D. (ed.) (1996), *Questioning the Secular State: The Worldwide Resurgence of Religion in Politics* (London: Hurst).

Westlake, J. (1904) *International Law: Peace*, 1st ed., vol. 1 (Cambridge: Cambridge University Press).

White, R. C. A. and C. Ovey (2010), *The European Convention on Human Rights*, 5th ed., (Oxford: Oxford University Press).

Whiting, A. and C. Evans (eds.) (2006), *Mixed Blessings: Laws, Religions and Women's Rights in the Asia-Pacific Region* (Leiden: Martinus Nijhoff Publishers).

Willer, D. E. (1994), 'Max Weber's Missing Authority Type', in J. Scott (ed.), *Power: Critical Concepts* (London, New York: Routledge), 131–139.

Wilson, A. J. (2006), 'Beyond Unocal: Conceptual Problems in Using International Norms to Hold Transnational Corporations Liable under the Alien Tort Claims Act', in O. de Schutter (ed.), *Transnational Corporations and Human Rights* (Portland, Oregon: Hart Publishing), 43–72.

Witte, J. Jr (1996), 'Introduction', in J. Witte Jr and J. D. van der Vyver (eds.), *Religious Human Rights in Global Perspective: Religious Perspectives* (The Hague: Martinus Nijhoff Publishers), ix–xxxv.

Witte, J. Jr (2000), 'A Dickensian Era of Religious Rights: An Update on Religious Human Rights in Global Perspective' 42 *William & Mary Law Review*, 707–770.

Wouters, J., et al. (2010), 'Accountability for Human Rights Violations by International Organisations: Introductory Remarks', in J. Wouters et al. (eds.) *Accountability for Human Rights Violations by International Organisations* (Antwerp: Intersentia), 1–20.

Young, S. E. and A. Shea (2007), 'Separating State from Church: A Research Guide to the Law of the Vatican City State' 99 *Law Library Journal* 3, 589–610.

Zappalà, S. (2001), 'Do Heads of State in Office Enjoy Immunity from Jurisdiction for International Crimes? The Ghaddafi Case Before the French Cour de Cassation' 12 *EJIL* 3, 595–612.

Ziegler, J. (2008), '"Die Gleichheit aller" versus "die Individualität eines jeden". Das Prinzip der Trennung von Kirche und Staat in Deutschland und Frankreich im Spiegel der Kopftuchdebatte', in F. Heidenreich, J. C. Merle, and W. Vogel (eds.) *Staat und Religion in Frankreich und Deutschland/L'Etat et la religion en France et en Allemagne* (Berlin: LIT Verlag), 158–175.

Ziemele, I. (2004), *Reservations to Human Rights Treaties and the Vienna Convention Regime: Conflict, Harmony or Reconciliation* (Leiden: Martinus Nijhoff).

Zolotov, A, (not dated) 'Russia, Defamation of Religion & Free Speech: Implications for Media', http://www.themediaproject.org.

Documents of United Nations treaty bodies, special procedures, and other mechanisms

Annual report of the Special Rapporteur on the right to education, Katarina Tomasevski, UN doc E/CN.4/1999/49, 13 January 1999

CEDAW Committee, Combined initial and second periodic reports of Saudi Arabia, UN Doc. CEDAW/C/SAU/2, 29 March 2007

CEDAW Committee, Concluding observations of the Committee on the Elimination of Discrimination against Women, Bahrain, UN Doc. CEDAWCEDAW/C/BHR/CO/2, 14 November 2008

CEDAW Committee, Concluding comments of the Committee on the Elimination of Discrimination against Women,: Niger, UN Doc. CEDAW/C/NER/CO/2, 11 June 2007

CEDAW Committee, Concluding observations of the Committee on the Elimination of Discrimination against Women, Nigeria, UN Doc. A/59/38, 2004

CEDAW Committee, Concluding observations of the Committee on the Elimination of Discrimination against Women, Nigeria, UN Doc. CEDAW/C/NGA/CO/6, 8 July 2008

CEDAW Committee, Concluding observations of the Committee on the Elimination of Discrimination against Women, United Arab Emirates, UN Doc. CEDAW/C/ARE/CO/1, 5 Febraury 2010

CEDAW Committee, *General Recommendation No. 3*, 6th session, 1987.

CEDAW Committee, *General Recommendation No. 19: Violence against women*, 11th session, 1992

CEDAW Committee, *General Recommendation No. 21: equality in marriage and family relations*, 13th session, 1994

CEDAW Committee, *General Recommendation No. 23: women in political and public life*, 16th session, 1997

CERD Committee, Consideration of State party reports: Holy See, CERD 28th, No. 18 UN Doc. A/9018, 1973

CERD Committee, Consideration of State party reports: Holy See, CERD 30th, No. 18 UN Doc. A/10018, 1975

CERD Committee, Consideration of State party reports: Holy See, UN Doc. A/32/18, 1977

CERD Committee, Consideration of State party reports: Holy See, UN Doc. A/36/18, 1981

CERD Committee, Consideration of State party reports: Holy See, UN Doc. A/37/18, 1982

CERD Committee, Consideration of State party reports: Holy See, UN Doc. A/40/18, 1985

CERD Committee, Consideration of State party reports: Holy See, UN Doc. A/42/18, 1987

CERD Committee, Consideration of State party reports: Holy See, UN Doc. A/45/18, 1990

CERD Committee, Consideration of State party reports: Holy See, UN Doc. A/48/18, 1993

CERD Committee, Consideration of State party reports: Holy See, UN Doc. A/55/18, 2000.

CERD Committee, Thirteenth, fourteenth and fifteenth periodic report (consolidated), Holy See, Committee on the Elimination of Racial Discrimination, UN Doc CERD/C/338/Add.11, 26 May 2000

CESCR, *General Comment No. 12: Right to adequate food*, UN Doc. E/C.12/1999/5

CESCR, *General Comment No. 13: The right to education (Art. 13)*, UN Doc. E/C.12/1999/10, 8 December 1999

CESCR, *General Comment No. 14: The right to the highest attainable standard of health (art. 12)*, 11 August 2000, UN Doc. E/C.12/2000/4

CESCR, *General Comment No. 19: The right to social security (art. 9)*, 4 February 2008, UN Doc. E/C.12/GC/19

CESCR, *General Comment No. 20: Non-Discrimination in Economic, Social and Cultural Rights (art. 2, para. 2)*, UN Doc. E/C.12/GC/20, 10 June 2009

CESCR, *General Comment No. 21: Right of everyone to take part in cultural life (art 15, para. 1 (a))*, 20 November 2009, UN Doc. E/C.12/GC/21

CRC Committee, Compte rendu analytique de la 255ème seance, Examen des rapports présentés par les Etats parties: Rapport initial du Saint-Siège, UN Doc. CRC/C/SR.255, 24 novembre 1995

CRC Committee, Concluding observations of the Committee on the Rights of the Child: Brunei Darussalam, UN Doc. CRC/C/133, 31 December 2003

CRC Committee, Concluding observations of the Committee on the Rights of the Child: Holy See, UN Doc. CRC/C/15/Add.46, 27 November 1995

CRC Committee, Concluding observations of the Committee on the Rights of the Child: Mauritania, CRC/C/MRT/CO/2, 17 June 2009

CRC Committee, Concluding observations of the Committee on the Rights of the Child: Oman, UN Doc. CRC/C/111, 2001

CRC Committee, Concluding observations of the Committee on the Rights of the Child: Syria, UN Doc. CRC/C/SYR/CO/3-4, 9 February 2012

CRC Committee, Concluding observations of the Committee on the Rights of the Child: United Arab Emirates, UN Doc. CRC/C/118, 2002

CRC Committee, Concluding observations of the Committee on the Rights of the Child: Yemen, UN Doc. CRC/C/15/Add.267, 21 September 2005

CRC Committee, Consideration of Reports Submitted by State Parties under Article 44 of the Convention, Concluding observations: Nigeria, UN Doc. CRC/C/NGA/CO/3-4, 11 June 2010

CRC Committee, Consideration of Reports Submitted by State Parties under Article 44 of the Convention, Concluding observations: Pakistan, UN Doc CRC/C/15/Add.217, 27 October 2003

CRC Committee, First periodic report, Saudi Arabia, Committee on the Rights of the Child, UN Doc. CRC/C/61/Add.2, 1998

CRC Committee, *General Comment No. 5: General measures of implementation of the Convention on the Rights of the Child*, UN Doc. CRC/GC/2003/5, 27 November 2003

CRC Committee, *General Comment No. 7: Implementing child rights in early childhood*, UN Doc. CRC/C/GC/7/Rev.1, 20 September 2006

CRC Committee, *General Comment No. 10: Children's rights in juvenile justice*, UN Doc. CRC/C/GC/10, 25 April 2007

CRC Committee, Initial Report to the Committee on the Rights of the Child on the Optional Protocol on the Sale of Children, Child Prostitution and Child Pornography, Holy See, UN Doc. CRC/C/OPSC/VAT/1

CRC Committee, Second Report to the Committee on the Rights of the Child on the Convention on the Rights of the Child, Holy See, UN Doc. CRC/C/VAT/2

CRC Committee, Summary Record of the 256th Meeting, Consideration of Reports of State Parties: Holy See (continued), UN Doc. CRC/C/SR.256, 17 November 1995

HRC, Concluding observations of the Human Rights Committee, Islamic Republic of Iran, UN Doc. CCPR/C/IRN/CO/3, 29 November 2011

HRC, Concluding observations of the Human Rights Committee: Nepal, UN Doc. CCPR/C/79/Add.42, 11 October 1994

HRC, Concluding observations of the Human Rights Committee: Sudan, UN Doc. CCPR/C/SDN/CO/3, 29 August 2007

HRC, Concluding observations of the Human Rights Committee: United States of America, UN Doc. A/50/40, 1995

HRC, Consideration of Reports Submitted by States Parties under Article 40 of the Covenant, Concluding observations: Morocco, UN Doc. CCPR/CO/82/MAR, 1 December 2004

HRC, *General Comment No. 11: Prohibition of propaganda for war and inciting national, racial or religious hatred (Art. 20)*, 29 July 1983

HRC, *General Comment No. 18: Non-discrimination*, 10 November 1989

HRC, *General Comment No. 22: The right to freedom of thought, conscience and religion (Art. 18)*, U.N. Doc. CCPR/C/21/Rev.1/Add.4, 30 July 1993

HRC, *General Comment No. 23: The rights of minorities (Art. 27)*, 8 April 1994

HRC, *General Comment No. 24: Issues relating to reservations made upon ratification or accession to the Covenant or the Optional Protocols thereto, or in relation to declarations under article 41 of the Covenant*, 4 November 1994, UN Doc. CCPR/C/21/Rev.1/Add.6

HRC, *General Comment No. 28: Equality of rights between men and women (article 3)*, UN Doc. CCPR/C/21/Rev.1/Add.10, 29 March 2008

HRC, *General Comment No. 29: States of Emergency (article 4)*, 31 July 2001, UN Doc. CCPR/C/21/Rev.1/Add.10

HRC, *General Comment No. 32*: Article 14: Right to equality before courts and tribunals and to a fair trial, 23 August 2007, UN Doc. CCPR/C/GC/32

HRC, *General Comment No. 34: Freedoms of opinion and expression*, 12 September 2011, UN Doc. CCPR/C/GC/34

HRC, Second periodic report, Egypt, Corrigendum, UN Doc. CCPR/C/51/Add.7/Corr.1, 19 July 1993

HRC, Second periodic report, Egypt, UN Doc. CCPR/C/51/Add.7, 2 September 1992

HRC, Summary Record of the 1252 Meeting: Iran (Islamic Republic of), UN Doc CCPR/C/SR.1252, 27 June 1994

HRC, Summary Record of the 2459th meeting: Sudan, UN Doc. CCPR/C/SR.2459, 31 July 2007

HRC, Summary Record of the 2460th meeting: Sudan, UN Doc. CCPR/C/SR.2460, 13 October 2008

ILC, First Report on the Law of Treaties by Sir Humphrey Waldock, UN Doc. A/CN.4/144 and Add.1, 1962

ILC, Fragmentation of International Law: Difficulties Arising from the Diversification and Expansion of International Law, Report of the Study Group of the International Law

Commission finalized by Martti Koskenniemi, UN Doc. A/CN.4/L.682, 13 April 2006

ILC, Report of the International Law Commission on the work of its 14th session, *Yearbook of the International Law Commission*, Vol. II, 1962

ILC, Report of the International Law Commission on the work of its forty-seventh session, UN GAOR 50th Sess., Supp. No. 10, UN Doc. A/50/10, 1995

ILC, Report of the International Law Commission on the work of its 52 session, Yearbook of the International Law Commission, Vol. I, 2000, UN Doc. A/CN.4/SER.A/2000

ILC, Report of the International Law Commission on the work of the sixty-third session, UN Doc. A/66/10/Add.1, 2011

ILC, Reservations to Multilateral Conventions, Mr J.L. Brierly, Special Rapporteur, UN Doc. A/CN.4/41, 1951

ILO, Digest of Decisions and Principles of the Freedom of Association Committee of the Governing Body of the ILO, 5th (revised) edition, (Geneva: ILO, 2006),

Rapport soumis par M. Abdelfattah Amor, Rapporteur spécial, conformément à la résolution 2001/42 de la Commission des droits de l'homme, Additif: *Etude sur la liberté de religion ou de conviction et la condition de la femme au regard de la religion et des traditions*, 5 avril 2002, UN. Doc. E/CN.4/2002/73/Add.2

Report of the independent expert in the field of cultural rights, Ms Farida Shaheed, submitted pursuant to the resolution 10/23 of the Human Rights Council, UN Doc. A/HRC/14/36, 22 March 2010

Report of the independent expert on the issue of human rights obligations related to access to safe drinking water and sanitation, Catarina de Albuquerque, Un doc A/HRC/12/24, 1 July 2009

Report of the Independent International Commission of Inquiry on the Syrian Arab Republic, UN Doc. A/HRC/19/69, 22 February 2012

Report of Special Rapporteur Abdelfattah Amor, Implementation of the Declaration on the Elimination of All Forms of Intolerance and of Discrimination Based on Religion or Belief, UN Doc. E/CN.4/1997/91, 30 December 1996

Report of the Special Rapporteur on freedom of religion or belief, Asma Jahangir, UN Doc. E/CN.4/2006/5, 9 January 2006

Report of the Special Rapporteur, Mr Nigel S. Rodley, submitted pursuant to Commission on Human Rights resolution 1995/37 B, UN Doc. E/CN.4/1997/7, 10 January 1997

Report of the Special Rapporteur on the promotion and protection of the right to freedom of opinion and expression, Ambeyi Ligabo, UN Doc. A/HRC/7/14, 28 February 2008

Report of the Special Rapporteur on the promotion of truth, justice, reparation and guarantees of non-recurrence, Pablo de Greiff, UN Doc. A/HRC/21/46, 9 August 2012

Report of the Special Rapporteur on religious intolerance, Mrs Elizabeth Odio Benito, U.N. Doc. E/CN.4/Sub.2/1987/26, 1987

Report of the Special Rapporteur on violence against women, its causes and consequences, Yakin Ertürk, UN Doc. A/HRC/11/6/Add.3, 14 July 2009

Report submitted by the Special Representative of the Secretary-General on human rights defenders, Hina Jilani, Addendum, Compilation of developments in the area of human rights defender, UN Doc. E/CN.4/2006/95/Add.5, 6 March 2006

Index